S0-CKG-743

Trading Blows

Trading

Blows

Party Competition and U.S. Trade Policy in a Globalizing Era

JAMES SHOCH

The University of North Carolina Press

Chapel Hill and London

382.30973
S55t

© 2001 The University of North Carolina Press
All rights reserved
Manufactured in the United States of America

The paper in this book meets the guidelines for
permanence and durability of the Committee on
Production Guidelines for Book Longevity of the
Council on Library Resources.

Library of Congress Cataloging-in-Publication Data
Shoch, James.
Trading blows : party competition and U.S. trade
policy in a globalizing era / James Shoch.
p. cm.
Includes bibliographical references and index.
ISBN 0-8078-2646-4 (cloth: alk. paper)
ISBN 0-8078-4975-8 (pbk.: alk. paper)
1. United States—Commercial policy. 2. Free trade—
Political aspects—United States. 3. Political parties—
United States. I. Title.
HF1455.S54 2001
382′.3′0973—dc21
2001027412

05 04 03 02 01   5 4 3 2 1

For Barbara, of course,
and my parents,
Gertrude Shoch and
the late David Shoch

University Libraries
Carnegie Mellon University
Pittsburgh, PA 15213-3890

Contents

Preface

This book, the first of its kind on the recent partisan politics of U.S. trade policy, has been a long time in the making. It has its origins in my years as an activist in the early and mid-1980s, when many of us on the Left debated how to advance our cause through the vehicle of the Democratic Party. These were years of soaring trade deficits and "deindustrialization"; thus one important area of concern to us was the Democrats' stance on trade and industrial policy.

The 1980s were hard on the Left, so in 1987 I decided to go to graduate school in the hope that if I could not change the world, I might at least better understand it. But I took my obsession with American party politics with me. As I searched for a dissertation topic, it appeared clear to me that party competition was to a significant degree driving U.S. trade policy, which at that time was focused on combating the mounting Japanese challenge, yet few scholars had noticed this. So I wrote a thesis on the party politics of American "economic nationalism" in the 1980s. Of course, the subsequent rise of concern over economic "globalization" and the great free-trade battles of the 1990s forced me to include analysis of these issues as I worked to turn my thesis into a book. Writing on this topic was thus like trying to hit a fast-moving target, and this slowed production of the manuscript.

The book was also delayed as I struggled both to grasp the fields of American politics and international political economy and to find my own scholarly voice through an integration of the heterodox political-economic views of my activist days with the more conventional political science that I absorbed in graduate school. Whether I have succeeded in producing the synthesis that I was searching for is up to the reader to decide.

For reasons that are not entirely clear to me, the writing of this book has been a somewhat more solitary process than I had expected. Perhaps this is in part because the project falls so squarely between two fields. Still, I have received indispensable professional and personal support along the way from a host of colleagues and friends, including Joanne Barkan, Suzanne Berger, Bill Bernhard, Fran Bernstein, Fred Block, Michael Bodaken, David Brady, Mlada Bukovansky, Andrew Bundy, Walter Dean Burnham, John Campbell, Jim Cronin, Kathy Donald, Barbara Fasher, Laura Frader, Amy Glasmeier, Peter Hall, Karen Hansen, Dave Hart, Chris Howard, Carole Ivin, Jane Jenson, Dave Kang, Elliott Lehman, Frances Lehman, Andy Martin, Cathie Martin, Jim Murphy, Tom Nichols, Ken Oye, Fran Piven, David Plotke, Andy Polsky, Darsie Riccio, Mark Ritchie, George Ross, Kay Schlozman, Stanley Schlozman, Joe Schwartz, Catherine Shapiro, Ken Sharpe, Gordon Silverstein, Bob Skomro, Dean Spiliotes, Charles Stewart III, Suzi Teegarden, Ruy Teixeira, Lowell Turner, Rick Valelly, Dirk Vandewalle, Margaret Weir, and Howie Winant.

I was assisted at various stages of this project by a number of diligent research assistants, the most outstanding of whom were Erin Green, Amy Semet, and Tamar Tal. At the University of North Carolina Press, I have had the good fortune to work with several fine (and patient!) editors, including Lew Bateman (before his departure), Kate Torrey, Paula Wald, and my crack copyeditor, Stevie Champion.

My biggest debt, however, is to the members of my most nontraditional family who have provided me with unstinting support over the years: my stepson Toby Gabriner, my daughter-in-law Mara Hook, and Toby's other parents Bob Gabriner and Eileen Goldman; my sister-in-law Margaret Baran; my nephew and niece Ben and Rebecca Rees; my father- and mother-in-law, Saul and Betty Baran; my brother John Shoch and my other sister-in-law Sheree Shoch; and, of course, my parents: my mother, Gertrude Shoch, and my late and much-missed father, David Shoch, who would have taken immense pride in this book, as he did in (almost!) all my accomplishments.

There is one person, though, to whom I owe everything: my wife and partner for virtually my whole adult life, Barbara Baran. Not only has she stuck with me through stunningly different and sometimes difficult phases of our lives; she also took precious time from her own demanding work to expertly edit my unmanageably long manuscript down to an almost readable length. As I write this I do not know where our lives will take us next, but I do know that we will make the journey together.

Trading Blows

Introduction

Since the late 1970s, and for the third time in the past one hundred years, the world has witnessed a major wave of economic "globalization"—of trade, production, and finance.[1] During this period, as both imports and exports grew as proportions of American national wealth creation, trade policy in particular was often forced to the top of the daily economic headlines and to the forefront of American political debate.

During the quarter-century-long "golden age" that followed World War II, the U.S. position as the world's dominant economic power allowed a succession of American governments to take the lead in promoting multilateral trade liberalization. But by the late 1960s, American firms found themselves increasingly challenged in domestic and global markets by Japanese and Western European producers, whose war-devastated home economies had been rebuilt. The resulting protectionist pressures were largely contained in the 1970s by the decline in the value of the dollar in the early part of the decade. But the soaring dollar of the first half of the 1980s combined with preexisting problems of competitiveness to produce an explosion of the U.S. trade deficit. Imports surged, especially from Japan and other newly industrializing East Asian countries, and exports sagged, contributing to the erosion of the nation's core mass production industries. This prompted widespread fears of "deindustrialization" and new demands for a tougher trade policy.

Much of this pressure in the early and mid-1980s was directed toward curbing the rising tide of imports. While various bills to limit the import of specific products either never passed both houses of Congress or were vetoed by President Ronald Reagan, a number of significant "voluntary restraint" and other agreements were reached with foreign countries to slow the import of cars, steel, textiles, machine tools, semiconductors, and lumber.

During the second half of the 1980s and continuing into the following decade, trade-related stress spread from the nation's basic industries to formerly competitive high-technology sectors, due in part to the inability of high-tech firms to penetrate the relatively closed Japanese market. The focus of U.S. trade policy now shifted toward the export side, as the government increasingly resorted to the practice of "aggressive unilateralism" or "aggressive reciprocity." Washington tried to pry open closed foreign markets through the threatened retaliatory imposition of U.S. import barriers if negotiations failed to convince other countries to reduce their own barriers. This principle was most famously embodied in the "Super 301" provision of the Omnibus Trade and Competitiveness Act of 1988. Under Super 301, Japan—whose growing economic might provoked considerable public and governmental anxiety—was cited in 1989 by President George Bush for its failure to open its markets for a number of goods to foreign producers. Such pressure on Japan, especially for access to its auto and auto parts markets, continued during the first three years of the Clinton administration, which during this time pursued what was termed a "results-oriented" trade policy.

Due both to the post-1985 fall in the value of the dollar and the restructuring and revived competitiveness of many American firms, the U.S. trade deficit declined in the late 1980s and early 1990s. As a result, U.S. trade policy saw another partial shift of focus, this time toward further trade (and investment) liberalization via the negotiation of regional and multilateral agreements, often with low-wage countries, which sparked furious battles over what was now widely called economic "globalization." Following an intense congressional struggle, in late 1993 the Clinton administration, strongly backed by internationally oriented business interests, won approval of the North American Free Trade Agreement (NAFTA) and then more easily a year later achieved ratification of a new General Agreement on Tariffs and Trade (GATT) treaty.

After the approval of the GATT deal, however, and with the trade deficit rising again, progress toward further trade liberalization stalled. In particular, two attempts to renew Clinton's "fast-track" negotiating authority—which require that free-trade agreements be awarded quick up-or-down votes in Congress, without amendments that could unhinge such pacts—were defeated in the House of Representatives in 1997 and 1998.

But in yet another turnaround that appeared to restore some momentum to the trade liberalization process, after another tough fight in the House, Congress in 2000 approved permanent normal trade relations (PNTR) with China,[2] a step thought to be necessary if American firms were to receive the wide range of market-opening and investment concessions made by Beijing in a recent agreement with the United States in order to get into the World Trade Organization (WTO).

The Changing Politics of Trade

The politics surrounding many of these issues has differed in important ways from that characteristic of trade policy-making before 1980. From World War II through the 1970s, U.S. trade policy was largely the preserve of a relative handful of affected business interests, executive branch officials, and congressional committee leaders. After 1980, however, trade was drawn into the realm of highly public "macropolitics," as conflict over import curbs, unilateral market-opening actions, fast-track proposals, and free-trade agreements often engaged the energies of the president, the entire Congress, a wide range of interest groups, and even sectors of the general electorate.

Most important for our purposes here, trade policy also became more partisan after 1980. Between the Civil War and the Great Depression, trade was the principal issue dividing Democrats from Republicans. Following the experiences of depression, world war, cold war, and postwar prosperity, however, a bipartisan consensus in support of liberal trade gradually emerged, especially at the presidential level, that lasted through the 1960s. But beginning in the early 1970s and notably in the 1980s, trade once again became the subject of intense partisan contention.

Analysts have identified a range of causal factors in determining recent American trade policy. International relations scholars have focused on "structural" or "systemic" factors, including the relative size and productivity of competing national economies, the international division of labor, interstate bargaining, international regimes and norms, and international security structures. Other observers, recognizing the limitations of such approaches, which treat the state as a unitary actor, have called for a "return to domestic factors" or the opening of the "black box" of domestic politics.[3] Thus, they have explored the influence in the trade policy-making process of economic interest groups and coalitions, the autonomy of state actors, the structure of electoral and state institutions, economic ideas, and even public or voter opinion.

Yet relatively little attention has been paid to the role of political parties.[4] This perhaps is not surprising, since until fairly recently most scholars have understood American parties in this century to be in secular, irreversible decline in the electorate, as organizations, and in government, while trade has been viewed as the preeminent nonpartisan issue since the end of World War II. The scant discussion of this topic that has occurred suggests that party competition has had little impact on U.S. trade policy choices or outputs since 1980.

This book is intended to fill the current gap in scholarship by examining the nature, determinants, and impact of party competition over U.S. trade policy during the past two decades. It joins with other recent works in arguing that although parties may have grown weaker in some respects, in other ways they have actually grown stronger in the past quarter century; party coalitions have become more socially and ideologically distinctive; the parties in government, or at least in Congress, have become more polarized; and national party organizations, again especially in Congress, have become more active and effective.[5] More specifically, I revise the widespread view that party competition has not much mattered to the conduct of U.S. trade policy.

Party Trade Policy Positions and Their Determinants

One of the reasons for the academic neglect of this subject may be that the dynamics of party competition over trade in the United States in the 1980s and 1990s have been disconcertingly diverse and complex. This has produced considerable disagreement among those few scholars who have studied the topic.

With respect to the evolution of party positions on trade, some scholars have been impressed by the degree to which U.S. trade policy since 1980 has remained relatively bipartisan in nature.[6] Noting opposition to product-specific protectionism and support for the NAFTA, GATT, and China accords by Reagan, Bush, and Clinton, many writers argue that U.S. presidents regardless of party are almost always free traders, due to their diverse national constituencies and their foreign policy responsibilities. Other analysts see presidential selection imperatives sometimes forcing both Democratic and Republican presidents to support protectionist or fair-trade policies, the latter intended to combat foreign "dumping,"[7] subsidies, and nontariff barriers (NTBS) to imports.[8]

Various authors have also noted the substantial support in Congress by both parties for the 1984 Trade Act, for the final version of the landmark 1988 Trade Act, for the 1988 Canada-U.S. Free Trade Agreement, for the 1994 GATT agreement, and at least in the Senate for PNTR with China, as well as for more aggressive executive action on imports and exports alike. Some are struck by the extent to which Republican as well as Democratic lawmakers continue to back an open, liberal trading order, due either to (1) the persisting "lessons" of the infamous Smoot-Hawley Tariff Act of 1930: that protectionism produces trade wars, economic collapse, and the repudiation of the party it is associated with,[9] or (2) pressure from internationally oriented business interests on both sides of the aisle.[10] Other analysts take note of growing bipartisan support for tougher trade policies and slowed trade liberalization.[11] In either case, ideological commitments and constituency pressures are said to have influenced legislators' trade policy preferences without respect to their party membership.

Still other scholars have underlined the significance of intraparty divisions and cross-partisan coalitions on trade, which are said to have regional, ideological, or institutional sources.[12] These splits and coalitions have been observed in congressional voting on commodity-specific legislation like the various textile quota bills of the 1980s or on George Bush's 1991 fast-track bill and the NAFTA, GATT, and China agreements, during the last four presidential primary campaigns, and between the pro–free-trade presidential and the more protectionist-leaning congressional wings of each party.

Against these views, although in agreement with still other authors, I will argue that since 1980 there has been a significant differentiation of the parties' trade policy stances, albeit much more in Congress and especially in the House, than at the executive level.[13] In Congress, the Democrats have fought for tougher fair-trade and even protectionist policies and against various trade liberalization initiatives, while the Republicans have more consistently backed free trade. Fairly sharp partisan divisions have been manifested, for example, during fights over the auto "domestic content" bill in 1982, various drafts of the Omnibus Trade and Competitiveness Act of 1988, and the 1997 and 1998 fast-track bills. Even voting on product-specific quota legislation and on the 1991 fast-track bill, the NAFTA agreement, and the PNTR bill was at least partially partisan in nature.[14]

Democratic and Republican presidents and White House candidates have similarly differed over trade, both on the campaign trail and in office, although such differences have been less sharp than those between the congressional parties. Democrat Bill Clinton initially assumed a tougher stance toward Japan than had his Republican predecessors Ronald Reagan and George Bush. The Clinton administration also helped pass a North American Free Trade Agreement that was accompanied by stronger labor and environmental side agreements than Reagan or Bush would have accepted and pushed (unsuccessfully) to add a fast-track plank with labor and environmental provisions to the 1994 GATT implementing bill. Finally, the Clinton administration slowed its drive for further trade liberalization in 1995–96 and backed away from launching a new round of international trade negotiations at a WTO meeting in Seattle in late 1999.

The sources of this new partisan division on trade, one that has actually involved a reversal of the parties' historic positions, lie in constituency pressures, personal ideologies, and partisan electoral ambitions. Before the 1930s, the Democrats had been the party of southern agricultural export interests and thus also of low tariffs, a stance the party continued to adhere to into the 1960s. But shortly thereafter and intensifying in the 1980s, the Democrats embraced an "economic nationalist" or even a protectionist position due to pressure from their core labor constituents, their ideological commitment to an active government role in the economy, and, during the Reagan-Bush years, their hopes that trade could work as a popular campaign issue to help their party strengthen its position in Congress and regain control of the White House. As for the Republicans, before the depression they had been the party of northern manufacturers and high protective tariffs. Following World War II, however, the Republicans became more closely tied to internationally oriented business interests and middle-class consumers and more ideologically committed to a more limited government economic role. Thus gradually since about 1950 and more decisively since 1970, the GOP has emerged as the party of free trade.

I would certainly not want to deny that the past two decades have seen important instances of bipartisanship on and intraparty conflict over trade policy. Instead, I will reconcile various apparently contradictory empirical findings by arguing first that for reasons of constituency, ideology, and campaign issue creation, the main tendency in Congress with respect to trade policy, again mainly in the House, has been toward partisan differentiation. The degree of differentiation has varied, depending on (1) the distributive characteristics of different policy proposals, and particularly the degree to which such proposals divide capital and labor, the core constituencies of the Republican and Democratic parties respectively, (2) the balance of business and labor influences inside *both* parties, (3) the salience of the proposals under debate to key swing constituencies, (4) the ideological composition of the two congressional party caucuses, (5) the propensity of members of the president's party to support, and of opposition party members to oppose, the president's position, (6) the related inclination of the president and members of the two congressional parties either to compromise or to pursue "strategies of disagreement," (7) the lobbying efforts of the president and congressional party leaders, and, sometimes, (8) whether partisan control of the White House and the two houses of Congress is unified or divided.

I will also contend that although there has been some partisan differentiation over trade policy at the executive level, this has been moderated on the one hand by the president's role as representative of the interests of the nation as a whole, which inclines him toward free trade, and on the other hand by electorally driven pressures on presidents of both parties to sometimes support protectionism or more often fair trade.

The Impact of Parties on Trade Policy Choices and Outputs

The preceding paragraphs have discussed only the determinants of party trade policy positions. In the American system of separated powers, party influence on trade policies themselves is institutionally mediated by the interaction between Congress and the executive. Here again, scholars disagree over the extent to which parties matter to actual trade policy choices and outputs.

Most of those authors who see no—or only rhetorical—differences in the parties' positions on trade or who mainly see intraparty divisions naturally also find no partisan policy effects.[15] Other analysts, perceiving more significant differences between the parties on trade, although usually only in Congress, have explored whether it matters to the substance of trade policies if partisan control of Congress and the executive is unified or divided. Some argue that divided government produces tougher or more restrictive policies than does unified government, while others find no consistent effects.[16]

In the following chapters I will both argue and demonstrate that since 1980 party competition has in fact significantly affected U.S. trade policy choices and outputs, albeit in different ways under varying determinant conditions. More specifically, the nature and magnitude of these partisan effects have depended on (1) the preferences of the president (not always for unmitigated free trade), (2) the preferences, size, and internal cohesion of the congressional party caucuses, (3) the willingness of the president and the congressional parties to compromise, and, under certain conditions, (4) whether control of government is unified or divided.

I will show first that under the conditions of divided government that prevailed during the Reagan-Bush years, strategic interaction between the parties produced a moderate but real toughening of U.S. trade policy. With the unraveling of the New Deal political order during the "stagflation" crisis of the 1970s and the subsequent explosion of the U.S. trade deficit in the early 1980s,[17] the Democrats embraced elements of an "economic nationalist" accumulation strategy to improve their sagging political fortunes. During this period Democrats sought both to defend their core labor constituents and, via a tactic I label "heresthetics," to exploit the trade issue for still wider partisan advantage among key swing voters and groups, including blue-collar "Reagan Democrats" and even some business interests, by raising the relative salience of the issue on the nation's political agenda. Toward these ends, Democratic presidential candidates pressed the trade issue on the hustings, while congressional Democrats used their control of one or both houses of Congress to introduce and actually pass popular trade bills.

Through a process of what I call "policy contagion," this Democratic pressure in turn forced reluctant Republican presidents to strategically retreat from their normal free-trade commitments. Thus, Reagan signed the Omnibus Trade and Competitiveness Act of 1988, and both he and Bush took import-curbing or market-opening administrative actions to reduce GOP electoral vulnerability and quell party-amplified pressures for still more protectionist actions.

The return of unified Democratic government during the first two years of Bill Clinton's presidency also had real if complex effects on the conduct of U.S. trade policy, as Clinton—"triangulating" or "tacking" between free and fair trade—pursued "export-led growth" as a central element of an activist new accumulation strategy that he hoped would revive the Democrats' fortunes. In interaction with the Democrat-controlled Congress, Clinton's induced and personal preferences produced trade policies that were paradoxically both more aggressive and more liberal than were the policies that the Reagan and Bush administrations pursued under divided government or that a second Bush administration could have followed had Bush been reelected.

On the one hand, Clinton launched a "results-oriented" Japan trade policy, intended to pry open Tokyo's unfairly closed markets, that at least from 1993 to 1995 was more aggressive than the one that either Reagan or Bush had conducted. Not a simon-pure free trader, Clinton was prompted to adopt such an approach by several party-related factors: the preferences of his own core labor backers along with those of the blue-collar swing voters who had supported Ross Perot or even George Bush, his desire to strengthen his relations with liberal congressional Democrats, his ideological commitments to an active government, and his personal belief that Japan was a "different" kind of industrial power.

On the other hand, in successfully pushing NAFTA (and *perhaps* the GATT treaty) through Congress, Clinton, presiding over a unified Democratic government, won a victory for trade liberalization that a Republican president at that time would probably have been unable to engineer. His tough Japan policy notwithstanding, with his presidential responsibility for the "national interest," Clinton was at heart a free trader, if not an unadulterated one. But as a Democratic president, and with the help of internationally oriented business interests, he was able to persuade at least some normally protectionist members of his congressional party, no longer inclined to posture against him as they had against his GOP predecessors, to join the Republicans and pro-trade New Democrats to provide the critical support necessary to pass NAFTA. This was a feat that neither Reagan nor Bush, facing the same Democrat-controlled Congress, would likely have been able to accomplish.

Also important, the NAFTA struggle continued a pattern begun during the 1991 fast-track fight and that would persist throughout the Clinton years in which the shifting fortunes of trade liberalization initiatives would be largely determined by the preferences and level of cohesion of House Democrats.

Following the Republican takeover of Congress in 1994, partisan factors continued to influence the conduct of U.S. trade policy. The shift to an "inverted" form of divided government did not initially strengthen support for free trade, as might have been expected with Republicans in charge of both the House and the Senate.

In 1995–96, looking toward the upcoming presidential election, Clinton hoped to win back those working-class Democrats and Perot voters who, disgusted by his strong support for the NAFTA and GATT accords, had either sat out the 1994 elections or voted for Republican candidates. The White House therefore escalated the U.S. dispute with Japan in the first half of 1995 and postponed further trade liberalization efforts until after the election.

With his reelection safely secured, Clinton then tried to restart the trade liberalization process with Republican support, but these efforts were blocked by mainly Democratic opposition. In late 1997 House Democrats, joined by a minority bloc of conservative Republican nationalists, united to defeat an administration-sponsored bill to renew Clinton's fast-track negotiating authority that contained no commitment to the inclusion of core international labor and environmental standards in any new free-trade agreements. The solid Democratic opposition was due to the loss of a substantial number of New Democratic seats in the 1994 elections, weak White House and business lobbying efforts, and above all the strong campaign by organized labor against the measure. A year later House Democrats similarly turned back another GOP-sponsored fast-track bill.

Toward the end of his presidency, Bill Clinton, hoping to lighten the stain of impeachment and burnish his historical legacy, launched a final, two-pronged offensive on behalf of free trade. First, in late 1999 he traveled to a WTO meeting in Seattle to start a new round of international trade negotiations. The meeting famously collapsed, again for mostly partisan reasons. With little business enthusiasm for a new round and organized labor still vociferously opposed to his trade agenda, Clinton, anxious to secure labor's support for the presidential campaign of his vice president, Al Gore, chose to blow up the meeting by urging the WTO to seriously address the issue of international labor standards, an idea strongly opposed by developing nations.

The next year, however, Clinton pushed hard on a trade issue that he viewed as sufficiently critical to his overall legacy that he was again willing to provoke a major split in his own party and risk Al Gore's presidential hopes: congressional approval of "permanent normal trade relations" with China. After a battle royal, PNTR was approved in the House thanks to the expanded ranks and activities of the New Democrats, an energetic administration lobbying effort, and especially the massive campaign waged by the business community. Together these forces overwhelmed a somewhat divided labor movement and fractured the Democratic caucus, producing enough Democratic support to pass the PNTR bill (the same measure was later easily passed by the Senate). Yet another restructuring of partisan forces gave new life, if perhaps only temporarily, to the process of trade liberalization.

In the rest of this book I will expand on and substantiate these arguments and claims. In the next chapter I provide a synthetic theoretical framework to help understand the dynamics and impact of party competition over trade policy. I then briefly apply this framework to the history of U.S. trade policy from the Civil War to Ronald Reagan's election as president in 1980. The next three chapters examine trade policy-making during the Reagan era, emphasizing the role of policy contagion in producing a "strategic retreat" from free trade. A similar analysis is then presented of the politics of trade policy during George Bush's presidency. Three chapters then follow on Bill Clinton's triangulations between free and fair trade and the recent congressional battles over trade liberalization. A final chapter summarizes and draws conclusions from the work.

1

Parties and Trade Policy

A Theoretical Framework

How can we understand the complex dynamics and policy impact of party competition over American trade policy since 1980? This chapter presents a theoretical framework to help answer this question.

In developing this framework, I have drawn on "realist" social theory, according to which events or states of affairs are determined by multiple and contingently interacting structures—rule-maintained social relationships that selectively distribute life chances and resources—and other generative mechanisms. These include both "deep" or relatively fixed economic, political, and cultural structures and more malleable, though still durable, institutions and ideas often embedded in them that to varying degrees influence actor identities, interests, and preferences and constrain and enable actor behavior and interactions. Causal power is also exercised by knowledgeable, reflexive, and often strategic individual and collective actors, whose activities—facilitated by the material, symbolic, and informational resources they command—both reproduce and sometimes transform deep structures, institutions, and ideas as well as their own agency.[1]

With respect to expressly political actors, I further posit, adopting a variable or context-dependent notion of rationality, that within the competitive representative institutions of advanced capitalist democracies, party officeholders should be viewed as purposive albeit cognitively limited, or "boundedly" rational, actors who simultaneously pursue reelection, institutional influence, and good policy. The less politically secure such officials are, however, the more likely they are to subordinate their other goals to the imperatives of reelection.

Guided by these broad conceptualizations, in what follows I will begin this study by reviewing, critiquing, and amending existing explanations of party trade policy positions that emphasize the influence of constituency pressures, ideology, and the party holding the presidency, approaches that all have explanatory value under certain determinant conditions. These factors generally produce at least some differentiation of party stances, although when trade issues are salient for key swing constituencies, including voters and organized interests, this can produce partisan convergence as well as hybrid forms of party competition identified as "policy contagion" and "triangulation." Finally, I show how electoral and political institutions mediate the influence of other factors on party trade policy positions, producing different levels of partisanship in the two branches of government, while sometimes internally fragmenting and at other times further polarizing the parties.

Next, to explain the influence of party competition on actual trade policy choices and outputs, I show how in the American system of separated powers, this influence is institutionally mediated by the interaction between Congress and the executive. Trade policies are mainly determined by the balance and unity of partisan forces in Congress in interaction with a president inclined toward liberal trade. But certain patterns of unified and divided control of government can have determinant effects on policy choices and outputs. Last, trade policy can take on a partisan cast due to direct constituent and ideological influences on the president.

I then demonstrate how party trade policy positions and choices are influenced and constrained by international economic, political, and security structures and institutions and by interstate bargaining processes. Finally, I embed the preceding arguments in a still more encompassing, temporally oriented theory of successive, provisionally integrated "political orders." The institutions, rules, and norms of such orders help to "regulate" the structures of the national economy, and these orders emerge and decline in complex conjunction with the periodic crises and transformations of the same structures. I show how party economic strategies and policies, including trade policies, shape and are in turn shaped by these political orders. The chapter concludes with an explanation of the narrative method employed in this work.[2]

Party Trade Policy Positions

In the scholarly literature, party trade policy positions are usually explained by one or more of three factors: constituency pressures, ideology, and which party controls the presidency.[3] In fact, all of these perspectives have value, depending in part on the distributive and other characteristics of the specific policy under debate.

In constituency-based views, party trade policy positions are determined by the preferences and political influence of competing coalitions of economic interests, including classes, industries or sectors, firms, or various categories of workers. These groups' preferences are in turn determined either by the relative abundance of capital or labor or by their locations in the international economy.[4] Their influence on party positions is wielded first through the voting strength of (1) their attentive members, mainly recipients of large, concentrated, and immediate policy benefits or costs, and secondarily (2) their more numerous but inattentive members, whose "potential" preferences lawmakers try to anticipate to forestall their activation at the next election. Formally organized interests exercise additional influence through their abilities to overcome collective action problems to (1) turn out voters to the polls, (2) make campaign contributions for the purpose of persuading inattentive voters, (3) engage in "inside" or direct lobbying to (a) convey to lawmakers interpretations of the likely consequences of proposed policies for their constituents or of those constituents' preferences themselves, (b) promise lawmakers campaign assistance or threaten its withdrawal,[5] and (c) shape lawmakers' personal policy preferences, and (4) undertake "outside" or grassroots and media lobbying to both influence public opinion and mobilize citizens to contact their representatives.[6]

Prominent among the proponents of constituency-based views are Ronald Rogowski and Stephen Magee, William Brock, and Leslie Young, who have separately argued that in the United States since World War II, the Democratic Party has supported protectionism due to its close ties to labor, which as a whole is hurt by the wage-depressing effects of imports, while the Republicans have backed free trade as a consequence of their political dependence on business, which again as a whole benefits from exports.[7]

Other scholars observe that in the present period, both labor and capital are often internally divided on trade issues due to different forms of exposure to the international economy. Some also argue that business and in some cases labor provide electoral and/or financial support for both Republicans and Democrats. Thus, these analysts maintain that party trade policy positions are determined by different intraparty balances of domestically oriented, import-competing interests and internationally oriented export and multinational interests, including their respective workforces.[8]

For example, in one of two hypothetical views he advances, Timothy McKeown assumes with Rogowski and with Magee, Brock, and Young that the two major political parties represent distinct classes—that is, the Republicans represent capital and the Democrats labor.[9] But he also assumes that both capital and labor are fractured along industry or sectoral lines over trade policy. This produces intraparty differences but also interparty division to the extent that the balance of strength differs between domestically and internationally oriented business and labor interests within the Republican and Democratic Parties respectively. In his second view, McKeown, joined in part by Michael Hiscox and David Vogel, sees both parties as cross-class sectoral coalitions, with each party including both domestically and internationally oriented sectors. The result again will be intraparty differences over trade policy along with interparty division to the extent that the balance between these sectors inside the two parties differs. Thomas Ferguson and Peter Gourevitch also see both parties as sectoral coalitions, but in their cases, domestically and internationally oriented sectors, or what Ferguson calls "investor blocs," are often in different parties. The result is intraparty unity and interparty conflict over trade policy.[10]

HETEROGENEOUS PREFERENCES, HETEROGENEOUS PARTIES

In my view, the second group of analysts is correct in regarding the trade policy preferences of both capital and labor in the current era as heterogeneous.[11] I would also suggest that the McKeown/Hiscox/Vogel variant of this perspective most accurately describes the influence of economic actors on party trade policy positions, although I think that these influences produce greater interparty differences over trade than these authors believe is the case.

Since the Civil War, businesses of all kinds have generally tilted toward the pro-market Republicans, especially in presidential contests.[12] Since the 1950s the influence within the party of expanding internationalist and thus pro-trade interests—exporters, multinational corporations, retailers selling imports, and manufacturing firms depending on imported inputs—has grown relative to that of once dominant, domestically oriented, and often protectionist concerns. The GOP also attracts substantial support from skilled manufacturing workers, who are disproportionately concentrated in competitive, internationally oriented businesses, and some, though much less, backing from unskilled and semiskilled workers, who are heavily concentrated in import-competing, domestically focused industries.

Unskilled and semiskilled workers have voted largely Democratic since the class-based New Deal realignment committed the Democratic Party to an active role for government in economic and social welfare policy. The relative influence of these workers within the party is amplified by their level of unionization, which is higher than that of those skilled workers in competitive sectors who also vote Democratic; by their disproportionate strength within labor's powerful umbrella organization, the AFL-CIO; and by the overwhelming tendency of the labor movement as whole to back Democratic candidates. Since the 1960s, unskilled and semiskilled workers and their unions in import-competing industries have turned away from free trade and toward protectionism and fair trade. Deploying its human and financial resources in both primary and general elections, labor has pushed the Democrats in the same direction.

Business support for the less ideologically sympathetic Democrats is usually relatively limited in presidential contests; in congressional races, it comes mostly from those access-seeking firms that pragmatically donate most of their campaign contributions to incumbents of both parties as well as to whichever party controls the two houses of Congress.[13] The effects of business support on Democratic trade policy preferences are mixed. Opposition to free trade inside the party is reinforced by the influence of some import-competing firms, while certain exporters and multinational corporations, geographically diffusing their activities throughout the country, including into formerly protectionist regions, apply counteracting pressure on the Democrats on behalf of free and sometimes fair trade.

The presence of internationally and domestically oriented interests within each party coalition creates internal conflict for cross-pressured lawmakers representing increasingly heterogeneous constituencies.[14] This often results in intraparty splits and cross-partisan coalitions on issues like product-specific quota bills, the North American Free Trade Agreement (NAFTA), and permanent normal trade relations (PNTR) with China, thus also limiting interparty differences over trade issues. The recent growth of internationalist influence inside the Democratic Party also mitigates that party's support for classic protectionism and contributes to the bipartisanship occasionally observed on moderate fair trade bills, like the Omnibus Trade and Competitiveness Act of 1988, or liberalizing legislation seen as doing little harm to labor's interests, like the 1994 bill to implement the treaty that concluded the Uruguay Round of the General Agreement on Tariffs and Trade (GATT).

But I would also argue that the dominance of internationalist business interests inside the Republican Party tilts the GOP toward reasonably consistent support for free trade, while contra Vogel in particular, organized labor retains sufficient strength relative to other forces within the Democratic Party such that the party remains considerably more critical of free trade than its Republican rival. The result is significant albeit variable core constituency-based partisan differences over trade policy, especially in the House of Representatives, and even on issues like NAFTA and PNTR with China.

Such differences will be greatest when (1) capital and labor are sharply and intensely, if never completely, divided on trade issues,[15] (2) business is solidly committed to the Republican Party, a condition that is likely to prevail when the GOP is firmly in control of Congress, leading access-oriented business interests to direct the bulk of their campaign contributions to the Republicans, thus reducing their leverage on Democratic lawmakers, (3) additional polarizing pressures are exerted during primary campaigns by ideologically extreme voters, activists, and donors, (4) there are credible, trade-related general election threats of abstention by Democratic labor activists and voters, and of the withdrawal of campaign funds by business and labor contributors to the Republicans and Democrats respectively, and (5) the number, attentiveness, or expected turnout of often-centrist swing voters is low,[16] thus putting a premium on energizing each party's base of activists and core supporters.[17]

THE ROLE OF SWING VOTERS AND INTERESTS

Sometimes, however, there are large blocs of swing voters for whom trade is or might become politically salient enough to determine how they will cast their ballots.[18] Blue-collar, mostly nonunionized Reagan Democrats in the 1980s, Ross Perot's supporters in the first half of the 1990s, and white-collar suburbanites working in high-technology export industries are examples of swing groups for whom trade policy has often been salient in recent years. On some occasions, an issue can become salient to even the normally inattentive median voter, who will almost certainly also be a swing voter. More commonly, such voters' preferences are latent or "potential," but as noted earlier, these preferences can sometimes be activated by various "instigators" at the next election if incumbents take actions opposed by newly aroused voters.[19]

Less frequently noted is the existence of swing business interests, wedded to neither and thus open to supporting either party, whose campaign contributions are determined not by broad ideology, incumbency, or majority status, but rather by party and candidate positions on specific issues, sometimes including trade. High-tech companies are currently the preeminent example of such swing business interests. For ease of exposition, I will often, if somewhat unhappily, refer to swing voters and business interests together as swing "constituencies."

In some circumstances, reelection-minded politicians of both parties will take trade policy positions that converge, either prospectively or adaptively, on those held by attentive and, to a lesser extent, potentially attentive swing or even median voters, or by swing business interests. Such partisan convergence is most likely to occur in individual electoral jurisdictions when (1) swing constituencies are numerous relative to committed partisan groups, (2) trade is a highly salient issue, most likely for policies expected to confer large, immediate, and concentrated effects, and for which the causal links between lawmakers, policies, and effects are clear, (3) swing constituency preferences are relatively homogeneous, and the polarization of the parties' core business and labor supporters over trade is low, both of which are most likely in the case of product-specific policies that concentrate *either* substantial benefits *or* costs, but not both, on firms and workers in a particular jurisdiction, and (5) elections are highly competitive or imminent.

On trade issues, the parties can converge in support of free trade if swing constituencies in a certain jurisdiction are concentrated in internationally oriented industries or, less commonly, if swing voters are attentive mainly to their preferences as consumers. Or the parties can both back "tough" trade policies if swing constituencies are instead concentrated in import-competing sectors or swing voters are principally attentive not to their narrow material interests but rather to their "social concerns" for low-wage workers or to their anxieties over the erosion of the nation's industrial base, the loss of national economic supremacy or sovereignty, and so forth. Such responsiveness to swing or median voter and group preferences may, for example, partly explain the substantial bipartisan support for the fair-trade approach contained in the mammoth Omnibus Trade and Competitiveness Act of 1988.

Ideology-Based Views

Proponents of ideology-based views argue that party trade policy positions are determined mainly by their members' shared normative and causal beliefs. Such beliefs are variously shaped by personal biography and experience, the prevailing economic and political culture, the interpretation of important historical precedents, and the ideas of policy intellectuals functioning in "epistemic communities" or "discourse coalitions," whose work is sometimes funded by corporate-backed policy planning groups and think tanks.

In some cases, party members' trade preferences may be determined mainly by their beliefs as to what constitutes good policy for the nation as a whole. These beliefs, however, will usually be congruent with the preferences of constituents. But in other cases, policy-seeking rather than vote-seeking behavior will put lawmakers at odds with their constituents, sometimes even producing a risk of electoral defeat. This kind of ideological "shirking" is most common when the political opportunity costs of such behavior are low, that is, when trade issues lack salience or constituency preferences are evenly divided,[20] or during a president's second term, when the pressure of campaigning for reelection is past.

For more consistently vote-seeking politicians, ideas may serve as "focal point" solutions in strategic situations of multiple equilibria; that is, they may use ideas to help them select from a set of equally viable or politically "efficient" choices. Alternatively, lawmakers may rely on ideology or ideas when they are otherwise unclear as to how to best advance their reelection prospects. Under conditions of high uncertainty, when politicians, economic actors, and voters are all unsure of their interests, reelection-minded lawmakers often draw on ideas to provide shared understandings of such things as (1) the depth, causes, and relative priority of different economic problems, (2) the appropriate technical policy solutions to these problems, including the severity of the exogenous structural constraints that may limit policymakers' options, (3) the likely consequences of various policies for different groups within the population, and (4) the actual preferences of their constituents. Policymakers may use ideas about such matters to shape distributive and allocative policies that will benefit attentive but uncertain core and swing constituencies. Or they may rely on a specific economic ideology to develop stabilization policies intended to win the support of more inattentive retrospective voters, sometimes even in the face of opposition from attentive core and swing constituencies, by producing strong aggregate economic performance. In either of these ways, ideas can serve lawmakers as cognitive "road maps" or guides for action.[21]

In the case of trade policy, ideological or ideational influences are likely to be greatest on generic legislation to reform the trade remedy laws rather than on product-specific or even trade liberalization measures that provide relief for or benefits to a number of industries. Because the widely dispersed benefits and costs conferred by generic legislation usually predominate over the kind of concentrated effects that spur interest group mobilization, lawmakers' voting will be influenced less by interest group pressures than by their ideologically colored perceptions of the likely impact of these measures on the welfare of both the nation and their various constituents.

For different scholars, however, ideology can contribute either to bipartisanship, interparty conflict, or intraparty division over trade policy. In the first of these camps, Judith Goldstein argues that during and after the Great Depression, members of both parties became convinced that the highly protectionist Smoot-Hawley Tariff Act of 1930 had either caused or at least deepened the depression and in so doing had contributed to the Republican rout in the 1932 election. Thus, in the half century after World War II, Democrats and Republicans alike eventually joined and maintained an institutionalized, bipartisan ideological consensus—in support of the view that liberal trade simultaneously promotes growth, efficiency, stable prices, and employment—that has largely survived the international economic upheaval and record trade deficits of recent years. Although since 1980 the Democratic Party in particular has sometimes postured on behalf of a tough trade policy for electoral advantage, neither party has sought a return to the discredited protectionist policies of the past, and party positions on trade have remained only marginally differentiated from each other.[22]

Other authors maintain, contra Goldstein, that at least since 1970, ideology has contributed to substantial partisan divisions over trade. For example, Stanley D. Nollen and Dennis P. Quinn, in their study of congressional voting on trade legislation during 1987–88, find evidence that the Democrats, as an adjunct to their pro-government Keynesian economic ideology, embraced either protectionism, fair, or "strategic" trade in order to foster short-term growth, employment, and consumption, while Republicans, as a complement to their pro-market, anti-interventionist, neoclassical views, backed free trade in the name of efficiency and stable prices.[23] Other analysts have also found independent, party-linked ideological effects on congressional voting on key trade issues in the 1980s and 1990s. Still other scholars point instead to the recent emergence of *intra*party ideological divisions between free traders and economic nationalists in both parties.

In the following chapters, I will argue that the bipartisan, antiprotectionist ideological consensus of which Goldstein writes has remained largely in force down to the present day. But at the same time, I see more partisan "conflict within consensus" than Goldstein finds, some of it due to the ideological divisions discussed by Nollen and Quinn, as well as the secondary importance of intraparty ideological disputes over trade policy.

The Endogenous Shaping of Preferences

Party elites have alternatives to either passively accommodating voter and group preferences or pursuing their own ideological beliefs. Instead, parties can try to endogenously influence the balance of political forces by employing a number of "preference-shaping" tactics.[24]

Ideologically oriented or policy-seeking politicians can try to strengthen their positions in at least three ways. First, via processes of "policy feedback," a governing party—in the United States, especially one in control of both branches of government—can use public policies to improve the circumstances, and thus win the retrospective support, of both its core supporters and swing constituencies, while often simultaneously weakening or shrinking its opponent's base of support.[25] Second, both parties in government, but above all the president, can attempt to mobilize supportive voters and organized interests to pressure lawmakers to back the parties' respective positions.

Third, employing media-assisted, symbol-laden problem, causal, and solution "stories" or "narratives," policy-seeking parties—especially the one occupying the White House—can undertake persuasive efforts to change the content or direction of swing constituency preferences (politicians also try to change each other's preferences through persuasion).[26] This can involve, for example, attempts to alter perceptions of the likely consequences, that is, the costs and benefits, of a proposed policy or to redefine or reframe what a specific issue is actually about.[27] Particularly in the United States, though, with its fragmented political institutions and independent media, the partisan manipulation of the preferences of either inattentive voters or attentive constituencies with strong, sometimes structurally determined views is not easy, and consequently the direction of these preferences on most issues tends to remain rather stable.[28]

More electorally minded or vote-seeking parties frequently employ a variant of another tactic that William Riker labels "heresthetics."[29] In a complex and uncertain world, with many issues competing for the attention of cognitively limited, boundedly rational voters and interests, parties often try to shape the field of political conflict to their advantage by influencing not the fairly stable *direction* of swing constituency preferences on various issues, but rather the relative *intensity* of those preferences. That is, parties will struggle over the relative salience of various issues by attempting to manipulate the political agenda. Such heresthetical maneuvering is an essential component of the third major explanation of party trade policy positions.

Incumbency-Focused Views

The last approach to explaining party trade policy positions is an incumbency-focused one in which party stances are determined by which party controls the presidency (the "in" party).[30] Proponents of this view begin by assuming that irrespective of his partisan attachments, the president supports free trade, because (1) representing a diverse national constituency—including diffuse consumer as well as concentrated producer interests—the president's political fortunes are tied to the overall health of the economy, which benefits from substantial gains from trade, and (2) the president is responsible for the peaceful conduct of U.S. foreign policy, which could be jeopardized by a trade war.[31]

Meanwhile, the vote-seeking "out" party, that is, the one not in control of the White House, will tend to posture against free trade. Sensing that the president's strong free-trade stance and record may be unpopular or at variance with the preferences of attentive swing or even median voters as well as certain business interests, the out party adopts the position held by these groups in an effort to dislodge the president's party from power. Beyond accommodating the preferences of attentive swing constituencies in this way, however, the out party is very likely to seek greater partisan advantage by engaging in heresthetical efforts to further heighten the relative salience of the trade issue for both actually and potentially attentive swing constituencies.

Building on work by Riker and E. E. Schattschneider on the maneuvers of political "losers," various contemporary analysts have argued that during periods of electoral "dealignment," a recently defeated out party will often launch a search for "wedge" issues that can be used to fracture the in party's electoral coalition, expand its own base of support, and thus help it regain majority status.[32] Focusing solely on voters, these analysts argue that during presidential and congressional campaigns as well as in Congress itself, the opposition party will attempt to introduce new issues onto the agenda or to raise the relative salience of or expand the scope of conflict over existing issues, debate over which may previously have been confined to insulated policy subsystems. In either case, the out party's aim is to use such issues to gain power by surfacing dissatisfaction with the in party among key groups of both actually and, perhaps even more important, potentially attentive swing voters, while retaining and ideally strengthening the support of the party's core constituents.

Given both their uncertainty as to the electorate's preferences and the heterogeneity of decision rules employed by voters,[33] heresthetically minded parties will experiment in an evolutionary, trial-and-error fashion with different kinds of issues. To appeal to relatively inattentive retrospective voters during electoral campaigns, an out party will often highlight the in party's performance failures on "valence" issues—typically peace and prosperity—especially in the wake of some "focusing" crisis or event.[34] To attract more attentive "directional" voters who support candidates who propose to move policy away from the status quo in a desired direction, the out party will sometimes stress "position" issues that the president's party appears to be on the "wrong" side of, while itself advocating the direction preferred by the majority of such voters.

Finally, to win the support of highly attentive "proximity" voters who back candidates whose views are spatially closest to their own, the out party will emphasize position issues on which the in party's stances are distant from the preferences of such proximity voters, while positioning itself closer to the views of these voters. This last type of issue can be used to win the votes of "issue publics" or "intense minorities" who benefit from or are harmed by policies conferring concentrated benefits or costs,[35] but also to attract campaign contributions from highly attentive business interests that are dissatisfied with the governing party's policies.

During the Reagan-Bush era, congruent with the predictions of both incumbency-focused and heresthetical approaches, out-party Democrats in Congress and on the campaign trail regularly assumed a tough, "economic nationalist" stance on trade issues in an effort to both strengthen their congressional position and recapture the White House from the more free-trading Republicans. For similar reasons, congressional Republican leaders attempted to delay voting on the Uruguay Round GATT agreement and the China PNTR bill, and longtime free trader and GOP presidential nominee Bob Dole assumed a slightly more aggressive trade posture during the 1996 presidential campaign. This approach, however, does not explain constituency and ideologically based GOP support for NAFTA, Clinton's 1997 fast-track proposal, and eventually the GATT treaty and the China bill.

The incumbency-focused view is really only one example of what John Gilmour calls a "strategy of disagreement," in which one party tries to exploit an unpopular stance assumed by its rival.[36] If due to core constituency or ideological commitments, it is the out party that takes a broadly unpopular position, the president, too, may seize the opportunity both to adopt the views of attentive swing groups on the issue and to heresthetically raise the salience of the issue in order to attract the support of other potentially attentive swing voters or interests.[37] During the 1992 presidential campaign, for example, George Bush pushed NAFTA as a wedge issue to break Hispanic voters in the Southwest away from the Democrats, while Bill Clinton—not an unmitigated free trader—later escalated a long-running trade dispute with Japan to firm up the support of his core labor constituents and win new backing from working- and lower-middle-class swing voters and certain export interests.

Hybrid Forms of Party Competition: Policy Contagion and Triangulation

The strategic interaction over time between two parties with preferences that for various reasons are initially differentiated can produce either continued partisan divergence, partisan convergence, bipartisan compromise, or intraparty divisions. But such strategic interaction can also eventuate in hybrid forms of party competition involving dynamics of both divergence and convergence.

One such hybrid is what, following Maurice Duverger, I call "policy contagion." Policy contagion results when an out party's position, arising from core constituency pressures, ideological commitments, or heresthetical maneuvering, either proves to be, or is thought likely to become, attractive to actually and potentially attentive swing voters. This forces the reelection-minded in party to adopt a weaker version of its opponent's position in order to undercut the out party's support and thus defuse the issue politically.[38] (In Congress, a similar process has been referred to as "mimicking.")[39] As demonstrated in the first half of this book, policy contagion played a key role in the conduct of U.S. trade policy throughout the Reagan-Bush years, when the Democrats regularly pressured the Republicans in Congress and the White House to at least moderately toughen their own trade policy positions.

A second hybrid form of party competition has come to be known as "triangulation," so labeled by a former adviser to Bill Clinton, Dick Morris. Often incorrectly described as simply a centrist strategy of adopting median voter positions, triangulation also includes (1) tacking or zigzagging between liberal and more conservative positions on alternating issues, (2) simultaneously advancing liberal and conservative policies, and (3) combining liberal and conservative ideas in the same policy proposal. Party candidates and officeholders will sometimes employ these tactics on issues that the large mass of median voters is inattentive to or confused about. Pursuing what is essentially a "coalition of intense minorities" strategy, politicians in these circumstances triangulate by cobbling together coalitions of, or zigzagging between, various attentive constituencies, including both core party supporters and swing groups.[40] As demonstrated in the second half of this book, during his presidency Bill Clinton regularly triangulated between free- and fair-trade positions.

The Influence of Institutional Factors

Patterns of party competition over trade policy become still more complex when the role of electoral and political institutions in mediating or refracting the influence of other factors on party trade policy positions is more fully considered. The separation of powers, bicameralism, federalism, single-member districts, winner-take-all elections, staggered terms, committee and congressional leadership structures, and so forth mostly fragment but sometimes unify the parties. In addition, and with some signs of reversal in recent years, the parties have been institutionally weakened or displaced in this century by (1) the rise of the civil service, the administrative presidency, the welfare state, the fiscal state, and the incumbency advantage, and (2) the advent of candidate-centered campaigning resulting from the expansion of direct primaries and an increased dependence on personally acquired campaign money, media, and consultants.

These institutional factors and developments have contributed to the evolution of parties that are best understood not as unified and tightly disciplined organizations but rather as loose "leadership coalitions," revolving around and largely directed by their principal public officeholders.[41] The positions of such parties can diverge or converge, to be sure, but intraparty divisions, including between coherent interest-and-ideology-based "factions,"[42] and cross-partisan coalitions are also common.

INSTITUTIONAL EFFECTS IN THE EXECUTIVE BRANCH

Since the 1930s the differentiation of the parties' stances on trade policy has been substantially less at the executive level than in Congress. Many authors, including proponents of the incumbency-focused view, argue that presidents of both parties, Democrats as well as Republicans, tend to be free traders due to the president's large, heterogeneous national constituency, which on the whole benefits from free trade, and to his foreign policy responsibilities. Thus, Presidents Reagan, Bush, and Clinton all supported a new GATT agreement, both Bush and Clinton backed NAFTA, and Clinton fought for PNTR with China. In Congress, on the other hand, Democrats since the 1960s have been more likely to be critical of free trade than Democratic presidents, thus producing greater interparty differences, because they represent smaller and disproportionately northeastern and midwestern districts and states, in many of which their core labor constituents have considerably greater influence than is the case in the nation as a whole.

The institutionalist account of the alleged preference of presidents of both parties for free trade has clear limits, however.[43] For reasons of constituency as well as ideology, Republican presidents before the Great Depression were strong proponents of high tariffs. And particularly since the 1960s, presidents and candidates of both parties, but primarily labor-backed Democrats, have also sometimes deviated from unqualified support for free trade, thanks in part to the influence of two other institutional factors: the presidential primary and the electoral college.

Pressure on Democratic candidates from organized labor during primary campaigns often produces commitments to trade policies that are less liberal than those advocated by more business-friendly Republican candidates (the same is true during congressional primary contests).[44] The tough trade policies toward Japan backed by Walter Mondale and to a lesser extent Michael Dukakis and Bill Clinton during the 1984, 1988, and 1992 presidential primary campaigns were largely motivated by their desire to curry favor with their core labor constituents.

The role of the electoral college sometimes inclines presidential candidates of both parties to promise support for trade policies, usually product-specific in nature, that appear likely to confer substantial benefits on, or "surgically" redistribute income to, employers and their employees in large, electorally competitive or swing states.[45] When a normally free-trading Republican president is pressured to make such promises during a campaign by a more protectionist or fair-trade-inclined Democratic candidate, as often occurred during the Reagan-Bush years, this can be understood as a case of policy contagion.

INSTITUTIONAL EFFECTS IN CONGRESS

The institutional structure of Congress similarly mediates the influence of other factors on the trade policy stances of the congressional parties.[46] Senators of both parties are more likely to support free trade than their counterparts in the House, resulting in narrower party differences in the upper chamber. This is because (1) states are larger than House districts, meaning that many House Democrats represent districts that have higher concentrations of protectionist-inclined workers than do the more diverse states represented by Senate Democrats, (2) relatively more agricultural and less unionized, and therefore more pro–free-trade, states are overrepresented in the Senate, meaning that free traders are also overrepresented in that chamber's Democratic caucus,[47] (3) senators have longer terms than do representatives, giving ideological free traders among Senate Democrats more leeway than similarly inclined House Democrats to resist pressure from their labor constituents, (4) party leadership in the House is stronger and more centralized than in the Senate, and (5) the Senate has foreign policy responsibilities not shared by the House.

Within the House and Senate alike, the fragmented nature of representation can either amplify geographically based intraparty divisions or encourage interparty conflict over trade issues. On the one hand, product-specific protectionist policies—for example, the textile quota bills of the 1980s—that concentrate substantial benefits on both employers and their workers in a distinct geographic area will usually be supported by members of both parties in that area. Conversely, such policies will be opposed by members of the two major parties in areas that are expected to bear the policies' concentrated costs, often meaning foreign retaliation against these areas' exports. The result will be the formation of cross-partisan coalitions on such issues.

Alternatively, the fragmented nature of Congress can contribute to partisan polarization on trade when, in keeping with their information-saving liberal and conservative images, the parties' bases of support are geographically differentiated in a manner that corresponds to or overlaps with the geographic distribution of different industrial sectors. Thus, the liberal voters who have disproportionate strength in the industrial Northeast and Midwest elect protectionist or fair-trade Democrats, while more conservative voters who predominate in the high-tech and agricultural areas of the West, the Plains states, and parts of the South elect free-trade Republicans.[48]

Electoral redistricting can also heighten geographically based, *intra*regional partisan differences over trade policy when blue-collar voters, often employed in import-competing industries, are "packed" into homogeneously Democratic districts, whereas white-collar voters working in export-oriented or non-traded sectors are packed into homogeneously Republican districts.[49]

Internal congressional structures can also magnify existing tendencies toward either partisan fragmentation or polarization. The decentralized committee system, responsive to localized interests, encourages fragmentation, again particularly on product-specific issues.

On the other hand, the power of the congressional majority party leadership, notably in the more centralized House, to reward and punish caucus members through committee appointments, bill referrals, legislative scheduling, influence on the rules under which bills are debated and voted on, the facilitation of intraparty logrolls, the use of its "whip" organization, the mobilization of external constituencies, the provision of campaign assistance, and so forth can be used to foster partisan polarization.[50] This is most likely to occur when "conditional party government" prevails, that is, when the preferences of the members of the majority party are already sufficiently homogeneous such that majority party members are willing to delegate substantial authority to party leaders.[51]

In these circumstances, the majority party leadership can heighten intra-party cohesion and sometimes interparty divisions through its efforts to increase the "brand-name" value of its party label. First and probably most important, majority party leaders can introduce onto the congressional agenda, or assist the introduction of, popular legislative proposals that unify their party caucus (and often elicit minority party opposition), while attempting to suppress proposals that split their party and measures backed by the minority party.[52] Congressional Democratic leaders pushed trade legislation in this way throughout the Reagan-Bush years. Second, to facilitate actual passage of its favored legislation and thereby establish a strong, information-saving, and thus electorally useful party "record," the leadership uses its powers to heighten internal party loyalty and discipline, thus moving the outcome of roll-call votes away from the chamber median toward the median of the governing party caucus.[53] In pursuit of their own electoral and policy goals, minority party leaders can also use their more limited powers, principally those of persuasion, to heighten the cohesion of their followers on roll-call votes, further increasing partisanship. Leaders of both parties regularly acted in these ways on trade issues in the 1980s and 1990s.

Bicameralism can either decrease or increase partisanship on trade issues.[54] For example, if the more pro–free-trade Senate and the more protectionist-leaning House disagree on a piece of trade legislation, bipartisan compromise may be necessary to pass some version of the bill, as was the case with the final version of the Omnibus Trade and Competitiveness Act of 1988. Alternatively, Democratic free traders in the House facing labor or other constituent pressure to back a protectionist bill can safely vote for and even help pass the measure, thus increasing party polarization over it, when they are confident that the Senate, especially if controlled by Republicans, will eventually kill the legislation. This occurred during House voting on both the domestic content bill of 1982 and early drafts of the 1988 trade bill.

THE EFFECTS OF INTERACTION BETWEEN THE BRANCHES

The separation of powers and the consequent interaction between the executive and legislative branches influences presidential and especially congressional party positions. First, in some policy domains, either in response to the complexities of governing or to avoid blame for possible policy failures, Congress has delegated considerable authority to the executive branch.[55] This is likely to depoliticize and thus reduce congressional partisan conflict in these policy areas, as it did during much of the post–World II era, when Congress, susceptible to pressure from powerful, import-competing producer interests, sought to avoid protectionist logrolls by delegating trade negotiating authority to the more insulated president. Of course, Congress can reclaim that authority, reopening party divisions in the process.

Intraparty unity across the branches and interparty division within Congress over trade are encouraged by the predisposition of members of the president's party to support him and of members of the out party to oppose him, a view that is consistent with an expanded incumbency-focused perspective. The president's partisans in Congress may sometimes back him on trade issues even if, for reasons of constituency or ideology, they do not share his pro–free-trade preferences.[56] This is because (1) they feel some personal loyalty to him as a fellow party member and do not want to embarrass him, (2) they want his support on more politically or personally important nontrade issues, (3) they want his personal campaign assistance, (4) their reelection prospects depend in part on his perceived record of accomplishment, and (5) he possesses substantial persuasive skills, which are most effectively deployed on issues he cares intensely about.[57] Considerations like this can explain the votes for NAFTA and PNTR by some congressional Democrats who would have opposed these deals had a Republican been in the White House instead of Bill Clinton.

Members of the opposition party in Congress, on the other hand, generally have few incentives to cooperate with the president, whose legislative success is often viewed as a threat to their electoral and policy goals.[58] This may be true of trade policy, as the incumbency-focused view suggests, when the president's free-trade views are out of sync with the preferences of key swing constituencies.

Still, because in the American separation of powers system, the president and members of Congress are elected separately, have staggered terms, and thus have different bases of political support, members of the president's party may oppose him on some issues due to strong pressures from their constituents or ideological commitments. This often forces the president to form ad hoc, cross-partisan coalitions with members of the opposition party who agree with him, also based on constituency or ideological considerations.[59] From 60 to 85 percent of House Democrats broke with Bill Clinton to oppose his various major free-trade initiatives, while from 67 to 75 percent of House Republicans regularly joined with the president to support these bills.

Finally, and again made possible by the separation of powers, patterns of congressional partisanship over trade policy may be affected by whether control of the executive and legislative branches is unified or divided. These effects, however, also depend on (1) how other factors combine to influence the preferences of the president and the congressional parties, and (2) the inclination of both sides to compromise, a propensity that is influenced by two additional institutional factors: the presidential veto and the Senate filibuster.[60]

Under unified government, interparty conflict will occur when both congressional parties are otherwise internally unified and externally opposed and the president's views reflect those of the dominant faction of his congressional party, and all sides prefer confrontation over compromise. On trade policy, such conditions are most likely to pertain when the more liberal party controls both branches of government. In these circumstances, constituency, ideological, and incumbency-focused influences will all tend to point in one direction within one party and in the opposite direction inside the other party.

Partisanship will be muted under unified government when the congressional parties are internally split, the president's preferences are at odds with those of the dominant majority party faction, and the parties prefer cooperation over conflict. Again on trade policy, these conditions are most likely to occur when it is the more protectionist party that exercises unified control of government. Assuming that the president is a free trader despite his party affiliation, incumbency-focused influences will reduce congressional partisanship, since at least some members of the generally pro-trade majority party will posture against the president's stance, while the president will usually be able to win some normally protectionist members of his party over to his position. During the unified government phase of his presidency in 1993–94, Bill Clinton's strong support for NAFTA contributed to splits in the Republican and above all the Democratic Party over the issue.

Party conflict is usually more intense under unified than divided government, since bipartisan or cross-partisan coalitions are more often required in the latter circumstances to enact legislation that both parties can claim credit for. But divided government can either foster or dampen party divisions under determinant conditions. The likelihood of either outcome will be influenced not only by the factors cited above, but also by the disagreement that often exists under divided government within both parties over whether there is more political support to be gained, especially from swing constituencies, by compromising to pass moderate legislation or by insisting on the enactment of less watered-down measures. In particular, the out party in control of Congress is likely to be divided over whether to pursue either "a bill or an issue."

When the more protectionist of the two parties controls Congress, the congressional parties are relatively homogeneous and opposed, the president is a committed free trader, and all sides opt for confrontation rather than compromise, divided government will magnify party conflict over trade policy. In an incumbency-focused variant of this case, an out party, to improve its electoral prospects with swing constituencies, may use its control of one or both houses of Congress to pursue a "strategy of disagreement" by heresthetically introducing, publicly posturing on behalf of, claiming credit for passing, or even provoking what has been termed a "blame game" veto of tough, popular trade legislation.[61] The Democrats pursued this kind of strategy on trade policy throughout the Reagan-Bush era of divided government, whereas congressional Republicans often rallied in support of GOP presidents, resulting in heightened partisanship.

Knowledge that a president under the preceding form of divided government will most likely veto any protectionist measures can also increase opposition party support for and thus party polarization over such legislation. Ideological free traders within the out party, pressured by core labor constituencies or hoping to score political points against the president's party, can vote for an otherwise objectionable bill, secure in the belief that the president's veto is unlikely to be overridden (although the president may be prodded via a process of policy contagion into taking tough administrative actions to avoid losing swing voter support). We saw such behavior by congressional Democrats in voting on the domestic content and textile bills of the 1980s and early versions of the 1988 Trade Act.

In other circumstances of divided partisan control, when the more free-trade–inclined party controls Congress, the two parties are again relatively homogeneous and opposed, the president is a strong free trader, and all sides resist compromise, divided government is still likely to be accompanied by party conflict over trade policy. Such divisions will probably be less sharp than in the previous case, however, since some members of the pro-trade majority party will posture against the president's position and some normally protectionist members of the president's party will support him. The partisan fight in Congress over Bill Clinton's 1997 fast-track proposal was waged under these kinds of conditions.

On the other hand, partisanship will be muted under divided government if the congressional parties are internally split, the president sometimes favors fair as well as free trade, or all sides are willing to compromise. This can lead to the formation of cross-party or bipartisan legislative coalitions as well as to executive-level policy contagion. Again, we saw occasional examples of this during the Reagan-Bush years. The somewhat dampened partisanship surrounding the PNTR fight also fits into this category.

Parties and Policy Choices

The discussion thus far has examined only the factors that explain party trade policy positions, not the supply of trade policies themselves. In the American system of separated powers, policies once again result from the interaction between Congress and the executive. What difference does party competition, mediated by this institutional interaction, make to actual trade policy choices and outputs?

Not much, say some of the most prominent analysts of U.S. trade policy. Drawing on ideology-based arguments, these scholars maintain that mindful of the disastrous Smoot-Hawley experience, legislators of *both* parties have delegated product-specific trade policy authority to the president, assumed to be a free trader, and executive branch agencies whose heads he appoints in order to deflect protectionist pressures. As incumbency-focused theories suggest, the out party may sometimes adopt a symbolically tough posture on trade to please its constituents and politically discredit the in party, as the Democrats regularly did during the Reagan-Bush years and the Republicans did to a much lesser extent during Clinton's presidency. But neither party, including the apparently more protectionist Democrats, has intended to overturn the existing liberal policy orientation.[62] Thus, the import-curbing and unilateral market-opening actions taken by the Reagan and Bush administrations in response to Democratic posturing only marginally toughened U.S. trade policy, and the return of a Democrat-led unified government in 1993 produced not backsliding into protectionism but rather approval of the liberalizing NAFTA and GATT agreements.[63]

I would argue, however, that by minimizing the degree to which legislators' constituents expect results rather than just agreeable positions, this view underestimates the extent to which Democratic pressure led to a tougher U.S. trade policy during the 1980s and cannot really explain why 60 and 65 percent of House Democrats respectively voted against Bill Clinton on NAFTA and PNTR and why 80 and 85 percent of House Democrats respectively opposed the 1997 and 1998 fast-track bills, enough to defeat both of them. This perspective also has difficulty accounting for why, for largely partisan reasons, the Clinton administration itself got tough with Japan in 1993–95, retreated from trade liberalization in 1995–96, and blew up a World Trade Organization (WTO) meeting in late 1999.[64]

Other analysts have explored the influence of parties on trade policy choices and outputs by focusing on the difference made by varying patterns of partisan control of Congress and the executive. Whereas most general studies have limited themselves to investigating the difference unified versus divided government makes to legislative productivity—variously concluding that divided government can produce gridlock, compromise, or even the competitive "bidding up" of public policy[65]—work in the area of trade policy has looked into the implications of different patterns of partisan control for the actual content of policies.

The best known, if problematic, view is that of Susanne Lohmann and Sharyn O'Halloran, who argue that divided government produces trade legislation that is more restrictive of executive authority and tariff levels that rise faster than is the case under unified government.[66] Along with most other analysts, they maintain that, regardless of party membership, all presidents are inclined toward free trade. Legislators, on the other hand, are said to be more protectionist than presidents, due to the small size and homogeneous nature of congressional districts, which allows great influence to concentrated producer interests. Again, chastened by the lessons of Smoot-Hawley, Congress has delegated tariff-setting authority to the executive to avoid protectionist logrolls. But under divided government, to prevent the president from helping his party's districts at the expense of those held by the majority party in Congress, the majority is forced to constrain the executive in order to produce at least the level of protection that it would have received under the logrolling outcome. The result, according to this variant of the incumbency-focused argument, is more restrictive trade legislation and more rapidly rising tariffs than unified government produces.

As David Karol contends in a recent article, however, Lohmann and O'Halloran's argument is fatally flawed by their assumption that congressional party differences arise only in reaction to which party controls the presidency.[67] Instead, constituency-induced partisan differences can outweigh the incentives for in-party members to support and out-party members to oppose the president on trade issues, incentives that are central to the incumbency-focused view.[68] Karol argues, therefore, that divided government has no consistent effect on trade policy, that is, its influence depends on the preferences of the congressional parties as well as on which party controls Congress. More specifically, and again assuming that the president is a free trader, divided government impedes trade liberalization when the more protectionist party controls Congress and facilitates it when the more liberal party is in control.

Karol's argument is mostly convincing. Yet he unduly minimizes the influence on the behavior of the congressional parties of which party holds the presidency. At the same time, despite his focus on Congress, he neglects the importance of the size and internal cohesion of the congressional party caucuses. By combining Karol's Congress-centered perspective, with the addition of attention to the size and unity of the congressional parties, and the incumbency-focused approach, we can make at least a few fine-grained if highly conditional statements on the effects of unified and divided government on trade policy choices and outputs.

First, trade policy is likely to be most liberal under a unified government controlled by the more pro-trade party holding a large and cohesive congressional majority. If, however, the governing party's congressional majority is narrow and internally divided while the more protectionist minority party is highly unified, trade liberalization will be impeded.

Second, a unified government controlled by the more protectionist party will slow trade liberalization when the ruling party's congressional majority is large and cohesive. This same form of unified government, however, may facilitate trade liberalization when the majority party in Congress is split. Among other reasons, this can occur because, as William Keech and Kyoungsan Pak suggest, the president may be able to persuade some normally protectionist members of his party, already disinclined to oppose him, to join minority party members whose pro-trade commitments outweigh their own inclinations to posture against the president.[69] Due to its majority status, there will likely be more such converts to free trade in the president's party than there will be minority party free traders who shift to a protectionist posture in order to discredit the president.[70] Thus, because Bill Clinton was able to convince some of his fellow Democrats to support NAFTA, the return to unified government in 1993 may have aided the pact's approval; had George Bush tried to push the agreement through the same but more hostile Democratic Congress, it might well have been defeated.[71]

Third, and the flip side of the second point, under a divided government in which the party in control of Congress is the more protectionist one and its majority is both large and internally unified, trade liberalization is likely to be slowed.[72] In these circumstances, members of the majority party will push for tough trade legislation to satisfy their constituents' or their own personal preferences or to heresthetically raise the relative salience of the trade issue to the point where it can serve as an effective congressional or presidential campaign issue. In most instances, some form of compromise legislation will pass, sometimes over the president's veto, or the president will be forced through a process of policy contagion to retreat from his free-trade views and take tough import-curbing or market-opening administrative actions of his own to keep his party from losing the support of key swing constituencies. Such dynamics were at work throughout the Reagan-Bush era, as divided government amplified Democratic pressure on free-trading Republicans in Congress and the White House, producing the massive Omnibus Trade and Competitiveness Act of 1988 and repeated episodes of administrative policy contagion.

If, however, under this same pattern of divided government, the more protectionist majority party in Congress is internally split, more liberal trade policies can result. In 1991 intra-Democratic divisions allowed George Bush to win the new fast-track authority he needed to begin negotiating NAFTA, although the Democrats forced Bush to produce an "action plan" to allay concerns that the proposed pact would not adequately protect workers, consumers, and the environment.

Finally, a divided government with a president from the more protectionist party and a large, unified liberal congressional majority will promote trade liberalization, especially if the president's congressional copartisans are divided, including by his persuasive efforts. These were the conditions that allowed the approval of PNTR in 2000. If under the same pattern of divided partisan control, however, the liberal congressional majority is narrow and not fully unified, the more protectionist minority party is highly unified, and the president's persuasive endeavors are relatively ineffective, then trade liberalization will be impeded, as it was during the fast-track fights of 1997 and 1998.

All of these analyses of partisan influences on trade policy choices and outputs underestimate the importance of another factor: presidents who occasionally deviate from their free-trade courses. Granted, it is unlikely that a contemporary president of either party will actually embrace out-and-out protectionism, although Republican presidents certainly did so before the Great Depression. But for reasons of constituency or ideology, a president from the less liberal party—in this era, the Democrats—may pursue at least fair trade rather than pure free trade or decline to pursue further trade liberalization. For instance, prompted by his own beliefs and a concern to firm up his working-class and other core support, Bill Clinton called for the negotiation of labor and environmental side agreements to accompany NAFTA, tried (unsuccessfully) to add a fast-track measure containing labor and environmental provisions to the GATT implementing bill, and conducted a "results-oriented" trade policy toward Japan that at least in 1993–95 was tougher than the Japan policies of Republicans Ronald Reagan or George Bush. For similar reasons, Clinton refrained from sending a new fast-track proposal to Congress in 1995–96 and torpedoed the 1999 Seattle WTO meeting, in the latter case to help Al Gore secure labor support for his upcoming presidential run.

Even presidents from the more liberal party may be forced by electoral imperatives—that is, fear of losing swing constituency support—to pursue fair-trade policies. We have already seen how this can occur under divided government due to pressure from the more protectionist majority party in Congress. Such policy contagion can also result directly from presidential campaigns, when pressure from the candidate of the more protectionist party forces the more liberal party's nominee to promise and then as president to deliver tougher trade policies. The Reagan and Bush presidencies provided examples of this kind of policy contagion, most famously when shortly before the 1984 election Ronald Reagan, under pressure from Democratic nominee Walter Mondale, announced and later followed through on his intention to negotiate voluntary restraint agreements with foreign steel producers.

Systemic Influences

The determinants of party trade policy positions and choices are not purely domestic in nature. Also significant are a number of international or systemic structures and processes that narrow but do not eliminate partisan differences over trade policy; such structures and processes thus limit but do not negate partisan effects on actual trade policy choices and outputs.[73] The most important of these systemic influences are the structures of the world economy, best understood in the present period as a "globalizing," though not yet fully global, configuration of arms-length market exchanges, multinational and transnational corporations, and interfirm networks, including horizontal "strategic alliances" and vertical "commodity chains," underpinned by a more thoroughly globalized financial system.[74]

A first international economic-structural influence would appear to privilege a liberal and bipartisan approach to trade policy. Some analysts argue that growing international market integration, arising from declining transportation and communications costs, has increased both the political salience of the trade issue and the efficiency, price, and employment opportunity costs of economic closure, especially if such closure provokes foreign retaliation.[75] The result is greater actual or potential median voter support for free trade and the consequent convergence of both parties toward a free-trade stance.

There are three problems with this argument. First, in nations like the United States that have large and still relatively closed economies, the opportunity costs of a limited dose of protectionism, or the benefits of a modest liberalization of trade policy, are apt to be rather small.[76] Consequently, median voter trade policy preferences in such countries may well be both weak and ambiguous, providing little centripetal pull on the two parties. Second, in the short run, and absent foreign retaliation, protectionist measures can actually raise domestic output and employment. Finally, recent developments in trade theory have demonstrated that although there may well be static or one-time gains from trade liberalization (in the form of lower prices, etc.), it is much less clear that trade is good for economic growth in the longer run.[77] Thus, whether the median voter on balance even benefits from freer trade is also unclear. For all these reasons, group, ideological, and incumbency influences of the kind discussed earlier are more likely than median voter preferences to determine party trade policy positions, with a correspondingly reduced likelihood of partisan convergence on trade issues.

Other authors argue that structural trends in the world economy have produced domestic *group* alignments that will likely eventuate in bipartisan support for liberal trade. The growing integration of the international economy or previous steps toward trade liberalization are said to have expanded the ranks of exporters, import-using firms, and multinational companies that benefit from and thus support free trade. Meanwhile, over time import-competing interests are either driven out of business or forced to adjust to more competitive market conditions, reducing their demand for protection.[78] This shifting balance of structurally determined group preferences is expected to translate into growing support for free trade inside both parties.[79]

This is likely to be a prolonged process, however; despite their attrition, some of the losers from free trade, especially segments of organized labor, may well be more effective in mobilizing their human and financial resources to oppose further liberalization than winners are in organizing to support it, as occurred during the 1997 fast-track fight. To the extent that internationally and domestically oriented interests give their allegiances to different political parties, as to an important degree business and labor do in the United States, the group-based partisan differences over trade policy will continue.

Internationalization or globalization produces another broad constraint on economic policy-making that can structurally privilege a liberal approach to trade: international capital mobility.[80] Theorists of the "structural dependence on capital" have argued for some time that the threat of an investment "strike" or the "flight" of productive capital can restrain governments from enacting policies that undermine "business confidence."[81] More recently, attention has focused on financial market confidence and the policy effects of the heightened mobility of financial capital.

Such capital mobility is most commonly viewed as a constraint on the autonomy of a nation's macroeconomic and especially its interest rate policy. But the threat or reality of capital mobility can also prevent or reverse aggressive, party-driven trade policies that financial and currency markets fear might spark an economically destabilizing trade war. In a flexible exchange rate system, such policies can produce a flight from, and thus a drop in the value of, the offending nation's currency, followed by a politically damaging rise in inflation and interest rates and perhaps eventually a recession. This kind of downward pressure on the dollar in part caused the Clinton administration to retreat from its tough, results-oriented Japan policy in 1994 and 1995. However, because the likelihood and adverse consequences of capital flight in response to tough trade policies are subject to debate, again mainly in relatively large, closed economies, some space will usually be left for constituency and ideologically driven partisan differences over trade policy.

Interstate interactions and bargaining over trade, though in part determined by domestic—including partisan—conflicts, can also react back upon or endogenously influence those conflicts.[82] First, the threat or reality of foreign retaliation against a nation's exports can reduce partisan-inspired pressure inside that country for a tougher trade policy. Second, if the concessions won by a nation's negotiators in an international trade agreement fall well within that country's "win-set," that is, if they are acceptable to the core constituencies of both out and in parties, party conflict is likely to be dampened. If, on the other hand, such concessions are deemed insufficient by key out party constituencies, party conflict may be intensified.

International institutions and "regimes"—specifically, the General Agreement on Tariffs and Trade and its successor, the World Trade Organization—have sometimes been conducive to the bipartisan conduct of American trade policy.[83] By reducing transaction costs, providing information about and policing countries' behavior, strengthening domestic free-trade coalitions, and encasing ideas and norms that influence the preferences of state actors, the GATT and the WTO have facilitated interstate cooperation on behalf of free trade, thus sometimes dampening domestic party conflict over trade issues. Yet the effectiveness of such institutions and regimes is usually due to the prior convergence of participating governments' preferences, which, in turn, are mainly influenced by domestic, including partisan, politics. Should GATT or now WTO constraints threaten the electoral interests of government leaders, a political backlash and heightened partisanship over trade policy may result.

International security structures can also mute partisan divisions over trade issues. The need to unite against a common military adversary may mitigate potential trade conflicts among rival economic powers.[84] One likely domestic consequence of this alliance imperative—experienced, for example, by the United States during the Cold War—is a bipartisan consensus in support of a liberal trade policy. Of course, should security tensions diminish, trade conflict among former military allies and domestic partisan divisions over trade policy may arise anew.

Periodizing Political and Economic Development: Toward a Theory of Political Orders

The dynamics and policy consequences of party competition over trade policy can vary by historical period. This section offers a general, synthetic approach to understanding the periodic nature of the evolution of American party competition and policy-making.

Political Orders and Party Strategies

Following a number of analysts, I would suggest that American political development has been characterized by a succession of relatively stable "political orders" linked by periods of disorder, partisan "realignment," and institutional transformation. At the metatheoretical level, the dynamics of these orders and the transitions between them can be illuminated with the help of Margaret

Archer's temporally oriented realist or "morphogenetic" approach to the agent-structure problem. According to this approach, (1) structures and agents are analytically separable and interact on a temporal basis, (2) structure necessarily predates the actions that transform it, and (3) structural transformation necessarily postdates those actions.[85] Of course, though informed by Archer's highly abstract view, the framework presented below will necessarily be developed at a more concrete level.

As explained by David Plotke, a political order—or what others call a partisan "regime"—is a durable, integrated mode of organizing and directing social life in an advanced capitalist society.[86] Influenced but not determined by the "deep structures" of the nation's economy, its constitutionally prescribed political institutions, and its political and industrial culture, each political order has its own party system, including dominant and minority parties and corresponding electoral coalitions, its own distinct policy agenda, and its own forms of state organization and political discourse.

The institutions of a political order are also central elements of what French "regulation" school theorists term a "mode of regulation," a wider ensemble or "matrix" of complementary norms, institutions, policy subsystems and networks, and other "governance" mechanisms, both public and private, including, for example, forms of corporate and labor market organization, consumption norms, and the industrial relations, monetary and financial, economic policy, innovation, educational, and social welfare systems. By securing property rights, establishing a stable structure of exchange relationships, providing public goods, and generally reducing uncertainty and social conflict, a mode of regulation fosters investor confidence and stabilizes an associated "regime of accumulation," a historically specific structure of production and consumption relations articulated to a relatively autonomous "technological paradigm" and linked to and influenced by the structures of the international economy.[87] To complete the circle, a well-functioning regime of accumulation generates increasing returns and a long wave of rapid investment and growth that firms up support for the prevailing political order and its dominant party.[88]

The various governance mechanisms of a political order and the wider mode of regulation with which that order is entwined do not, however, automatically stabilize the regime of accumulation. Rather, at least a core of often abrading and even colliding institutions and subsystems must be provisionally integrated through the activities of officials of the dominant party, which usually holds unified control of government. These officials' positions as ambition-and-ideology-driven "macro-actors," sitting atop multiple institutions, give them the autonomy, reflexivity, access to resources, and incentives to overcome collective action problems necessary to undertake such an "order-building" task.[89]

Principal among these integrative activities are the formulation, implementation, and institutionalization by governing party officials—assisted by top state administrators, policy experts, and supportive interest groups—of several types of projects and strategies that help unify both public and private actors, thus also facilitating the cohesion of the mode of regulation. These include what British state theorist Bob Jessop calls "hegemonic projects,"[90] which secure broad public consent by articulating compelling visions of both the "good society" or the "national interest" and the state's role in achieving these goals, and "state projects," which unify state and other actors around internal efforts at governmental organization and reform.[91]

Most important for our purposes, however, are interlocking sets of economic ideas that Jessop terms "accumulation strategies." An accumulation strategy simultaneously includes an overarching "economic ideology," influenced by both general party ideology and specific currents of professional economic thought, which in turn subsumes a number of partial but complementary "policy paradigms" that operate in discrete macroeconomic, regulatory, industrial, and, of particular concern to us here, trade policy subsystems.[92] Such ideologies and paradigms help cognitively limited, boundedly rational actors to develop shared perceptions and understandings of the causal dynamics of the economy, the severity and sources of its problems, appropriate policy goals and techniques, and the likely consequences of various policies. An accumulation strategy also includes a corresponding "policy package," the elements of which are implemented inside the various subsystems, which consists of a specific mix of macroeconomic stabilization policies, allocative policies that affect the overall size of government, and distributive policies, including trade policies, that influence the distribution of income and wealth.[93] Finally, an accumulation strategy includes a set of policy discourses or "frames" intended to shape public and group preferences.

In the relatively stable or "normal" phase of a political order, inside each subsystem, the prevailing policy paradigm and its associated policies will vertically unite a dominant "advocacy coalition," including public officials, experts, and interest group representatives, that is more or less aligned with the governing party.[94] At the same time, intersubsystem conflict and abrasion are reduced and horizontal coordination and integration aided by the governing party's general economic ideology and the bargains it facilitates.[95]

A successful accumulation strategy, however, must also help bind together broader, durable electoral and governing coalitions. While resonating with the prevailing political culture or "universe of political discourse," such a strategy— including its economic ideology; its allocative, distributive, and, secondarily, its stabilization policies; and its policy frames—will express or, under conditions of high uncertainty, discursively constitute the preferences, coordinate the behavior, and foster the coalition-maintaining partisan loyalty of key private and public actors.[96] These include (1) core party constituents, activists, and donors, including business and labor interests, (2) certain attentive swing voters and economic interests, and (3) executive branch officials, especially top political appointees, and governing party congressmembers. Such a strategy will also usually involve concessions to the opposition party and its supporters, notably under divided government.

Reflecting the conflicts out of which a political order arises, in "normal" times a successful accumulation strategy becomes institutionalized inside the state as a set of weighted or asymmetrical social as well as intraparty and interparty compromises that may outlast the evolving balance of underlying social forces.[97]

Finally, a successful, institutionalized strategy will eventually earn the dominant party broad support within the electorate as a whole. As noted above, in helping to forge viable electoral and governing coalitions, such a strategy also helps to cohere the mode of regulation, that is, it facilitates what David Lockwood famously called both "social" and "system" integration.[98] In turn, the mode of regulation, especially its macroeconomic policy routines, stabilizes the regime of accumulation, fostering a long period of economic growth that wins the governing party widespread support among less attentive, mostly retrospectively oriented voters. During such relatively stable, institutionalized, and prosperous periods, the moment of "order" and "structure" eventually dominates that of "disorder" and "agency," and a durable, integrated political order can be said to exist.

Some would argue that American parties are too fragmented and undisciplined to undertake the integrative or unifying tasks discussed above. But, to the contrary, I maintain that because such parties are so open and porous, they can and do serve as arenas or contested terrains in or on which party officials, officeholders, candidates, and factions, assisted by supportive experts and interest groups, formulate economically, administratively, and politically viable strategies and policies through processes of argument, compromise, and experiment.

Stability, Crisis, and the Search for New Strategies and Institutions

A new political order usually commences during a "critical juncture" or "constitutive moment" when a political party, resting on a distinct coalitional base and in control of both the White House and Congress, implements a new accumulation strategy that contributes to the construction of a new mode of regulation and regime of accumulation, thus lifting the nation out of a long period of economic stagnation. As the new, long wave of growth gathers speed, the new political order is consolidated as its institutions are "locked in" by path-dependent, self-reinforcing, or positive feedback processes involving (1) increasing returns to institutions—due to large set-up costs, learning effects, and network externalities—which raise the cost of switching to an alternative set of institutional arrangements, (2) the strengthened position of vested interests that benefit from the new institutions,[99] and (3) the rigid "mental models" of public officials who become cognitively biased in favor of institutionally embedded and apparently successful economic ideologies and policy paradigms.[100]

Following an initial phase of sharp party conflict, during the prosperous, institutionally facilitated normal stage of the political order, economic issues decline in salience and divisiveness, as even the minority party gradually comes to support a weaker version of the majority party's successful accumulation strategy. Economic policy is now formulated and implemented in an evolutionary and incremental way within insulated policy subsystems by dominant advocacy coalitions in interaction with subordinate competitors. In the fragmented U.S. political system, cross-partisan legislative coalitions over a wide range of issues become more common.

At some point, however, the wave of growth ends as a result of endogenously generated contradictions or exogenous shocks, either domestic or international in origin.[101] Sometimes marked by a full-blown economic collapse that "punctuates" the prevailing path-dependent equilibrium, a long "crisis of regulation" begins.[102] As anomalies or intractable economic problems pile up and the flow of benefits to key majority party constituencies slows, the authority and coherence of the majority party's accumulation strategy are eroded; social, intraparty, and interparty conflict erupts; the dominant electoral coalition fractures or even collapses; and the institutions of the wider political order, along with the compromises embedded in them, begin to weaken or unravel. The moment of disorder and agency comes to dominate that of order and structure.

Various private and public actors now begin an intense search for viable new or transformed strategies, policies, and institutions. Economically, this involves or eventuates in the restructuring of capital-labor relations and forms of market competition, the geographic reorganization of production and exchange, the emergence of a new technological paradigm, and the decline of old industrial sectors and the rise of dynamic new ones.

Politically, the crisis simultaneously raises the salience of economic issues, "dealigns" or loosens the partisan commitments of voters and economic interest groups, and produces frequent episodes of divided government. As economic debate spills out of insulated subsystems into the realm of public macropolitics, leaders of both parties, including competing intraparty factions, begin their own search for accumulation strategies, policies, and institutions that can help them build winning new party coalitions and a durable new political order.

At some point during the long downturn, dissatisfied retrospective voters are likely to give the old minority party control of all or most institutions of government. If this occurs in the wake of an economic crash or a severe recession or an electoral landslide that allows the party to claim a political mandate, the new majority party will try to reverse certain policies and dismantle or restructure various institutions of the old order and to begin building new institutions and a new order of its own. In these circumstances, the old majority party will be split between a "restorationist" faction defensive of the old order and a younger faction (or factions) committed to a significant revision of party doctrine to regain power.[103]

For both parties, the development of new strategies and policies will be influenced by novel economic theories and other ideational factors as well as by the clear, intense preferences of attentive core partisan and swing constituencies. Included among these groups are powerful economic interests, whose fortunes rise or fall with the transformation of the economy; such interests often convert and mobilize their human and financial resources to press their views upon policymakers.

In such periods of crisis, the two major parties try to improve their positions using the various kinds of preference-shaping tactics described earlier. This can involve policy and institutional changes to strengthen or weaken various party-aligned groups, the mobilization of some of these same groups on behalf of the parties' goals, or, when the preferences of other dealigned swing constituencies are highly uncertain, persuasive efforts to reconstitute or change the direction of voter and group preferences.[104]

Also common are partisan attempts to heresthetically influence the relative *intensity* of the preferences of swing constituencies holding clear but weak opinions. During presidential and congressional campaigns as well as in Congress itself, members of both parties, but mainly the out party, will try to introduce new economic issues and proposals onto the government agenda, or to raise the relative salience of existing issues on which they believe they hold an electoral advantage. Although parties often will emphasize noneconomic issues during periods of prosperity, once the economic boom peaks and a crisis of regulation begins, both parties will redirect their energies back to economic issues. This hunt for specific, salient, and politically useful economic issues is an important element of the parties' wider search for economically and politically viable new accumulation strategies.

The Emergence of Successful Strategies, Institutions, and Political Orders

At some point there emerges a particular partisan accumulation strategy that helps to integrate at least a core of institutions at the heart of a new mode of regulation, thus stabilizing a new regime of accumulation, facilitating a long-term revival of the economy, and contributing to the consolidation of a new political order. The complex process through which these outcomes are produced is simultaneously and in varying degrees (1) *intendedly rational*, involving conscious planning and design based on coherent economic theory, (2) *evolutionary*, involving either adaptive processes of trial-and-error learning or processes of variation, selection, and retention in economic, administrative, and electoral markets, (3) *imitative or emulative* of the experiences of others, (4) *conflict-ridden*, involving bargaining and compromise both within and between the (nonunitary) parties and their allied constituencies, and (5) *regenerative*, involving the alternation of partisan control of the different branches of government.[105]

In the transition to a new political order, it is important to recognize that even if a crisis of regulation largely destroys the old order's electoral underpinnings and brings to power a party committed to overthrowing that order, it is by no means the case that all of the old institutions and policy paradigms embedded in them are also necessarily uprooted and replaced in toto. Instead, due to path-dependent rigidities, some existing institutions inertially withstand the pressure of hard times, others are transformed—either recombined or rearranged in new ways or "functionally reconverted" to new purposes—while in yet other instances, new institutions are layered on top of old ones.[106]

Finally the accumulation strategy, specific policies, and institutions that eventually emerge from this complex process to stabilize a new political order will be "structurally privileged," though not uniquely determined, by several factors. Among them are the particular constraints of and problems besetting the domestic and international economies, the shifting balance of strength between rising and declining economic sectors and the workers/voters employed in them, and broad demographic shifts.[107]

The actual manner in which a new political order is established can vary. For example, what I call the "Order of '96" (covered in the next chapter) emerged at the end of a prolonged, late-nineteenth-century regulation crisis and period of partisan contestation that was abruptly punctuated by the depression of 1893–97, a collapse that, along with the Democrats' lurch to the left, finally destroyed the closely balanced electoral alignment of the Civil War Order, if not all of that order's institutions. At this critical juncture, the Republican Party won control of the White House and Congress, after which its monetary, tariff, and regulatory policies were popularly credited with producing a sustained revival of the economy and accelerated the interregional transfer of income from the agricultural South to the industrializing North. The result was a performance- and regionally based partisan realignment, or a durable shift in the balance of party strength, and the inauguration of a stable Republican-dominated political order.

The process that culminated in the consolidation of the New Deal Order, on the other hand, *began* with an economic crash that punctuated a long period of rapid growth and destroyed the electoral foundations of the Order of '96. The Great Depression, a critical juncture if ever there was one, triggered a lengthy new regulation crisis, brought unified Democratic control of government, and initiated a conflict-ridden period of economic policy search and experimentation. By the late 1940s the Democrats' "commercial Keynesian" accumulation strategy had helped to integrate the two core institutions of a new mode of regulation, the Keynesian Welfare/Warfare State and the new system of collective bargaining, which in turn had stabilized a new "Fordist" regime of accumulation combining mass production and consumption. The growth fostered by the new institutions and the particular benefits directed toward the expanding industrial working class consolidated a performance-and-class-based realignment and the New Deal political order.

The current period is a perplexing one. The regulation crisis of the 1970s broke up the "Keynesian consensus" and undermined the New Deal Order. But due to institutional inertia and other obstacles and the absence of a punctuating crash, I do not believe that either Republican presidents Ronald Reagan and George Bush or Democrat Bill Clinton were able to consolidate a successor to the New Deal Order. The near future is thus likely to see the persistence of the current state of partisan dealignment and disorder as two almost evenly balanced parties with continuing but narrowed differences struggle for primacy. In the longer run, we may—emphasize *may*—see the the emergence—via a novel, protracted, and evolutionary process of search and strategic interaction—of a new majority coalition and a new political order adapted to the requirements of an "information" or "post-Fordist" age.[108]

Trade Policy and the Struggle for New Political Orders

The partisan search for new accumulation strategies during crises of regulation will likely include a quest for new trade policies, as rising unemployment and the growth of surplus capacity generate demands to both close domestic markets and open foreign ones.[109] Import-competing firms, exporters, multinational companies, importers, import-using firms, and workers in all these kinds of enterprises will battle over the nation's orientation toward the international economy. These conflicts and the shifts in the relative economic and political strength of various industries that underlie them disrupt the existing trade policy paradigm and the compromises that were institutionalized in the old mode of regulation. This, in turn, contributes to the wider crisis of the party system and political order.

As part of their efforts to fashion new accumulation strategies and rebuild

crumbling electoral coalitions, the parties will back trade policies thought capable of securing the support of key industrial sectors and voting groups.[110] As we
shall see in the next chapter, this was the case during the earlier regulation crises
of the late 1800s and the 1930s.

In the 1970s the crisis of Fordism together with the rise of foreign competition not only eroded the New Deal Order; they also called into question
the prevailing liberal trade policy paradigm and provoked battles over import
curbs, unilateral market-opening tactics, and regional and multilateral free-
trade initiatives.

At various points over the past two decades, Republicans and Democrats have
made trade policy an important element of the accumulation strategies that
they have developed in an attempt to build new electoral and governing coalitions and a successor to the New Deal Order. Due to path-dependent, self-
reinforcing processes that have both strengthened the influence of internationally oriented interests and cognitively entrenched free-trade ideas, the dominant
World War II liberal trade policy paradigm and the institutions in which it is
embedded have for the most part inertially withstood the recent domestic and
international economic turmoil that has helped to transform other institutions
and paradigms. But I will show how, during this period, the parties' search for
economically and politically viable new strategies has nevertheless had a significant effect on the conduct of U.S. trade policy.

A Methodological Note on Analytic Narratives

The remainder of this book employs the framework developed in this chapter
to explain the complex dynamics and impact of party competition over American trade policy, first in a short historical chapter, then in much greater depth
for the period since 1980.

This work takes the form of an "analytic narrative," which I use neither just
for descriptive purposes, nor in the postmodernist or interpretivist sense as a
way to explain the social narratives that people employ to describe and construct their reality, but rather as a method of causal analysis.[111] In recent years,
following the earlier revival of narrative among historians,[112] growing numbers
of social scientists have turned to narrative methods in the belief that "history
matters," that is, that time must be incorporated into social explanation.

According to Andrew Sayer, a narrative is "an account of some process or
development in terms of a story, in which a series of events are depicted chro-
nologically. . . . Its power derives from the way in which putting things in
chronological order, in a story, gives the appearance of a causal chain or logic in
which each event leads to the conclusion."[113] Thus, the central focus of narra-

tivists is on actions, events, and temporal sequences. Their principal claim is that the temporal order in which causal factors occur within a sequence of events will affect outcomes.

The danger involved in the narrative approach is that one can lapse into mere storytelling. For this reason, narrative must also be accompanied by "analysis," defined by Sayer as "the explanation of concrete cases by the direct application of abstractions or theoretical models of what are believed to be widely replicated structures and mechanisms."[114] Analysis tends to abstract from particular historical sequences.

Narrativists have drawn on various types of analysis or theory to construct their explanatory narratives. Historical institutionalists within political science, joined by some historical sociologists, have combined narrative methods with theories of critical junctures (or constitutive moments) and path dependence, which posit that events or key actions in the distant past can affect later periods by pushing history down one path and foreclosing others.[115] This coupling of narrative and theory has been fruitfully employed to explain dramatic moments of institutional origin and subsequent periods of institutional stability or inertia. But such overly structuralist accounts are less successful in comprehending the often "agential" sources of the political and institutional changes that do take place either during noncrisis or normal times or during other less stable periods that are nevertheless characterized by gradual or evolutionary rather than abrupt or punctuated forms of institutional transformation. Such views, in other words, tend to take the politics out of political science.[116]

Rational choice analysts, again including political scientists and sociologists, have begun to combine narrative methods with extensive form game theory in order to bring actors, their preferences, and their behavior back into historical analysis. In their work these authors demonstrate how some events or phenomena are the consequence of sequences of action and reaction, that is, of the temporally ordered strategic interaction between purposive actors.[117] This way of joining narrative and theory is useful in explaining the strategic behavior of political actors within stable institutional settings. Yet the well-known weaknesses of game theory, especially the prevalence of multiple equilibria, suggest that the use of a more informal type of rational choice theory may often be more appropriate to the construction of such "actor-centric" narratives.

Finally, some "critical realists" use a narrative approach to illuminate the causal interaction between structures and agents. In her morphogenetic approach, Margaret Archer argues that given its inherently temporal character, this interaction can be grasped only through the construction of rich analytic narratives.[118]

As this discussion should make clear, I find it useful to employ narrative methods in conjunction with elements of all of these theoretical approaches, which I believe to be compatible in important ways, in order to illuminate the dynamics of both stable political orders and the "disorderly" transitions between them. Narrative analysis can help to explain the nature and consequences of the strategic interaction over time between party elites and their various constituencies, and between the parties themselves, as these interactions unfold within, are constrained by, and sometimes influence the economic, political, and cultural structures and institutions of a given political order during stable or normal times. And because it is well suited to the study of agency, narrative analysis is perhaps even more useful during crises of regulation, when the old order and its institutions are eroding or breaking down, and party elites and other political actors are struggling to build a new order.

The following chapters combine narrative and analysis in a form of historical "process tracing" to explain the dynamics and policy consequences of party competition over U.S. trade policy across several political orders—first from the Civil War to Ronald Reagan's election and then in much greater detail for the period since 1980—as this competition was mediated by America's unique political institutions and influenced by other domestic and international structures and processes.

Trade Policy and Party Politics
from the Civil War to 1980

As background to the detailed analysis of the period since 1980, presented in the balance of this book, and to demonstrate the general utility of aspects of the periodized theoretical framework developed in the last chapter,[1] this chapter considers the history and consequences of party competition over U.S. trade policy before 1980. Specifically, it examines the party politics of trade policy under what I have identified as three distinct political orders: the Civil War Order, the Order of '96, and, at greater length, the New Deal Order.

The Civil War Order

The emergence of trade as a focus of partisan contention in the 1980s and 1990s marked the return to prominence of an issue—then called the "tariff question" —that had been the most important subject of party competition during the period running from the Civil War through the Great Depression.[2] In these years, which spanned two political orders, the tariff was an important tool of national economic policy, and the parties fought furiously over the level of duties intended to protect nascent American industry from foreign competition. During most of this era, due to constituency-based and ideological influences, the Republicans backed high tariffs, whereas the Democrats favored lower ones. The congressional parties correspondingly became sharply polarized over the tariff issue; tariff levels rose when Republicans controlled both branches of government and fell when the Democrats were in power. During the first half of this period, from 1860 to 1896, the Civil War Order structured the nation's politics, including its trade politics.

The victory of the Union in the Civil War secured the industrial future of the United States.[3] Industrial capitalism was already developing before the conflict, founded on a regime of accumulation at the heart of which was a new technological paradigm based on the steam engine and machinofacture, railroads and steamships, and the telegraph. The Civil War helped to consolidate the emerging industrial order by facilitating the institutional transformations that had been blocked by the conflict between capitalism and slavery.

Many of these institutional changes were the work of the Republican Party. Following the realignment that was triggered in the 1850s by the crisis of slavery and consolidated by the successful conduct of the Civil War, the GOP assumed unified control of the national government until 1874. During the war and the period of Reconstruction that followed it, the GOP pursued a developmentalist and mercantilist accumulation strategy that was intended to cement a political coalition between the manufacturers and workers of the industrial North and the farmers of the agricultural West. Toward this end, the party fostered the development of a new mode of regulation—including an unregulated national market for labor and production, adherence to the international gold standard, a national banking system, looser immigration laws, an expanded federal role in education, and higher tariffs on manufactured goods—to promote northern industrialization. The Republicans also legislated land grants, railroad subsidies, and river and other internal improvements to encourage western agriculture and to link it to northern ports and cities.

Under the second or Jacksonian party system from 1832 to 1860, the GOP's forerunner, the commercially oriented Whig Party, had supported high protective tariffs to encourage industrial development. The more agrarian-based Democrats, fearing both expensive imports and foreign retaliation against U.S. cotton exports, favored free trade or lower tariffs for "revenue only."

During and after the war, the newly formed Republicans continued to back a high tariff to protect war-spawned industries plagued by inefficiency and excess capacity and thus to secure votes in northern manufacturing states, as well as to raise revenues to fund wartime public works and later Civil War pensions. The vanquished Democrats, now largely confined to the secessionist and agricultural South, continued to support a tariff mainly for revenue purposes.[4]

The depression of 1873–77 allowed the Democrats to regain lost ground in the North. Together with the readmission of the South into the Union, this resulted in both a Democratic takeover of the House of Representatives in 1874 and the revival of the party's broader political hopes. In fact, the depression—which was caused by falling prices, the result of improved production and transportation technologies, and increasing wages that together squeezed profits—marked the end of the long, Civil War–spurred upswing of capital accumulation and signaled the start of a lengthy, deflationary "crisis of regulation" that economic historians have termed the "Great Depression" of 1873–97. The long downturn disrupted existing political coalitions and institutions and inaugurated a period of closely balanced party competition—or what Tom Terrill has called a partisan "equipoise"—that lasted from 1875 to 1996. The period saw six different presidents from both parties chosen in six elections, as well as frequent episodes of divided partisan control of both branches of government and the two houses of Congress.[5]

In these conditions of marked instability, both Republicans and Democrats sought politically and economically viable accumulation strategies that, by distributing benefits to favored constituents and restoring more rapid rates of economic growth, could help them break the stalemate to become the dominant party. As the parties oscillated in their control of the various institutions of government, it was their position on the tariff, an important instrument of national economic management, that Republicans and Democrats relied on in their search for political advantage.[6]

Dueling over Trade

The differentiated tariff positions taken by the parties during this period were in part determined by their traditional, mercantile-era constituency and ideological commitments.[7] These were then reinforced by Civil War–generated sectional cleavages between North and South. The Republicans, politically reliant on import-competing northern manufacturing industries and their workers and ideologically inclined toward government activism to promote industrialization and protect workers' wages, generally continued to favor high tariffs on imported industrial goods. The Democrats, on the other hand, linked to southern agricultural export interests and ideologically supportive of limited government, the protection of consumers against corrupt monopolies, states' rights, and agrarianism, held to their low-tariff position. At this stage, however, both parties contained opposition factions on the tariff issue that would prevent a truly sharp partisan polarization over trade policy until about 1887.

Although core constituency and ideological influences were important in determining party positions, each party also believed that its tariff stance could earn it broader electoral favor among swing voters and regions. With other matters either settled, lacking appeal, or too divisive, the tariff, promising prosperity and social harmony, appeared to be a salient, unifying issue. As such, it was capable of overcoming the party system's locally rooted centrifugal tendencies and bridging sectional, ethnic, and religious divisions to win the support of voters in every economic and geographic category.[8]

After 1874, the GOP took the initiative on trade. Defending the need for high tariffs, Republicans spoke of the threat to American workers and manufacturers from products produced by European "pauper" labor. But the GOP also advocated the "home market thesis," according to which industrialization and accompanying urbanization would provide domestic markets for surplus-ridden midwestern and Plains states farmers, reducing their need for agricultural exports. Republican leaders also promised that their high-tariff policies would facilitate southern industrialization.[9]

For their part, the Democrats insisted that high tariffs exploited farmers and workers alike. They embraced tariff reduction first to hold or win the support of both southern cotton planters and consumers of finished products. But by the early 1880s the Democrats had also begun to stress the importance of tariff reduction to the expansion of foreign trade, arguing to midwestern farmers that lower tariffs would increase agricultural exports and to northern and eastern export industries that lower tariffs on raw materials would boost manufacturing exports. Democratic tariff reductionists attempted to cut tariffs but were blocked by Republicans in the White House (1884) and Congress (1886), in alliance with a faction of protectionist congressional Democrats.

With the defeat of Republican tariff reductionist and Democratic protectionist factions by the late 1880s, a long period of heightened interparty division and intraparty cohesion on trade began, one that would continue beyond the Great Depression of the 1930s (see Figures A.1 and A.2).[10] In 1888 the Democrat-controlled House and the GOP-controlled Senate each passed bills along almost straight party lines that respectively cut and raised tariffs. The ensuing House-Senate stalemate prevented any bill from passing.

Meanwhile, the tariff was central to the 1888 presidential campaign. Republican Benjamin Harrison's victory over Democratic incumbent Grover Cleveland, together with the simultaneous Republican capture of the House and Senate, was interpreted by GOP leaders as a mandate to raise tariffs. Thus in 1890, again along sharply partisan lines, the Republicans passed the McKinley Tariff, which raised duties on industrial and certain agricultural products to their highest levels since the Civil War. This revived an earlier pattern that would continue up to World War II in which tariffs rose and fell under unified Republican and Democratic governments respectively (see Figure A.3).[11]

The McKinley bill also included a "reciprocity" provision to help export-oriented manufacturers and farmers dispose of troublesome agricultural and industrial surpluses. By reciprocity, however, the GOP meant not the reciprocal exchange of market concessions by the United States and its trading partners but rather the use of unilateral threats to close the American market to those nations that refused to lower their barriers to U.S. goods.[12]

Two years later, popular discontent with inflation and the Republican tariff, currency, and trust policies that were thought to have caused it gave the Democrats control of both Congress and the White House for the first time since before the Civil War. With the onset of the depression of 1893, congressional Democrats enacted the Wilson-Gorman Tariff Bill in 1894. The bill modestly cut tariffs on raw materials to obtain export markets for depression-plagued industries and farms. It also repealed the McKinley bill's reciprocity provision.[13]

Unfortunately for the Democrats, the depression deepened and thereby "punctuated" the precarious partisan equilibrium of the Civil War Order. In the 1894 congressional elections the GOP regained control of the Senate and won a plurality of seats in the House. The rout of the Democrats was completed with the election of 1896, when, after the party had turned sharply to the left to nominate William Jennings Bryan, the agrarian populist and free trader was trounced by the high-tariff candidate of northern manufacturing interests, Republican William McKinley. Bryan dragged Democratic congressional candidates down to defeat with him, and thus unified Republican control of government was restored.

The election of 1896 broke the partisan stalemate of the late-nineteenth-century Civil War Order and together with various institutional and policy developments, which accelerated the transfer of income and wealth from the agricultural South to the industrializing North, fully realigned the party system along sectional or regional lines. The Republicans became politically dominant in the North and West, while Democratic strength was confined to the South and to a lesser extent the border states. This electoral earthquake ushered in the Order of '96—an era of Republican supremacy—during which the GOP, resting on a cross-class coalition of northern industrial capitalists and workers, held unified control of both branches of government for most of the next thirty-six years.[14]

The Order of '96

With the defeat of the populist threat in 1896, the triumph of the advancing industrial capitalist system over the declining agrarian order was cemented. The turn of the century saw the transition to a regime of accumulation based on the mass production, though not yet the mass consumption, of industrial goods and propelled by a new technological paradigm revolving around electric power and heavy engineering. The core institutions of a new mode of regulation helped to consolidate the new regime of accumulation, launching another long upswing of economic growth.[15]

This institutional core included first and foremost the new, oligopolistically concentrated structure of industry produced by the great merger movement of

1898–1902, which kept prices from falling as they had during the long down-turn of 1873–97. But government interventions facilitated by the Republican landslide and realignment of 1896 played a role, too. The Republicans modern-ized their developmentalist and mercantilist accumulation strategy and con-tributed to the construction of a new mode of regulation with policies that included the transformation of corporate jurisprudence to facilitate the merger movement, the court-enforced repression of labor unions to keep worker mili-tancy and wages in check, an aggressively expansionist foreign policy, and strengthened U.S. adherence to the gold standard.

Most important for this study, however, was the continued commitment of the Republican Party, whose backbone remained the dominant import-competing manufacturing sector, to high protective tariffs and reciprocity poli-cies.[16] Both were embodied in the Dingley Tariff Act of 1897, which again passed both houses of Congress on sharply partisan votes. The economic recovery that followed hard on the heels of the enactment of the Dingley bill, though not due to that measure, further legitimated protectionism, and the tariff remained in effect for the next twelve years of unified Republican control.[17] Thus, while old institutions were being transformed and new ones built to underpin the new Order of '96, the old protectionist trade policy paradigm and system—core components of the post–Civil War mode of regulation—inertially withstood the transition to the new political order to become important elements of the new mode of regulation.

The tariff issue took center stage again in the 1908 and, more importantly, the 1910 elections.[18] In 1910, after fourteen years in the political wilderness and with the economy in serious trouble, the tariff issue helped the Democrats take control of the House of Representatives and win additional seats in the Senate. Then in the 1912 presidential race, Democrat Woodrow Wilson mobilized vot-ers around tariffs, while differences over the tariff and related issues led Theo-dore Roosevelt and other progressive Republicans to bolt their party and form the Bull Moose Party. The split in Republican ranks threw the election to Wilson, producing a "mini" realignment within the Order of '96. Once in office, Wilson pressed Congress to pass the liberal Underwood-Simmons Tariff Act of 1913, again along party lines, which substantially lowered tariffs.[19]

World War I briefly reconciled protectionists to the Democrats, due both to the need for national unity and bipartisan cooperation during the conflict and to the fact that the war probably curbed imports more effectively than a higher tar-iff would have. But with peace restored, protectionist pressures reemerged. The small, inefficient, labor-intensive infant industries that had sprung up during the war—the so-called war babies—needed protection to remain viable. The nation's sense of self-sufficiency had grown during the conflict, U.S. agriculture was in a depression, and foreign currencies had depreciated relative to the dollar.

With the end of wartime cooperation, the Republicans recaptured control of both houses of Congress in 1918 and once again tried to revise tariff levels upward. Wilson vetoed two such GOP-sponsored bills, giving the Republicans an issue to campaign on in the 1920 presidential race.

Warren Harding's victory gave the GOP unified command of government. With agricultural prices and thus farmers especially hard hit by the recession of 1920–21, the Republicans fulfilled their campaign pledge by raising agricultural and other tariffs with the passage of the Emergency and the Fordney-McCumber Tariff Acts of 1921 and 1922 respectively. Prosperity followed for all but the farm sector, which remained depressed for most of the decade.

In response to pressure from Farm Belt Republicans, presidential candidate Herbert Hoover promised new agricultural tariffs during the 1928 campaign. Hoover's landslide victory, coupled with significant GOP gains in both the House and Senate, resulted in the Tariff Act of 1930—more famously known as the Smoot-Hawley Tariff Act after its congressional cosponsors. Tougher than the new president intended, Smoot-Hawley raised the average ad valorem rates on dutiable imports to a formidable 52.8 percent.[20] Although responsiveness to constituent economic interests as well as logrolling played a role in the bill's enactment,[21] Smoot-Hawley passed the Senate and House along clear partisan lines, with Republicans decisively for the measure and Democrats overwhelmingly opposed.[22] (The Democrats did not, however, dispute the right of industry to at least some protection.)

Politicians and scholars have debated Smoot-Hawley's contribution to the economic crash that followed its passage. Whatever the truth, congressional Democrats heresthetically tried to make Republican protectionism an issue in the 1930 and 1932 elections,[23] even though the Democrats themselves had recently drifted from their low-tariff roots in pursuit of support from the growing numbers of immigrant industrial workers and hard-pressed midwestern farmers. During the 1932 presidential campaign, Democrat Franklin Roosevelt zigzagged or straddled the tariff issue as he struggled to balance the concerns of nationalist and internationalist interests.

Roosevelt, of course, defeated Hoover in a crushing landslide. Just as the depression of 1893–96 had destroyed the electoral underpinnings of the old Civil War Order, so the depression of the 1930s dynamited the Order of '96. The latter crisis, together with a series of dramatic institutional and policy changes that both revived the economy and funneled benefits to urban workers, precipitated a largely class-based Democratic realignment and the construction of the New Deal political order. The new order rested on a coalition of unionized labor, urban ethnics, southerners, northern blacks, and middle-class liberals and was opposed by a diminished Republican coalition of representatives of big and small business and members of the upper middle class. Among its other accomplishments, the New Deal Order would bring forth a new era of, and eventually a bipartisan consensus on, liberal trade.

The New Deal Order

Regulation and other theorists argue that the Great Depression was caused by the failure of workers' wages to rise as fast as productive capacity during the 1920s.[24] Out of the wreckage of the crisis, a new Fordist regime of accumulation eventually emerged; combining the mass production and consumption of standardized commodities, it was based on a new technological paradigm at the core of which were the petrochemical, automobile, airplane, and consumer durable industries. The Fordist regime was stabilized by a new mode of regulation that institutionalized a series of compromises between the major societal actors: business, labor, and agriculture.[25] By preventing another collapse of demand, this new mode of regulation contributed to a sustained upswing of capital accumulation that lasted until the late 1960s or early 1970s.

Two institutions—both prefigured to a degree during World War I—were at the core of the new order. The first, a new collective bargaining system that helped raise wages in step with productivity increases, was given legal form by the Wagner and Taft-Hartley Acts of 1935 and 1947 respectively. The second, the Keynesian Welfare/Warfare State (KWWS), boosted demand via social welfare, infrastructure, and military spending.[26] These institutions and the New Deal coalition that supported them were integrated and unified by the deployment of what has been termed a business-oriented "commercial Keynesian" accumulation strategy. Synthesizing Keynesian ideas and classical economics, this strategy involved the use of countercyclical policies and later tax cuts and investment support to stimulate consumer demand and increase growth.

The Fordist era also saw the discrediting and dismantling of the old protectionist trade policy paradigm and many of its associated institutions. Over time these were replaced by a new, liberal trade policy paradigm and by new international and domestic institutions that fostered demand and economic growth by facilitating the development of an open world economy. These additional elements of the new mode of regulation included a set of multilateral trade, aid, and monetary regimes—the General Agreement on Tariffs and Trade (GATT), the World Bank, and the International Monetary Fund (IMF)—and an executive-centered system of domestic policies and institutions that fostered trade liberalization while deflecting and containing protectionist pressures.[27]

Many of these stabilizing institutions and policies, including the new liberal trade policy system, emerged through a simultaneously intentional, conflict-ridden, and evolutionary search process undertaken by Roosevelt and other Democratic architects of the New Deal Order in the 1930s and 1940s.[28] In seeking first to end the depression, then to win World War II, and finally to reconstruct the postwar world economy, these leaders also sought to consolidate the rule of the Democratic Party.[29]

The Democrats Begin to Construct a Liberal Trade System in the 1930s

Early New Deal foreign economic policy, congruent with Roosevelt's straddling of trade issues during his presidential campaign, was an odd and shifting amalgam of internationalist and nationalist elements that was actually weighted toward the latter. This reflected the continuing economic nationalism of most people in business and many midwestern farmers who sought to insulate domestic markets from overseas competition, as well as the administration's initial priority to seek passage of its domestic recovery program.[30]

Soon, however, Roosevelt reversed course and began to move toward the more internationalist positions that he personally appeared to favor. In early 1934 he submitted to Congress what became the Reciprocal Trade Agreements Act (RTAA), a measure that established the basic structure of trade legislation for the next quarter century.[31]

To facilitate both tariff reduction and export expansion, the RTAA shifted de facto tariff-setting power from Congress to the more insulated president, who was granted the authority for a specified period to negotiate bilateral reciprocal trade agreements and then to lower tariffs by up to 50 percent by executive proclamation alone. Although the RTAA did not contain any proposed tariff cuts that might have injured politically influential industries, the dramatic change in the institutions and process of tariff setting eventually had a profoundly liberalizing effect and therefore marked the beginning of a new era of steadily declining tariffs. The so-called bargaining tariff authorized by the RTAA was the first element of the liberal postwar trade policy system.

The initiative behind the RTAA came from Secretary of State Cordell Hull, a longtime leader of free-trading southern Democrats, and other State Department officials, for all of whom freer trade and world peace were inextricably linked. But why did Roosevelt, who had initially rejected Hull's internationalism for political reasons, now reverse himself and support the RTAA? One reason may be, as "business conflict" theorists argue,[32] that Roosevelt wished to win the support of internationally oriented industrial and financial interests,[33] although there is little evidence that these interests actively backed the RTAA, and most U.S. industries, still nationalist in orientation, opposed the bill.[34] More important was the president's growing belief, influenced by underconsumptionist thinking,[35] that (1) the revival of industrial and especially agricultural exports, which had collapsed with the onset of the depression, was crucial to the recovery of the economy and thus to his reelection hopes, and (2) the RTAA was important to the revival of exports.[36] Thus, in early 1934, with certain import protections for industry, labor, and agriculture approved as part of its domestic recovery program, the Roosevelt administration submitted the RTAA to Congress. The bill was passed late that year.

Another question now presents itself: Why, after controlling trade policy since the founding of the republic, did Congress agree to delegate considerable trade policy authority to the president? Most analysts argue that the answer lies in the shock of the depression and the associated lessons of Smoot-Hawley. In this view, Congress tried to protect itself against often politically irresistible pressures from import-competing interests by delegating tariff-setting authority to the president, who, in representing a large, heterogeneous national constituency, was thought more likely to ward off such pressures.[37]

But this argument implies that the RTAA should have commanded substantial bipartisan majorities when, in fact, it passed both houses of Congress along almost totally partisan lines, with Democrats in favor and Republicans opposed.[38] Further, voting on subsequent renewals of the trade agreements program remained highly partisan until the end of World War II. The lessons of Smoot-Hawley gained bipartisan endorsement only in the prosperous 1950s, when the benefits of free trade had become clearer.

A more convincing explanation of why Congress passed the RTAA is a partisan one linked to the trauma of the depression. During the years of Republican domination before 1934, protectionist GOP Congresses had been reluctant to grant the president control of trade negotiations. But after the depression and the political realignment it triggered, the now greatly expanded Democratic congressional majority was willing to delegate considerable authority in a range of policy domains to a Democratic president in order to resolve the economic crisis.[39]

In the case of trade, low-tariff congressional Democrats hoped that the delegation of trade-negotiating authority to a president of their own party would lead to reciprocal tariff reductions, resulting not only in lower domestic tariffs and prices but also in increased exports and employment, particularly in the agricultural sector, all of which would redound to the Democrats' political benefit.[40] This delegation was made easier by the fact that key House and Senate committees were now in the hands of a group of aging southern congressmen, who, by reason of either long-standing ideological conviction or ties to the region's dominant agricultural export interests, were among their party's strongest advocates of lower tariff barriers.[41]

Cautious throughout the depression about antagonizing still powerful domestic industries, the Democrats did not really take the offensive in support of liberal trade until near the end of World War II. During the final stages of that conflict, the American and British governments began negotiations that both hoped would lead to the construction of a new open and nondiscriminatory international economic order. A key aim of Roosevelt and Truman administration officials—assisted by corporate-sponsored policy planning groups like the Council on Foreign Relations and the Committee for Economic Development, pillars of the wider elite "Establishment"[42]—was to further revive U.S. exports, prevent a return to depression and war, and, not incidentally, help secure the future of the Democratic Party.[43]

The first fruits of these efforts were the Bretton Woods agreements of 1944 that established a fixed exchange rate system, the International Monetary Fund, and the International Bank for Reconstruction and Development (IBRD). In 1947 the United States also helped to form the General Agreement on Tariffs on Trade, which addressed traditional concerns of commercial policy like tariffs and quotas.[44] Through a series of multilateral negotiations held under its auspices, the GATT helped to reduce tariff barriers throughout the postwar period. At the same time, the reciprocal trade agreements program begun in 1934 was periodically renewed and the president granted new tariff-cutting authority to allow the United States to participate in this continuing process of trade liberalization.

These new monetary and trade regimes by no means involved a simple return to the gold standard or an unqualified embrace of free trade, which would have undermined the effectiveness of New Deal employment and welfare policies. Instead, the design of the Bretton Woods and GATT institutions accommodated the popular demand throughout the industrial world for state intervention in domestic economies to stabilize employment and prices and to achieve various social welfare objectives. The postwar period thus saw the institutionalization of, in John Ruggie's words, the "compromise of embedded liberalism."[45] Domestically this meant an accommodation between major social groupings—capital, labor, and agriculture—and between export-oriented and import-competing industries. Internationally, the United States and Britain reached an understanding on acceptable forms of domestic intervention.[46] Taken together these compromises, premised on a "politics of productivity" in which economic growth superseded class conflict,[47] allowed the simultaneous pursuit of international openness and substantial autonomy in domestic policy.

With respect to trade policy, the result was "liberal" or "freer," rather than unqualified "free" trade. During World War II, "escape clause" provisions, permitting temporary protection of industries injured by liberalizing concessions, were written into reciprocal trade agreements. After the war, this practice became the rule. GATT agreements to eliminate or reduce quotas, tariffs, and other barriers to trade were predicated on the ability of member countries to employ various import-limiting safeguards, exceptions, exemptions, and restrictions to protect social policies, industries and workers from injury resulting from past tariff concessions, and participating countries from balance-of-payments problems arising from full employment policies. Agriculture was exempted entirely from GATT obligations.

In the United States, the ensemble of institutions and practices that I. M. Destler has termed the executive-centered trade policy "system" embodied a conflict-dampening compromise between export-oriented and import-competing interests.[48] This system simultaneously facilitated the liberalization of trade and the acceptance of global economic change by threatened domestic groups by helping to contain and socialize the costs of adjustment.

In addition to the "bargaining tariff" established by the RTAA, elements of this system would eventually or at various times include (1) rules or quasi-judicial procedures through which industries could receive limited administrative, rather than legislative, relief from injury caused by either fairly traded imports (the escape clause and "peril point" laws, the latter only until 1962) or unfair foreign trade practices (antidumping, counterveiling duty, and other laws),[49] (2) "special deals"—including voluntary export restraint and orderly marketing agreements—to curb imports in especially sensitive sectors, like textiles, steel, and automobiles, in order to deter the formation of broader protectionist coalitions, and (3) specific institutions, created and encouraged by Congress to absorb or deflect protectionist pressure on its members, including (a) the U.S. International Trade Commission, a "nonpolitical" regulatory agency that administers the trade relief rules, (b) the U.S. Department of Commerce, which enforces the antidumping and counterveiling duty laws, and (c) the U.S. trade representative, placed by Congress in the White House to act as an overall trade broker, balance competing interests, manage trade issues, and draw heat away from Congress, and (4) strong, pro-trade congressional committees, which regularly killed protectionist legislation before it reached the floor of the House or Senate.

The move toward a more open world economy predated but was reinforced by the Cold War. Until the late 1950s, the United States opened its markets to and even encouraged imports from Japan and Europe, while allowing those countries to discriminate against American exports, in order to help get these nations back on their feet and thus to ward off internal communist threats and contain the threat of Soviet expansion.[50]

The Decline of Partisanship over Trade

Also important to the maintenance of the liberal postwar trading order, as well as a product of it, was the eventual decline of partisanship surrounding the making of trade policy.[51] Throughout the depression trade policy had continued to sharply divide the parties. In congressional voting on proposed extensions of the trade agreements program in 1937 and 1940, Democrats were overwhelmingly supportive, while virtually all Republicans remained opposed. But after World War II, these divisions began to fade, and by about 1960 a largely bipartisan consensus in support of a new liberal trade policy paradigm had emerged.

This consensus was the product of numerous factors, including (1) sustained prosperity, attributed in part to the expansion of world trade, which appeared to confirm the lessons of Smoot-Hawley,[52] (2) the expansion of U.S. export interests whose success had been fostered by the RTAA, leading them to pressure officials of both parties to support continued trade liberalization,[53] (3) the embedded liberal compromise, including the executive-centered domestic trade policy system, which helped to defuse residual protectionist opposition to trade liberalization, (4) the liberalizing influence of the GATT regime, (5) the imperatives of the Cold War, which led control of trade policy to be delegated to the State Department, and (6) the replacement of the tariff by the income tax as the main source of federal revenue and the emergence of Keynesian demand management as the main instrument of national economic policy-making,[54] thus reducing the salience of trade issues, confining them to an insulated policy subsystem, and allowing party elites to pursue liberal trade even though the general public remained more protectionist in its sympathies.[55]

The process by which the new bipartisan trade consensus emerged was complex and not without conflict. Party presidential platforms converged most fully, a process that was completed by about 1960. In Congress, beginning in 1943 but more clearly after 1950, Republicans began to join with Democrats in supporting liberal trade legislation, at least on final passage (see Figures A.1 and A.2).[56] Intraparty splits also became more important. Thus, the overall levels of both interparty division and intraparty cohesion on trade issues steadily declined until the early 1980s.[57] Whereas congressional voting on trade had been more partisan than overall voting in the 1930s and 1940s, during the next three decades, trade voting was much less partisan.[58] Nevertheless, from 1945 to 1962 the Republicans often only supported what were on balance liberal trade bills because restrictive amendments had been included to strengthen the generic procedures by which industries were eligible for import relief. And party conflict over various restrictive and liberalizing amendments and motions was often intense.[59]

Congressional party divisions over trade did decline further in the 1960s. But in the early 1970s, after new protectionist pressures had arisen, the parties' historic trade positions were partially reversed on several key votes, as a majority of Republicans supported free trade, while a majority of Democrats took the more protectionist side. This trend abated for the remainder of the decade, only to strongly reassert itself in the 1980s.

Just as wider political orders, including the Democratic regime, contain moments of both partisan conflict and *dis*order, so, too, did the post–World War II American trade policy system. The pattern of party competition over trade policy during the period up to 1980 can be characterized as one of growing bipartisan consensus on a new liberal trade policy paradigm at the presidential level, often combined with partisan conflict within, or over the ground rules of, that consensus in Congress.[60]

What impact did these evolving dynamics of party competition at the presidential and congressional levels have on actual trade policy choices or outputs during this period? From the passage of the RTAA in 1934 through 1946, tariffs declined sharply under unified Democratic government. Divided government then slowed the process of tariff reduction in 1947–48. Tariffs continued to decline gradually during the next three decades, but with the growth of bipartisanship on trade during this period, the differences in tariff levels that can be explained either by whether a Democrat or a Republican occupied the White House, or by whether partisan control of government was unified or divided, were modest (see Figure A.3).[61]

But in the 1950s and 1960s partisanship did influence the development of the rules and procedures governing postwar trade liberalization. Given the liberal trade commitments of presidents of both parties, the partisan influence was determined mainly in Congress by the parties' trade positions, their relative strength, and their internal cohesiveness. The party affiliation of the president also played a role in shaping the behavior of congressional party members, as incumbency-focused theories suggest.[62]

From 1945 to 1962, then, general trade bills were sometimes tilted in a restrictive direction due to the efforts of large, cohesive Republican congressional contingents, sometimes allied with a faction of protectionist Democrats. Conversely, general trade legislation was less restrictive when congressional Democrats had greater strength, sometimes in coalition with liberally inclined Republicans. After the 1960s, as the parties began to reverse their historic positions, the partisan sources of more or less restrictive provisions in general trade bills were also reversed.[63]

Continuing Partisan Conflict, 1945–1950

The half decade from 1945 to 1950 saw the continuation, especially in the House, of the highly partisan conflict that had characterized congressional voting on the RTAA renewals of 1937 and 1940.[64] The Democrats were still ideologically committed to trade liberalization, politically dependent on both their traditional base of southern agricultural exporters and their new base within a then pro-trade labor movement,[65] and intent on winning the support of internationally oriented industrial and financial interests. Meanwhile, the Republicans were still largely wed to protectionist ideology and the import-competing northern manufacturing interests it served, although the growing influence within the party of export interests that had benefited from the RTAA did begin to moderate GOP protectionism.[66]

In 1945, with the Democrats firmly in control of Congress, Roosevelt's bill requesting further tariff reduction authority was enacted without major change. Voting in the House was highly partisan, while Senate Republicans were split, though still marginally opposed.

Partisan tensions over trade were ratcheted up a notch and trade policy made more restrictive when the Republicans captured both the House and the Senate in 1946, ushering in a two-year period of divided government. GOP pressure kept President Harry Truman from submitting the first GATT agreement to Congress for formal ratification and forced him to issue an executive order calling for the inclusion of an escape clause in all future trade agreements, which would prohibit concessions on imports that injured or threatened to injure domestic industries.

By the time of the RTAA's renewal in 1948, the Republicans had come to accept the trade agreements program, due to rising influence of export interests and emerging Cold War concerns. But the GOP congressional majority, opposed by Democrats in both houses, would agree only to a one-year extension of the act; it also restricted the executive's discretionary authority by modifying the legislation to include the establishment of minimum tariff peril points below which no future tariff concessions could be negotiated if such reductions were anticipated to seriously injure domestic industries. Rather than let the trade agreements program expire, Truman reluctantly signed the bill. In 1947–48, then, with the more protectionist party in control of Congress, divided government slowed the process of trade liberalization.

In 1948 Truman was reelected and the Democrats unexpectedly recaptured both houses of Congress. With a second round of GATT negotiations approaching, Congress in 1949 repealed the Trade Agreements Act of 1948, including its peril point clause, and extended the president's negotiating authority for three years from the original 1948 expiration date. In both the House and the Senate Democrats were overwhelmingly supportive of the extension, whereas the Republicans were divided, as more party members joined the emerging liberal consensus. GOP motions in the House and Senate to reintroduce the peril point were defeated on sharply partisan votes. Thus, the return of unified government with a strongly liberal Democratic congressional majority also produced a return to more liberal trade.

Conflict within Growing Consensus, 1951–1961

The decade of the 1950s saw the emergence of new, complex patterns of partisanship on trade issues.[67] Largely liberal bills to renew the trade agreements program were now regularly passed with substantially bipartisan support. But partisan battles continued to be fought over various secondary amendments and motions, and divisions emerged within each party, especially over these same amendments and motions. Democrats from import-sensitive parts of New England, the South, and other regions began to question the value of liberal trade, while the GOP was sometimes split between its traditional protectionist and newer free-trade wings.[68]

In 1951, with Truman still presiding over a unified Democratic government, the RTAA was extended for two more years. This time, however, congressional support for the renewal was substantially bipartisan, in part because the highly unified Republicans, with the help of some southern textile-state Democrats, were able to force the inclusion in the bill of both peril point and escape clause provisions. Nevertheless, the House struggle over these restrictive planks was still highly partisan.

In 1952 the Republicans captured control of both branches of government for the first time since the years of the Hoover administration. Many GOP observers predicted a return to protectionism, but this did not occur. Instead, President Dwight Eisenhower assumed a liberal trade policy stance. This was due both to Cold War imperatives and to pressure from the expanding ranks of internationally oriented business interests that,[69] alienated by Democratic economic and social welfare policies, had decisively shifted their allegiances to the Republicans, at least at the presidential level.

In 1953 and 1954, however, reflecting the continuing strength of GOP protectionists, Eisenhower won only one-year extensions of the RTAA with no new tariff-cutting authority. Both bills passed Congress by large partisan majorities, although liberalizing Democratic motions were defeated on highly partisan votes.

On balance, both bills remained liberal in character, but contrary to the views of Susanne Lohmann and Sharyn O'Halloran, this was in spite of, rather than because of, unified government.[70] The measures actually passed with disproportionate Democratic support and only after they had been tilted in somewhat restrictive directions by pressure from or concessions to the protectionist Republican congressional majority. Had the Democrats controlled Congress under divided government, the two bills would probably have been even more liberal.[71]

In 1955 and 1958, with Democrats back in control of both houses, Eisenhower was able to win the first new tariff-cutting authority to be added since 1945, although his bills were modified in Congress to make them more restrictive. The measures' liberalizing and restrictive features together allowed them to win substantial bipartisan support. Restrictive GOP-sponsored motions and amendments were defeated by the new Democratic congressional majorities on mostly partisan votes.

Despite the shift from unified to divided government in 1955, the impact of party competition on the content of the trade bills of 1955 and 1958 does not seem very different from its influence on the legislation of 1953 and 1954. In some ways the two later bills were more liberal and in other ways less liberal than the earlier pair. The more restrictive provisions of the two later bills cannot be attributed to divided government, as Lohmann and O'Halloran imply, since most Democrats opposed them. Had the Republicans controlled Congress as well as the White House, the 1955 and 1958 bills would have been even more restrictive.

The Trade Expansion Act of 1962: The Triumph of Liberalism

In 1962 newly elected President John Kennedy was presiding over a once more unified Democratic government. Kennedy, a committed liberal trader, sought to replace the reciprocal trade agreements program that was due to expire with a new one that would allow him greater negotiating powers. His particular aim was to bargain down the common external tariffs of the recently formed European Community (EC).

In the Trade Expansion Act (TEA) of 1962, Kennedy asked for the unprecedented authority to cut tariffs generally by up to 50 percent over five years and to reduce or eliminate tariffs on imports in cases where the United States and the EC together accounted for 80 percent or more of total free world trade. In return, the president pledged to protect U.S. industry from trade-related injury, but he sought new, more liberal means to accomplish this, proposing to eliminate the peril point provision and weaken the escape clause, and to instead compensate firms and workers injured by imports with other forms of aid through a new program called Trade Adjustment Assistance (TAA).[72]

With few major legislative wins in his first year in office, Kennedy made the liberal TEA a major part of his agenda. He was backed in this endeavor by export-oriented manufacturing and agricultural interests, whose numbers and enthusiasm for liberal trade had grown considerably since the war, thanks in part to the successful operation of the trade agreements program.[73] Many industrial unions and labor's umbrella organization, the AFL-CIO, also supported the TEA, due to the benefits from trade that labor had enjoyed since World War II, the labor leadership's support for trade liberalization as a bulwark against the spread of communism, and the inclusion in the bill of the TAA program.[74]

Of course, interest groups were not unanimously supportive of Kennedy's bill. Import-competing firms in labor-intensive industries continued to oppose trade liberalization. Similarly, whereas the AFL-CIO supported the TEA, individual unions representing workers in import-competing industries did not.

Kennedy's efforts were rewarded when the Democratic Congress made only minor changes in his comparatively liberal bill and then passed it with relative ease. Partisanship nevertheless dogged the legislation. The Senate vote in favor of the bill on final passage was strongly bipartisan, but in the House, while Democrats decisively supported the measure, the GOP was badly split, and in the end, a small majority of Republicans voted against it. In both chambers, restrictive Republican-sponsored motions and amendments were defeated on partisan votes by large and cohesive Democratic congressional majorities.

With the passage of the Trade Expansion Act, which authorized U.S. participation in the five-year Kennedy Round GATT negotiations, the high point of liberal trade in postwar America had been reached.[75] This accomplishment was due in no small part to the emergence of a consensus on liberal trade between the Democratic and Republican Parties. Members on both sides of the aisle increasingly understood that trade contributed to economic efficiency and national security. Nevertheless, the parties continued to differ over the conditions or rules under which trade should be liberalized.

The Rise of Protectionist Pressures and Bipartisan Concern

It was not long before new challenges to the liberal trade regime arose. Already by 1960, the relative position of American industries in the world economy had begun to decline due, among other factors, to the reconstruction of the war-devastated Western European and Japanese economies and the asymmetrically free access other nations' producers were allowed to the American market. By 1959 the U.S. share of world exports had dropped to 18.7 percent, from 29.4 percent in 1953.

The American economy's gradual competitive decline was accelerated in the late 1960s with the onset of the "crisis of Fordism."[76] The Democrats' Keynesian accumulation strategy, so vital in solving earlier demand-side problems, now contributed to supply-side difficulties. Rising Vietnam War and Great Society social spending, which President Lyndon Johnson refused to finance with a tax increase, tightened labor markets, pushing up wages. At the same time the growth rate of domestic productivity began to decline, for a series of still poorly understood reasons. The resulting rise in unit labor costs simultaneously fueled inflation and cut into corporate profitability. As inflation gathered strength, progressively overvaluing the dollar, the challenge from the rebuilt Western European and Japanese economies intensified, ultimately producing a trade deficit in manufactured goods in 1971 for the first time since 1888.

Protectionist pressures in light or labor-intensive industries like textiles, apparel, footwear, mining, and chemicals had increased in the mid- and late 1950s. By the late 1960s a much broader group of heavy or capital-intensive Fordist mass production industries—including steel, automobiles, and consumer electronics—had begun to experience heightened import pressures. In response, the steel industry began to seek protection in 1968. Other industries soon followed.[77]

Probably the most significant new protectionist pressures came from the onetime bastion of liberal trade: organized labor. In the late 1950s unions representing unskilled or low-end semiskilled workers in light, labor-intensive industries turned to protectionism. Then, as imports flooded the U.S. market from about 1968 to 1974, labor organizations representing semiskilled workers, beginning with the United Steel Workers and later including the AFL-CIO and many of its constituent unions, joined the protectionist ranks.[78]

Not all firms or unions, of course, embraced protectionism. Multinational corporations with extensive intrafirm trade and export-oriented capital-intensive and high-tech firms continued to support trade liberalization. Unions representing high-end semiskilled and professional workers in most of these same industries also continued to back free trade. In the late 1960s and early 1970s, however, the forces of protectionism appeared to be gaining strength and threatened to undermine the liberal trade policy paradigm. Deluged by complaints about unfair foreign trade practices, members of Congress of both parties began to support import quota legislation to buffer domestic industries.

In 1967–68 the vast majority of these measures were bottled up in the House Ways and Means and Senate Finance Committees by their pro-liberal trade chairmen, while President Johnson, another Democratic liberal trader, threatened to veto any protectionist legislation. Thus, none of these bills was approved. But protectionist sentiment in both parties in Congress was strong enough to prevent passage of administration-sponsored legislation to implement parts of the tariff-cutting agreement that concluded the Kennedy Round GATT negotiations in 1967.[79]

The Revival of Trade Partisanship: The Parties Begin to Reverse Their Positions

In 1968 Republican Richard Nixon was elected president, as southern and white working-class voters turned against the party that they held responsible for the racial and cultural turmoil of the 1960s. A new period of divided government began. Nixon's presidency also saw the strongest protectionist pressures of the postwar era until that time, as well as the renewal of partisan divisions over trade policy.

In late 1969 Nixon, preoccupied with domestic economic problems, submitted a modest trade bill to the Democratic Congress that called for additional tariff-cutting authority and other liberalizing measures. The next summer the House Ways and Means Committee, under strong protectionist pressure, then combined Nixon's measure with other proposals that, on balance, left the bill restrictive in nature. The House passed the bill on a partially partisan vote, but now the parties were beginning to reverse their historic positions: the Republicans becoming the defenders of liberal trade and the Democrats assuming a more protectionist stance.[80] The bill died in the Senate.

During the next year inflation accelerated and the U.S. trade position deteriorated, leading to the nation's first trade deficit since 1888. Compounded by U.S. overseas military spending and growing foreign investment, the rising trade deficit also caused severe balance-of-payments problems and a consequent speculative attack on the dollar. In response, and hoping to improve his reelection chances, Nixon in August 1971 dramatically announced a wage-price freeze, a 10 percent import surcharge, and, most important, an end to the convertibility of dollars into gold. This was followed in December by the famous Smithsonian Agreement in which the United States formally agreed to devalue the dollar in order to make American goods more competitive.

Over the next six months, the overall improvement in the balance-of-payments deficit was disappointing. In February 1972 the administration announced that Nixon would ask Congress to authorize another devaluation of the dollar. He also sent Capitol Hill a bill requesting the authority over a five-year period to adjust tariff and, for the first time, nontariff barriers in another upcoming GATT round. The final bill passed by the Democratic Congress—the Trade Reform Act of 1974—gave Nixon almost all the authority he sought.[81]

Although the president's discretion was restricted in a number of important ways, considering the seemingly protectionist mood of the country, what was in the end a fairly liberal bill passed the House and the Senate by impressive margins.[82]

Partisan divisions were again evident in congressional voting on the bill, as the parties continued to switch positions. On final passage in the House, the Republicans favored the liberal bill by a decisive margin of 160–19, while the Democrats marginally opposed it 112–121. Although the Senate passed the final bill in 1974 with an overwhelming bipartisan majority, an amendment to limit the president's tariff-cutting power was defeated in a more partisan vote. Thus, the enactment of the liberal Trade Reform Act of 1974 can be attributed to the support of the cohesive House and Senate Republican minorities, in coalition with a still significant faction of Democratic liberal traders.

On the GOP side, some partisanship over the 1974 trade bill was due to Nixon's prestige with congressional Republicans. Across the aisle, Democratic opposition to the bill resulted in part from the fact that congressional Democrats were voting on the program of a Republican president.[83] Ideology also influenced the new partisan alignment on trade. Since the New Deal, the Democrats had been committed to government intervention in the marketplace to reduce economic instability and redress social inequities; Republicans had favored a much less intrusive government role. On trade, however, these positions had been reversed. Now, in the early 1970s, the parties began to bring their respective trade policy stances into correspondence with their broader ideological views of the proper function of government.[84]

Most important in explaining the new partisan division over trade, however, were the historic shift in the geographic bases of the two parties, produced by exogenous political factors, and regional industrial changes.[85] Before the 1950s, Republican strength was concentrated in the industrial Northeast and Midwest, and the party backed the high tariffs advocated by the regions' manufacturing interests. The Democratic Party found its base mainly in the South among export-oriented agricultural interests and thus supported lower tariffs. But after the New Deal and later the racial and cultural upheavals of the 1960s had clarified the parties' national images, the Democrats began to dominate among the industrial workers, minorities, and liberals of the Midwest and Northeast, while the Republicans gained strength among conservatives in the South and the Mountain West.

At the same time, regional industrial structures and import sensitivities were also changing, shifting the trade policy preferences of economic actors in those regions. Following their migration from New England, the textile and apparel producers of the Southeast were threatened by imports in the 1950s. By the end of the 1960s or the early 1970s, the competitiveness of Fordist mass production industries in the Northeast and Midwest had also begun to decline. Consequently, capital and labor in these various sectors turned toward protectionism. Meanwhile, agricultural producers in the South, West, and particularly the Plains and Rocky Mountain states were becoming increasingly efficient, and dynamic new high-tech sectors were beginning to emerge in parts of the West, predisposing these areas toward liberal trade.

In about 1970 the geographic shift in the parties' bases of support and reinforcing regional industrial shifts began to produce a slow, incremental reversal of the parties' trade policy positions, evident to a small extent in party presidential platforms, but to a greater degree in congressional roll-call voting. Although the Democrats' traditional southern base was slowly eroding, much of the region's still substantial Democratic congressional delegation represented districts, especially in the Southeast, that were now dependent not so much on agricultural exports as on import-competing industries like textiles, apparel, and shoes. Beginning in the 1950s, this pushed some southern Democrats toward support for protectionism.[86] At the same time, the Democrats became relatively more dependent on the historically and now once again protectionist Northeast and Midwest. In particular, they relied increasingly on the votes, volunteers, and money of organized labor, which was becoming steadily more protectionist in outlook.[87] Labor aggressively fought the liberal Trade Reform Act of 1974, and its influence was felt in congressional, notably House, voting on the bill. Only 17 of 149 House Democrats from northern industrial states supported the legislation, thanks largely to pressure and campaign contributions from the AFL-CIO and its member unions.[88] Labor's turn to protectionism prompted a similar move by northern Democrats.

Meanwhile, the Republicans reduced their dependence on the historically protectionist industrialists of the Northeast and Midwest and instead became more closely allied with southern, western, Plains states, and Rocky Mountain agricultural interests, western high-tech sectors, and the rapidly expanding multinational corporate community. All of these interests were export and internationally oriented, and so the GOP gradually severed its protectionist roots and embraced liberal trade.

The result of these various trends was slowly growing partisan conflict over trade in Congress and to a lesser extent on the presidential campaign trail, but with a reversal of the parties' historic positions.

The Search for New Strategies in the 1970s

Through the 1970s but especially after the oil shock of 1973, the crisis of the Fordist regime of accumulation deepened, and the Fordist mode of regulation and the capital-labor, welfarist, and embedded liberal compromises inscribed in it were eroded. This ended the postwar boom and inaugurated a long era of economic stagnation, or at least markedly slower growth. The end of the boom also signaled the beginning of the crisis of the New Deal Order.

In the sphere of production, Fordist firms tried to reverse their declining rate of profits by holding the line on wage increases, rationalizing employment, increasing employment flexibility, introducing new labor-saving technologies, geographically redeploying their assets toward low-wage developing countries or parts of the American Sun Belt, adopting new intrafirm organizational arrangements, and redefining their relationships with their subcontractors and markets.[89]

At the level of the state, presidents of both parties continuously adjusted their accumulation strategies, alternately experimenting with expansionist and restrictive macroeconomic policies as they sought to hold or win the support of an increasingly dealigned electorate. Along with the Watergate crisis, the inability of President Nixon and his Republican successor, Gerald Ford, to end stagflation gave the Democrats another chance to govern, this time under Jimmy Carter. Carter's failure to resolve the economic crisis—indeed, it worsened in the late 1970s, when the second oil shock produced a new burst of stagflation—further undermined the New Deal coalition and order.

On the trade front, though, Carter—another Democratic liberal trader—was considerably more successful. Although the trade deficit and protectionist pressures had been checked in the mid-1970s by the declining dollar and continued agricultural and high-tech export growth, by the end of the decade imports were pouring in again from Europe and Japan and now the advanced developing countries. Carter defused some of the new protectionist pressure by negotiating or imposing a variety of import curbs.

Protectionism was also braked, and the further repolarization of the parties over trade policy was temporarily reversed by the passage of the liberal Trade Agreements Act of 1979. In April 1979 the Tokyo Round GATT negotiations, U.S. participation in which was authorized by the Trade Reform Act of 1974, were successfully concluded. The new agreement called for substantial further reduction in tariff rates and, more significant, for the reduction and regulation of various nontariff barriers.[90]

In the summer of 1979, President Carter submitted a bill to the Democratic Congress to codify the Tokyo Round into law. Although the AFL-CIO opposed the bill as too liberal—for reasons that included the new "fast-track" provision of the 1974 trade act, which mandated regular consultation between the executive and Congress during trade negotiations, and the willingness of some protectionist Democrats to defer to the wishes of a free-trading president of their own party—the measure passed with overwhelming bipartisan majorities.

Before the Great Depression, trade played the key role in structuring American party alignments. In the post–World War II period, however, the public salience of the trade issue and the level of partisan conflict over it both declined as a bipartisan consensus on liberal trade gradually took hold. Under the New Deal Order, Keynesian demand management emerged as the nation's main tool of national economic policy, and budget and social welfare policies, not trade policy, principally divided the parties.

In the early 1970s the partisan trade fires began to burn anew, with the parties' historic positions now reversed, although by the end of the decade, the fires had been contained. Soon enough, however, the smoldering embers would again burst into flame.

The First Reagan Administration

Democratic Pressure and White House Retreat

In November 1980 Ronald Reagan was swept into the White House by an electoral college landslide. The Republicans also captured the Senate for the first time since 1954 and strengthened their position in the House of Representatives. The once-mighty Democratic coalition and political order were crumbling. Nonetheless, the Democrats did manage to retain control of the House, producing a new episode of divided government and the further dealignment of the political system.

The Republican Takeover and the
Struggle for a New Political Order

The Democratic presidential majority, if not yet the wider New Deal Order, had been weakened as early as 1948 by the party's internal struggle over civil rights, which alienated southern white Democratic voters.[1] The racial, social, and cultural upheavals of the 1960s drove the Democrats still further to the left, producing a more substantial defection of southern and white ethnic working-class voters in the elections of 1968 and 1972. Reagan was then helped to victory in 1980 by yet another wave of popular opposition to crime, welfare, affirmative action, busing, and abortion, as well as by the mounting tax revolt, the mobilization of conservative intellectuals and especially the business community against the welfare and regulatory state, and the Iranian hostage crisis.

Most central in propelling Reagan into office, however, was the intensifying "stagflation" of the last years of the Carter administration, which was the product of two interrelated trends. First, the dual crisis of Fordism and the Democrats' Keynesian accumulation strategy resulted in a further slowing of productivity growth and continued wage and labor market rigidity, which raised prices while reducing corporate profitability, competitiveness, and investment. Second, the rapid globalization of trade, investment, and finance—begun in the 1950s and 1960s, interrupted during much of the 1970s, but under way again by the end of the decade—rendered the U.S. economy more vulnerable to external disturbances. These included the two oil shocks of 1973 and 1979, a new surge in manufacturing imports, and heightened capital mobility and exchange rate instability, which also squeezed profits and investment and contributed to higher prices and unemployment.

These problems were compounded in 1979, when Federal Reserve chairman Paul Volcker raised interest rates to combat inflation and defend the value of the dollar, a policy turn that in the short run only further depressed employment without having much immediate impact on inflation. Thus, in November 1980, with unemployment, inflation, and interest rates all at or near postwar highs, the retrospectively minded American electorate rejected the incumbent Democratic president whom it rightly or wrongly held responsible for these ills.

Transitions to Post-Fordism

At the end of the 1970s, the economic problems that wrecked Jimmy Carter's presidency and brought Ronald Reagan to power were by no means uniquely American. Most advanced industrial economies had gone into crisis earlier in the decade for similar domestic and international reasons. In particular, basic mass production industries appeared to be in decline or at least under serious threat. In response, business and political leaders began a process of economic and industrial restructuring to restore conditions of profitability and national competitiveness. This has produced a gradual and still incomplete "quintuple transition," underpinned by the emergence of an "information technology paradigm":[2]

> 1. A transition from Fordist regimes of accumulation based on mass production by big firms using dedicated machinery, scale economies, and mass consumption to post-Fordist regimes based on more flexible forms of production by smaller networked firms, economies of scope, innovation rents, and more rapidly changing and differentiated patterns of consumption.[3]
> 2. A transition among industrial sectors from basic manufacturing or "sunset" industries like automobiles and steel to new information and high-tech or "sunrise" industries, including computers, software, microelectronics, telecommunications, robotics, biotechnology, and, of course, the Internet.

3. A shift from a manufacturing-based industrial society to a service-oriented postindustrial society.

4. A transition from an international to a globalizing economy, best understood as a configuration of electronically integrated arms-length market exchanges, multinational and transnational corporations, and interfirm networks, including horizontal strategic alliances and vertical commodity chains, underpinned by global financial flows.[4]

5. A more recent—and, in light of the 2000 Nasdaq collapse, possibly reversible—transition to a "financialized capitalism" in which (a) the stock market and venture capital partially supplant banks as sources of investment funds, especially in the high-tech sector, and (b) consumption levels are increasingly determined by the technology-influenced movement of stock prices.[5]

As much for ease of exposition as anything else, I shall subsume these five related shifts under the single, widely used if admittedly inadequate, rubric of the transition from Fordism to post-Fordism.[6]

This fundamental economic transition has been assisted by institutional and policy changes, that is, by the development of elements of a new mode of regulation. The principal component of the mode of regulation that corresponded to the Fordist regime was the Keynesian Welfare State (KWS) (or more accurately in the United States, the Keynesian Welfare/Warfare State), with liberal or laissez-faire, corporatist or social-democratic, and statist or developmental variants. The KWS promoted full employment in the relatively closed postwar economies mainly through demand management and new forms of collective consumption. During the Fordist Golden Age, most of the advanced industrial nations also pursued more or less liberal or freer trade policies to foster expanded global demand and thus economic growth.

A key element of the new mode of regulation is what Philip Cerny and others have termed the "competition state," which, in contrast to the demand-side focused KWS, is a supply-side oriented state form structurally privileged by globalization and the stagflation crisis of the 1970s. It is true that recent years have seen the displacement of some governance functions upward to supranational organizations, downward to regional and local entities, and sideways to various public-private networks and partnerships. Nevertheless, the national state retains a significant, if transformed, role in promoting innovation and the economy's overall structural competitiveness to make it an attractive site for domestic and inward foreign investment, while subordinating welfare policy to the demands of competitiveness and labor market flexibility.[7]

Bob Jessop has identified three ideal-typical forms of the competition state—neoliberal, neocorporatist, and neostatist—each with distinct, corresponding sets of institutions and policy packages, including trade strategies.[8] *Neoliberalism* promotes a market-led transition to post-Fordism, emphasizing privatization, deregulation, and a generally limited government role in the economy. National competitiveness emerges from entrepreneurial innovation and the decisions of individual firms, not from government intervention. Neoliberalism also correspondingly supports freer trade, on either a regional or multilateral basis, to promote the more efficient allocation of resources and thus to further enhance competitiveness and national welfare. *Neocorporatism* fosters innovation, production and labor market flexibility, and competitiveness through the institutionalization of continuing, negotiated concertation among key economic and political actors, especially at the level of the firm and the locality. Generally liberal trade is nevertheless regulated to reduce the threat of job loss and downward pressure on wages, taxes, and labor and environmental standards. *Neostatism* advances market-conforming but state-sponsored programs—including active labor market, infrastructure, innovation, technology, industrial restructuring and promotion, and other policies—to increase flexibility, efficiency, and competitiveness. Neomercantilist or economic nationalist trade policies, including selective import protection and unilateral market-opening tactics, are also employed to defend key emergent or "strategic" high-tech industries, which often need large markets to achieve economies of scale.

As Jessop notes, none of these ideal-typical variants of the competition state are likely to be found in pure form within any single nation. During crises of regulation, as dominant strategies fail and social compromises and institutions are eroded, new coalitions or constellations of economic and political interests advance and struggle over contending accumulation strategies, or what a number of authors call "competitive strategies" to emphasize their international dimensions.[9] Through processes of conscious design, conflict, and trial-and-error experiment, mixed and often internally contradictory strategies usually emerge; these strategies embody or reflect compromises between the various contending social and political forces and become institutionalized within the structures of the state, resulting in new hybrid state forms.

In the years after Ronald Reagan took office in 1981, the struggle over the direction and structure of the U.S. economy included proponents of various neoliberal, neocorporatist, and neostatist strategies of transition to post-Fordism. But it also included defenders of the old Fordist order and its dominant Keynesian accumulation strategy, who had by no means been driven from the political scene.

To an important degree, this struggle was fought out in the arena of trade policy. Supporters of competitive, export-oriented post-Fordist sectors who nevertheless differed over the appropriate post-Fordist trade strategy did battle with each other as well as with defenders of Fordism, who often advocated protectionism or fought trade liberalization initiatives to arrest the decline of beleaguered mass production industries. These competing interests fought over import curbs in the early 1980s, unilateral market-opening measures from the mid-1980s through the mid-1990s, and various trade liberalization proposals throughout the 1990s.

Political parties play a key role in formulating, organizing conflict over, and implementing different accumulation or competitive strategies. Parties, including internal party factions, develop and deploy such strategies, both in campaigns and in office, to appeal to their core supporters—organized labor and the poor for the Democrats, business and the upper middle class for the Republicans—as well as to swing voters and interests. In the United States since 1980, swing constituencies have included various layers of the white-collar middle class, whose ranks have expanded with the transition to post-Fordism, and nonunionized, blue-collar Reagan Democrats, who are no longer reliable supporters of the party of Roosevelt. In competitively pursuing their politically driven accumulation strategies during the past two decades, the Democratic and Republican Parties and their respective factions have decisively influenced the process of transition to a new post-Fordist mode of regulation and regime of accumulation.

The rest of this volume shows how, since 1980, party competition has played a central role in one particularly important aspect of this process: the development of U.S. trade policy. This chapter begins the detailed narrative by charting the reemergence of trade as a subject of partisan contention during the first Reagan administration.[10]

Reagan in Power: Ideology and Pragmatism

Although he did not conceptualize his goal in precisely these terms, on taking office in 1981 Ronald Reagan set out to accomplish nothing less than the erosion or even the dismantling of many institutions of the New Deal Order and the consolidation of a durable new conservative Republican political order via the construction of a dynamic post-Fordist regime of accumulation and mode of regulation.[11] Toward this end, Reagan boldly began to pursue what was essentially a neoliberal strategy, intended to restructure and revitalize the economy, and thus also to promote his reelection, by unleashing what he called the "magic of the marketplace."

Amid Republican claims of "mandate" and "realignment," Reagan moved quickly to implement his supply-side strategy. This strategy was actually a hybrid combining Paul Volcker's tight money policy both to combat inflation and prop up the value of the dollar; corporate tax reductions and deregulation to disencumber the private sector and thus unleash investment; personal tax cuts tilted toward the upper brackets to encourage individual work effort; and social spending cuts to help balance the budget and thus reduce the "crowding out" of private investors from the capital markets. Not formally part of his program but essential elements of it nevertheless were a substantial increase in military spending and a weakening of organized labor in order to drive down business wage costs.

Reagan's strategy had a number of sources. Probably most important were his own strongly antistatist ideological beliefs, rooted in his disillusionment as a former Democrat with the New Deal and its legacy and his subsequent immersion in the conservative movement.[12] Reagan's economic advisers and interlocutors—true supply-siders, monetarists, and conservative fiscalists in the White House, the academy, think tanks, and the press—also influenced his thinking. Further, the new president wanted to attract and hold the support of the business community, including the Sun Belt entrepreneurs, small business owners, and middle managers who were his earliest backers, but also bigger, internationally oriented corporate interests who rallied to his side after he won the nomination and expressed his support for cutting corporate taxes. These various business interests had taken a "right turn" in the late 1970s in mobilizing to rein in the Keynesian welfare and regulatory state, and Reagan promised to move public policy in this direction.[13] Finally, his program was designed to appeal to middle- and working-class voters, including the blue-collar swing voters later known as "Reagan Democrats," who were tired of stagflation and rising taxes and the "Big Government" that was thought to have produced them.[14]

Reagan aggressively fought for and won passage of his tax and budget programs in the spring and summer of 1981. In this he received surprising support from Democrats, especially southern "boll weevils," who were intimidated by the scale of his election victory and his initial popularity. The steep recession of 1981–82, however, diminished that acclaim, increased the Democratic House majority by twenty-six seats in the midterm elections, and stiffened Democratic resistance to his subsequent budget requests. Although the economy recovered strongly enough for Reagan to win reelection in 1994, he was forced to give ground in negotiations with the Democrats over the budget. Less ideological and more pragmatic than some analysts would have it, and always looking to claim even small-scale political victories, Reagan agreed to modest tax increases and more federal spending than he preferred. His goal was to maintain the support—for himself and Republicans in Congress[15]—of both influential business interests, who were alarmed at the burgeoning budget deficit, and key groups of swing voters who worried that the growing deficit would eventually force severe cuts in retirement and other social programs.[16]

Congruent with his strong antistatist beliefs, Reagan was also an ideological free trader, his views rooted largely in his personal depression-era experiences and his conviction that the crash was caused or at least deepened by the Smoot-Hawley Tariff Act.[17] Reagan's free-trade stance was later reinforced by his ties to internationally oriented business interests and by the influence of State and Defense Department officials, who maintained control of trade policy during the president's first term.

By relying on the combined forces of "free markets and free trade" to heighten competitive pressures on U.S. manufacturers, the Reagan administration hoped to accelerate the process of post-Fordist restructuring and thus improve the competitiveness of the U.S. economy. But Reagan's initial program actually made little mention of trade or other forms of international economic policy, since the president and his advisers' top priority was to get the country's own economic house in order.[18]

Soon after Reagan took office, with the American economy already mired in the worst economic downturn since the Great Depression, the U.S. trade deficit exploded. This was due to an overvalued dollar, declining industrial competitiveness, the rise of new (particularly East Asian) competitors, and foreign industrial policies and unfair trade practices. For the first time since World War II, manufacturing employment declined for three consecutive years (1980–82). In the same period, imports, which usually fall during a recession, actually grew by 8.3 percent, while exports declined by 17.5 percent.[19]

Seeking an economically and politically viable accumulation strategy with which to oppose Reaganomics, the Democrats seized on the administration's neglect of international economic policy, which had provoked demands from business and labor for import curbs and action to open closed foreign markets, and began to advocate "economic nationalism" as part of the solution to the nation's trade and competitiveness problems. Their proposed solutions included tougher trade policies as well as interventionist industrial policies.[20] As *Business Week* noted, by the end of 1982, such policies had become "central to the 'alternative' economic strategies" that the Democrats were "shaping as their answer to laissez-faire Reaganomics."[21]

Both on the campaign trail and in Congress, where they still controlled the House, the Democrats tried to heresthetically raise the salience of, or expand the scope of conflict over, the trade issue by pulling it out of its insulated subsystem and propelling it into the realm of macropolitics. Their goals were to protect their core labor constituents employed in import-battered Fordist mass production industries, rebuild their fractured coalition (including among swing Reagan Democrats during the 1982 and 1984 elections), and dislodge the Republicans from their hold on the Senate and the White House. Accordingly, the Democrats pressed for the passage of domestic content legislation to help the automobile industry in 1982 and 1983 and an omnibus trade bill in 1984. They also tried to make a presidential campaign issue of a mid-1984 ruling by the U.S. International Trade Commission (ITC) that found that imports were injuring the domestic steel industry and issued recommendations for quotas and tariffs.

This Democratic pressure contributed to the renewal of partisan divisions in Congress over domestic content and other trade issues. It also forced Reagan, through a process of policy contagion, to begin what Council of Economic Advisers (CEA) chairman William Niskanen would later call the administration's "strategic retreat" from free trade.[22] Just as Reagan pragmatically struck deals with congressional Democrats on the budget, so he repeatedly compromised his free-trade principles to retain the political support, for both himself and congressional Republicans, of firms and workers, especially swing Reagan Democrats, in the nation's threatened mass production industries.

Murmurings of Partisan Trade Warfare, 1981–1982

The Auto Agreement

Almost immediately on taking office, Reagan confronted his first big trade challenge, one involving a country—Japan—and an industry—automobiles— that would preoccupy American trade policymakers in the White House and Congress into the mid-1990s.[23] Moreover, this episode would signal the beginning of Reagan's politically driven "strategic retreat" from free trade.

In early 1981 the continuing flood of Japanese auto imports was battering America's premier Fordist industry. In the wake of the oil shocks of 1973 and 1979, there was a surge in foreign and notably Japanese imports as U.S. automakers failed to anticipate and adapt to the public's growing demand for smaller, more fuel-efficient cars. In the summer of 1980 the United Auto Workers (UAW) and the Ford Motor Company had reluctantly abandoned their traditional free-trade positions and submitted a petition to the U.S. International Trade Commission—filed under Section 201 (the escape clause) of the Trade Act of 1974—alleging that imports of light cars and trucks were causing "substantial" injury to the U.S. auto industry. When the ITC unexpectedly rejected the UAW/Ford petition in November, the defeated Jimmy Carter left the politically sensitive issue to his successor.

Despite his free-trade views, during the fall presidential campaign Reagan had made promises of protection or other assistance to trade-battered firms and workers in the textile, steel, and auto industries. In particular, he had pledged to politically powerful Michigan autoworkers that he would slow the torrent of automobile imports. After his election the president needed to reconcile this assurance with his long-standing free-trade commitments. His situation was further complicated by bipartisan congressional support for legislation to impose quotas on Japanese auto imports. After a heated intra-administration debate, Reagan reluctantly decided to press Tokyo for a voluntary export restraint agreement (VRA), which was announced in May.

In this case the two congressional parties did not divide over the auto issue— the influential automobile industry had defenders in both parties—but, nevertheless, partisan considerations were involved in Reagan's decision. Had he refused any import restrictions, he was guaranteed a bruising battle with Congress. This, in turn, could have jeopardized his economic recovery program and dimmed Republican chances for gaining an even stronger congressional base in the 1982 midterm elections.[24]

Reciprocity and Domestic Content

Anxious to combat the perception that in agreeing to the auto VER it had abandoned the principles of free trade, the Reagan administration generally paid little attention to the growth of imports during the rest of 1981. But in the summer and fall, imports continued to pour into the country. Concurrently, the Volcker/Reagan tight money policy drove up interest rates and thus the value of the dollar, compounding problems of competitiveness, while the recession triggered by this same policy worsened. As a consequence, the trade deficit surged, especially with Japan, and protectionist pressures steadily grew in the steel, textile, and semiconductor industries.

To deflect this protectionist threat, and in reaction to the emergence of nontariff barriers (NTBs) as the main obstacle to international trade as tariffs continued to fall, the administration modestly changed course and revived an old issue in U.S.-Japan trade relations and an old Republican theme: reciprocity.[25] Earlier in the year, the White House had indicated its intent to press Japan to open its markets to various U.S. products, but there had been no follow-up. Now the United States made a formal request that Japan begin to open up, warning of a likely protectionist backlash in Congress if it failed to comply.

In pursuing this strategy the White House was playing a new version of the old game of "export politics," in which executive branch trade officials attempt to contain domestic protectionist pressures by building coalitions of export interests to open foreign markets. In the postwar period, this had been done through the multilateral negotiation of reciprocal tariff concessions. The new reciprocity strategy was designed to accomplish the same goal through bilateral, sector-specific negotiations to reduce mostly nontariff barriers, backed up by at least the threat of retaliation.[26]

Beyond its concern to blunt protectionist pressures, the White House cautiously took up the banner of reciprocity to undermine Democratic attempts to exploit the trade issue for partisan advantage. Democrats were starting to attack not only the administration's trade policies but also its macroeconomic policies that were driving up the value of the dollar. Further, Congressional Democrats charged that the executive was unwilling to employ "structural" policies to boost the nation's sagging productivity growth rates, viewed as one source of declining American competitiveness.[27]

The White House attempted to deflect these partisan criticisms by arguing that the real problem was closed Japanese markets, not the strong dollar or uncompetitive American products.[28] But the disappointingly limited Japanese response to the administration's mild market-opening efforts produced heightened protectionist pressures in Congress, as White House officials had feared. It was then the turn of Senate Republican leaders to take up the cause of reciprocity. John Danforth (R-Mo.), chairman of the Senate Finance Subcommittee on International Trade, introduced a bill that called for negotiations with and retaliation against those countries that refused to reduce their barriers to U.S. exports. In truth, however, Danforth and other congressional supporters of reciprocity legislation did not intend to throw up import barriers but rather to defuse protectionist pressures and to neutralize any Democratic attempt to exploit the trade issue in the 1982 midterm election.[29]

Domestic Content Legislation

In fact, the GOP's reciprocity campaign did neither. Many congressional Democrats, finding the moderate Danforth bill far too weak a response to the mounting trade crisis, instead supported the UAW-backed "domestic content" bill. The Fair Practices in Automotive Products Act, introduced in the House the previous December by Richard Ottinger of New York, was intended both to curb car and auto parts imports and to encourage foreign companies to produce automobiles in this country. The bill would have prescribed the share of parts that had to be produced in the United States and Canada for automobiles, light trucks, and spares.

With Republicans in control of the Senate, the Reagan administration had never taken the domestic content bill seriously. But as the recession and the overvalued dollar continued to pound American industry, in the summer of 1982 domestic auto sales plummeted, autoworker unemployment rose, and import market shares in this key sector grew. Throughout Rust Belt midwestern and northeastern states, more generalized fears were developing that the country was "deindustrializing," heightening protectionist sentiment in Congress. This was particularly true of Democrats dependent on labor votes, volunteers, and money, since not only the UAW but also the AFL-CIO had made the domestic content bill their top legislative priority. The Reagan administration, supported by most Congressional Republicans, blasted the legislation as unacceptably protectionist.

Campaigning on Trade, Defusing Threats

The partisan fires were also fanned by the winds of presidential politics. In late September 1982, Edward Kennedy and Walter Mondale delivered a pair of highly publicized speeches to the United Steel Workers convention as they sought labor support for their bids for the Democratic presidential nomination.

In the 1970s the AFL-CIO, though not some of its more progressively inclined member unions, had reduced its involvement in presidential politics.[30] Having played a key role in brokering the choice of Democratic presidential nominees in the preprimary era, the AFL was angry at the success of socially and culturally liberal, middle-class "New Politics" activists in reforming the party's nominating process after the tumultuous 1968 Democratic convention and then in winning the nomination for George McGovern in 1972. Thus, the federation refused to endorse McGovern in the general election. Four years later the AFL remained neutral during the primary campaign, although it did support the eventual Democratic nominee, Jimmy Carter, in the general election. In 1981, however, in response to the previous year's election debacle and the devastation of the unions by the Reagan recession, surging imports, administration and employer attacks, and long-term economic-structural changes, the AFL-CIO had embarked on a plan to become the dominant financial and political force within the Democratic Party. The federation's aim was to block a Republican takeover of Congress in the 1982 elections and, by making an unprecedented endorsement of a presidential candidate before the 1984 primaries, to once again play a pivotal role in choosing the Democrats' nominee that year.

With long-standing ties to the labor movement, Kennedy and Mondale had already voiced support for import curbs, including passage of the domestic content bill, and for pressure on Japan to open its markets, both top labor priorities. Now, in their much-reported speeches to the steelworkers, they talked even tougher on trade.[31]

Kennedy and Mondale's speeches also spurred efforts by Democratic congressional and gubernatorial candidates to raise the salience of the trade issue during the last weeks of the fall campaign, as evidence mounted that the public was turning increasingly protectionist.[32] The Democrats saw a real political opportunity in the lingering recession, but they were afraid to attack Reaganomics head-on, and they still lacked a comprehensive economic strategy of their own to replace discredited Keynesian thinking. Thus, in states like Connecticut, Michigan, Ohio, and Missouri, Democratic candidates, many with strong UAW support, attacked Reagan administration trade policies, especially toward Japan, for contributing to the nation's unemployment woes.[33] In particular races, they also criticized their Republican opponents for opposing the domestic content bill.

With some of his fellow partisans in trouble on trade, and with Democratic presidential candidates all backing the Senate version of the domestic content bill, Reagan took several steps to defuse the issue in what can be understood as textbook cases of policy contagion. On October 19, 1982, Senator Danforth, locked in a close race with a challenger who had attacked his opposition to the domestic content bill, was allowed to announce that Japan would be pressed to extend the auto voluntary restraint agreement for a third year.[34] Two days later, Reagan disclosed that European carbon steel producers had "voluntarily" agreed to limit their steel exports to the United States. Presidential press secretary Larry Speakes explained the political considerations that lay in part behind the agreement: "Our judgment is that this will give us a boost in Youngstown and other hard-pressed steel-producing cities."[35]

On another front, the White House hoped to launch a new round of international trade negotiations at a late November ministerial meeting of the General Agreement on Tariffs and Trade (GATT) in Geneva, Switzerland.[36] In proposing a new round, U.S. Trade Representative (USTR) William Brock, a committed free trader, wanted to open new markets for American agricultural, service, and other producers. But Brock was also playing export politics. He hoped that engaging internationally oriented business interests in a new GATT round would help to contain the forces of global and domestic protectionism and head off the domestic content bill. Further, as a former Republican National Committee chairman, Brock had a more partisan goal in mind: to defuse the Democratic trade threat to Reagan and congressional Republicans.[37]

The outcome of the Geneva meeting was disappointing to both the White House and congressional members of the U.S. delegation. Talk of a possible trade war and heightened congressional protectionism was widespread.

Domestic Content Again

In fact, following the failed GATT meeting, and despite the administration's earlier actions to curb auto and steel imports, the House Democratic leadership kept the pressure on, bringing the domestic content bill to a vote in early December 1982.[38] The vote was a payback to the United Auto Workers for the help it provided to many of the party's candidates in the recent elections, in which the Democrats made a net gain of 26 House seats. Despite widespread media criticism of the measure and an intensified lobbying campaign by groups opposed to it, the House voted 215–188 to approve the domestic content bill.

The vote was a fairly partisan one; Democrats supported the measure by a 171–58 margin, while Republicans opposed it 44–130. To some extent, the partisan split can be explained by the regionally differentiated nature of the parties' bases of support. The Democrats' strength was increasingly concentrated in the import-sensitive and hence protectionist industrial Northeast and Midwest. The Republicans, on the other hand, were relatively stronger in the Pacific and Mountain West, the Plains states, and the South, regions that were more favorably disposed to free trade by virtue of their dependence on agricultural and high-technology exports.[39] But other, nonregional or intraregional sources of partisan division were important, too.

Ideological and cognitive differences between the congressional parties over trade were one such additional factor. Some Democrats were convinced that the bill would mainly produce general benefits such as an increase in aggregate employment and a slowing of deindustrialization. Republicans saw the bill as more likely to result in general costs such as reduced economic efficiency and even perhaps a trade war and depression.

But the partisan division over the domestic content bill was due mostly to House members' attentiveness to the preferences of their core reelection constituencies. Most broadly, Democrats backed the bill to defend or improve the employment situation of blue-collar workers in the auto and related industries. Republicans, on the other hand, opposed the measure to hold down car prices for middle-class consumers, who were much better informed about the price of an automobile than they were about the cost of other consumer goods.[40]

More important, however, were the actual lobbying efforts of organized interests, which mobilized in response to the perceived incidence of the bill's benefits and costs. Internationally oriented business interests pressured Republicans to oppose the measure.[41] The effectiveness of this lobbying was magnified by the growing dependence of Republican congressional candidates on business campaign contributions. This dependence was due to (1) a massive increase in total corporate political action committee (PAC) spending after 1974, (2) a rise in the share of that spending that went to GOP candidates, both incumbents and challengers, beginning in the 1978 midterm elections, as business took an ideological right turn in seeking to help the Republicans win control of both houses of Congress,[42] (3) the much smaller increase in spending by labor PACs during this period, and (4) the tiny fraction of labor PAC money given to Republican candidates.[43]

Conversely, organized labor successfully lobbied Democrats to back the domestic content bill. Labor's influence on the Democrats was strengthened by its extensive involvement on behalf of Democratic candidates in the recently concluded midterm elections. The AFL-CIO's Committee on Political Education (COPE) coordinated registration drives that added at least 3 million members of union households to the voter rolls. An estimated 150,000 COPE volunteers and several thousand paid staffers canvassed union neighborhoods and organized get-out-the-vote drives, assisted by COPE's computerized data on almost 15 million union members. Individual unions, prominently including the United Auto Workers, also undertook their own independent activities. With the UAW leading the way, labor substantially increased its campaign contributions to Democratic candidates, much of it directed to challengers and open-seat contenders, to offset business's increased financial support for the Republicans.[44]

Labor's efforts paid off. Union members cast 35 percent of the vote, though they made up only a quarter of the electorate, and more than two-thirds of them voted Democratic. This was a big change from the relatively high defection rate in 1980. Sixty-three percent of COPE-backed House candidates (237 of 376) were elected. More specifically, thirty-four of the fifty-seven new Democrats in the House were elected with the help of the UAW. Democratic challengers supported by the UAW upset nineteen House incumbents, whereas only one challenger upset a UAW-backed incumbent.[45]

When the domestic content bill hit the House floor in early December 1982, the UAW and other labor lobbyists called in their campaign debts and implicitly raised the threat of primary challenges to members who opposed the measure. The Democrats responded with strong support for the bill.[46]

Party divisions over the legislation also stemmed from the general propensity of House Republicans to support, and of Democrats to oppose, the positions of a sitting GOP president. The partisan split over the domestic content bill was further exaggerated by the institutional realities of divided government and divided partisan control of Congress. Many House Democrats, still gripped a half century later by the experience of Smoot-Hawley, agreed with their GOP colleagues that the domestic content bill was a bad piece of legislation. But these Democrats could vote for the bill, thus signaling their toughness on trade to their labor backers and Japan and helping to discredit Reagan administration policies with the wider electorate, because they knew that the measure would either be defeated in the GOP-controlled Senate or vetoed by the president. As one top House Democratic aide recalled, "A lot of those votes were free votes in the sense that they knew it was not going to pass."[47]

In an end-of-the-year analysis of the reemergence of trade as a partisan issue, *Business Week* observed that "Protectionism, consigned to the back burners of U.S. politics for 50 years, is suddenly a live issue for leading Democrats."[48] This was due both to Democratic ideological convictions and, more important, to pressure from the import-battered labor movement, a core party constituency. As Hodding Carter III, an assistant secretary of State in the Carter administration, explained, "support for protectionism translates into money and votes for Democrats and a big leg up on labor support for the would be Democratic presidential nominee perceived as standing toughest on the issue."[49]

But encouraged by leading party pollsters and strategists, some Democrats regarded what would soon be widely called "economic nationalism" as a component of a new Democratic accumulation strategy. In this view, trade and industrial policies could be used to simultaneously help arrest the decline of key mass production industries, strengthen the Democrats' position in the House, and dislodge the Republicans from their control of the Senate and the presidency. Thus, as *Business Week* noted, the "new mood" had become "central to the 'alternative' economic strategies that both Mondale and other Democratic hopefuls are shaping as their answer to laissez-faire Reaganomics."[50]

The Republicans were forced to respond to the Democrats' trade push, and thus began a decade-long pattern of strategic interaction between the parties. "Out" party Democrats heresthetically pressed trade as both a "valence" and a "position" issue in order to end GOP-led divided government. This, in turn, compelled the White House to politically neutralize the issue by taking moderately tougher trade actions, especially just before elections or key congressional trade votes that the Democrats hoped to use as campaign issues.

The Industrial Policy Interlude

The year 1982 ended with the ranks of congressional protectionists expanded by the recent election and with both the overall American and U.S.-Japan trade deficits still rising. Thus, 1983 was widely predicted to be the "year of trade" in Washington. This, however, did not prove to be the case. Pummeled by the White House, congressional Republicans, and the media for supporting the domestic content bill, Democrats became concerned that their party had become too closely identified with protectionism. For this reason, in 1983 many Democrats turned from trade policy to "industrial policy"[51] as a more forward-looking response to the trade deficit and to America's apparent competitive decline.[52]

The Democrats' interest in industrial policy began in late 1981 or early 1982,[53] when the recession and the U.S. trade deficit were both worsening. Influenced by and responding to Japan's industrial targeting and subsidization policies, Democratic politicians, searching for electorally useful alternatives to both Keynesianism and an apparently failing Reaganomics, began to explore the value of industrial policy as the core of a neostatist strategy of transition to post-Fordism. Hopefully, such a strategy would be capable of restoring American competitiveness and economic growth and, perhaps more important, rebuilding the fractured Democratic coalition and driving the Republicans from power.

The party, however, was not united on the issue. Some Democrats from the northern liberal/labor wing or faction of the party were attracted to investment banker Felix Rohatyn's proposed Reconstruction Finance Corporation, modeled on the New Deal institution of the same name, to help revive the nation's mass production industries. But the real interest in industrial policy was among the party's relatively youthful "neoliberals," who called for a reorientation of Democratic strategy and policy to allow the party to regain and expand its support, especially among the growing ranks of the suburban-based professional and managerial middle class.[54]

Influenced by the writings of economist Lester Thurow and public policy analyst Robert Reich, the neoliberals argued that the United States had entered a new era of global competition and technological change. The resulting transition to an information and service-based postindustrial society had rendered old liberal politics and policies obsolete. To restore growth in the economy, they placed priority on capital formation, investment, and productivity improvement ahead of increased consumption and expanded social welfare. The neoliberals were also adamant free traders who believed that protectionist efforts to shield American industries and workers against the forces of global competition would only mire the economy in inefficiency and stagnation.[55]

The neoliberals were elected in the post-Watergate Democratic surge from formerly Republican, middle-class suburban and Sun Belt areas with little basic industry, and thus they had few ties to organized labor. As such, they were particularly enamored of high technology and supported a variety of industrial policies intended to facilitate the transfer of resources from "sunset" to "sunrise" sectors. The neoliberals considered a pro–high-tech politics ideal for solidifying and expanding their own electoral base, as well as that of the entire Democratic Party.[56] There was also possible business support to be won from newly politically active high-tech executives, who despite their apparent affinity for Republican tax cutting were critical of the Reagan administration's close ties to traditional business leaders. High-tech officials were markedly exercised about and open to proposals to counter Japan's industrial targeting policies, leading the neoliberals to hope that their advocacy of a high-tech industrial policy would prove attractive to Silicon Valley leaders.[57] Their efforts bore fruit in September 1982, when the House Democratic caucus released the report of the Committee on Party Effectiveness, which had been formed in early 1981 to explore ways to strengthen the party and return it to power. Among other proposals, the report recommended a high-tech–tilted industrial policy.

Although the neoliberals were the most energetic proponents of industrial policy, more traditional liberals began to embrace a version of the concept, albeit one more oriented toward rebuilding basic industries. The AFL-CIO began to call for the reindustrialization of the nation, while Edward Kennedy and Walter Mondale, both traditional liberals and strong supporters of labor, also endorsed the concept of industrial policy, which Kennedy called the possible "basis of a Democratic alternative" to "the schizophrenic non-economic policy of the president."[58]

During the first half of 1983, with Reaganomics apparently crumbling under the weight of recession and massive budget and trade deficits, interest in the new strategy spread rapidly. By midyear, all the leading Democratic presidential contenders except John Glenn had embraced some form of industrial policy.[59]

In the spring the industrial policy debate had moved out of the agenda-setting stage and into the policy-formulation stage, as detailed legislative blueprints began to appear. In mid-May Representatives Stanley Lundine (D-N.Y.) and David Bonior (D-Mich.) introduced the National Industrial Strategy Act, which reflected Rust Belt priorities in its inclusion of a National Industrial Development Bank.[60] In June Representatives Tim Wirth (D-Colo.) and Dick Gephardt (D-Mo.) produced a neoliberal bill intended principally to promote dynamic new technologies.[61] There was no mention of a bank.

Lingering economic difficulties and a Democratic attempt to exploit the competitiveness issue for partisan advantage put pressure on the Reagan administration to develop some kind of competitiveness policy of its own. As one "nervous Reaganite" explained, industrial competitiveness "is the most explosive issue for 1984 and could blow us out of the water if we're not careful."[62] In the summer and fall, the White House announced a number of modest competitiveness initiatives.

During the summer, however, opposition to the concept of industrial policy had been building in several quarters. Business leaders who only a few months earlier had been open to general proposals to improve competitiveness now came out against the idea of a bank designed to channel capital toward targeted sectors, arguing that it was impossible to pick "winners" and "losers."[63] At the same time, mainstream economists, already vocal in their criticism of industrial policy, launched a frontal assault on the idea.

By the fall, the withering criticism of industrial policy from the Reagan administration, academe, the business community,[64] and the media; analyses of public opinion that found little popular support for a coordinated industrial policy;[65] and the economic recovery that had begun some months earlier—all of these factors had combined to erode support for the concept. Tension grew within the Democratic Party over the idea along ideological, class, and regional lines.

By early November, the tide had turned, and the Democratic retreat from an interventionist industrial policy began in earnest. In Spring 1984 an industrial policy bill sponsored by Representative John LaFalce (D-N.Y.) that included a development bank died in committee when House Democrats split over the measure.[66] By the time of the general election, the concept had virtually receded from sight. The Democratic platform, drafted with considerable input from labor, did call for a very mild form of industrial policy. But except for the fall announcement of a plan to revitalize the steel industry, Mondale made little mention of the idea during the presidential campaign. Thus, in late October 1984, just before the general election, *Congressional Quarterly Weekly Report* commented in a legislative wrap-up, "Industrial policy, which at times in 1983 looked as if it might become a rallying cry for Democrats, instead remained largely a collection of ideas looking for supporters."[67]

Trade Policy and Presidential Politics, 1983–1984

While the industrial policy debate slowly died out in 1984, the trade issue was revived by presidential politics. At the end of 1983 and in early 1984, with the U.S. recovery and the overvalued dollar continuing to suck in imports at a record rate, and with the presidential election only a year off, trade politics began to heat up again. This was especially the case in three crucial industrial sectors—automobiles, textiles, and steel.

On November 1, 1983, the United States and Japan agreed to extend the auto VRA for still another year. This was both to head off another Democrat-led House effort to pass domestic content legislation and because "1984 [was] an election year," as former CEA chairman William Niskanen recalled being reminded by White House officials.[68] Both U.S. auto companies and the UAW criticized the agreement for raising the quota level too high, however, and the union pressed hard for passage of the domestic content bill. On November 3 the House passed the measure by a fairly partisan vote of 219–199. Democrats voted 187–68 for the bill, and the Republicans opposed it 32–131. As in 1982, many Democrats only voted for the bill because they knew it would never pass the Senate. They again opted to back the measure to ensure labor support in the upcoming election year.

Meanwhile, since the signing of the new U.S.-China bilateral textile agreement the previous July, anger had been building within the U.S. textile and apparel industries over China's alleged subsidization of its textile and apparel imports via exchange rate manipulation. When it appeared in mid-December that the administration was about to reject increased protection for the U.S. industries, the already active textile lobby and its congressional supporters swung into action. In particular, Senator Strom Thurmond (R-S.C.) went to the White House to remind presidential advisers James Baker and Edwin Meese "of the South's importance to Reagan's reelection bid."[69] In mid-December Reagan outlined additional criteria for restricting imports of textile and apparel goods from all countries, not just China.

At the end of 1983 protectionist pressures also began to emerge from the steel industry, which despite the year-old economic recovery, was still depressed and under attack from low-cost foreign imports. On the same day in early November, the House Steel Caucus, backed by the industry, introduced a steel quota bill, and U.S. Steel announced that it was filing a number of antidumping and countervailing duty complaints. Then, in late January 1984, the Bethlehem Steel Corporation and the United Steelworkers of America jointly filed a Section 201 escape clause petition, one of the largest such suits ever initiated. Other U.S. manufacturers responded to the tide of imports with a torrent of demands for import protection.

As Nixon administration trade negotiator William N. Walker noted, the steel and other actions were all timed to coincide with the upcoming presidential campaign. Industry leaders believed that during the campaign the Reagan administration would be "responsive to domestic industry pressures so that Democrats [wouldn't] be able to call them soft on trade."[70]

The Steel Decision

On June 12 and 14, 1984, the issues of trade and protectionism erupted into the presidential contest. On the first date, the ITC surprised the Reagan administration by ruling that imports were injuring the domestic steel industry. A month later it proposed a five-year import relief program for steel consisting of tariffs and quotas. Reagan was forced to decide whether to accept the recommendations by September 24, just six weeks before the election. Two days after the steel ruling, the ITC found that imports were also injuring U.S. copper producers and presented another recommendation for escape clause relief the next month.

The copper case was resolved first. On September 6, after intense intra-administration debate, Reagan denied relief to the copper industry in a decision that was made principally on political grounds. The president was already electorally strong in the Rocky Mountain states in which copper production was concentrated, so import relief was not viewed within the administration as a political necessity. On the other hand, there were five times more copper fabricating industry workers than there were copper miners, and they were located in states that Mondale had some chance to carry, states that controlled more electoral votes than did the copper producers.[71]

Reagan also took a free-trade stance on copper to give himself some maneuvering room on the politically more important steel case.[72] The president faced a number of dilemmas as he grappled with the steel problem. On the one hand, he needed to provide the industry with enough relief to allow him to fend off steel quota legislation and, more important, partisan attacks from Walter Mondale and congressional Democrats, who were calling for stiff quotas in an effort to create a major campaign issue. With 225 of the 470 electoral votes necessary for victory in the presidential race held by the nine major steel-producing states—California, Illinois, Indiana, Kentucky, Michigan, New York, Ohio, Pennsylvania, and Texas—the Republicans were fully aware of the high stakes involved. "Reagan must carry at least two of the major 'rust belt' states to win in November," one senior administration official noted.[73] Senator John Heinz (R-Pa.) warned that an adverse decision in the steel case "could be politically harmful in Pennsylvania and many other key states."[74]

On the other hand, Reagan was concerned that tighter steel quotas might lead to Common Market retaliation against U.S. agricultural exports, alienating increasingly active farm interests just before the election. Major steel users also opposed steel import restraints, and Reagan worried about losing votes from workers in these sectors, too. Finally, the president feared that the imposition of new steel quotas might gravely damage broader U.S. trade and political relations with Europe and the Third World.[75]

As election day drew closer, Mondale kept up the pressure on the steel issue. On September 17 he announced a plan to limit steel imports to 17 percent of the U.S. market, half the current figure at the time, for five years to allow the industry a chance to modernize. The next day, in another significant example of policy contagion, Reagan finally announced his own less restrictive plan to help the steel industry. Although rejecting the ITC's proposed package of tariffs and quotas, the president opted to seek politically useful voluntary restraint agreements with countries responsible for surges in U.S. steel imports.[76] As William Niskanen remembered, "of course, political considerations were dominant in September, when some of the steel-producing states were considered uncertain. It is much less clear whether the administration would have made the same decision in 1983 or 1985."[77]

By choosing VRAS over more restrictive quotas, Reagan achieved what one commentator called "something of a political miracle."[78] While granting the steel industry some of the relief it sought, thus cooling the issue and the threat from Mondale in the steel-producing states, Reagan was able to portray his rejection of quotas as a victory for free trade, thereby allaying the fears of trade-dependent interests.

The Omnibus Trade Bill

With the tricky steel decision behind him, one final obstacle remained to Reagan's successful marginalization of trade as a campaign issue: an omnibus trade bill whose various components Congress had been working on for months.[79]

The Ninety-eighth Congress of 1983–84 was mostly unproductive, as the White House and the unified Democratic House majority deadlocked over the budget. Hoping to claim some credit on another front, many House Democrats, with labor's strong support, pressed their leaders in early 1984 to draft legislation to strengthen the nation's trade remedy laws both to protect constituents threatened by imports and to elevate trade as an issue in the upcoming campaign. Signaling this interest, a year-old House Democratic Task Force on Trade in early March presented its report calling for trade law reform. Outlining the report, Representative Stan Lundine (D-N.Y.), cochairman of the task force, said that he expected the mounting trade deficit to play an important role in the presidential campaign, since "it is an issue that people can understand and one in which the Reagan administration is very vulnerable."[80]

In response to rank-and-file Democratic pressure, House Ways and Means Trade Subcommittee chairman Sam Gibbons developed a trade reform bill to counter a variety of unfair foreign trade practices. Although supported by a large group of major corporations and business associations, the bill was opposed by the Reagan administration and a group of internationally oriented firms and associations.[81] A weakened, compromise version of the bill was passed by the House in late July by a 295–95 margin, with Democrats in favor 193–24 and Republicans opposed 66–71.[82] In late August the Republican-controlled Senate unanimously passed a catchall trade bill that included reciprocity and other unfair foreign trade provisions. The House approved similar measures in early October.

The House also passed a bill to curb steel imports more sharply than would Reagan's announced plan. After his steel decision, many Democrats denounced the president's action as a purely political move, intended "to get Mr. Reagan by the election," as Mondale put it.[83] In a Democrat-backed effort to keep the issue alive in the presidential campaign, in late September Dan Rostenkowski (D-Ill.) introduced a plan that conformed to Mondale's proposal to restrict steel imports to 17 percent of the U.S. market, less than the 20 percent that Reagan sought. The full House approved Rostenkowski's bill by a fairly partisan vote of 285–314. The Democrats overwhelmingly backed the measure by a 222–36 margin; most Republicans opposed it (63–98), except for those from Pennsylvania, Ohio, and other steel states.[84]

A few days later a House-Senate conference committee agreed to the major provisions of an omnibus trade bill, to which Gibbons's trade remedy reform measure was attached. After skillful lobbying by USTR William Brock, a host of tariff and other import restrictions that the White House found objectionable were struck from the legislation. As well, the House steel measure was weakened by making it a nonbinding "sense of the Congress" that steel imports should be cut back by 17–20 percent. The final, largely nonprotectionist bill—the Trade and Tariff Act of 1984—including the watered-down steel provision, was then overwhelmingly passed by both houses on October 9.

Brock's accomplishment in forging a nonprotectionist, bipartisan compromise was striking. During most of 1983–84, congressional voting on other trade issues had been generally partisan, due to ideological differences, polarizing constituency pressures, especially from labor and internationally oriented business interests, and the Democrats' greater willingness under divided government to oppose the policies of a Republican president.[85]

A number of factors contributed to Brock's success in persuading Democrats to moderate their positions and to strip out or weaken the bill's most protectionist provisions, including the threat of a presidential veto, organized labor's preoccupation with Walter Mondale's presidential campaign,[86] and lobbying by increasingly active antiprotectionist business interests.[87]

Related to this last point, a moderating role may have been played by a partial shift of corporate campaign contributions back to the Democrats. Recall that before 1978, most business PACs pursued a pragmatic, access-oriented strategy of contributing to incumbents of both parties. But during the 1978, 1980, and 1982 campaigns, business took an ideological right turn, substantially shifting their contributions to Republican incumbents and challengers. Beginning in the 1982 midterm elections, labor tried to at least partly make up the Democrats' shortfall, but the slow growth in the number of union PACs and campaign contribution limits that they regularly encountered left congressional Democrats desperately short of funds to conduct their increasingly media and consultant-intensive campaigns.

The Democrats were thus forced to adopt new tactics to win back business support. After the 1980 campaign and especially after the successful 1982 midterm elections, Democratic Congressional Campaign Committee (DCCC) chairman Tony Coelho argued to prospective business donors that since his party would almost certainly retain control of at least the House and its committees for the foreseeable future, they would be well advised to shift some of their contributions back to the Democrats if they hoped to get a fair hearing in the

House. Democratic Senatorial Campaign Committee chairman Lloyd Bentsen of Texas also dunned business for more money.[88]

These efforts proved successful, and in 1984 business PACs returned to their pragmatic habit of contributing to both parties, but especially to incumbent House Democrats and the DCCC, since the Democrats appeared to be securely in control of that chamber.[89] Thus, for example, the Democratic share of total business PAC donations to House candidates rose from 40 to 48 percent between 1982 and 1984.[90] Senate Democrats' share of business money rose, too.

Both contributing to and a consequence of this shift was greater Democratic responsiveness to business's policy concerns in the House and Senate.[91] To the extent that most of the business community still opposed protectionism, this may well have contributed in late 1984 to the willingness of some Democrats, hopeful of receiving even more substantial business contributions, to support the weakening of the omnibus trade bill.

In the end, trade did not figure prominently in the presidential election. Reagan's September steel decision, the passage of the omnibus trade bill, the muting of Mondale's once tough trade policy rhetoric in the face of media and business criticism,[92] and the general economic recovery together politically defused the issue, even in the trade-impacted industrial heartland. Reagan did, however, impose or extend restrictions on the import of cars, steel, and textiles to neutralize the real or potential threat from the Democrats in the Michigan auto corridor, in midwestern steel-producing states, and in southeastern textile states. Election-year pressures thus produced important new instances of trade policy contagion and further "strategic retreat" from free trade by the Reagan administration.

With Ronald Reagan's smashing victory over Walter Mondale, it might have been thought that trade issues had been put to bed. But as 1984 ended, Japan's trade surplus with the United States and the rest of the world was soaring, and U.S.-Japan tensions were rising. Unless progress in opening Japan's markets was made soon, Commerce Under Secretary for International Trade Lionel Ulmer warned in December, instead of a light at the end of the tunnel, the United States and Japan might be looking at "an oncoming train."[93] The train was not long in arriving, and, as we shall see, a partisan fireman stoked its engine.

Partisanship Heats Up

The Trade Policy Explosion of 1985–1986

During his 1984 reelection campaign Ronald Reagan proclaimed that it was "morning in America again," but he offered no real second-term agenda. Even with his landslide victory, Reagan could claim no policy mandate, especially since voters also kept the Democrats in control of the House of Representatives.[1] Reagan and Senate Republicans respectively did take the initiative on the two major policy achievements of the Ninety-ninth Congress—the 1986 tax reform bill and the Gramm-Rudman-Hollings balanced budget proposal. The Democrats' more limited role was to refashion these proposals to make them more acceptable.[2] But on other issues, House Democrats began to play a more assertive role.

The potential for a stronger role for the House Democratic leadership in the agenda-setting and legislative processes lay in a number of antecedent developments in the 1970s and early 1980s that raised Democratic lawmakers' expectations of their leaders.[3] First, the difficulty of enacting legislation favored by Democrats was markedly increased by (1) the decentralizing House reforms of the 1970s, which led to a decline in intercommittee reciprocity and a rise in floor amending activity that hindered the production of good policy, and (2) the hostile political climate of the 1980s, including huge budget deficits and control of the Senate (through 1986) and especially the White House by conservative and combative Republicans. By the early 1980s, Democratic lawmakers began to demand that their leaders use the resources that other centralizing provisions of the 1970s reforms had bequeathed them, including greater committee appointment, referral, scheduling, and procedural powers, to facilitate passing the legislation that members wanted.

The Democrats' willingness to have their leaders play a more active role was also heightened by the increased ideological homogeneity of the members of the Democratic caucus. In fact, both parties became more internally homogeneous and more externally polarized after about 1982, producing a rise in party conflict (although less so around issues of general concern to the parties' business contributors).[4] GOP lawmakers became more conservative with the growth of southern Republicanism and the increasing conservatism of GOP activists. Democrats, on the other hand, became more uniformly liberal, due mainly to the continued exodus of white southern conservatives from the party, which lessened the differences between the constituencies of northern and southern congressional Democrats.[5]

During Ronald Reagan's first term, House Democrats had already begun to use retreats and task forces, including those on trade and competitiveness issues, to develop alternatives to Reaganomics.[6] Now at the beginning of Reagan's second term, the House Democratic leadership, under pressure from its more likeminded members to help them realize their less easily attainable policy goals, engaged still more energetically in agenda-setting and legislative activities. Trade policy was one of the main areas in which Democratic leaders became more active.

In early 1985 the U.S. trade deficit ballooned while Reagan, freed of reelection pressures, largely neglected the problem. After briefly ceding leadership on the trade issue to Senate Republicans, the Democrats again attempted to make trade a central issue in the 1986 congressional elections. Using retreats and task forces to develop new legislation, the Democrats introduced, supported, and even forced vetoes of bills to toughen U.S. policy, including an early House draft of the future Omnibus Trade and Competitiveness Act of 1988 and a restrictive textile quota bill.

This strategy produced regional but also sharply partisan patterns of congressional conflict depending in part on the perceived incidence of the benefits and costs of the legislation being considered. It also led to significant instances of policy contagion—including new or tightened restrictions on machine tool, lumber, textile, semiconductor, and other imports but also an aggressive new White House effort to pry open closed foreign markets—as the Reagan administration again sought to head off passage of tough legislation as well as to prevent the Democrats from exploiting the trade issue for partisan advantage.

Democratic Heresthetics and the Reagan Administration's Turn toward International Economic Activism

In early 1985 the U.S. trade crisis deepened. In particular, the flood of Japanese imports was still rising, while Tokyo remained unwilling to open its markets to

American goods. Although U.S.-based transnational corporations and agricultural exporters continued to back free trade, business anger at Japan was no longer limited to import-battered Fordist industries like textiles, automobiles, steel, and consumer electronics. A much broader array of industries was now up in arms about surging imports and especially the many formal and informal barriers to their penetration of Japan's markets. High-technology sectors like telecommunications and semiconductors, characterized by large economies of scale, high research and development costs, and steep learning curves that required growing volumes of sales to remain competitive, railed at the ability of Japanese firms to dominate their closed "sanctuary" markets while continuing to export relatively freely to the United States.[7]

Yet Reagan, now freed of trade-related election pressures, appeared mostly indifferent to the mounting crisis. With trade policy still largely in the hands of State Department officials and their Pentagon allies, who sought above all to avoid disrupting the U.S.-Japan security relationship, the president rejected suggestions by the Commerce Department and the U.S. Trade Representative (USTR) that he press Tokyo to set specific targets for buying more American manufactured goods. More explosively, in March 1985 Reagan declared his intention to let the Japanese auto voluntary restraint agreement (VRA) lapse, a move that was followed by Tokyo's announcement that it would hike automobile exports to the United States in the coming year by 25 percent.[8] Both the Senate and the House reacted immediately by overwhelmingly passing nonbinding resolutions urging the president to retaliate against Japan unless it bought enough U.S. goods to offset its increases in automobile shipments.

Party Politics Renewed: A Return to Historic Positions?

As congressional trade activism rose in the spring of 1985, the issue once again began to take on a partisan cast. This time, however, the parties appeared to be returning to their historic, pre-1930s positions.[9] It was actually Senate Republicans, with twenty-two of their members up for reelection in 1986, who now demanded a more aggressive U.S. trade posture. With new sectors of the heavily Republican business community, including politically "hot" high-tech firms, moving away from pure free trade,[10] and with public opinion shifting in a more protectionist direction,[11] Senate Republicans felt the need to beat the Democrats to the "toughness" issue. As Mark Bisnow, a former aid to Majority Leader Bob Dole, recalled, "In the spring of 1985, [Senator John] Danforth convinced Dole that Democrats would inevitably take the lead on trade issues unless the Republicans beat them to it."[12]

The Democrats were, in fact, exploring the political potential of the trade issue. In the winter and spring of 1985, Senate and House Democratic task forces were formed to study the trade problem.[13] At this stage, however, Democrats had no unified position on trade policy. While some supported various forms of retaliatory legislation, many others felt that Walter Mondale's rout the previous November had discredited the tough, labor-backed positions he had sometimes advocated. "We have the stigma of protectionism," Representative Don Bonker of Washington complained, "which comes by way of our closeness to labor and sponsorship of the domestic content bill." Bonker and other Democrats were eager to pin the protectionist label on the Republicans.[14]

Rather than address trade policy directly, the Democrats began to argue that the source of the trade deficit lay in the faulty budget and currency policies of the Reagan administration. This position dovetailed nicely both with the more general fiscal conservatism of many suburban and Sun Belt neoliberals and with the views of important sectors of the business community whose support the Democrats sought.[15] As the spring wore on and a deal to cut the budget deficit appeared more remote, the Democrats began to place greater stress on the importance of exchange rate policy as a "second best" option, and in late April, the Senate and House Democratic trade policy task forces called for currency market intervention to help reduce the trade deficit.[16]

Reagan Ignores Trade, Turns to Tax Reform

Despite the rising trade deficit and growing demands for protection and action to open Japanese markets, trade remained on the legislative back burner for most of the late spring. Congress at this time was tied up with the budget and hearings on Reagan's proposals on another issue: tax reform.

Following Reagan's landslide reelection victory, there was much talk in Republican circles about the prospects for a partisan realignment, that is, a durable shift in the balance of partisan identities and political power toward the GOP. Republican strategists sought a second-term Reagan program to consolidate this realignment and a wider conservative political order.[17] After an intra-administration debate in which he rejected a proposed emphasis on tougher trade policy,[18] Reagan opted instead for tax reform.[19]

Reagan's plan, unveiled in late May, called for a substantial reduction in individual taxes. Designed to benefit working-class families—"the final backbone of the Democratic coalition," as a top administration official put it[20]—the plan was introduced as a heresthetical maneuver intended to further weaken the Democrats. But the proposal also favored the high-tech, entrepreneurial sector of the economy, located mainly in suburban and Sun Belt areas of Republican growth, while striking hardest at capital-intensive industries located in the predominantly Democratic regions of the urban Northeast and Midwest.[21]

Critics blasted Reagan both for advancing a plan that was likely to weaken the competitiveness of capital-intensive industries and for continuing to ignore the whole wider question of the skyrocketing trade deficit. "Rome's burning and we're fiddling with the tax code," fumed Chrysler chairman Lee Iacocca.[22]

Democratic Initiative, Republican Response

Under these conditions of administration neglect, congressional trade activism intensified. Although two major trade bills were introduced in Congress in June and July with bipartisan support, the trade issue soon assumed a partisan complexion as the Democrats sensed a political opening. In mid-July, abandoning their party's politically unsuccessful attack on the budget deficit and undertaking a heresthetical maneuver of their own, three leading congressional Democrats—House Democratic caucus chairman Dick Gephardt of Missouri, House Ways and Means Committee chairman Dan Rostenkowski of Illinois, and Senate Finance Committee chairman Lloyd Bentsen of Texas—introduced an import surcharge proposal. The measure would have required the addition of a 25 percent levy on products from Japan, Taiwan, South Korea, and Brazil—countries with "excessive" trade surpluses with the United States—unless they took steps to open their own markets to U.S. products. The measure was widely viewed as likely to end up as "the Democratic battle plan in what could be an intensely partisan competition over trade issues."[23]

The proposal was designed to win business support for the Democrats from import-competing interests and exporters denied access to Japan. But buoyed by public opinion polls that showed voters—especially Republicans and conservatives—in a more protectionist mood,[24] the three Democrats also introduced their proposal with the aim of increasing the relative salience of the trade issue, displacing public attention from Reagan's tax reform plan, and thus hopefully disrupting the broader Republican electoral coalition. "I think [the trade issue] is here and I think it is exploding," Bentsen declared.[25]

Dick Gephardt, who was the driving force behind the surcharge proposal, had additional motives of his own for introducing it. A leading neoliberal in the early 1980s, Gephardt was the first chairman of the Democratic Leadership Council, formed after the 1984 election debacle by a group of moderate elected officials, mostly from the South and West, who hoped to loosen the grip of labor and other so-called special interests on the party and to move it back to the political center. But in the spring of 1985 Gephardt was already exploring a possible presidential campaign and beginning to modify his political positions in the process. Attuned to the growing public concern with trade, and especially mindful of the key role played by the protectionist-leaning labor movement in

Democratic presidential primaries and caucuses, Gephardt obtained a seat on the House Ways and Means Trade Subcommittee, declaring, "It would do the Democrats good to be identified as the party of fair trade."[26] The import surcharge proposal was the first substantive result of Gephardt's new interest in trade policy.

The GOP responded in a number of ways to the Democrats' trade initiative. Senate Republicans sought to politically neutralize the issue by intensifying their earlier push to open Japanese markets and by urging Reagan to modify his free-trade stance. "This issue is becoming more partisan than it has been in the past," said a Finance Committee staff member. "The Democrats have realized that the Administration is vulnerable, and the Republicans have realized that the Administration's vulnerability may be rubbing off on them."[27]

The White House response was complex. Publicly, the administration attacked the surcharge measure. Behind the scenes, however, Treasury Secretary James Baker took control of trade policy from the State and Defense Departments, and the cabinet-level Economic Council, which he chaired, began work on a new administration trade strategy. Baker also accelerated unobtrusive consultations between the United States and its industrial allies on macroeconomic and exchange rate coordination to reduce international economic imbalances.

The Reagan administration had long been reluctant to acknowledge exchange rate problems, suggesting instead that the strong dollar reflected investor confidence in the U.S. economy. An emergent element of Reagan's accumulation strategy, the White House stance had both ideological and political roots. The noninterventionist, strong-dollar strategy simultaneously (1) was congruent with Reagan's general antistatist convictions, (2) helped to combat the politically deadly inflation that had sunk Jimmy Carter's presidency, (3) facilitated the financing of large federal budget deficits by widening the trade deficit, which in turn led foreign bankers to recycle their dollar holdings into the purchase of U.S. treasury securities,[28] (4) earned Reagan support from the financial community, which was concerned about maintaining the value of its vast dollar reserves, and (5) fostered the transition to a post-Fordist economy by accelerating the shift of capital from basic to more competitive high-tech sectors or by forcing older industries to restructure in order to improve productivity and competitiveness.[29]

On taking his Treasury job in early 1985, however, Baker had realized that the overvalued dollar, by slowing economic growth and exacerbating protectionist pressures, could damage Republican prospects in 1986.[30] Thus, Baker quietly began to plan a retreat from the administration's hands-off exchange rate policy. Negotiations toward this end were begun with the Japanese finance minister in Tokyo in late June and were intensified in early August after a midsummer rise in the value of the dollar.

A Texas Special Election Fans Democratic Hopes

Further raising Democratic hopes of exploiting the trade issue and spurring Republican efforts to defuse it were developments in a hotly contested special election to fill a House seat in northeastern Texas held by the Democrats for more than a century. Ever since the Dixiecrat walkout from the Democratic convention in 1948 and especially after the civil rights revolution of the 1960s, the Republicans had been making steady inroads into the once solidly Democratic South. By 1984 only a little more than one-fourth of white southerners voted for the Democratic presidential ticket, prompting analysts to write of a regional partisan realignment.[31] Recognizing the centrality of this trend to their broader realignment hopes, GOP leaders now aimed to consolidate and expand their southern gains by extending their party's strength to the congressional and state levels.[32]

The key to the GOP's southern strategy was Texas, where the party had recently won significant victories. Thus, the national party funneled resources from all over the country into the special election race. The Democrats understood the importance of holding the seat if they were to block the Republicans' strategy, and the Democratic Congressional Campaign Committee (DCCC), chaired by the aggressive Tony Coelho of California, also poured resources into the Texas campaign.[33]

In mid-July, after a Democratic poll of the district's voters surprisingly found that trade ranked second only to social security among their concerns, the Democratic candidate, Jim Chapman, began to campaign hard on the issue. When his opponent was quoted as saying that he did not know what trade policies had to do with bringing jobs to East Texas, Chapman pounced on his rival's apparent insensitivity.

In early August Chapman eked out a narrow, come-from-behind victory. Immediately pronouncing Republican realignment hopes dead, numerous Democratic officials and strategists concluded that trade had played a key role in deciding the race and would remain important in the upcoming national election cycle.[34] This conviction was reinforced for many Democratic lawmakers by their experiences during the August recess, when they found their constituents clamoring not for Reagan's cherished tax reform but for action on the trade front. Moreover, the president's late August rejection of a recommendation by the International Trade Commission (ITC) for quotas on shoes created an uproar in Congress.

As Congress reconvened in September, there was widespread speculation that the president was losing control of the overall political agenda. The Democrats, generally forced to react to Republican initiatives during Reagan's first term, were now taking the offensive on a range of issues.

The hottest issue on the congressional agenda was trade. Several hundred more or less protectionist bills were pending in both houses, the most prominent of which were the import surcharge proposal and the textile quota bill that had been introduced the previous spring. Although congressional sentiment for a tougher trade policy was bipartisan, the issue was being driven by the Democrats, whose protectionist and free-trade factions were for the moment united around an aggressive market-opening stance.

The Democrats stressed the trade issue in part because of continued pressure from organized labor. Despite its steady decline since the mid-1950s and its tarring as a "special interest" during the 1984 presidential campaign, labor still provided indispensable electoral and financial support to Democratic candidates. In the fall of 1985, comprehensive trade law reform was the AFL-CIO's immediate legislative priority.

But in emphasizing trade, the Democrats also sought to appeal to the business community, whose support the party had been concertedly pursuing since 1982. A year earlier, most of the business community had opposed the protectionist provisions of the Trade and Tariff Act of 1984, contributing to the willingness of House Democrats to eliminate most of them. In the fall of 1985, however, the center of gravity within the business community was shifting toward a much tougher stance on trade. Thus, DCCC chairman Tony Coelho and other Democrats pressed the trade issue to win political and financial support from both import-competing and export-oriented manufacturing interests. As Jack Albertine, president of the American Business Conference, an association of fast-growing, medium-sized firms, explained, the Democrats saw trade as driving a wedge between the administration and its traditional business supporters: "The manufacturing community, which normally supports Reagan, is off the wall on this issue."[35]

But the Democrats had even grander ambitions. Many believed that the trade issue could have widespread voter appeal, especially if it was packaged in a new language—that of "economic nationalism." By 1980 the Democratic Party suffered from at least two major problems: it had lost its postwar mantle as the party of jobs and growth, and since the Vietnam era it had become widely perceived as "soft" on defense. Now the Democrats were hopeful that the trade issue could give them a way to fuse popular concerns over economic and national security into a compelling nationalist discourse that could help them regain the support of patriotic blue-collar and southern voters—the swing "Reagan Democrats." "This is the same sort of nationalism you see in demands for a stronger defense," Representative Vic Fazio (D-Calif.) observed. "It's economic nationalism."[36] "It's a powerful issue for us," said a Democratic congressional official. "It's a jobs issue—we're protecting jobs. And at the same time, it's a nationalist issue."[37]

The Democrats, employing both heresthetical and persuasive tactics, attempted to raise the relative salience of the trade issue by using economic nationalist imagery to alter popular perceptions of the effects of both Reagan's trade policies and their own tougher alternative proposals. Instead of stressing only the concentrated geographic or group costs and benefits of these policies in terms of lost or protected jobs and sales, the Democrats emphasized the *general* costs and benefits involved by blasting Reagan's policies for contributing to a generalized decline of the American economy. In this way, the party made a concerted effort to symbolically construct the trade issue as one of national "strength." Calling trade a "Democratic macho issue," Tony Coelho declared, "We're for American strength."[38]

In the fall of 1985, the Democrats' approach was a multilevel one. To appeal to the highly attentive "issue public" or "intense minority" that was preoccupied with trade, mostly concentrated groups of workers and employers in trade-sensitive industries, the Democrats assumed a tough, spatially specific position on the trade issue. To attract the support of less attentive directional voters, the party proposed to move trade policy in a tougher general direction. And to win the backing of a wider group of still less attentive, retrospectively minded voters, the Democrats spotlighted performance failures of Republican trade policy.

Congressman Don Bonker (D-Wash.), chairman of the House Democratic task force on trade policy, concisely explained the political appeal of a tougher stance on trade policy for members of his party at this time: "It allowed them to identify with economic problems in their districts, expanding their support among business leaders. And it provided them with a viable campaign issue at a time when Democrats had few alternatives to offer to President Reagan's economic policies."[39]

Fearful of being outflanked by the opposition on a popular issue in the 1986 elections, many normally free-trading Republicans now began to toughen their own positions. Representative Edwin V. Zschau ruefully observed that his GOP colleagues were being driven "to adopt the Democrats' approach. They said, 'yeah, we know this is wrong, but we can't be viewed as doing nothing.'"[40] To protect their members, Republican leaders in Congress threatened to draft their own trade legislation and pressed the White House to take more aggressive action. "Republicans are not going to stand by and be rolled over by the Democrats on trade issues," Senate Majority Leader Robert Dole vowed.[41]

The Administration Acts to Defuse the Crisis

After months of resistance, the Reagan administration finally moved to slow the protectionist momentum and defuse the Democratic threat. First, on September 7, the president announced the the USTR's initiation of some new Section 301 unfair trade cases against Brazil, South Korea, and Japan—not coincidentally, three of the four countries explicitly targeted in the Democrats' import surcharge bill. This was the first time the USTR had ever used its authority to open such cases.

Two weeks later, the White House officially announced its change of course in international economic strategy. The administration was politically unable to attack the macroeconomic roots of the trade gap through tax hikes or spending cuts and unwilling either to compromise ideological commitments to free trade, antagonize trade-dependent business interests, or run the risk of a trade war by resorting to outright protectionism. Instead, the White House devised a two-track strategy to force others to adjust through dollar devaluation and a policy of so-called aggressive reciprocity, that is, market-opening pressures accompanied by threats of retaliation in sectors where U.S. firms remained competitive.

On September 22 the United States and four key economic allies—West Germany, France, the United Kingdom, and Japan—agreed at a meeting at the Plaza Hotel in New York City to work together to reduce the value of the dollar against other currencies.[42] The next day, again resorting to the tactic of "export politics," Reagan reluctantly outlined the administration's Trade Policy Action Plan, intended to address the problems of exporters and thus to divide them from and isolate protectionist interests. The plan called for the creation of a $300 million "war chest" to help counterveil foreign export subsidies, the formation of a government "strike force" to uncover and combat unfair trading practices, and, most important, a new emphasis on the self-initiation by the USTR of Section 301 cases against countries unfairly closing their markets to U.S. goods.

Although the administration's new two-pronged dollar and trade initiative is often viewed as an attempt to defuse congressional protectionism, it was also expressly designed to blunt the Democratic *partisan* threat. This was indicated by the addition of a "fair" trade emphasis to the stress on "free trade" in the final draft of Reagan's September 23 speech. The change was made, according to a GOP adviser to White House chief of staff Donald Regan, to provide "political cover" for congressional Republicans who were under constituent and Democratic pressure to back a tougher U.S. trade posture.[43] *Business Week* similarly reported that the administration believed that the new exchange rate and trade strategy had "given the Republicans a shield to fend off Democratic attacks."[44]

In announcing its plan, however, the White House had a still larger partisan goal in mind. Administration leaders also "wanted to get trade behind them," one trade official explained, in order "to get back to taxes," the issue they were convinced could help cement a Republican realignment.[45]

The important Fall 1985 White House shift on currency and trade policy was yet another product of partisan interaction and policy contagion at the congressional and executive levels. Party competition, by threatening to expand the scope of the conflict over trade, amplified the protectionist pressures then emanating from the trade-impacted sectors of the economy. This forced the administration to move to lower the value of the dollar and to adopt a portion of the Democrats' trade program, albeit in weaker form. It was an effort not only to quell rising congressional protectionism, but also to undermine the Democrats' appeal to trade-sensitive sectors of the business community and to swing voters and thus to defuse the trade issue as a threat both to congressional Republicans and to Reagan's longer-term partisan agenda.

Following the administration's September policy turn, the fires of protectionism and Democratic trade militance did begin to cool. As intended, Reagan's actions themselves slowed the drive for a tougher trade policy by partially co-opting the issue. Further, the elite press heatedly attacked bills seen as unacceptably protectionist, including the Democrats' import surcharge proposal and especially the textile bill then making its way through Congress.[46]

Democratic apprehensions of overly tough trade restrictions began to reassert themselves. Members from states or districts with export- or import-dependent firms and industries shied away from protectionism.[47] And, once again, Smoot-Hawley fears resurfaced.[48] Republican Representative Trent Lott of Mississippi accurately captured some of the Democrats' mixed feelings on trade: "The Democrats see trade as a good political issue, but they're holding their breath. They hope the president won't let it happen. They want the issue but not the results."[49]

By late September, the Democrats' enthusiasm for tough import surcharge or product-specific trade legislation was waning. Instead, during the rest of the fall, members of both parties in both houses of Congress turned to the drafting of more comprehensive "generic" legislation, that is, measures addressing the basic procedures and standards that undergird U.S. trade policy. The Democrats continued to pursue partisan advantage, while the Republicans sought protective cover.[50]

Trade Policy in an Election Year:
Omnibus Legislation and Tangling over Textiles

Interest in the trade issue was rekindled in early 1986, when it was announced that in 1985 the U.S. merchandise trade deficit had reached an all-time high—$148.5 billion, up from $123 billion in 1984. Members of Congress were particularly angry about the huge bilateral deficit with Japan, which accounted for about one-third of the total U.S. deficit. In reaction to these staggering figures, members of both parties renewed their calls for passage of new, nonprotectionist generic trade legislation.

The Democrats once again took the lead. Exercising his strengthened agenda-setting and bill management powers, in late February Speaker Tip O'Neill convened a meeting of the chairmen of all committees with some jurisdiction over trade to announce his intent to try to move omnibus trade legislation to the floor of the House during the week of May 12. He assigned Majority Leader Jim Wright to plot overall strategy for the bill. Reflecting the ascent of the Democratic leadership, O'Neill also tasked Wright with containing tensions between powerful committee chairmen.[51]

Democratic leaders, pursuing what John Gilmour has termed a "strategy of disagreement,"[52] hoped to use their control of the House under divided government to pass and then confront the Republican Senate and the White House with a popular "fair trade" bill. If the Senate failed to come up with a bill of its own, or produced a weak one, Democrats planned to attack the Senate GOP leadership. If Reagan vetoed a trade bill, Democrats would challenge the president during the fall campaign.[53] "The House Democrats will send us a bill," said a staff member for a Republican senator. "And the Republican Senate may mess it up and give them a campaign issue, or the president may veto it and give the Democrats an issue."[54] In either case, the Democrats hoped to use the trade issue to strengthen their position in the House and to regain control of the Senate in the 1986 elections. Trade is a "key jobs and pro-America issue for the Democrats in 1986," reiterated Tony Coelho.[55]

On March 20–21 the House Ways and Means Trade Subcommittee began the formal process of writing a new trade bill. As anticipated, the measure appeared designed to toughen the U.S. stance toward unfair foreign trade practices without including outright protectionist proposals. Among the many changes put forward in the draft were proposals calling for (1) revision of Sections 201 and 301 to transfer from the president to the USTR the authority to make escape clause decisions and findings of whether foreign practices met statutory criteria, (2) expansion of the definition of foreign trading practices that might trigger U.S. retaliation, and (3) mandatory retaliation against countries that discriminated against U.S. exports. The framework for the draft legislation was largely provided by a 1984 bill written by the Labor-Industry Coalition for International Trade. Organized labor, in particular, was gearing up for a campaign to toughen U.S. responses to unfair trade practices. "If there is one issue that is the hot button for labor all across the country, it's trade," said Brian Turner, legislative director of the AFL-CIO's Industrial Union Department.[56]

Other sympathetic witnesses testified at the hearings on the draft bill on behalf of trade-sensitive business interests. Most internationally oriented or competitive business interests, however, opposed the House draft, fearing the disruption of world trade that such a bill might produce.[57]

Reagan Tries—and Fails—to Stop the Bill

The Reagan administration had little enthusiasm for a major trade bill. The only trade item that it considered essential was negotiating authority for a new round of the General Agreement on Tariffs and Trade (GATT), and that could wait until the following year when, the White House believed, the trade deficit would be smaller and the partisan protectionist pressures of an election year would be diminished. The administration thus attacked the Ways and Means Trade Subcommittee's draft bill, and the threat of a presidential veto hung over all discussions of the measure.

In deciding whether or not to veto a trade bill, however, Reagan had to weigh the importance of keeping the Senate in Republican hands. USTR Clayton Yeutter discussed the electoral and policy trade-offs that the administration would consider in developing its position: "There is a great desire on the part of the administration to aid those [Republican] senators [up for reelection]. But we cannot afford to have legislation that will devastate the international trading environment in order to gain votes in November."[58]

To avoid having to decide at some later date whether to issue a possibly politically damaging veto of a tough trade bill, the administration on March 31 again took a number of steps to simultaneously tone down or perhaps even block passage of such a measure, neutralize the Democratic political threat, and help Farm Belt Republicans in an election year. Thus, the White House announced curbs on imports from the European Community (EC),[59] an investigation of whether a new EC meat directive would hurt U.S. exports, and an investigation of Taiwan's export performance requirements.

Reagan's actions did not stop the progress of the House bill, however. On April 23 and May 1, House Democrats edged closer toward a major political confrontation with the administration when first the Ways and Means Trade Subcommittee and then the full Ways and Means Committee, on party-line votes, approved drafts of an omnibus trade bill. Subcommittee and committee Democrats voted down repeated efforts by Republicans to make the bill more acceptable to themselves and the president. "I think we have lost whatever spirit of bipartisanship existed," said Bill Frenzel (R-Minn.). "This has become a Republican-Democratic scrap."[60]

Some Republicans had been initially sympathetic to portions of the bill, but partisanship sharpened on April 30, when Ways and Means approved, along almost straight party lines, an amendment, similar to the old import surcharge proposal, that would have singled out countries maintaining large trade surpluses with the United States and other nations.[61] The amendment was offered by Dick Gephardt, who was now running hard for the Democratic presidential nomination. Gephardt knew that a tough stand on trade policy would help win him (1) crucial support from the United Auto Workers (UAW) and other unions in the Iowa caucuses and in later industrial state primaries and (2) support among textile and shoe industry workers in early caucus and primary states in New England, in Georgia and Alabama, and perhaps in North and South Carolina, Virginia, Tennessee, and Missouri.[62]

As the House vote on the omnibus trade bill approached, Reagan and his top advisers worried over the Democrats' plans to campaign on the bill and the wider trade issue in the November elections.[63] To head off passage of the bill and defuse the threat from the Democrats, the administration took still another spate of trade actions.

Just hours before the House started debate on the omnibus trade bill, Reagan initiated one of his strongest actions to date, announcing that he would ask four nations—Japan, West Germany, Taiwan, and Switzerland—to voluntarily cut their exports of machine tools to the United States. American trade officials denied that the president's announcement was designed to influence the vote on the House trade bill, but other informed observers were dubious.[64] Recently resigned Council of Economic Advisers member William Niskanen later wrote unequivocally that the machine tool decision "was clearly timed to affect the vote on the omnibus trade legislation that was being considered in the House."[65]

On May 22, the day of the House vote, Reagan slapped a 35 percent tariff on Canadian red cedar shake and shingle imports under the escape clause provision of the Trade Act of 1974. Finally, the administration blasted Brazil's informatics policy of protecting its computer industry and threatened to place a 200 percent tariff on European pasta and cheese unless a pasta-citrus dispute was resolved. Vice President George Bush later explained that all these actions were intended "to derail the protectionist juggernaut now sweeping through the United States Congress."[66]

The administration's actions and continued veto threats failed to stop House enactment of the bill, in part because despite a 30 percent drop in the value of the dollar since the previous November, the U.S. trade deficit was still rising. On May 22, after a debate filled with mostly Democratic references to national "muscle-flexing," the House passed the sweeping omnibus trade bill by a vote of 295–115. All but 4 Democrats supported the measure. More surprisingly, 59 GOP members, nearly one-third of the House Republican contingent, also voted for the bill. A Republican substitute for the bill was defeated on a largely party-line vote of 145–265.[67] Three Republican amendments aimed at eliminating various provisions of, and thus weakening, the bill were opposed by all but a handful of Democrats as well as by 44, 65, and 95 GOP members respectively.

As a result of the perceived geographic distribution of the bill's likely benefits and costs, opposition to the weakening amendments and support for the overall measure was strong among members of both parties from the Northeast, the East, the South, and the Midwest, regions with industries—such as textiles and heavy manufacturing—that were being hard hit by imports.[68]

Despite its regional character, House voting also had a strong partisan dimension, due both to the regionally differentiated nature of the parties' bases of support and to members' attentiveness to the preferences of their core reelection constituencies, that is, blue-collar workers for the Democrats and the upper middle class for the Republicans. But more important, again, were the actual lobbying efforts of organized interests. Earlier in the year, Tony Coelho had dunned union officials for contributions to the DCCC's Capital Trust and other soft money projects.[69] Now labor, backed by Coelho, successfully pressured the Democrats to return the favor by voting for the trade bill. In fact, despite its business support, the bill was largely a labor-sponsored initiative, and its passage was generally portrayed by the news media as a triumph of labor.[70]

Bickering among business lobbyists limited their overall influence relative to labor in the debate. But the Republicans were heavily pressured to oppose the bill by internationally oriented business interests—industrial and agricultural exporters, import-using firms, and transnational corporations—that feared both import curbs and foreign retaliation against U.S. exports. Thus the division between organized labor and most of business over the bill once again contributed to the partisan nature of the vote.

Partisanship was further heightened by lawmakers' ideologically colored perceptions of the bill's general benefits and costs, which due to the measure's generic rather product-specific nature, predominated over concentrated group and geographic effects.

Party conflict over the bill also stemmed from the general propensity of House Republicans to support, and of Democrats to oppose, the positions of a sitting GOP president. These predispositions were reinforced by the bargaining and persuasive efforts of the president and the House Democratic leadership.

Finally, divided government, along with divided partisan control of Congress, played a role in hardening partisan divisions over the bill. Many House Democrats who wanted to pass a bill either to show their support for labor or to create a campaign issue, but who feared that the measure was too protectionist, were assured by party leaders that the legislation would never survive the gauntlet of a GOP-controlled Senate or a presidential veto. "Our bill won't become law," Tony Coelho predicted.[71]

The Senate Tries to Begin Work on a Bill, but Reagan Resists

The passage of the House bill and the Democrats' subsequent aggressive use of trade as a campaign issue in various parts of the country put pressure on the Senate Republican leadership to come up with a trade initiative of its own to demonstrate to the voters that Republicans were not soft on trade. Majority Leader Bob Dole was concerned that without a bill, the trade issue might cost the GOP its control of the Senate. As a presidential hopeful, Dole also wanted to pass a bill to demonstrate his leadership abilities. Cooperation with the Reagan administration was seen as key.

The White House at this stage, however, had little or no interest in a trade bill of any kind, still preferring to wait until the following year to pursue legislation to renew the president's negotiating authority. In the face of the administration's seeming intransigence, sectors of the business community began to mobilize to put further pressure on Reagan to compromise with Congress. A number of influential business organizations, although opposed to all or part of the House bill, nevertheless found the White House too passive in the face of the trade problem and at the same time feared more extreme protectionist measures if the administration continued to block any bill whatsoever.[72]

The White House initially resisted this new pressure for a change in strategy. But with business frustration mounting, in mid-July Donald Regan told representatives of a number of major business organizations that the administration would reverse its position and work with the Senate. By now, however, Congress's tight legislative calendar had become another obstacle to the passage of a trade bill in 1986. Moreover, Congress was preoccupied with tax reform, and the Gramm-Rudman deficit reduction bill and the budget resolution still lay ahead.

Despite little progress toward a Senate trade bill, Democratic congressional candidates wasted no time in taking the trade issue onto the campaign trail. In the immediate aftermath of the House vote, Democratic Senate candidates emphasized industry-specific trade themes in North Carolina (textiles), Alabama (textiles and steel), Georgia (textiles), Pennsylvania (steel), and Missouri (shoes). Specific U.S. dealings with Canada over forest products were a major concern in Idaho, Oregon, and Washington. Slumping U.S. agricultural exports were a key issue in Farm Belt races, particularly in North and South Dakota.[73]

With House Speaker Tip O'Neill's support, DCCC chairman Tony Coelho, using the trade bill as a central piece of his strategy, targeted a dozen races where he thought the trade issue might swing elections in November. Committee staff members spent much of their time helping Democratic candidates to exploit the controversy: "Textiles in North Carolina and South Carolina, steel in Pennsylvania, Illinois. The Republicans can Polyanna on this, but we aren't going to Polyanna it: When we're talking trade, we're talking jobs," Coelho said.[74] Elsewhere, Coelho rejoiced that "we've put the Republicans on the defensive" on the trade issue.[75]

In focusing on trade, the Democrats hoped for gains in states like Maine, Pennsylvania, and North and South Dakota. But it was to the South that they looked for their biggest trade-related political victories. The Democrats were aware that, given the country's shifting demographics, they could no longer rely on their base in the thirteen states of the Northeast and the Midwest to win presidential elections and control of Congress. They would have to look either West or South for more votes. And with the Mountain West emerging as a solidly conservative region, many Democrats had become convinced that they had to win back the South to regain national dominance.[76]

The Democrats had high hopes that the trade issue could help them reverse the GOP tide in the South, first in the 1986 congressional races, then perhaps in the 1988 presidential campaign. Party strategists believed that an emphasis on trade concerns could work in Missouri, Louisiana, and the southeastern textile states—Georgia, Alabama, South Carolina, and especially North Carolina, where an open Senate seat was up for grabs and all five Republican House seats were thought to be in danger.[77] Democratic candidates throughout the region pounded their GOP opponents for failing to persuade a Republican administration to change its disastrous trade policies. "This is the kind of issue," said Democratic Representative Charlie Rose of North Carolina, "that can send a message to all those nouveau Republicans in the South that their gods have let them down and they better return to the religion of their forefathers."[78]

Not all Democrats agreed that a tough trade stance was the path to renewed strength in the South. The moderates of the Sun Belt–based Democratic Leadership Council (DLC) played a major role in reorienting the party toward rebuilding its position in the South. But the DLC saw the region's future lying in its rapidly growing, high-tech, internationally competitive areas—like the urban centers of Houston, Dallas, Atlanta, Miami, and North Carolina's Research Triangle (Raleigh, Durham, and Chapel Hill)—rather than in the declining, import-battered southeastern textile districts.[79] In 1985 leading DLC members barnstormed the Sun Belt talking about growth, opportunity, improved productivity, and expanded trade without protectionism. And in early 1986 congressional DLC members introduced an omnibus trade bill that was considerably more moderate than the Democratic-sponsored measure that passed the House later that spring.[80] As we shall see, this split between the DLC and more liberal Democrats would reemerge in the 1990s over various trade liberalization initiatives.

The Textile Bill and the Battle for the South

The DLC's reservations notwithstanding, the Democrats' southern hopes soon became entwined with the House battle to override Reagan's veto the previous December of the restrictive textile quota bill. The measure had been introduced in Congress in the spring of 1985 by sponsors who believed that the Multi-Fiber Arrangement, due to expire on July 31, 1986, was not being used to protect U.S. textile manufacturers from a surge of imports. When Congress returned from its summer recess the following September, of the hundreds of pieces of proposed trade legislation awaiting action, the textile bill, backed by the House Democratic leadership, had the widest support and greatest momentum behind it.[81]

Convinced that the Democrats had "won the Texas [special] election as a result of trade dominating the debate,"[82] Tony Coelho thought that the textile bill could be helpful to the party elsewhere in the South, especially among white men. "In every poll," Coelho said, "the biggest problem Democrats have had is with white males in the South. The whole textile issue appeals to Southern white males, and I think the Administration is blowing it."[83] Democratic leaders also viewed the textile bill as a vehicle for enlisting still wider popular support among those concerned with America's economic decline. In explaining his endorsement of the bill, for example, Tip O'Neill attacked Reagan for "being willing to preside over the deindustrialization of America."[84]

Although interest in the bill waned in the fall as the protectionist fever cooled, it nevertheless passed the full House in early October, the Senate in mid-November, and the House again in early December.[85] Given the geographic concentration of the likely benefits and costs of the bill, it is not surprising that the voting was regional in nature. Lawmakers from southern textile states, regardless of party, overwhelmingly backed the measure, whereas those from trade-dependent states, particularly on the Pacific Coast and in the Farm Belt, were solidly opposed.

At the same time, for reasons of constituency, ideology, and campaign issue creation, voting on the textile bill had a partisan character, especially on the Democratic side. Divided government again played a role in heightening partisanship over the bill by allowing Democrats of all stripes, including free traders, to support the measure in order to score political points in the South, knowing that a Reagan veto would not likely be overridden. As Democratic Representative Donald Pease of Ohio, an opponent of the legislation, remarked, "A lot of people are eager to get this bill to the president, are eager to have him veto it and are eager to have the veto sustained—all for next year's election."[86]

In mid-December, despite warnings from Senators Strom Thurmond (R-S.C.) and Jesse Helms (R-N.C.) that a veto of the textile bill would hurt Republican candidates in the South in 1986, Reagan rejected the measure. Freed from his own reelection worries and with protectionist pressures lessening, the president could now more easily buck southern textile interests to defend free trade than he could during his first term.

Recognizing that they did not have the necessary two-thirds majority in both the House and the Senate to surmount the veto, House supporters of the bill won approval of a motion to push back an override attempt until August 1986. By that date the international negotiations to renew the Multi-Fiber Arrangement would be well under way and the 1986 elections would be only three months ahead. The bill's sponsors hoped that this timing would force the White House to take a stronger stance in the upcoming talks and induce more members to vote to override in order to demonstrate "toughness" on trade to their constituents. Many Democrats also planned to use the override to score points in the fall elections.[87]

In the summer of 1986 the battle was rejoined. In the month and especially the week before the vote, the Reagan administration took a flurry of new trade actions to see the veto sustained, to block Senate passage of the omnibus trade bill, and to provide political cover on the trade issue for GOP incumbents. First, the USTR announced that Hong Kong, Taiwan, and South Korea, the three primary targets of the textile bill, had agreed to limit exports to the United States of fabric and apparel goods not previously restricted by bilateral agreements. Second, trade officials from fifty-four countries, including the United States, agreed on a five-year extension of the Multi-Fiber Arrangement that called for tighter limits on some textile imports. Finally, the White House took several nontextile trade actions, the most important of which was the announcement of a precedent-setting market-sharing or "managed trade" agreement with Japan to enhance the sale of U.S. semiconductors in that country and to prevent dumping of chips by Japanese firms in both U.S. and third-country markets.[88]

Lobbying on the override was exceptionally intense. Textile and apparel interests were, of course, highly visible in their support of the override, whereas retailers and farm groups, the latter fearing foreign retaliation against U.S. exports, worked actively against it. Hoping both to defeat the textile bill and to discourage the Senate from passing omnibus trade legislation, the Reagan administration lobbied vigorously against the override, focusing on wavering Republicans who were torn between regional interests and party loyalties.

In the end, the efforts of the administration and other opponents of the bill paid off. On August 6 the override attempt came up short, the count being eight votes shy of the two-thirds needed to block the veto. Two hundred five Democrats, 82 percent of those who voted, went against Reagan, but only 71 Republicans opposed him—40 percent of those voting. As in earlier votes on the bill, the override had both regional and partisan characteristics.

Many nontextile state Republicans rallied to Reagan's side, thanks to his lobbying blitz, pleas for party loyalty, and trade policy handouts; the usual pressures from internationally oriented business interests; attentiveness to consumer interests; and ideological commitments to free trade. Meanwhile, many Democrats from the same nontextile states joined Democrats from import-sensitive regions of the South and the Northeast to back the bill, because they were either heavily lobbied by organized labor, attentive to blue-collar job concerns, ideologically committed to defending the American industrial base, hoping to create a campaign issue in the South and perhaps elsewhere, or pressured by House leaders who sought to maintain the Democrats' majority status by boosting the reelection prospects of the party's southern members.[89]

Immediately after the House vote, the Democrats attempted to turn Reagan's veto and the failed override into a campaign issue, especially in the South. "There will be another trade vote on November 4," Tip O'Neill declared.[90]

The Fall Campaign

Democratic candidates campaigned hard on the trade issue in a number of states in the late summer and early fall. Fusing populist and economic nationalist appeals, the candidates and party congressional leaders stressed the role of trade competition in the creation of both an alleged middle-class "decline" or "squeeze" and a "bicoastal economy," in which recent growth had been confined to the high-tech and service-oriented states of the East and West Coasts at the expense of the industrial and agricultural "heartland."[91]

Contrary to Democratic hopes, however, the trade issue caught on in only a few races.[92] In export-dependent parts of the country, especially the Pacific Coast, Reagan's free-trade stance was actually popular. In other areas, voters were of two minds, favoring the protection of American goods but also wanting access to cheap foreign products. Even in import-competing states, Republican candidates were able to ward off Democratic attacks by taking tough trade positions themselves. For most voters, though, the trade issue simply was not very salient.[93]

Leaving nothing to chance, however, the administration took yet another set of election-eve actions in October to toughen its trade posture and blunt the Democratic threat. For one thing, the White House announced a cut in certain Japanese textile imports and reached an agreement, intended in part to prevent the "loss of Republican seats in the Senate," whereby Tokyo promised to eliminate barriers to U.S. cigarette sales.[94] In its most significant move, the administration slapped a preliminary 15 percent tariff on some Canadian lumber imports, the biggest such tariff in decades. As William Niskanen explained, the determination "was clearly timed to save several Republican Senate seats in the timber-producing states" of the Northwest and the South.[95]

Also intended to defuse Democratic pressure on trade was the launching of the Uruguay Round GATT talks in late September. After the failure of the 1982 GATT ministerial meeting, the White House revived the idea of a new GATT round in 1985, hoping to lower trade barriers in "new" areas, that is, those not covered by existing GATT rules, where American producers were most competitive, like agricultural goods and business services. But as the Uruguay Round began in the fall of 1986, the White House further hoped "to score political points for its pro-trade efforts before November's congressional elections, aiding Republican candidates who are being harassed by Democrats over the U.S. trade problems."[96]

When the September trade figures were released on October 30 showing a $760 million decline in the trade deficit—the second straight month of decline—Democratic hopes of making the trade issue central in more than a few races were finally dashed. Even though the party recaptured the Senate and netted an additional five House seats, the role of trade policy in producing these gains was limited.[97]

The decline in the apparent salience of the trade issue also contributed to the diminished interest of Senate Republicans in pushing a tough trade bill through Congress in 1986. Finance Committee work on such a measure was abandoned.

Despite the fact that trade in the end played a fairly minor role in the midterm elections, party competition to an important extent drove the making and further strengthening of U.S. trade policy during the years of the Ninety-ninth Congress. This would continue to be the case in the now fully Democratic-controlled One-hundredth Congress.

The One-hundredth Congress

Trade Legislation and Presidential Politics

The Democrats did surprisingly well in the 1986 congressional elections, recapturing the Senate and netting five House seats. That victory altered the context in which party competition influenced trade policy during the One-hundredth Congress. In the previous Congress, the Democrats had generally found themselves either obstructing the Reagan program or introducing popular bills that they thought Senate Republicans would likely kill, thus creating issues for the 1986 campaign. Now, however, the Democrats were again in a position to actually legislate, and while some party members still wanted to posture on trade and other issues to embarrass the Republicans, many others were eager to produce a record of accomplishment that both they and their party's presidential nominee could campaign on in 1988.[1]

At the top of their ambitious legislative agenda was a new omnibus trade bill, which many Democrats still hoped to turn into a campaign issue. Throughout much of 1987–88, in a process that did, in fact, become thoroughly entangled with the electoral cycle, the One-hundredth Congress labored over and finally produced the mammoth Omnibus Trade and Competitiveness Act of 1988, which moderately strengthened the nation's trade laws. The bill was ultimately enacted with substantial bipartisan majorities in both houses and signed by President Reagan. But its development was again largely driven by the Democrats, especially in the House. Along the way there were episodes of sharp partisan conflict and of bipartisan cooperation, as well as new cases of policy contagion.

Getting Serious about a Trade Bill

As the fully Democrat-controlled One-hundredth Congress began its work, Ronald Reagan appeared uninterested in domestic policy and in any event was weakened by the mounting Iran-Contra scandal. Seizing the initiative, Democratic leaders in both houses moved quickly and aggressively to formulate and pass a sweeping legislative program.[2]

The process actually began in December 1986, when the House Democratic caucus chose Jim Wright of Texas, a quasi-populist who retained a New Deal commitment to active government, as the new speaker. Newly elected Senate Majority Leader Robert Byrd of West Virginia wielded considerably less power than Wright, due to the more individualistic character of the Senate. But Byrd worked to the best of his ability with the speaker to develop a coherent congressional agenda for their party.

In their late January response to Reagan's State of the Union address, Wright and Byrd jointly outlined an ambitious ten-point Democratic legislative agenda, focusing on domestic issues, headed up by trade, farm relief, and education. Janet Hook of *Congressional Quarterly Weekly Report* explained the political logic that lay behind this agenda: "Even if those initiatives do not become law, many Democrats hope their legislative menu will serve as a rough draft of their party's 1988 platform."[3]

Heading the new Democratic leadership's agenda in both the House and the Senate was, perhaps surprisingly, a new trade bill. Calling such legislation the "first imperative" of the new Congress, Speaker Jim Wright, with the support of more than 180 House Democrats, introduced on January 6 a measure—H.R. 3, the third to be introduced that session—that mirrored the omnibus trade legislation passed by the House the previous May. The next day Majority Leader Robert Byrd similarly declared that trade would be one of the Senate's top priorities.

This Democratic emphasis on trade may seem hard to understand, since the trade issue appeared to have had little impact on the 1986 congressional elections. Part of the explanation lies in the Democrats' continuing attempts to retain or win business and labor support. As *Fortune* observed, "Democrats see the trade issue as a winner. It lets them appeal to a broad spectrum of business and labor leaders who are impatient with what they consider the Administration's lack of aggressiveness on trade."[4]

Since the meeting the previous summer between White House officials and a number of major business organizations, internationally oriented business interests had become even more frustrated by the administration's unwillingness to work with Congress to develop a moderate trade bill.

On the labor side, the AFL-CIO and its member unions continued to give top priority to a tough trade bill. Labor had not fared well politically during the first half of the 1980s. But after the 1986 elections, at least in the House, labor's influence was revived by (1) a heightened internal unity within the labor movement, (2) an improved union national and grassroots lobbying capacity, (3) the continued dependence of many congressional Democrats, especially in cities of the industrial Northeast and Midwest, on labor money, manpower, and votes, (4) the diminished role of anti-union southerners within the congressional party, and (5) Jim Wright's personal inclination to cooperate closely with labor on behalf of a progressive agenda.[5] At the AFL-CIO's annual meeting in mid-February, House Democratic leaders pledged that they would address the first concern of labor—a tough trade bill.

Democrats still harbored the hope that the trade issue could be of more general value in the 1988 elections. Party members differed, however, on whether to seek "a bill or an issue."[6] Some key Democrats urged their colleagues to cooperate with the Republicans in order to produce a bipartisan compromise trade bill that they could claim at least partial credit for.[7] But other Democrats still favored a "strategy of disagreement." Either responding to the preferences of their core labor constituents for a tough bill or convinced that the best way to win swing voter support on the issue was to dramatize their differences with the unpopular free-trade views of the Republicans, these Democrats were disinclined to work toward compromise trade legislation. Many in this group instead hoped to provoke a Reagan "blame game" veto of a popular bill that they could use as a campaign issue. The "real battle that is shaping up," explained a Senate Democratic staff member, "is not between Congress and the White House, but between the Democratic leadership—Jim Wright and Bobby Byrd—who might prefer a White House veto, and guys like Rostenkowski who really want a bill that can become law."[8]

Competing over "Competitiveness"

The year 1986 had left some Democrats gun-shy. Stung by the unfavorable reaction to the 1986 House bill, many Democrats, especially party moderates, backed away from supporting new legislation that could be viewed as protectionist. Instead, they turned to "competitiveness" policy, still ill-defined, as a nonprotectionist approach to the trade problem.[9]

Although industrial policy had been driven from the political agenda with Ronald Reagan's rout of Walter Mondale, the underlying concern—the relative decline of American industry's competitiveness in world markets—remained alive. By the summer and fall of 1986, a consensus was reemerging within the trade policy community—including important business interests—that the U.S. economy was beset by long-term structural problems. Sensing another opening, the Democrats began to test the political appeal of "competitiveness."[10] House and Senate Democrats developed new competitiveness proposals, while Democratic presidential hopefuls talked up the concept. The free traders of the Democratic Leadership Council were particularly active in promoting the political value of a focus on competitiveness as an alternative to protectionism.

Reagan was by no means oblivious to this Democratic maneuvering. In mid-February, in a classic case of policy contagion, the White House sent a modest competitiveness package to Capitol Hill. No longer able to count on a GOP-controlled Senate to bury House-passed trade legislation, the White House now resolved to work with congressional leaders to shape a new trade bill. Their goals were to seize the competitiveness issue from the Democrats, prevent passage of a protectionist trade measure, obtain authority to negotiate a new multilateral trade agreement, and deflect public attention from the emerging Iran-Contra scandal.[11]

Most of the president's plan, however, consisted of a repackaged laundry list of ideas repeatedly submitted by the White House in recent years and repeatedly rejected by Congress. In addition, urged by both business and labor to concentrate on trade law reform, congressional Democrats had begun to conclude that "competitiveness" was an elusive concept that did not forthrightly tackle America's trade problems. Thus their response to Reagan's package was tepid, and they refocused their efforts on strengthening the trade laws well beyond what Reagan was proposing.

The House Drafts and Passes a Bill

In the House, H.R. 3 had been referred to six committees. The biggest part of the bill went to the Ways and Means Committee, chaired by Dan Rostenkowski. Nonetheless, Jim Wright made sure that the House Democratic leadership would retain control over the bill as a whole rather than Rostenkowski, who, despite his earlier cosponsorship of the original import surcharge proposal, was considered too much of a free trader by the many Democratic trade hawks.[12]

Despite his free-trade views, Rostenkowski believed that the Reagan administration had been lax in combating unfair foreign trade practices. In his committee, he hoped to strike a bipartisan compromise between his colleagues, including Wright, who backed Dick Gephardt's call for tough limits on imports from countries with large trade surpluses with the United States, and the White House, which wanted continued flexibility to negotiate open markets for U.S. goods.

On March 10 and 25 respectively, the Ways and Means Trade Subcommittee and then with minor changes the full committee reported out a moderate package of amendments to H.R. 3. The most important provision of the committee bill required the president to retaliate when another nation was found engaging in unfair trade practices, but it left the form of retaliation up to him. The Gephardt excess trade surplus amendment was replaced by a more moderate substitute, and many other provisions of H.R. 3 that administration and business critics said were extreme or in violation of international trade agreements were modified or dropped. As Rostenkowski later explained, "I chased away all the things that were visibly objectionable, not just to the administration but to the business community."[13] Both the White House and internationally oriented business interests were generally pleased with the committee draft.

On the other hand, organized labor and its Democratic supporters, who favored tough retaliatory sanctions against unfair foreign traders, were unhappy about the changes in the bill and its resulting mild character. After the trade subcommittee had dropped the Gephardt amendment from its draft, labor had pressed the lawmaker to fight to reinstate it in the full committee version of the bill. But concluding that he did not have the votes to do so, Gephardt chose instead to wait to offer a somewhat more moderate version of his amendment when the measure reached the House floor in April. Jim Wright, committed to repaying labor for its earlier help in overriding Reagan's veto of a key highway bill, promised Gephardt his support for the new version of the amendment at the floor stage.

Conflict with Japan Fans the Flames—Again

As the trade bill worked its way through various House subcommittees and committees during March, congressional Democrats' resolve to pass an aggressive trade bill was strengthened by a new flare-up with Japan. In the spring of 1987, the U.S.-Japan semiconductor market-sharing pact negotiated the previous summer was unraveling as evidence mounted that Japan was continuing to dump chips into third-country markets and had failed to increase the foreign share of its semiconductor market. When public White House preparations to retaliate produced no change in Japanese policy, the Senate on March 19, by a vote of 93–0, passed a nonbinding resolution urging the president to take forceful action to gain Japanese compliance with the pact. Congress also indicated that new support for the Gephardt amendment might be generated if Tokyo did not relent.

After much fretting, the Reagan administration was forced to act. On March 27 it announced, and then on April 17 actually imposed, 100 percent tariffs on $300 million worth of Japanese products. These were the harshest trade sanctions that the United States had slapped on the Japanese since the end of World War II.

The White House decision was prompted by a number of factors, including bipartisan congressional anger with Japan,[14] bipartisan support for the nation's pivotal high-tech sector, and the administration's concern over widespread public anxiety that the United States's superpower status was eroding. But once again the administration acted in part to undermine Democratic efforts to exploit the trade issue for partisan purposes. As Hobart Rowen of the *Washington Post* observed, the decision to impose sanctions was a victory for "the protectionist-minded among [Reagan's] advisers who see the Democrats coming out ahead in election-year Japan-bashing sweepstakes."[15]

Battling over the Gephardt Amendment

Contrary to White House hopes, however, the imposition of sanctions against Japan did little to erode Congress's determination to pass a trade bill. At the same time, there was no congressional unity on the Gephardt amendment, which the Missourian was still pushing to boost his presidential chances. Congressional Republicans almost unanimously opposed the proposal, and the Democrats were split.

Democratic divisions over the amendment reflected the broader cleavage within the party between traditional liberals and moderates, the latter including members of the Democratic Leadership Council. Liberals backed the measure due to ideological conviction, dependence on or loyalty to labor constituents, or, according to House Majority Leader Tom Foley, to provoke a Reagan veto of a tough trade bill, which, especially if not overridden, would help "sustain the issue into a driving force for the 1988 election."[16] On the other hand, moderate opponents of the amendment included ideological free traders and Democrats from export-oriented high-tech and agricultural regions who feared retaliation against goods produced in their districts. Additionally, as Rostenkowski explained, many of his Democratic colleagues were "afraid . . . of the atmosphere of Smoot-Hawley" and thus did not want a "protectionist label around them."[17] Although polls consistently found that voters favored limiting imports to protect American jobs even if this meant higher prices, surveys showed that the public rejected solutions labeled "protectionist."[18] Finally, there were those, like Rostenkowski himself, who believed that their party could claim more credit by initiating "good legislation" that the president would feel compelled to sign than it could by "establishing an issue."[19]

Throughout April, conflict raged between two coalitions.[20] The pro-Gephardt coalition, backed by most of the House leadership and mobilized by task forces coordinated by new Democratic Whip Tony Coelho, included the labor move-ment, especially the United Auto Workers (UAW) and the AFL-CIO, and some powerful, mostly import-competing businesses in the automobile, textile, steel, and electronics industries. These interests anticipated that most countries run-ning chronic trade surpluses with the United States, notably Japan, would be unable to comply with the requirements of the Gephardt amendment, thus triggering its retaliatory provisions.

The anti-Gephardt coalition was supported and even organized by Rosten-kowski and the Ways and Means staff. It included internationally oriented business, farm, and consumer groups. Retailers took the lead among business interests, but high-tech and other manufacturing exporters, importers, import-using firms, and transnational corporations were also involved in the coali-tion, which eventually included more than seventy-five trade groups and firms. These interests feared that the Gephardt amendment, if enacted, would most likely lead to higher import prices and foreign retaliation against U.S. exports.

As the House vote on the trade bill approached, a potentially disastrous intra-Democratic battle was averted when Rostenkowski decided to back off from an open confrontation with Jim Wright over the Gephardt amendment. The Reagan administration however, again backed by the elite media, showed no such restraint. Nonetheless, after a suspenseful vote count, the measure passed by a narrow 218–214 margin. As usual, the vote had something of a regional character, as to a modest extent, members of both parties from the industrial Northeast and Midwest opposed those from the West Coast.[21] But the vote was also a highly partisan one. Democrats voted for the measure 201–55, whereas Republicans opposed it 17–159.[22]

To some extent, this sharp partisan division can again be explained by the regionally differentiated nature of the parties' bases of support. But because the benefits and costs of the generic Gephardt amendment were of a mostly general character, voting on Gephardt's measure was more ideologically partisan than had been the case on product-specific measures, like the textile bill, whose effects were more geographically concentrated.[23]

The usual constituency and ideological influences, along with White House pressure, kept more wavering Republicans from defecting to support Gephardt. Given their earlier split over the amendment, however, the Democrats' strong roll-call support for the measure is surprising. Some Democratic trade hawks backed the Gephardt amendment due to a genuine constituency or ideologi-cally driven desire to toughen U.S. trade policy. Other Democrats, who person-ally found the measure overly aggressive, voted for it because they wanted to send a signal to Japan or to blue-collar voters.[24] Still others hoped to provoke a Reagan veto and thus create a campaign issue. And there were those who backed the amendment simply out of loyalty to Gephardt and his presidential campaign.

As before, the vote for the amendment by Democrats who thought it to be bad legislation was again facilitated by bicameralism and divided government. As Rostenkowski later explained, some of his fellow party members supported the amendment as "kind of a free vote" for "labor and Dick Gephardt" in the belief that "when it gets to conference it will be dropped because the Senate has strong opposition to it."[25] If somehow the amendment survived the conference, members knew that the wider bill would most certainly be vetoed by the president.

Passing the Bill, Moving toward a Fair-Trade Consensus

The vote on final passage of the omnibus bill, 290–137, was less partisan than the vote on the Gephardt amendment. Forty-three Republicans, fearful of being outflanked on an electorally popular issue by their Democratic rivals, joined all but six Democrats to approve the bill.[26] Both Republican and Democratic critics of the Gephardt amendment and other potentially protectionist provisions knew they would get another look at the measure after the Senate acted on it and a conference committee worked out differences between the two chambers.[27]

Before the final vote, the acrimonious debate on the Gephardt amendment had masked an emerging if incomplete bipartisan consensus in support of fair trade and reciprocity. Although the vote did pit almost all Democrats against about three-quarters of House Republicans, the Democrats were not as protectionist as their vote for the Gephardt amendment made them appear, and many Republicans who opposed the overall bill did so only because it included the Gephardt measure. Democrat Charles Schumer of New York observed that "both sides are moving toward reciprocity. The free traders now know something has to be done, and the out-and-out protectionists know that's not where the consensus is."[28]

Part of the reason for this growing consensus lay in the constraining legacy of the Smoot-Hawley Act and the continued resilience of the liberal trade policy paradigm, which was particularly important in keeping Democratic protectionist tendencies in check. Also important were the evolving views of internationally oriented business interests, which, despite their opposition to the Gephardt amendment, had reversed their earlier resistance to a bill of any kind and now supported passage of a moderate, market-opening, and competitiveness-promoting fair-trade bill. This development pushed Democrats and especially business-oriented Republicans toward support for such a centrist measure.[29]

Finally, the emerging consensus on "free but fair trade" was also a product of more expressly electoral dynamics. To maintain or win the support of pivotal swing voters who sought more aggressive trade policies, the Republicans were slowly prodded by their Democratic rivals, via a process of contagion or mimicking, into assuming a tougher trade position. At the same time, the Democrats moderated their own views to avoid being labeled "protectionists."[30] Still, this consensus remained a partial one. For constituency, ideological, and incumbency-based reasons, congressional Democrats continued to back tougher trade policies than those favored by their Republican rivals.

The Senate Takes Its Turn, Then on to the Conference

On May 7, a week after the House passed its version of the omnibus trade bill, the Senate Finance Committee, chaired by Lloyd Bentsen, reported out its own measure. Repeatedly insisting that he wanted "a result, not an issue,"[31] Bentsen, who like his House counterpart Rostenkowski was a free trader, strove to maintain his committee's traditional bipartisan approach to trade and to produce a generic bill that could command sufficient support from members of both parties to survive a possible Reagan veto.

Bentsen's bill thus included a proposed ten-year extension of the president's authority to negotiate international trade agreements and provisions to pressure the president to retaliate against unfair practices by foreign trading partners, to streamline the antidumping laws, and to increase import relief. There was no Senate version of the Gephardt amendment. Despite compromises made to allay White House objections, the administration suggested that the Finance Committee bill might face a veto.

Over the next month and a half, other committees worked on their contributions to the Senate version of the omnibus bill. In mid-May the Senate Labor and Human Resources Committee approved a controversial provision requiring plants to give employees advance notice before they laid off large numbers of workers or closed down. The measure was backed by labor and the Democrats and strongly opposed by most of the business community, congressional Republicans, and the administration. A month later, another amendment was approved, also strongly opposed by the White House, granting the president authority to block foreign takeovers, mergers, and joint ventures involving U.S. firms if he decided such actions could harm national security

On June 25, after nine committee bills had been rolled together, the Senate finally began consideration of its omnibus trade bill. The voting on the bill and its key amendments would see complex patterns of partisanship and interaction between Congress and the White House. In one effort to avoid a presidential veto, the Senate tabled by a bipartisan 69–27 vote an amendment offered by Arlen Specter (R-Pa.) and opposed by Reagan that was thought to be a test of whether senators would favor tough restrictions on imports. Similarly, the Senate by a 55–41 vote approved an amendment to strike from the bill a provision, sponsored by Lloyd Bentsen and also opposed by the president, curbing oil imports.

There were limits, however, to the Democrats' willingness to accommodate the White House. After a heated debate, by a vote of 41–55 that was both regional and partisan in nature, senators rejected an amendment by Robert Packwood (R-Oreg.), strongly backed by the administration and most of the business community, that would have allowed the president to refuse industry requests for temporary protection under Section 201 if the action would harm the overall economy more than it would aid the industry seeking help.

The most pitched battle was fought over plant closings. The original Senate language was repeatedly watered down to erode support for a Republican amendment to strike the provision from the bill. The move to strike was then defeated on a highly partisan vote, and the plant closing amendment was passed by voice vote.

The expected partisan combat and confrontation with the president over the Gephardt amendment never materialized. By an overwhelming 87–7 margin, the Senate passed a compromise "leadership" measure, drafted by Senators Don Riegle (D-Mich.) and John Danforth (R-Mo.). Nicknamed "Super 301," the measure required the White House to take "mandatory but waivable" steps to reduce certain unfair trade barriers maintained by targeted countries, while avoiding the linking of such action to large bilateral trade surpluses with those countries, as did the Gephardt amendment.[32] "This is not son of Gephardt," said Majority Leader Byrd, who had been anxious to avoid a divisive intra-Democratic floor fight over the Gephardt language.[33] The White House indicated that it would "reluctantly accept" the Riegle-Danforth measure, but administration officials objected to many of the bill's other provisions, and veto threats remained in the air.

On July 21 the Senate finally passed its version of the omnibus trade bill by a fairly partisan vote of 72–27.[34] Democrats backed the measure 50–0, whereas Republicans opposed it 19–27. Partisanship in the voting was exacerbated by White House officials, who appealed to Senate Republicans to vote as a block against the measure to show the Democrats that they lacked the majority necessary to override a presidential veto of any product emerging from the upcoming conference. Such an en masse "no" vote, the officials argued, would give the administration more bargaining leverage in the conference.

Not all Republicans were persuaded by these arguments. Indeed, some felt that the bill contained many positive, bipartisan elements and that a large-scale vote against it could both reduce Republican influence in the conference and hand the trade issue to the Democrats. Consequently, nineteen GOP senators voted for the bill. But the president did win the support of 60 percent of the Republicans, especially those who had been angered by the Democrats during the fight over the plant closing amendment.

The Democrats, having made a series of concessions in the bill, were infuriated by the White House's position, concluding that the administration planned to approach the conference with an inflexible veto strategy. Thus, all fifty Democratic senators in attendance angrily voted with one voice. With all sides claiming victory, the bill was sent to conference.

The Conference Begins: Conflict, Crash, and Retreat

As the October 21 starting date for the massive House-Senate conference approached, it appeared that heightened conflict between the parties might prevent agreement on a moderate compromise that the president could sign. Congressional partisanship had been rising steadily since the early 1980s, especially in the House, but by mid-1987 conflict had escalated to new heights. The Democrats had gotten off to a quick start in the One-hundredth Congress, decisively passing a number of their priority bills and easily overriding Reagan's vetoes on highway and water project measures. By midyear the Democrats had turned to a still more divisive, labor-backed agenda that was strongly opposed by business and its GOP allies, slowing the legislative momentum. Bills passed in the House under Wright's firm guidance foundered in the Senate, where the Republicans rediscovered the filibuster. Reagan repeatedly used the veto threat to influence pending legislation.[35] By the fall, policy-making was paralyzed by partisan conflict both in Congress and between Congress and the White House.[36]

This climate of conflict threatened to intrude into the conference on the trade bill. Many Democrats remained convinced that the trade issue was a political winner. The still-soaring trade deficit had Republicans on the defensive, and opinion polls revealed an angry electorate, which seemed to clear the way for tough trade legislation. *Business Week* reported: "Many Democrats, including Wright and Senate Majority Leader Robert C. Byrd (D., W. Va.), think that the best course would be to send Reagan a bill he would veto, then to override him."[37] Even trade moderate Rostenkowski was torn between his desire to be seen as an effective legislator and his role as a party leader. "If we get a bill acceptable to the Administration," the Ways and Means chairman said, "we dull the sharpness of this as a political issue."[38]

The possibility of producing bipartisan compromise legislation was also diminished by the administration's intensified criticism of various provisions of the bill, criticism that was fueled by White House and Republican perceptions that Wright and Byrd sought a campaign issue rather than a bill that Reagan could sign.

Then, on October 19—"Black Monday"—the stock market crashed, falling five hundred points or 22.6 percent in a single day. Although a number of explanations were offered for the collapse, some analysts put part of the blame on the pending trade bill. Wall Street and other observers immediately drew parallels with the stock market crash of 1929 and the Smoot-Hawley Act.[39] The White House seized the opening to pressure Congress to pass a moderate trade bill.

By the end of October, administration, Wall Street, media, and academic warnings that a tough trade bill would further destabilize the U.S. and world economies had taken their toll. Fearing that the voters might blame them for a possible recession, the Democrats began to slowly back off from a confrontational stance and to talk of the need for a more moderate bill.

The Conference—Eventually—Produces a Bill

As the second session of the One-hundredth Congress began in January 1988, congressional Democrats were committed to recovering the momentum they had lost during the second half of 1987. Jim Wright and Robert Byrd planned to push their party's leftover agenda items though to final action both as legacies of a "can-do" Congress and, as a leadership aide explained, to give "the Democratic presidential candidate a record he can run on."[40]

Once again at the top of the list of leadership priorities was passage of the omnibus trade bill. The trade bill conference did not actually reconvene until late February, delayed by lingering stock market anxieties and the press of other work. But early in the year, optimism was growing that the White House and the Democratic Congress would eventually reach agreement on a moderate compromise bill, possibly by early spring. Not the least of the reasons for this optimism was the apparently foundering state of Dick Gephardt's presidential campaign.

The Bill Becomes Entangled with Primary Politics

During the 1988 Democratic presidential primary contest, the leading candidates—Gephardt; Governors Michael Dukakis of Massachusetts and Bruce Babbitt of Arizona; Senators Paul Simon, Joseph Biden, and Albert Gore of Illinois, Delaware, and Tennessee respectively, and the Reverend Jesse Jackson—advanced surprisingly similar economic views. Drawing on the earlier industrial policy debate and advised by Democratic policy intellectuals, the candidates all propounded variants of what some analysts called "investment economics." Hoping to bridge the blue collar/white collar and liberal/moderate divides within the party, they spoke of the need to encourage private investment but also called for more public investment in education and training, infrastructure, and the development of new technologies to restore American growth and competitiveness.[41]

Trade policy, however, was one issue on which the Democratic contenders disagreed. During the previous summer and fall, the candidates had spiritedly debated the trade issue, especially in unemployment-battered Iowa, site of the first-in-the-nation Democratic caucuses. The trade deficit was seen as one of the few weak links in Reagan's economic record, the issue gave the candidates something to disagree about, and the political geography of the primary campaign favored an emphasis on trade. Iowa's February 8 caucuses were closely followed by the March 8 Super Tuesday primaries in southern textile states, which in turn were followed by primaries in the midwestern industrial states.[42]

Gephardt had staked out the toughest trade position of the candidates, painting a dark picture of America as a declining nation of boarded-up factories and failing farms. His targets included the estimated 20 percent of Iowa caucus attendees, mainly union members, who were eager for aggressive trade policies. Gephardt's candidacy in Iowa had been given a boost the previous spring by House passage of his trade surplus amendment.[43] Among the other Democrats, Dukakis had assumed the closest thing to a free-trade position in the debate, presenting an optimistic message of revival based on the example of the high-tech-driven "Massachusetts Miracle." The other candidates held intermediate views.

Despite the Democratic candidates' efforts to raise the salience of the trade issue, with economic growth steady and unemployment falling the electorate as a whole remained largely uninterested. In fact, late December polls showed that Gephardt had sunk from 24 percent to a meager 6 percent of the vote in Iowa.[44] But then, in a stunning development that for a time blocked further progress toward a compromise trade bill, Gephardt's campaign suddenly caught fire. In January he surged to the lead and then won the Iowa caucuses with 31.3 percent of the vote.

Pressed by his Iowa UAW backers, Gephardt in December had embraced what one observer called a hard-hitting "populist economic nationalism."[45] Borrowing influential arguments from Paul Kennedy and other so-called declinist authors,[46] Gephardt spoke everywhere of the need to reverse America's economic decline. In particular, he turned up the heat under unfair foreign traders.[47]

The apparent centrality of the trade issue to Gephardt's come-from-behind victory in Iowa led many Democrats to believe that a tough, patriotic trade message could finally win working- and lower-middle-class white Reagan Democrats back to their party.[48] It also stalled progress on the omnibus trade bill until the popularity of Gephardt's stance was more fully tested.

As Super Tuesday approached, the campaign turned to the import-battered South. There, however, Gephardt won only about 13 percent of the vote in fourteen primaries, leading critics to argue that his protectionist views had been repudiated.[49] Nonetheless, as the campaign shifted into the traditionally pivotal states of the industrial heartland, all the Democratic candidates, including front-runner Michael Dukakis, adopted some of Gephardt's economic nationalist themes.[50] But Gephardt's own candidacy had been badly damaged on Super Tuesday. When Jesse Jackson won the Michigan caucuses, Gephardt was forced to drop out of the race.

The Bill Moves Again, and the Conference Nears a Bipartisan Compromise

With Gephardt defeated and his particularly aggressive trade stance seemingly rejected by the voters, the omnibus trade bill began to move again. In mid-March House Ways and Means and Senate Finance conferees, led by Rostenkowski and Bentsen, began to exchange offers on core provisions of the bill.[51] Visible progress was also made in negotiations with a newly cooperative White House.

As the conferees broke on March 31 for the Easter recess, they were close to finishing what was shaping up as a nonprotectionist, bipartisan compromise measure. The Reagan administration and its congressional Republican allies, who at different points had opposed any bill, now reluctantly accepted provisions they had long rejected. The most important of these were (1) limits on the president's discretion in granting import relief recommended by the ITC in Section 201 escape clause cases and (2) the transfer from the president to the USTR of the authority to decide whether to initiate investigations of unfair foreign trade practices under Section 301.

Congressional Democrats made even bigger concessions, despite the continuation of pressure from organized labor for a tough bill and their own interest in using trade as a campaign issue.[52] First, the Gephardt amendment was replaced by the more moderate Riegle-Danforth Super 301 provision, which the labor movement was unable to strengthen once Gephardt's presidential campaign had faltered. Rostenkowski and Bentsen also agreed to leave Section 201 authority in the hands of the president rather than the USTR, to make USTR action in Section 301 cases subject to presidential discretion, and to eliminate dozens of special interest provisions from the bill.

What explains the compromise? On the Republican side, the White House could no longer defer its request for Uruguay Round negotiating authority, and

Congress would grant such authority only in return for administration acquiescence to other trade policy reforms. Also, GOP supporters among internationally oriented sectors of business now supported passage of a moderate bill. The centrist business organizations—especially the Business Roundtable and the Emergency Committee for American Trade, both representing major multinational corporations—played a key role in prodding a reluctant Reagan administration to back a moderate bill as well as in shaping the content of the legislation.[53] Finally, Republicans in both branches of government feared that if they refused agreement on a compromise bill, during the fast-approaching 1988 election campaigns the Democrats would successfully blame them for doing nothing to reduce the trade deficit.

The Democrats, for their part, were also led to compromise by a number of factors in addition to the failure of Gephardt's presidential candidacy. First, the trade balance had finally begun to improve, thanks to the falling dollar and the export boom it had triggered. Second, strong economic growth and declining unemployment diminished the impact and salience of the remaining trade deficit. Third, the Reagan administration continued to take a tougher stance toward foreign trading partners.[54] Fourth, the Japanese had assumed a more conciliatory position in a number of simmering disputes.[55] Fifth, the Democrats were subjected to moderating pressures from the centrist business organizations, which played an important role in stripping potentially protectionist measures out of the bill,[56] and from the growing ranks of their business donors. Sixth, the media continued to hammer away at provisions of the bill thought to be protectionist.[57] Seventh, despite the partial revival of its influence in the One-hundredth Congress, organized labor lacked the social and political weight needed to compel the Democrats to continue to insist on a tougher bill.[58] Eighth, the October 1987 stock market crash revived memories of Smoot-Hawley and the electoral fate of Republicans held responsible for that act.[59] Finally, facing a free-trading Republican president armed with the supermajoritarian veto weapon, most Democrats had by now concluded that in an election year, their party could claim more credit for passing a moderate, bipartisan, compromise bill, thus demonstrating their ability to govern "responsibly," than from making a campaign issue of a Reagan veto of a stronger bill. "It's a leadership bill for Democrats," said Senator Max Baucus (D-Mont.).[60]

The Final Battle over Plant Closings

Congress returned from the Easter recess having reached bipartisan agreement on most of the main trade-related issues of the omnibus bill. The battle over the final shape of the legislation now focused on two nontrade issues—the plant closing section and a provision that would have required disclosure of foreign ownership of 5 percent or more of publicly or privately held U.S. businesses or real estate.[61] These Democratic-sponsored measures were strongly opposed by the U.S. business community and provoked veto threats from the White House. Many observers assumed that both of these contentious partisan provisions would ultimately be dropped from the bill, especially since Dan Rostenkowski and Lloyd Bentsen were reluctant to see their hard work threatened by two nontrade issues.

There was a serious obstacle, however, to dropping the plant closing and foreign investment provisions: the labor movement. Organized labor was quite disappointed with the near-final conference product. Its chief priority in the bill, the Gephardt amendment, had been stripped out, and other labor-backed sections had been watered down. Although labor found some of the remaining provisions useful, most were too intangible for rank-and-file unionists to get excited about. Labor officials thus seized on the plant closing measure—and, to a lesser extent, the foreign investment disclosure provision—as readily understandable victories they could take back to their members. The plant closing provision was also important to labor precisely because business was so opposed to it. "The plant-closing bill has become an article of principle with the business community," a UAW official explained. "As a result, it's become a sort of holy grail for the labor, too."[62]

On April 13 House and Senate Democratic leaders held a highly unusual meeting with labor leaders to convince them to support the trade bill without the plant closing and foreign investment measures. But labor was adamant on retaining the provisions. The White House, on the other hand, would not guarantee that Reagan would sign the bill even if the disputed sections were removed. Under these circumstances, Wright and Byrd decided that the final conference agreement would include both measures. The fate of the foreign investment disclosure provision was decided on April 19, when it was left out of the conference report due to the inability of the subconferees with jurisdiction over the measure to agree to its inclusion. That left only the plant closing provision in dispute.

The day before the April 21 House vote on the conference report, things looked grim for the Democrats, as conservative southerners were joining the Republicans in strong criticism of the plant closing measure. With its collective back to the wall, the Democratic leadership swung into action. To representatives of southern oil states, Wright and others argued that a reopened conference could not be limited to the plant closing issue; it might also take up the bill's provision to repeal the "windfall" tax on oil revenues. To lawmakers from textile states, the leadership argued that the time had come to repay Rust Belt members for their earlier support on textiles.[63]

These leadership efforts paid off, and the next day, after a failed GOP motion to drop the plant closing provision, the omnibus trade bill passed by a surprisingly strong 3–1 margin. The final vote was 312–107, 23 more than needed to override a veto. Sixty-eight out of 173 Republicans joined all but 2 Democrats in voting for the measure. Despite the growing bipartisan consensus on trade policy proper, the vote was quite partisan, due to the continued inclusion in the bill of the plant closing plank.

On April 27 the Senate also passed the bill, but only by a 63–36 margin, three votes short of the two-thirds majority needed to withstand a promised Reagan veto. Again the vote was partisan: Democrats backed the measure 52–1, whereas Republicans opposed it 11–35. The margin of victory was eroded by continuous White House and business lobbying of undeclared GOP senators and by a last-minute dispute over a little-noticed restriction on oil exports from a proposed Alaskan refinery.

In the days immediately following the Senate vote, Reagan several times reiterated his intention to veto the bill. In citing almost exclusively his objection to the plant closing and Alaska oil export provisions, the president did not want to appear to be opposing the bill's popular trade-specific proposals in an election year. He also hoped with his narrow veto threats to send an election-year message of solidarity to the GOP's loyal business constituents, who forcefully opposed the plant closing measure but supported the rest of the trade bill.[64]

In Congress, leading Democratic trade moderates like Lloyd Bentsen, Dan Rostenkowski, and Sam Gibbons indicated that they might be willing to support a bill without the plant closing provision, but Robert Byrd and Jim Wright sent no such signals. In the late spring and early summer of 1988, congressional Democratic leaders were pressing a broad new labor-backed agenda intended to make the Republicans look heartless in an election year.[65] With polls showing that over 80 percent of the public favored advance notification of plant closures,[66] Byrd, Wright, and other Democratic leaders were now enthusiastic about the issue's appeal to the public's sense of fairness and thus about its potential to help win back defecting blue-collar voters without driving away conservative southern Democrats. Even if they failed to override Reagan's veto, the Democrats would have created a powerful campaign issue. "We want the bill," said an aide to a key Democratic lawmaker. "But even if we don't get the bill, we've got the issue."[67]

Meanwhile, out on the primary trail the remaining Democratic presidential candidates, Michael Dukakis and Jesse Jackson, were already energetically campaigning on the plant closing issue throughout the industrial heartland, finding it more politically potent than trade. And many Republicans, including presidential candidate George Bush, now worried that opposition to the plant closing provision would hurt them in the fall by portraying them as captives of business and, as Robert Dole put it, as "being against the poor working man and woman."[68]

Despite this widespread concern, on May 24 Reagan vetoed the omnibus trade bill, as he had long promised to do. Hours later the House voted 308–113 to override the veto. Sixty reelection-minded House GOP members joined all but one Democrat to support the override. The Senate, however, with only one-third of its members up for reelection in November, was unable to override the veto; it was sustained on a partisan vote of 61–37, five votes short of the two-thirds majority necessary to override. Ten Republicans voted with the Democrats, and two Democrats abstained.

Jim Wright was still intent on claiming trade as an issue for his party in the fall elections. On June 10, after a divided meeting with House Democratic leaders, he announced a clever two-track strategy. First, a new trade bill would be introduced but stripped of the plant closing plank (and the Alaskan oil provision). Second, the plant closing provision would be offered as a free-standing piece of legislation. The strategy's supporters reasoned that faced with two separate bills, Reagan would be forced to sign what was, after all, a moderate, bipartisan trade measure whose main provisions he had already accepted. At the same time, the Democrats hoped to sustain plant closings as a campaign issue by forcing a politically embarrassing veto of a free-standing advance notification bill.[69]

On July 6 the Senate approved the plant closing and mass layoffs bill by a vote of 72–23, more than enough to override a still-anticipated Reagan veto. The declining partisanship surrounding the issue was evidenced by the nineteen Republicans who voted for the legislation, many of whom were facing reelection in November.

Now the focus shifted back to the House. On July 13, following another administration veto threat, the plant closing bill passed the House by a 286–136 vote. Democrats backed the measure 232–16, whereas Republicans opposed it 54–120. Only sixteen House Democrats, mostly conservative southerners, voted against the measure, thanks to hard lobbying by organized labor and Tony Coelho's Democratic whip organization.[70]

Hours after the plant closing measure was approved, the House passed the new omnibus trade bill by an overwhelming bipartisan vote of 376–45. Partisan convergence was still not complete, however; Democrats continued to give stronger support to the legislation, voting 243–4 for it, while Republicans backed the measure by a smaller 133–41 margin.

Supported by business, an intransigent Ronald Reagan planned to veto the plant closing measure. But it was clear that the Democrats had won the battle to frame the issue for the public. The Republicans "decided plant closing was a labor issue," said Tony Coelho, "but it's come off as a fairness issue and it's really boomeranging on them."[71] Michael Dukakis, now the Democratic presidential nominee, had been effectively raising the issue in every speech, and the constant Democratic pounding appeared to be hurting Republican candidates with Reagan Democrats in the Midwest and the Northeast.[72]

In the last two weeks of July, congressional Republicans strongly lobbied the president to let the bill pass into law. George Bush also urged his boss not to veto the bill. "It's fair to say that the vice president would like the president to find a way to sign the bill," admitted an administration official with close ties to the Bush campaign.[73] On August 2, after a fierce White House debate, Reagan announced his intention to let the plant closing bill go into law without his signature.

With the plant closing issue at last disposed of, the Senate gave final approval to the omnibus trade bill on August 3. The bipartisan vote on H.R. 4848 was 85–11, with ten Republicans and one Democrat opposing the measure. Three weeks later, on August 23, President Reagan finally signed into law the Omnibus Trade and Competitiveness Act of 1988.

In 1985, in what was in part a heresthetical maneuver under divided government to improve their party's fortunes in the 1986 and later the 1988 elections, congressional Democrats launched a complex legislative process that culminated three years later in the passage of the omnibus bill. Driven by the Senate and especially the House Democratic leadership, the process involved both sharp party conflict and bipartisan compromise, with the former gradually giving way to the latter as the parties converged toward support for fair trade and reciprocity.

But party differences remained. Statistical analyses of a wide range of role-call votes on trade measures in the One-hundredth Congress have found that, due to constituency and ideological differences and to Democratic electoral maneuvering, Democrats in both houses voted more consistently for protectionist and fair-trade legislation than did Republicans.[74] Thus the eventual enactment of the 1988 trade bill, like many of the administrative trade actions taken by the White House along the way, can be understood as the result of policy contagion. Using their House and Senate floor majorities, the Democrats prodded free-trading Republicans in Congress and the White House into supporting a compromise fair-trade bill they had initially opposed in order to avoid the loss of swing voter and business support on a potentially salient issue in the 1988 elections.

Trade and the General Election

With the trade bill finally out of the way, the issues of trade and competitiveness played only a modest role in the rest of the 1988 election campaigns. Congress did grapple with the latest incarnation of an old trade issue—a new textile quota bill—that congressional Democrats again hoped to use for partisan advantage. A textile measure had passed the House in 1987 and a companion bill had been reported by the Senate Finance Committee in the same year without recommendation and without a committee report. Democratic leaders had promised the sponsors of the textile bill a clear shot at passage in return for their pledge to keep the controversial measure out of the omnibus trade bill.

In late July 1988 Ernest Hollings (D-S.C.) introduced a bill to replace the earlier Senate version, and in September the upper chamber passed the bill on a vote that, like all others on the measure that fall, had both regional and partisan characteristics. House Democratic leaders then skipped the usual conference committee meetings to prevent delays that could allow Reagan to avoid a veto and thus deprive the Democrats of another campaign issue, especially in the South.[75]

On September 23 the House voted to accept the Senate amendments to the textile bill passed by the House the previous year. The bill was then sent to the president, who quickly vetoed it, an action that pleased those Democrats who sought a campaign issue. On October 4 the House sustained Reagan's veto on a vote that was eleven short of the two-thirds majority needed to override.

Until this point, Michael Dukakis had been slow to pick up on the trade issue, which sounded too much like Japan-bashing to him. But now there was only a month left in the campaign and Dukakis was faltering under Bush's damaging attacks on his liberalism and his patriotism. Desperate, Dukakis took a leaf from Dick Gephardt's book and embraced the populist economic nationalism that his advisers had been urging on him for weeks. Dukakis's strategists hoped that his new position on trade would make him look tough to pivotal blue-collar workers. "Our message is going to make sense to Joe Six-pack, because it's an issue of national pride, of jobs," said issues director Christopher Edley.[76]

Though George Bush did not make trade issues central to his campaign, he did respond to Dukakis's economic nationalist turn by making a number of election-eve trade pronouncements and promises of his own in key states. He announced his endorsement of an unfair trade practices petition filed by the U.S. rice industry against Japan, a move clearly intended to win him support in the big rice-producing states of California and Texas.[77] Just days before the election, Bush also backed renewal of the steel voluntary export restraints that were due to expire in September 1989 to boost his prospects in several closely contested midwestern steel-producing states, including Pennsylvania, Ohio, Illinois, and Michigan.[78]

Of course, Dukakis did not win the 1988 election, but he did gain momentum in the last few weeks of the campaign, cutting into Bush's margin of victory. Most polling results did not indicate that Dukakis's last-minute adoption of a populist economic nationalist campaign "frame" had much to do with his final run at Bush.[79] Nevertheless, a number of influential Democratic strategists continued to believe otherwise.[80] During the next four years of George Bush's presidency, the Democrats would continue to play the economic nationalist card, producing new episodes of policy contagion.

The Bush Years

Opening Japan, Negotiating NAFTA

George Bush's presidency has generally been described as one of "continuity and consolidation."[1] This was certainly true in the area of trade policy. With the steady if uneven decline of both the overall U.S. trade deficit and the U.S.-Japan trade gap during Bush's term of office, the trade issue lost some of its political salience. But business, labor, and popular pressure for a tougher U.S. trade policy, especially toward Japan, by no means completely dissipated. Thus the Democrats, in Congress and on the presidential campaign trail, continued to exploit the issue for partisan advantage. As during the Reagan years, this produced new cases of policy contagion, as Bush sought to provide political cover for both himself and congressional Republicans. The most important of these actions were the 1989 citing of Japan for failing to open its markets under the retaliatory "Super 301" provision of the 1988 Trade Act and early 1992 agreements in which the Japanese promised to buy more American auto parts and other goods.

With the Democrats continuing to push him on U.S.-Japan trade, Bush tried to deflect this partisan pressure, regain the political initiative on trade policy, and enhance his reelection prospects by proposing that the United States enter into negotiations with Mexico and Canada on a North American Free Trade Agreement (NAFTA). By splitting the Democrats, Bush won the first battle in his campaign for NAFTA in the spring of 1991, when he gained congressional approval of a proposal to extend his fast-track trade negotiating authority. Although he was defeated by Bill Clinton in 1992, pressure from Bush did force his rival to support NAFTA, albeit with conditions that were intended to help hold the disparate "old" and "new" Democratic elements of Clinton's electoral coalition together.

The Growth of Economic Nationalism and
the Struggle to Open Up Japan

Despite the apparently limited role of trade in the 1988 presidential election, when George Bush took office in early 1989, trade was by no means a dead issue. The main focus remained Japan, whose growing dominance in many high-technology sectors was particularly worrisome.[2]

American anger at Japan's many formal and informal import barriers remained high. But early 1989 saw the continued growth among both elites and the public of more general "economic nationalist" sentiments. This included concern not only for Japan's unfair trade practices, but also for American industrial competitiveness, the decline of which appeared to help explain why the U.S. trade deficit remained so high despite the steep fall in the value of the dollar. There was also apprehension about the alleged threat to the U.S. economy posed by the rising tide of foreign investment, again especially from Japan.

Support for economic nationalism came from diverse quarters. Within the business community, influential interests pressed for a tougher U.S. trade policy toward Japan. Some major business groups, including the blue-ribbon President's Advisory Committee for Trade Policy and Negotiations (ACTPN), which mainly represented internationally oriented firms, went so far as to call for "managed trade" agreements under which Japanese import levels would be negotiated on either an overall or a sectoral basis.[3] Similarly, high-tech executives, predominantly in the electronics industry, responded to the still-mounting Japanese challenge by pushing for a new "industry-led policy," involving the formation and public funding of research and production consortia, to help commercialize new technologies.

Complementing these business pressures were the publications and advocacy of various groups and organizations of policy intellectuals.[4] These analysts contributed to the outlines of a neostatist, post-Fordist accumulation strategy and, more specifically, to a neomercantilist or economic nationalist trade and competitiveness policy paradigm.

"Declinist" writers like Paul Kennedy continued to stress the relative erosion of American economic power, especially vis à vis Japan.[5] An influential group of so-called revisionists, the most prominent of whom in early 1989 was former Reagan administration trade negotiator Clyde Prestowitz, argued that Japan was a different kind of industrial power, organized to privilege production over consumption, to promote exports, and to restrict imports in order to catch up with and surpass the West. These analysts correspondingly backed both the negotiation of sector-specific managed trade agreements to guarantee U.S. firms access to the Japanese market and an industrial policy to make U.S. industries more competitive with their Japanese rivals.[6]

In a related argument, academic proponents of the new "strategic trade theory" suggested that the assumptions of free trade theory did not hold in high-tech industries characterized by imperfect competition, economies of scale, learning curve effects, and positive externalities or spillovers. As a result, competitive advantage could be created and the national welfare enhanced by selectively protecting these advanced industries, by prying open foreign markets closed to their exports, or by using industrial or technology policies to subsidize some of their research and development costs.[7]

Public opinion also appeared to be moving in a nationalist direction. In particular, with the waning of the Cold War, polls found that Americans increasingly viewed Japanese economic power as a greater threat to national security than Soviet military strength.[8]

Some Bush administration officials were more responsive to such influences than their predecessors in the Reagan White House. Heading agencies with close and long-standing ties to the business community, Secretary of Commerce Robert Mosbacher and U.S. Trade Representative (USTR) Carla Hills both advocated a more aggressive strategy toward Japan than the Reagan administration had pursued. Similarly, the Commerce and Defense Departments indicated their intentions to markedly increase their support for key high-tech industries.

Others in the Bush administration, however, opposed tougher trade action and interventionist industrial policies. The doubters included the president himself, State and Defense Department officials who were fearful of jeopardizing the strategic relationship with Japan, and especially the "troika"—Chief of Staff John Sununu, Office of Management and Budget director Richard Darman, and Council of Economic Advisers chairman Michael Boskin—whose top trade-related policy priority was not getting tough or competing more effectively with Japan, but rather the successful conclusion of the Uruguay Round General Agreement on Tariffs and Trade (GATT) negotiations.

The Democrats Embrace Economic Nationalism

As the 101st Congress began in January 1989, optimistic congressional Democrats hoped to seize the political initiative from George Bush, who had presented no agenda of his own during the 1988 campaign. The Democrats planned to greet the new president with an aggressive program that would include a host of housing, environmental, health care, employee benefits, minimum wage, and other proposals.

Trade, competitiveness, and foreign investment issues were also a part of their new agenda. Following the 1988 election, a number of leading Democratic lawmakers and strategists insisted that Michael Dukakis's late surge was due in part to his belated turn toward populist economic nationalism. They urged continued emphasis on such themes—especially to appeal to hard-pressed, patriotic, working-class voters, including swing Reagan Democrats—during the run-up to the 1990 congressional elections and the 1992 presidential race.[9]

The Democratic standard-bearer for economic nationalism was again Dick Gephardt, who made increasingly sophisticated use of the trade issue as he searched for a new accumulation strategy and an electoral strategy for his party. Throughout 1989 Gephardt, in speeches he delivered all over the country, proposed a neostatist and economic nationalist approach to reviving American economic strength. Recognizing the merits of this approach, House Speaker Jim Wright, in March, appointed Gephardt chairman of a twenty-six-member House Trade and Competitiveness Task Force, charged with developing and coordinating legislative efforts to address America's trade problems.[10]

Implementing Super 301: Targeting Japan

With the Democrats often leading the charge, in the spring of 1989 Congress pressed the Bush administration on a number of difficult issues relating to trade, competitiveness, and foreign investment. On competitiveness, for example, when the Bush administration's early interest in industrial policy began to wane, the Democrats escalated their own support for what they termed an "industry-led policy," intended to win the support of both voters and high-tech executives for their efforts to assist the "industries of the future."

In U.S.-Japan relations, the most contentious issue was the implementation of the Super 301 provision of the 1988 Trade Act.[11] On April 28 USTR Carla Hills released a 214-page list of foreign trade barriers in which Japan's offenses were highlighted. The next month saw a fierce debate take place among Bush's top economic advisers over which countries and practices to actually target for negotiations and possible retaliation. On one side, Budget Director Richard Darman and Economic Adviser Michael Boskin opposed broadly targeting Japan as a "priority" violator, fearing that this would hinder U.S. foreign policy and risk starting a trade war. Darman and Boskin proposed instead that only individual egregious trade practices be designated. On the other side, Hills and Commerce Secretary Mosbacher urged that Japan be broadly cited, arguing that a failure to do so could cause a backlash in Congress and lead to new protectionist legislation.

Until shortly before Bush announced his decision, it appeared that he was leaning against naming Japan as a priority country, despite intensified pressure from Congress, the Commerce Department, business, and organized labor. In the end, however, he yielded to the trade hawks of both parties, naming Japan to the priority country "hit list" on May 25. But then he moved quickly to soften the blow in two ways. First, the administration cited Japan for failing to buy the products of only three U.S. industries: processed lumber, satellites, and super-computers.[12] And second, it also cited Brazil and India as priority countries to avoid isolating Japan.

Bush was also spurred to address the broader concerns within the business community, Congress, and the administration itself over Japan's import-restrictive generic trade practices, and to provide an alternative to ideologically unacceptable managed trade proposals. To this end, the president called for separate but simultaneous talks outside the coercive Super 301 framework—termed the "Structural Impediments Initiative" (SII). This would involve top-level negotiations with Tokyo to eliminate its "structural" barriers to trade, that is, those deeply embedded ways of doing business and forms of personal be-havior that thwarted U.S imports but that did not violate international law.[13]

Although the congressional anger that contributed to Bush's decision to cite Japan and to launch the SII initiative was brought to bear by Republicans and Democrats alike, partisan considerations again played an important role in the process. First, congressional Democrats were more numerous and vocal in expressing their concerns than their Republican rivals.[14] Second, those GOP members who did pressure the White House did so in part because they feared that not naming Japan would hurt the Republicans with key swing voters. "I can see trade being *the* issue in the 1992 election," said Senator John Heinz (R-Pa.).[15]

Partisan concerns also deeply influenced the tougher trade stance assumed by George Bush, who like Ronald Reagan was a committed Republican.[16] Trea-sury Secretary Nicolas Brady and Secretary of State James Baker reportedly convinced the president that failing to take action against Japan "might cost Republicans seats in the 1990 elections."[17] "The Bush Administration will not get positioned as being soft on trade," one White House political strategist declared later. "We are not going to let this issue slip away."[18]

The Democrats Keep Pushing

Over the next ten months, with the annual U.S. trade deficit with Japan stuck at about $50 billion and progress in both the Super 301 and SII negotiations exceptionally slow, U.S.-Japan relations deteriorated and economic nationalist sentiment remained strong.

American business interests continued to press for greater access to the Japanese market as the second mid-July, Super 301 deadline approached. A long list of U.S. industries, including auto parts and semiconductors, urged that Japan be redesignated under the law to open markets for their products. Protesting the Bush administration's continued retreat from any federal role in encouraging high technology, Silicon Valley executives intensified their call for a new strategic partnership between the electronics industry and government.

Meanwhile, policy intellectuals labored to provide new analytic support for the now widely debated concept of managed trade,[19] as well as for industrial and technology policies. Polls found continued public concern that Japan had surpassed the United States economically and considerable support for both prying open Japanese markets and curbing Japanese imports.[20] Congressional pressure for action grew, often spearheaded by the Democrats.

Despite the Democrats' early hopes of controlling the political agenda during 1989, George Bush held the upper hand for most of the year. Thrown into disarray in the House by an ethics crisis that brought down Jim Wright and Majority Whip Tony Coelho, congressional Democrats were regularly out-maneuvered by the veto-wielding Bush. As the second session of the 101st Congress began, they were looking for new themes and a legislative agenda to further define their differences with a still very popular president in advance of the 1990 midterm elections and the 1992 presidential race.

Lacking other compelling campaign issues and encouraged by the results of polling and focus groups, many Democrats, with Dick Gephardt again in the lead, turned to the themes of trade, competitiveness, foreign investment, and a new issue, foreign lobbying, which were now regularly bundled together under the label of "economic nationalism."[21] For example, with the Bush administration deaf to the pleas of the electronics industry for help in doing battle with the Japanese, the Democrats saw an opening to win support in traditionally Republican Silicon Valley and developed a raft of legislation aimed at making U.S. technology companies more competitive.[22]

The slow pace of the Super 301 and SII negotiations with Japan was exasperating to members of Congress, especially the Democrats. In late March Max Baucus (D-Mont.), chairman of the international trade subcommittee of the Senate Finance Committee, introduced three bills: one to force the Bush administration to get tougher with Japan over forest products and the other two to expand the president's power to retaliate against unfair trade. A companion bill was introduced in the House by Representative Frank Guarini (D-N.J.).

The White House worried that Congress might in fact demand retaliation against Tokyo in the absence of significant Japanese concessions in the Super 301 and SII negotiations. To avert this threat and accelerate the negotiations, Prime Minister Toshiki Kaifu was summoned to a March 2–3 meeting in Palm Springs, California. "If Bush and Kaifu fail to create movement," *Business Week* observed, "the Democrats could cash in later this year in congressional elections."[23]

To derail the Democrats, Bush pressed for and received a pledge from Kaifu that Tokyo would ease restrictions on U.S. imports. Then, to the surprise and delight of administration officials, the prime minister delivered. On March 23, April 3, and April 25, the three Super 301 negotiations were successfully concluded, as deals were struck to open the Japanese supercomputer, satellite, and wood products markets. In an April 5 interim report on the SII negotiations, Japan committed itself to eliminate various structural barriers to trade.

With these modest Japanese concessions in hand, the White House felt politically emboldened to remove Japan from its list of problem trading partners. Secretary of State James Baker argued that congressional reaction to that decision would be relatively subdued, and his prognostication proved to be correct.[24]

From mid-1990 until the November congressional elections, the Democrats focused on attempting, with little success, to make campaign issues of declining U.S. competitiveness, the rising tide of foreign investment, and the involvement of overseas investors in the U.S. political process. Trade policy did not further engage the attention of lawmakers until the Uruguay Round negotiations collapsed.[25]

The Collapse of the Uruguay Round Triggers New Democratic Pressures

The breakdown of the talks came on December 7, when the European Community (EC), supported by Japan and South Korea, refused to cut agricultural subsidies. The failure to find common ground prompted fears in some quarters of a new wave of protectionism, if not a global trade war.

In the United States, congressional Democrats took the lead in calling for tougher trade policies. The timing seemed propitious. In late 1990 the Democrats were on the rebound. After forcing Bush to sign off on a budget deal that increased the relative tax burden on the wealthy, the Democrats took the populist issue of tax fairness to the voters in the last weeks of the congressional campaign. The payoff was a bigger-than-expected nine-seat gain in the House and one additional Senate seat. In the aftermath of the election, the Democrats sought to press their newly won advantage.

No sooner had the GATT negotiations broken down, than Gephardt, Baucus, and other mostly Democratic lawmakers called for new legislation targeting unfair foreign traders. Once again, the Democrats' main focus was on Japan. Anger in Washington ran high as a result of Tokyo's contribution to the collapse of the Uruguay Round, its refusal to open the Japanese rice market, its reluctance to award large public works contracts to U.S. construction firms, and its slowness in complying with prior agreements to reform the country's distribution system and to buy American computers and satellites.

Although the outbreak of the Gulf War against Iraq in mid-January 1991 pushed other issues into the background for the next six weeks, trade did not disappear from the political agenda. In fact, Democratic attempts to strengthen U.S. trade policy, especially toward Japan, were actually spurred by the war, or more precisely, by growing congressional resentment against what many saw as Tokyo's halfhearted support for Operation Desert Storm.[26] Assessing recent developments in U.S. trade policy and politics in mid-February, *Business Week* concluded that with "the President pinned down in the gulf and with the Administration's lofty plans for a new world order for trade in shambles, this could be the year that Democrats' oft-repeated promises to toughen U.S. trade policy finally turn into action."[27]

NAFTA: Bush Tries to Regain the Initiative

Even as the Gulf War continued, Bush attempted to recapture the initiative on trade policy, and thus both head off the threat from the Democrats and boost his reelection prospects, by shifting the fight for trade liberalization to a new front. Responding to a proposal from Mexican President Carlos Salinas de Gortari, and hoping to expand the Canada-U.S. Free Trade Agreement approved by Congress with little controversy in 1988,[28] Bush announced his intention to press ahead with negotiations on a new North American Free Trade Agreement with Mexico and Canada.[29]

To facilitate these negotiations as well as the eventual resumption of the GATT talks, the White House sent a bill to Capitol Hill on March 1 requesting a two-year extension of the president's fast-track negotiating authority, under which Congress would vote to approve or disapprove legislation implementing either agreement up or down without amendment within ninety days.[30] Although NAFTA would be a regional accord, Bush's action marked the first volley in a lengthy war over what would become the dominant trade issue of the 1990s—the now widely labeled process of economic "globalization"—and more specifically, trade and investment relations with low-wage developing nations.[31]

In deciding to pursue the trade pact, Bush had a number of goals in mind. First, he hoped to use the negotiations on a North American accord to jumpstart the stalled GATT talks. If these talks ultimately failed and the GATT regime continued to erode, NAFTA could serve as a regional alternative.

NAFTA in its own right held considerable appeal for the president and his advisers. They believed that such an agreement could help stabilize Mexico politically and slow illegal Mexican immigration to the United States. More fundamentally, Bush saw a regional trade deal as an international adjunct to the neoliberal accumulation strategy that he had carried over from the Reagan era. Lower trade barriers would hopefully lead to increased U.S. exports and thus high-wage jobs, larger markets for U.S. firms seeking to achieve economies of scale, and heightened competition in the domestic market, which would put pressure on U.S. firms to adopt efficient new technologies and managerial strategies.

Still more important, reduced *investment* barriers, like export restrictions and domestic content rules, would make it easier for U.S. manufacturers to relocate their plants in Mexico to take advantage of its lower labor costs.[32] Although this would mean the loss of some low-wage American jobs, by further improving the competitiveness of U.S. companies, other higher-wage jobs would be preserved that might otherwise have been lost to European and Japanese firms.

Bush also hoped to derive personal political advantage from a free-trade deal. On the one hand, he sought the financial support of exporters and multi-national firms that figured to benefit from an agreement. The negotiation of such a treaty "means dollars, fund raising" for Bush, said GOP pollster Vince Breglio.[33]

On the other hand, Bush thought that the pact could boost his reelection chances in California and the economically depressed southwestern border states, where the prospect of increased commerce with Mexico made the idea very popular. In particular, the White House and other Republicans sought to heresthetically exploit the proposed agreement as a "wedge issue" to disrupt the Democratic coalition by pitting Hispanic-American voters in Texas, California, and elsewhere, who were likely to favor such a deal, against organized labor, which was almost certain to oppose it. "Just think of the politics down the road," said the White House communications director, David Demarest. "This puts the Democratic party in a very odd position."[34]

The Lineup of Forces

The battle lines that emerged in the spring conflict over Bush's fast-track request had actually been forming for some months.[35] On the pro-NAFTA side were competitive agricultural exporters, especially grain and oilseed producers. Also backing an agreement were high-tech and other manufacturing exporters in imperfectly competitive sectors whose competitiveness depended on their ability to achieve economies of scale, in part by engaging in specialized intra-industry trade. NAFTA promised to help these firms achieve scale economies by creating a regionally enlarged market for their exports.[36]

The strongest business proponents of fast track and an eventual deal, however, were U.S.-based multinational corporations (MNCS), which had provided the initial impetus for such a pact in the early 1980s.[37] More than trade liberalization, these firms sought the liberalization of Mexico's investment rules.[38] Some MNCS, mainly Fordist mass producers of labor-intensive consumer goods, anticipated that the agreement would enable them to more easily tap Mexico's vast pool of cheap labor, thus helping to improve their international competitiveness vis à vis their European and especially their Japanese rivals.[39] At the same time, corporations could use the increased *threat* of flight to Mexico to force workers in their American plants to make wage and work rule concessions.[40] Other post-Fordist, "flexible," or "lean" producers, whose orientation toward rapidly shifting niche markets and reliance on "just-in-time" inventory systems required proximity to both customers and suppliers, supported NAFTA to facilitate the development of new regional rather than global markets and production and sourcing networks.[41] In March 1991 pro-NAFTA business interests formed the Coalition for Trade Expansion, consisting of major corporations and business associations like the Business Roundtable, the U.S. Chamber of Commerce, and the National Association of Manufacturers, to lobby on behalf of fast track.

Other labor-intensive, domestically oriented agricultural and industrial interests, however, including southern producers of warm-weather fruits and vegetables and various small manufacturers, strongly opposed an agreement, fearing a wave of cheap imports. The most concerted opposition to a regional trade pact, however, was mounted by the American labor movement. Members of industrial unions, who had often allied with their employers in efforts to curb imports, now worried that liberalizing *both* trade and investment rules would intensify the actual and threatened flight of import-sensitive manufacturing firms to Mexico in search of cheap labor, thus eliminating U.S. jobs and undercutting the bargaining power and wages of American workers.[42] Although unionized workers employed in companies threatened by either imports or capital flight represented only a fraction of the labor force, their influence in the anti-NAFTA fight was magnified by the mostly unorganized status of workers employed in industries likely to benefit from NAFTA, the still-dominant position of the industrial unions within the AFL-CIO, and the ability of the industrial unions to enlist the support of public and other service-sector unions in the fight against NAFTA.

Initially joining labor in its opposition to an agreement were groups new to the trade issue. Environmentalists worried that pollution-intensive firms would relocate manufacturing operations to northern Mexico to take advantage of the country's weakly enforced environmental laws, thus exacerbating environmental problems along the border and undercutting U.S. environmental standards.[43] Human rights groups also feared that an agreement would encourage a repressive regime to perpetuate low wages and unsafe working conditions for Mexican workers in order to attract U.S. investment.

The Democrats See Another Opportunity

A large majority of congressional Republicans quickly declared their support for NAFTA and the renewal of Bush's fast-track authority. On the other side of the aisle, despite the mobilization against NAFTA by labor and other core Democratic constituencies, some Democratic lawmakers and activists also supported the proposed pact. In particular, in early May the eight hundred delegates to the convention of the moderate Democratic Leadership Council (DLC), chaired that year by Governor Bill Clinton of Arkansas, endorsed Bush's fast-track request.[44] The DLC's endorsement was another maneuver in the organization's ongoing campaign both to reduce organized labor's influence within the party and, in this case, to win support from internationally oriented business interests and upper-middle-class suburbanites.

Most congressional Democrats, however, especially those with strong ties to labor, opposed the president's fast-track proposal. In the aftermath of the successful U.S. conduct of the Gulf War, George Bush's popularity skyrocketed. Searching for a comeback agenda for the 1992 election, at a late March meeting, Democratic National Committee (DNC) members, joined by a number of leading congressional Democrats, began once again to stress the theme of economic nationalism. The DNC thus adopted a resolution denouncing a U.S.-Mexico free-trade agreement as a "disaster for workers in both countries."[45] Participants also stressed the importance of reestablishing American economic preeminence, notably vis à vis Japan.[46]

With the submission of Bush's fast-track proposal, congressional Democrats saw an opportunity to toughen U.S. policy toward Japan and other countries by linking the granting of fast-track authority to provisions that would have limited the president's flexibility on certain trade issues. Later, as the late May House and Senate votes on fast track approached, the Democrats, joined by some Republicans, pressed hard in two areas where Japan had reneged on past trade agreements: construction and semiconductor chips.[47]

White House Maneuvers Carry the Day

In early March organized labor and its allies moved aggressively to line up congressional opposition to Bush's fast-track request. In response, and with the support of the administration and congressional Republicans, the free-trading chairmen of the Senate and House panels with trade jurisdiction, Senator Lloyd Bentsen (D-Tex.) and Representative Dan Rostenkowski (D-Ill.), asked Bush for an "action plan" to allay concerns that the proposed agreement would not adequately protect workers, consumers, and the environment, and to undercut the criticisms of House Majority Leader and NAFTA skeptic Dick Gephardt. With the Democrats in control of both houses of Congress under the prevailing conditions of divided government, Bush had to comply with Bentsen and Rostenkowski's request if he hoped to win sufficient Democratic support to see his fast-track proposal passed. On May 1 the White House produced a plan that committed Bush to a pact that cushioned workers and upheld environmental standards.

In other actions intended to defuse pressure from the Democrats and win the fast-track extension, the Bush administration, in another case of policy contagion, announced that the United States, after a public-comment period of thirty days, would bar Japan from bidding on federally supported U.S. construction projects in retaliation for Tokyo's refusal to open its public-works construction market. In separate actions, USTR Hills also cited China, India, and Thailand for inadequate protection of intellectual property rights and promised to hang tough on other trade disputes with Japan and Europe.[48]

Although Bush's NAFTA action plan was insufficient to change labor's position on fast track, it did help him split the environmental movement. Together with his actions against Japan and other unfair foreign traders, Bush's plan also helped win the congressional Democratic leadership's endorsement of NAFTA. To labor's dismay, among these endorsers was Dick Gephardt, who was trying to shed his protectionist reputation as he contemplated another campaign for the presidency in 1992.[49]

With this new support in hand, the Bush administration was able to push the fast-track bill through both houses of Congress.[50] Driven by ideological conviction, their ties to internationally oriented sectors of business, and administration lobbying, about 85 percent of Republicans in both houses supported the extension.[51] The Democrats, on the other hand, were seriously divided. Because of their personal ideologies, the existing and potential preferences of their blue-collar constituents in the Rust Belt and southeastern textile states, organized labor's substantial campaign contributions and lobbying efforts, or hopes of creating a campaign issue, about 65 percent of House and 60 percent of Senate Democrats opposed fast track.[52] But sizable minorities of Democrats in both houses, disproportionately from competitive, nonunion, and urbanized parts of the South, supported Bush's request,[53] beginning a pattern in which the size of intra-Democratic divisions would mainly determine the fate of trade liberalization initiatives.

Although NAFTA's Democratic opponents were disappointed by the approval of the president's bill, their strategy of linking the granting of fast-track authority to the White House's assumption of a tougher U.S. posture toward Japan did produce results. On June 1 Tokyo reversed its prior position and acceded to U.S. demands to allow foreign companies to bid on a variety of big construction jobs. Three days later, the two countries agreed to extend the 1986 semiconductor pact for another five years, stating specifically that foreign chip makers should gain 20 percent of the Japanese market by the end of 1992.

Despite these victories, during the late spring and summer of 1991 the Democrats sank into a state of political depression in the face of George Bush's sky-high job approval ratings. The Democratic presidential campaign was late in starting, as the party's most prominent potential contenders either hung back or declined to take Bush on, leaving long-shot former Massachusetts senator Paul Tsongas as the lone declared Democratic candidate by Labor Day.

On Capitol Hill, the Democrats were deeply divided. On the one hand, there were those who hoped to strengthen their hold on Congress and elect a Democratic president by acting as a "party of opposition," that is, by passing and, if necessary, forcing Bush vetoes of sharply partisan legislation. On the other hand, growing numbers of less partisan Democrats had come to believe that cooperation and compromise with the Bush administration were essential if the Democrats hoped to win credit from the voters for acting responsibly as a "party of government."[54] Many within this group were gradually becoming resigned to continued Republican domination of the presidency, or to the notion, as Representative Robert Torricelli (D-N.Y.) put it, that "Congress is ours and the White House is theirs."[55]

Trade Politics and the 1992 Election Cycle: Targeting Japan

As both the summer and the recession that had begun the previous year wore on, however, public dissatisfaction with George Bush's handling of the sluggish economy grew. Yet the president, resting on his Gulf War laurels, continued to pursue his foreign policy priorities despite the end of the Cold War two years earlier, while advancing only a minimal domestic agenda. Sensing renewed possibilities, the Democrats' spirits revived. In both the presidential campaign and in Congress, they launched appeals to aggrieved working- and middle-class voters emphasizing job protection, tax relief, health care, education, and economic nationalism.

In the fall of 1991, the U.S. trade deficit was on the rise after three years of decline. Two-thirds of that deficit was due to the trade gap with Japan. Thus, after a summer of reduced U.S.-Japan tensions, the reenergized Democrats again turned up the heat on Tokyo.[56] On the presidential campaign trail, almost all of the declared and undeclared Democratic candidates began to trumpet economic nationalist themes.[57]

In Congress, the Democrats introduced a number of trade bills, some of which were expressly intended to push the trade issue into the center of the 1992 presidential campaign. In a well-publicized speech on September 10, Dick Gephardt attacked Japan's system of "adversarial capitalism" and declared his intention to "put teeth" in the Super 301 provision of the 1988 Trade Act.[58] Gephardt and Sander Levin (D-Mich.) in the House and Don Riegle (D-Mich.) in the Senate also developed legislation to impose new limits on the sale of cars that were either imported from Japan or produced in the United States at Japanese-owned "transplant" factories. And on November 4, Gephardt and Levin introduced the tougher version of the Super 301 law promised by Gephardt two months earlier.

Calling trade "the important issue" for the presidential election now exactly one year away, Gephardt argued that Bush had failed "miserably" on trade and other economic issues and "would be held to account for that failure in November 1992."[59] He added that many people would be watching the special Senate election in Pennsylvania, on the same day, where Bush's trade policy had become a major campaign issue.

Much to the Democrats' delight and to the Republicans' dismay, in the Pennsylvania race the underdog Democratic challenger, Harris Wofford, upset the heavily favored former GOP governor of the state, Dick Thornburgh, by a ten-point margin. In his campaign, the labor-backed Wofford played to economically anxious voters by stressing issues like national health insurance, middle-class tax relief, extended unemployment benefits, and—of particular interest here—trade policy.[60]

Bush Changes Course

While the Democrats hailed Wofford's victory as a harbinger of things to come, George Bush panicked. Already facing public and Democratic criticism for spending too much time on foreign policy at the expense of economic issues at home,[61] Bush abruptly canceled a late November trip to Asia intended to firm up long-term American strategic and political ties with that region. The president declared that he wanted to stay in Washington to tend to the sluggish economy and other domestic concerns while Congress remained in session.

Two weeks later the president rescheduled the visit for early January. But now he portrayed the trip as a mission to fight for trade concessions from Japan and thus to create "jobs, jobs, jobs."[62] Underlining the point, Commerce Secretary Robert Mosbacher suggested that Japan's closed markets had contributed to the length and severity of the recession.

To heighten the political value of the trip, in early December Bush invited twenty-one American business executives to accompany him, mostly from old-line industries that had complained about being denied access to Japanese and other Asian markets. Mosbacher, who was preparing to depart for his new job as general chairman of Bush's reelection drive, persuaded the president to invite the executives "to signal everyone—that we've got a new relationship—that business is going to get tangible help from the Government in selling its goods."[63] Of particular significance was the inclusion in Bush's delegation of the top executives of the U.S. automobile and auto parts industries.

In late 1991 the American auto industry was reeling, due both to buyers' recessionary fears and to an enormous worldwide excess of automaking capacity, most of it owned and aimed at the rich American market by Japan-based car companies and Japanese-owned transplants in the United States. The American automakers' problems were compounded by their continuing inability to penetrate the protected Japanese car market, which contributed to a deficit with Japan in automobiles and auto parts that totaled almost three-quarters of the ballooning U.S. merchandise trade deficit with that country.[64]

In part, auto executives were invited to help firm up the president's support among industry leaders. Bush also hoped to undermine congressional backing for restrictive, Democrat-sponsored auto legislation. More important still was the signal the White House hoped to send to a key electoral bloc—voters in the "Auto Belt" states of Illinois, Indiana, Ohio, and especially, of course, Michigan. Bush had carried these states in 1988, and with seventy-three electoral votes, they were "the ones likely to tip the balance one way or the other" in the 1992 general election.[65] The president promised to use the trip to press Japan to open its car and car parts markets in order, in his words, to create "thousands of jobs in Michigan" and the other Auto Belt states.[66] The automobile executives who accompanied him were intended to be a symbol of this commitment. As a White House staffer explained, Mosbacher had been told that the only way Bush could win Michigan in 1992 was "to demonstrate the president was doing something about the auto problems and this [invitation to the automobile industry leaders] would be a good way to do something about it."[67]

Under Attack from Both Left and Right, Bush Brings Home Some Bacon

As the president prepared for his trip, the Democrats kept the heat on his trade policy. Most of the leading Democratic presidential contenders hammered away at his handling of U.S.-Japan trade relations, and in Congress Gephardt and Levin introduced their tough Trade Enhancement Act aimed at Japan.

By now, however, the attack on Bush's trade policy was coming not only from the Democratic left; surprisingly, the Republican right had also entered the lists. At the end of the 1980s, with the end of the Cold War and huge budget deficits discrediting Reaganomics, the conservative movement began to crumble. Four loose factions began to contend for primacy within the Republican Party: (1) budget-balancing, internationalist, culturally conservative "traditional Republicans"; (2) tax-cutting, free trading, culturally moderate, "libertarian supply-siders"; (3) culturally conservative, mostly southern, "religious rightists"; and (4) antistatist, culturally conservative, economic nationalist, "populist conservatives."[68]

The economic nationalists among the new Republican populist conservatives are of most interest here.[69] In the second half of the nineteenth and the first half of the twentieth centuries, the Republican Party, largely representing northern manufacturing interests, had supported a high tariff in order to protect the nation's industries against more powerful British and other competitors. But in the 1950s, the GOP gradually entered into a bipartisan consensus on liberal trade. In the 1970s, with the reconstruction of the West European and Japanese economies and the emergence of a number of newly industrializing countries in East Asia, conservative Republican businesses in import-battered industries like textiles and steel began to lobby for protection against a rising tide of imports. In the mid-1980s these interests found expression in the U.S. Business and Industrial Council, an old-right group that now began to make the case against free trade.[70]

Meanwhile, by the mid- or late 1980s, the alliance of elite economic conservatives and working-class social conservatives that had brought the Republicans to power at the beginning of the decade was beginning to fragment. With the end of the unifying force of the Cold War, many so-called Reagan Democrats began to look toward populist and economic nationalist, though not liberal, solutions to the wage stagnation and job loss that had begun to plague them.[71]

Among party leaders, economic nationalism found support in Congress from Senators Jesse Helms and Strom Thurmond from the textile states of North and South Carolina respectively, as well as from other conservative Republicans like Representatives Helen Bentley of Maryland, Duncan Hunter of California, and Don Ritter of New Jersey. But the most prominent Republican economic nationalist was former Reagan speechwriter Patrick Buchanan.

When Buchanan left the White House in 1987, he was still a free trader. But by 1991, after several years of prodding by the Business and Industrial Council, he was openly defending what he called a "protectionist" strategy. In mid-

December, Buchanan declared his candidacy for the GOP presidential nomination. Hearkening back to Republican isolationists of the 1930s and 1940s, Buchanan promised to put "America First" by breaking with the free trade and internationalist foreign policies of the Bush administration.

As Bush set off on his twelve-day Asian journey, he indicated that he intended to use his trip to defuse criticism of his trade policies from Democrats and now even some Republicans. "Let me make very clear the focus of this trip," the president said. "My highest priority is jobs . . . for American workers."[72] Just before reaching Japan, Bush himself acknowledged that "It's politics—it's politics from tomorrow on."[73] As the president had explained a few days earlier, "I will do what I have to do to be re-elected."[74]

In his negotiations with Japanese leaders in Tokyo, Bush was able to win some modest concessions. In an "action plan" issued by the two countries at the conclusion of the talks, Japanese auto manufacturers promised to buy $19 billion in auto parts from the United States by fiscal 1994, up from $10 billion in 1990, and to sell U.S.-made cars in their dealerships. The Japanese also pledged to find ways to purchase more American computers, glass, and paper.

On returning to Washington Bush tried to put an optimistic gloss on his trip, with little success. Unemployment had risen to 7.1 percent in December, the highest rate in six years. The public and the media were skeptical of the value of the Asian jaunt, and U.S. automakers were harshly critical of the agreements struck with the Japanese. Democratic presidential candidates, seconded by Pat Buchanan, and leading congressional Democrats rapped Bush for going begging, "hat-in-hand," to the Japanese for what in the end were only minor concessions.

Dueling over Japan in the Presidential Primaries

Smelling blood, the newly feisty Democrats took the offensive against Bush when Congress reconvened in late January. Their goal was to end the divided government regime that was blocking the passage of substantial legislation. In the wake of the president's failed Asian trip, many were convinced that trade had suddenly become the No. 2 issue behind only recession fighting in political importance.

Intraparty disagreements, however, kept the Democrats from taking up trade legislation until early May, and thus the main political battles over trade in early 1992 were fought out—in both parties—on the presidential campaign trail, especially in New Hampshire's crucial primary races. Drawing on over a decade's worth of work by Democratic policy intellectuals and encouraged by the growing support among high-tech and other business interests for a more active government role in promoting national competitiveness, the Democratic candidates supported new technology policies as well as increased spending on education, training, and infrastructure.

With few other points of disagreement among them, the candidates argued over trade policy. In so doing, they were continuing the intra-Democratic debate, begun in the early 1980s, between traditional and neoliberals, over both party strategy and the contours of the nation's economic future. Senator Tom Harkin of Iowa and Senator Bob Kerrey of Nebraska assumed the toughest trade policy stances. Their target was recession-weary New Hampshire voters and, more generally, blue-collar workers in the nation's struggling mass production industries.[75] At the opposite pole of the argument, former senator Paul Tsongas, of Massachusetts, targeting suburban white-collar workers and executives in post-Fordist, high-tech industries, vigorously opposed protectionism and supported reduced consumption and a pro-business industrial policy.

Governor Bill Clinton of Arkansas, former chairman of the moderate DLC and a self-styled "New Democrat," tried to stake out a middle-ground position in the debate, one that could appeal to various factions within his party. As an ideological free trader who also sought the support of college-educated, upper-middle-class suburbanites and internationally oriented business interests,[76] Clinton opposed protectionism and instead offered a "national economic strategy" to encourage growth and restore competitiveness. But to attract the support of both noncollege-educated, working-class economic nationalists and export-dependent business interests who chafed at closed foreign markets, Clinton also called for "tough trade policies," including the use of the Super 301 mechanism to retaliate against Japan and other unfair traders.

On the Republican side of the New Hampshire primary race, Pat Buchanan campaigned under the banner of "America First" and continued his assault on Bush's liberal trade policies. George Bush, in response, warned against the "siren's call of protectionism."

On primary day, Tsongas and Bush emerged as the victors, defeating the "trade hawks" in their respective parties. Harkin and Kerrey were forced to drop out of the Democratic contest. As the campaign headed south for Super Tuesday, trade temporarily disappeared as a campaign issue, for the region was becoming less dependent for employment on import-competing industries like textiles and more reliant on export-oriented, high-tech firms and inward foreign investment.[77]

When the primary campaign turned back north in mid-March to the key industrial states of Michigan and Illinois with Clinton and Bush the clear front-runners, the trade issue regained importance, but the terrain had shifted. Rather than pivoting around Japan, the debate among Democrats now centered on the proposed free-trade agreement with Mexico, which Clinton and Tsongas supported and the former California governor Jerry Brown opposed as he sought the votes of embattled auto and other industrial workers. As for the Republicans, the fading Buchanan continued to rail at Bush's Japan policies, while the president himself now attacked his opponent for driving a German car.[78]

Predictably, Bush did what he could to undercut his rivals' criticisms and to weaken support for the Democrats' tough trade legislation. In mid-January the United States and China struck a deal to provide greater protection for American products against illegal copying in China. In late February, the USTR announced that trade sanctions would be imposed on the European Community if the EC implemented a law giving preference to European manufacturers in government purchases of telecommunications equipment. The same day, the USTR also announced a series of agreements to open up South Korea's market for telecommunications. And in early March the Commerce Department issued a preliminary report that Canada's provincial governments unfairly subsidized softwood lumber sales to the United States.

Finally, in what *Newsday* termed "signs of an election-year get-tough approach to Japanese business,"[79] the White House initiated a modest package of actions to aid U.S. carmakers in their struggle with their Japanese rivals. The move, according to Bruce Stokes of the *National Journal,* appeared to be "designed to get the Bush reelection campaign through the primaries."[80]

In the end, relative free traders carried the day in both parties' primary contests. Clinton and Bush won decisive victories in Michigan and Illinois, then marched with little difficulty toward their respective parties' nominations. Trade policy played little role along the way. It appeared that enough voters were either attentive to their interests as consumers or dependent for their jobs on exporters and Japanese transplants to keep U.S.-Japan trade from becoming the "hot button" issue that Democratic and now Republican trade hawks hoped that it might. But the partisan maneuvering in the primary campaign did force some strengthening of U.S. trade policy by a Bush administration intent on providing itself with political cover.

The Action Shifts Back to Congress:
The House Passes a Bill, but the Senate Does Not

With the nomination for president of two relative free traders, the trade policy action shifted back to Congress. In early May House Democratic leaders, sensing a new opportunity, convinced Ways and Means Committee Chairman Dan Rostenkowski to introduce a tough new trade bill to draw voter attention to Bush's neglect of unfair trade practices by U.S. competitors, especially Japan. Many Democrats were eager to force Bush to veto a popular trade bill during the fall election campaign.[81]

The multipart bill was an attempt to bridge the divide within the Democratic Party between free traders and those favoring a more retaliatory posture. The legislation reauthorized for five years the Super 301 provision of the Trade Act of 1988, although it gave the USTR latitude about what countries to name and even more latitude about imposing sanctions. On the controversial question of auto trade, the bill sought to cap U.S. sales of Japanese cars, including those made in American transplants.

The Bush administration blasted the House Democrats' bill as protectionist, and congressional Republicans predicted that the president would veto it. The business community was split over the measure. Some Democrats who supported the bill sought changes in it, fearing in particular that its transplant provision would threaten American jobs. Thus, while the House Ways and Means Committee approved the bill, it did so only after deleting the measure's restrictions on sales of Japanese cars in the United States. With this, despite a last-minute surge of administration lobbying and a veto threat, the full House passed the bill by a 280–145 vote. Surprisingly, a new version of Dick Gephardt and Sander Levin's relatively tough measure on autos and auto parts was adopted as an amendment by a rather comfortable 260–166 vote. The voting on the overall bill was regional and ideological, but it was also substantially partisan. Democrats favored the legislation 245–15, whereas Republicans opposed it 34–130.

On the Republican side, traditional factors like pressure from internationally oriented business interests; sensitivity to the existing and potential preferences of workers in export industries, employees of Japanese-owned transplants, and middle-class consumers; free-trade ideology; and White House lobbying—all contributed to GOP opposition to the bill. As for the Democrats, their votes were also influenced by traditional factors like pressure from the labor movement and perhaps from Chrysler, Ford, and other-import competing business interests; fair trade ideology; and the activities of the Democratic leadership.

Probably most important under the prevailing conditions of divided government, though, were Democratic hopes of forcing Bush into, and profiting from, a politically unpopular veto shortly before the November election.[82] These hopes were fueled by the apparent public support for independent presidential candidate Ross Perot's tough trade stance toward Japan.[83] At the same time, those Democrats who sought to use the bill to send signals to either Japan, their labor backers, or their wider constituents, but who also worried that the legislation—especially its transplant provision—was overly restrictive, could still safely vote for the measure. They knew that even though it had comfortably passed the House, it would almost certainly never be enacted into law, either because it would not pass the Senate, where no comparable bill had even been introduced and where the autumn legislative calendar was already crowded, or because it would not survive a Bush veto.[84]

In fact, in 1992 the Senate never did produce its own trade bill thanks largely to the unwillingness of Senator Lloyd Bentsen, the influential Democratic Finance Committee chairman, to move such a measure through his committee. On July 1, eleven Senate Democrats, led by Majority Leader George Mitchell of Maine, did present an election-year package of thirty trade and competitiveness proposals, intended to dramatize Bush administration failings in these areas.[85] Bill Clinton, the Democratic presidential nominee who had called for some of these same programs, and who was now under pressure from independent candidate Ross Perot to adopt a "harder" economic nationalist stance, publicly endorsed the Senate plan.

But Lloyd Bentsen worried that passing such a measure would make it harder to approve a Mexican free-trade agreement, which was sure to benefit a border state like Texas.[86] With Japan having unilaterally agreed in the spring to tighten its voluntary limits on auto exports to the United States, the auto industry's electoral clout shrinking,[87] and the Big Three carmakers actually beginning to recover their cost competitiveness, there was insufficient political pressure on Bentsen to force him to introduce a new fair-trade bill. In the late summer and fall of 1992, the Democrats' election-year legislative initiative on trade quietly died.

Nor, contrary to the earlier hopes of many congressional and other Democrats, did U.S. trade policy toward Japan play much of a role in the general election phase of the presidential campaign. Clinton did allege that Bush had failed to be tough enough on Japan and Germany, and he reiterated his support for the reinstatement of the Super 301 law. But with no Democrat-sponsored trade bill awaiting a possible Bush veto, and with free trader Clinton disinclined to attack Japan too sharply, the U.S.-Japan trade gap was not a major point of contention. Although USTR officials proposed new sanctions against Japan, they were overruled by top White House officials, who felt no urgent political need to take such steps.[88] Instead, Bush announced a now-typical spate of smaller trade-related actions to help secure his reelection, including increased wheat export subsidies, the sale of fighter jets to Taiwan and Saudi Arabia, and an agreement with China to lower barriers to a variety of American export goods.[89]

NAFTA in the Presidential Campaign

What debate there was on trade policy during the campaign centered on the proposed North American Free Trade Agreement, which Bush enthusiastically embraced, Clinton reservedly accepted, and Ross Perot vociferously attacked. The president attempted to make NAFTA an important element of his reelection campaign, arguing that the proposed pact would create more jobs for American workers. In promoting the treaty, Bush campaign officials continued to pursue what they called their "Southwest strategy."[90] They were still convinced that NAFTA could be a political winner, especially among Hispanics and business interests, in the vote-rich border states of Texas and California.[91] The pact was also thought likely to help Bush widen his national business support.[92]

After Bush regrouped to turn aside Pat Buchanan's economic nationalist challenge following the surprisingly strong showing of the "America First" candidate in the New Hampshire primary, White House trade negotiators pressed hard to finish the NAFTA treaty before the August Republican convention, where the administration hoped to showcase the deal. A preliminary free-trade agreement was announced on August 12 and touted with much fanfare at the GOP convention the next week.[93]

Although polling evidence indicated that the agreement was unpopular in the politically vital industrial Midwest,[94] with the president slumping in the polls, administration and campaign officials hoped that the announcement of the new pact would give their man a badly needed boost. "The two big issues in presidential campaigns are now one: peace and prosperity. Almost nothing illustrates that better than Nafta," said campaign chairman Robert Teeter.[95] Beyond trumpeting his support for NAFTA and its job-creating potential, again especially among Hispanics in the Southwest,[96] Bush also attacked his Democratic opponent, Bill Clinton, for failing to endorse the agreement for fear of offending organized labor.

At heart Clinton was a free trader, a conviction he had adopted when as governor of Arkansas he had led campaigns both to win foreign markets for his state's products and to attract foreign investment to Arkansas. As the presidential nomination campaign heated up in late 1991, Clinton used NAFTA to cast himself as a "New Democrat." The liberal Senator Tom Harkin of Iowa had made opposition to the pact a centerpiece of his campaign as he sought labor support in the primaries. To appeal to business and upper-middle-class suburbanites, Clinton backed NAFTA in part to demonstrate his willingness to stand up to the labor movement and to break with traditional liberal policies.[97]

Clinton's stance wavered just before the March primaries in Michigan, however. In a speech to a UAW local in Flint, he defended his general support for a free-trade agreement, but added that he doubted he could support a pact that George Bush had negotiated. The maneuver worked; Clinton won the Michigan primary and subsequently the Democratic nomination. Throughout the summer Clinton continued to support the principle of free trade with Mexico. But sensitive to the opposition among key sectors of the electorate, particularly in the pivotal midwestern industrial states, Clinton expressed skepticism about the actual pact that Bush was working on.

In mid-August NAFTA's role in the campaign was elevated when Bush pressed Clinton to stop straddling the issue and to endorse the preliminary agreement that his negotiators had produced. Clinton procrastinated, saying that he could not evaluate the treaty until its full text was released and Congress had held hearings on it.

After weeks of intense debate inside the Clinton camp, in late September the Democratic candidate convened a large meeting of advisers to help him hammer out a position on NAFTA.[98] Some advisers opposed an endorsement of the pact, worried that it could cost Clinton votes in key industrial states, especially in pivotal Michigan. Others, though agreeing with these concerns, thought that Clinton could benefit politically from backing NAFTA by sharpening his New Democrat image. This would help him more in states like California, with big blocs of independent, upper-middle-class voters, than it would hurt him in the industrial states. Still other advisers argued that Clinton should endorse NAFTA to put himself on the same side as Bush, thus politically neutralizing the issue and allowing him to remain focused on the economy.

In characteristic fashion, Clinton tried to bridge the two poles of the debate. Thus, he rejected the option backed by much of organized labor and many liberal congressional Democrats: opposing NAFTA but with a promise to negotiate a new agreement. Instead, on October 4, only a month before the election, Clinton announced his decision to support NAFTA as it stood, but only if Mexico and Canada promised to negotiate side agreements to deal with core labor standards—including laws on worker health and safety, child and prison labor, and the rights of unions to organize—the environment, and the threat of sudden import surges. He also insisted on retraining programs for workers who lost their jobs due to NAFTA.

In the end, then, there was both convergence and divergence in the candidates' positions. Personal ideology, the gains likely to accrue to the national constituency whose votes they both sought, and their quest for business and middle-class support led both Republican George Bush and Democrat Bill Clinton to support NAFTA. But party-linked influences produced some differentiation of their positions. To appease his party's core labor and other liberal constituents, Clinton conditioned his support for the treaty on the negotiation of a number of side agreements.

As some of his advisers had hoped, Clinton's endorsement took NAFTA off the table, and it did not appear to play much of a role in the November presidential balloting. The issue certainly did not *help* Bush or Clinton as supporters of the pact, since popular opposition to the agreement rose throughout the presidential campaign. By election day exit polls showed that a majority of

Americans opposed NAFTA, even in Texas and California.[99] If any candidate benefited from the NAFTA debate it was Ross Perot, a militant opponent of the pact, who famously predicted that it would produce a "giant sucking sound going south." But a year later, the issue would dramatically return to the center stage of American politics, accompanied by both interparty and intraparty conflict.

History records, of course, that thanks mostly to voter perceptions of a weak economy and to his mantralike invocation of change, Bill Clinton captured the November election and the presidency, ending the twelve-year-era of divided government. At the same time, in a development that would be of great significance to the conduct of trade policy during Clinton's presidency, Ross Perot won an impressive 19 percent of the vote.

Although the trade issue ultimately played only a minor role in the presidential campaign, to a significant degree, party competition had driven the making of trade policy throughout the Bush administration. As occurred many times during Ronald Reagan's two terms in office, the Democrats attempted to use their congressional majorities under divided government to pressure Bush on U.S.-Japan trade for partisan advantage; similarly, Democratic presidential candidates tried to discredit Bush on the issue. When this Democratic pressure was intense, it once again produced new episodes of policy contagion, as the White House was forced to take a tougher line with Tokyo—for example, on Super 301 implementation in 1989 and in separate negotiations on semiconductors, construction, and autos and auto parts—than might otherwise have been the case. When Democratic pressure slackened, however—after the negotiation of Super 301 and SII agreements with Japan in 1990, and after Senate Democrats failed to produce a trade bill in the fall of 1992—the White House was able to lighten up on Japan.

Even as his Democratic rivals pressured him, George Bush attempted to seize the initiative on trade policy from the Democrats and to boost his reelection prospects with his 1991 fast-track proposal and his strong support for the recently concluded NAFTA pact during the general election phase of the 1992 campaign. Bush was able to split the Democrats to win approval of his fast-track bill, but not without making concessions to his adversaries on labor, the environment, and U.S.-Japan trade. His strong advocacy of NAFTA could not save his bid for a second term, but he did force Bill Clinton to adopt a compromise position on the pact in order to hold the disparate "old" and "new" elements of his electoral coalition together. Clinton's continuing efforts toward this end would shape the making of trade policy throughout his presidency.

7

Clinton's First Two Years in Office
Trade Activism on All Fronts

Bill Clinton's victory in the 1992 presidential election ended the twelve-year-old, Republican-led era of divided government and in so doing changed the partisan dynamics of trade policy-making. As the preceding chapters have shown, the Reagan-Bush era saw growing group and ideology-based party divisions over trade policy, especially in Congress, that were complicated in ways suggested by an incumbency-focused view. To secure their hold on Congress and drive the Republicans from the White House, the "out"-party Democrats, already predisposed to support protectionism or at least fair trade by pressure from their core labor constituents and by their pro-government ideology, heresthetically attempted to raise the electoral salience of the trade issue by calling for a tougher U.S. stance toward foreign trading partners.

The result in Congress was mainly increased party conflict but also some instances of bipartisanship, produced by GOP "mimicking," and cross-partisan coalition formation. At the executive level, the result time and time again was "policy contagion," as free-trading presidents tried to undercut or neutralize the Democrats' maneuvers by themselves assuming tougher positions on trade. The actual consequence of all this was a modest legislative and administrative strengthening of U.S. trade policy for both imports and exports.

Bill Clinton, like all post–World War II presidents, was a free trader (albeit not an unadulterated one). Although congressional Democrats often opposed his trade liberalization initiatives, they naturally did not do so with the aim of dislodging him, a fellow Democrat, from the White House. With a few exceptions, however, the now opposition Republicans also refrained from such heresthetical maneuvering on trade throughout Clinton's presidency. The GOP was predisposed against such behavior by its ties to internationally oriented business interests and its free-trade ideological commitments.

Thus, White House and congressional party positions on trade as well as actual policy choices and outputs during the Clinton years were influenced mainly by personal ideology, group pressures, and bargaining and interaction between the president and the two congressional parties. Administrative actions were largely determined by the president's personal and induced preferences, although there were a few cases of policy contagion. In Congress, the big battles of the period were fought not over Democrat-sponsored fair-trade bills, but rather over Bill Clinton's free-trade initiatives. The outcomes of these fights were determined both by the balance of seats held by the two congressional parties and by the parties' internal cohesion, with the latter in turn determined by the constituency, ideological, leadership, and interinstitutional factors discussed below.

Before proceeding to a detailed examination of trade policy-making during Bill Clinton's first two years in office, it will be helpful to review the political context and calculations that shaped Clinton's evolving trade strategy as well as the congressional politics of trade during his administration.

"Clintonism," Congress, and Trade

Reorienting the Democratic Party

As had been the case a dozen years earlier when Ronald Reagan defeated Jimmy Carter, Bill Clinton's victory over George Bush in 1992 was due largely to the retrospective judgment by the electorate that Bush had mismanaged the economy. But Clinton's campaign strategy and positions also helped him with prospective issue voters.

In all advanced capitalist societies, post-Fordist and postindustrial restructuring has shrunk the traditional blue-collar base of parties of the left, forcing them to broaden their support within the expanding new middle strata, especially professionals and routine white-collar workers.[1] The decline of the Democrats' reliable union base was compounded in the 1980s and early 1990s by the defection to the Republicans of many of the party's remaining white, male, nonunionized blue-collar supporters—the so-called Reagan Democrats.[2] Clinton thus campaigned in part as a New Democrat to win the support of what he termed the "forgotten middle class," made up of the nonrich and the nonpoor. To Clinton and other like-minded Democrats, this broadly included middle-income and middle-education workers, both blue- and white-collar, as well as many professionals and managers.

Michael Lind has usefully distinguished between two layers of this broad, mostly white "middle class."[3] The first—the "moderate middle"—includes up-scale, college-educated, outer suburban professionals and managers who generally favor social liberalism, economic conservatism, and free trade. The second—the "radical center"—is comprised of more economically downscale and insecure, noncollege-educated, urban and inner suburban, blue-collar and lower-level white-collar workers who incline more toward social moderation or conservatism, economic liberalism, and protectionism or fair trade.[4] Since Ronald Reagan's election in 1980, different intra-Democratic factions have variously targeted these two segments of the white middle class—both swing groups—as they have sought to recapture the White House.[5]

In the early 1980s Democratic "neoliberals" attempted to reorient the party toward the expanding, relatively affluent "moderate middle" layer of the middle class. They rallied behind Colorado Senator Gary Hart in the 1984 Democratic presidential primaries and Massachusetts Governor Michael Dukakis in the 1988 primaries and general election. The neoliberals called for a new centrist economics based on growth rather than redistribution, fiscal restraint, and free trade, while reaffirming their support for traditional Democratic social and foreign policy liberalism.

A new attempt was made to reorient the party toward the middle class following the rout in the 1984 presidential election of the Democratic "regular" Walter Mondale, whose candidacy was propelled by organized labor, minorities, and other liberal interests. This time the effort was spurred by moderate and conservative Democratic elected officials, mostly from the South and Midwest. In early 1985 the Democratic Leadership Council (DLC) was formed to wrest control of the party from "liberal fundamentalists" and "special interests," especially organized labor, and to move the party back to the "center."[6] More than the neoliberals, the DLC sought to attract the support of both layers of the middle class. At the same time, the heavily corporate-funded DLC also attempted to regain business support for the wider party.[7]

On the one hand, to appeal to the economically liberal but often socially conservative downscale radical center, including the Reagan Democrats, the DLC initially promoted a progressive economics stressing security, public investment, and fighting inequality, coupled with a greater emphasis on mainstream cultural values that was intended to inoculate the Democrats against Republican attacks. On the other hand, to attract the support of the upscale moderate middle and various internationally oriented business interests, the DLC (1) called for a leaner, more efficient, and more market-oriented government, and (2) opposed protectionism while backing both moderate fair-trade measures and new trade liberalization initiatives. In the late 1980s and early 1990s, however, the early progressive elements of the DLC's economic program were increasingly displaced by more moderate, business-oriented ideas.[8]

As governor of Arkansas Bill Clinton chaired the DLC from 1990 to 1991, and he accepted much of the organization's thinking. During his presidential campaign, he thus called for social moderation, a tougher crime policy, welfare reform premised on personal responsibility, fiscal restraint, and a "reinvented" government. But Clinton also knew that to claim the presidency he would have to retain the support of the core Democratic constituencies—union members, minorities, urban liberals, and so forth. To appeal to these groups as well as to economically insecure Reagan Democrats and other downscale radical centrists, on the campaign trail Clinton also advocated both a mild economic populism and a tinge of economic nationalism.[9]

The centerpiece of Clinton's effort to unite both old and new Democratic constituencies was his "national economic strategy," which called for increased public investment in education and training, infrastructure, and new technologies in order to revitalize the relatively declining American economy. Although he mostly tried to duck divisive trade issues, his positions on trade were also designed to attract the support of both new and old Democrats. Clinton thus both supported the North American Free Trade Agreement (NAFTA) and promised to get tough with Japan and other unfair traders.

His synthetic strategy helped carry him to victory, although competing Democratic factions disagreed over why he won, as they would over the meaning of every election during his presidency.[10] The Democratic Leadership Council argued that Clinton prevailed because he had campaigned as a moderate or centrist New Democrat, which allowed him to extend his support well beyond his party's historical New Deal core to win a clear majority of the two-party middle-class vote.[11] Liberals, however, pointed out that with independent Ross Perot winning 19 percent of the vote, Clinton was unable to make absolute inroads into the middle class beyond those forged by Dukakis four years earlier. The key to his victory was the strong support his populist and economic nationalist campaign themes won for him among traditional core Democratic constituencies.[12] In fact, Clinton's campaign had combined both "old" and "new" themes,[13] and "Clintonism" in power would remain a compound of these two elements, with consequences for the pattern of policies he would pursue, including his trade policies.

Another aspect of the 1992 campaign would also have important consequences for Clinton's trade and other policies: Ross Perot's strong showing among very disparate constituencies. The Texan's balanced budget advocacy won him support from both conservative Republicans and upscale moderate middle Democrats. But Perot also ran well among downscale radical centrists, including blue-collar Reagan Democrats and even some union members,[14] who were attracted to his tough positions on trade. The behavior of and struggle to win over both groups of Perot's supporters would profoundly color much of Clinton's first term in the White House.

Clinton in Office

Once in office, Clinton continued to try to appease both wings of his party.[15] The first two years of his presidency did see something of a tilt toward the Democrats' liberal or populist faction. With the return of unified government, Clinton tended to eschew bipartisan coalitions in favor of close cooperation with the liberal Democratic congressional majority, especially in the House, in order to break the legislative gridlock of the later Bush years. Clinton signed the Family and Medical Leave Act, expanded the Earned Income Tax Credit, increased taxes on business and the wealthy, and proposed a sweeping reform of the nation's health care system. But his first two years in office also saw him press a number of more centrist, bipartisan, New Democrat-style initiatives, including a shift to an emphasis on budget deficit reduction, a crime bill to put more police officers on the street, increased defense spending, "reinventing government," NAFTA, and a new General Agreement on Tariffs and Trade (GATT) accord.

After the debacle of the 1994 congressional midterm elections, in which the Republicans captured control of both houses of Congress, Clinton essentially adopted the DLC's view that his party had been repudiated by the voters because he had governed as an "old" culturally and fiscally liberal Democrat. He therefore moved further to the center, famously declaring that "the era of big government is over" and working with the Republicans to pass important legislation, notably the welfare reform bill of 1996 and the balanced budget agreement of the next year. But the post-1994 period also saw Clinton battle Republican-proposed cuts in Medicare in 1995–96, back increases in the minimum wage, and propose modest new spending initiatives during the last three years of his second term as budget surpluses began to mount.

To some observers Clinton appeared to govern through a chaotic, indecisive process of ad hoc, issue-by-issue coalition building that was determined by the prevailing context of secularly weakening political parties.[16] But Clinton's governing style actually involved a more systematic process of what his controversial, sometime political adviser Dick Morris called "triangulation." For most commentators, triangulation simply meant that on every important issue Clinton positioned himself in the center between liberal congressional Democrats to his left and conservative Republicans to his right, thus essentially adopting the views of the median voter. On certain highly salient issues, this was in fact the course that Clinton chose. But in general, Clinton's practice was more complex. Frequently, as Morris explained, he pursued his political objectives by regularly "tacking" or zigzagging between liberal and more conservative positions on alternating issues, ending up "where he wanted to be, in the middle."[17] On other occasions, he would simultaneously advance liberal and conservative policies or a combination of liberal and conservative ideas in the same policy proposal.[18]

Clinton's triangulations have been explained in various ways by political scientists. Painting on a broad historical canvas, Stephen Skowronek argues that Clinton was a "third way" or "preemptive" president who served during a strong conservative Republican policy "regime" but who was not himself affiliated with that regime. Clinton was forced to practice "an unabashedly mongrel politics" that combined elements of the agendas of both the dominant Republican regime and its liberal Democratic opponents into a hybrid, middle-ground, and not particularly partisan governing approach.[19]

Bert Rockman puts somewhat more emphasis, appropriately I think, on the imperatives of electoral coalition construction and maintenance. He argues that Clinton triangulated because on all but a handful of highly salient issues, there is no real or effective political center. Although moderate mass publics do occupy the spatial center, they are usually indifferent to or confused about most issues. Thus, successful party candidates and officeholders—in this case, Clinton—have to pursue a "coalition of intense minorities" strategy, cobbling together coalitions of or zigzagging between various attentive constituencies, including both core party supporters and groups of swing voters.[20]

One area in which Clinton persistently practiced triangulation was trade policy.[21] Although Clinton's trade policy choices were influenced by his own somewhat ideologically ambivalent or eclectic views on trade policy, as well as those of his sometimes-divided economic advisers, narrower political or constituency considerations were also at work. As the next three chapters show, Clinton consistently triangulated on trade as he variously (1) pressed to open Japanese and other closed foreign markets in order to appeal to organized labor, the radical centrist followers of Ross Perot, and certain export interests, (2) worked to secure congressional approval of liberalizing trade legislation— that is, the NAFTA and GATT agreements, the renewal of his fast-track trade negotiating authority, and permanent normal trade relations (PNTR) with China—to attract the support of upscale, moderate middle voters and other internationally oriented business interests, and (3) refrained from pursuing, or insisted on including labor and environmental standards in, liberalizing agreements or legislation to appease critics of free trade.

The big trade battles of the Clinton years were fought in Congress, or more precisely in the House of Representatives, between but also within the two parties over a series of presidential trade liberalization initiatives: NAFTA, the Uruguay Round GATT accord, fast-track legislation, and PNTR with China.

Throughout this period the congressional party divisions that had begun to widen in the early 1980s, especially in the House, continued to do so, thanks to (1) the centralizing Democratic reforms of the 1970s and the subsequent reforms that followed the GOP takeover of Congress in 1994, (2) the continuing exit of white southern conservatives from the Democratic Party, which reduced the differences between the constituencies of northern and southern congressional Democrats, (3) the growth of southern Republicanism, paradoxically aided by redistricting efforts aimed at ensuring the election of black candidates, and the increasing conservatism of GOP activists, which together led to the election of greater numbers of avid Republican conservatives to Congress, (4) low voter turnout, which led the parties to emphasize the targeting and "activation" of their core constituents, who often held extreme policy preferences,[22] and (5) impeachment-fueled Republican anger at Bill Clinton.[23]

These congressional party divisions were also evident in trade policy conflicts, with the Republicans as usual supportive of free trade and the Democrats generally opposed. Unlike fights on most other issues, however, in which Bill Clinton cooperated with and was supported by House Democrats in the face of strong GOP opposition, on trade Clinton usually allied with the Republicans against the majority of the members of his own party.[24]

Interparty divisions over trade policy were also somewhat more variable in depth or intensity than was the case on other issues, and this had important policy consequences. Due again to ideological commitments, their ties to internationally oriented business interests, and GOP leadership efforts, two-thirds to three-quarters of House Republicans regularly supported trade liberalization initiatives during the Clinton years; they were opposed by a smaller bloc of conservative nationalists and other free-trade critics.

Democratic opposition to free trade was still more variable, however, because of (1) electorally induced changes in the relative size of "old" and "new" Democratic congressional factions, (2) shifting balances of labor and business influences on party members, in part determined by (3) differences in the perceived magnitude, incidence, and certainty of the benefits and costs of particular policies, (4) the ebb and flow of Democratic leadership cohesion, and (5) the uneven energy and quality of Bill Clinton's bargaining and persuasive efforts. It was the waxing and waning of intra-Democratic divisions over trade that mainly explains the shifting fate of trade liberalization proposals during the Clinton years, that is, the passage of the NAFTA and GATT accords in 1993 and 1994 respectively, the defeat of fast-track legislation in 1997 and 1998 (the latter a GOP initiative), and the approval of PNTR with China in 2000.

The rest of this chapter explores the dynamics and consequences of party competition over trade policy during Bill Clinton's first two years in office, when after the failure of his initial "investment" program, he embraced a strategy of "export-led growth." During this new period of Democrat-led unified government, Clinton's triangulations on trade resulted in policies that were paradoxically more aggressive and more liberal than those pursued by the Reagan and Bush administrations under divided government or that a second Bush administration would have been able to pursue had George Bush been reelected.

On the one hand, Clinton's results-oriented Japan policy, backed by fellow Democrats in control of both houses of Congress, was initially more aggressive than the one that either Reagan or Bush had conducted. On the other hand, with help from business and New Democrats, Clinton fought for and won approval of the liberalizing NAFTA and GATT agreements, in the first case by sharply splitting his own congressional party.[25] These were feats that, especially in the case of NAFTA, a Republican president facing the same, but more hostile Democratic Congress under divided government probably would have been unable to accomplish. Before addressing the party politics of trade policy during these two years, however, it will be helpful to review the formation and fate of Clinton's wider "national economic strategy."

The Rise and Demise of Clinton's "Investment" Strategy

The regulation crisis of the 1970s undermined both the "Keynesian consensus" and the New Deal Order. But despite the establishment during the Reagan-Bush era of certain elements of a new mode of regulation—including changes in corporate governance and financial institutions, shifts in labor-management relations, slowed government spending, and deregulation[26]—which contributed to improved rates of economic growth, contrary to Skowronek and other authors,[27] a thoroughgoing Republican realignment and the construction of an unmitigatedly conservative new political order were blocked by a number of path-dependent and other factors. Among these were (1) the weakening of party loyalties, the rise of candidate-centered campaigning, and the growth of the "personal vote" and the "incumbency advantage," which together increased split-ticket voting and produced a long period of divided government, during which the Democrats retained control of one or both houses of Congress, (2) the increasingly "hyper-pluralist" character of U.S. politics, in which powerful interest groups that benefit from the status quo mobilize at the fragmented American state's many "veto points" to block proposals for significant change, (3) continued popular support for the core programs of the welfare state, (4) the general "thickening" of the institutions of government, and (5) the absence, thanks to the operation of various economic stabilizers, of a true "punctuating" crash during the Carter years, which might have more fully disrupted or dislodged the institutions of the New Deal Order.[28]

When Bill Clinton took office in early 1993 committed to what he repeatedly referred to as a "comprehensive national economic strategy," his aim, like any first-term president, was to produce enough economic growth to guarantee his reelection. But he also hoped to rebuild, albeit on partly new foundations, a Democratic political order. Departing from his party's traditional reliance on Keynesian demand-stimulus nostrums and drawing on over a decade's worth of work on industrial policy and competitiveness by Democratic policy intellectuals, Clinton and his advisers initially advocated what they called an "investment" strategy to revitalize the American economy by improving its conditions of supply through greatly expanded public and private investment.

Clinton believed that a neostatist accumulation strategy was necessitated by the dramatic changes—globalization and post-Fordist restructuring—that were under way in the U.S. and world economies. To both facilitate and cushion the transition to a new, more internationally competitive economic order, Clinton, influenced in particular by the recent work of his longtime friend Robert Reich,[29] advocated increased public investment in physical and human capital in a twenty-two-page plan released in June 1992—"Putting People First." A technology plan followed in mid-September.

The education and infrastructure spending proposals in "Putting People First" were attractive to black, urban, and labor Democrats—core party constituencies—as well as to blue-collar Reagan Democrats and suburban white-collar workers and professionals, all key swing groups. At the same time, reflecting the influence of other more moderate Clinton advisers, his plan also called for halving the deficit within four years and certain spending cuts, both of which appealed to affluent, suburban New Democrats and some of Ross Perot's potential supporters.

Finally, Clinton's investment strategy—along with his general pro-market, pro–free-trade, New Democrat outlook—was attractive to elements of corporate America, including high-tech and internationally oriented interests, that had become disenchanted with George Bush's management of the economy.[30] In fact, while building on the Bush-era efforts of his vice presidential running mate Al Gore and other congressional Democrats, Clinton's technology plan was essentially developed by key industry leaders, many of them Republicans and many of whom publicly endorsed him.[31] "This is the first time where I have seen a significant section of the business community, before the election, coming out in favor of a Democratic candidate," said William T. Archey, the U.S. Chamber of Commerce's senior vice president for policy and congressional affairs. "That's particularly true of high-tech industries and industries that are particularly capital-intensive or that have R&D costs and are heavily involved in international trade."[32]

Clinton in Power: The Demise of the Investment Strategy

Even before election day, Clinton's investment strategy ran into trouble. In mid-October the already shaky, deficit-and-inflation-averse bond market shuddered after word leaked that Clinton might be considering a short-term economic stimulus package on top of the investment program he had been promoting. To assuage bond market concerns after his election, Clinton appointed deficit "hawks" to most of the top economic posts in his administration.

As Clinton and his advisers pulled together the economic plan that they intended to submit to Congress, the president's initial investment strategy was transmuted into a markedly different "financial markets" strategy. The new approach, dubbed the "Wall Street–Pennsylvania Avenue Accord" by economists Barry Bluestone and Bennett Harrison, stressed deficit reduction over public investment, primarily to foster bond market confidence and thus lower interest rates and secondarily to appeal to the concerns of Ross Perot's deficit-conscious supporters. To reach its deficit reduction goal, the plan called for tax hikes for upper-income households and business, a broad-based energy tax, and defense and domestic spending cuts. The investments proposed in "Putting People First" were cut in half.[33]

Although Clinton's plan was initially well received by much of the general public and the business community, over the next five months support deteriorated as the president came increasingly to be seen as a "tax-and-spend" liberal, a view that was echoed by some New Democrats.[34] Sensing an opportunity to make gains with swing voters, especially Perot backers, and to strengthen their business support, congressional Republicans opposed Clinton at every turn of the budget battle, refusing to give the president a single vote on the floor at any stage of the process. In late April 1993 Senate Republicans, armed with the supermajoritarian weapon of the filibuster, were able to kill Clinton's $16.3 billion economic stimulus package, which contained a number of his proposed investments.

Strenuous appeals by the White House and congressional leaders to save Clinton's presidency and the Democratic Party from a humiliating defeat helped keep the great majority of Democrats in both houses in line on floor voting on the budget resolutions and the budget reconciliation bills. But given the unified GOP opposition to Clinton's plan and the slim Democratic majorities in both House and Senate, the administration was forced to make substantial concessions to Democratic moderates and conservatives. In the final House-Senate conference report, Clinton's investment agenda was once again cut roughly in half.

By as early as mid-1993, then, Bill Clinton's once-promising investment strategy had essentially been defeated by the combined forces of the persistent budget deficit, faltering bond market confidence, fiscally moderate White House economic advisers, mounting public and business opposition to Clinton as a tax-and-spend liberal, institutional obstacles and veto points, wall-to-wall Republican hostility, and the compromise-forcing role of moderate and conservative congressional Democrats.[35]

Clinton's Export Strategy

With the demise of his investment program, Clinton was left with an essentially neoliberal, Republican-like financial markets strategy that counted on deficit reduction and an attendant lowering of long-term interest rates to produce the economic growth necessary for his reelection. There were risks to such an approach, however, since deficit reduction by itself would have contractionary effects, with no guarantee that interest rates would fall or that declining rates would boost investment and consumption.

Beyond this, Clinton recognized that the introduction of new productivity-enhancing technologies to improve business competitiveness would likely reduce the demand for labor. The increase in unemployment, together with the resulting downward pressure on wages, would in turn reduce consumer demand, thus further slowing both job and income growth. One key element of the solution to this problem, Clinton argued, was to raise demand by increasing exports. "If you want productivity . . . to lead to higher wages and more jobs," he explained, "you must have more customers. . . . The only way for a wealthy nation to grow richer is to export."[36]

After the gutting of his investment program and as a complement to his risky financial markets strategy, in mid-1993 Clinton, now convinced of the "increasing primacy of economics" in the post–Cold War era,[37] turned to a strategy of "export-led growth" to help secure his reelection. As *Business Week* reported, "Administration officials now concede that the key to the President's pledge to create millions of new, better-paying jobs depends on finding new markets overseas. . . . Clinton has embarked on a high-risk strategy to make trade a centerpiece of his economic policy." The Clintonites based their hopes on two central facts: First, since 1987, exports had accounted for more than one-third of U.S. economic growth and two-thirds of all new domestic jobs. Second, jobs created by exports, especially in the high-tech and service sectors, paid 13 percent more than jobs rooted solely in the domestic economy.[38]

Clinton's new export strategy would be multipronged. One element of it was aggressive export promotion. In late September the Commerce Department unveiled a long-awaited "National Export Strategy," the most important aspects of which were a sweeping rollback of controls on exports of high-tech equipment to the former Soviet bloc and China and a commitment to help U.S. companies win major overseas contracts, principally in the ten "big emerging markets" of the developing world.

Still more important to the new export strategy was the administration's intensified and simultaneous pursuit of unilateral, bilateral, regional, and multilateral market-opening initiatives and agreements. More specifically, the White House escalated efforts begun by previous administrations to pry open Japan's closed markets, committed itself to winning congressional ratification of the North American Free Trade Agreement, encouraged other regional free-trade initiatives in Asia and the Americas, and pledged to successfully conclude and win congressional approval of a new GATT agreement.[39]

Clinton's enthusiasm for his new export strategy stemmed in part from a long-standing ideological commitment to free trade tempered by a willingness to "get tough" with unfair foreign traders like Japan. But political considerations were even more important. Part of the electoral logic underlying the administration's trade initiatives was outlined by Clinton ally Senator Bill Bradley (D-N.J.). The NAFTA and GATT deals, Bradley said, "tie into job creation through exports, which is tied to people's perception of their own well-being, which is tied to [Mr. Clinton's] re-election campaign in '96."[40]

Such trade initiatives were not undertaken merely to win the support of retrospectively minded voters in 1996 by contributing to strong U.S. macroeconomic performance. They were also intended to maintain and strengthen the president's coalition by appealing to particular groups with different trade-specific concerns. First, as part of his effort to reach for support beyond working- and middle-class electoral constituencies, Clinton pursued his various market-opening initiatives to win the backing of both export-dependent and more fully multinational business interests. Second, he used his trade policies to maintain the support of the two major wings of his party. Throughout his presidency Clinton triangulated between old and new Democratic factions and constituencies by alternately getting tough with Japan or slowing the trade liberalization process and then turning around and working to secure congressional approval of liberalizing trade legislation.

Getting Tough with Japan: Act 1

On taking office, Clinton was immediately confronted by a darkening trade picture. In early 1993, with the U.S. trade deficit on its way back up to a projected $110 billion for the coming year, a host of industries and their unions were pleading or getting set to plead for protection from imports or for help in opening closed foreign markets. Clinton's most important early trade policy challenge was how to deal with Japan. In 1992 Japan had run its largest overall trade surplus ever, $124 billion, while Tokyo's bilateral surplus with the United States accounted for two-thirds of the total U.S. trade gap, fueled by a hefty increase in sales of cars, car parts, and semiconductors.

In March an interagency group was formed under the auspices of the Clinton's new National Economic Council to draft a "Policy Review Document" on Japan. After two months of debate Clinton signed off on something of a centrist approach to dealing with Tokyo.[41] Though ruling out protectionism and automatic retaliation against Japan for failing to meet import targets, the administration moved the United States considerably closer to a managed trade or results-oriented stance. This included calling for the achievement of both overall surplus reduction and sector-specific market access goals, progress toward which would be measured by various numerical benchmarks.

The Clinton administration's decision to seek new managed trade arrangements with Japan was influenced by a number of factors, some of which were distinctly partisan in nature. First, there was the ascent since the late 1980s of revisionism, whose proponents, the most influential of whom remained Clyde Prestowitz, maintained that Japan's state-sponsored capitalism was fundamentally different from the more market-dominated American version, not least because it was structured to keep imports out. The revisionists argued that rather than try to reconstruct Japan in America's image, the United States should instead set trade targets and quotas for Japan and then let Tokyo figure out how to meet them.[42] Even some leading mainstream economists had been forced to acknowledge that a certain measure of managed trade might be needed to whittle down the U.S. trade deficit with Japan.[43]

Through his own experience in leading trade missions to Japan as governor of Arkansas and his reading of revisionist works, Bill Clinton himself came to share the revisionists' view that Japan was "different" and to support their correspondingly tough trade policy prescriptions.[44] On taking office, Clinton guaranteed such views a prominent place in his administration with the appointment of a leading revisionist, Laura Tyson of the University of California at Berkeley, as chair of his Council of Economic Advisers.[45] The flexible, results-oriented approach toward Japan approved by Clinton in mid-June largely reflected Tyson's influence.

It was no accident that revisionism and secondarily, strategic trade theory, found support at the highest levels of a Democratic, rather than a Republican, administration. Congruent with the Democrats' general pro-government ideological beliefs, revisionism and strategic trade theory provided a party-linked justification for a results-oriented Japan policy that White House officials believed could contribute to economic growth and thus also to Clinton's eventual reelection.

Clinton's tough Japan policy was further intended to fulfill campaign pledges made to, and thus to consolidate and expand his support among, various economic and political interests. The main guardian of Clinton's political interests in the domain of trade policy was U.S. Trade Representative (USTR) Mickey Kantor, a former Democratic National Committee chairman and the national chairman of the Clinton-Gore '92 Campaign. Shortly after his appointment, Kantor reportedly declared that his primary trade policy objective was to "get Clinton reelected."[46]

The White House was eager to win the political support of those many export-oriented business interests that were still frustrated by their inability to gain access to the Japanese market. In February 1993 the prestigious Advisory Committee for Trade Policy and Negotiations—which included chairmen of some of the nation's largest corporations—issued a report urging that, in cases involving high-tech "strategic industries," the new Clinton administration should press Tokyo to set quantitative goals to measure progress toward achieving an open Japanese market. The significance of the report was not lost on the White House. As one administration official noted, "the fact that this group of export-oriented, strong free-trade multinational corporations would propose this is indication that the center of gravity has changed in U.S.-Japan relations."[47]

The administration also used its Japan policy to curry favor with organized labor, which had long favored getting tough with Tokyo and which had been alienated by Clinton's support for NAFTA.[48] Finally, White House officials believed that a tough stance toward Japan would play well with key swing voters, including Ross Perot's economic nationalist supporters.[49] Such a position, it was hoped, would help offset the decline of Clinton's popularity due to his liberal social positions, some of his appointments, and the perception that his economic program constituted a return to "tax-and-spend liberalism."[50]

Following Clinton's mid-June approval of the new Japan policy, bilateral meetings were held between Washington and Toyko to work out a negotiating framework. During these meetings the Japanese government angrily rejected the American proposals, which it decried as managed trade. With Japan's dependence on the U.S. market greatly reduced by its exporters' recent switch to Asia, U.S. leverage on Tokyo had correspondingly declined. Japanese leaders were now determined to never again be forced into signing market-sharing deals like the 1986 semiconductor and 1992 auto agreements.

The Clinton administration's efforts to reach an agreement with Japan appeared to be on the brink of failure until a last-minute compromise deal, or "framework agreement," was struck at the Tokyo G-7 summit in early July. Japan agreed to significantly reduce its trade surplus, but without setting specific numerical targets. The two countries also agreed to talks in five broad categories and to the use of unspecified qualitative and quantitative objective criteria, rather than clear numerical benchmarks, to measure progress toward market access. Vague and weak as this framework agreement undoubtedly was, it did constitute a step toward a more results-oriented U.S. trade policy than either Reagan or Bush had conducted. Thus, the return of unified Democratic government did bring with it a tougher U.S. posture toward Tokyo than produced by the previous Republican-led divided government regime.

The Fight to Approve NAFTA

During the seven months of negotiations that followed the signing of the framework agreement, U.S.-Japan tensions subsided and NAFTA took center stage.[51] Despite subsequent politically driven flare-ups with Japan, the NAFTA fight marked a shift in the focus of U.S. trade policy in the 1990s away from bilateral market-opening issues. From now on the fiercest battles would be waged over proposals to liberalize trade, especially with the developing world, on a regional or multilateral basis. More fundamentally, these were struggles over the allocation of the costs and benefits of what would increasingly be termed economic globalization.

Despite his get-tough attitude toward Japan, Clinton, like most presidents, remained a free trader. Following the politically damaging budget fight that saw the gutting of his investment initiatives, he turned to a more active advocacy of free trade both to promote export-led growth and to burnish his credentials as a New Democrat. Thus in the fall of 1993, after some initial doubt and delay, Clinton fully engaged himself in the fight to approve NAFTA.

Negotiating the Side Agreements

In mid-March 1993 negotiations began with Mexico and Canada on the NAFTA side agreements that Clinton had promised during the presidential campaign.[52] In intra-administration debate preceding the negotiations, USTR Mickey Kantor and Secretary of Labor Robert Reich and other Labor Department officials, hoping to mollify liberal critics of the pact with what were in essence "side payments,"[53] called for strong agreements to protect American workers and the environment. They proposed commissions that could impose trade sanctions against countries and businesses that violated their own labor and environmental standards. But influential Treasury, State, and National Economic Council officials feared that intrusive side agreements would antagonize business and congressional Republicans. Thus, the initial U.S. proposals deprived the labor and environmental commissions of the power to investigate complaints or enforce their findings.

NAFTA critics strongly protested the weak proposals, and congressional Democrats warned the administration that the House would not approve a trade pact lacking strong side agreements. In mid-May the White House reversed course and presented tougher proposals to Mexican and Canadian negotiators. But the Mexican and Canadian governments strongly resisted the new U.S. proposals, and business and Republican backing for NAFTA eroded. At the same time, the AFL-CIO declined to play a role in developing the labor side agreement. As a result, in mid-August the Clinton administration backed away from its May proposals and agreed to a much weaker set of enforcement procedures, chiefly with respect to labor standards. The weakened side agreements reassured nervous business groups and Republicans whose support Clinton would need to pass the treaty. But the many NAFTA critics within and outside Congress, especially organized labor and its supporters, were deeply dissatisfied.

In 1993 opposition to NAFTA had been spearheaded by the labor movement, grassroots environmental groups, and the Citizens Trade Campaign (CTC), an umbrella coalition of more than seventy labor, environmental, consumer, farm, human rights, and religious organizations.[54] Signaling a new stage in the adoption by interest groups of sophisticated grassroots mobilization and media— or "outside lobbying"—strategies,[55] these anti-NAFTA forces, reinforced by the efforts of Jerry Brown, Pat Buchanan, and above all Ross Perot's United We Stand organization, employed rallies, protests, press conferences, media ads, petitions, letters to Congress, and educational caravans. Thanks to these forces, by the summer of 1993 public opinion had turned against NAFTA.[56] With the announcement of the weak side agreements, opponents escalated their attacks, creating a nationwide firestorm of protest against the pact in congressional districts during the three-week August recess.

Reflecting the anti-NAFTA preferences of their core constituents, especially union members, as well as wider public sentiment, the Democrats' opposition to NAFTA had been building from the time Clinton assumed office, particularly in the House, where the 1992 elections had shifted the Democratic caucus to the left. When they learned of the side agreements, liberal congressional Democrats intensified their criticism of NAFTA. House Majority Leader Dick Gephardt, regarded as a fence-sitter, stunned White House officials when he vehemently denounced the side agreements and then came out against NAFTA. House Majority Whip David Bonior, a pro-labor liberal from a suburban Detroit district in which the Big Three automakers were the largest employers, said he planned to use the resources of the whip's office to organize opposition to the pact. Some House Democratic leaders, however, including Speaker Tom Foley, did back NAFTA and Clinton. In fact, the ten-member majority leadership was split right down the middle on the issue, unable even to discuss the pact among themselves.

Clinton Finally Commits Himself: Triangulating to the Right

In the fall of 1993 the anti-NAFTA forces appeared to have the upper hand. As interest group, public, and congressional opposition to the pact mounted, the treaty's supporters did relatively little to promote it. In particular, Bill Clinton was largely absent from the fight during early and mid-1993.[57] There were several reasons for this. First, the White House could not risk losing Democratic votes for its budget plan by pushing the divisive NAFTA agreement too early. Second, Clinton and his political advisers hoped to avoid for as long as possible a damaging confrontation with organized labor and other core Democratic constituencies. Third, Hillary Rodham Clinton and key presidential political aides wanted to put off dealing with NAFTA until health care reform legislation had been passed.

In mid-August, however, Clinton finally decided to abandon his cautious stance and to commit himself to the fight for NAFTA's approval. Two main considerations appear to have been responsible for this shift. First, as we have seen, following the defeat of his investment-oriented economic strategy, Clinton embraced an export-led growth strategy, of which NAFTA was now viewed as an important element. And second, during the budget battle Clinton saw his middle-class and business support decline as he was tagged as a traditional tax-and-spend liberal. To regain this support, Clinton was convinced by other key advisers that he had to return to, or triangulate, or tack back toward his moderate, New Democrat roots, a course of action that was also backed by the leaders of the Democratic Leadership Council. Thus, in the fall of 1993, Clinton committed himself to building bipartisan coalitions in support of New Democrat goals and initiatives like reinventing government, immigration and welfare reform, crime prevention, and NAFTA.[58]

Rather than accept the advice of liberal Democrats who urged him try to win over labor and downscale radical centrist Perot voters by edging away from NAFTA, Clinton instead sided with those of his advisers like White House congressional liaison Howard Paster, who told him, "If you abandon NAFTA, Mr.

President, there goes New Democrat."[59] Thus, both seeking the support of moderate middle voters and, according to political adviser Carter Eskew, feeling "the power of corporate America getting behind this thing,"[60] Clinton threw himself into the fight for the pact's ratification.

The Final Conflict Is Joined: The Lineup of Forces

The fall battle over NAFTA was concentrated in the House. Although certain senators were quite vocal in their opposition, the treaty's prospects in that chamber were reasonably good. Most senators represented fairly large, heterogeneous constituencies, including internationally oriented interests that could be expected to counterbalance the views of domestically oriented, anti-NAFTA interests. In addition, the Senate overrepresented more agricultural and less unionized states in which support for NAFTA was relatively strong.[61] The prospects for NAFTA in the House, with its smaller and more homogeneous districts and its greater representation of anti-NAFTA interests, were decidedly poorer.

The armies that lined up against each other during the last months of the NAFTA fight—competing coalitions that would battle each other throughout the Clinton years—were varied in composition. On the pro-NAFTA side, after its delayed start, the Clinton administration waged an energetic fight for the deal's approval under the leadership of NAFTA czar William Daley. Administration officials, including cabinet members, intensively pressured representatives in Washington and their home districts through personal lobbying, the mobilization of business interests, and public events. But the heaviest lifting was done by President Clinton, who feverishly bargained with and persuaded undecided and wavering House members, especially Democrats, who were often cross-pressured by competing import-sensitive and export-oriented interests in their districts.[62]

In the NAFTA implementing bill that he sent to Congress on November 3, Clinton provided cover for members with political problems with the pact by including dozens of specific deals or side payments to curb imports of a variety of goods.[63] A North American Development Bank to help finance an array of development projects along the border and a new worker retraining program were among other promises made by the White House to win over undecided members. Clinton also went public with eighteen events and personally phoned and met with lawmakers on hundreds of occasions. According to House Speaker Thomas S. Foley, a thirty-year veteran of Congress, Clinton "worked harder . . . than any president I've seen on any issue."[64] Finally, the administration sought to weaken the influence of the two strongest anti-NAFTA forces when Clinton criticized organized labor for its "roughshod, muscle-bound" attempts to intimidate House members and Vice President Al Gore bested Ross Perot in a nationally televised debate on the pact.

The business community, which saw large, concentrated benefits in NAFTA, also threw itself into the fight after a slow start. Although in October 1992, four hundred major trade associations, corporations, and business coalitions had formed USA*NAFTA to defend the deal,[65] a number of factors, especially an unwillingness to act before the side agreements were finished, kept business from mobilizing effectively during much of 1993.[66] In mid-September, however, internationally oriented business interests finally engaged themselves seriously in the battle. The moribund USA*NAFTA, with four thousand member companies and trade associations by the time of the House vote, revived and launched a two-pronged strategy involving both "inside" and "outside" lobbying tactics, that is, traditional Washington lobbying, an $8 million media campaign, and the grassroots mobilization of executives and factory workers to contact members in their states and districts.[67] "I think we've done more on Nafta than on any legislative issue in history," said Lawrence A. Bossidy, chairman of Allied Signal Inc., and the head of USA*NAFTA.[68] Export-oriented agricultural interests also actively supported the pact.

Although many grassroots environmental organizations opposed the agreement, some national organizations did endorse it, arguing that NAFTA set an important precedent that would lead to the incorporation of environmental concerns into future trade agreements. Contrary to the original expectations of many observers, the Hispanic community was also split over NAFTA, but the treaty did find considerable support among Hispanic business leaders. The elite national media and the vast majority of mainstream academics—including those affiliated with think tanks like the Institute for International Economics, the Brookings Institution, and the Heritage Foundation—were strongly behind NAFTA. Moreover, Mexico's government and industry continued to lobby heavily on its behalf.

On the anti-NAFTA side, organized labor remained the most formidable opponent; indeed, labor leaders viewed the battle over the pact as crucially important to the movement's future.[69] By 1993 labor had been in serious decline for several decades, as the percentage of the nonagricultural workforce represented by unions had been falling steadily since the mid-1950s.[70] With the erosion of labor's structural position and resources came the weakening of its political influence.

In addition to attacks from the Republican Reagan and Bush administrations, labor suffered from the erosion of its influence within the Democratic Party. Labor's impact on the Democratic presidential nominating process had diminished following the 1984 Mondale debacle. Labor's influence on congressional Democrats was also reduced when party leaders successfully used their control of the House and its committees to pressure business political action committees (PACs) to hike their contributions to the party. This diversification of the Democrats' funding base reduced the party's historic dependence on organized labor and rendered congressional Democrats more supportive of business on a wide range of issues, including trade policy.

Nevertheless, labor looked at Bill Clinton's election in 1992 with hope.[71] Although the AFL-CIO Executive Council had voted to abstain from an early endorsement and many industrial unions had backed Senator Tom Harkin of Iowa in the primaries, Clinton received strong support from some of the major public and service sector unions, which appreciated his commitment to an activist government. Labor as a whole united behind Clinton in the general election. When 55 percent of union voters, who made up a quarter of the electorate, cast their ballots for the Arkansas governor, helping to deliver the crucial swing states of Ohio, Michigan, and Pennsylvania for him, the unions had reason to believe that, despite his New Democratic posture and his endorsement of NAFTA, they would be able to call in their debts when Clinton took office. Adding to this optimism, the AFL-CIO had endorsed 248 successful House candidates in the election.

In fact, labor fared relatively well during the first year of the Clinton administration. The president signed the Family and Medical Leave Act, endorsed a bill to bar the permanent replacement of strikers, and proposed a dramatic overhaul of the health care system. Still, labor worried that Clinton and congressional Democrats remained too influenced by business and the moderates of the Democratic Leadership Council.

For labor, the defeat of NAFTA was crucial in two respects. First, in a period of "jobless growth," it was hoped that the pact's demise would slow globalization and trade liberalization, processes that were thought to threaten not only American workers' jobs and wages, but also the very existence of unions. Second, the labor movement sought to use an expected victory in the fight to rebuild its political strength within and beyond the Democratic Party.

Toward these twin ends, labor waged a multilevel, inside and outside lobbying campaign against NAFTA, its biggest on any issue since the 1930s. State and local union affiliates mounted an unprecedented grassroots mobilization against the agreement. The AFL-CIO funded a TV, radio, and print media blitz against the pact. A number of leaders of major international unions vowed to make a congressmember's vote on NAFTA a litmus test for financial and other support in the 1994 elections.[72] "It's got a lot of members worried," acknowledged Representative Robert T. Matsui (D-Calif.), an organizer of the pro-NAFTA forces.[73] Labor's position was also strengthened by the movement's internal unity; public sector unions, the one expanding part of the labor movement, joined the fight in solidarity with the embattled industrial unions, although their opposition was naturally not as passionate.

Labor found allies among the grassroots-oriented environmental and consumer groups, prominently including the Sierra Club and Ralph Nader's Public Citizen, who together formed the Citizens Trade Campaign, by then up to three hundred member organizations. Some Hispanic and black organizations also came out against the agreement, fearing its employment effects on working-class members of their communities. A few liberal think tanks like the Economic Policy Institute and the Institute for Policy Studies produced analyses critical of NAFTA. A number of import-competing agricultural interests and small manufacturing concerns, the latter represented by the U.S. Business and Industrial Council, also opposed the pact. In addition, a network of conservative activists were against NAFTA, both because they viewed it as a threat to American sovereignty and because they expected it to increase immigration and the flow of drugs from Mexico. Finally, Ross Perot and his United We Stand organization campaigned fervently against NAFTA toward the end of the fight.[74]

Interparty and Intraparty Divisions

The divide over NAFTA between these two competing coalitions of forces was reflected in splits both between and within the parties, splits that were exacerbated by individual members' ideological commitments. The Republicans, however, were less divided than the Democrats.[75] Because free trade was so central to the GOP's upper-income and business supporters, as well as to the party's ideology, a large majority of Republican members of Congress were predisposed to back NAFTA.

At the level of constituency-induced Republican preferences, support for NAFTA was particularly strong among GOP lawmakers from areas with high concentrations of export-oriented agricultural and high-technology production: the Sun Belt, the Plains states, the Mountain West, and the Pacific Coast. Most Republicans opposed to the pact, on the other hand, hailed from midwestern and northeastern industrial areas, southeastern textile states, or, at least until the end of the fight, Sun Belt citrus and vegetable-producing states whose industries and workers were likely to be hardest hit by the lowering of trade and investment barriers.

At the ideological level, the pro-NAFTA constituency influences felt by many Republicans were reinforced by their personal beliefs in free trade. On the other side of the issue, some anti-NAFTA House Republicans resisted the treaty for ideological as well as constituency-based reasons. Specifically, they shared the economic nationalist views championed by Pat Buchanan. In the fall of 1993 the former GOP presidential candidate continued to denounce NAFTA as a sellout of

American workers and a threat to U.S. sovereignty. At stake, Buchanan declared, was nothing less than "the character of the Republican Party and the conservative movement in the post–Cold War era." Republican free traders agreed. "In some ways this is a struggle for the heart and soul of the Republican Party," said NAFTA backer Senator John McCain of Arizona.[76]

Early in the fall of 1993, there were also four groups of wavering or undecided Republicans: (1) many of the forty-eight GOP freshmen and some thirty former supporters of the agreement, all of whom had been elected by narrow margins from districts where support for Ross Perot had been strong, (2) some representatives of industrial states who were pressed by organized labor, (3) those who balked at supporting the administration's NAFTA financing package, and (4) those who considered opposing NAFTA to prevent Clinton from winning a substantial political victory.[77]

House Minority Leader Robert Michel (R-Ill.) and Whip Newt Gingrich (R-Ga.) delayed their efforts to bring their wavering members into line until the president allayed their doubts about his commitment to NAFTA. By the end of the struggle, however, with Clinton and pro-trade House Democrats fighting hard for the pact's approval, the House Republican leadership was also working diligently and successfully to pull the GOP waverers and undecideds into the pro-NAFTA camp.

On the Democratic side, strong constituent opposition to NAFTA forced a majority of House Democrats to break with Clinton over the issue. And as with the Republicans, constituency-based cleavages over the agreement were amplified by ideological differences. Thus the divisions among congressional Democrats over NAFTA were severe.[78] Predictably, Democrats from northeastern and midwestern industrial areas with firm ties to organized labor tended to oppose the pact, whereas their colleagues from more competitive Sun Belt, Pacific Coast, and other regions where organized labor was weak were inclined to support it.

But this intra-Democratic split was also a manifestation of a deeper, decade-old divide within the party. The NAFTA fight was a new battle in the ongoing conflict over the restructuring of the American economy that was being forced by the dual processes of globalization and post-Fordist transition.[79] On one side, "old" Democrats, led by Whip David Bonior and less actively by Majority Leader Dick Gephardt, continued to try to slow and cushion the impact of these dislocating changes. Advocating an essentially neosocial-democratic reorganization of international trade, they called for improved protections of worker rights, the defense of independent union activity, and higher wages in those foreign countries with which the United States signed trade agreements. The aim was to help foreign workers while simultaneously reducing wage-based competitive threats to the jobs and incomes of American workers.

On the other side, the New Democrats sought to encourage growth and efficiency-inducing economic restructuring in order to reach out to business and the growing ranks of middle-class suburbanites, often employed in competitive high-tech industries, whose backing the party would need to retain its majority status.[80] "NAFTA recognizes the reality of today's economy—globalization and technology," said Senator John Kerry (D-Mass.).[81] Instead of rejecting trade liberalization, these moderate Democrats called for a range of education, training, and other programs to prepare workers to compete in the new economy.

The efforts of New Democratic NAFTA supporters in Congress and the White House were reinforced by those of the Democratic Leadership Council, which turned its back on the radical centrists it had once tried to court, siding instead with the business and upscale "moderate middle" supporters of the pact. While the DLC could unite with liberal Democrats behind attempts to pry open closed foreign markets, the organization stood four-square in support of NAFTA. DLC leaders thus saw the fight over the pact, in the words of executive director Al From, as a "battle for the heart of the Democratic Party."[82] The council launched its first corporate-backed, grassroots lobbying and communications effort on behalf of the pact.

NAFTA Supporters Carry the Day: The Role of Partisanship

By November 17, when the measure came up for a House vote, the pro-NAFTA forces had reversed the earlier course of the battle on three fronts. First, public opinion moved from solid opposition to the agreement in September to roughly an even split in mid-November.[83] Second, whereas mail and phone calls to Congress were running 100–1 against NAFTA through mid-October, thanks to the aggressive grassroots campaign waged by business and other NAFTA supporters toward the end of the fight, by the time of the House vote the mail was coming in equally heavily on both sides of the issue. This allowed NAFTA backers to influence the lawmakers' *perceptions* of the direction of public opinion. Finally, the pro-NAFTA forces were able to persuade at least some undecided or wavering House members that NAFTA was actually good policy.[84]

On the seventeenth NAFTA supporters claimed their hard-fought victory when the House voted to approve the treaty by the surprisingly wide margin of 234–200. (Three days later the Senate also passed the measure by a still more decisive vote of 61–38.) With real and perceived public opinion neutralized on the issue, members' votes on the pact were influenced by a range of constituency, ideological, and other factors.

The House vote did have a partisan character: Republicans backed the agreement 132–43, while Democrats opposed it 102–156.[85] But intraparty divisions, reflecting those discussed above as well as the expected incidence of the more narrow distributive benefits and costs of the pact, were also important, especially on the Democratic side. As in the 1991 fast-track vote, this intra-Democratic split was key to NAFTA's approval.

Based on the twenty-five roll-call analyses of the House vote that I have located, a number of conclusions can be drawn with respect to the role of partisanship.[86] For one thing, the 25 percent of House Republicans who voted against NAFTA (1) resided mostly in the Northeast or Southeast, although GOP support for the pact in both regions was still strong, (2) represented relatively blue-collar, low-income, or noncollege-educated constituencies that were disproportionately employed in import-sensitive industrial and agricultural sectors, or (3) were ideologically moderate to liberal. The 75 percent of GOP members who provided NAFTA its biggest bloc of support (1) hailed from all regions of the country, particularly the West and Midwest, (2) represented relatively white-collar, high-income, or college-educated constituencies that were employed in agricultural, high-tech, or export-dependent industries, (3) received substantial business PAC contributions and little labor PAC money, (4) were ideologically conservative, or (5) were successfully lobbied by the House Republican leadership.

Democratic opposition to NAFTA, comprising 60 percent of the Democratic caucus, was concentrated among party members who (1) came from the industrial Northeast and Midwest, (2) had strong backing from organized labor, both electoral and especially financial,[87] (3) were ideologically liberal, and (4) represented districts in states that gave Clinton strong support in 1992. Conversely, the 40 percent of House Democrats whose support for NAFTA provided the crucial margin of victory for the agreement generally (1) hailed from the Pacific Coast and the Sun Belt, particularly the nonsoutheastern South, (2) received at least as much funding from business as from labor PACs (with the rise in the business share of House Democrats' total PAC receipts from 41 to 54 percent between 1982 and 1992 and the corresponding decline of labor's share from 43 to 33 percent,[88] the number of these business-dependent Democratic lawmakers had expanded substantially),[89] (3) were ideologically moderate to conservative, and (4) were elected from districts in states in which Clinton had fared poorly in 1992.[90]

Also important in winning support for NAFTA from about fifty undecided and wavering Democrats were Bill Clinton's lobbying efforts.[91] Many of these Democrats were southerners who may have faced constituency pressures to oppose NAFTA, but who were also responsive to appeals from Clinton as a fellow southerner, especially on an issue that was compatible with their own and moderate or conservative leanings.[92] Several major quantitative studies of presidential influence on Congress have concluded that the president has only a marginal impact on congressional decision-making. The president's bargaining and persuasive skills are said to be less important than the partisan and ideological makeup of Congress or the president's public approval ratings.[93] But on issues that the president cares most about, he can influence Congress's behavior. Clinton came to care intensely about NAFTA, and his lobbying of Democrats on the issue was correspondingly effective.[94]

Although Clinton was opposed by 60 percent of House Democrats, his success in winning over many of his fellow party members suggests that central to NAFTA's victory was the return to unified government following the 1992 election. Had George Bush been reelected, he almost certainly would have been unable to win enough Democratic support for the agreement to ensure its approval. With Bush still in office, some of the ambivalent or cross-pressured Democrats who rallied to Clinton's side at the end of the fight out of loyalty to a Democratic president would have had less reason to risk a loss of their own political support by backing the agreement. Other Democrats might have voted against NAFTA with the hope of exploiting Republican backing of the accord, which remained unpopular among key swing constituencies, in the 1994 congressional or 1996 presidential elections. In either case, USTR Mickey Kantor was probably right when he said that "George Bush could never have passed NAFTA. No Republican President could have, because he couldn't have brought [along] enough Democrats."[95]

Clinton Gets Tough with Japan: Act 2

Immediately on the heels of his dramatic NAFTA victory, Bill Clinton completed what White House officials touted as a November–December free-trade "triple play." Signaling his interest in expanding U.S. trade with the booming economies of Asia, Clinton, on November 20, hosted a meeting in Seattle of the leaders of the fifteen member nations of the Asia-Pacific Economic Cooperation forum. Then in mid-December, the Uruguay Round GATT negotiations were successfully concluded. The administration also began to aggressively implement its new "National Export Strategy," including a sweeping rollback of export controls on high-tech equipment and a major Commerce Department–led effort to help U.S. firms penetrate the so-called Big Emerging Markets. By the end of 1993, Clinton's export-led growth strategy was in full swing.

In early 1994, though, administration trade officials refocused their energies on an old problem—Japan's closed markets. In the seven months that followed the July 1993 signing of the framework agreement between the United States and Japan, negotiations between the two countries did not go well. With the new government of Prime Minister Morihiro Hosokawa preoccupied with political reform, the Japanese economy mired in a persistent slump, and with corporate profits being hammered by the strong yen, Tokyo was in no mood to expose its manufacturers to a wave of imports.

Faced with Japanese intransigence, and with the U.S.-Japan trade gap having risen 20 percent in 1993, the Clinton administration once again turned up the heat on Tokyo. On the eve of a February 11 trade summit between Clinton and Hosokawa, USTR Mickey Kantor suspended the negotiations between the two nations to signal the United States's displeasure with the pace of the talks and to put maximum pressure on Tokyo to make concessions. Five days later, U.S. officials elevated an existing dispute by declaring that Tokyo had violated a 1989 deal promising Motorola access to the Japanese cellular telephone market.

On March 3 Clinton signed an executive order reinstating a weakened version of the Super 301 provision of the 1988 Trade Act. Kantor said that on March 31 the White House would issue a preliminary list of what it considered unacceptable foreign trade barriers and would follow up by September 30 with a final list subject to investigation under 301 rules. If the investigation revealed that the trade barriers had not been lifted, sanctions could be imposed.

The administration's hardened stance toward Japan can be explained by a number of factors. Most immediately, Clinton and other U.S. officials had simply lost patience with Tokyo. But political considerations also underlaid the administration's renewed toughness. Clinton sought to preserve his credibility with export interests, which worried that he might be losing his nerve in the gradually escalating test of wills with Japan.[96] More important, though, Clinton was attempting to heal the wounds opened within the Democratic Party by the bitter NAFTA fight.

During the fight over the pact, Clinton built social and congressional coalitions unlike those that he had previously relied on. At the societal level, Clinton aligned himself with the business and moderate middle beneficiaries of globalization and post-Fordist transition, most of whom had not supported him in the 1992 election.[97] At the congressional level, Clinton similarly found support for NAFTA mainly among members from centrist and Sun Belt districts that had provided him little previous electoral or legislative backing. Meanwhile, liberal members from traditional Democratic strongholds that were critical both to Clinton's election and to his earlier legislative victories opposed the pact.[98]

The question following the NAFTA fight was whether Clinton was going to try to further burnish his centrist, New Democrat credentials, return to a more partisan advocacy of liberal policies, or try to find continued legislative success through the construction of a series of ad hoc, issue-by-issue coalitions.[99] In fact, Clinton continued to triangulate between the two major wings of his party, which in early 1994 meant tacking toward the populist faction. Organized labor and its liberal Democratic congressional sympathizers had been deeply affronted by Clinton's energetic and successful campaign on behalf of NAFTA, and especially by his sharp criticism of the movement's tactics at the end of the struggle. Labor was also angry at the moderate congressional Democrats who voted for the pact. Immediately after the NAFTA vote, the AFL-CIO decided to cut off all financial support to Democratic campaign committees for at least the next three months. A number of individual labor leaders vowed to withdraw financial support from, and in some cases to back primary challenges to, Democrats who had voted for the agreement.[100] Although these labor leaders eventually backed off from their threats of retaliation, unwilling to break with the Democrats and sacrifice their broad agenda for NAFTA alone,[101] in early 1995 the Clinton administration could not be certain of labor's continuing support. Beyond this, though Clinton's overall popularity had rebounded after the NAFTA fight, as the president's more moderate advisers had hoped would be the case, it had declined among blue-collar workers and Perot supporters.

In early 1994 Clinton's more liberal political advisers persuaded him to make a top priority of mending his relations with organized labor, blue-collar workers more generally, and the liberal Democratic congressional majority. Toward this end, with Labor Secretary Robert Reich as the prime mover, Clinton proposed a modest "economic security system" for the nation's working people and their families.[102] Most important, he recommended a universal lifetime health insurance program, a principal concern of labor for decades.

In the area of trade policy, Clinton triangulated to the left as well, which in early 1994 meant getting tougher with Japan. The administration's more aggressive posture was intended first of all to quiet organized labor's anger with the president and those congressional Democrats who had voted for NAFTA. The goal here was to keep labor in the Democratic fold in the 1994 congressional and 1996 presidential election campaigns. USTR Mickey Kantor was particularly hopeful that new pressure on Tokyo would help make peace with union leaders. Secondarily, Clinton remained convinced that a tough stance toward Japan was also favored by key groups of swing voters, including Reagan Democrats and Perot backers.[103]

Clinton also turned up the heat on Japan in response to demands from liberal and labor-backed congressional Democratic trade hawks, although with a Democrat in the White House, this pressure was less intense than had been the case during the Reagan-Bush era. Clinton's tougher stance toward Tokyo, including his reinstatement of a moderate version of the original Super 301 law, was intended in part to preempt passage of Democratic-sponsored market-opening legislation.[104] But in addition, Clinton needed to appease powerful congressional Democrats who had opposed him on NAFTA, but whose loyalty was required in an uphill battle for his domestic legislative agenda, notably health care reform.[105]

Clinton Reverses Course: The Power of the Financial Markets

No sooner had the administration escalated its trade conflict with Japan than it surprisingly appeared to reverse course. In late March 1994, under the recently renewed Super 301 law, the White House released its list of countries erecting egregious trade barriers, singling out Japan as the worst offender. But administration officials said they were not, for the moment, contemplating any new sanctions against Tokyo. Two months later, the two countries decided to resume their stalled trade talks after the Clinton administration agreed in writing not to demand that Japan set specific numerical import goals for a number of products. During the subsequent negotiations, the United States gave up on slashing Japan's $121 billion global trade surplus, focusing instead on opening markets sector by sector.

What explains this rapid softening of the U.S. position toward Japan? Although a number of factors were at work, the most important were international economic structural constraints. First, the growing interdependence between the American and Japanese economies prompted some U.S.-based multinational corporations, especially those involved in complex alliances with Japanese firms and companies dependent on the import of intermediate goods from Japan, to urge the White House to deescalate the conflict between the two countries.[106]

Second, and more important, was the role played by world financial markets.[107] During the last twenty or so years, it has become widely recognized that the growing interrelationship between the international foreign exchange market and national bond markets has constrained the autonomy of states in the conduct of their monetary policies by limiting their ability to raise and lower interest rates in response to purely domestic conditions. Less well understood is the way global financial market volatility can constrain a nation's trade policy. It did so in the spring of 1994, when the threat of a trade war between the United States and Japan led to a plunge in the value of the dollar relative to the yen, as currency speculators and investors assumed that Washington sought a yen appreciation to punish Tokyo for its intransigent opposition to opening its markets. The result was higher inflation and interest rates and a bond market collapse in the United States at a time when the White House was already forecasting an economic slowdown that could adversely affect Clinton's re-election prospects.

As Thomas Friedman of the *New York Times* aptly put it, the Clinton administration discovered that its get-tough policy toward Japan "played well on Main Street but bombed on Wall Street." Consequently, the White House and the Treasury Department pressed for a cooling of the dispute, with Deputy Treasury Secretary Roger Altman at one point warning a hawkish Mickey Kantor that "if the market turns against you, it will squash you like a bug." Kantor himself finally came around to this point of view. "Mickey is finally starting to get the message that he can't keep up this yowling on trade and not expect an impact on interest rates and exchange rates," said a top Clinton adviser.[108]

On October 1 a modest deal was struck with Japan. But little progress was made on the most important issue—automobiles and auto parts, which accounted for nearly two-thirds of the $60 billion U.S. trade deficit with Japan— even though mostly Democratic auto industry supporters in Congress had pressured the White House to take a hard line on this front. With midterm congressional elections looming, administration officials were unwilling to risk setting off another financial crisis, choosing instead to claim some political credit for the modest concessions they had actually won.[109]

Ratifying the Uruguay Round GATT Accord

During much of 1994, while Clinton was engaged in his bilateral dispute with Japan, he also pursued further multilateral trade liberalization via the implementation of the Uruguay Round GATT accord, concluded in mid-December of the previous year. This was not simply a case of the president tacking back toward support for New Democratic constituencies and policies. Rather, he *simultaneously* tried to triangulate between the two major wings of his party by pushing *both* for the treaty's approval *and* for the inclusion in the implementing bill of a long-term extension of fast-track procedures that required the principal negotiating objectives of future trade talks to include the protection of workers' rights and the environment, key elements of the "new trade agenda."

The level of partisanship varied across different parts of the implementing bill as it passed through the "non-markup" process, but it was probably highest over the proposed renewal of Clinton's fast-track authority. Intense business and Republican opposition to the proposal and the refusal by labor and its congressional Democratic allies to back a watered-down alternative eventually led the White House to abandon its fast-track plan. With labor now largely standing on the sidelines, following a series of mostly Republican tactical maneuvers, Clinton finally won approval of the GATT accord, this time with big bipartisan majorities in both the House and the Senate.

Concluding the Round and Sparring Over the Implementing Legislation

The Uruguay Round, of course, was not Bill Clinton's initiative; rather, it was Republican-inspired. The negotiations had begun and most of the tough issues had been resolved during the Reagan and Bush administrations, although the talks had bogged down as Bush left office. Despite these origins, Clinton was pledged to finishing up the negotiations. Initially he tried to jump-start the flagging talks by asking Congress to extend his fast-track negotiating authority through December 15, 1993. Organized labor and environmental groups were critical of the proposed extension, but congressional Democratic opposition was muted by the narrowness of the proposal and by a concern to avoid undermining a Democratic president.[110] In late June the fast-track bill passed both chambers by comfortable bipartisan majorities, although a substantial number of House Democrats did oppose the measure.

Clinton's effort to prod the GATT talks along worked. At the Tokyo economic summit in early July, the leaders of the G-7 industrialized nations agreed to new cuts in tariffs on industrial goods. Then, in mid-December in Brussels, Washington was finally able to reach agreement with its trading partners on a new GATT treaty after a flurry of last-minute negotiations. Among other provisions, the sweeping accord cut industrial tariffs, brought agriculture under GATT for the first time, provided protection for trade-related intellectual property rights, established new rules to govern trade in services, and replaced the GATT with a new, more powerful World Trade Organization (WTO).[111]

Unlike NAFTA, the GATT accord produced little controversy in the United States, mainly because its economic effects were generally viewed as being more evenly spread across income groups than were those of NAFTA.[112] For instance, House Majority Leader Dick Gephardt, a leading opponent of NAFTA, endorsed the GATT deal within a week of its signing. Over the first eight months of 1994, however, negotiations on the implementing legislation between the USTR and Capitol Hill proceeded fitfully, and a final draft of the measure was not actually submitted to Congress until September 27. During this period White House and congressional negotiators grappled with a number of significant provisions of the implementing bill, generating varying patterns of party competition.

The contentious issue of dumping was resolved in a bipartisan manner that largely favored import-competing firms. The matter of industrial subsidies initially produced a sharper partisan division, as Republican senators worried that in agreeing to loosen the rules allowing nations to subsidize private sector research and development (R&D), Clinton was trying to solidify his allegiances with the politically powerful high-tech community. The issue was resolved with language that narrowly defined which subsidies were acceptable.[113]

Party conflict also emerged over the financing of the new GATT agreement. Initial White House proposals to raise taxes to pay for the accord were met by Republican attempts to tar the administration in an election year with the tax-and-spend label. The administration finally offered a compromise plan.

It was the Clinton administration's proposed extension of fast-track procedures that provoked the sharpest partisan conflict, one that would periodically resurface in subsequent years. The focus of controversy was White House efforts to include the protection of workers' rights and the environment as principal negotiating objectives in future trade talks.[114]

In the first half of 1994, as part of its wider move to triangulate back toward, or to make amends with, the liberal-labor wing of the Democratic Party that had been aggrieved by Clinton's strong support for NAFTA, the administration undertook a two-pronged initiative to integrate labor and environmental standards into the conduct of international trade policy.[115] First, it launched a drive to put labor standards, along with the environment and other issues, high on the agenda of the new WTO. More important, in mid-June the White House unveiled a proposed seven-year extension of fast-track procedures, which it sought to incorporate into the GATT implementing bill to facilitate the launch of negotiations on a Free Trade Area of the Americas at a December summit in Miami. Now, though, hoping to appease its free trade critics, the White House made labor and environmental standards two of its seven main trade negotiating objectives. While the administration attempted to steer down the middle with its fast-track proposal, business and its GOP allies reacted strongly against the White House's new push on labor and the environment.

Ideological and constituency-based influences were responsible for some of the partisan differences over issues in the implementing bill. But these were amplified by the broader sparring between the parties that emerged as the 1994 midterm elections approached. With Clinton's top political priority—health care reform—faltering under business and Republican attacks by the summer of 1994, White House officials began to view approval of the GATT accord as something the administration could claim credit for before the fall elections. Conversely, congressional Republicans sought to deprive Clinton and pro-GATT Democrats of another trade policy triumph. "Republicans may not want to hand the President another win before the election," a House staff aide said.[116]

But despite their posturing, most Republicans remained supportive of free trade in general and the GATT accord in particular. As an out party, however, the GOP sought to use criticisms of the agreement to undermine support for the party in control of the executive branch, as incumbency-focused theories of trade policy suggest.[117]

After two weeks of formal deliberations, on August 2 the Senate Finance Committee gave tentative approval to an implementation bill, but the panel left out several provisions sought by the White House. Most important, committee chairman Daniel Patrick Moynihan (D-N.Y.)—caught between business and labor—dropped the extension of fast-track negotiating authority.

The House Ways and Means Committee completed its own work on the implementing legislation on August 17. In a compromise brokered by the administration that angered House liberals, the committee agreed to a three-year extension of fast-track rules while removing language pertaining to labor and environmental standards.

Despite his best efforts during the next month, USTR Mickey Kantor was unable to develop a fast-track compromise that was acceptable to both business-oriented Republicans and labor-backed Democrats. With the stalemate threatening to stall the implementing legislation, on September 13 the administration announced that it would drop the fast-track extension in exchange for commitments from the Finance and Ways and Means Committee chairmen that Congress would take up a fast-track renewal bill in early 1995. Thus, intracongressional partisan polarization resulted in gridlock over the fast-track issue.[118]

With the major obstacle to a compromise removed, members of the "mock" House and Senate conference announced on September 20 that they had reached agreement on the draft GATT bill. A week later Clinton submitted the final version of the draft to Congress.

The GATT Battle Is Joined, and the Parties Appear to Reverse Sides

For over a year Clinton had considered the GATT accord to be a central element of his export-led growth strategy and thus also of his reelection strategy. Now, however, the agreement assumed even greater, short-term political importance. With the collapse of his prized health care reform plan in September under the weight of withering new Republican attacks on him as a tax-and-spend liberal, Clinton was badly in need of another major New Democrat–style legislative success that he could claim for himself and for Democratic incumbents running in the November elections. For that reason, the president began to tout GATT as a big generator of jobs, income, and profits.[119] White House lobbying of Congress on behalf of the accord escalated.

As on NAFTA, the administration's lobbying efforts were closely coordinated with those of the business community, which under the umbrella of the Alliance for GATT NOW almost monolithically backed the deal.[120] The opposition to the pact on the left was spearheaded by the Citizens Trade Campaign and included Ralph Nader's Public Citizen, organized labor, environmental groups, liberal religious groups, and populist farm organizations. Various conservative individuals and organizations, including Pat Buchanan, Senator Jesse Helms (R-N.C.), and the U.S. Business and Industrial Council also opposed the treaty, fearing that the new World Trade Organization would infringe on American "sovereignty." Ross Perot and his United We Stand organization were against the deal as well.[121]

Yet both support for and opposition to the Uruguay Round agreement was not nearly as vocal as had been the case on NAFTA. Business found the benefits from the treaty to be fairly modest, while the predominantly general rather than income-group-specific effects of the agreement resulted in less opposition from the left than had been true of NAFTA, which labor and other critics feared would produce a devastating flight of capital to Mexico. Instead, the strongest opposition to the treaty actually came from the nationalist right.[122]

As the fight over GATT entered the home stretch in late September and early October, some members of both congressional parties assumed surprising stances on the agreement.[123] If only briefly and partially, and especially on the GOP side mostly for tactical or incumbency-focused reasons, the parties actually seemed to be reversing their recent positions and reverting to their pre-1930s views, with Democrats supporting the accord and Republicans at least threatening to oppose it.

It is true that some Rust Belt Democrats simply rejected the GATT deal outright. Others, fearful of offending labor shortly before the midterm elections, called for a delay of the vote. But the congressional Democratic leadership and other party members, including traditional trade hawks like Dick Gephardt, strongly supported both the GATT accord and an early vote on it. Facing little labor or other opposition, they accepted Clinton's position that the agreement would expand market opportunities for U.S. exporters and create many new jobs for American workers.

On the other side of the aisle, many Republican free traders with ties to internationally oriented business interests continued to give strong support to the GATT agreement. But other, often younger, rank-and-file GOP members, influenced by the ideas of Pat Buchanan and Ross Perot or elected with the support of Buchanan and Perot backers, opposed the accord.

Still other Republicans, while remaining committed to the principle of free trade, sought for various reasons to delay voting on the GATT deal. Some GOP leaders did not want to jeopardize the party's increasingly good chances of taking control of both houses of Congress by having their members forced to cast a vote for free trade that might alienate Buchanan and Perot supporters before the elections. In addition, sensing victory at the polls, Republican leaders in both houses increased their obstructionism as they sought to deny Clinton and congressional Democrats any politically useful legislative successes. "There are a bunch of Republicans who would just as soon not give a victory to the president," said Jim Kolbe (R-Ariz.).[124]

In the end, stymied by election-year politics, and despite objections from and intensified lobbying by pro-GATT business interests, the House Democratic leadership on October 5 decided to postpone a vote on the agreement until after the November elections to prevent an embarrassing setback for President Clinton and Democratic supporters of the accord.

After the Elections: House Republicans Cease Their Maneuvering, Bob Dole Does Some of His Own, and the Agreement Is Finally Approved

On November 8 the Republicans won a stunning electoral victory, taking control of both houses of Congress for the first time in forty years. Some observers argued that trade policy per se, including popular opposition to either the NAFTA or GATT agreements, did not play much of a role in producing the GOP takeover.[125] But polls suggested that a not insignificant fraction of Republican voters had doubts about the value of free trade in general and the GATT deal in particular. And many Republicans were convinced that they triumphed because they finally had won over white, noncollege-educated males whose incomes had stagnated during the previous decade, due at least in part to the downward pressure exerted on wages by cheap foreign imports.[126]

Whatever the precise contribution of trade issues to the GOP victory, a new crop of "America First" Republicans was swept into office, especially from southern textile states. With the fate of the GATT accord in increasingly nationalist Republican hands, free traders were worried.

As it happened, with the elections behind them, House Republican leaders largely ceased their tactical maneuvering against the GATT treaty, fearful of being blamed for a GOP-led gridlock. Instead, Republican opposition to, or at least reservations about, the agreement were concentrated in the Senate, where the leading GOP waffler was the unlikely Robert Dole, the soon-to-be majority leader from Kansas.[127] Dole worried that backing the WTO would damage his presidential prospects among conservative nationalists and that supporting the budget waiver necessary to finance the pact would leave him vulnerable to attacks for being soft on the deficit by his then leading opponent for the nomination, Senator Phil Gramm of Texas. After frantic lobbying by internationally oriented business interests, Dole finally came around, clearing the way for both houses of Congress to approve the GATT accord.

On November 29 the House overwhelmingly passed the agreement by a bipartisan vote of 288–146. Republicans supported the deal by a 121–56 margin, while Democrats backed it 167–89. Two days later the Senate also passed the agreement by a much wider bipartisan margin than expected, 76–24. Three-quarters of the senators from each party backed the GATT deal.

On the Democratic side, some liberal and labor-oriented representatives and senators predictably opposed the GATT accord.[128] Along with other Democratic activists, they worried that Clinton's support for the pact and other free-trade initiatives were hurting their party with noncollege-educated, working-class voters who had deserted the Democrats in the November election or who had not voted at all.[129] But with much of organized labor on the sidelines during the fight, most Democrats, including many who had previously sided with labor on NAFTA and other trade issues, accepted the Clinton administration's promises of booming U.S. export and job growth resulting from the GATT pact.[130]

On the GOP side, where opposition to GATT had been stronger, some members in both houses did vote against the pact due either to constituent pressures, economic nationalist ideological commitments, or a desire to score political points against a Democratic president.[131] But a number of factors combined to limit the number of Republicans who rejected the agreement to embarrass Bill Clinton.

First, traditional GOP free traders sided with Clinton because they agreed with him on the merits of the pact. Second, other Republicans were persuaded by business and other GATT supporters that the defeat of the accord would send shock waves through U.S. and world financial markets. Third, despite its late and poorly organized start, the business community was fully mobilized in support of the pact by the end of the fight. Fearing the loss of vital campaign contributions, many Republicans who had flirted with opposing the agreement or further delaying the vote on it were whipped back into line by this pressure from their core business supporters.[132] Finally, GOP leaders worried that should the GATT deal be defeated, their party would be blamed by the voters for perpetuating gridlock rather than applauded for embarking on a new era of accomplishment.

Thus, almost exactly a year after his hard-fought NAFTA victory, Clinton won yet another major free-trade battle. This second triumph came more easily than the first. Apparent opposition to the GATT accord among many normally free-trading Republicans had been more tactical than substantive in nature. For the most part, GOP members sought not to kill the pact but rather to delay a vote on it until after the November elections. Across the aisle, the limited mobilization by organized labor against the pact allowed normally protectionist-minded congressional Democrats to support it. Lobbying by Clinton and White House officials also won over some wavering Democrats. Had George Bush still been in office in 1994 presiding over a divided government, he would have had more trouble gaining the Democratic votes needed to approve the deal.[133]

During the first two years of his presidency, a new period of unified Democratic government, Bill Clinton pursued his export-led growth strategy by systematically triangulating on trade policy, alternately getting tough with Japan and pushing for congressional approval of free-trade agreements. This resulted in trade policies that were simultaneously more aggressive and more facilitative of trade liberalization than the policies pursued under divided government by Republicans Ronald Reagan and George Bush or that a second Bush administration would have been able to pursue had he been reelected. Clinton's results-oriented Japan policy was tougher than his GOP predecessors'—at least until financial market constraints and other factors forced Clinton to back off from his confrontation with Tokyo. At the same time, backed by business and New Democrats, Clinton was able to secure approval of the NAFTA agreement by winning the support of a crucial bloc of congressional Democrats. George Bush, facing a more hostile Democratic Congress, would likely have failed in this endeavor. It is even possible that Bush would have been unable to get the GATT treaty through a Democrat-controlled Congress.

How, then, can we say that parties mattered to the conduct of U.S. trade policy in the transition between the Republican-led divided governments of the Reagan and Bush years and the unified Democratic government of Clinton's first two years in office? The answer to this question lies in recognizing that policy choices depend not only on whether control of government is unified or divided, but also on the configuration of a range of other factors, the most important of which, of course, are the preferences of the president and members of the congressional parties.

The decisive factor that explains the Clinton administration's somewhat contradictory Japan and NAFTA/GATT positions is Bill Clinton's personal and induced preferences. On the one hand, and contrary to the views of those analysts who see presidents of both parties as unadulterated free traders, Clinton pursued a tough market-opening stance toward Japan. This was because (1) he accepted the revisionist argument that Japan was a different kind of industrial power, and (2) he hoped to strengthen his position with organized labor and other working-class, radical centrist voters and key export-dependent business interests. On the other hand, Clinton fought for approval of the NAFTA and GATT agreements (while also backing labor and environmental measures opposed by Republicans) due to his essential ideological commitment to free trade, his institutional position representing a large national constituency, and his concern to expand his support among moderate middle voters and the most internationally oriented sectors of the business community.

Of course, Clinton's actual success in these free-trade battles depended on the size and preferences of the congressional party caucuses and, at least in the case of NAFTA, on the ability of Clinton, aided by the efforts of internationally oriented business interests and New Democrats, to convince enough Democratic lawmakers to join with more free-trade-inclined Republicans to approve the agreement. In fact, the NAFTA fight continued a pattern, begun in the 1991 fast-track controversy and persisting throughout Clinton's presidency, in which, with two-thirds to three-quarters of House Republicans consistently supportive of free trade, the outcomes of a series of subsequent trade liberalization battles—over the GATT agreement, two more fast-track proposals, and

PNTR with China—were largely determined by the shifting preferences and internal cohesion of House Democrats.

During Clinton's first two years in office, then, years of Democratic-led unified government, Clinton's preferences, in interaction with those of the congressional parties, produced trade policies that differed in significant ways from those pursued by his predecessors under Republican-led divided governments.

Trade Liberalization Grinds to a Halt, 1995–1998

Following the successful fight to approve the Uruguay Round GATT accord, the White House continued to vigorously pursue its export-led growth strategy, both to regain the political initiative after the humbling November elections and to boost Bill Clinton's reelection prospects. At a mid-November summit in Indonesia, the eighteen members of the booming Asia-Pacific Economic Cooperation forum (APEC) agreed to establish a free-trade and investment area by 2020. A few weeks later, a hemispheric Summit of the Americas was held in Miami to launch negotiations on the expansion of NAFTA into a Free Trade Area of the Americas.

Although the White House would go on to conclude a number of global market-opening deals in telecommunications, financial services, and information technology during the next several years, Clinton's success in the GATT fight would be his last major free-trade victory until the fight over China's entry into the World Trade Organization (WTO) in the last year of his presidency. The Republican takeover of Congress in the 1994 midterm elections and the return to an "inverted" form of divided government might have been expected to strengthen support for free trade, but initially this was not the case.

To be sure, there was no reversion to old-fashioned, product-specific protectionism. With the major exception of the steel industry, protectionist pressures generally subsided or were contained during the 1990s because

1. the trade deficit first declined as a proportion of national income, and when it increased again to near-record levels by the end of the decade, due to a rising dollar and faster growth in the United States than abroad, the econ-

omy was so strong and unemployment so low that the trade gap did not cause as much pain as it had in the 1980s;

2. American exporters and multinational companies continued to expand and to geographically diffuse across the United States, including into once solidly protectionist areas like the Northeast, the industrial heartland, and the southeastern textile states;

3. protectionist firms in industries like textiles, automobiles, and steel had either declined in economic and political strength or had responded to diminished possibilities for winning protection by opting for alternative strategies of domestic adjustment or the foreign sourcing or off-shoring of production; and

4. the establishment of foreign-owned "transplants" inside the U.S. market had rendered protectionism a less viable strategy for domestically oriented American firms.[1]

What suffered in the period from 1995 to 1998, however, was the process of regional and multilateral trade liberalization, which ground to a halt for mostly party-related reasons.[2]

In 1995–96, looking toward the upcoming presidential election, the White House was concerned with recapturing the backing of those economic nationalist working-class Democrats and Perot backers who, disgusted by Clinton's strong support for the NAFTA and GATT accords, had either sat out the 1994 elections or had voted for Republican candidates. Thus, rather than push for new fast-track authority to permit Clinton to negotiate new free-trade agreements, in the spring of 1995 the administration escalated the bilateral dispute with Japan over autos and auto parts, although it soon backed off from that confrontation. Then, after failed negotiations over a Republican fast-track proposal, the White House postponed further trade liberalization efforts until after the election to avoid alienating labor and environmental interests. Instead, it took a number of trade-restrictive actions as well as new steps to combat unfair foreign trade practices. Both types of actions were intended to secure the support of various targeted electoral constituencies and to ward off criticism of Clinton's trade policies from Republican presidential candidate Bob Dole.

With his reelection safely secured, Clinton tried to restart the trade liberalization process with Republican support, but his efforts were blocked mainly by Democratic opposition. Under intense pressure from organized labor, which massively mobilized on behalf of Democratic candidates in the 1996 and 1998 elections, and backed by a core of conservative Republican nationalists, congressional Democrats overwhelmingly and successfully opposed fast-track renewal bills in late 1997 and the fall of 1998 that contained inadequate commitments to the inclusion of strong international labor and environmental standards in any new free-trade agreements.

Japan—Act 3: Fighting over Autos

In early 1995 it appeared that Japan was no longer central to the Clinton administration's market-opening strategy. The White House had tired of two relatively unproductive years of fighting with that country over trade issues and consequently was not inclined to draw attention to the U.S.-Japan trade gap by picking a new fight with Tokyo. Administration officials worried that they would be unable to bring the bilateral deficit down much by the 1996 presidential election.

In the spring of 1995, however, the focus of U.S. trade policy shifted back to Japan. U.S. officials were fuming at Tokyo's refusal to budge in the recent talks on auto and auto parts trade that the Japanese had invited the United States to resume at the end of 1994. After twenty months of fruitless negotiations, cars and auto parts still accounted for nearly 60 percent of Tokyo's $66 billion trade surplus with the United States. The biggest sticking point was Japan's unwillingness to increase U.S. auto part purchases by a specific amount.

In mid-April the White House decided to warn Tokyo that it would move to impose several billion dollars in punitive sanctions unless major progress was made in the next three weeks in opening Japan's auto and auto parts markets. A month later the administration lived up to its threat by placing a 100 percent tariff, the largest ever imposed by the United States against any trading partner, on thirteen Japanese luxury car models that had accounted for $5.9 billion in sales in the United States in 1994. Administration officials also said, however, that the sanctions would be rescinded if Tokyo and Washington could reach an accord by June 28.

Why did the Clinton administration choose to renew this conflict, especially at a time when it had been widely observed that U.S. productivity and competitiveness had been revitalized, whereas Japan's economy was in a deepening crisis? A number of factors were at work. First, revisionist thinking was still influential among key administration officials, including U.S. Trade Representative (USTR) Mickey Kantor and even to a certain degree Robert Rubin, who had replaced Lloyd Bentsen, an opponent of large-scale retaliation against Japan, as Treasury secretary. Second, support from at least some U.S. business interests for pressure on Japan to open its markets remained strong. The Big Three auto companies were particularly active in helping to develop and line up political support for the U.S. position.[3]

Most important in explaining the administration's tough stance in the auto fight was the White House's concern to (1) consolidate its political support among core Democratic constituencies, especially unionized industrial workers, (2) win the backing of key swing voters, notably Reagan Democrats and Perot supporters, and (3) defuse problems in its relations with liberal congressional Democrats.

Many analysts have argued that following the devastating congressional midterm elections in 1994, Bill Clinton quickly shifted back to the political center. This is not quite true. After an intense intra-Democratic debate, what emerged, at least through the first half of 1995, was not an unqualified shift to the center, but rather a synthetic approach that mixed both liberal and moderate initiatives. It was only in June 1995, when Clinton embraced the Republican call for a balanced budget, that his move to the center became clear.

During the postelection debate, New Democrats and other moderates, including the operatives of the Democratic Leadership Council (DLC) and top Clinton policy advisers, argued that middle-class independents and other swing voters had turned against the Democrats largely because, although Clinton had been elected as a New Democrat, he had governed as a cultural and tax-and-spend liberal. The moderates correspondingly called for Clinton to shift back to the center.[4]

On the other hand, liberal or "populist" Democrats, as they were termed, prominently including Labor Secretary Robert Reich and Clinton's political advisers, told a competing story. Noting that moderate members of the DLC-linked Mainstream Forum lost at higher rates than did the rest of the House, the liberals argued that the Democrats' problems were principally ones of performance, not ideology. In 1992 downscale, noncollege-educated, working- and lower-middle-class radical centrists, a key swing group, had voted for Clinton and especially Ross Perot because their wages had stagnated or even declined during George Bush's presidency. In 1994 these same members of what Reich called the "anxious class" turned against the Democrats, now in control of both branches of government, when the party was judged to have failed to raise living standards.[5]

The populists argued as well that in 1994 the Republicans also benefited from a low turnout of the Democrats' demoralized base of poor and working-class voters, including union members disillusioned by Clinton's aggressive support for the NAFTA and GATT agreements and the failure of health care reform.[6] In the 1992 presidential and congressional elections, exit polls showed that 19 percent of the electorate was from union households. Two years later, as discouraged union activists largely sat on the sidelines, the union share of the turnout had dropped to only 14 percent. The populists concluded that to reverse such trends among both core Democratic and swing voters, Clinton would have to use government power more aggressively to raise wages and living standards.

Pressure on Clinton to move left was intense from liberal congressional Democrats, whose strength had increased due to the November defeat of a number of southern moderates and conservatives.[7] Beyond this, the liberalism of this group had been heightened following the election when business political action committees (PACs), seeking influence with the new GOP-controlled Congress, shifted some of their campaign contributions from the Democrats to the Republicans. This left congressional Democrats relatively more dependent on organized labor and other liberal groups for campaign financing.[8] Markedly vocal at this time was House Minority Leader Dick Gephardt, who gave a series of speeches simultaneously intended to push the president toward a populist agenda, develop an independent platform for congressional Democrats to run on in 1996, and keep his own presidential options open.[9]

During the first half of 1995, President Clinton attempted to synthesize or triangulate between New Democratic and populist strategies as he sought to find what he called the "dynamic center" of American politics. On the one hand, reflecting New Democrat concerns, he called for a bipartisan approach to solving the nation's problems, spoke of values and the need for community, and pressed for welfare reform and new "reinventing government" initiatives. On the other hand, to appeal to the Democratic base, especially organized labor, and head off a primary challenge from Gephardt, Jesse Jackson, or another liberal Democrat, Clinton called for a hike in the minimum wage, issued an executive order prohibiting federal contractors from permanently replacing striking workers, and promised to veto any GOP-passed measure to weaken the Davis-Bacon Act, which boosted wages on government contracts.[10] Finally, the White House promoted a number of what it referred to as "web issues"—a middle-class tax cut, education, job training, and crime fighting—that it believed could appeal to both core Democratic constituencies and the middle class.

Political Benefits and Easing Constraints

In May 1995 USTR Mickey Kantor and political adviser Dick Morris persuaded Bill Clinton that the U.S.-Japan auto conflict could be another such web issue, capable of uniting both core Democratic and radical centrist swing voters, while appeasing the concerns of liberal congressional Democrats.[11] The showdown with Tokyo had the additional advantage of allowing Clinton to appear strong at a time when he had little chance of moving an agenda through the GOP-controlled Congress. It was this political utility of the issue that mainly explains why his administration cranked up the auto dispute in the spring of 1995.

White House officials were particularly hopeful, as John F. Harris of the *Washington Post* reported, that "the tough stance with Japan [would] shore up Clinton's support with organized labor, a crucial part of the Democratic coalition." The Democrats in 1994 had suffered serious losses in the industrial heartland, especially in the auto states of Michigan, Missouri, and Ohio.[12] Some administration officials believed that this was because many workers who had been angered by Clinton and some Democrats' approval of NAFTA had either voted Republican or stayed home and perhaps also because the AFL-CIO had withheld its endorsement of some incumbent Democratic NAFTA supporters.[13] With his backing in the South disintegrating, Clinton had no hope of reelection unless he could firm up his labor support in the Rust Belt. One way to do this, House Democratic Whip David Bonior of Michigan suggested in the spring of 1995, was to "take on some trade policy with the Japanese, who have been screwing us for a while." The auto dispute was such an issue.[14]

The Clinton administration was convinced that its tough stance toward Japan would also play more broadly with key swing groups, especially backers of Ross Perot. White House officials pointed to polls showing that over 70 percent of the American public supported the administration's position in the dispute with Japan. Basking in poll results like these, one White House aide exulted that the "politics" of the auto dispute were "excellent."[15]

Finally, the administration's Japan posture was intended to deal with a number of problems in its relations with liberal congressional Democrats. The White House hoped to appease unhappy Democrats who worried that their support for NAFTA and GATT had cost them votes in the November elections. It also wanted to preempt any effort by potential presidential candidate Dick Gephardt to "out-tough" Clinton on Japan.[16]

The Clinton administration's decision to escalate the auto dispute by imposing sanctions on Japan was facilitated by the apparent easing of earlier constraints on tough action. First, the sanctions were carefully limited to luxury cars made in Japan with few American parts, thus threatening fewer than 17,000 American jobs at U.S. dealerships that sold Japanese vehicles. And because these cars were priced beyond the reach of most middle-class Americans, the administration was unconcerned about a consumer backlash.[17]

Second, Japanese auto companies had greatly slowed their investment in the United States, thus reducing the resistance to sanctions from lawmakers who might otherwise have hoped to attract Japanese factories to their districts.[18]

Third, and perhaps most important, the state of world financial markets appeared to be more favorable to the imposition of sanctions than it had been a year earlier. Since late 1994, in the wake of collapse of the peso and the subsequent U.S. bailout of the Mexican economy, the yen had appreciated 20 percent against the dollar, leading some Japanese exporters who were being priced out of the American market to pressure their government to reduce Japan's trade surplus in order to drive down the value of the yen. Trade officials in the Clinton administration believed that this would give them additional leverage in negotiations with their Japanese counterparts.[19] As for concerns that the threatened U.S. sanctions might roil the financial markets and cause the dollar to actually collapse against the yen, Treasury Secretary Robert Rubin assured the president that currency traders had already discounted the dollar in anticipation of the sanctions.[20]

The Auto Deal

Despite fears of a trade war, on June 28 the U.S.-Japan auto dispute ended with a familiar last-minute deal in which Tokyo agreed to make the Japanese car and parts markets marginally more open to imports. Although the White House claimed that the United States had won a historic victory, in fact it failed to win commitments to measurable results from either the Japanese government or its carmakers.

Why did the administration accept such a limited deal? First, and probably most important, the Japanese were intransigent in their resistance to U.S. demands.[21] Also, U.S. auto dealers selling Japanese cars lobbied against the sanctions, foreign governments and leading newspaper editors and economists criticized Clinton's approach to Japan, and some State Department and other administration officials feared that a prolonged trade fight could damage the U.S.-Japan security relationship.

And once again, bond and currency market volatility played a key role. Despite Secretary Rubin's assurances, after the small rise in the value of the dollar that immediately followed the threat of U.S. sanctions, by the end of May currency traders had grown more worried about the possibility of a worsening trade war. Thus, the dollar resumed its downward fall relative to the yen, taking a steep plunge at the end of May. With the Japanese economy and banking system driven to the edge of collapse by the rising yen, an ensuing sell-off of the country's huge U.S. assets could have precipitated a further dramatic decline in the dollar's value, an upsurge of inflation, higher interest rates, and possibly a recession in the United States. With the presidential election only eighteen months away, the Clinton administration now reversed direction on two fronts: it began to cooperate with Japan and Germany to drive down the yen (and the

Deutschmark) and push up the dollar, and, more important to us here, it backed away from its trade confrontation with Tokyo.[22]

The auto dispute proved to be the last big trade conflict with Japan during the Clinton years. Trade tensions between the two countries ebbed for a number of reasons. These included (1) the WTO's stronger enforcement powers, which encouraged both the United States and Japan to rely on it for resolution of trade disputes, (2) Japan's resistance in the mid-1990s to U.S. demands, based in part on the deepening Japanese economic crisis, (3) conversely, the subsequent gradual opening of the Japanese market to U.S. goods and investment and the growth of strategic alliances between U.S. and Japanese firms—all encouraged by Japanese officials who, in a turnabout, hoped that increased competition would help revive the country's slumping economy—which reduced pressure from U.S. business and unions for a tougher stance toward Tokyo, (4) the reviving U.S. economy, which allayed American fears of Japan, (5) continuing concerns that the threat of a trade war might undermine Japan's already fragile banking system and throw world financial markets into turmoil, and (6) the emergence of China and North Korea as possible security threats, bolstering the importance of the U.S.-Japan security alliance. Moreover, Clinton's political advisers worried that during the presidential campaign, new trade battles with Japan would undermine the president's claim that he had fulfilled his campaign promise to open Japanese markets. Instead, the White House declared victory.[23]

Campaign '96: Reelecting Clinton, Slowing Trade Liberalization

The White House's retreat from trade confrontation with Japan paralleled the administration's more general decision in the summer of 1995 to tack more clearly to the center. Rejecting liberal advice urging him to adopt a "downscale" strategy aimed at restoring Democratic loyalties among less well-off working- and lower-middle-class white voters, Clinton instead embraced an "upscale" strategy of accommodation with the Republicans, advocated by strategist Dick Morris and new pollsters Mark Penn and Doug Schoen and seconded by DLC leaders, that called for a focus on economically optimistic middle- and upper-middle-income swing voters.[24] The shift was also intended to win back the support of disaffected business interests that were cheering GOP plans to cut taxes, spending, and regulations, but whose financial backing Clinton would need in the upcoming presidential election.[25]

Clinton thus began to triangulate to the right, starting with his decision, which followed a furious intra-administration debate between traditional and

New Democrats, to break with his congressional party and join with Republicans in calling for a balanced budget by 2002. He also repudiated his own 1993 tax hike and famously declared in his January 1996 State of the Union address that "the era of big government is over."

Through the spring of 1996, however, Clinton did occasionally tack back to the left. Rejecting Dick Morris's plea to strike a budget deal with the Republicans, he instead successfully battled Republican efforts to cut popular entitlement programs, especially Medicare. He also joined with congressional Democrats to win a hike in the minimum wage, defended the earned-income tax credit, and backed the Kennedy-Kassebaum health insurance reform bill. But as the economic recovery and the presidential campaign both picked up steam in the late spring and summer of 1996, Clinton resumed his New Democratic shift to the right. To preempt the GOP on traditionally Republican social and cultural issues, Clinton signed a tough new immigration law, the Defense of Marriage Act to prevent states from recognizing gay and lesbian unions and, most important, a modified version of the Republicans' welfare reform bill. On the campaign trail, based on polls by Penn and Schoen, he spoke less about the economy and more about "values."

The August Democratic convention provided clear evidence that victory in the ongoing intraparty debate had at least temporarily gone to the New Democrats. The platform adopted at the convention—drafted by moderate White House officials and organized around the concepts of "opportunity," "responsibility," and "community"—was a thoroughly New Democratic document.[26]

The ascent of New Democratic influence within the White House and the wider party in 1995–96 did not immediately translate into a push for additional regional or multilateral trade liberalization, although this was a central tenet of New Democratic thinking. Instead, in a prolonged example of triangulation, the trade liberalization process was put in a holding pattern during the run-up to the 1996 presidential election. This was done to avoid further inflaming core Democratic constituencies that were already uneasy with Clinton's shift to the center.

As the election approached, USTR Mickey Kantor, though a key player in winning congressional approval of the NAFTA and GATT agreements, was anxious to mend relations with those Democrat-aligned labor and environmental groups that had been affronted by the administration's strong push for the two free-trade accords. He knew that they would support only a new fast-track bill that included strong labor and environmental standards, but such a measure was unlikely to pass the Republican-controlled Congress. Thus, despite its free-trade commitments, and even as it was tacking in a rightward direction on budget and other issues, the White House never produced a fast-track proposal for congressional consideration during the two years that preceded the 1996 election.

In the fall of 1995, however, the Republican-controlled House Ways and

Means Committee approved its own "clean" fast-track proposal, that is, one that essentially ruled out labor and environmental standards. The administration opposed the measure, and the full House never voted on it.[27]

During the next year, when Clinton sought to build on his victory in the epoch fight with the Republicans over the 1996 budget and thus salvage his presidency and his reelection prospects, partisan pressures led the White House to continue retreating from its earlier priority of trade liberalization.

With new fast-track legislation on hold, in December Mickey Kantor attempted to fix some political problems for the administration caused by NAFTA. First, eyeing Florida's twenty-five electoral votes, Kantor pushed several bills or actions that would have held up tomato and other vegetable imports from Mexico that competed with Florida-grown produce. Then, at the behest of the powerful Teamsters union, Kantor engineered a delay in a long-scheduled liberalization of trucking rules that would have allowed Mexican-owned-and-driven cargo trucks access to U.S. highways throughout electoral vote-rich Texas, California, and other border states.[28]

The already simmering trade issue briefly came to a boil in late February when Pat Buchanan stunned the political world by besting Senate Majority Leader and longtime free trader Bob Dole in the New Hampshire Republican presidential primary. Tapping into middle-class job and income insecurity, Buchanan revisited the economic nationalist themes of his 1992 campaign. As it turned out, however, Buchanan's New Hampshire triumph was the high point of his campaign. Dole defeated him in the March 2 primary in South Carolina, where the continuing decline of the textile industry and the growth of employment in foreign-owned businesses left voters less responsive to Buchanan's nationalist trade message. Dole's subsequent clean sweep of the primaries in the industrial Midwest further indicated the limited mobilizing power of the trade issue. Nevertheless, Buchanan's surprising victory in New Hampshire brought a number of developments in its wake. With polls finding considerable skepticism toward free trade among an economically worried public,[29] Buchanan's brief success provoked an intense media discussion of trade policy and the wider question of middle-class economic anxiety.

On the presidential campaign trail, while rejecting protectionism, Bob Dole moderately toughened his own positions on the World Trade Organization, NAFTA, and U.S. trade relations with Japan and China. This was partly to stave off Buchanan's challenge but also to score points against Bill Clinton.

Even as trade issues and the wider problem of economic anxiety seemed to fade in the primary campaign, the White House still felt it necessary to stiffen its posture on trade to prevent any possible hemorrhaging of support to Dole. In early March administration officials filed a complaint with WTO charging that Canada's tax policies were unfairly keeping American magazines out of the

Canadian market. At the same time, the White House successfully pressured the Canadian federal government to agree to impose a national tax on provincially subsidized softwood lumber exports to the United States. In early May U.S. trade negotiators rejected as inadequate a proposed international telecommunications agreement.[30] In June the United States and China reached agreement on combating Chinese counterfeiting of CD-ROMs and recorded music, an issue that was of major importance to the computer and music industries, both centered in California, a state that White House officials had long recognized as crucial to Clinton's reelection.[31]

For reasons discussed earlier, one country that the Clinton administration chose not to confront during the spring primary season was Japan. Thus, in an April meeting in Tokyo with Japanese prime minister Hashimoto, Clinton emphasized security, not trade issues. In late June, however, the White House briefly reversed course and once again stepped up its criticism of Japan, as President Clinton fired off a letter to Prime Minister Ryutaro Hashimoto citing roadblocks put up by Tokyo in negotiations over semiconductor sales, insurance access, and U.S. airline landing rights. Clinton's political advisers and other White House officials feared that the lack of agreements on these key issues might soon become entangled in presidential politics. In late March Bob Dole had written Clinton a letter urging him to renew the semiconductor pact; more recently Dole had sent his own letter to Hashimoto urging him to abide by the agreement to give U.S. insurance companies more access to the Japanese market. Clinton's aggressive new posture toward Tokyo was thus partly intended to head off further Republican charges that the administration was soft on Japan.[32] In early August the United States and Japan reached a vague, largely unenforceable agreement in the semiconductor dispute. Some Clinton administration officials privately admitted that the sole reason for negotiating another agreement was politics: the White House wanted to shore up Clinton's support in California, where many high-tech companies were based.[33]

For much of the summer, Dole continued to criticize the Clinton administration's record on trade as he courted the still-potent bloc of swing voters who had supported Pat Buchanan and Ross Perot. After the Republican convention, however, Dole backed off from the trade issue due both to his selection of longtime free-trade advocate Jack Kemp as his vice presidential running mate and to protests from free-trading economists and corporate supporters.[34]

Despite the muting of Dole's criticism of him, Clinton refrained from trumpeting his free-trade accomplishments during the fall campaign, mostly to avoid antagonizing organized labor.[35] Under the vigorous leadership of the new AFL-CIO president, John Sweeney, the unions had undertaken a massive mobilization of activists and money on behalf of the president and Democratic congressional candidates. Clinton had no interest in undermining this effort by rubbing his free-trade victories in labor's face.

Instead, as election day approached, the White House took a number of actions to demonstrate that it could be tough on trade. For example, in early September, in a move to win the president labor and southern support, the USTR's office reduced China's 1996 textile quotas by $19 million to punish Beijing for "transshipping," or sending goods made in China through another country to evade U.S. limits on the Chinese imports. A month later, Commerce Secretary Mickey Kantor won a tentative agreement with Mexico to keep a floor under the price of Mexican tomatoes shipped to the United States, thus easing the competitive threat faced by Florida growers. The issue was a major one in Florida, a hotly contested state that was still in play as the election approached. "The math was pretty simple," an administration official said. "Florida has 25 electoral votes, and Mexico doesn't."[36]

Bill Clinton, of course, was reelected in 1996. He benefited first and foremost from a strong economic recovery and secondarily from Republican overreaching in Congress. But administration trade policy played some modest role in the victory. Getting tough with Japan and putting trade liberalization on hold before the election reduced or prevented the further alienation of core Democratic constituencies as well as Reagan Democrats and other swing voters, all of whom had been angered by Clinton's forceful efforts to pass the NAFTA and GATT accords.

During the campaign, the White House also used targeted trade policies to "surgically redistribute" income to concentrated interests located mostly in populous states, rich in electoral college votes. This last group of actions, rare examples during the Clinton years of policy contagion, provided the president with what Commerce Secretary Mickey Kantor understatedly called "incidental political benefits."[37] These maneuvers helped to blunt criticism of Clinton's trade policies from "out"-party candidate Bob Dole, criticism predicted by incumbency-focused theories of the role of party competition in the trade policy-making process.

The Return to Trade Liberalization: The 1997 Fast-Track Battle

Having secured a comfortable victory over Bob Dole, Clinton now felt freer to resume pursuit of his ambitious trade liberalization goals. In short order, the administration signed a number of market-opening agreements and launched a campaign to renew Clinton's fast-track authority so he could begin to negotiate free-trade deals with Latin American and Asian countries.

Clinton's Strengthened Commitment to Free Trade: The New Democrats and Postindustrial Transition

As his second term began, Bill Clinton's commitment to free trade, originally born of ideology, ties to internationally oriented business, and the interests of moderate middle voters, had been strengthened by his new understanding of the role of his presidency in America's evolving, post-Fordist political economy. His ideas in this regard were influenced by new thinking from the Democratic Leadership Council, *Business Week*, and others on the much-hyped, technology-driven "New Economy."[38]

As early as 1990, revisiting some of the ideas raised by the neoliberals in the early 1980s, the DLC had begun to argue that the United States was in transition from a national and industrial to a global and postindustrial economy, although at the time this theme was relatively muted. By the mid-1990s, however, the council was forcefully insisting that "the old industrial order of American politics" was "crumbling" and that the backbone of the New Deal coalition— the industrial working class—was being replaced by a new, more affluent class of "knowledge" or computer-linked "wired" workers.[39] DLC leaders pushed the wider party to orient itself strategically to these new, prosperous, suburbanized, and often independent swing voters of the moderate middle by adopting policies to speed up the transition to the "Information Age" or what they would soon call the "New Economy," just as Theodore Roosevelt, Woodrow Wilson, and other turn-of-the-century Progressives had similarly encouraged the earlier shift from farm to factory. The DLC thus called for a market-oriented "third way" between old Democratic liberalism and the new Republican conservatism, an approach that included continued trade liberalization, from which knowledge or wired workers benefited as consumers and often as employees in competitive, export-oriented, high-tech industries.[40]

The Democratic Leadership Council once again saw confirmation of its views in the 1996 election results.[41] Based on a postelection survey conducted by Clinton pollster Mark Penn, it argued that the president's victory was due mainly to support from relatively upscale middle-class families who liked his tack to the center. Moreover, the council maintained that congressional Democrats failed to regain a majority precisely because they had not moved to the center as clearly as Clinton had. Immediately after the election, DLC leaders called on Clinton to continue to try to strike bipartisan, market-oriented compromises with the Republican congressional majority on issues like social security, Medicare, and reform of education.

Populist Democrats, including members of the House Democratic leadership but also some of Clinton's more liberal political advisers, opposed the DLC's analysis and prescriptions. They agreed that the nation was in transition to some kind of a new political-economic order (although many were cool to the idea of a New Economy), but they insisted that government's role was less to facilitate that transition than to slow it and to cushion its dislocating impact on the country's workers and communities, just as the old Progressives had attempted to put boundaries around the market with various forms of regulation and other measures. Among other protections for working people, the populists, reminiscent of Theodore Roosevelt, called for a "New Nationalism," including curbs on the power of multinational corporations, fair or managed trade, and the insertion of international labor and environmental standards in trade agreements to prevent a "race to the bottom."[42]

The populists also thought that the New Democrats' proposed strategic focus on suburbanized knowledge or wired workers was bad politics, both because exit polls tended to seriously exaggerate their numerical importance and because this relatively comfortable sector of the electorate showed little evidence of Democratic sympathies.[43] For the Democratic left, the main challenge was still to use populist economic themes to regain the support of those downscale, noncollege-educated radical centrists—especially white, blue-collar men—who had abandoned the party in 1994.

Liberal or populist Democrats naturally disagreed with the DLC over the meaning of the 1996 elections. Drawing on another postelection survey conducted for the liberal Campaign for America's Future by former Clinton pollster Stanley Greenberg, they argued that most of Clinton's new 1996 voters were lower-income, noncollege-educated whites—particularly women—who were attracted to his values agenda, but who were primarily motivated by a perception that the economy was improving and by Clinton's defense of Medicare, Medicaid, education, and the environment.[44] Populists also maintained that the increase in votes for House Democrats since 1994 was even more skewed toward downscale voters and that the Democrats had actually come quite close to taking back the House. The populists pushed the president to aggressively confront the GOP with proposals to alleviate job insecurity, stagnant wages, and widening inequality.

Although Clinton had some sympathy for the populists' arguments, he eventually adopted more of the DLC's "transition story."[45] When he took office in 1993, Clinton had initially modeled his presidency after Franklin Roosevelt's, attempting to push a large agenda through Congress. But after the defeat of his health care plan and the devastating 1994 congressional elections, Clinton, according to his aides, concluded that his was not a presidency of crisis like FDR's but rather of transition like those of Theodore Roosevelt and Woodrow

Wilson.[46] By the fall of 1995, Clinton had come to believe more strongly than ever that the United States was in the midst of an epochal, inexorable transition to an information-based postindustrial society. Like the DLC, Clinton compared the wrenching changes the country was going through to those experienced during the Progressive Era at the turn of the twentieth century. As his second term began, he resolved to both facilitate and to a lesser extent cushion the transition to post-Fordism, or what he, too, now called—most dramatically in his second inaugural address—the New Economy.[47]

Clinton's beliefs were reinforced, through a process of evolutionary learning, by both the apparent success of his policies in fostering a technology-driven economic boom and by the seeming crisis of Japan's state-led development model. He correspondingly heightened his commitment to a neoliberal accumulation strategy supported by and intended to benefit a "coalition of the center," mainly though not exclusively including the New Economy's winners. On the one hand, Clinton stuck both to his deficit reduction course, eventually reaching a balanced budget agreement with the Republicans in the summer of 1997, and to his strong-dollar policy, adopted in mid-1995. With the economy heating up, both were intended to keep inflation in check and interest rates low to help sustain investment and consumption. By fueling the stock market boom, these policies further boosted consumption via the "wealth effect" characteristic of the new "financialized capitalism."[48]

Clinton's strategy also included the resumption of his earlier drive for exports, for he agreed with a postelection editorial by the New Economy enthusiasts at *Business Week* that "it is exports of high-tech goods and services that are the elixir of New Economy health. . . . Barriers that deprive the U.S. of exports directly hurt the New Economy."[49] Because the strong dollar widened the U.S. trade deficit, Clinton's new export push may also have been intended to offset this influence. Clinton viewed his free-trade victories as great personal achievements, and he hoped to strengthen his legacy as a champion of free trade during his second term.

Back on the Fast Track

Despite its scope, the Uruguay Round agreement had actually done relatively little to open foreign markets for the high-tech and service industries that were at the heart of the New Economy. "It's yesterday's agreement," said Gary Hufbauer of the Institute of International Economics.[50] With active U.S. participation, three New Economy–oriented sectoral negotiations left over from the Uruguay Round were successfully concluded within only about a year after Clinton's reelection: information technology in December 1996, basic telecommunications services in February 1997, and financial services in December 1997.

Much more controversial, however, was Clinton's 1997 campaign to win new fast-track authority.[51] Clinton's immediate aim in seeking such authority was to expand NAFTA to include Chile, but his broader ambition was to negotiate still other free-trade agreements with nations in Latin America and Asia. With the election over, the administration was willing to consider a "clean" bill with no significant labor and environmental provisions in order to gain business and Republican support.

The new White House strategy was based on the crucial calculation that the labor movement would not make trade a top priority in 1997. New AFL-CIO president John Sweeney, formerly president of the Service Employees International Union (SEIU), and his close advisers all came out of the service and public sectors. As such, they tended to care less about trade than did the old-line industrial unions.[52] But the administration was mistaken about labor's intentions. Under pressure from the industrial unions, the AFL-CIO, at its annual February meeting, denounced any NAFTA expansion agreement that did not include provisions to raise foreign wages and labor standards.[53]

Presidential election politics also intruded into the debate. The split between Old and New Democrats that had to some extent been deferred by the 1996 election resurfaced over fast track as the two camps already began to look ahead toward the 2000 campaign. "This is a defining issue for the party," said Representative Robert T. Matsui of California.[54]

Potential presidential hopeful and leading populist Democrat Dick Gephardt, now calling for "rules for globalization—not resistance to it," aligned himself with the unions, attaching a wide range of labor, environmental, and political conditions to any new free-trade agreement. Vice President Al Gore, a New Democrat, a New Economy booster, and the odds-on favorite for his party's nomination in 2000, had been a strong supporter of Bill Clinton's trade liberalization program. But Gore had been courting organized labor for the past year, and he urged at least a delay in the submission of the fast-track proposal to Congress to allow him more time to talk with the unions about the issue.

With additional delay caused by the summer negotiation of a bipartisan balanced budget agreement that Clinton now saw as essential to his legacy, it was not until September 16 that he finally unveiled his fast-track plan while offering fulsome praise for the emerging New Economy.[55] In the proposal, the White House attempted to find a middle ground between Democrats and Republicans. Labor and environmental standards were among the "negotiating objectives" set out in the bill. But these standards were to be included in trade pacts only if they were "directly related to trade." Moreover, their enforcement was assigned to multilateral trade institutions like the World Trade Organization, which in the past had objected to linking labor standards and trade.

Commercial issues, however, such as intellectual property, trade in services, and agriculture, were to be addressed in core trade agreements, where sanctions could be used to enforce them.

Clinton's plan initially satisfied no one. Labor and its liberal Democratic allies thought the labor and environmental provisions too weak, whereas business and Republican critics decried the fact that they had received any attention at all. By the time of the October 1 markup of the bill by the pro-trade Senate Finance Committee, the White House, convinced that the fate of its fast-track proposal lay in Republican rather than Democratic hands, had agreed to weaken its labor and environmental provisions enough to mollify most GOP concerns. The bill was passed by the committee with only one opposing vote. A week later, after another round of negotiations with the administration, the House Ways and Means Committee approved a similar version. But heralding the partisan battle to come, only four of the panel's sixteen Democratic members voted for the measure.

The Battle Is Joined

During the next two months another NAFTA-like battle royal was waged between the supporters and opponents of further trade liberalization. Once again, the fight was focused on the House.

As usual, internationally oriented business interests, including the high-tech firms of the New Economy, were the strongest fast-track backers. In June Americans Lead on Trade (ALOT), a coalition including the Business Roundtable, the National Association of Manufacturers, the U.S. Chamber of Commerce, and about 550 other trade associations and companies, was formed to build support for the renewal of fast-track authority. Fearing that Clinton's fast-track proposal might include unacceptable labor and environmental provisions, the coalition refused to endorse the measure until it saw the final Senate and House language, and thus it really did not start working the bill until late October. But the business push for fast track during the last weeks of the fight was substantial, as ALOT funded and coordinated the production of television ads, Washington lobbying by member company chief executive officers and employees, and grassroots lobbying.[56] Business was again joined in its support for fast track by the elite media and the great majority of professional economists.

The lobbying efforts of the pro–fast-track coalition were reinforced by those of Newt Gingrich and the rest of the House Republican leadership. As is often the case under divided government, GOP leaders had to decide whether there was more to be gained for their party by cooperating or fighting with the president. But after extracting a series of trade and budget concessions from the White House, the GOP leadership threw itself into the fight for fast track with a lobbying effort that several party members described as the most intense they had seen.[57]

On the Democratic side, the moderates of the Democratic Leadership Council and their congressional allies, the members of the recently formed New Democrat Coalition,[58] waded into the fight. Armed with a Mark Penn poll showing that Democratic voters were more educated, more female, more middle class, more suburban, and less unionized than in 1980, and thus supported "free trade, as long as there is reciprocity,"[59] the New Democrats warned that the labor and other liberal opponents of the fast-track bill were threatening the party's future. The DLC gathered the signatures of more than one hundred state and local officials on a petition supporting fast track and spent $200,000 on a TV ad campaign in favor of the bill.[60] Finally, after a slow start, at least toward the end of the controversy, Bill Clinton worked hard to win on fast track, bargaining with and trying to persuade House members to back his proposal. Among other things, he promised a $4 billion job retraining package and other aid for communities that lost jobs to trade.

Organized Labor's Campaign

In the opposing trenches, the fight against fast track was again led by organized labor, whose forces had been revitalized by the election in late 1995 of a dynamic new AFL-CIO leadership team headed by John Sweeney. The "Sweeney rebellion" had a number of causes: the growth of the liberal public sector unions, the growing number of women and minority union members, and, not least, the electoral debate of 1994, which produced a call for strong and sophisticated labor leadership to help pro-union Democrats regain power, leadership that the increasingly lackluster AFL president, Lane Kirkland, no longer seemed capable of providing.[61]

Two years after his reenergizing victory, labor led what Sweeney called a "progressive internationalist" campaign against fast track, attempting to turn the debate into a referendum on NAFTA, which, labor argued, had cost the United States hundreds of thousands of jobs. The union offensive employed a wide range of "inside" or Washington-based and "outside" or grassroots and media-oriented lobbying strategies. But to an important extent, labor's influence in the battle was made possible by its unprecedented grassroots and financial involvement in the 1996 congressional races, which marked a new level of interest-group participation in electoral politics.[62]

Shortly after the Republican takeover of Congress in 1994, which was followed by a multipronged GOP campaign against organized labor, the unions had launched a concerted campaign—"Labor '96"—to help the Democrats recapture control of at least the House of Representatives. Individual unions provided tens of thousands of volunteers to the campaigns of the candidates they supported. Beyond this, the AFL-CIO waged a $35 million campaign on behalf of Democratic candidates. It spent $10 million on an ambitious grass-roots field campaign, which included the hiring of 135 full-time political coordinators to direct the efforts of volunteers in registering, educating, and turning out members to vote in 105 congressional districts around the country. The remaining $25 million was spent on an issue advocacy campaign that included TV and radio attacks on the records of vulnerable Republican incumbents as well as the distribution of voter video guides. In addition to the special $35 million fund, labor stepped up other forms of campaign spending.

Labor's intensified efforts in 1996 achieved a greater return than seen in previous campaigns. In 1992, 19 percent of the electorate was from union households. Two years later, angered by their loss to Clinton on NAFTA, union activists largely sat out the midterm elections, producing a decline in the union share of the turnout to 14 percent. But in 1996, turnout among union households jumped to 23 percent of the electorate. Further, whereas 40 percent of union members had voted for Republican House candidates in 1994, this figure dropped to 32 percent in 1996.

Labor's campaign contributions also played an important role in 1996. Business, as usual, substantially outspent labor in PAC and individual contributions, this time by a margin of 7–1.[63] But this year, pragmatic, access-oriented business PACs shifted their contributions to Republicans in order to retain their influence with GOP members following the party's takeover of Congress in 1994. Thus, whereas business PACs made 44 percent of their contributions to Republican House candidates in the 1993–94 election cycle, that figure rose to 68 percent in 1995–96. Together with an increase in labor PAC contributions to Democratic candidates, this business shift left the Democrats more dependent on union money. Labor PAC contributions to Democratic House candidates, which totaled roughly 36 percent of all PAC donations to such candidates in 1994, rose to about 48 percent of the total in 1996.[64]

Labor's education, registration, and turnout drives, along with its PAC contributions, paid real dividends in the 1996 elections. Democratic House candidates defeated 45 of the 105 Republicans targeted by the AFL-CIO. Federation-endorsed challengers defeated GOP incumbents in 18 of 57 races, a success record of 31.2 percent, which is impressive considering that incumbent reelection rates are usually well above 90 percent.[65]

During the fast-track fight a year later, labor sought to capitalize on the political influence that it had established through its work in 1996. Patterning its inside and outside lobbying campaign after that election-year effort, the AFL-CIO in 1997 coordinated an exceptionally effective grassroots and advertising offensive against fast track in targeted congressional districts. Several federation affiliates—especially the Teamsters, the Steelworkers, and the Union of Needle-trades, Industrial, and Textile Employees (UNITE)—undertook their own independent anti–fast-track activities.[66]

Union members who opposed fast track sent hundreds of thousands of letters and postcards to their representatives, placed over ten thousand telephone calls to Congress, made hundreds of visits to congressional district offices, distributed thousands of anti–fast-track videos and booklets, and held dozens of teach-ins and rallies on trade. The AFL-CIO spent about $2 million on TV and radio ads in twenty congressional districts. Labor was also active inside the Washington Beltway. Throughout the fight, but most intensely in early November, labor lobbyists regularly met with and pressed House members—mostly Democrats, but also some Republicans—to oppose fast track. Drawing on the political capital they had accumulated, labor leaders bluntly warned that lawmakers supporting fast track could not expect union manpower or money for their 1998 campaigns, even if that meant some Democrats might lose.[67]

Even more than during the fight against NAFTA, labor cooperated in the battle against Clinton's fast-track proposal with other members of the Citizens Trade Campaign—a broad coalition of labor, environmental, consumer safety, and civil rights organizations—that remained highly critical of NAFTA and its weak side agreements. The anti–fast-track cause was also strengthened by a modest shift in expert opinion since the NAFTA fight. A number of studies questioned the degree to which that agreement had benefited the country or different groups within the population.[68] Still other analyses argued more broadly that globalization had negatively affected the wages of certain sectors of the labor force as well as the distribution of income.[69] Finally, labor and its allies enlisted the active support of key House Democratic leaders, especially Minority Leader Dick Gephardt and Minority Whip David Bonior, who worked hard to convince undecided Democrats to come out against fast track.

The Fast-Track Bill Is Withdrawn as the Parties Polarize

Although the traditionally pro-trade Senate would have passed its version of the fast-track bill,[70] this time labor and its allies emerged victorious in the House. After a vote on the measure was delayed twice, Clinton was forced to withdraw his proposal when it became clear that he lacked the votes in the House to pass it. The House was sharply divided along partisan lines. A number of tallies suggested that fast track would have received the support of about 70–75 percent of House Republicans but only about 20 percent of House Democrats.[71]

On the Republican side of the aisle, conservative economic nationalist influences, both electoral and ideological, contributed to the decision of some GOP members to oppose fast track. The 1994 elections had sent a wave of radical populist and nationalist Republicans into the House, helping the GOP capture control of Congress. Elected with the help of Buchanan and Perot supporters, these firebrands in many cases replaced marginal Democrats, especially in the South, whose support for NAFTA and free trade more generally had alienated blue-collar voters. Overlapping this group were newly elected social conservatives, mostly from the South and West, who opposed fast track because it would prevent them from adding antiabortion and religious right amendments to trade agreements. Thus, over one-third of the ninety-one Republicans first elected to the House in 1994 and 1996 opposed the fast-track bill.[72] Other moderate Republicans from swing northeastern and midwestern states, mainly those experiencing NAFTA-related job loss,[73] opposed the administration's proposal to avoid offending their blue-collar constituents and organized labor. Still others wanted to inflict a defeat on Clinton while dividing the Democrats.[74] In the end, though, 70–75 percent of the House Republican caucus, wedded to free trade by ideology, the preferences of their disproportionately export-dependent constituents, or their reliance on business campaign contributions, or lobbied heavily by the House GOP leadership, supported the fast-track bill, close to the same proportion that had backed NAFTA in 1993.[75]

As for House Democrats, whereas 60 percent of them had voted against NAFTA in 1993 (and 65 percent had actually *supported* the GATT treaty in 1994), 80 percent of them opposed fast track in 1997. It was this shift in Democratic sentiment that mainly doomed Clinton's proposal.

To an important extent, the more unified Democratic opposition in 1997 was an artifact of the more liberal composition of the House Democratic caucus.[76] A substantial number of moderate and conservative, pro-trade and pro-NAFTA Democrats retired or were defeated in the Democratic rout of 1994. Continuing a well-established trend, most of these losses were in the South, where House Democrats had been much more supportive of NAFTA than their colleagues in the rest of the country.[77] More southern conservatives retired or were beaten in the 1996 elections, while at the same time, the great majority of the forty-one new Democratic lawmakers elected that year were northern liberals and moderates from districts where opposition to free trade was stronger.

But this heightened Democratic cohesion on fast track does not explain why among the ranks of Democratic fast-track opponents there were both nineteen former NAFTA supporters and some newly elected nonsouthern moderates. Included in these two groups were half of the forty-one members of the moderate New Democrat Coalition. Several other factors were at work.

First, despite a late burst of activity, the business campaign on behalf of fast track was not as well organized and was less energetic than the one for NAFTA. Unlike NAFTA, which provided a wide range of businesses with immediate, significant, and concentrated benefits, the procedural fast-track measure offered benefits that were much more long-term, dispersed, and uncertain. Moreover, business underestimated the strength of the opposition to the fast-track bill.[78]

Second, Bill Clinton's efforts in support of the measure were also less concerted and effective than they had been during the NAFTA battle. Clinton mistakenly assumed that business and the Republicans would enthusiastically fall in line behind his bill, while at the same time he underestimated the pressure to oppose fast track that House Democrats of all stripes would feel from organized labor. And, not wanting to further offend labor, whose support Al Gore would need in the 2000 presidential campaign, Clinton never took his case to an anxious public, which remained highly skeptical of the value of liberalized trade. Instead, he relied exclusively on an "inside-the-beltway" strategy, promising members of Congress a flurry of last-minute concessions in return for their votes. But this time his deal making did not work. Clinton's credibility had been diminished by his failure to deliver on most of the promises he had made during the NAFTA fight.[79] Beyond this, he had antagonized House Democrats with the balanced budget deal that he had struck with Republicans the previous summer.

Labor's Pivotal Role

The most important factor underlying the Democrats' solid opposition to fast track, however, was the structurally enabled "agency" of organized labor. It is true that labor's secularly deteriorating structural position had not improved since 1993, when 40 percent of House Democrats voted for NAFTA. Despite the AFL-CIO's heightened commitment to organizing under its new president John Sweeney, union membership had been down in both relative and absolute terms since early 1996. But labor was able to marshal and strategically deploy the human and financial resources it did possess during the fast-track struggle. Thomas Edsall went so far as to suggest that the "unions' formidable efforts to block the 'fast track' trade bill shows that organized labor has more influence than at any time since 1968, when it nearly elected a president."[80]

Labor's grassroots mobilization and issue advocacy campaign, which included the use of persuasive narratives of NAFTA-related and future job loss, lower wages, and environmental degradation, expanded the scope of the fast-track conflict, shifted public opinion against Clinton's proposals, particularly in heavily unionized Democratic congressional districts, and conveyed information about the public's preferences on the issue to lawmakers. By late 1997, now convinced that NAFTA had been a failure, the American public was solidly opposed to renewing Clinton's fast-track authority and had grave concerns that trade liberalization was adversely affecting American jobs and living standards.[81]

Still, the role of general public opinion in this regard should not be exaggerated. Government officials have often pursued free-trade policies even when those policies were unpopular. This is likely to occur when the public's preferences are not intense, as appears to have been the case on fast track, which voters found less salient than NAFTA.[82] Had public opinion as a whole played a predominant role in the demise of fast track, more than 25–30 percent of House Republicans should have opposed it.

More critical than generalized public opinion was the scale of labor's grassroots mobilization in both the 1996 elections and the fast-track fight. This led many Democrats—moderates as well as liberals—to fear that their support for fast track could provoke union activists to sit out the 1998 congressional races, once again depressing labor turnout.[83] Particularly important in explaining Democratic opposition to fast track was the heightened threat posed by a loss of union *money* in 1998, a threat that stemmed from a significant shift in the sources of Democratic campaign funds.[84]

It will be recalled that during the 1978, 1980, and 1982 congressional campaigns, business PACs, hoping to scale back the New Deal social welfare and regulatory state, moved the bulk of their contributions to Republican incumbents and challengers to help the GOP secure control of the White House and both houses of Congress. Under the prodding of Democratic Congressional Campaign Committee chairman Tony Coelho and his successors, however, during the remainder of the 1980s and the early 1990s, business PACs were persuaded to shift some of their spending back to incumbent Democrats who appeared securely in control of the House.[85]

This shift in the Democrats' base of financial support had rendered Democratic members of Congress more supportive of business and less responsive to labor on a range of issues, including trade policy. This partly explains why 40 percent of House Democrats voted for NAFTA in the face of strong opposition from labor.

The 1994 elections produced yet another shift in the structure of campaign finance, also with corresponding policy consequences.[86] After the Republican takeover of Congress, business PACs, pressured by the new GOP congressional leadership, again reduced their contributions to the Democrats while substantially increasing their donations to the now majority Republicans. Meanwhile, labor PACs boosted their contributions to Democratic candidates. Union PAC contributions thus rose from 36 percent of all PAC donations to Democratic House candidates in 1994 to about 48 percent in 1996.[87]

The Democrats had once again become heavily dependent on organized labor for campaign funds. This dependence was compounded by the Democratic fund-raising scandals stemming from the 1996 elections. Abandoned by many of its major donors, the Democratic National Committee was $15 million in debt, leaving it unable to aid party candidates with unregulated or soft money, which can be used to finance so-called party-building activities and issue advertising campaigns that do not directly advocate the election of specific candidates.[88]

This increased Democratic dependence on labor money and the threat of the loss of those funds in the 1998 midterm elections greatly contributed to the defeat of Clinton's fast-track proposal.[89] "Labor has obviously increased its influence in the Democratic Party since we've become the minority and the business community is either less engaged or less influential with us than ever before," said one senior House Democrat. A House Democratic leadership aide observed, "Your average House Democrat is thinking, 'The DNC is broke, Clinton is helping Gore, Big Business is with the Republicans, all we've got is labor.'" "This is a $200,000 vote for me," another Democrat reportedly told a Clinton aide, explaining why he might not vote for fast track even though he had voted for NAFTA.[90]

It is important to be clear that during the fast-track fight, labor's financial clout gave the movement influence with Democrats of various ideological stripes, not just pro-union liberals. Looking to labor for help, fully half of the DLC sympathizers in the New Democrat Coalition planned to vote against the fast-track bill. "The business community really has to think very hard about ignoring House Democrats," said DLC president Al From, bemoaning the extent of New Democratic opposition to fast track.[91]

The 1998 Fast-Track Fight:
The Democrats Sink a Republican Proposal

Many observers saw the fast-track controversy as a harbinger of upcoming battles between the administration and liberal congressional Democrats as well as of a bitter presidential primary contest between Old Democrat Dick Gephardt and New Democrat Al Gore.[92] In particular, another battle over a new White House proposal on fast track was widely expected.

In fact, the anticipated intra-Democratic conflict over fast track and other issues never materialized. As 1998 began, Clinton hoped simultaneously to reinvigorate his presidency, repair fractured relations with organized labor and liberal congressional Democrats before heading into the fall midterm elections, and smooth the way to the White House for Al Gore, who would need labor and liberal votes, manpower, and money. With the federal budget deficit surprisingly all but eliminated and his poll numbers as strong as ever, Clinton tacked slightly back to the left by proposing an activist agenda for 1998 that included a raft of progressive if modest new policies.[93] Congressional Democrats, their expectations finally lowered in response to the change in the balance of political power, embraced Clinton's new initiatives.

Throughout the rest of 1998, both Clinton and Gore spent considerable energy working to repair their ties to the liberal-labor wing of the Democratic Party. Of considerable significance, Clinton warned his allies in the Democratic Leadership Council to let up in their attacks on labor, which they eventually agreed to do.[94]

Republican Fast-Track Heresthetics

Also important to Clinton's rapprochement with his party's populist faction was his decision to hold off on sending another fast-track proposal to Congress until after the November elections, thus avoiding another politically damaging intra-Democratic fight. Instead, it was Republican Speaker of the House Newt Gingrich who in late June surprised observers by announcing a late September vote on a new fast-track proposal containing no strong labor and environmental provisions.[95] Gingrich's motives appear to have been partisan ones. In a typical out-party heresthetical maneuver under divided government, albeit this time in support of free rather than fair trade, Gingrich introduced his fast-track bill in order to (1) exploit differences on trade among labor, House Democrats, and the White House just before the fall midterm congressional elections, (2) mend political fences with farmers, hit hard by shrinking foreign markets and falling prices due to the year-old Asian financial crisis, who were angry at the GOP for phasing out the farm subsidies that once cushioned price drops, and (3) allay the concerns of business interests disaffected by the Republicans' apparent neglect of or even opposition to the corporate agenda. This last point is worth a bit more discussion.

By the spring of 1998, many corporate leaders had come to believe that business had made a mistake in so dramatically shifting its support from Democratic to Republican incumbents after the 1994 midterm elections.[96] These leaders worried that the Republicans were now too strongly influenced by southern and western social conservatives, small business populists, and economic nationalists, leading the party to focus on social issues and on cutting "corporate welfare," while abandoning Big Business on taxes, health care, in some cases trade, and so forth. Most distressing was the GOP's apparent retreat from an internationalist foreign economic policy. Under pressure from conservative nationalists and religious conservative critics of foreign human rights abuses and abortion practices, many Republicans opposed top business priorities like the renewal of China's most-favored-nation (MFN) status and new funding for the International Monetary Fund (IMF). As we have seen, 25–30 percent of House Republicans opposed the extension of Bill Clinton's fast-track authority.

Angry business interests—including the U.S. Chamber of Commerce and the Business-Industry Political Action Committee (BIPAC), a group that counsels about a thousand PACs as to which candidates are good bets for business—threatened to reduce or cut off funds to Republican lawmakers if they did not pay closer attention to corporate positions on key issues. "We can no longer restrict ourselves to one or two political options in our quest to assure a genuinely and reliably pro-business majority in Congress," BIPAC officials wrote in a controversial March memorandum, implying that business should consider supporting pro-business Democrats on some occasions.[97]

Some business interests, including the Chamber of Commerce and the editors of *Business Week*, explicitly called for a shift of some campaign donations back to the Democrats. In a closely balanced Congress controlled by not-always-reliable Republicans, these interests recognized that business would need at least some Democratic allies if it hoped to win on issues like fast track in the future.[98] This required that the pro-business, pro-trade "New Democratic center" be bolstered and, conversely, that labor's current position of strength within the party, a result in part of business's abandonment of the Democrats after the 1994 GOP takeover of Congress, be weakened or offset. This, in turn, called for a rebalancing of business contributions to the two parties.[99]

Such business reorientation was encouraged by the New Democrats, who in mid-1996 formed the New Democrat Network (NDN), a political action committee philosophically aligned though not formally affiliated with the Democratic Leadership Council. The NDN's aim was to help push the Democratic Party in a moderate, pro-business, and pro–free-trade direction by raising more corporate money, especially from high-tech firms, for ideologically sympathetic Democratic candidates, thus weaning the party away from its heavy dependence on labor union contributions.[100]

In fact, business did begin to rebalance its financial support for the parties. As of June 30, 1998, in the 1997–98 electoral cycle, the Democrats had received 37 percent of all business PAC contributions to House and Senate candidates, up from 30 percent for the whole of the 1996 campaign.[101] "I know of some PAC managers who have already told [GOP] candidates, 'Sorry, not this year,' " said BIPAC president Charles S. Mack. "The business community doesn't feel any great debt to Republican leaders in the House."[102]

Battling Over and Defeating the Republican Fast-Track Proposal

Republican congressional leaders angrily fired back at their critics, but in an attempt to regain business support, an effort that in fact slowed or even partly reversed the shift of PAC contributions to the Democrats,[103] they reassured the business community that they would take up key elements of its agenda. In what was dubbed the "Treaty of K Street," GOP leaders promised support for a capital gains tax cut, liberalized immigration quotas for high-tech workers, and three foreign economic policy items: continuation of MFN for China, funding for the IMF, and, of special concern here, new fast-track legislation. "It's really an issue for the business community and an issue for our farmers," Georgia Republican John Linder said of fast track. "We have to give them a vote." GOP leaders pressed toward a late September vote on Newt Gingrich's bill, hoping to use the issue against Democratic fast-track opponents who hailed from districts with concentrations of export-dependent agricultural interests.[104]

The Republicans' usual allies in trade conflicts for the most part deserted the front. Bill Clinton and many New Democrats opposed what they saw as an obvious GOP attempt to embarrass and divide their party before the November elections. In addition, Clinton had no wish to again antagonize liberal Democrats, whose support he would need to fend off impeachment over the escalating Monica Lewinsky scandal.

The business community was split. Some business and farm groups, employing both inside and outside lobbying tactics, pressed hard for a vote at all costs to put House fast-track opponents on record, thus allowing business to respond by withholding financial support in the upcoming elections. But other business interests thought the timing of the vote was bad and backed away from the measure as its prospects dimmed.[105]

Organized labor, of course, attacked and mobilized against Gingrich's bill, with the Steelworkers Union playing a particularly active role. At the same time, wanting to prevent the election of a filibuster-proof Republican Senate, labor mounted another major effort in support of Democratic candidates in the upcoming congressional races. This time, though, labor was (1) not satisfied with the results of its media "air war" in 1996, (2) confronted by a business community that was both massively outspending the unions and directing at least some of its campaign contributions back to the Democrats,[106] (3) facing the threat of a low turnout of its members, who along with other Americans had become increasingly alienated from politics by a succession of scandals, and (4) coming off a highly successful grassroots campaign in California against Proposition 226, a ballot measure intended to curb union spending of dues money on political activities. Thus, labor decided that in 1998 its route to greater electoral effectiveness lay in a full-scale, grassroots, get-out-the-vote "ground war."[107] The strategy was also designed, of course, to increase labor's influence in Congress, beginning immediately with the Republican fast-track bill.

On September 25 the House decisively defeated the GOP bill by a vote of 180–243, a substantially greater margin than the one by which Clinton's fast-track proposal had been rejected the year before. Once again, the vote was fairly partisan. On the Republican side, 151 members, or about 68 percent, voted for the measure, while 71 voted against it. Only 29 Democrats, or about 14 percent, voted yes this time, while 171 voted no.[108]

As always, GOP fast-track supporters included ideologically conservative or pro-business lawmakers, those representing less unionized and more prosperous districts, and those highly dependent on business campaign contributions.[109] The ranks of Republican fast-track opponents, mostly conservative nationalists and lawmakers from more blue-collar districts, were somewhat increased on this vote by the reluctance of certain GOP lawmakers to give Bill Clinton new negotiating authority at the very time that he was about to be impeached by the Republican Senate.

As for the Democrats, ideologically liberal or pro-labor party members voted against the bill, as did Democratic lawmakers from districts with high proportions of unionized and less-educated workers. Reflecting the success of labor's strategy, both traditional union supporters and other more moderate Democrats opposed the bill, hoping to retain the support of grassroots union activists to avoid another depressed labor turnout in the elections now only six weeks away. Some Democrats also again voted against the fast-track bill to avoid losing future labor campaign contributions, which remained vital despite the shift of some business money back to the Democrats.[110] Other moderate Democrats in safe seats nevertheless opposed Gingrich's measure out of anger at the GOP attempt to split their party shortly before the election.

From 1995 to 1998 partisan pressures persistently blocked the trade liberalization process. After intracongressional partisan polarization had frustrated Mickey Kantor's attempt to include new fast-track authority in the GATT implementing bill in 1994, the political strength of the liberal-labor wing of the Democratic Party led Clinton to delay the introduction of a new proposal until after the 1996 elections. The same faction, with secondary help from Republican critics of free trade, then defeated Clinton's 1997 fast-track bill, kept the White House from sending a new proposal to Congress, and finally defeated a Republican-sponsored measure in 1998.[111]

At the three-quarters mark of Bill Clinton's presidency, trade liberalization had ground to a halt due largely to renewed partisanship at both the presidential and especially the congressional levels. Senator Daniel Patrick Moynihan (D-N.Y.) went so far as to claim that the old free-trade coalition had been "shattered," most importantly by organized labor's shift to protectionism together with its revived influence within the Democratic Party.[112] In fact, the Democrats had not reverted to advocating a pre-1930s form of protectionism. But the post–World War II bipartisan consensus on liberal trade had certainly frayed, with apparent adverse consequences for further progress toward trade liberalization.[113]

Trade Liberalization Set Back Again, Then Renewed?

The Battle in Seattle and PNTR with China

During his last two years in office, Bill Clinton was preoccupied with securing his presidential legacy. Above all, this meant removing or at least lightening the stain of impeachment, in part through the enactment and implementation of new policy initiatives in areas like education, health care, and children's issues. But with spending possibilities still limited by his growing neoliberal commitment to use mounting budget surpluses to preserve the solvency of the social security system and to reduce the national debt, Clinton once again turned to a cheaper way to burnish his legacy: a renewed, two-pronged offensive on behalf of free trade.

In late November 1999 the president traveled to a meeting of the World Trade Organization (WTO) in Seattle with the hope of launching a new "Millennium Round" of international trade negotiations. Amid dramatic street protests, however, the conference collapsed, due in good measure to Clinton's concern for two other elements of his legacy: the election of his vice president, Al Gore, as his successor in 2000 and the fate of a trade-and-investment-liberalizing agreement struck with China only two weeks earlier to facilitate China's entry into the WTO. Anxious to help Gore gain the active backing of organized labor in both the primaries and the general election and to reduce labor opposition to the China deal, and finding only modest business support for a new round of trade talks, Clinton proposed that the WTO establish a working group on international labor standards. He even suggested that the organization might eventually need to use sanctions to enforce compliance with such standards. But the developing nations took great exception to these ideas, so the WTO meeting fell apart.

Having triangulated to the left in an attempt to appease labor, Clinton now tacked back in the other direction to pursue his more important trade policy goal: the opening of the China market. This would require Congress to award China "permanent normal trade relations" (PNTR). The spring of 2000 thus saw another bitter but familiar trade struggle in the House of Representatives over Clinton's PNTR bill. This time, however, labor, liberal Democratic, and conservative Republican opponents of the measure were defeated by the massive inside and outside lobbying campaign undertaken by its business, White House, Republican, and moderate Democratic backers. The pro-PNTR forces won by restructuring the balance of partisan forces surrounding the issue; they held the support of a big majority of House Republicans while badly dividing the Democratic caucus.

In early September, after several months of partisan maneuvering, PNTR with China was finally approved when the Senate passed Clinton's bill with a substantial bipartisan majority. As Bill Clinton's presidency drew to a close, it appeared that the forces of internationalism and free trade had regained the initiative.

Clinton the Free Trader: The New Democrats, the New Economy, and the High-Tech Sector

Clinton's strengthened commitment to free trade during his last two years in office had two related sources: his growing belief in the reality and political significance of the information-based New Economy and the heightened political activity of the high-tech sector at the core of this economy. Although his evolving ideas on the New Economy were influenced by a number of sources, he was eminently impressed by the ongoing work of the Democratic Leadership Council (DLC) and its affiliated Progressive Policy Institute (PPI). In the summer of 1998 the DLC and the PPI jointly began a campaign to more fully understand, accelerate, and help the Democrats benefit politically from the transition to the New Economy.

PPI's Technology Project produced a New Economy Index intended to illuminate the structural changes under way in the U.S. economy.[1] The institute's New Economy Task Force, including high-tech entrepreneurs and Democratic officeholders, was formed to deepen links between centrist New Democrats and the increasingly powerful and politically active high-tech industry. DLC supporters explored the emerging New Economy and its political implications in a new magazine—*Blueprint: Ideas for a New Century*—where contributors argued that the key to the Democratic Party's future was its ability to expand its support among the centrist swing voters of the growing, upscale, educated, suburbanized "learning class," including its computer-using "wired workers."[2]

The DLC claimed vindication of its views in the 1998 congressional midterm elections, in which the Democrats picked up five House seats. DLC leaders argued that the party's success was due to its nomination of centrist candidates who ran well among middle- and upper-middle-class voters—the moderate middle—in suburban and southern districts.

Liberal and labor Democrats continued to dispute the DLC's economic and political analysis.[3] These critics argued that the Democrats' success in 1998 was due less to gains among upscale voters than to the mobilization of the party's traditional base of unionized and black voters in a low turnout election. To actually recapture control of Congress the Democrats would have to expand their support not within the learning class, but rather among the true swing voters, the downscale members of the radical center, who in many ways had failed to benefit from the New Economy.[4]

Although acknowledging elements of the liberal view, Bill Clinton remained more intellectually sympathetic to the DLC's analysis. Indeed, during his last two years in office he was more committed than ever to the pursuit of an accumulation strategy favorable to the New Economy, its firms, and its politically pivotal wired workers.[5] This included a strengthened belief in the importance of expanded trade, a belief that was reinforced by new arguments advanced by Treasury Secretary Lawrence Summers. Summers maintained that exports were of great importance to the New Economy, because, by enlarging markets, they helped high-tech firms to (1) achieve the economies of scale necessary to rapidly amortize their high research and development (R&D) and other fixed costs, and (2) benefit from "network effects," that is, from the increase in the value of their products arising from the use of these goods by larger networks of people.[6]

Clinton's enthusiasm for both the New Economy and free trade was further heightened by the increased political activism in the late 1990s of the high-tech sector, whose support he had already courted in his two presidential campaigns.[7] As previous chapters have shown, beginning in the early 1980s, some high-tech firms had become politically active around U.S.-Japan trade and technology policy issues. But most high-tech executives had libertarian sensibilities and remained wary of political involvement.

All this changed in 1996, when Silicon Valley electronics firms were forced to mobilize to defeat Proposition 211, which would have made the filing of often frivolous shareholder suits easier in California state courts. The imperative of politics became still clearer with the emergence of the World Wide Web, which rendered the high-tech sector more vulnerable to government intervention and regulation; the passage of the Telecommunications Act of 1996; and the federal government's antitrust suit against Microsoft. By the late 1990s, high-tech firms, including the new Internet companies, trade associations, and organizations like Silicon Valley's Technology Network (or "TechNet"), the industry's first broad-based political action committee (PAC), had expanded or opened new offices in Washington, D.C., and were regularly lobbying Congress and the White House on a wide range of issues. Moreover, the high-tech sector sharply increased its campaign contributions to pro-technology presidential and congressional candidates of both parties.

During the late 1990s newly politically active high-tech firms sought to rapidly amortize high fixed costs and to benefit from network effects by expanding foreign markets via either exports or direct investment. They joined other established exporters and multinational corporations in making both trade and investment liberalization a top priority. This reinforced the Clinton administration's own commitments in this area.

Toward a New Trade Round: The "Battle in Seattle"

The first of Clinton's final trade liberalization initiatives was his call for a new round of international trade negotiations. In addition to restoring momentum to his postimpeachment presidency, Clinton hoped to head off a global protectionist backlash in response to the Asian financial crisis that had begun in the summer of 1997, boost U.S. exports and thus reduce the U.S. trade deficit that the administration's strong-dollar policy had contributed to, and prevent a collapse of the dollar and the ensuing inflation, higher interest rates, and possible recession that a widening trade gap might eventually produce.[8] To defuse opposition to a new trade round, Clinton also reiterated the White House's earlier call for the WTO to work to raise labor and environmental standards.

After fending off an industry and union-backed, Democrat-sponsored steel quota bill during the first half of 1999,[9] and hoping to contain any new outburst of protectionism through the tried-and-true tactic of "export politics," Bill Clinton journeyed to the WTO ministerial meeting in Seattle in late November with the aim of launching what some called a new "Millennium Round" of global trade negotiations.[10] Supported, if not vigorously, by internationally oriented agricultural and business interests and bucked up politically by pro-trade New Democrats both within and outside Congress,[11] the Clinton administration had a wide range of commercial items on its proposed agenda for the round, including ending European farm subsidies and further reducing tariffs on goods and services. Most important to the United States, however, reflecting both the White House's embrace of New Economy thinking and the advocacy of the high-tech community, was the administration's e-commerce agenda: extending the existing moratorium on Internet tariffs and loose regulation of Internet sales.[12]

U.S. hopes were frustrated as the WTO meeting collapsed amid the "Battle in Seattle": several days of demonstrations organized by many of the same Internet-linked forces of "global civil society" that had fought the North American Free Trade Agreement (NAFTA) and fast track and in late 1998 had helped derail negotiations on a Multilateral Agreement on Investment (MAI). About 30,000 union members protested trade-related job losses that they attributed in part to the WTO's refusal to implement international labor standards. Another 10,000 environmental and human rights activists decried the alleged trade-and-WTO-abetted corporate depletion of the earth's dwindling resources and trampling on the world's poor.

The protests did reflect a real public unease over the impact of globalization and free-trade agreements.[13] But with the overall U.S. economy booming, these were not strong sentiments. A larger contributor to the breakdown of the talks were the disagreements among the participating governments over such issues as the elimination of agricultural subsidies, the weakening of antidumping laws, new investment rules, and developing nations' demand for a greater role in WTO decision-making.[14]

The greatest cause of the breakdown, though, was the U.S. proposal that the WTO establish a working group on international labor standards and especially Clinton's suggestion that sanctions might eventually be needed to enforce compliance. The developing nations took great offense at these proposals, viewing them as a thinly veiled attempt by the United States to exclude Third World goods from American markets.

The White House provoked the collapse of the WTO meeting to avoid jeopardizing two goals seen as more important to Clinton's legacy than a new trade round: the election of Al Gore as his successor and congressional approval of permanent normal trade relations with China, thought to be necessary if U.S. firms were to reap the benefits of a trade and investment accord struck with Beijing in mid-November to facilitate China's entry into the WTO. Toward these ends, before and during the Seattle meeting, the White House sought to appease labor and environmentalist critics of free trade.

Most critical to Clinton's calculations was the labor movement. At the urging of President John Sweeney, at its national convention in mid-October 1999, the AFL-CIO, which had not endorsed a candidate in a presidential primary since Walter Mondale in 1984, had backed Gore over his opponent, former New Jersey senator Bill Bradley. Gore had worked hard for the endorsement, recognizing that labor's volunteers and money would be crucial in the spring's frontloaded primary process, notably in the key early states of Iowa and New Hampshire.[15]

The industrial unions were much less enthusiastic about the vice president's candidacy than the public and service sector unions, due to his strong support for the administration's free-trade initiatives. In fact, despite Gore's promise at the AFL convention that he would insist on workers' rights as part of any new trade agreements, the United Autoworkers and the Teamsters, unions with substantial membership in the electorally pivotal industrial states, refused to support his endorsement.[16] The two unions later condemned the Clinton administration's negotiating objectives in Seattle.

Then in mid-November, only weeks after the AFL-CIO's endorsement of Gore, the White House concluded its deal with China.[17] Labor leaders were outraged that the administration had signed the agreement without securing Beijing's agreement to allow independent trade unions and to free imprisoned labor leaders. They feared that if China were allowed into the WTO, labor standards would never be incorporated into global trade rules. Finally, they were convinced that China's repressive labor and human rights policies would encourage a flight of manufacturing capital to China to take advantage of its cheap labor, with a corresponding loss of American jobs.

Responding to the fury of the industrial unions and feeling personally betrayed, John Sweeney denounced the Clinton administration as "disgustingly hypocritical," vowed to fight the China deal and PNTR, and suggested that the agreement would further reduce labor's enthusiasm for Gore's candidacy. Sweeney called on the White House to scuttle the upcoming WTO talks unless negotiators first took steps toward protecting workers' rights, including endorsing the use of trade sanctions against countries that violated basic labor standards. Two weeks later, labor took its concerns into the streets of Seattle.

In these volatile circumstances, White House officials worried, a WTO negotiating agenda that failed to include labor standards might so enrage the unions that they would escalate their denunciations of the administration, soften their support for Gore, and divert their money and manpower from Gore's race to a fight against Clinton's more important trade priority, PNTR with China. At the same time, most U.S. businesses, despite formal expressions of support, were relatively indifferent to the launching of a new trade round, as the booming domestic economy made greater access to foreign markets seem less pressing than during more difficult times. The big exception was the China deal, for which corporate enthusiasm ran high.[18]

Rather than agreeing to launch a politically risky new trade round in the face of considerable union opposition and with little business support, the Clinton administration opted to blow up the Seattle meeting. "The only thing worse than no agreement," one official explained, "was the agreement it looked like we might get," a sentiment that almost exactly mirrored John Sweeney's warning to the White House that no deal was better than a bad deal.[19]

The PNTR Fight: The Last Great Trade Struggle of the Clinton Years

During the first five months of 2000, Bill Clinton waged a concerted campaign on behalf of his second and more important trade priority: the China deal. Undeterred by the Seattle fiasco, administration officials employed the logic of triangulation in hoping that Clinton's actions at the WTO meeting would actually help with the China vote by showing that the president shared the protesters' goals.[20]

The China Deal and PNTR

Kept out of the WTO's predecessor organization, the General Agreement on Tariffs and Trade (GATT), by the Cold War and then by its crushing of the Tiananmen Square protests of 1989, China made a push to join the WTO as the organization's January 1, 1995, founding date approached. But with the sudden emergence of a big U.S. trade deficit with China, the Clinton administration, strongly backed by the U.S. business community, opposed Beijing's bid for membership until the country committed itself to eventually meeting WTO standards.[21]

China did not get serious about discussing the necessary concessions until 1997, and it was not until early January 1999 that Chinese Prime Minister Zhu Roghji signaled that his government was ready to offer huge openings of its markets in return for entry into the WTO. A deal was almost reached in April, when Zhu traveled to Washington, but Clinton backed away from a proposed agreement, convinced that it was not strong enough to allow a bill giving China permanent normal trade relations to pass Congress. Business outrage prompted the president to try to renew the talks, but opposition in Beijing and the bombing of the Chinese embassy in Belgrade by North Atlantic Treaty Organization planes during the Kosovo conflict torpedoed the negotiations.[22]

The talks finally began again in October, and an agreement was reached in mid-November that was similar to the package that Clinton had rejected the previous April. The deal involved significant benefits for American firms. China agreed, among other things, to cut average tariffs from 24 to 9 percent by 2005, eliminate import quotas and licenses, reduce taxes on imported cars and permit foreign automakers to sell to Chinese customers and to finance their purchases, open up its retail market by allowing foreigners to set up wholly owned distribution and sales subsidiaries, allow minority ownership of securities houses, and stop discriminating against foreign banks.

Particularly important to the Clinton administration was the significant reduction in barriers to U.S. firms' access to the Chinese high-tech sector. With some analysts predicting that China was about to become the world's second largest market in telecommunications and personal computers, Beijing agreed to eliminate by 2005 all tariffs on computers, semiconductors, and other high-tech products and to allow foreigners to invest in Chinese telecommunications, computer, Internet, and software businesses. In return for all these Chinese concessions, the United States had to agree only to phase out quotas on Chinese textile imports by 2005 and to forgo its ability to impose unilateral trade sanctions on Beijing, benefits to which all WTO members were entitled under the organization's founding Uruguay Round accord.

As an executive agreement rather than a treaty, the China pact itself did not require congressional approval. But as noted earlier, for American firms to actually realize the gains promised in the agreement, Congress would have to abandon its annual review of what the White House termed China's "normal trade relations" (NTR)—formerly, "most favored nation" (MFN)—status, which accorded Beijing the same trading privileges extended to America's other trading partners.[23] Instead, Congress would have to grant China permanent normal trade relations.

Every year since the Tiananmen Square events, congressional critics of Beijing had attempted to deny China MFN or NTR privileges. Each time, Presidents Bush and Clinton and their business allies beat back these challenges.[24] American business had hoped since the early 1990s to end the annual review of China's trade status. Now with the signing of Clinton's deal with China, the battle would finally be joined.

The Partisan Context

The years of the 106th Congress, 1999–2000, were generally ones of sharp partisanship.[25] Angered by Clinton's victory in the impeachment struggle, congressional Republicans, especially in 1999, opposed almost anything Clinton supported. On the other side of the aisle, Clinton and congressional Democrats, united by both the impeachment experience and the recent moderation of the Democratic caucuses, for the most part worked together harmoniously. Pointing toward the 2000 elections, the Democrats' joint aim was to occupy the political center by advancing a moderate, popular agenda while portraying the Republicans as right-wing extremists, and to block GOP accomplishments while denouncing the "do-nothing" Republican Congress.

Further, Bill Clinton issued a wide range of directives and executive orders and took other administrative actions, including on the trade front, that were intended in part to boost Al Gore's prospects, as well as those of congressional Democrats.[26] For example, in early January 2000, citing safety concerns, the administration surprisingly decided to delay opening all states to Mexican trucks and buses, as called for by NAFTA. A month later, Clinton imposed tariffs on $410 million worth of wire rod and steel pipe imports. In late July, the administration announced a new plan, developed with the United Steelworkers, to protect domestic steel producers from import surges by speeding up its use of antidumping measures and providing faster relief for companies and workers. As White House officials acknowledged, these moves were intended to win Vice President Gore the endorsement of the Teamsters and shore up his support among the Steelworkers, two unions with considerable strength in the pivotal industrial heartland that had been alienated by the administration's trade policies.[27]

By early 2000, however, Clinton had come to view the China deal as sufficiently critical to his overall legacy that he was willing to work with the Republicans, themselves now somewhat more open to such cooperation; provoke a major split in his own party; and risk Al Gore's presidential hopes in the pursuit of congressional approval of PNTR.[28] Thus, in early January Clinton announced an "all-out effort" to win permanent normal trade relations status for China, making the issue his top remaining legislative priority. The actual PNTR bill was introduced in early March.

The Battle Is Joined, the Administration Mobilizes

The late winter and spring of 2000 saw the most furious battle yet in the decade-long conflict over globalization. Deploying narratives that variously emphasized the economic, human rights, and national security implications of the China deal, PNTR supporters and opponents undertook massive inside and outside lobbying efforts to win public opinion to their side, mobilize constituents to contact their representatives, convey interpretations of constituent preferences to often cross-pressured and uncertain lawmakers, and sway legislators' personal beliefs on the issue. Private lobbyists more nakedly pressured House members through the promise of campaign contributions and volunteers and the threat of their withdrawal.

Chief among PNTR's supporters, of course, was Bill Clinton, ably assisted by cabinet members—Commerce Secretary William Daley again coordinated the White House effort—and other administration officials and aides, including the 150-member China Trade Relations Working Group.[29] Energized in a way more reminiscent of his efforts on behalf of NAFTA than fast track, Clinton repeatedly spoke out in favor of PNTR, prodded business leaders into greater lobbying activity, traveled to congressional districts in California and the Midwest, held often intense meetings with over 100 undecided and cross-pressured House members, especially Democrats, and made scores of phone calls to other members.[30]

Clinton and administration officials tried to influence public, group, and congressional opinion on the China bill with two kinds of arguments. With respect to the economic merits of the deal, they maintained that China had made almost all the concessions; the United States had won access to rich new export markets, which would translate into high-wage jobs for American workers; and if PNTR were defeated, U.S. firms would lose those markets to companies in other nations.

Shifting to a greater emphasis on national security concerns during the last month of the fight, Clinton and foreign policy officials argued that WTO membership and greater trade openness would promote the spread of the market and thus also democracy, the rule of law, and improved human rights in China, whereas the defeat of PNTR would damage the prestige of Chinese reformers, resulting in greater strength for hard-liners and a drift toward conflict and instability in Asia. Finally, and more parochially, as in earlier trade fights, if less than on NAFTA, Clinton again provided side payments to, or political cover for, certain vulnerable legislators by promising them various forms of help for their districts or reelection campaigns.[31]

Largely missing in action during the fight, it should be noted, was the Clinton administration's number-two man, Al Gore, who found himself caught between business supporters and labor opponents of the PNTR bill.[32] Gore did speak out publicly in support of the measure on several occasions, including to union audiences, and he apparently lobbied a small number of House members. But his efforts were perfunctory at best. Beholden to labor for its decisive contributions to his victories over Bill Bradley in the Iowa caucuses and the New Hampshire primary, counting on continued labor support in the general election, particularly in the crucial swing states of the Industrial Belt, and still hoping to win the endorsement of the Teamsters and the United Auto Workers (UAW), two militant opponents of the China deal, Gore found it politically expedient to keep a low profile in the controversy.

The Business Campaign

As for private actors, the pro-trade elite media and most of the economics profession again provided their usual support for the China deal, as did at least some environmentalists. Bill Clinton's strongest ally in the PNTR fight, however, was almost the whole of the American business community, which was dazzled, as U.S. commercial interests had been a century earlier, by the lure of the fabled China market. In their public arguments on behalf of PNTR, business lobbyists emphasized the beneficial effect the agreement would have on U.S. exports. They played down its likely impact on investment for fear of sounding supportive of union arguments that the deal would prompt companies to move U.S. production to China. But in fact, as with NAFTA, for business the China deal was more about liberalizing investment than trade rules. "This deal is about investment, not exports," explained Joseph Quinlan, an economist with Morgan Stanley Dean Witter and Company.[33] Some firms, primarily service businesses needing immediate proximity to their customers and consumer goods producers seeking to cut transportation costs, planned to supply the domestic Chinese market from new branches and plants inside China.[34] Other companies intended to tap the country's vast reserves of cheap labor by producing goods in Chinese factories for export back to the United States and other nations.[35]

In 2000 PNTR was the American business community's top legislative priority. Enthusiastic about the China deal, which unlike the more procedural fast-track bills involved large, concentrated benefits for a host of industries, but also fearful of being outgunned again by labor, business overcame standard collective action problems and mounted a much more extravagant campaign for PNTR than it had for fast track.[36]

The business effort was months in planning but only became fully operational in the two months preceding the vote, when it appeared that labor and broader public opposition might sink PNTR. The business campaign combined a wide range of inside and outside lobbying tactics, mostly aimed at undecided Democrats. Although there was plenty of traditional Washington lobbying, awakened to the power of grassroots pressure by its defeat at labor's hands in the fast-track fights and by the recent events in Seattle, business was no longer content simply to twist arms on Capitol Hill. Firms now also prodded their employees, retirees, suppliers, and subcontractors to make their own visits and phone calls to congressional offices, both in Washington and out in the districts. Wherever and however they lobbied, business-mobilized PNTR supporters, again learning from their adversaries, stressed the specific benefits the China deal would produce for lawmakers' constituents.[37]

The pro-PNTR business campaign engaged an exceptionally wide range of participants, including agribusiness interests, financial services companies, the film industry, and manufacturers of all kinds. Overseeing the enterprise was an umbrella group, the Business Coalition for U.S-China Trade, which included such major organizations as the Business Roundtable, the Emergency Committee for American Trade, the National Association of Manufacturers, the U.S. Chamber of Commerce, and dozens of large companies. The Roundtable, which alone spent up to $10 million during the fight, led the coalition's advertising campaign, running television, radio, and print ads. In addition, several dozen Roundtable chief executive officers (CEOS) intensively lobbied on Capitol Hill, while coalition members flew thousands of other company executives and workers to Washington to press lawmakers on the issue. At the grassroots level, taking a leaf from labor's book, the Roundtable and the U.S. Chamber of Commerce divided up responsibilities for working the districts of over 150 undecided members, who were lobbied heavily during the spring recess.[38]

Business also used its vast financial resources to influence the PNTR vote. The 1999–2000 election cycle saw an explosion of campaign contributions from the business community. During the first half of 2000, business interests wrote checks to and organized fund-raisers for members of both parties, especially those in close races, who were either committed to voting for the China deal or considered persuadable. Conversely, business lobbyists sometimes threatened to withhold campaign contributions from members who voted against PNTR. "If somebody's on the margin and they screw up on this vote, they'd better not look to me for money," warned Chamber of Commerce president Thomas Donohue.[39] Companies also increased their soft-money contributions to party committees in part to sway the PNTR votes of House members who stood to benefit from the expenditure of those funds.

The high-tech sector made a substantial contribution to the wider business campaign for PNTR, in contrast to the industry's relative inactivity during the fast-track fights.[40] In fact, PNTR had become high technology's number one legislative priority and perhaps its most important concern since the U.S-Japan trade conflicts of the 1980s.[41]

Two major high-tech industry coalitions lobbied heavily for PNTR: (1) the U.S. High-Tech Coalition on China, an older organization of Washington-based trade groups led by the American Electronics Association that also included the Electronics Industry Alliance, the Semiconductor Industry Association, and seven other trade associations, along with their member companies, and (2) and the Internet Coalition for China PNTR, a coalition of computer and Internet companies formed by America on Line that claimed AT&T, Microsoft, and Motorola among its members.[42]

Again focusing on undecided Democrats—in this case, in tech-heavy states like California—high-tech firms and groups bought newspaper and radio ads, held press conferences, sent out information packets, made speeches, signed letters, and buttonholed legislators. In addition to flying dozens of its top executives to Washington, the Electronic Industries Alliance, with 2,100 member companies, waged an exceptional grassroots campaign in the districts of a few dozen wavering legislators by holding town hall meetings and using industry trade shows to generate 11,000 computer-assisted letters to lawmakers. Individual companies used e-mail to solicit thousands of letters from their employees.

The high-tech sector also deployed its financial clout during the PNTR fight. The industry's campaign contributions had mushroomed since about 1997. Individual, PAC, and soft-money donations from computer-related companies to national party organizations and candidates leaped from a little over $9 million in the 1997–98 election cycle to nearly $24 million as of June 30, 2000, in the next cycle, putting the high-tech industry on a par with such other big donors as the energy, insurance, pharmaceutical, and banking industries.[43] In the first half of 2000, high-tech firms directed campaign funds to pro-PNTR lawmakers, and industry lobbyists made it clear to House members that their votes on PNTR would be strongly considered when it came time to dole out further contributions.[44]

The House Republican Leadership

As in earlier trade fights, Bill Clinton's principal ally in the House was not the leadership of his own party, but rather the GOP leadership. Although Republican lawmakers opposed him on most other issues, they generally welcomed the PNTR debate, seeing in it an opportunity both to shore up their business support and to deflect attention from issues like health care, minimum wages, and gun control, on which the Democrats had set the tone the previous year.

For two reasons, however, GOP leaders were initially hesitant to schedule an early vote on the PNTR bill and to forcefully advocate its passage. First, until late March they worried that the White House was not working the bill hard enough and that if PNTR consequently passed with overwhelming Republican support but only limited Democratic backing, GOP members would be vulnerable to partisan attacks in the November elections. Second, tempted as an opposition party under divided government to pursue a "strategy of disagreement," GOP leaders wanted to delay a vote on PNTR until the eve of the Democratic National Convention. Their aim was to drive a highly public and embarrassing wedge between Democrats, including Al Gore, and their labor supporters, who fervently opposed the China deal. As a House GOP aide explained, the PNTR vote will help the Republicans because "it will lead to disarray among the Democrats" and their union allies.[45]

Republican leaders only finally abandoned their delaying tactics in mid-April, after a delegation of top business executives read the riot act to GOP Whip Tom DeLay of Texas and insisted that a date be set for the PNTR vote.[46] By this time, the White House had begun to lobby House Democrats more aggressively, thus reassuring Republican leaders that support for PNTR would be at least somewhat bipartisan. The PNTR vote was quickly scheduled for late May, and the GOP leadership began to build support for the bill among its followers.

Although House Democrats were unified on most issues in 2000, trade once again emerged as a deep fault line within the party. While the Democratic leadership opposed PNTR, New Democrats in their various guises—the Democratic Leadership Council, the New Democrat Network (NDN), and the House-based New Democrat Coalition (NDC)—successfully waged an all-out effort to line up a significant minority of House Democrats in support of the China deal.[47]

New Democrats remained ideologically committed to free trade, but they also believed that the China deal would benefit members of the upscale learning class, whose support they viewed as key to the Democrats' political fortunes. New Democrats thus lobbied their fellow party members, published studies and polls, and enlisted the backing of moderate Democratic mayors and county officials.

The New Democrats' most important contribution to the China fight, however, was their two pronged-effort to win greater business financial assistance for party candidates, thus lessening their dependence on labor for campaign funds and reducing their own electoral risk of bucking the unions to vote for PNTR. On the one hand, New Democrats worked to develop, and pushed their more liberal colleagues to adopt, moderate, business-friendly positions, including support for PNTR. On the other hand, the New Democrats themselves, through the vehicle of the New Democrat Network, raised business money for moderate, pro-trade candidates.

The NDN set out to raise $5.5 million in business contributions to the 2000 campaigns of moderate, internationalist Democrats. One piece of this effort was a "Trade Fundraising Series" of a dozen events that netted $250,000 for ten pro-PNTR Democratic incumbents and candidates. NDC cochairman Cal Dooley of California explained the strategy underlying the New Democrats' trade-related fund-raising endeavors: "We have been trying to demonstrate to Democrats who are willing to vote in a pro-trade fashion that could cause problems with traditional bases of support like labor, we have our independent support system. . . . [For] Democrats [who] do embrace a pro-trade policy, there is political support within the business community."[48]

The New Democrats focused intently on building support for their party within the high-tech sector. During the late 1990s both congressional parties energetically competed for the favor of high-tech interests in a quest for campaign contributions as well as the politically beneficial cache derived from being associated with the industries of the future.[49] But just as the neoliberals and the DLC had played key roles on competitiveness and technology issues in the 1980s, so it was the New Democrats, both within and outside Congress, who now most avidly courted the high-tech sector.

Inside Congress, NDC leaders brokered high-tech bills and pushed the Democratic leadership to take high-tech issues more seriously. Outside Congress, the DLC and its affiliated Progressive Policy Institute formed the New Economy Task Force to build bridges between Democratic elected officials and high-tech executives, and the DLC and the NDN sponsored meetings on the New Economy in Boston and San Jose. Not least important, the New Democrat Network raised campaign funds from high-tech interests. "By working with the high-tech community and the new economy businesses, we're trying to build a new pool of money for Democrats," said NDN president Simon Rosenberg.[50]

Since the high-tech industry's top legislative priority in 2000 was approval of PNTR, the New Democrats embraced the issue with special fervor. They lobbied more liberal party colleagues on the issue and held fund-raisers with high-tech interests to raise money for vulnerable pro-PNTR lawmakers who were under pressure from labor to oppose the measure.

Organized Labor and Other PNTR Opponents

Leading the forces on the other side of the barricades was, of course, the labor movement. As it had on NAFTA, labor argued, and business representatives privately conceded, that the key elements of the agreement were those that would liberalize China's investment rules. Drawing on studies produced by the Economic Policy Institute (EPI), union leaders insisted that the deal would result in both a real and a threatened flight of manufacturing capital to China to take advantage of its cheap, repressed labor force. The result for the United States would be a bigger trade deficit, lost jobs, and a decline in workers' bargaining power and wages.[51] Labor also worried that if China was allowed into the World Trade Organization, leverage on Beijing to improve labor and human rights would be lost, and the WTO would never seriously address the wider issue of global labor standards. In fact, labor saw the China vote as "a proxy for all our concerns about globalization," according to AFL-CIO spokeswoman Denise Mitchell.[52]

The labor movement waged a powerful campaign against PNTR, led by the industrial unions—especially the United Autoworkers, the United Steelworkers, the Teamsters, the Machinists, and the Union of Needletrades, Industrial, and Textile Employees (UNITE).[53] In Washington, labor leaders and lobbyists met repeatedly with House members, mostly Democrats, often joined by religious leaders, environmentalists, and exiled Chinese dissidents. On April 12, 15,000 union members turned out for an anti-PNTR rally on the steps of the Capitol followed by a day of lobbying.

Outside the Washington Beltway, the AFL-CIO put full-time coordinators in the districts of thirty-two undecided House members, where they organized demonstrations and candlelight vigils, arranged meetings with lawmakers, facilitated letter-writing efforts, and took cell phones to factories so union members could inundate House offices with about thirty thousand phone calls over the course of the campaign. This grassroots lobbying was markedly intense during the two weeks of Congress's spring recess, when union members handed out one million pieces of literature and joined multistate "fair-trade" caravans organized by the Citizens Trade Campaign. At the same time, the AFL-CIO ran about $2 million worth of television ads in fifteen congressional districts urging viewers to lobby lawmakers to vote against PNTR.

In its anti-PNTR lobbying drive, which was directed mostly toward undecided Democrats, labor tried to trade on (1) its perceived success in turning out its members in the 1998 midterm elections,[54] (2) its key contribution to Al Gore's victory in the Democratic presidential primary campaign, chiefly in the decisive Iowa and New Hampshire contests,[55] (3) the AFL-CIO's planned $46 million grassroots mobilization in the 2000 congressional races on behalf of candidates, all but one of them Democrats, in seventy-one swing districts in twenty-five states,[56] an effort that figured to be significant in what was anticipated to be another low turnout election, and (4) to a lesser extent, its increased campaign contributions, donated almost entirely to Democrats, including record amounts of soft money, much of which went to the Democratic Congressional Campaign Committee (DCCC) to help the party recapture the House.[57]

As the China vote approached, some labor leaders bluntly warned undecided House Democrats that PNTR supporters could not count on union backing, either financial or grassroots, in the fall elections. "We expect congressmen with a tight race to vote for us," said Teamsters president James P. Hoffa, a fierce critic of the China deal. "I have delivered the message to them. There are no free votes. This is the line in the sand."[58]

In its opposition to PNTR, labor was, as usual, joined by groups like the National Farmers Union, whose family farm members along the Canadian and Mexican borders most acutely felt the effects of NAFTA; environmental associations, such as the Sierra Club and Friends of the Earth, that feared China's entry into the WTO would undermine protections of the atmosphere and animals of other countries; and human rights and church organizations that were concerned about political and religious repression in China. Many of these groups worked in coalition with labor unions under the umbrella of the Citizens Trade Campaign, which put together a number of fair-trade caravans during the spring congressional recess. Among the more conservative PNTR opponents were the textile industry, which worried that it would lose 150,000 more jobs to imports while China would not open its own markets to U.S. textile exports; other small, import-competing domestic manufacturers; conservative religious organizations appalled by China's human rights record; and conservative groups, activists, and writers troubled by China's growing military might.

In Congress, the fight against PNTR was again led by House Minority Whip and strong labor ally David Bonior, of Michigan, working with other Democratic labor and human rights supporters and a few party members with national security concerns. Republican opposition to PNTR was led this time not mainly by conservative economic nationalists sympathetic to Pat Buchanan, as in the NAFTA and fast-track fights, but rather by GOP lawmakers with their own human rights and national security worries.

Why Did PNTR Pass?

On May 24, after two months of intense lobbying on both sides of the issue, the House passed Bill Clinton's PNTR bill by a vote of 237–197. With this victory by internationalist forces, the process of trade liberalization appeared to have been renewed.

The internationalists' revived fortunes were largely attributable to changes on the Democratic side of the aisle. Despite the presence in their ranks of a core of conservative economic nationalists and other free-trade critics from mostly blue-collar districts, throughout the preceding decade and continuing with the PNTR vote, House Republicans remained generally supportive of free trade. From two-thirds to three-quarters of GOP lawmakers supported NAFTA, the GATT agreement, and the two fast-track bills. In voting for PNTR 164–37, GOP members again backed free trade by almost a 3–1 margin.

It is, therefore, the Democrats' behavior that explains the waxing and waning of congressional support for free trade. Although about 40 percent of House Democrats joined with Republicans to approve NAFTA and fully 65 percent of Democrats backed the GATT accord, only 20 and 15 percent of Democratic lawmakers supported the 1997 and 1998 fast-track bills respectively, sending those measures down to defeat. On PNTR however, Democrats again opposed the bill by a smaller margin of 188–73; that is, almost 35 percent supported free trade, enough to give Clinton and his allies another victory. To better understand this outcome, let us take a closer look at Republican and especially Democratic voting on PNTR.

The Republicans

About one-quarter of Republicans voted against PNTR, either because they had blue-collar constituents, because they had human rights or national security concerns, or in a few cases because they hoped to deny Bill Clinton a political victory.[59]

Yet almost three-quarters of House Republicans supported PNTR, due either to (1) ideological commitments to free trade, (2) the disproportionately white-collar, wealthier, agricultural, and export-oriented nature of the districts they represented,[60] (3) loyalty to or inside and outside lobbying by their core business constituents, (4) their dependence on business campaign contributions,[61] (5) the passage in early May of a bill liberalizing trade with Africa and the Caribbean basin that was supported by cotton growers and textile workers in North and South Carolina and Texas, key constituents of GOP lawmakers in those states,[62] and (6) the concerted whipping efforts of the House Republican leadership.[63]

Finally, it appears that about ten Republicans concerned about human rights were persuaded to support PNTR by the addition to the bill of a proposal developed by Democrat Sander Levin of Michigan and Republican Doug Bereuter of Nebraska. The proposal called for a commission to monitor China's performance on human rights, as well as for assistance to U.S. workers hurt by a surge in Chinese imports and sanctions on China if Beijing violated international trade rules.[64]

Anti-PNTR Democrats

On the Democratic side, reflecting the continued division between the parties over trade policy and globalization, over 65 percent of House Democrats opposed PNTR, including 42 percent of the members of the New Democrat Coalition. Some party members voted against PNTR due to ideological commitments to fair rather than free trade or to continued use of the annual review of China's trade status as leverage on Beijing's human rights and military policies. But for most Democrats opposed to PNTR—and those supporting it, too—the vote was not mainly about ideas and ideology. "This is not an intellectual debate," said Electronic Industries Alliance head and former Democratic congressman Dave McCurdy. "The China debate is pure politics."[65]

Most Democrats, including many who privately supported the China deal because it appeared to involve so few U.S. concessions, voted against PNTR mainly for political reasons. These included (1) the disproportionately blue-collar, unionized, and poorer character of their districts,[66] (2) the inside and outside lobbying efforts of organized labor, (3) their continued dependence on labor for manpower and campaign funds,[67] and (4) the related fear, held even by many moderates and members with safe seats, that if marginal Democrats risked the loss of labor support by voting for PNTR, most business donors, rather than replace withheld labor campaign contributions, would still back these Democrats' generally more pro-corporate Republican opponents in November, thus jeopardizing the party's chances of recapturing the House.[68]

Despite such compelling political reasons to oppose PNTR, however, almost 35 percent of House Democrats did back the bill, providing its margin of victory. What explains the increase in Democratic support for free trade since the fast-track fights?

Pro-PNTR Democrats: The Negligible Role of Public Opinion

There was certainly no wave of intense public support for PNTR to offset the strong opposition of labor and its allies. Depending on how questions were worded, some polls found support for PNTR, others opposition.[69] A series of Gallup Polls conducted between November 1999 and May 2000 that asked respondents only whether they favored or opposed a PNTR bill that would allow China to join the WTO found a decline and then a rise in support for the measure, the latter coming in the six weeks preceding the vote.[70] This suggests that as on NAFTA, proponents of the China deal were successful in moving public opinion in their direction toward the end of the fight.

The main thing to be said, however, is that the public paid little attention to the PNTR controversy. PNTR "is a big deal for the business and labor elites," said Democratic pollster Mark Mellman, "but it is not a very salient issue for the general public."[71] Though there was still public unease about globalization and its effects,[72] the booming economy and attendant low unemployment levels reduced the salience of both the general issue and the China agreement specifically.

A More Moderate Democratic Caucus

Part of the increased Democratic support for PNTR compared to fast track lay in the changing composition and orientation of the House Democratic caucus. Although the Democrats were routed in the 1994 congressional races, the result paradoxically was a more liberal Democratic caucus, since most of the party's losses were in marginal southern districts represented by relatively conservative Democrats. The 1996 congressional elections modestly reinforced this trend, as more conservative southerners were defeated, while liberal and moderate Democratic candidates won some new GOP-held and open seats in the North. As we have seen, this liberalization of the House Democratic caucus contributed to the demise of fast track in 1997 and 1998.

But some of the freshman Democrats elected in 1996 and most of those elected in 1998 were young, pro-business moderates from marginal, upscale suburban districts, notably in the Northeast. Many were elected with assistance from the New Democratic Network; 15 of 26 and 26 of 34 NDN-backed challengers won in 1996 and 1998 respectively. Whereas only 25 percent of freshman Democrats elected in 1994 later joined the moderate New Democrat Coalition, formed in late 1996, 68 and 75 percent of those first elected in 1996 and 1998 respectively signed up.[73] At the same time, even some traditional liberal Democrats, including strong labor allies like Minority Whip David Bonior and Minority Leader Dick Gephardt, were adopting more moderate views, now convinced that Bill Clinton's conservative fiscal and welfare policies were working.[74]

. Thanks to these two developments, the NDC grew from 41 members at the time of the 1997 fast-track vote to 65 members by the time of the PNTR vote, making it the largest caucus in the House. The Democratic caucus as a whole had become more centrist and thus at least somewhat more open to free-trade initiatives like the China deal.[75]

These changes in the Democratic caucus, however, do not alone explain why seventeen former Democratic NAFTA opponents still in the House supported PNTR or why 58 percent of NDC members voted for PNTR, up from the 50 percent who backed fast track in 1997.

Weaknesses in Labor's Mobilization

Most important in explaining the victory of PNTR was the shifting balance of forces surrounding the issue. First, despite the intensity of its effort, the labor movement's opposition to PNTR was not as effective as it might have been because (1) labor had little presence in the expanding industries of the New Economy, (2) unions "maxed out" their campaign contributions too early in the electoral cycle, preventing them from punishing members who then turned against labor on PNTR,[76] and (3) labor was not fully united in the struggle. While the industrial unions' international offices fought furiously against the China deal, the public and service sector unions, representing workers in nontraded sectors, were more indifferent to the agreement.[77] Moreover, dozens of major union locals in eighteen states representing workers in trade-dependent firms in the longshore, machine tool, steel, auto, engineering, and aerospace industries broke with their internationals and actually supported the deal.[78]

For related reasons, organized labor's fight against PNTR was not as spirited as many observers had expected it to be. As important as the issue was to much of labor, especially the industrial unions, the movement as a whole—including the AFL-CIO and its president, John Sweeney, who came out of the service sector—had a still higher priority in the spring of 2000: helping the Democrats recapture the House and holding onto the presidency. As the fall elections approached, labor had many other nontrade-related policy goals, such as raising the minimum wage and protecting Medicare and Social Security, all of which required Democratic control of as many branches of government as possible.

Reluctant to threaten Al Gore's candidacy or the Democrats' hopes of recapturing the House by waging an overly divisive fight against PNTR, much of organized labor, according to many observers, pulled its punches toward the end of the battle. Although Teamster and UAW leaders continued to promise reprisals against Democrats who voted for PNTR, AFL-CIO political director Steve Rosenthal spoke for most of labor when he said that the federation would not make the PNTR vote "a litmus test" for supporting Democrats in the fall elections.[79] Thus, some Democrats called labor's bluff and voted for PNTR, convinced that most of the movement would stick with the party rather than jeopardize its chances in November.

Persuasion, Bargaining, and Political Cover

On the other side, the mobilization of pro-PNTR forces was much more effective in winning over undecided and cross-pressured lawmakers, primarily Democrats, than had been the case on fast track. In the White House, Bill Clinton's energetic persuasion and bargaining, though less successful than on NAFTA, did swing some key votes, mainly by putting a focus on the overall course of U.S.-China relations.[80] In Congress, the House Republican leadership kept most of its members in line, while pro-PNTR Democratic leaders, including prominent New Democrat Coalition lawmakers, helped win crucial support from members of their party.

In addition to their persuasive efforts, the Clinton administration and pro-PNTR members of Congress worked separately and together to provide various forms of political cover for Democratic lawmakers who were personally inclined to support PNTR but fearful of the electoral consequences of doing so. Clinton's deal making was useful in this regard. Perhaps still more important was the addition to the PNTR bill of the Levin-Bereuter proposal, supported by the White House, that called for a commission to monitor China's human rights, assistance to U.S. workers hurt by import surges from China, and sanctions on China if it violated international trade rules. Some observers suggested that the inclusion of the proposal, which despite being labeled a "figleaf" and "toothless" by labor reflected the movement's continuing influence, won the votes of twenty Democrats who were worried about the loss of U.S. jobs and union support.[81]

Business Mobilization and Money Make the Difference

Probably most important in producing the PNTR victory, however, was the business community's massive inside and outside lobbying campaign, costing ten times what labor spent during the fight, which helped offset pressure from the unions and other PNTR opponents on Democratic lawmakers caught between competing interests in their districts.[82] Business lobbyists effectively made the case that, unlike the procedural fast-track bills, the China deal would produce billions of dollars in benefits for U.S. industries. The lobbying efforts of high-tech firms and organizations were particularly effective in swaying undecided and cross-pressured Democrats. "Obviously they played a huge role," said Representative Patrick Kennedy, of Rhode Island, chairman of the Democratic Congressional Campaign Committee and an opponent of the bill.[83]

In addition to its various lobbying activities, the business community influenced Democratic voting on PNTR by continuing to reorient its campaign contribution strategies. Through 1994, when the Democrats still controlled both houses of Congress, business directed a small majority of its campaign contributions to the Democrats, but after the GOP capture of Congress, business decisively shifted its donations to the GOP. Following their 1997 fast-track defeat, however, many corporate leaders concluded that they had erred in so dramatically shifting their support to the not fully reliable Republicans, while at the same time leaving even pro-business Democrats short of cash and thus too dependent on labor money. Consequently, business began to rebalance its financial support for the parties.

During the 1999–2000 election cycle, this trend continued. Whereas in 1997–98, 34 percent of business PAC contributions to individual congressional campaigns went to Democratic House and Senate candidates, through June 30, 2000, of the 1999–2000 cycle, this figure rose to 40 percent.[84] Similarly, while in 1997–98, 37 percent of individual, PAC, and soft-money donations by business to House campaign committees went to the Democratic Congressional Campaign Committee, through June 30, 2000, of the next cycle, this figure rose to 52 percent.[85]

The Democrats made impressive fund-raising inroads into the high-tech sector. Through August 2000 of the 1999–2000 election cycle, $11.9 million of the $21.9 million in individual, PAC, and soft-money contributions made by computer-related companies to national party organizations and candidates went to Democrats.[86] During roughly the same period, the Democratic House and Senate campaign committees took in nearly $17.7 million in hard and soft money from the electronics and communication industries, over $3 million more than their Republican counterparts, who had received $14.3 million.[87]

The growth of business contributions to the Democrats outpaced the increase in labor's donations, helping to shift the balance of power within the party. For example, in mid-2000 labor contributions to the DCCC were holding steady as a percentage of overall donations, while business contributions had increased to 75.2 percent of all donations, up from 69.7 percent in the 1998 elections.[88]

The Democrats' new success in raising money from business was due in part to their five-seat pickup in the House in 1998 and to business's inclination to hedge its bets on a possible Democratic takeover of the chamber in November. But this was not the whole story. Business also increased its contributions to the Democrats because—thanks in good measure to the efforts of the various New Democratic groupings (the DLC, the NDC, and the NDN), prominently in the high-tech sector—it perceived the party as becoming more friendly to business. For example, the U.S. Chamber of Commerce intended to give some money to pro-business Democrats in the fall. The organization's spokesman, Frank Coleman, explained why: "The Chamber supports Democrats, not in anticipation of the party taking over Congress, but because some of them have begun to vote more pro-business than in the past."[89]

By boosting their donations to the Democrats, and thus counterbalancing labor's influence within the party, business hoped both to encourage this general pro-corporate trend and to influence Democratic lawmakers' votes on specific issues. In the spring of 2000, this above all meant PNTR. As we have seen, business interests, especially high-tech firms, both directed campaign contributions to pro-PNTR legislators and threatened to withhold funds from those who opposed the China bill. This carrot-and-stick approach contributed to the decision of almost 35 percent of the members of the House Democratic caucus to ally with business and buck organized labor by voting for PNTR.[90]

Business was an effective force in the PNTR fight not only for what it did, but also for what it did not do. Three years earlier, business had vehemently insisted on a "clean" fast-track bill with no labor or environmental provisions attached, a position that had contributed to the measure's defeat. Now, having learned from that failure, business assumed a more flexible stance, acquiescing to the inclusion of the Levin-Bereuter proposal in the PNTR bill to protect a number of Democrats against union criticism.[91]

Dick Gephardt's Role

This discussion of Democratic support for PNTR cannot be concluded without noting the crucial and complex part that Minority Leader Dick Gephardt played in the fight. Although Gephardt opposed the China bill, his political tightrope walking on the measure was central to its passage. The key to comprehending his role was his single-minded commitment to recapturing the House for the Democrats. Some context is required to show how PNTR figured into these ambitions.

Through 1997, as the House's leading liberal and economic nationalist, Gephardt was one of Bill Clinton's toughest critics, battling the president over the balanced budget and fast-track bills of that year as he prepared to challenge Al Gore from the left for the 2000 Democratic presidential nomination. But with Clinton's strong commitment to defend social security in his 1998 State of the Union address and then Republican attempts to impeach the president over the Monica Lewinsky scandal, Gephardt muted his criticisms of Clinton. Finally, following the Democrats' unexpectedly strong showing in the 1998 midterm races, Gephardt abandoned his plan to seek the presidency and instead set about to help the Democrats regain control of the House in 2000 and make himself Speaker.[92] Accomplishing these goals, Gephardt understood, would require three things: party unity, votes, and money. The pursuit of these resources prompted Gephardt to begin a move to the political center.

With the expansion of the New Democrats' ranks following the 1998 elections, Gephardt, convinced that party unity was essential to recapturing the House in 2000, formed a 50–60 member leadership group that included Democratic lawmakers from all points on the political spectrum and worked to develop a consensus, centrist agenda for the upcoming campaigns.

Beyond this, Gephardt himself had come to recognize that suburban districts like those represented by the New Democrats were critical to the party's future. "They're more moderate, and if we're going to win the majority and hold the majority, we've got to have more representatives win in those districts," he said. Concluding that the Democrats had to "lead from the middle," Gephardt now personally endorsed a balanced budget, national debt reduction, and other New Democratic positions that he had long rejected. "Dick has not only listened and responded positively to moderate and conservative Democrats," said an appreciative Representative Tim Roemer, of Indiana, a New Democrat Coalition cochairman, "but increasingly he has incorporated our ideas into his messages and his speeches and his legislation."[93]

Gephardt's centrist turn was reinforced by his aggressive solicitation of business money to finance the Democrats' 2000 campaigns.[94] Galvanized by the results of the 1998 elections, Gephardt, already a top fund-raiser, essentially took over the Democratic Congressional Campaign Committee, transferring almost all his political operation to the committee. Capitalizing on donor anger at the GOP over impeachment, the momentum generated by the recent election gains, and the solid prospect that the Democrats might retake the House in 2000, Gephardt criss-crossed the country raising unprecedentedly large sums of hard and above all soft money.[95] Business interests responded to Gephardt's efforts and, as discussed earlier, began to evenly split their contributions between the two House party committees.

Among the various reasons for this increased giving to the DCCC was the more business-friendly face of the party, a development that the former populist Gephardt now did much to encourage. "We're treating [business contributors] much more like customers and shareholders," said DCCC spokesman Erik Smith. "We're . . . making the point that we're protecting the resources they give us." The New Democrats appreciated the change. "Dick Gephardt has done a very successful job of listening to and often responding to the business community," said NDC cochairman Tim Roemer.[96]

Gephardt was conspicuously solicitous of the interests—and the money—of high-tech firms, thanks to pressure from the New Democrats. He made technology the focus of the Democratic caucus's February retreat and invited key high-tech leaders to join party members at an early May congressional business summit. Most dramatic, in a major speech in late March to the Information Technology Association of America, Gephardt endorsed a list of industry policy priorities that he had developed in private meetings with high-tech CEOs.[97]

This is the wider context in which Gephardt's role in the PNTR fight must be understood. Due to his long-standing ties to organized labor, most observers expected Gephardt to eventually oppose the China bill, but until mid-April he said little at all about the issue. He did so to avoid splitting the Democratic caucus before the fall elections and angering high tech and other business interests that had made approval of PNTR their top 2000 legislative priority. Instead, Gephardt tried to broker a compromise with the White House, said that caucus members should vote their consciences or whichever way would help them win and thus help the Democrats recapture the House in November, told both labor and business that he would not whip the issue, and urged unions not to punish those Democrats who did vote for PNTR. New Democratic and business leaders praised his restraint.[98]

On April 19 Gephardt finally announced his opposition to PNTR, an action that initially angered some high-tech executives, especially since it came only a week after a DCCC fund-raiser in Silicon Valley. But during the last five weeks of the PNTR fight, Gephardt launched no public assault on the bill, and he continued to refrain from whipping the issue, rebuffing labor pressure to do so and urging unions not to retaliate against PNTR supporters in November. "I have not talked with one Member who told me that Gephardt has talked to them about anything," said Cal Dooley. Gephardt's relative inactivity on the issue made it easier for cross-pressured Democrats to eventually come down in support of PNTR. "I think that went a long way toward allowing enough Democrats to [to vote for PNTR] so that it could win in the House," said TechNet head and Democratic operative Jeff Modisett.[99]

After the House had approved the PNTR bill, Bill Clinton and the business community pressed for its quick passage in the Senate, where at least seventy members were estimated to support the measure, before it became further entangled with election-year politics. But partisan maneuvering delayed the vote until early September.

GOP Majority Leader Trent Lott of Mississippi put off the vote for several reasons.[100] First, most Republicans did not want consideration of the PNTR bill to delay voting on the chamber's thirteen appropriations bills. They worried that a drawn-out PNTR debate would leave them with a backlog of spending measures to deal with after the August recess, once again putting them at Bill Clinton's mercy during an election-eve budget battle. Second, Republicans used the threat to delay voting on PNTR in an effort to extract spending concessions from Senate Democrats, who feared that postponing the vote until after the Democratic convention, at which a range of possibly embarrassing protests were planned, might turn the China deal into a damaging election issue. Third, at least some GOP senators wanted to delay the PNTR vote precisely to create difficulties for Democrats who were counting on labor support in the November elections.

Finally, Lott put off the vote to give him time to work out an agreement on how to deal with a potential amendment to the PNTR bill, cosponsored by Senators Fred Thompson (R-Tenn.) and Robert G. Torricelli (D-N.J.), that was intended to combat weapons proliferation by China by imposing sanctions on Chinese companies if they were caught exporting nuclear, chemical, or biological weapons or long-range missiles. The White House and the business community vehemently objected to the measure, fearing that its sanctions requirement would wreak havoc on trade relations with China and punish U.S. businesses. They also were concerned that if the legislation were attached to the PNTR bill as an amendment, forcing a conference committee on the amended bill and then a second House vote, the result would be further delay, perhaps beyond the November elections, or even the defeat of the measure.

The Senate finally began debate on permanent normal trade relations with China in early September. Bill Clinton, top administration officials, and business groups like the U.S. Chamber of Commerce and the Business Roundtable all lobbied heavily against the Thompson-Torricelli amendment, which opponents had been unable to keep off the bill. Chamber president Thomas J. Donohue publicly warned of retribution against senators who supported the amendment.[101]

The Senate easily dispatched some twenty amendments, most of them centered on human rights concerns, and then on September 13 defeated the more contentious Thompson-Torricelli amendment on a bipartisan vote of 65–32.[102] A week later the Senate approved the PNTR bill by a resounding vote of 83–15, with only 8 Republicans and 7 Democrats opposed. Pro-trade Republicans were reluctant to antagonize their business backers in a hotly contested election year. Democrats, for their part, felt little pressure from labor leaders, who never believed that they could win enough Democrats over to defeat the bill in the Senate, a body more traditionally supportive of free trade than the House, as we have seen.[103] Thus, labor had long ago shifted its focus to the November elections. Moreover, despite some union warnings after the House vote in May, few Democratic PNTR supporters in the House were known to have lost labor backing for their fall campaigns, and none was believed to be in serious political difficulty because of his or her vote.[104] The China deal had largely dissipated as a campaign issue, while labor expended its energy on other priority issues like health care and raising the minimum wage.[105]

Business hailed the PNTR vote as a victory for economic internationalist over antiglobalist forces and a welcome return to bipartisanship in trade policy. "This historic trade legislation clearly is setback for the forces of protectionism and reestablishes important bipartisan support for global trade expansion," proclaimed Jerry Jasinowski, president of the National Association of Manufacturers.[106]

Following the demise of the first of his final two trade liberalization initiatives, a new WTO negotiating round, amid the tear gas of Seattle, Bill Clinton triumphed in the more important fight for congressional approval of his China bill. As in the earlier free-trade battles of the 1990s, the PNTR victory was the result of the shifting balance of inter- and intra-partisan forces in the House of Representatives. More precisely, changes inside the Democratic Party were once again the most significant, since despite the presence within their ranks of a bloc of free trade critics—including conservative nationalists, allies of the textile and other import-competing industries, and representatives of blue-collar districts—two-thirds to three-quarters of House Republicans remained supportive of trade liberalization throughout the various conflicts.

The principal factors contributing to the ebb and flow of the Democrats' support for free trade were electorally induced changes in the relative size of Democratic congressional factions, the varying magnitude and effectiveness of Bill Clinton's persuasive and bargaining efforts, and, probably most important, the shifting balance of strength within the party between internationally oriented business interests and organized labor. PNTR with China was approved in the House thanks to the expanded ranks and activism of moderate New Democrats, the efforts of a reenergized Clinton White House, and especially the campaign waged by the business community, which saw vast concentrated benefits in the China deal and whose forces were swelled by the new activism of high-tech firms. Learning from its 1997 fast-track defeat, business deployed its structurally generated resources to overwhelm its somewhat divided union adversaries with a massive inside and outside lobbying effort and campaign contributions distributed more evenly to both parties, thus reducing the Democrats' financial dependence on labor. Together these three factors fractured the Democratic caucus, producing enough Democratic support to carry PNTR to victory. The subsequent Senate approval of the bill produced the final triumph of internationalist forces on the issue.[107]

As Bill Clinton's presidency approached its conclusion, then, yet another reconfiguration of party coalitions on trade policy helped, at least temporarily, to unblock the stalled process of trade liberalization.

Although the dynamics and impact of party competition over U.S. trade policy after 1980 were highly complex, we can nevertheless draw some general conclusions from this study. Despite the view of many political analysts that American parties remain in secular decline and that party politics has had little effect on U.S. trade policy, party competition has significantly influenced the way we have dealt with our foreign trading partners and will in all likelihood continue to do so.

Party Positions on Trade

Parties and Presidents

A first conclusion is that partisan differences over trade at the presidential level remained relatively modest. As conventional wisdom would have it, most presidents, irrespective of party affiliation, are free traders as a result of their heterogeneous national constituencies, which on the whole benefit from free trade, and their foreign policy responsibilities. These factors, together with their search for support from upscale voters and internationally oriented business interests, led Ronald Reagan, George Bush, and Bill Clinton—two Republicans and a Democrat—to generally oppose product-specific protectionism and to support bilateral, regional, and multilateral trade liberalization initiatives like the North American Free Trade Agreement (NAFTA), the Uruguay Round accord of the General Agreement on Tariffs and Trade (GATT), and permanent normal trade relations (PNTR) with China.

In some circumstances, though, presidents or candidates of both parties supported tougher trade policies. In the case of Republican presidents, such toughening was often caused by pressure from Democrats on the campaign trail and in Congress. Ronald Reagan and George Bush, two committed free traders, were sometimes forced via a process of policy contagion to adopt fair-trade positions toward Japan and other countries to avoid losing swing voter and group support, thus narrowing their differences with their Democratic adversaries.

Still, there was some differentiation of party positions on trade at the executive level, especially during presidential campaigns, but also in the White House. Thus, during their presidential primary and general election races, Walter Mondale, Michael Dukakis, and Bill Clinton all assumed somewhat tougher postures on trade than did their GOP rivals as they sought both the support of their core blue-collar constituencies and a wider campaign issue to win the backing of key swing constituencies, including Reagan Democrats.

Once in office, Bill Clinton "triangulated" between free and fair trade. He took a tougher stance toward Japan, at least in 1993–95, than had either Ronald Reagan or George Bush, pushed for NAFTA labor and environmental side agreements that, however weak, Bush would not have backed, and pressed (if unsuccessfully) to include a fast-track measure with labor and environmental provisions in the 1994 GATT implementing legislation. Clinton subsequently slowed further progress toward trade liberalization in 1995–96 to avoid antagonizing labor and other liberal interests before the 1996 presidential election. He similarly blew up the World Trade Organization (WTO) talks in Seattle at the end of 1999 to avoid souring labor on Al Gore's presidential campaign.

The Congressional Parties (Often) Divide over Trade

At the congressional level, there were considerable differences between the parties on important trade legislation like domestic content, early drafts of the 1988 Trade Act, and the 1997 and 1998 fast-track bills. In fact, party divisions over trade were surprisingly pronounced.

Simple quantitative evidence for this split has been compiled by the Competitive Enterprise Institute (CEI). During the ten years from 1985 to 1994, the CEI produced an annual index rating lawmakers' support for free-market principles. In addition to an overall rating for each member of Congress, the CEI calculated ratings in specific policy areas, including trade policy. The score for each member, both overall and in individual policy areas, represents the percentage of votes cast by the member that were "promarket" from among the votes sampled. On trade policy, a "promarket" vote was one in support of free trade.[1]

As the graphs produced from the CEI indexes show (Figure A.4), party divisions over trade during this ten-year period were substantial, both in the House and more surprisingly in the Senate, as Republicans were consistently more supportive of free trade.[2] The average annual House Republican rating on trade during this decade was 67, compared to only 28 for the Democrats.[3] Subsequent House voting on trade issues—including the 1997 and 1998 fast-track bills and even permanent normal trade relations with China—remained partisan.

In the Senate, the average annual rating from 1985 to 1994 was 70 for Republicans and 34 for Democrats. Thus, partisan divisions over trade during this period, which included Reagan's second term and all of Bush's presidency, were almost as sharp in the Senate as in the House. Senate voting on trade throughout the Clinton years, however—including on NAFTA, PNTR, and the 1997 fast-track bill if a vote had been taken—was less partisan.

Also surprising, partisan divisions over trade in both chambers were comparable in depth to the overall divisions between the parties. The average annual overall rating for House Republicans during 1985–94 was 67, identical to the party's average trade rating. The average overall House Democratic rating was 19, not dramatically lower than the party's average trade rating. The average annual overall rating for Senate Republicans was 66, whereas for Democrats it was 24, again similar in both cases to the parties' average trade ratings (see Figure A.5). It appears, then, that in recent years, particularly in the House, trade has to an important extent been drawn into the single dimension of conflict around which congressional voting in general has increasingly been organized since the 1960s.[4]

The most important sources of partisan differences over trade were polarizing pressures from core constituencies: from protectionist or fair-trade–inclined unions on the Democrats and from pro-trade, internationally oriented business interests on the Republicans.[5] Ideological differences also contributed to party divisions, notably on generic measures thought likely to produce dispersed benefits and costs like the early drafts of the 1988 Trade Act. Democrats supported such legislation in the name of increased employment and consumption, while Republicans opposed it on behalf of efficiency and price stability.

This constituency- and ideologically induced differentiation of congressional party positions on trade actually involved a secular reversal of the parties' historic postures. Before the 1930s, the Democrats had been low-tariff advocates, due to their dependence on southern agricultural export interests and to their agrarian, antistatist ideological outlook. They continued to adhere to this stance into the 1960s, when pressure from labor and their own post–Great Depression embrace of a more positive attitude toward government led them to begin supporting tougher trade policies. The Republicans, on the other hand, had been the party of northern manufacturers, active government (at least until the 1920s), and thus high protective tariffs. But after World War II, as the Republicans became both more closely tied to internationally oriented business interests and ideologically committed to a more limited role for government, they gradually emerged as the party of free trade.

In the Reagan-Bush era, constituency- and ideologically induced partisan splits in Congress were reinforced by incumbency-focused influences.[6] In the early 1980s, the New Deal coalition and political order were in disarray, undermined by the dual crisis of Fordism and Keynesianism. At the same time, declining American industrial competitiveness, the overvalued dollar, unfair foreign trade practices, and Ronald Reagan's neglect of international economic policy combined to produce a "focusing crisis" in the trade sphere. Seeking an economically and politically viable alternative to Reaganomics, the Democrats—now the "out" party in a period of divided government—seized on the trade issue, along with competitiveness, in a heresthetical attempt to fracture the Republican coalition and dislodge it from control of the White House and Senate, while keeping the House of Representatives in Democratic hands.

Although a majority of Americans has regularly backed the imposition of tariffs to protect U.S. jobs as well as efforts to open foreign markets seen as unfairly closed to U.S. producers, up through the 1970s the public had never considered trade an uncommonly salient issue.[7] With the explosion of the U.S. trade deficit in the early and mid-1980s, however, and the concomitant rise in demands for protectionist and fair-trade policies from sectors of business and labor, the Democrats had reason to believe that trade could become of much greater concern to the wider electorate. Democratic congressional leaders now attacked Republican performance failures on trade while advocating a tougher general direction for, and specific spatial position on, trade policy to simultaneously appeal to relatively inattentive retrospective voters and more attentive directional and proximity voters. In pursuing this "strategy of disagreement," which included attempts to provoke "blame game" vetoes of tough trade legislation, the Democrats hoped both to raise the relative salience of the trade issue and to spotlight and isolate the Republicans for their unpopular free-trade stance.[8]

Toward these ends, the Democrats stressed more than the concentrated benefits of a tougher trade policy in the form of preserved jobs. In fusing economic and patriotic elements into an "economic nationalist" discourse, they also emphasized the general benefits to be derived from using government power to restore American national strength, while downplaying the potential costs of a tougher policy in the form of increased consumer prices or reduced economic efficiency. The Democrats hoped that this would expand the scope of conflict over the trade issue, thus drawing it out of its traditional policy subsystem into the realm of partisan macropolitics and attracting swing and even traditionally Republican constituencies without driving away core Democratic supporters.

It does not appear that the Democrats succeeded in making trade policy central to any but a few congressional races—during the 1980s, no more than 5 percent of those polled by the Gallup organization ever rated trade as the nation's most important problem,[9] and most voters actually favored the GOP on the matter—but this was clearly their intent in pressing the issue.

What Did the Democrats Want?

Some authors, including I. M. Destler and Judith Goldstein, argue that partisan differences in Congress over trade policy during the Reagan-Bush years were due mostly to Democratic attempts to score political points against the free-trading Republicans, not to any Democratic desire to fundamentally alter the liberal direction of U.S. trade policy.[10] Still traumatized by the lessons of Smoot-Hawley, the Democrats had no interest in legislating protection for specific industries. Rather, in pressing the trade issue, they were merely posturing for partisan advantage. This was a politically useful tactic, maintains Destler following David Mayhew, because voters are necessarily more attentive to legislators' announced positions than they are to actual policy outcomes, which are more difficult to observe.[11] The Democrats cast "free" votes for product-specific protectionist legislation, like the domestic content and textile bills, and tough generic measures like the 1986 House bill and the Gephardt amendment to signal support for their core labor constituents or to discredit the Republicans more broadly, knowing full well that these bills would never become law, thanks to the institutional realities of bicameralism and the veto.

It is true, as Destler argues, that most Democrats had no wish to see product-specific protectionist measures enacted into law. Although other factors, notably pressure from internationally oriented business interests that pragmatically contributed to incumbents of both parties,[12] moderated Democratic support for protectionism, normative and especially cognitive constraints of the kind stressed by Destler were undoubtedly important. Engaging in what Stephen Majeski has termed a process of "precedent-based reasoning"—in which boundedly rational actors simplify complex problems by using information-saving precedents and analogies to perceive and interpret current situations[13]—congressional Democrats anxiously remembered the Smoot-Hawley experience, especially following the November 1987 stock market crash. Recalling the Republicans' fate in the 1932 election after passage of Smoot-Hawley two years earlier, Democratic legislators adopted atypically long "time horizons" or low future "discount rates," seeing not just short-term political gain in voting for tough trade legislation in the 1980s, but also possible adverse medium-term electoral consequences should an economic crisis appear to be the result.[14]

This does not mean that the Democrats were merely posturing for electoral advantage when they advocated tough trade policies. As several authors have argued, voters, or at least interest groups and other attentive "issue publics," possess more information on policy outcomes than Mayhew and Destler would have it, while at the same time, in an evermore complex world, they are increasingly uncertain about the links between policies and outcomes. Some constituencies are thus often more attentive to policy outcomes than to legislators' announced policy positions.[15] This means that when Congress delegates trade policy authority to the president, it does not intend to prevent any action whatsoever. Organized interests and voters are not so inattentive to policy outcomes that they cannot see through such a ruse; if they were, such protective delegation would not be necessary in the first place.[16]

Hence, during the Reagan-Bush era Democratic votes in Congress for tough trade bills were genuinely intended to strengthen U.S. trade policy both to aid the Democrats' core labor backers and to attract wider business and popular support to the party. Such strengthening could come either through the actual enactment of generic or perhaps even product-specific legislation or through the use of threats to pass both kinds of measures in order to generate "anticipated reactions" from the executive branch in the form of administrative trade actions intended by the White House to cool protectionist pressures.[17]

Bipartisanship and Cross-Partisanship in the Reagan-Bush Era

Despite the general tendency in Congress toward partisan division on trade during the Reagan-Bush years, this period did see some examples of bipartisanship, including on relatively nonsalient issues like the 1984 Trade Act and the Canada-U.S. Free Trade Agreement, neither of which sharply divided business and labor. More significant was the bipartisan—or seemingly bipartisan—final vote in both houses on the Omnibus Trade and Competitiveness Act of 1988.

This bill was not quite the bipartisan product that some observers thought it to be. The Democrats drove the legislative process in the face of GOP opposition to early drafts of the measure; the Republicans only went along with the final version to avoid losing support among key swing constituencies in the approaching 1988 elections. It is true that the Democrats moderated their own stance to avoid being labeled protectionist, suggesting that both parties may have been converging on the position held by moderate swing voters or internationalist business interests. But it is also the case that Ronald Reagan's vetoes and veto threats, more than constituency-induced preference shifts, motivated some Democrats to agree to the final compromise version. In the end, substantially more Democrats than Republicans voted for the legislation. Thus, a process of strategic interaction between the two congressional parties whose ideal positions remained only partially convergent—that is, a process of intracongressional "mimicking" or "policy contagion"—produced the apparent bipartisan support for the 1988 Trade Act.[18]

The Reagan-Bush era also saw important cases of intraparty division and cross-partisan coalition formation. This occurred mostly on product-specific legislation like the textile quota bills of the 1980s, but also to some extent on various drafts of the more generic 1988 trade bill and on the 1991 fast-track bill, all of which were eventually expected to produce some regionally differentiated benefits and costs. The result was bipartisan support for these bills in some regions, bipartisan opposition in other areas, and cross-partisan coalitions in Congress. But voting on all of this legislation, even product-specific measures, had something of a partisan character, due to group, ideological, and incumbency-focused considerations.

Patterns of Partisanship during the Clinton Era

With Bill Clinton's election as president in 1992, the relative importance of the various determinants of congressional party positions on trade policy shifted. In particular, the impact of incumbency-focused influences changed dramatically. With a member of their own party in the White House, the Democrats had fewer incentives to pursue a strategy of disagreement, or to engage in heresthetical maneuvering, by posturing on behalf of a tough trade policy. Instead, otherwise protectionist-minded Democrats were susceptible to Clinton's persuasive attempts to win their support for his free-trade initiatives. Meanwhile, with the partial exception of their behavior on the GATT accord, the now opposition Republicans were predisposed against pursuing a strategy of disagreement, even after they captured control of Congress in 1994, by virtue of their ties to internationally oriented business interests and their free-trade ideological commitments.

Abetted by the revival of the American economy and the concomitant decline of Japan's, the big congressional trade battles during the Clinton years were not fought over Democrat- or Republican-sponsored, heresthetically inspired fair-trade bills. Instead, the main battles were over Bill Clinton's free-trade initiatives, especially toward low-wage developing countries, which emerged as key elements of the president's accumulation strategy and resulted in agreements that are, in fact, components of a new post-Fordist mode of regulation. Congressional party positions on these issues were influenced mainly by group pressures, lawmakers' personal ideology, leadership whipping, and bargaining and interaction with the president.

The cumulative effect of such influences, at least on high-salience issues that intensely divided labor from much of business, was the continued differentiation of congressional party positions over trade policy, at least in the House (the Senate is discussed separately below). Two-thirds to three-quarters of House Republicans regularly supported trade liberalization proposals during this period. On the other side of the aisle, Clinton's election did reduce incumbency-focused sources of Democratic opposition to trade liberalization. But except for the 1994 GATT agreement, more or less substantial majorities of House Democrats opposed Clinton's major free-trade initiatives (and one GOP-sponsored measure)—60 percent on NAFTA, 80 and 85 percent on the 1997 and 1998 fast-track bills respectively, and 65 percent on PNTR—primarily to protect the perceived interests of their core labor supporters, who felt threatened by the prospect of further trade liberalization and the wider processes of economic globalization.[19]

As the preceding figures indicate, however, the level of House partisanship on trade issues was quite variable, with substantial intraparty divisions, especially on the Democratic side, contributing to the formation of cross-partisan coalitions and one bipartisan alliance. Republican free traders, backed by the GOP leadership, were consistently opposed inside their own party by a smaller bloc of conservative nationalists, textile and other import-competing industry allies, and representatives from blue-collar districts who together comprised 25–33 percent of the Republican caucus on different issues. More important, Democratic opponents of trade liberalization had to contend with a bloc of Democratic free-trade supporters, whose size varied significantly from issue to issue, because of (1) shifting balances between "old" and "new" Democratic factions, (2) the waxing and waning of business and labor influences on party members, determined in part by (3) differences in the perceived magnitude, incidence, and certainty of the benefits and costs of various policies, (4) variations in the cohesion and energy of Democratic leaders, and (5) the fluctuating intensity and effectiveness of Bill Clinton's bargaining and persuasive efforts.

Forty percent of House Democrats backed NAFTA due to the substantial group of moderate, pro-trade New Democrats in the House in 1993; effective lobbying by and campaign contributions from a business community motivated by the promise of large, concentrated benefits; and the energetic efforts of the Clinton administration. A year later, 65 percent of House Democrats supported the GATT agreement, which labor found much less threatening than NAFTA.

In 1997 and 1998, on the other hand, 80 and 85 percent of House Democrats respectively opposed two fast-track proposals, thanks to big New Democratic losses in the 1994 congressional elections; a shift of corporate campaign contributions to the Republicans following those elections, which reduced business's leverage on the Democrats; a more unified Democratic leadership; half-hearted lobbying by business, stemming in part from the uncertain benefits to be derived from the procedural measures, as well as by the White House; and a major mobilization of labor's human and financial resources, building on its extensive and successful efforts on behalf of Democratic candidates in 1996 and 1998.

The balance of intra-Democratic forces shifted again in 2000, when 35 percent of House Democrats supported PNTR with China. This can be attributed to several factors—the expansion of New Democratic ranks in 1998; a massive corporate mobilization and a shift of campaign contributions back to the Democrats by a business community that saw vast, concentrated benefits in the China deal; a somewhat divided labor campaign against PNTR; renewed Democratic leadership splits; and another energetic White House effort.

However variable the level of partisanship may have been in the House, in the Senate the Clinton presidency did see a decline in party conflict over trade.[20] This would appear to indicate that the kind of posturing or heresthetical maneuvering predicted by the incumbency-focused approach was a relatively more important determinant of Senate Democrats' tough trade views during the Reagan-Bush era than it was of the positions of their House colleagues. With Clinton's election, Democratic posturing declined, and institutional factors— larger electoral jurisdictions, the overrepresentation of agricultural and less-unionized states, longer terms of office, weaker party leadership, and greater foreign policy responsibilities—produced less partisanship on trade in the Senate than prevailed in the House. Senate Democrats split down the middle on NAFTA and provided substantial bipartisan support for both the GATT and China deals, as there would have been for the 1997 fast-track bill had it been brought to a vote.

Despite the complex patterns of party competition over trade policy that have prevailed since 1980, it seems fair to conclude that, to different degrees at different times, constituency, ideology, and incumbency-based influences—sometimes, though not always amplified by the lobbying of the White House and congressional party leaders—together produced considerable partisan conflict over trade in Congress.[21] Although the bipartisan consensus on liberal trade did not crack during these years, it certainly suffered a number of significant stress fractures.

Taking a still broader view, we might say that the combination of an executive that pursues a largely nonpartisan or bipartisan approach to trade policy and a Congress that is substantially differentiated along party lines exemplifies the workings of what Gerald Pomper has termed America's "semi-responsible" party system.[22]

The Policy Consequences of Party Competition over Trade

The complex dynamics of party competition over trade since 1980 also have had important consequences for policy. In other words, during this period parties mattered to U.S. trade policy choices and outputs.

The Reagan-Bush Era of Divided Government

In the Reagan-Bush era of divided government, strategic partisan interaction and Democratic-driven policy contagion contributed to a real if incremental toughening of U.S. trade policy. Legislatively, the period saw the passage and presidential signing of the sweeping Omnibus Trade and Competitiveness Act of 1988, which strengthened U.S. trade remedies and laws to deal with unfair foreign trade practices. More important were White House administrative actions. The Reagan and Bush administrations imposed or renewed a significant set of import limits on automobiles, steel, machine tools, textiles, semiconductors, lumber, and so forth. Probably more significant was the U.S. turn toward "aggressive reciprocity" in its approach to prying open closed foreign markets.

Some scholars dispute the role of party competition in the policy shift of the Reagan-Bush years. Proponents of the leading "inter-branch" view, including Destler, maintain that these changes were agreed to or taken by the White House to quell bipartisan congressional demands for still stronger action, demands that were in turn generated by pressure on lawmakers of both parties from labor and import-competing and export-oriented business interests.[23]

To a significant extent, however, these policy changes were also the products of the strategic interaction at both congressional and executive levels between two parties whose ideal positions on trade were not fully convergent. Heresthetical maneuvers by the more fair-trade–inclined Democrats "amplified" the demands for a more aggressive commercial policy that were then emanating from trade-impacted sectors of the economy.[24] This enabled congressional Democrats, after retaking control of the Senate in the 1996 midterm elections and putting a new trade bill at the top of their agenda, to force an eventual compromise on the 1988 trade bill upon its Republican adversaries in Congress and the White House. Similarly, White House administrative actions on both the import and export sides—the "anticipated reactions" sought by Democrats—were also the result of strategic interaction between the parties. In what I have termed a process of policy contagion, Republicans in both branches of government were forced to adopt a portion of the Democratic trade program, albeit in weaker form, not only to subdue rising congressional protectionism, but also to defuse the trade issue as an electoral threat to the GOP among swing constituencies.

Counterfactual reasoning suggests that had the Democrats not pressed the issue, White House action on trade would have been considerably weaker during this period than was in fact the case. This action would have been even more restrained had the Republicans had unified control of both branches of government, since the Democrats could not have used command of one or both houses of Congress to threaten the Reagan and Bush administrations with the passage of politically embarrassing trade legislation.

Scholars also question the actual scope and significance of the policy changes made during the Reagan and Bush presidencies.[25] For the most part, neither congressional party sought to pass product-specific protectionist legislation. Even as substantial changes were being wrought in various policies and institutions of the Fordist mode of regulation, the liberal trade policy system largely withstood the economic turmoil of the 1980s.

The limited shift toward a greater emphasis on fair trade can be understood as a form of path-dependent policy change. As argued in the third chapter, through a process of policy feedback, the institutions and processes of the liberal trade policy system formed after World War II became self-reinforcing. First, the lessons of Smoot-Hawley together with subsequent postwar prosperity, attributed in part to the liberalization of world trade, entrenched an elite normative and cognitive consensus on a liberal trade policy paradigm, institutionalized in both the presidency and Congress,[26] that inertially constrained lawmakers' perceptions and beliefs. Second, the members of Congress who represented trade-dependent businesses and constituencies that had benefited from the system were politically rewarded for supporting liberal trade.[27] Both factors allowed lawmakers to resist protectionist pressures until they finally abated in the late 1980s, thus obviating the need for a radical departure in policy.

But this dual path-dependence argument should not be taken too far. In pressing for tougher trade policies, the Democrats were more than merely posturing for electoral advantage. They also sought actual results to satisfy the demands of their trade-battered labor and business constituencies.[28] Although it shied away from product-specific legislation, the Democrat-led Congress did pass and force President Reagan to sign the 1988 Trade Act in a genuine attempt to compel the White House to take tougher administrative actions against unfair foreign traders. The bill would have been tougher still had Democrats not been forced to agree to a compromise to avoid a Reagan veto. Democratic presidential candidates added their own pressure on Reagan and Bush.

The results of this Democratic legislating and prodding were first that during the early and mid-1980s, Ronald Reagan, according to Secretary of State James Baker, "granted more import relief to U.S. industry than any of his predecessors in more than half a century." The share of imports subject to some form of restraint increased from 12 percent in 1980 to 24 percent in 1989. These import curbs produced a slower growth of trade than would otherwise have resulted from the reduced communications and transport costs of the period. This contributed to a stagnation or even a decline in the ratio of U.S. trade to output, relative to the 1970s and to the world as a whole. Perhaps still more significant was the U.S. turn in the second half of the 1980s toward an aggressive stance on market access. This produced a sharp increase in the investigation and self-initiation of cases of unfair foreign trade practices under Section 301.[29]

Although the dominant liberal trade policy paradigm and the institutions in which it was encased remained largely intact during the Reagan-Bush era, they were incrementally but significantly modified in the direction of fair trade, due in large measure to the pressures of party competition.[30] Or perhaps more accurately, they were recombined with or rearticulated to a strengthened set of fair-trade institutions and practices that had been at the core of American trade law before World War II.[31]

The Clinton Era

Partisanship continued to influence U.S. trade policy in complex ways after the election of Bill Clinton as president in 1992 and the Republican capture of both houses of Congress in the 1994 midterm elections. With the return of unified Democratic government in 1993, U.S. trade policy paradoxically became both tougher and more liberal than had been the case during the Reagan-Bush era of divided government.

Clinton's election produced a decline in heresthetical posturing on trade and thus also less policy contagion. Nevertheless, the "results-oriented" policy that the new president at least initially pursued toward Japan was tougher than the approach that the Democrats had forced Reagan and Bush to adopt.[32] Clinton opted for this stance because he was both ideologically committed to activist government and convinced that Japan was an exceptionally unfair trader, but also because he hoped to firm up his support among blue-collar Democrats and swing groups. Similar political concerns prompted him to seek the NAFTA labor and environmental side agreements and the inclusion of similar provisions in the fast-track measure that he unsuccessfully tried to append to the GATT agreement implementing bill.

At the same time, on other issues Clinton was essentially a free trader, a commitment that was reinforced by his search for additional political support among the suburban upper middle class and internationally oriented business interests. Like his immediate Republican predecessors, Clinton supported new trade liberalization initiatives, including the NAFTA and GATT agreements, which he hoped to make an important part of his presidential legacy.

It appears likely that Clinton's role at the head of a unified Democratic government helped him to win a victory on NAFTA that George Bush, facing the same Democratic Congress, would probably have failed to secure. As the expanded incumbency-focused view suggests, with help from business and pro-trade New Democrats, Clinton was able to persuade some protectionist House members of his own party to back the accord. These same Democrats, little inclined to support a Republican president, would probably have opposed the deal had Bush still occupied the White House. In the case of NAFTA, then, the prevailing form of unified government, controlled by the more protectionist-oriented party, was probably more facilitative of liberal trade than the specific type of divided government that preceded it would have been, led as it was by a president from the more pro–free-trade party.

The NAFTA struggle also continued a pattern, begun with the 1991 fast-track fight and present throughout the Clinton presidency, in which, with two-thirds to three-quarters of House Republicans consistently supporting free trade, the fate of a succession of trade liberalization proposals was determined mainly by the waxing and waning of intra-Democratic divisions over these measures. Thus, a year after NAFTA's approval, the Uruguay Round GATT treaty was overwhelmingly ratified thanks to the support of 65 percent of House Democrats.

The capture of Congress in 1994 by the more pro–free-trade Republicans might have been expected to smooth the way for further trade liberalization, especially with American economic growth and competitiveness recovering smartly. Instead, the trade liberalization process ground to a halt, due again to partisan influences. With his reelection campaign fast approaching, Clinton in mid-1995 escalated a long-standing auto dispute with Japan to appease union and other working-class voters who had been angered by his strong support for NAFTA and GATT. The White House also postponed any new free-trade initiatives until after the election to avoid further alienating labor, environmental, and other Democratic-aligned liberal interests.

Having comfortably secured his reelection, Clinton then tried to restart the trade liberalization process with Republican support when he sent a fast-track bill to Congress in the fall of 1997. But for reasons discussed above, principally the reinvigorated labor movement's energetic and skillful mobilization of its human and financial resources, 80 percent of House Democrats, joined by conservative Republican nationalists and other GOP free-trade critics, sank Clinton's proposal. A Republican-sponsored fast-track bill, this time opposed by 85 percent of House Democrats as well as by Clinton himself, met a similar fate ten months later.

At a WTO meeting in Seattle in late 1999, Clinton essentially sabotaged his own efforts to launch a new round of international trade negotiations, when he urged the World Trade Organization to take up the issue of international labor standards, an idea that developing nations quickly rejected and over which the meeting in part broke up. Clinton apparently had partisan concerns in broaching this issue; he hoped to assuage organized labor's anger at his administration's trade liberalization agenda in order to help Al Gore gain union support for his upcoming presidential campaign.

In the last year of his presidency, however, Clinton made one final attempt to secure his legacy as a champion of free trade when he pushed for congressional approval of PNTR with China. After a fierce struggle, PNTR was approved in the House and then more easily in the Senate four months later, imparting renewed if perhaps temporary momentum to the trade liberalization process. Once again, the key to the hard-fought victory in the House was a shift in Democratic voting: 35 percent of Democratic caucus members voted in favor of the China deal, up from the 20 and 15 percent who had supported the 1997 and 1998 fast-track bills respectively. This realignment was due to various factors discussed earlier, but especially to the massive business lobbying effort directed mainly toward undecided and wavering Democrats and to the partial shift of corporate campaign contributions back to Democratic candidates.

A Look toward the Future

What are the prospects for U.S. trade policy in the aftermath of the astounding 2000 presidential and congressional elections? What role will partisanship play? At least to some extent, the answers to these questions depend on an understanding of the current state of the closely balanced American party system.

Some analysts might see the installation of a (barely) unified Republican government for the first time since 1954 as the continuation of a GOP political order that had its origins in 1968 or perhaps 1980.[33] Others argue that in light of Bill Clinton's two victories, Al Gore and Ralph Nader's joint popular majority in 2000, and steady Democratic gains in the House and Senate following the debacle of the 1994 congressional elections, the party system has actually been realigning toward the Democrats throughout the 1990s, and they expect the party to capture unified control of government within the next eight years.[34] Still other authors see regional realignments in different directions: toward the Republicans in the South and Mountain West, toward the Democrats in the Northeast and on the Pacific Coast. Some maintain that we may be in transition to a novel form of political order endorsed or led by either party or by an alliance of both. Yet others view the 1990s as a new "critical era" following the demise of the sixth "candidate-centered" party system that emerged from the earlier critical era of the 1960s. Finally, there are observers who contend that the party system remains in an uncertain state of dealignment or disorder.[35]

I would put myself in the last camp. With the dead-even presidential vote in

November 2000 and with the new Senate split 50–50 and the Republicans holding onto a slim, 221–212 majority in the House as of January 2001, the two parties are now at virtual parity. Fundamentally, this is so because neither party has yet been able to construct a successor to the New Deal coalition and political order that is appropriate to the ongoing transition from Fordism to post-Fordism.[36] In important respects, the current conjuncture most nearly resembles the 1870s and 1880s, a period of economic transition—from agrarianism to industrialism—and close partisan balance. As in that earlier period, we should expect the parties to struggle to tip the balance of forces in their favor as they strive to build new electoral and governing coalitions and a new political order.

It is unclear, however, to what degree the parties will find cooperation or conflict to be more in their interest as they pursue durable majority status.[37] Following the election, some observers predicted that aided by centrist public opinion and a permissive fiscal environment, George W. Bush and moderate congressional Republicans might try to build "floating" bipartisan coalitions on issues like education and prescription drugs with moderate New Democrats and more conservative, mostly southern "Blue Dog" Democrats, whose ranks were expanded in the 2000 elections.[38]

Instead, backed by conservative Republicans, Bush has pushed a highly partisan agenda, especially on tax cuts, but also on the environment and labor issues. White House efforts at bipartisanship have thus for the most part amounted only to attempts to pick off the support of a few conservative and moderate Democrats. In these circumstances, both old and new congressional Democrats, already angry at Bush's alleged "theft" of the election, under pressure from organized labor and minority groups that turned out their members in huge numbers on behalf of Democrats, and tempted to pursue a strategy of disagreement toward Bush and the Republicans in the run-up to the 2002 midterm elections, have mostly united to oppose Bush's proposals, producing sharp party conflict. There have been instances of bipartisanship—on the bankruptcy bill and the final Senate budget resolution—but these have resulted from the initiatives of centrists in both congressional parties (reopening intra-Democratic rifts in the process), not from White House efforts.

Trade Policy Prospects

What does this mean for U.S. trade policy? If the current economic showdown turns into the first recession of the New Economy, a number of simmering trade disputes, particularly with the European Union, may become more contentious, and product-specific protectionist pressures may arise again, most likely from the embattled steel industry.[39] Nevertheless, absent a deep (and unlikely) economic crisis that threatens the still-dominant liberal trade policy paradigm, U.S. commercial policy will continue to emphasize trade liberalization over the next few years.

The first such issues include congressional approval of trade agreements signed by the Clinton administration with Vietnam and Jordan. Votes may also be taken on other deals still being negotiated with Singapore and Chile.[40] The most significant battle, however, will be waged over congressional approval of new fast-track authority to allow the White House to complete by 2005 stalled negotiations on a Free Trade Area of the Americas (FTAA). Bush and the business community back the FTAA to gain wider access to Latin American markets and labor and to counter moves by Europe and Canada to cut free-trade deals with the region's nations, while Bush also hopes to use a deal to expand his support among the rapidly growing Hispanic electorate.

The trade issue actually played little role in the 2000 presidential campaign, and during his first days in office Bush seemed inclined to stress national security over foreign economic policy.[41] But at the protest-ringed, 34-nation Summit of the Americas in Quebec City in April 2001, the president voiced his strong support for the FTAA and promised to send Congress later in the year a bill to renew his fast-track authority, now renamed "trade promotion authority" and called a "top legislative priority" by White House officials.[42]

Bush, most congressional Republicans, and most business leaders would ideally prefer a "clean" fast-track bill, that is, one without labor and environmental provisions. But such a proposal would almost certainly be defeated by the vociferous opposition of organized labor, environmentalists, and the large majority of both House and Senate Democrats, including New Democrats, who are now also committed to the incorporation of some kind of labor and environmental standards in future trade agreements.[43]

More uncertain would be the fate of a compromise fast-track proposal that did call for such standards to be included in the FTAA, albeit without providing for the use of trade sanctions as an enforcement mechanism. Recognizing the need for a new consensus on trade, the Bush administration's new U.S. trade representative, Robert Zoellick, is talking with members of both congressional parties and certain newly pragmatic business interests about a compromise fast-track bill that would contain provisions for the use of incentives and monetary fines instead of trade sanctions to produce compliance with labor and environmental standards.[44] Labor, most environmentalists, and liberal Democrats would continue to oppose this kind of proposal, however, especially one introduced by a Republican president, demanding that trade sanctions be among the penalties available to enforce violations of these standards.

With the most ardent GOP critics and defenders of free trade also likely to oppose such a compromise measure, the outcome of this fight would be determined by the behavior of the growing bloc of Blue Dogs and New Democrats. On the one hand, rewarded financially and in other ways by various business interests for their support of PNTR,[45] cognizant of the fact that labor did not actively oppose pro-PNTR Democrats in 2000, and convinced by familiar Democratic Leadership Council (DLC) arguments that Al Gore lost in part because the populist rhetoric he adopted at the Democratic Convention failed to appeal to the growing ranks of the upscale, educated, suburban, and "wired" workers of the New Economy, moderate and conservative Democrats might opt to approve a compromise fast-track bill of the type described above, particularly if the economy stays out of recession.[46]

On the other hand, some moderate Democrats did benefit from the massive turnout drive mounted by the labor movement,[47] which retains significant political clout.[48] The business community may fail to enthusiastically mobilize for what will be a procedural measure without immediate or concrete benefits. Finally, Democrats of all stripes, angry at the way Bush pushed his tax plan through Congress, may look to score political points by opposing a potentially unpopular Republican free-trade initiative as the 2002 midterm elections approach. In such circumstances, enough moderate Democrats could join with their more liberal colleagues to again derail a compromise fast-track bill containing only weak labor and environmental provisions.

The long-term fate of future trade liberalization initiatives, including eventual congressional approval of a treaty concluding a new round of international trade negotiations that may be launched in the next year or two, will continue to depend on the evolving balance of ideologies and interests inside the two parties. More accurately, developments within the Democratic Party will as usual be decisive, since most Republicans are likely to remain wedded to free trade by virtue of their ideological convictions, their close ties to and financial dependence on internationally oriented business interests, and, at least during the administration of George W. Bush, their loyalty to a president of their own party.

Some observers have claimed in the wake of the PNTR fight that Bill Clinton helped move the Democratic Party, however haltingly, "from reflexive mistrust of trade and globalization to an acceptance of it."[49] If the economy quickly regains its late 1990s momentum, the ranks of New Democrats in Congress keep expanding, business continues to mobilize on behalf of unfettered free trade while funneling campaign contributions to both parties, and labor's strength is further reduced by structural and other factors,[50] it is possible that future trade liberalization agreements with only token labor and environmental standards will be approved with bipartisan support. On the other hand, and especially if economic conditions deteriorate, even if most Democrats are no longer "reflexively" opposed to trade liberalization, it may well be a mistake to underestimate either the consensus that is building among various Democratic factions for trade deals that include serious labor and environmental standards or the ability of organized labor and its allies to mobilize their human and financial resources to block agreement without such standards.

If forced to hazard a prediction, I would bet that in the long run neither labor and its mostly Democratic supporters nor business and its mainly Republican allies are likely to have sufficient strength to win unqualified victories over their opponents. Rather, I think it is more likely that both sides in the continuing battle, together with various developing nations, will eventually agree to compromise on modest but in some way enforceable labor and environmental standards that, for example, might gradually rise from low initial starting levels in step with improvements in productivity.

One thing does appear clear, however. Despite much commentary on both the decline of American political parties and the irrelevance of party competition to U.S. trade policy, party politics has mattered in the conduct of that policy. The conditions of this partisan influence are admittedly complex, depending on (1) the constituency- and ideologically induced preferences of the president, (2) the size, preferences, and internal cohesion of the congressional party caucuses, (3) the inclination of the president and the congressional parties to compromise, and, under some circumstances, (4) whether control of government is unified or divided. But under determinant conditions, party competition has predictable consequences. There is every reason to believe that party politics will continue to influence the making of American trade policy.

Appendix

FIGURE A.1. Tariff Levels and Major Trade Acts by Partisan Control, 1820–1990

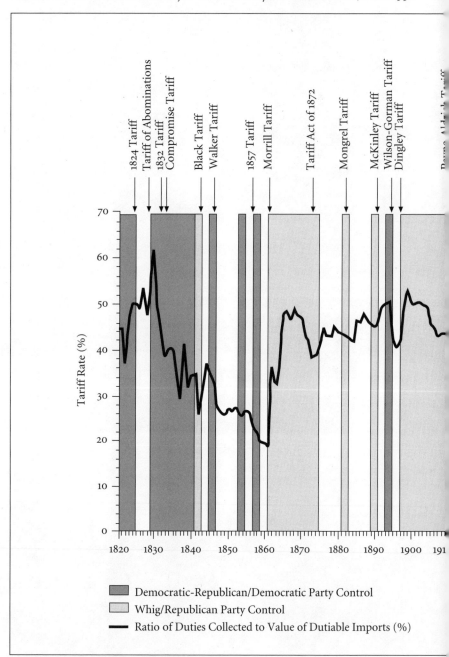

Source: Wendy L. Hansen and Thomas J. Prusa, "The Role of the Median Legislator in U.S. Trade Policy: A Historical Analysis," *Economic Inquiry* 35, no. 1 (January 1997): 100.

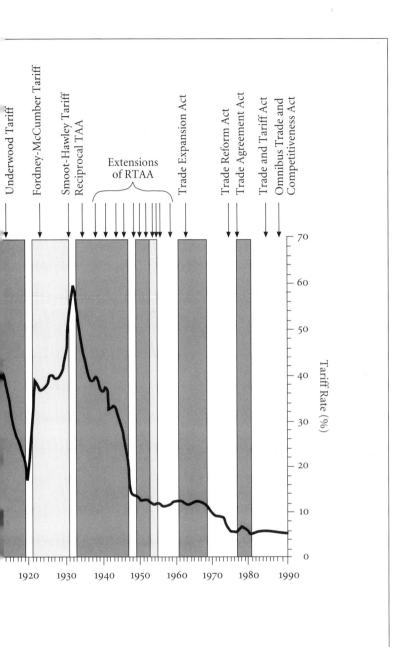

Underwood Tariff

Fordney-McCumber Tariff

Smoot-Hawley Tariff
Reciprocal TAA

Extensions
of RTAA

Trade Expansion Act

Trade Reform Act
Trade Agreement Act

Trade and Tariff Act
Omnibus Trade and
Competitiveness Act

Tariff Rate (%)

70

60

50

40

30

20

10

0

1920   1930   1940   1950   1960   1970   1980   1990

FIGURE A.2. Percentage of Party Members Voting for Freer Trade, 1870–1994

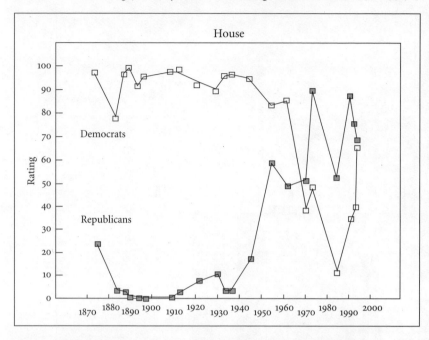

Source: Michael J. Hiscox, "The Magic Bullet? The RTAA, Institutional Reform, and Trade Liberalization," *International Organization* 53, no. 4 (Autumn 1999): 681; © 1999 IO Foundation and Massachusetts Institute of Technology.

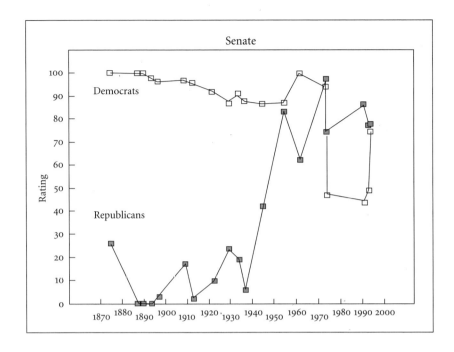

FIGURE A.3. Party Cohesion on Trade Votes in Congress, 1870–1994

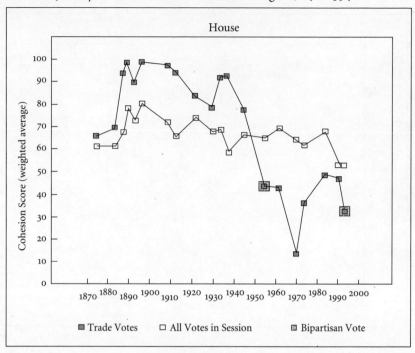

Source: Michael J. Hiscox, "The Magic Bullet? The RTAA, Institutional Reform, and Trade Liberalization," *International Organization* 53, no. 4 (Autumn 1999): 688; © 1999 IO Foundation and Massachusetts Institute of Technology.

Note: The Rice index used here is the absolute difference between the percentages of party members voting "yea" and "nay" and thus ranges from 0 to 100, with 0 representing a total absence of cohesion (50 percent of party voting on opposite sides) and 100 representing perfect cohesion (all party members voting the same).

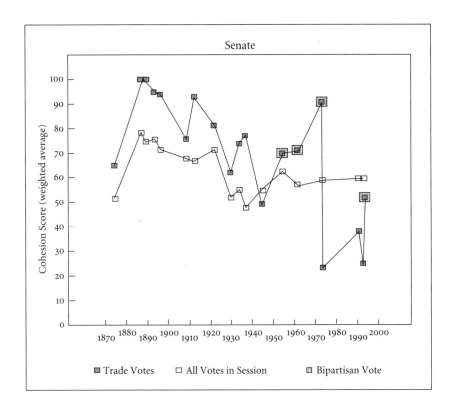

Senate

Cohesion Score (weighted average)

■ Trade Votes   □ All Votes in Session   ▣ Bipartisan Vote

FIGURE A.4. Percentage of "Promarket" Votes Cast by Members of Congress on Trade and All Issues, 1985–1994

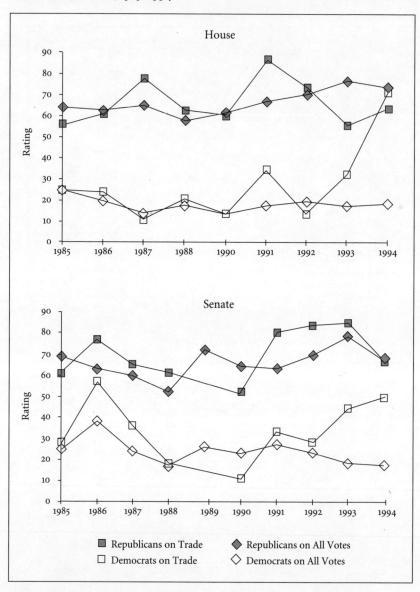

Source: *Competitive Enterprise Index, 1985–1994* (Washington, D.C.: Competitive Enterprise Institute, 1985–94).

Note: On trade issues, a "promarket" vote is a vote in support of free trade. There were no significant trade votes in 1989.

FIGURE A.5. Difference in "Promarket" Ratings between Republicans and Democrats on Trade and All Issues, 1985–1994

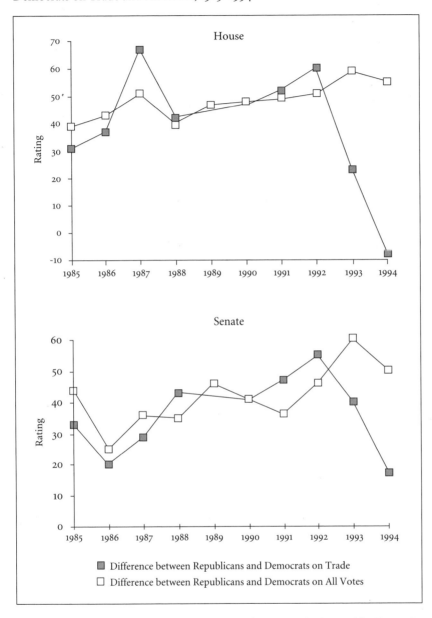

Source: Competitive Enterprise Index, 1985–1994 (Washington, D.C.: Competitive Enterprise Institute, 1985–94).

Note: On trade issues, a "promarket" vote is a vote in support of free trade. There were no significant trade votes in 1989.

Notes

Introduction

1. The first wave of globalization took place during the fifty or so years that ended with World War I. The second wave occurred in the 1950s and 1960s. See Charles Oman, "Globalization, Regionalization, and Inequality," in Andrew Hurrell and Ngaire Woods, eds., *Inequality, Globalization, and World Politics* (New York: Oxford University Press, 1999), 36–65.

2. PNTR did away with Congress's annual vote on China's "normal trade relations," or what used to be called "most-favored-nation" (MFN) status, a Cold War practice intended to pressure Beijing to improve its record on human rights.

3. Peter B. Evans, Harold K. Jacobson, and Robert D. Putnam, eds., *Double-Edged Diplomacy: Bargaining and Domestic Politics* (Berkeley: University of California Press, 1993); Andrew Moravcsik, "Taking Preferences Seriously: A Liberal Theory of International Relations," *International Organization* 51, no. 4 (Autumn 1997): 513–53; John Kurt Jacobsen, "Are All Politics Domestic? Rethinking the National-International Connection," in Jacobsen, *Dead Reckonings: Ideas, Interests, and Politics in the "Information Age"* (Atlantic Highlands, N.J.: Humanities Press, 1997), 188–212; Helen Milner, *Interests, Institutions, and Information* (Princeton, N.J.: Princeton University Press, 1997); James D. Fearon, "Domestic Politics, Foreign Policy, and Theories of International Relations," *Annual Review of Political Science* 1 (1998): 289–313.

4. But see Charles F. Doran and Gregory P. Marchildon, eds., *The NAFTA Puzzle: Political Parties and Trade in North America* (Boulder, Colo.: Westview Press, 1994), and Martha L. Gibson, *Conflict amid Consensus in American Trade Policy* (Washington, D.C.: Georgetown University Press, 2000).

5. For a recent, comprehensive collection on the state of U.S. parties, see L. Sandy Maisel, ed., *The Parties Respond: Changes in American Parties and Campaigns*, 3d ed. (Boulder, Colo.: Westview Press, 1998).

6. Most notably, see I. M. Destler, *American Trade Politics*, 3d ed. (Washington, D.C.: Institute for International Economics and Twentieth Century Fund, 1995), and Judith Goldstein, *Ideas, Interests, and American Trade Policy* (Ithaca, N.Y.: Cornell University Press, 1993).

7. "Dumping" is the sale of a product in foreign markets at a price that is lower than either the product's cost of production or its home market price.

8. Pietro S. Nivola, *Regulating Unfair Trade* (Washington, D.C.: Brookings Institution, 1993).

9. Again see Destler, *American Trade Politics*, and Goldstein, *Ideas, Interests*.

10. David Vogel, "The Triumph of Liberal Trade: American Trade Policy in the Postwar Period," in Morton Keller and R. Shep Melnick, eds., *Taking Stock: American Government in the Twentieth Century* (Cambridge: Woodrow Wilson Center Press and Cambridge University Press, 1999), 35–53.

11. Nivola, *Regulating Unfair Trade*.

12. Michael J. Hiscox, "The Magic Bullet? The RTAA, Institutional Reform, and Trade Liberalization," *International Organization* 53, no. 4 (Autumn 1999): 669–98.

13. See Gibson, *Conflict amid Consensus*; Stanley D. Nollen and Dennis P. Quinn, "Free Trade, Fair Trade, Strategic Trade, and Protectionism in the U.S. Congress, 1987–1988," *International Organization* 48, no. 3 (Summer 1994): 491–525; and William R. Keech and Kyoungsan Pak, "Partisanship, Institutions, and Change in American Politics," *Journal of Politics* 57, no. 4 (November 1995): 1120–42.

14. The "domestic content" bill would have required that high proportions of American-made parts and labor for foreign cars be sold in the United States.

15. Destler, *American Trade Politics*; Goldstein, *Ideas, Interests*.

16. For these two positions, see respectively Susanne Lohmann and Sharyn O'Halloran, "Divided Government and U.S. Trade Policy: Theory and Evidence," *International Organization* 48, no. 4 (Autumn 1994): 595–632, and David Karol, "Divided Government and U.S. Trade Policy: Much Ado about Nothing?," *International Organization* 54, no. 4 (Autumn 2000): 825–44.

17. "Stagflation" is the simultaneous occurrence of slow economic growth and high unemployment and inflation.

Chapter 1

1. There are many versions of philosophical realism. The one all too briefly presented here is rather unconventionally influenced by both "critical" and rational choice–oriented realism. For an excellent collection of critical realist writings, see Margaret Archer, Roy Bhaskar, Andrew Collier, Tony Lawson, and Alan Nourrie, eds., *Critical Realism: Essential Readings* (New York: Routledge, 1998). See also Paul Lewis, "Realism, Causality, and the Problem of Social Structure," *Journal for the Theory of Social Behaviour* 30, no. 3 (September 2000): 249–68. For an example of rational choice–oriented realism (or realist-influenced rational choice theory), see Daniel Little, *Microfoundations, Method, and Causation: On the Philosophy of the Social Sciences* (New Brunswick, N.J.: Transaction Publishers, 1998).

Most critical realists strongly oppose the "methodological individualism" of rational choice theory, which they maintain reduces structures and institutions to the choices of current actors. Rational choice theorists do stress, correctly I think, the importance of providing the individual-level microfoundations of social phenomena. But not all of them consider themselves methodological individualists. In Little's "methodological localism," for example, individuals are the engines of change, but only in circumstances in which long-established social entities and structures affect individual choice, preferences, and beliefs. Little, *Microfoundations*, 198. Alternatively Peter Hedstrom calls for a "weak" methodological individualism, arguing that although all social institutions in principle can be explained only by the intended and unintended consequences of individual actions, the causal histories of existing institutions are so long and complex that, for the sake of realism, they should be taken as given and often unexplained components of concrete phenomena. Hedstrom, "Social Mechanisms: An Introductory Essay," in Hedstrom and Richard Swedberg, eds., *Social Mechanisms: An Analytical Approach to Social Theory* (Cambridge: Cambridge University Press, 1998), 12–13. These views are not so different from the perspective of a critical realist like Margaret Archer, who writes that the past activities of individual agents create inertial structures that condition the practices of current agents. See Archer, *Realist Social Theory: The Morphogenetic Approach* (Cambridge: Cambridge University Press, 1995).

My analytic framework is also influenced by the several "new institutionalisms"—rational choice, historical, and sociological—now current in political science. For perhaps the best of many reviews of these approaches, see Peter A. Hall and Rosemary C. R. Taylor, "Political Science and the Three New Institutionalisms," *Political Studies* 44 (1996): 936–57. But much of this work is paradoxically too structuralist and yet not structuralist enough, in that it too often minimizes the causal importance of both strategic action, or "politics," and the "deep" structures of capital accumulation. For these two opposed criticisms of the new institutionalism, see respectively Andrew J. Polsky, "The New 'Dismal Science'? The Lessons of American Political Development for Politics Today," *Polity* 32, no. 3 (Spring 2000): 303–8, and Paul Cammack, "The New Institutionalism: Predatory Rule, Institutional Persistence, and Macro-Social Change," *Economy and Society* 21, no. 4 (November 1992): 397–429.

2. In developing and testing the multilevel analytic framework presented in this chapter, I have pursued an essentially "retroductive" research strategy. Whereas positivist induction starts with observations and ends with generalizations that it claims provide explanations, and rationalist deduction begins with a fully worked-out theory from which hypotheses can be drawn and empirically tested, realist retroduction commences with observed regularities, proposes hypothetical models of hidden structures and mechanisms to explain them, and then calls for further research on additional phenomena to confirm the existence of these structures and mechanisms. I should add, however, that although preferable to induction, which describes surface regularities rather than unearthing their underlying causes, and deduction, which relies on overly parsimonious theorizing, retroduction has its limits as a research strategy. For realists, the social world, unlike the laboratory, is an "open system" with multiple, often countervailing structures and mechanisms whose causal powers are sometimes unexercised. Thus, decisive, controlled testing of retroductively generated hypotheses cannot be undertaken, the empirical verification or falsification of these hypotheses can only be tentative, and prediction is difficult. For an accessible discussion of these issues, see Norman Blaikie, *Approaches to Social Enquiry* (Cambridge, England: Polity Press, 1993), esp. 168–70 and 204–5.

3. For this classification, see Charles F. Doran, "Trade and Party: Flip-Flops and Causal Linkages," in Doran and Gregory P. Marchildon, eds., *The NAFTA Puzzle: Political Parties and Trade in North America* (Boulder, Colo.: Westview Press, 1994), 227–37.

4. Although under conditions of uncertainty, corporate and worker preferences can also be shaped by (1) participation in business associations and labor unions, (2) private policy professionals, (3) the persuasive activities of public officials (more on this point later), and (4) policy legacies. On many of these issues, see Cathie Jo Martin, *Stuck in*

Neutral: Business and the Politics of Human Capital Investment Policy (Princeton, N.J.: Princeton University Press, 2000), esp. 33–45.

5. Although studies have concluded that individual political action committee (PAC) contributions often have limited effects on congressional roll-call voting, on certain kinds of issues—those that do not elicit much public attention, involve opposing groups and coalitions, or evoke intense partisan or ideological divisions—such contributions can have a significant influence. Perhaps more important, broad aggregations of corporate or labor PAC contributions can affect voting on issues of general concern to business and labor. On these points, including evidence from congressional voting in the early 1990s, see Robert E. Baldwin and Christopher S. Magee, "Is Trade Policy for Sale? Congressional Voting on Recent Trade Bills," *Public Choice* 105, nos. 1–2 (October 2000): 79–101. For a recent review of the general literature on the influence of corporate PAC spending on congressional voting, see Jeffrey Milyo, David Primo, and Timothy Groseclose, "Corporate PAC Campaign Contributions in Perspective," *Business and Politics* 2, no. 1 (April 2000): 75–88.

6. The propensity of such groups to engage in these various forms of collective action is determined by such factors as the resources they possess; levels of industry and geographic concentration; the magnitude, incidence, and certainty of the benefits and costs of different policies; and lobbying activity by one set of groups, which provokes "counteractive" lobbying by still other groups. For an extensive overview of the literature on interest groups, see Frank R. Baumgartner and Beth L. Leetch, *Basic Interests: The Importance of Groups in Politics and Political Science* (Princeton, N.J.: Princeton University Press, 1998).

7. These authors derive their views from the Heckscher-Ohlin model of international trade and its Stolper-Samuelson corollary, in which broadly defined factors of production, including labor and capital, are assumed to be highly mobile across industrial sectors. In such circumstances, an increase in protection will raise the income of a nation's relatively scarce and thus expensive factors and lower the income of its relatively abundant and hence cheap factors. Thus, scarce factors will support protection, while abundant ones will oppose it. In the case of a capital-abundant, labor-scarce country like the United States, trade conflicts will be fought along class lines, as workers will favor protection and capitalists, free trade. With the additional key assumption that parties are politically supported by distinct production factors, Rogowski and Magee, Brock, and Young argue that since World War II, the Democrats, representing labor, a relatively scarce factor, have been the party of protection, while the Republicans, representing capital (and for Rogowski, also agriculture), an abundant factor, have been the party of free trade. See Ronald L. Rogowski, *Commerce and Coalitions: How Trade Affects Domestic Political Alignments* (Princeton, N.J.: Princeton University Press, 1989), and Stephen P. Magee, William A. Brock, and Leslie Young, *Black Hole Tariffs and Endogenous Policy Theory* (Cambridge: Cambridge University Press, 1989), chap. 13.

8. Most of these works do not rely on formal theories of international trade, but they are all compatible with alternatives to Stolper-Samuelson two-factor models that see both business and labor trade policy preferences as heterogeneous. For example, Paul Midford's "multi-factor" model differentiates capital, labor, and land into eight separate production factors that are mobile only within clusters of similar industries, generating trade policy conflicts between factors employed in these clusters. See Midford, "International Trade and Domestic Politics: Improving on Rogowski's Model of Politi-

cal Alignments," *International Organization* 47, no. 4 (Autumn 1993): 535–64. Other "Ricardo-Viner" or "specific factors" models assume that at least one production factor is completely immobile between sectors. Under such conditions, capitalists and workers employed in high-cost, import-competing industries will gain from protection, whereas capitalists and workers in competitive, export-oriented industries will be hurt, producing intersectoral conflicts over trade policy.

Relaxing standard assumptions of constant production functions, constant or declining returns to scale, geographically immobile production factors, and fully informed and rational corporate decision makers produces still other theories that predict intra-industry, *firm*-level differences in the degree of international competitiveness, export dependence, and multinationality and thus also firm-level differences in trade policy preferences. See Helen V. Milner, *Resisting Protectionism: Global Industries and the Politics of International Trade* (Princeton, N.J.: Princeton University Press, 1988). Numerous "business conflict," "neo-Gramscian," and other Marxist-influenced analysts have also highlighted the importance of conflict between transnational and domestically oriented capitalist interests or "fractions" in determining a nation's trade policies. For a range of "business conflict" views, see Ronald W. Cox, ed., *Business and the State in International Relations* (Boulder, Colo.: Westview Press, 1996). For various neo-Gramscian views, see Stephen Gill, ed., *Gramsci, Historical Materialism, and International Relations* (Cambridge: Cambridge University Press, 1993).

Finally, proponents of these various heterogeneous factor models disagree over how to characterize the trade policy preferences of producers of nontraded goods. For example, in their revised Stolper-Samuelson model, Kenneth Schreve and Matthew Slaughter distinguish between skilled workers in traded and nontraded sectors, who as members of an abundant production factor in the United States favor free trade, and unskilled workers in both sectors, who as members of a scarce factor support protection. See Kenneth F. Schreve and Matthew J. Slaughter, "What Determines Individual Trade Policy Preferences?," *NBER Working Paper Series*, no. 6531 (April 1998). Adherents of specific-factor models, however, argue that producers of nontraded goods usually support free trade, reflecting their status as consumers or users of imported intermediate goods. Although Schreve and Slaughter produce polling evidence to support their view and, as we shall see, public-sector unions did ally with the industrial unions during the free-trade battles of the 1990s, the trade issue was much more salient and the level of mobilization much higher among industrial workers in import-competing industries than was the case among workers in nontraded sectors.

For a review and extensions of various theories of actor trade policy preferences, see James E. Alt, Jeffry Frieden, Michael J. Gilligan, Dani Rodrik, and Ronald Rogowski, "The Political Economy of International Trade: Enduring Puzzles and an Agenda for Inquiry," *Comparative Political Studies* 29, no. 6 (December 1996): 689–717.

9. Timothy McKeown, "What Forces Shape American Trade Policy?," in Doran and Marchildon, *The NAFTA Puzzle*, 65–85.

10. Michael Hiscox, "The Magic Bullet? The RTAA, Institutional Reform, and Trade Liberalization," *International Organization* 53, no. 4 (Autumn 1999): 669–98; David Vogel, "The Triumph of Liberal Trade: American Trade Policy in the Postwar Period," in Morton Keller and R. Shep Melnick, eds., *Taking Stock: American Government in the Twentieth Century* (Cambridge: Woodrow Wilson Center Press and Cambridge University Press, 1999), 35–53; Thomas Ferguson, *Golden Rule: The Investment Theory of Party*

Competition and the Logic of Money-Driven Political Systems (Chicago: University of Chicago Press, 1995); Peter Gourevitch, *Politics in Hard Times: Comparative Responses to International Economic Crises* (Ithaca, N.Y.: Cornell University Press, 1986).

11. These preferences and the coalitions they give rise to will vary with the perceived incidence of the effects of different proposed policies. Thus, for example, product-specific legislation like domestic content or quota bills usually appears to confer concentrated benefits on firms and workers in particular import-competing industries, while often imposing concentrated costs on specific importers, import-using industries, or export-oriented industries that are hurt by foreign retaliation. The result will be relatively narrow industry or sectoral coalitions. On the other hand, implementing legislation intended to liberalize trade with and investment in low-wage developing nations is usually perceived as likely to distribute large, concentrated benefits across a broad range of internationally oriented business interests, while distributing costs across different groups of industrial workers in the form of job and income losses due to both increased imports and the reality and threat of capital flight. The result in this case will be coalitions that, although not fully factoral in character, will nevertheless encompass a wider array of business and labor interests on opposite sides of the issue than is the case with product-specific measures. Other issues will produce still other patterns of preferences and coalitions. For similar arguments, see William H. Kaempfer and Stephen V. Marks, "The Expected Effects of Trade Liberalisation: Evidence from US Congressional Action on Fast-Track Authority," *World Economy* 16, no. 6 (November 1993): 725–40; Timothy J. McKeown, "The Global Economy, Post-Fordism, and Trade Policy in Advanced Capitalist States," in Herbert Kitschelt, Peter Lange, Gary Marks, and John D. Stephens, eds., *Continuity and Change in Contemporary Capitalism* (Cambridge: Cambridge University Press, 1999), 31–32.

12. See G. William Domhoff, "Which Fat Cats Support Democrats?," in Domhoff, *The Power Elite and the State: How Policy Is Made in America* (New York: Aldine De Gruyter, 1990), 225–55. In congressional races, some especially ideological firms donate the bulk of their campaign contributions to Republicans, including GOP challengers, but a larger number of more pragmatic, access-oriented interests give money to incumbents of both parties.

13. On the financial benefits of majority status in the House, see Thomas J. Rudolph, "Corporate and Labor PAC Contributions in House Elections: Measuring the Effects of Majority Party Status," *Journal of Politics* 61, no. 1 (February 1999): 195–206, and Gary W. Cox and Eric Magar, "How Much Is Majority Status in the U.S. Congress Worth?," *American Political Science Review* 93, no. 2 (June 1999): 299–309.

14. On such cross-pressuring, see Richard L. Hall, "Heterogeneous Preferences and the Practice of Group Representation in U.S. Trade Policy," in Alan V. Deardorff and Robert M. Stern, eds., *Constituent Interests and U.S. Trade Policies* (Ann Arbor: University of Michigan Press, 1998), 108–19.

15. An example is legislation of the kind discussed in note 11 that is intended to liberalize trade and investment relations with developing countries.

16. Such swing voters, i.e., independents and weak partisans who shift back and forth between the parties from election to election, often provide the margin of victory or defeat. Though mostly centrist in outlook, they may hold off-center positions on particular issues.

17. Among the myriad works on the dynamics of party competition, see Bernard Grofman, "Toward an Institution-Rich Theory of Political Competition with a Supply

Side Component," in Bernard Grofman, ed., *Information, Participation, and Choice* (Ann Arbor: University of Michigan Press, 1993), 179–93, and Morris P. Fiorina, "Whatever Happened to the Median Voter?" (paper presented at the annual meeting of the Midwest Political Science Association, Chicago, April 1999).

18. For a strong argument on the pivotal importance to two-party competition of swing voters, see Fritz W. Scharpf, *Games Real Actors Play: Actor-Centered Institutionalism in Policy Research* (Boulder, Colo.: Westview Press, 1997), 184–87.

19. On the concepts of "potential" preferences and "instigators," see R. Douglas Arnold, *The Logic of Congressional Action* (New Haven: Yale University Press, 1990).

20. Lawmakers also are able to pursue their own personal preferences when they can use their powers of incumbency, including constituency service, to make their seats safe from challenge and when they can package policies in ways that obscure attributes opposed by their constituents.

21. See Judith Goldstein and Robert Keohane, eds., *Ideas and Foreign Policy: Beliefs, Institutions, and Political Change* (Ithaca, N.Y.: Cornell University Press, 1993). See also Peter Hall, ed., *The Political Power of Economic Ideas: Keynesianism across Nations* (Princeton, N.J.: Princeton University Press, 1989), and most recently John C. Campbell, "The Problem of Ideas in Institutional Analysis," Department of Sociology, Dartmouth College, August 2000.

22. Judith Goldstein, *Ideas, Interests, and American Trade Policy* (Ithaca, N.Y.: Cornell University Press, 1993). See also I. M. Destler, *American Trade Politics*, 3d ed. (Washington, D.C.: Institute for International Economics and Twentieth Century Fund, 1995). Goldstein has recently stressed the role of export interests in buttressing free trade.

23. Stanley D. Nollen and Dennis P. Quinn, "Free Trade, Fair Trade, Strategic Trade, and Protectionism in the U.S. Congress, 1987–88," *International Organization* 48, no. 3 (Summer 1994): 503–4.

24. On preference-shaping tactics, see Patrick Dunleavy, *Bureaucracy, Democracy, and Public Choice* (New York: Harvester/Wheatsheaf, 1991).

25. On policy feedback, see Paul Pierson, "When Effect Becomes Cause: Policy Feedback and Political Change," *World Politics* 45, no. 4 (1993): 595–628.

26. See Lawrence R. Jacobs and Robert Y. Shapiro, *Politicians Don't Pander: Political Manipulation and the Loss of Democratic Responsiveness* (Chicago: University of Chicago Press, 2000), 44. For further discussion of the role of persuasion and argument in politics, see Diana C. Mutz, Paul M. Sniderman, and Richard A. Brody, eds., *Political Persuasion and Attitude Change* (Ann Arbor: University of Michigan Press, 1996).

27. Some analysts, however, consider these tactics to be examples of what William Riker has termed "heresthetics," discussed in the next paragraph.

28. John Zaller argues that persuasion is only effective in shifting the opinions of attentive constituencies with weak and uncertain preferences. Such conditions are most likely to pertain for policies with widely dispersed, late-order effects for which responsibility cannot be easily attributed. Zaller, *The Nature and Origins of Mass Opinion* (Cambridge: Cambridge University Press, 1992). On the limited empirical evidence for the success of persuasive tactics, see Mutz, Sniderman, and Brody, *Political Persuasion*, and George C. Edwards, "Building Coalitions," *Presidential Studies Quarterly* 30, no. 1 (March 2000): 47–78. Patrick Dunleavy has argued that American parties, in contrast to parties elsewhere, generally adopt "preference-accommodating" rather than "preference-shaping" tactics. Dunleavy, *Bureaucracy, Democracy*, chap. 5. For a theoretical critique of extreme forms of "social constructionism," see Andrew Sayer, "Essential-

ism, Social Constructionism, and Beyond," *Realism and Social Science* (London: Sage Publications, 2000), 81–104.

29. See William H. Riker, *The Art of Political Manipulation* (New Haven: Yale University Press, 1986).

30. Doran, "Trade and Party," 234–37.

31. The implications of this view for the behavior of members of the president's party in Congress are unclear, although it may be assumed that they will be predisposed to support him for reasons explained later.

32. See E. E. Schattschneider, *The Semi-Sovereign People: A Realist's View of Democracy in America* (New York: Holt, Rinehart, and Winston, 1960); Edward G. Carmines and James A. Stimson, *Issue Evolution: Race and the Transformation of American Politics* (Princeton, N.J.: Princeton University Press, 1989); and Bryan D. Jones, *Reconceiving Decision-Making in Democratic Politics: Attention, Choice, and Public Policy* (Chicago: University of Chicago Press, 1994).

33. See Douglas Rivers, "Heterogeneity in Models of Electoral Choice," *American Journal of Political Science* 32, no. 3 (August 1988): 737–57.

34. On focusing crises or events, see John W. Kingdon, *Agendas, Alternatives, and Public Policies* (New York: Little, Brown, 1984).

35. On the attraction of such groups to vote-seeking politicians, see Robert A. Bernstein, "Directing Appeals Away from the Center: Issue Position and Issue Salience," *Political Research Quarterly* 48, no. 3 (September 1995): 461–78; Peter H. Aranson, "Electoral Competition and Entrepreneurship," *Advances in Austrian Economics* 5 (1998): 199.

36. John B. Gilmour, *Strategic Disagreement: Stalemate in American Politics* (Pittsburgh: University of Pittsburgh Press, 1995).

37. On the heresthetical maneuvers of governing parties, see Jack H. Nagel, "Populism, Heresthetics, and Political Stability: Richard Seddon and the Art of Majority Rule," *British Journal of Political Science* 23, pt. 2 (1993): 139–74.

38. On what he actually called "contagion from the left," i.e., the politically driven spread of ideas from mass-based leftist parties to parties of the center and right, see Maurice Duverger, *Political Parties*, 3d ed. (London: Methuen, 1974). See also François Petry, "The Policy Impact of Canadian Party Programs: Public Expenditure Growth and Contagion from the Left," *Canadian Public Policy* 14, no. 4 (December 1988): 376–89. I believe that such contagion can operate from right to left, as well, e.g., on tax issues; hence my more nondirectional term. See also Gilmour's (*Strategic Disagreement*) similar notion of "excessive compromise to avoid the issue," a tactic frequently used by presidents, and Tim Groseclose and Nolan McCarty, "The Politics of Blame: Bargaining before an Audience," *American Journal of Political Science* 45, no. 1 (January 2001): 100–119.

39. Melissa Collie, "Universalism and the Parties in the U.S. House of Representatives, 1921–1980," *American Journal of Political Science* 32, no. 4 (November 1988): 877–88.

40. See Bert A. Rockman, "Leadership Style and the Clinton Presidency," in Colin Campbell and Rockman, eds., *The Clinton Presidency: First Appraisals* (Chatham, N.J.: Chatham House Publishers, 1996), 325–62.

41. For parties as leadership coalitions, see Gerald M. Pomper, *Passions and Interests: Political Party Concepts of American Democracy* (Lawrence: University Press of Kansas, 1992), 115–16.

42. For evolving Democratic and Republican factions since World War II, see Nicol C.

Rae, "Party Factionalism, 1946–1996," in Byron E. Shafer, ed., *Partisan Approaches to Postwar American Politics* (New York: Chatham House Publishers, 1998), 41–74.

43. See Hiscox, "Magic Bullet?"

44. On the polarizing role of primary elections, see John Aldrich, *Why Parties? The Origin and Transformation of Party Politics in America* (Chicago: University of Chicago Press, 1995).

45. Susanne Lohmann and Mohan Penubarti, "The Politics of Section 301: On the Strategic Design of Trade Policy Instruments" (paper presented at the annual meeting of the American Political Science Association, San Francisco, 1996). On such preelection handouts or "surgical" redistribution to "special interests," see Susanne Lohmann, "An Information Rationale for the Power of Special Interests," *American Political Science Review* 92, no. 4 (December 1998): 821. On the role of the electoral college in influencing presidential campaign strategy, see Scott C. James and Brian L. Lawson, "The Political Economy of Voting Rights Enforcement in America's Gilded Age: Electoral College Competition, Partisan Commitment, and the Federal Election Law," *American Political Science Review* 93, no. 1 (March 1999): 115–31.

46. The relevant literature is vast, but see David Rohde, *Parties and Leaders in the Postreform House* (Chicago: University of Chicago Press, 1991); Patricia A. Hurley, "Parties and Coalitions in Congress," in Christopher J. Deering, *Congressional Politics* (Chicago: Dorsey Press, 1989), 113–34; and David W. Brady and Kara M. Buckley, "Coalitions and Policy in the U.S. Congress: Lessons from the 103rd and 104th Congresses," in L. Sandy Maisel, ed., *The Parties Respond: Changes in American Parties and Campaigns*, 3d ed. (Boulder, Colo.: Westview Press, 1998), 286–315.

47. On the overrepresentation in the Senate of states with low levels of unionization, see Daniel Wirls, "The Consequences of Equal Representation: The Bicameral Politics of NAFTA in the 103rd Congress," *Congress and the Presidency* 25, no. 2 (Autumn 1998): 129–45.

48. Meengon Kim, "United States Trade Policy and Party Politics in the House of Representatives, 1934–1988" (Ph.D. diss., University of Iowa, 1994). To the extent that in recent years internationally oriented business interests have diffused their activities throughout the country, this has reduced such regionally based partisan divisions over trade policy. See Vogel, "Triumph of Liberal Trade."

49. Again, to the extent that internationally oriented firms operate in many of a given region's congressional districts, increasing the heterogeneity of lawmakers' constituencies, this will reduce district-based partisan conflict over trade policy. See Hall, "Heterogeneous Preferences."

50. For a good review of current debates on the role of congressional parties, see Steven S. Smith, "Positive Theories of Congressional Parties," *Legislative Studies Quarterly* 25, no. 2 (May 2000): 193–215.

51. See John H. Aldrich and David W. Rohde, "The Consequences of Party Organization in the House: The Role of the Majority and Minority Parties in Conditional Party Government," in Jon R. Bond and Richard Fleisher, eds., *Polarized Politics: Congress and the President in a Partisan Era* (Washington, D.C.: CQ Press, 2000), 31–72.

52. Aldrich, *Why Parties?*, 218–20; John B. Bader, *Taking the Initiative: Leadership Agendas and the "Contract with America"* (Washington, D.C.: Georgetown University Press, 1996); Gary W. Cox, "Agenda Setting in the U.S. House: A Majority-Party Monopoly?" (paper presented at the annual meeting of the American Political Science Associa-

tion, Atlanta, September 1999). I might add that in his well-known argument that congressional parties do not much matter in Congress beyond aggregating the induced and personal preferences of their individual members, Keith Krehbiel ignores the agenda-setting role of congressional party leaders, which, as the next section argues, can also affect policy. Krehbiel, *Pivotal Politics a Theory of U.S. Lawmaking* (Chicago: University of Chicago Press, 1998).

53. Aldrich, *Why Parties?*; Gary W. Cox and Matthew D. McCubbins, *Legislative Leviathan: Party Government in the House* (Berkeley: University of California Press, 1993).

54. See George Tsebelis and Jeannette Money, *Bicameralism* (New York: Cambridge University Press, 1997).

55. See David Epstein and Sharyn O'Halloran, *Delegating Powers: A Transaction Cost Politics Approach to Policy Making under Separate Powers* (New York: Cambridge University Press, 1999).

56. On the following points, see Jon R. Bond, Richard Fleisher, and Glen S. Krutz, "An Overview of the Empirical Findings on Presidential-Congressional Relations," in James A. Thurber, ed., *Rivals for Power: Presidential-Congressional Relations* (Washington, D.C.: CQ Press, 1996), 124–25, and Barbara Sinclair, "Trying to Govern Positively in a Negative Era: Clinton and the 103rd Congress," in Campbell and Rockman, *The Clinton Presidency*, 89–91.

57. The empirical evidence that a skilled president can persuade party members to support his policies is based mostly on case studies. The quantitative evidence is much more limited.

58. See Sinclair, "Trying to Govern Positively," 90.

59. Charles O. Jones, *The Presidency in a Separated System* (Washington, D.C.: Brookings Institution Press, 1994); Lester G. Seligman and Cary R. Covington, *The Coalitional Presidency* (Chicago: Dorsey Press, 1989).

60. For the following discussion, see Rohde, *Parties and Leaders*, 139–41, 168.

61. See Gilmour, *Strategic Disagreement*, 119–31. On the opposition party strategy of provoking "blame game" vetoes under divided government, see Tim Groseclose and Nolan McCarty, "Politics of Blame," and Charles M. Cameron, "Bargaining and Presidential Power," in Robert Y. Shapiro, Martha Joint Kumar, and Lawrence R. Jacobs, eds., *Presidential Power: Forging the Presidency for the Twenty-First Century* (New York: Columbia University Press), 63–64.

62. For some authors, the Democrats' disinclination to break with liberal trade was reinforced by the growing influence within the party of internationally oriented business interests. See Vogel, "Triumph of Liberal Trade."

63. See Goldstein, *Ideas, Interests*; Destler, *American Trade Politics*.

64. I. M. Destler notes the role of partisanship in producing recent setbacks for free trade. See Destler, "Congress, Constituencies, and U.S. Trade Policy," in Deardorff and Stern, *Constituent Interests*, 93–108.

65. For a recent review and extension of this literature, see John J. Coleman, "Unified Government, Divided Government, and Party Responsiveness," *American Political Science Review* 93, no. 4 (December 1999): 821–35.

66. Susanne Lohmann and Sharyn O'Halloran, "Divided Government and U.S. Trade Policy: Theory and Evidence," *International Organization* 48, no. 4 (Autumn 1994): 595–632.

67. David Karol, "Divided Government and U.S. Trade Policy: Much Ado about Nothing?," *International Organization* 54, no. 4 (Autumn 1994): 825–44.

68. In her book, Sharyn O'Halloran actually recognizes that the congressional parties have consistently differed over trade policy since World War II, with the Republicans advocating freer trade than the Democrats. See O'Halloran, *Politics, Process, and American Trade Policy* (Ann Arbor: University of Michigan Press, 1994), 179.

69. William Keech and Kyoungsan Pak, "Partisanship, Institutions, and Change in American Trade Politics," *Journal of Politics* 57, no. 4 (November 1995): 1139.

70. David Karol ("Divided Government," 834–35) acknowledges this possibility for this particular form of unified government, although he maintains that in many cases the president's persuasive efforts may repel as many members of the opposition party from his position as they attract representatives of his own party, thus producing no net gain in support for trade liberalization. (This argument is made more generally by Calvin Mouw and Michael MacKuen in "The Strategic Configuration, Personal Influence, and Presidential Power in Congress," *Western Political Quarterly* 45 [September 1992]: 579–608.)

71. Karol admits that Clinton persuaded more Democrats to support NAFTA than he drove Republicans to oppose it.

72. See Helen V. Milner, *Interests, Institutions, and Information: Domestic Politics and International Relations* (Princeton, N.J.: Princeton University Press, 1997), 140, 214, 151. According to Karol, Milner, like Lohmann and O'Halloran, erroneously claims that divided government consistently impedes international cooperation, including on trade liberalization, irrespective of the constituency-induced preferences of the congressional parties and which party controls Congress. See Karol, "Divided Government," 829. But Karol misunderstands Milner's concept of divided government, which is an unconventional one. Most scholars, Karol included, regard divided government as a dichotomous variable; either the party in control of the executive also controls the legislature, or it does not. Milner instead suggests that divided government should be treated as a continuous variable. When the preferences of the executive and the median legislator, regardless of party, diverge, control of government is considered to be divided. The more divergent these preferences, the more divided government is. Milner adopts this notion in recognition of the reality that parties are often internally divided. Thus, if the majority legislative party also controls the executive but lacks party discipline or is internally split, then even so-called unified government may appear divided. See Milner, *Interests, Institutions*, 37–38. I employ the standard definition of divided government, but in arguing that trade policy is restrictive under divided government only when the more protectionist party controls Congress with a large and unified majority or when the more liberal party controls Congress with only a narrow and divided majority, I am conceding the importance of Milner's point.

73. Here, of course, I am entering the ever-widening debate on the extent to which economic and other forms of "globalization" constrain the policy autonomy of the nation-state. For a balanced discussion of this issue that threads its way between the views of "hyper-globalists," who see globalization as both far advanced and highly constraining, and "globalization skeptics," who doubt both of these claims, see David Held, Anthony McGrew, David Goldblatt, and Jonathan Perraton, *Global Transformations: Politics, Economics, and Culture* (Stanford: Stanford University Press, 1999).

74. From an exponentially growing literature, see Stephen J. Kobrin, "The Architec-

ture of Globalization: State Sovereignty in a Networked Global Economy," in John H. Dunning, ed., *Governments, Globalization, and International Business* (New York: Oxford University Press, 1997), 146–71; Peter Dicken, *Global Shift: Transforming the World Economy*, 3d ed. (New York: Guilford Press, 1998); Jonathan Perraton, "What Are Global Markets? The Significance of Networks of Trade," in Randall D. Germain, ed., *Globalization and Its Critics: Perspectives from Political Economy* (New York: St. Martin's Press, 2000), 164–82. Note that the concept of structure used here is very different from that propounded by purely or predominantly systemic international relations theories like neorealism, neoliberal institutionalism, and constructivism. In assuming that the state is a unitary actor, all of these theories conflate the state and the nation, thus inexcusably minimizing the role of domestic politics of the kind that I am concerned with in this book.

75. Jeffry A. Frieden and Ronald Rogowski, "The Impact of the International Economy on National Policies: An Overview," in Robert O. Keohane and Helen V. Milner, eds, *Internationalization and Domestic Policies* (Cambridge: Cambridge University Press, 1996), 31–36.

76. Despite the undeniable growth of economic interdependence, it is unclear that market integration has proceeded as far or as rapidly as some "hyper-globalists" would have it.

77. See Geoffrey Garrett, "The Causes of Globalization," *Comparative Political Studies* 33, no. 6–7 (August–September 2000): 941–91.

78. See I. M. Destler and John S. Odell, *Anti-Protection: Changing Forces in United States Trade Politics* (Washington, D.C.: Institute for International Economics, September 1987); Michael Lusztig, "The Limits of Rent Seeking: Why Protectionists Become Free Traders," *Review of International Political Economy* 5, no. 1 (Spring 1998): 38–63; and Oona A. Hathaway, "Positive Feedback: The Impact of Trade Liberalization on Industry Demands for Protection," *International Organization* 52, no. 3 (Summer 1998): 575–612.

79. See Hiscox, "Magic Bullet?," and Vogel, "Triumph of Liberal Trade."

80. On the policy impact of capital mobility, see David M. Andrews, "Capital Mobility and State Autonomy: Toward a Structural Theory of International Monetary Relations," *International Studies Quarterly* 38, no. 2 (June 1994): 193–218, and Thomas Oatley, "How Constraining Is Capital Mobility? The Partisan Hypothesis in an Open Economy," *American Journal of Political Science* 43, no. 4 (October 1999): 1003–27

81. For an interesting counterargument, see Mark A. Smith, *American Business and Political Power: Public Opinion, Elections, and Democracy* (Chicago: University of Chicago Press, 2000), chap. 7.

82. See Milner, *Interests, Institutions*, 65–66, and Peter B. Evans, Harold K. Jacobson, and Robert D. Putnam, eds., *Double-Edged Diplomacy: International Bargaining and Domestic Politics* (Berkeley: University of California Press, 1993). International relations specialists will criticize the present work for focusing exclusively on the partisan determinants of national preferences over trade policy *outcomes*, while neglecting the fuller determinants of preferences over bargaining *strategies*, which include the behavior of other states. In other words, they will argue that I should pay more attention to the international side of "two-level" bargaining games. But I agree with James Caparaso, who, in comparing the strengths and weaknesses of general and partial equilibrium analyses, maintains that "partial models provide one way to build comprehensive models, and that such an approach may be more practically attainable than models that are comprehensive from the start." James A. Caparaso, "Across the Great Divide: Integrating

Comparative and International Politics," *International Studies Quarterly* 41, no. 4 (December 1997): 573.

83. See Judith Goldstein, "International Institutions and Domestic Politics: GATT, WTO, and the Liberalization of Internationalization of Trade," in Anne O. Krueger, ed., *The WTO as an International Organization* (Chicago: University of Chicago Press, 1998).

84. See Joanne Gowa, *Allies, Adversaries, and International Trade* (Princeton, N.J.: Princeton University Press, 1994), and Edward Mansfield, *Power, Trade, and War* (Princeton, N.J.: Princeton University Press, 1994).

85. Archer, *Realist Social Theory*. See also Roy Bhaskar's Transformational Model of Social Action (TMSA), elaborated, among other places, in his *Dialectic: The Pulse of Freedom* (London: Verso, 1993). Archer's theory differs in important ways from the apparently similar "structurationism" of Anthony Giddens. See his *The Constitution of Society* (Cambridge, England: Polity Press, 1984). Whereas Archer insists on a "dualism" or analytic separation of structure and agency, Giddens tries to overcome such a dualism with his concept of the "duality of structure," whereby structures and agents are simultaneously and mutually constitutive. But as Archer points out, Giddens's approach underestimates the constraining aspect of structure and does not permit us to understand the temporal interplay *between* analytically distinct structures and agents.

86. David Plotke, *Building a Democratic Political Order: Reshaping American Liberalism in the 1930s and 1940s* (New York: Cambridge University Press, 1996), 1. See also Stephen Skowronek, *The Politics Presidents Make: Leadership from John Adams to Bill Clinton* (Cambridge: Belknap/Harvard University Press, 1997); Karen Orren and Stephen Skowronek, "Regimes and Regime Building in American Government: A Review of Literature on the 1940s," *Political Science Quarterly* 113, no. 4 (1998–99): 689–702; Andrew J. Polsky, "Why Regimes? Ideas, Incentives, and Policies in American Political Orders," *Polity* 29 (Summer 1997): 625–40, and "When Business Speaks: Political Entrepreneurship, Discourse, and Mobilization in American Partisan Regimes," *Journal of Theoretical Politics* 12, no. 4 (October 2000): 455–76; Robert C. Lieberman, "Political Time and Policy Coalitions: Structure and Agency in Presidential Power," in Shapiro et. al., *Presidential Power*, 274–310; and Edward Greenberg, *Capitalism and the American Political Ideal* (Armonk, N.Y.: M. E. Sharpe, 1985). For a useful application of the "regime" concept to Japan, with comparative material on other countries, including the United States, see T. J. Pempel, *Regime Shift: Comparative Dynamics of the Japanese Political Economy* (Ithaca, N.Y.: Cornell University Press, 1998).

87. From the diverse and rapidly growing corpus of works by regulation theorists, see Robert Boyer, *The Regulation School: A Critical Introduction* (New York: Columbia University Press, 1990); Adam Tickell and Jamie A. Peck, "Social Regulation *after* Fordism: Regulation Theory, Neo-liberalism, and the Global-Local Nexus," *Economy and Society* 24, no. 3 (August 1995): 357–86; Bob Jessop, "Twenty Years of the (Parisian) Regulation Approach: The Paradox of Success and Failure at Home and Abroad," *New Political Economy* 2, no. 3 (November 1997): 503–26; and Jacques Mazier, Maurice Basle, and Jean-François Vidal, *When Economic Crises Endure* (Armonk, N.Y.: M. E. Sharpe, 1999). For related views, see David M. Kotz, Terrence McDonough, and Michael Reich, eds., *Social Structures of Accumulation: The Political Economy of Growth and Crisis* (Cambridge: Cambridge University Press, 1994); Douglass C. North, *Institutions, Institutional Change, and Economic Performance* (Cambridge: Cambridge University Press, 1990), 95; Bruno Amable, "Institutional Complementarity and Diversity of Social Systems of Production and Innovation," *Review of International Political Economy* 7, no. 4 (Winter

2000): 645–87; and Peter A. Hall and David Soskice, "An Introduction to Varieties of Capitalism," Department of Government, Harvard University, August 1999. On the relation between theories of regulation and governance, see Bob Jessop, "The Regulation Approach, Governance and Post-Fordism: Alternative Perspectives on Economic and Political Change?," *Economy and Society* 24, no. 3 (August 1995): 307–33.

88. A number of other authors have based their analyses of party systems and the political "realignments" that link them on various theories of capitalist periodization. Plotke and Terrence McDonough both rely on "social structures of accumulation" theory, whereas Brian Berry and his collaborators utilize the neo-Schumpeterian "techno-economic paradigm" approach. See Plotke, *Building a Democratic Political Order*, 40–42; Terrence McDonough, "The Construction of Social Structures of Accumulation in US History," in Kotz, McDonough, and Reich, *Social Structures of Accumulation*, 101–32; and Brian J. L. Berry, Euel Elliott, Edward J. Harpham, and Heja Kim, *The Rhythms of American Politics* (Lanham, Md.: University Press of America, 1998). For other attempts to link party systems, realignments, and economic conditions, see David W. Brady, *Critical Elections and Congressional Policy Making* (Stanford: Stanford University Press, 1988), and Jerome M. Clubb, William H. Flanagan, and Nancy Zingale, *Partisan Realignment: Voters, Parties, and Government in American History* (Beverly Hills: Sage Publications, 1980). David Mayhew has recently authored a wide-ranging theoretical and empirical critique of realignment and party systems theory. See David R. Mayhew, "Electoral Realignments," *Annual Review of Political Science* 3 (2000): 449–74, and my comments in n. 12 of Chapter 2.

89. On "macro-actors," see Nicos Mouzelis, *Back to Sociological Theory: The Construction of Social Orders* (London: Macmillan, 1991), 107. Although in "Regimes and Regime Building" (1998–99) Orren and Skowronek are critically sympathetic to the concept of a partisan "regime," in influential earlier work they mounted a strong criticism of the idea of successive, integrated, institutionalized political orders. They argued instead for a notion of "intercurrence," or "patterned anarchy or disorder" among abrading institutions with independent logics and temporalities. Karen Orren and Stephen Skowronek, "Beyond the Iconography of Order: Notes for a 'New Institutionalism,'" in Lawrence C. Dodd and Calvin Jillson, eds., *The Dynamics of American Politics: Approaches and Interpretations* (Boulder, Colo.: Westview Press, 1994). I believe that any given historical period is characterized by *both* a moment of institutionally integrated order and stability, or "structure," and a moment of disorder, conflict, and strategic maneuver, or "agency." In some periods, the moment of order or structure is dominant. Conflict remains, to be sure, and some institutions continue to abrade against each other. But the deployment by party leaders of successful strategies and projects can reduce such conflict and institutional abrasion to the point where it is possible to speak of a political order, with at least a "core" of several integrated institutions securely in place. In other periods of crisis and instability, the moment of disorder, conflict, and agency is dominant, although certain structures remain in place. For the argument that a "core" of integrated institutions within a wider but not yet fully established mode of regulation (or what he calls a "social structure of accumulation") can suffice to launch a long wave of economic growth, see David Kotz, "Interpreting the Social Structures of Accumulation Theory," in Kotz, McDonough, and Reich, *Social Structures of Accumulation*, 50–71. See also Amable, "Institutional Complementarity," 659–60.

90. Bob Jessop, *State Theory: Putting Capitalist States in Their Place* (University Park: Pennsylvania State University Press, 1990). Jessop's "hegemonic projects" are similar to

the "public philosophies," "governing ideas," "societal paradigms," and "party narratives" described by other authors.

91. Ibid. Jessop has tried to fill in the political dynamics that are largely absent from the first generation of regulation school writings. See also Colin Hay, "Crisis and the Structural Transformation of the State: Interrogating the Process of Change," *British Journal of Politics and International Relations* 1, no. 3 (October 1999): 317–44, and Jonathan Joseph, "A Realist Theory of Hegemony," *Journal for the Theory of Social Behaviour* 30, no. 2 (June 2000): 178–202.

92. On policy paradigms, see Peter A. Hall, "Policy Paradigms, Social Learning, and the State: The Case of Economic Policymaking in Britain," *Comparative Politics* 25, no. 3 (April 1993): 275–96.

93. On this distinction between stabilization, allocative, and distributive policies, see M. Stephen Weatherford and Lorraine M. McDonnell, "Do Presidents Make a Difference in the Economy? (And If So, How?)" (paper presented at the 1997 Annual Meeting of the American Political Science Association, Washington, D.C., August 28–31, 1997).

94. On such advocacy coalitions, see Paul Sabatier and Hank Jenkins-Smith, "The Advocacy Coalition Framework: An Assessment," in Sabatier, ed., *Theories of the Policy Process* (Boulder, Colo.: Westview Press, 1999), 117–66.

95. See B. Guy Peters, "Managing Horizontal Government: The Politics of Co-Ordination," *Public Administration* 76, no. 2 (Summer 1998): 295–311.

96. Pertinent to this last point, M. Stephen Weatherford argues that the president's economic ideology can help bind together support coalitions by heightening coalition members' party loyalty, thereby discouraging them from free-riding or defecting from their party's program to pursue short-term interests, which can undermine aggregate economic performance and thus also their party's long-run prospects. In Weatherford's game-theoretical terms, a prisoner's dilemma game in this way is transformed into an assurance game. Weatherford, "*An Economic Theory of Democracy* as a Theory of Policy," in Grofman, *Information, Participation, and Choice*, 209–30.

97. At the same time, the successful implementation of an accumulation strategy requires the state to have adequate administrative capacity and a sufficient degree of centralization and autonomy from societal actors. On institutions as products of compromises among organized interests, see Terry Moe, "Institutions: The Neglected Side of the Story," *Journal of Law, Economics, and Organization* 6, Special issue (1990), and Jack Knight, *Institutions and Social Conflict* (Cambridge: Cambridge University Press, 1992).

98. David Lockwood, "Social Integration and System Integration," in G. K. Zollschan and H. W. Hirsch, eds., *Explorations in Social Change* (Boston: Houghton Mifflin, 1964).

99. These vested interests may mobilize at the decentralized American state's many "veto points" to block proposals for radical institutional change.

100. For a thorough, sophisticated discussion of these and other types of path dependence, all of which he unfortunately classifies under the rubric of "increasing returns," see Paul Pierson, "Increasing Returns, Path Dependence, and the Study of Politics," *American Political Science Review* 94, no. 2 (June 2000): 251–67. On the cognitive variant of path dependence, see Arthur Denzau and Douglass North, "Shared Mental Models: Ideologies and Institutions," *Kylos* 47 (1994): 3–31, and Jack Knight and Douglass North, "Explaining Economic Change: The Interplay Between Cognition and Institutions," *Legal Theory* 3 (1997): 211–26.

101. See David M. Gordon, " 'Inside and Outside the Long Swing': The Endogeneity/ Exogeneity Debate and the Social Structures of Accumulation Approach," *Review* 14,

no. 2 (Spring 1991): 263–312. For a historical institutionalist discussion of the importance of endogenous, "negative feedback" mechanisms of institutional change, little considered by most theorists of path dependence, see Kathleen Thelen, "Historical Institutionalism in Comparative Politics," in Nelson Polsby, ed., *Annual Review of Political Science* 2 (1999): 369–404. As examples of endogenously generated contradictions, (1) inertially rigid institutions may be unable to adapt to new economic circumstances, (2) the ambiguous and weighted compromises inscribed in state institutions as solutions to old problems may eventually disrupt the efficient operation of the mode of regulation, or (3) the dominant party's strategies and projects may fail to contain inter-institutional abrasion, resulting in the disarticulation of the institutions of the mode of regulation. See Moe, "Political Institutions," and Orren and Skowronek, "Beyond the Iconography of Order."

102. Here I draw on "punctuated equilibrium" theories of biological evolution that historical institutionalists have borrowed to explain processes of political and institutional development.

103. On this point, see Paul S. Herrnson and Kelly D. Patterson, "Toward a More Programmatic Democratic Party? Agenda-Setting and Coalition-Building in the House of Representatives," *Polity* 27, no. 4 (Summer 1995): 607–28.

104. Again, interest groups with strong preferences will also engage in such persuasive efforts to win public officials, other groups, and voters over to their positions.

105. This typology is based on Hugh Ward, "The Possibility of an Evolutionary Explanation of the State's Role in Modes of Regulation," in Jeffrey Stanyer and Gerry Stoker, eds., *Contemporary Political Studies* (Belfast: Political Studies Association of the United Kingdom, 1997); James G. March, *A Primer on Decision Making: How Decisions Happen* (New York: Free Press, 1994), 23–35; Jack Levy, "Learning and Foreign Policy: Sweeping a Conceptual Minefield," *International Organization* 48, no. 2 (Spring 1994): 279–312; and Knight, *Institutions and Social Conflict*.

106. For a similar argument, see Orren and Skowronek, "Regimes and Regime Building." For a more general discussion of institutional evolution and change from which the terms "functional reconversion" and "layering" are taken, see Kathleen Thelen, "Timing and Temporality in the Analysis of Institutional Evolution and Change," *Studies in American Political Development* 14, no. 1 (Spring 2000): 101–8. See also Thelen, "Historical Institutionalism."

107. On "structural privileging," see Geoffrey Garrett, "The Politics of Structural Change: Swedish Social Democracy and Thatcherism in Comparative Perspective," *Comparative Political Studies* 25, no. 4 (January 1993): 521–47, and Ward, "Possibility of an Evolutionary Explanation," 125–37. See also Carles Boix, "Partisan Government, the International Economy, and Macroeconomic Policies in Advanced Nations, 1960–1993," *World Politics* 53, no. 1 (October 2000): 38–73.

108. For a critique of the punctuated equilibrium model of institutional change and an argument for the possibility of more gradual or incremental change, see Philip Genschel, "The Dynamics of Inertia: Institutional Persistence and Change in Telecommunications and Health Care," *Governance* 10, no. 1 (January 1997): 43–66, and Kathleen Thelen, "How Institutions Evolve: Insights from Comparative-Historical Analysis," Department of Political Science, Northwestern University, 2000.

109. See Giulio M. Gallarotti, "Toward a Business Cycle Model of Tariffs," *International Organization* 39 (1985): 155–87, and John J. Coleman, "Bipartisan Order and Partisan Disorder in Postwar Trade Policy," Department of Political Science, University

of Wisconsin at Madison, 1997. Coleman notes, however, that a crisis with a predominantly inflationary character will elicit demands solely for the opening of the domestic market to imports.

110. On the particular role of trade policy in such circumstances, see Michael Lusztig, *Risking Free Trade: The Politics of Trade in Britain, Canada, Mexico, and the United States* (Pittsburgh: University of Pittsburgh Press, 1996).

111. On these distinctions, see Joseph M. Bryant, "On Sources and Narratives in Historical Social Science: A Realist Critique of Positivist and Postmodernist Epistemologies," *British Journal of Sociology* 51, no. 3 (September 2000): 489–523.

112. See Peter Burke, "History of Events and the Revival of Narrative," in Burke, ed., *New Perspectives on Historical Writing* (University Park: Pennsylvania State University Press, 1992).

113. Andrew Sayer, *Method in Social Science: A Realist Approach*, 2d ed. (New York: Routledge, 1992), 259.

114. Ibid.

115. See, e.g., Pierson, "Increasing Returns."

116. For a critique of historical institutionalism on this point, see Polsky, "New 'Dismal Science'?" See also Thelen, "How Institutions Evolve," who adds, however, that such theories often paradoxically posit too much contingency or indeterminacy during critical junctures, when, despite the tumult, some particularly inertial institutions continue to resist and constrain the process of change.

117. For examples from both disciplines, see Robert H. Bates, Avner Greif, Margaret Levi, Jean-Laurent Rosenthal, and Barry R. Weingast, *Analytic Narratives* (Princeton, N.J.: Princeton University Press, 1998), and Edgar Kaiser, "The Revival of Narrative in Historical Sociology: What Rational Choice Theory Can Contribute," *Politics and Society* 24, no. 3 (September 1996): 249–71.

118. Archer, *Realist Social Theory*. For a similar view from historical sociology, see Larry J. Griffin, "Temporality, Events, and Explanation in Historical Sociology," *Sociological Methods and Research* 20, no. 4 (May 1992): 403–27.

Chapter 2

1. Some elements of the theoretical framework only apply to the New Deal Order and its aftermath.

2. For general analyses of American trade politics from the nineteenth century to the Great Depression, see Frank Taussig, *The Tariff History of the United States*, 8th ed. (New York: G. P. Putnam's Sons, 1931); Sidney Ratner, *The Tariff in American History* (New York: Van Nostrand, 1972); Tom Terrill, *The Tariff, Politics, and American Foreign Policy, 1874–1901* (Westport, Conn.: Greenwood Press, 1973); Alfred E. Eckes Jr., *Opening America's Market: U.S. Foreign Trade Policy since 1776* (Chapel Hill: University of North Carolina Press, 1995), 1–77; Judith Goldstein, *Ideas, Interests, and American Trade Policy* (Ithaca, N.Y.: Cornell University Press, 1993), 23–115; Sharyn O'Halloran, *Politics, Process, and American Trade Policy* (Ann Arbor: University of Michigan Press, 1994), 45–85; Daniel Verdier, *Democracy and International Trade: Britain, France, and the United States, 1860–1990* (Princeton, N.J.: Princeton University Press, 1994), 70–82, 108–25; Richard Franklin Bensel, *The Political Economy of American Industrialization, 1877–1900* (Cambridge: Cambridge University Press, 2000); Morton Keller, "Trade Policy in Historical Perspective," in Keller and R. Shep Melnick, eds., *Taking Stock: American Govern-*

ment in the Twentieth Century (Cambridge: Woodrow Wilson Center Press and Cambridge University Press, 1999), 15–34; and Charles W. Calhoun, "Political Economy in the Gilded Age: The Republican Party's Industrial Policy," *Journal of Policy History* 8, no. 3 (1996): 291–309.

3. For the next two paragraphs, see Richard Franklin Bensel, *Political Economy of American Industrialization* and *Yankee Leviathan: The Origins of Central State Authority in America, 1859–1877* (Cambridge: Cambridge University Press, 1990), 64; Michael Reich, "How Social Structures of Accumulation Decline and Are Built," in David M. Kotz, Terrence McDonough, and Michael Reich, eds., *Social Structures of Accumulation: The Political Economy of Growth and Crisis* (Cambridge: Cambridge University Press, 1994), 30–31; Marc Alan Eisner, *The State in the American Political Economy* (Englewood Cliffs, N.J.: Prentice-Hall, 1995), 77–78; David Brady, *Critical Elections and Congressional Policy Making* (Stanford: Stanford University Press, 1988); 20–22, 49; and Edward Greenberg, *Capitalism and the American Political Ideal* (Armonk, N.Y.: M. E. Sharpe, 1985), 53–73.

4. As postwar industrialization and prosperity continued, however, the apparent success and popularity of the Republicans' higher tariff policies forced the Democrats to acknowledge at least some "incidental" role for tariffs in fostering industrial development. This has led Judith Goldstein (*Ideas, Interests*) to argue—somewhat excessively, I think—that the postbellum era saw the emergence of a bipartisan political and cognitive consensus on a protectionist trade paradigm that would persist until the 1930s. Within the parameters of this consensus, the parties battled over just how high tariff rates should actually be set. See also Calhoun, "Political Economy," 295.

5. Terrill, *The Tariff, Politics*, 3–16; Paul Kleppner, *The Third Electoral System* (Chapel Hill: University of North Carolina Press, 1979).

6. Terrill (*The Tariff, Politics*) and Bensel (*Political Economy of American Industrialization*) forcefully make this point.

7. See John Gerring, *Party Ideologies in America, 1828–1996* (Cambridge: Cambridge University Press, 1998), 11, 68–69, 167.

8. Terrill, *The Tariff, Politics*, 7–12, 25, 32, 210, 213–14.

9. In his stimulating new book, Richard Bensel argues that although the promotion of an unregulated national market for labor and production and adherence to the international gold standard were the economically essential elements of the Republicans' developmentalist accumulation strategy, the protective tariff was politically essential as the popular backbone of the party's program. Not only did the "tariff policy complex," as Bensel calls it, guarantee high profits and wages for manufacturing firms and workers; it also became the most important source of politically stabilizing "side payments," providing revenue for a vast system of pensions for Civil War veterans and protection for wool-producing farmers throughout the nation. Bensel, *Political Economy of American Industrialization*, xviii–xix.

10. Based on an analysis of congressional voting on eight key trade bills from 1890 to 1937, Michael Gilligan finds only ideological, rather than coalitional or interest-based sources of these party divisions. Gilligan, *Empowering Exporters: Reciprocity, Delegation, and Collective Action in American Trade Policy* (Ann Arbor: University of Michigan Press, 1997), 93–118. David Epstein and Sharyn O'Halloran, however, examining instead the effects of variations in party control of government on tariff levels for different commodities from 1877 to 1934, demonstrate that the parties differed significantly in how they treated different commodity groupings, with the Republicans enacting higher tar-

iffs in every case. They conclude, contra Gilligan, that different coalitions of constituent interests, rather than ideology, underlay the parties' contrasting preferences for high and low tariffs. Epstein and O'Halloran, "The Partisan Paradox and the U.S. Tariff, 1877–1934," *International Organization* 50, no. 2 (Spring 1996): 301–24. Morton Keller ("Trade Policy"), Charles Calhoun ("Political Economy"), and John Gerring (*Party Ideologies*) all stress the dual roots of the parties' trade policy positions in both ideology and interests.

11. Due to the sharp partisan differences over trade, the advent of divided government usually brought no significant shift in tariff policy. The party that had last been able to impose a major revision in tariff levels was able to veto any substantial new changes. See Epstein and O'Halloran, "Partisan Paradox," and Wendy L. Hansen and Thomas J. Prusa, "The Role of the Median Legislator in U.S. Trade Policy: A Historical Analysis," *Economic Inquiry* 35, no. 1 (January 1997): 97–107.

12. On the Republicans' push for reciprocity in the 1890s (which he may exaggerate relative to the party's traditional protectionist concerns), see Peter Trubowitz, *Defining the National Interest: Conflict and Change in American Foreign Economic Policy* (Chicago: University of Chicago Press, 1998), 77–91.

13. On trade politics during the depression of 1893–97, see Gerald T. White, *The United States and the Problem of Recovery after 1893* (University: University of Alabama Press, 1982).

14. On the realignment and Order of '96, see Brady, *Critical Elections*, 50–83; Paul Kleppner, *Continuity and Change in Electoral Politics, 1893–1928* (Westport, Conn.: Greenwood Press, 1987); and Walter Dean Burnham, "The System of 1896: An Analysis," in Paul Kleppner, ed., *The Evolution of American Electoral Systems* (Westport, Conn.: Greenwood Press, 1981).

15. For this and the following paragraph, see Brady, *Critical Elections*, 50–83; Reich, "Social Structures of Accumulation," 33–36; Terrence McDonough, "The Construction of Social Structures of Accumulation in U.S. History," in Kotz, McDonough, and Reich, *Social Structures of Accumulation*, 103–14; Greenberg, *Capitalism*, 74–92; Walter Dean Burnham, "Periodization and Party Schemes and 'Party Systems': The 'System of 1896,' as a Case in Point," *Social Science History* 10 (Fall 1986): 263–314; and Gerald Berk, "Corporate Liberalism Reconsidered: A Review Essay," *Journal of Policy History* 3, no. 1 (1991): 70–83. In a compelling recent article, David Mayhew launches a frontal assault on the entire realignment edifice, heavily resting his case on a detailed empirical criticism of the realignment and system of 1896. Among other things, Mayhew disputes the extent of both the electoral and policy shifts alleged to have accompanied this realignment. David R. Mayhew, "Electoral Realignments," *Annual Review of Political Science* 3 (2000): 449–74. Obviously I have no space here for a full reply to Mayhew's sweeping argument. But for a critique of some of the electoral data and analysis on which he relies, see Kleppner, *Continuity and Change*. Peter Nardulli also finds evidence of a "Republican industrial realignment" in the North that had significant national impact. Peter F. Nardulli, "The Concept of a Critical Realignment, Electoral, Behavior, and Political Change," *American Political Science Review* 89, no. 1 (March 1995): 10–22.

As for the policy shifts, it is true that they were not on the scale seen during and after the Civil War or during the New Deal. But as argued in the first chapter, the institutions of a new mode of regulation that in turn help to constitute a new political order are not just public in nature; private institutions are important, too. Thus, as I argue below, the core institution of the mode of regulation of the Order of '96 was not a public one, but rather the new structure of private industry. A new Republican political order was consolidated, however, after the electorate fortuitously attributed credit to the Republicans for the recovery from the depression of 1893–97 and the subsequent long economic boom of 1897–1929 fostered by this new industrial structure.

16. Although many U.S. firms had become increasingly competitive, they remained domestically oriented—at least until the Great Depression—and were little concerned about foreign retaliation against high U.S. tariffs. Even some large multinational corporations lost interest in the tariff debate, as they made foreign investments to counter the consequence of retaliatory tariffs. Thus, protectionist interests continued to determine Republican tariff policy during this period. See Gilligan, *Empowering Exporters*, 6, and William H. Becker, *The Dynamics of Business-Government Relations: Industry and Exports, 1893–1921* (Chicago: University of Chicago Press, 1982).

17. White, *Problem of Recovery*, 70.

18. After the 1908 election, the new Republican president and "revisionist" tariff reformer, William Howard Taft, demanded tariff reductions, taking his case to the people and splitting his party over the issue in the process. But congressional Republicans were slow to abandon a successful policy, and the Payne-Aldrich Tariff Act of 1909 did little to lower tariff rates.

19. Although as Goldstein (*Ideas, Interests*) contends, the Democrats continued to support a "competitive tariff," with rates just high enough to allow domestic firms to compete with foreign rivals.

20. For a classic study of the process that produced Smoot-Hawley, see, of course, E. E. Schattschneider, *Politics, Pressures, and the Tariff: A Study of Free Enterprise in Pressure Politics, as Shown in the 1929–1930 Revision of the Tariff* (New York: Prentice-Hall, 1935).

21. See, e.g., Douglas A. Irwin and Randall S. Kroszner, "Log-Rolling and Economic Interests in the Passage of the Smoot-Hawley Tariff," *Carnegie-Rochester Conference Series on Public Policy* 45 (December 1996): 173–200.

22. Ninety-two percent of House Republicans and 78 percent of GOP senators supported Smoot-Hawley, while 91 percent of House Democrats and 86 percent of Senate Democrats opposed it. See Robert Pastor, *Congress and the Politics of United States Foreign Economic Policy, 1929–1976* (Berkeley: University of California Press, 1980); Colleen M. Callahan, Judith A. McDonald, and Anthony Patrick O'Brien, "Who Voted for Smoot-Hawley?," *Journal of Economic History* 54, no. 3 (September 1994): 683–90; and Richard T. Cupitt and Euel Elliott, "Schattschneider Revisited: Senate Voting on the Smoot-Hawley Tariff Act of 1930," *Economics and Politics* 6, no. 3 (November 1994): 187–99.

23. Having won control of the House and almost the Senate in 1930, the Democrats attempted to embarrass Hoover and his party for their high-tariff stance by passing and then forcing Hoover to veto the Collier Tariff Act of 1932, which called upon the president to negotiate liberalizing reciprocal trade agreements with foreign governments. Eckes, *Opening America's Market*, 97.

24. This, of course, is a controversial proposition among economists, most of whom believe monetary policy errors or other factors to be more important sources of the depression. For a regulationist discussion of the depression, see Jacques Mazier, Maurice Basle, and Jean-François Vidal, *When Economic Crises Endure* (Armonk, N.Y.: M. E. Sharpe, 1999), 87–98.

25. On the role of the depression as a "defining moment" that altered "the basic rules, institutions, and attitudes governing the economy," see Michael D. Bordo, Claudia

Goldin, and Eugene N. White, eds., *The Defining Moment: The Great Depression and the American Economy in the Twentieth Century* (Chicago: University of Chicago Press, 1998).

26. Institutional reform of the banking system and financial markets was also important. See Reich, "Social Structures of Accumulation," 36–39; McDonough, "Social Structures of Accumulation," 114–23; Greenberg, *Capitalism*, 93–178; and Stephen A. Marglin and Juliet B. Schor, eds., *The Golden Age of Capitalism: Reinterpreting the Postwar Experience* (New York: Oxford University Press, 1990).

27. I. M. Destler, *American Trade Politics*, 3d ed. (Washington, D.C.: Institute for International Economics and Twentieth Century Fund, 1995), 11–38. More on the elements of this system appears below.

28. World War II and the immediate postwar period were especially important in consolidating the mode of regulation of the New Deal Order. See McDonough, "Social Structures of Accumulation," 123, and Brian Waddell, "Corporate Influence and World War II: Resolving the New Deal Political Stalemate," *Journal of Policy History* 11, no. 3 (1999): 224–57.

29. For some useful recent literature on the New Deal Order, see Brady, *Critical Elections*, 84–114; Eisner, *The State in the American Political Economy*, 160–285; Alan Brinkley, *The End of Reform: New Deal Liberalism in Recession and War* (New York: Knopf, 1995); David Plotke, *Building a Democratic Political Order: Reshaping American Liberalism in the 1930s and 1940s* (New York: Cambridge University Press, 1996); and Kenneth Finegold and Theda Skocpol, *State and Party in America's New Deal* (Madison: University of Wisconsin Press, 1995).

30. On the politics of foreign economic policy-making during the New Deal, see, e.g., Thomas Ferguson, "From 'Normalcy' to New Deal: Industrial Structure, Party Competition, and American Public Policy in the Great Depression," in Ferguson, *Golden Rule: The Investment Theory of Party Competition and the Logic of Money-Driven Political Systems* (Chicago: University of Chicago Press, 1995), 113–72; Peter Gourevitch, *Politics in Hard Times: Comparative Responses to International Economic Crises* (Ithaca, N.Y.: Cornell University Press, 1986), 147–53; Stephan Haggard, "The Institutional Foundations of Hegemony: Explaining the Reciprocal Trade Agreements Act of 1934," *International Organization* 42, no. 1 (Winter 1980): 91–119; Jeff Frieden, "Sectoral Conflict and U.S. Foreign Economic Policy, 1914–1940," *International Organization* 42, no. 1 (Winter 1988): 59–80; Kenneth Oye, *Economic Discrimination and Political Exchange: World Political Economy in the 1930s and 1980s* (Princeton, N.J.: Princeton University Press, 1992); and Ronald W. Cox and Daniel Skidmore-Hess, *U.S. Politics and the Global Economy: Corporate Power, Conservative Shift* (Boulder, Colo.: Lynne Rienner Publishers, 1999), 17–26.

31. On the politics of the RTAA, see esp. Karen S. Schnietz, "The Institutional Foundation of U.S. Trade Policy: Revisiting Explanations for the 1934 Reciprocal Trade Agreements Act," *Journal of Policy History* (Fall 2000): 417–44. See also Ferguson, "From 'Normalcy' to the New Deal"; Haggard, "Institutional Foundations"; Oye, *Economic Discrimination*; Pastor, *Congress*; and Michael Lusztig, *Risking Free Trade: The Politics of Trade in Britain, Canada, Mexico, and the United States* (Pittsburgh: University of Pittsburgh Press, 1996), 49–70.

32. See Ferguson, "From 'Normalcy' to New Deal"; Frieden, "Sectoral Conflict"; Gourevitch, *Politics in Hard Times*, 147–53; Lusztig, *Risking Free Trade*, 49–70; Cox and Skidmore-Hess, *U.S. Politics*, 19.

33. There is evidence that Cordell Hull, a former Democratic National Committee

chairman, envisioned using the tariff-reduction issue to create a new internationalist, export-oriented coalition or bloc of support for the Democrats that would link efficient new mass producers in the automobile and related industries with traditional southern agricultural export interests. See Eckes, *Opening America's Market*, 95.

34. The overwhelming majority of those testifying at congressional hearings on the RTAA opposed it. See Schnietz, "Institutional Foundation"; Haggard, "Institutional Foundations," 98–99; Meengon Kim, "United States Trade Policy and Party Politics in the House of Representatives, 1934–88" (Ph.D. diss., University of Iowa, 1994), 64–72.

35. On these influences, see Brinkley, *End of Reform*.

36. See Schnietz, "Institutional Foundation," and James Hearden, *Roosevelt Confronts Hitler: America's Entry into World War II* (DeKalb: Northern Illinois University Press, 1987), 22–51.

37. Most prominently, see Destler, *American Trade Politics*; Pastor, *Congress*; and Goldstein, *Ideas, Interests*.

38. Ninety-six percent of House Democrats and 93 percent of Senate Democrats voted for the RTAA, while 98 percent of House Republicans and 85 percent of Senate Republicans opposed it. Only 2 of the 86 Republican representatives and senators who voted for Smoot-Hawley in 1930 and were still in Congress in 1934 voted for the RTAA. See Schnietz, "Institutional Foundation," and Michael J. Hiscox, "The Magic Bullet? The RTAA, Institutional Reform, and Trade Liberalization," *International Organization* 53, no. 4 (Autumn 1999): 669–98.

39. This was consonant with Roosevelt's attempt to centralize authority within the executive branch to overcome what he felt were impediments created by state and locally based congressional parties to the exercise of effective national leadership. See Sidney M. Milkis, *The President and the Parties: The Transformation of the American Party System since the New Deal* (New York: Oxford University Press, 1993).

40. Gilligan, *Empowering Exporters*, 70; Schnietz, "Institutional Foundation"; Douglas A. Irwin, "From Smoot-Hawley to Reciprocal Trade Agreements," in Bordo, Goldin, and White, *Defining Moment*, 340. Gilligan, Schnietz, and Bailey, Weingast, and Goldstein go further to argue that pro-free trade-congressional Democratic leaders saw the RTAA as a way to institutionalize a low-tariff policy that could survive a future return to unified Republican control of government. First, due to the president's heterogeneous constituency, a tariff-setting process controlled by a Republican president would result in lower rates than a process controlled by a GOP Congress. Second, the elimination of Senate approval of trade agreements would make obtaining such agreement easier. Finally, "bundling" lower U.S. tariffs with reduced foreign rates would give American exporters an incentive to lobby against future Republican attempts to raise tariffs. Gilligan, *Empowering Exporters*, 70; Schnietz, "Institutional Foundation"; Michael A. Bailey, Judith Goldstein, and Barry R. Weingast, "The Institutional Roots of American Trade Policy," *World Politics* 49, no. 3 (April 1997): 309–38. Only Schnietz tries to provide evidence that congressional Democrats were thinking in this way when they approved the RTAA, and most of the individuals she quotes were either Roosevelt administration officials, business representatives, or congressional Republicans. As Douglas Irwin ("From Smoot-Hawley to Reciprocal Trade Agreements," 342) and Michael Hiscox ("Magic Bullet?") have argued, there was no guarantee that the RTAA would succeed; if the Republicans had returned to power, at least in the near term, they could easily have overturned the act, as they vowed to do in their party platforms until the early 1940s. In the long run,

however, I believe that the RTAA did help to expand the ranks of export interests, which in turn became important defenders of the liberal postwar trade order.

41. Raymond Vernon and Deborah Spar, *Beyond Globalism: Remaking American Foreign Economic Policy* (New York: Free Press, 1989), 41.

42. On this Establishment, comprised of internationally minded men drawn from the leading financial and business institutions, law firms, Ivy League universities, major foundations, and the East Coast media, see Priscilla Roberts, " 'All the Right People': The Historiography of the American Foreign Policy Establishment," *Journal of American Studies* 26, no. 3 (December 1992): 409–34, and John B. Judis, *The Paradox of Democracy: Elites, Special Interests, and the Betrayal of Public Trust* (New York: Pantheon, 2000).

43. Among the many studies of postwar planning, all of which stress to one degree or another the involvement of business and the importance of export expansion, see Hearden, *Roosevelt Confronts Hitler*, 223–45; Cox and Skidmore-Hess, *U.S. Politics*, 27–66; Lloyd C. Gardner, "The New Deal, New Frontiers, and the Cold War" in David Horowitz, ed., *Corporations and the Cold War* (New York: Monthly Review Press, 1969), 105–41; and G. John Ikenberry, "Creating Yesterday's New World Order: Keynesian 'New Thinking' and the Anglo-American Postwar Settlement," in Judith Goldstein and Robert O. Keohane, eds., *Ideas and Foreign Policy: Beliefs, Institutions, and Political Change* (Ithaca, N.Y.: Cornell University Press, 1993), 57–86. For two detailed discussions of the formation of early postwar trade policy, see Susan Aaronson, *Trade and the American Dream: A Social History of Postwar Trade Policy* (Lexington: University of Kentucky Press, 1996), 34–142, and Thomas W. Zeiler, *Free Trade, Free World: The Advent of GATT* (Chapel Hill: University of North Carolina Press, 1999). On the hopes of Roosevelt and Truman administration officials that the construction of a liberal new international economic order would contribute to the consolidation of a Democratic political order, see Plotke, *Building a Democratic Political Order*, 266–67.

44. The United States also proposed a more powerful International Trade Organization (ITO), but business groups found its charter too grandiose and ambitious, and the Truman administration finally withdrew the proposal from Congress in 1950.

45. John Gerard Ruggie, "International Regimes, Transactions, and Change: Embedded Liberalism in the Postwar Economic Order," *International Organization* 36 (Spring 1982): 379–415, and *Winning the Peace: America and World Order in the New Era* (New York: Columbia University Press, 1996), 35–39.

46. In its negotiations with the British, the United States pushed for only limited restrictions on trade and capital mobility, hoping that the resultant export expansion would create additional growth and employment sufficient to quiet the demand for domestic planning and income redistribution. The British, on the other hand, backed more substantial international controls to allow them greater freedom to pursue their domestic policy objectives. A compromise was eventually struck between the two positions. Among many sources, see Georg Schild, *Bretton Woods and Dumbarton Oaks: American Economic and Political Postwar Planning in the Summer of 1944* (New York: St. Martin's Press, 1995).

47. Charles S. Maier, "The Politics of Productivity: Foundations of American International Economic Policy after World War II," in Peter J. Katzenstein, ed., *Between Power and Plenty: Foreign Economic Policies of Advanced Industrial States* (Madison: University of Wisconsin Press, 1978), 23–49.

48. Destler, *American Trade Politics*, 11–38.

49. The continued use of antidumping and countervailing duty laws enacted during the protectionist era leads Goldstein (*Ideas, Interests*) to conclude that the old protectionist policy paradigm and institutions were not completely destroyed, but rather that a liberal paradigm and liberal institutions were "layered" on top of the them after the Great Depression.

50. Eckes (*Opening America's Market*) and Verdier (*Democracy and International Trade*), among others, give particular emphasis to the role of the Cold War in fostering a liberal trading order.

51. This section is drawn from Destler, *American Trade Politics*, 5–8, 30–32; Kim, *Trade Policy*; William R. Keech and Kyoungsan Pak, "Partisanship, Institutions, and Change in American Trade Politics," *Journal of Politics* 57, no. 4 (November 1995): 1130–42; and John J. Coleman, "Bipartisan Order and Partisan Disorder in Postwar Trade Policy," Department of Political Science, University of Wisconsin, 1997.

52. Pastor, *Congress*; Destler, *American Trade Politics*; Goldstein, *Ideas, Interests*.

53. Douglas A. Irwin and Randall S. Kroszner, "Interests, Institutions, and Ideology in Securing Policy Change: The Republican Conversion to Trade Liberalization after Smoot-Hawley," *Journal of Law and Economics* 42 (October 1999): 643–73. These first two factors can be understood as path-dependent processes. The RTAA system became self-reinforcing, as positive policy feedback strengthened both the elite free-trade cognitive consensus and the position of business interests benefiting from and thus supportive of trade liberalization, in both cases helping to "lock in" the system.

54. Coleman, "Bipartisan Order."

55. On postwar public opinion on trade, see Aaronson, *Trade and the American Dream*, esp. 59–60, 99–100.

56. From 1943 to 1958 Republicans in both houses of Congress supported thirteen of sixteen final passage roll calls on major trade legislation.

57. According to John Coleman, from 1947 to 1964, 60 percent of *all* trade-related votes in the House were "party votes," i.e., votes where a majority of one party opposes a majority of the other. This figure dropped to 49 percent from 1965 to 1972 and to 44 percent from 1976 to 1982. John J. Coleman, *Party Decline in America: Policy, Politics, and the Fiscal State* (Princeton, N.J.: Princeton University Press, 1996), 26–28. See also Hiscox, "Magic Bullet?"

58. Kim, *Trade Policy*, 150.

59. For an important analysis of party conflict over what she calls the "ground rules" governing trade liberalization during this period, see Martha L. Gibson, *Conflict amid Consensus in American Trade Policy* (Washington, D.C.: Georgetown University Press, 2000), 74–99.

60. Gibson, *Conflict amid Consensus*; Coleman, "Bipartisan Order."

61. Susanne Lohmann and Sharyn O'Halloran find that a shift from unified to divided government, on average, increases the tariff level by only 0.24 percent. Lohmann and O'Halloran, "Divided Government and U.S. Trade Policy: Theory and Evidence," *International Organization* 48, no. 4 (Autumn 1994): 595–632. For further evidence of the limited partisan impact on tariff rates after 1934, see Hansen and Prusa, "Role of the Median Legislator."

62. On these points, see Robert E. Baldwin, *Trade Policy in a Changing World Economy* (Chicago: University of Chicago Press, 1988), 50. On the role of the party affiliation of the president, see Keech and Pak, "Partisanship, Institutions," and Kim, *Trade Policy*, 132–43.

63. This account relies heavily on the *Congressional Quarterly Almanac* and *Congress*

and the Nation, published annually and quadrennially respectively by Congressional Quarterly Press. I have also drawn on Baldwin, *Trade Policy,* 97–120; O'Halloran, *Politics, Process,* 87–104; Gibson, *Conflict amid Consensus;* and Charles K. Rowley, Willem Thorbecke, and Richard E. Wagner, *Trade Protection in the United States* (Brookfield, Vt.: Edward Elgar, 1995), 164–88.

64. On this period, see Baldwin, *Trade Policy,* 50–51; Gibson, *Conflict amid Consensus,* 74–78; Aaronson, *Trade and the American Dream;* Zeiler, *Free Trade, Free World;* and Joe R. Wilkinson, *Politics and Trade Policy* (Washington, D.C.: Public Affairs Press, 1960).

65. The American Federation of Labor (AFL) first endorsed an RTAA renewal in 1943. On labor's pro-trade views in the 1943–62 period, see Peter Donohue, " 'Free Trade' Unions and the State: Trade Liberalization's Endorsement by the AFL-CIO, 1943–1962," *Research in Political Economy* 13 (1992): 1–73.

66. On this last point, see Irwin and Kroszner, "Interests, Institutions."

67. For this period, see Baldwin, *Trade Policy,* 52–56; Gibson, *Conflict amid Consensus,* 78–85; and Wilkinson, *Politics and Trade Policy.*

68. On the intraparty splits, see Richard A. Watson, "The Tariff Revolution: A Study of Shifting Party Attitudes," *Journal of Politics* 18, no. 4 (November 1956): 678–701.

69. According to polls examined by *Fortune* in 1955, in a fifteen-year period executives favoring the lowering of tariffs almost doubled, while the percentage supporting an increase in duties dwindled from 31.5 to 5.0 percent. Watson, "The Tariff Revolution," 693. On the role of business, especially the Committee for Economic Development (CED) and its unofficial lobbying arm, the Committee for a National Trade Policy (CNTP), in shaping Eisenhower's trade policies, see Cox and Skidmore-Hess, *U.S. Politics,* 90–93.

70. Lohmann and O'Halloran, "Divided Government."

71. See David Karol, "Divided Government and U.S. Trade Policy: Much Ado about Nothing," *International Organization* 54, no. 4 (Autumn 2000): 825–44.

72. On the Trade Expansion Act of 1962, see Baldwin, *Trade Policy,* 56–57; Gibson, *Conflict amid Consensus,* 85–91; Gilligan, *Empowering Exporters,* 75–77; and Thomas W. Zeiler, *American Trade and Power in the 1960s* (New York: Columbia University Press, 1992), 47–158.

73. On the substantial role of business, again including the CED and the CNTP, in developing and passing the TEA, see Cox and Skidmore-Hess, *U.S. Politics,* 106–14.

74. See Donohue, " 'Free Trade' Unions."

75. As a result of the six GATT negotiating rounds from 1947 to 1962 authorized by the various RTAA extensions, U.S. trade policy was substantially transformed in a liberal direction. Tariffs on dutiable imports had dropped from an average of 35 percent in the early 1940s to only about 7 percent by the end of the 1960s.

76. Among many sources, see Michael Dunford, "Globalization and Theories of Regulation," in Ronen Palen, ed., *Global Political Economy: Contemporary Issues* (London: Routledge, 2000), 154–56.

77. For this and the next two paragraphs, see Paul Midford, "International Trade and Domestic Politics: Improving on Rogowski's Model of Political Alignments," *International Organization* 47, no. 4 (Autumn 1993): 538–39, 555–57.

78. Another cause of this shift within the AFL-CIO was disappointment with the TAA program. Following its establishment in the 1962 trade bill, not a single TAA decision favorable to labor was made until late 1969.

79. Gibson, *Conflict amid Consensus,* 91–95.

80. Although both parties were internally split, the Republicans opposed the measure by a 78–82 margin, while the Democrats backed it 137–83.

81. On this bill, see Baldwin, *Trade Policy*, 61–70; O'Halloran, *Politics, Process*, 96–101; and Pastor, *Congress*, 136–85.

82. Among other things, the bill mandated that international agreements would henceforth require congressional approval under the so-called fast-track procedures, through which presidential trade proposals would be considered by an up-or-down vote without amendment.

83. Baldwin, *Trade Policy*, 61.

84. Destler, *American Trade Politics*, 179; Kim, *Trade Policy*, 213.

85. For by far the best analysis of the repolarization of the parties over trade policy, see Kim, *Trade Policy*. See also Destler, *American Trade Politics*, 176–78.

86. Vernon and Spar, *Beyond Globalism*, 51.

87. In 1970 labor strongly backed a textile quota bill, and in 1971–72 it promoted but failed to achieve passage of the Burke-Hartke bill to impose across-the-board import quotas and regulate foreign investment, which was seen as another major cause of job loss.

88. In a quantitative study of House voting on final passage of the bill, Robert Baldwin found that the larger the contributions received from labor unions and the greater the proportion of constituents employed in import-competing industries, the more inclined members were to vote against the legislation. Democrats were also more likely than Republicans to oppose the bill. Baldwin, *Trade Policy*, 64–70.

89. See Dunford, "Globalization."

90. The nontariff barriers included subsidies and countervailing duties, antidumping duties, customs valuations, government procurement requirements, and various technical barriers to trade.

Chapter 3

1. For a this and the next two paragraphs, see, among many sources, David G. Lawrence, *The Collapse of the Democratic Presidential Majority: Realignment, Dealignment, and Electoral Change from Franklin Roosevelt to Bill Clinton* (Boulder, Colo.: Westview Press, 1997).

2. For a recent, thorough discussion of this transition, see Manuel Castells, *The Rise of the Network Society* (Oxford: Blackwell Publishers, 1996), vol. 1 of his magisterial three-part work, *The Information Age: Economy, Society, and Culture* (Oxford: Blackwell Publishers, 1996, 1997, 1998).

3. See the essays in Ash Amin, ed. *Post-Fordism: A Reader* (Cambridge, Mass.: Blackwell, 1984).

4. On this point, in addition to Castells's work, see Stephen J. Kobrin, "The Architecture of Globalization: State Sovereignty in a Networked Global Economy," in John H. Dunning, ed., *Governments, Globalization, and International Business* (New York: Oxford University Press, 1997), 146–71; Peter Dicken, *Global Shift: Transforming the World Economy*, 3d ed. (New York: Guilford Press, 1998); and Jonathan Perraton, "What Are Global Markets? The Significance of Networks of Trade," in Randall D. Germain, ed., *Globalization and Its Critics: Perspectives from Political Economy* (New York: St. Martin's Press, 2000), 164–82.

5. See Robert Boyer, "Is a Finance-Led Growth Regime a Viable Alternative to Fordism? A Preliminary Analysis," *Economy and Society* 29, no. 1 (February 2000): 111–45.

6. For a comprehensive overview, see Bob Jessop, "What Follows Fordism? On the Periodization of Capitalism and Its Regulation," in Robert Albritton, eds., *Phases of Capitalism and Development: Perspectives at the Year 2000* (New York: St. Martin's Press, 2001). As an alternative to post-Fordism, Castells (*Rise of the Network Society*) suggests the in many ways more accurate and useful term "informational capitalism," which is both more substantive and less manufacturing-centric than post-Fordism. In this book, post-Fordism refers merely to the range of economic and technological structures that are emerging *after* Fordism, and I use the concept mainly to preserve a certain terminological symmetry.

7. Philip G. Cerny, "Restructuring the Political Arena; Globalization and the Paradoxes of the Competition State," in Germain, *Globalization*, 117–38; Ronen Palan and Jason Abbott with Phil Deans, *State Strategies in the Global Political Economy* (New York: Pinter, 1996). See also Carles Boix, *Political Parties, Growth, and Equality: Conservative and Social Democratic Economic Strategies in the World Economy* (Cambridge: Cambridge University Press, 1998). For a thorough discussion of contemporary debates on "governance," see Jon Pierre and B. Guy Peters, *Governance, Politics and the State* (New York: St. Martin's Press, 2000).

8. Jessop actually calls what I have labeled the competition state, the "Schumpeterian Workfare State," but the two terms are virtually the same. In identifying three forms of the competition state, Jessop is siding with those analysts who see not convergence, but rather the persistence of several "varieties of capitalism" in the face of advancing globalization. See Bob Jessop, "Towards a Schumpeterian Workfare State? Preliminary Remarks on Post-Fordist Political Economy," *Studies in Political Economy*, no. 40 (Spring 1993): 7–39. For a discussion of what he refers to as neoliberal, neomercantilist, and social-democratic trade policy strategies, which can be viewed as the trade adjuncts to Jessop's three broader competition state strategies, see Gregory P. Marchildon, "Trade and Political Party Orientation in North America," in Charles F. Doran and Marchildon, eds., *The NAFTA Puzzle: Political Parties and Trade in North America* (Boulder, Colo.: Westview Press, 1994), 9–31.

9. On competitive strategies, see Palan and Abbott with Deans, *State Strategies*, and Boix, *Political Parties*.

10. In constructing this account and analysis, I owe an enormous debt to the steady stream of writings produced over the years by I. M. Destler. See in particular his pioneering book, *American Trade Politics*, 3d ed. (Washington, D.C.: Institute for International Economics and Twentieth Century Fund, 1995).

11. On Reagan as a "reconstructive" president, see Stephen Skowronek, *The Politics Presidents Make: Leadership from John Adams to Bill Clinton* (Cambridge: Belknap/ Harvard University Press, 1997), 409–29. See also Martin Shefter and Benjamin Ginsberg, "Institutionalizing the Reagan Regime," in Ginsberg and Alan Stone, eds., *Do Elections Matter?* (Armonk, N.Y.: M. E. Sharpe, 1986), 191–203.

12. On the ideological roots of Reaganomics, see M. Stephen Weatherford and Lorraine M. McDonnell, "Ideology and Economic Policy," in Larry Berman, ed., *Looking Back on the Reagan Presidency* (Baltimore: Johns Hopkins University Press, 1990), 122–55, and Thomas L. Langston, *Ideologues and Presidents: From the New Deal to the Reagan Revolution* (Baltimore: Johns Hopkins University Press, 1992), 135–64.

13. On the corporate right turn of the late 1970s and the role played by elements of the business community in Reagan's political rise and in support of his economic program, see Thomas Ferguson and Joel Rogers, *Right Turn: The Decline of the Democrats and the*

Future of American Politics (New York: Hill and Wang, 1986), 78–137; Sidney Blumenthal, *The Rise of the Counter-Establishment: From Conservative Ideology to Political Power* (New York: Times Books, 1986), 55–86; David Vogel, *Fluctuating Fortunes: The Political Power of Business in America* (New York: Basic Books, 1989), 240–89; and Cathie Jo Martin, *Shifting the Burden: The Struggle over Growth and Corporate Taxation* (Chicago: University of Chicago Press, 1991), 107–58.

14. On the electorally driven aspects of Reaganomics, see Blumenthal, *Rise of the Counter-Establishment*, 197–203, and Paul J. Quirk, "The Economy, Economists, Electoral Politics, and Reagan Economics," in Michael Nelson, ed., *The Elections of 1984* (Washington, D.C.: CQ Press, 1985), 164.

15. On Reagan as a committed Republican, see Sidney M. Milkis, "The Presidency and Political Parties," in Michael Nelson, ed., *The Presidency and the Political System*, 6th ed. (Washington, D.C.: CQ Press, 2000), 388–92.

16. On Reagan's efforts to balance ideology with pragmatism, see John W. Sloan, *The Reagan Effect: Economics and Presidential Leadership* (Lawrence: University Press of Kansas, 1999), esp. 266–69, and Lou Cannon, *President Reagan: The Role of a Lifetime* (New York: Simon and Schuster, 1991), 185–86.

17. Lou Cannon, *Reagan* (New York: Perigee Books, 1982), 324. See also Gerald M. Boyd, "Basing National Policy on Personal Experience," *New York Times*, August 3, 1986.

18. Sloan, *The Reagan Effect*, 196; William Niskanen, *Reaganomics: An Insider's Account of the Policies and the People* (New York: Oxford University Press, 1988), 6.

19. David Vogel, "The Triumph of Liberal Trade: American Trade Policy in the Postwar Period," in Morton Keller and R. Shep Melnick, eds., *Taking Stock: American Government in the Twentieth Century* (Cambridge: Woodrow Wilson Center Press and Cambridge University Press, 1999), 42.

20. Insofar as the trade deficit and the consequent pressures for a tougher trade policy were due to the soaring dollar, which itself was partly a product of the Reagan's administration's unusual policy mix of tight money and budget deficits, we might say that the macroeconomic policy subsystem "collided" with, or that problems in that subsystem "spilled over" into, the trade policy subsystem. For these concepts, see Karen Orren and Stephen Skowronek, "Beyond the Iconography of Order: Notes for a 'New Institutionalism,'" in Lawrence C. Dodd and Calvin Jillson, eds., *The Dynamics of American Politics: Approaches and Interpretations* (Boulder, Colo.: Westview Press, 1994), 311–30, and Paul A. Sabatier and Hank C. Jenkins-Smith, "The Advocacy Coalition Framework: An Assessment," in Sabatier, ed., *Theories of the Policy Process* (Boulder, Colo.: Westview Press, 1999), 117–66.

21. "The New Politics of U.S. Protectionism," *Business Week*, December 27, 1982, 38–39.

22. Niskanen, *Reaganomics*, 137.

23. On this episode, see Douglas R. Nelson, "On the High Track to Protection: The U.S. Automobile Industry, 1979–1981," in Stephan Haggard and Chung-in Moon, eds., *Pacific Dynamics: The International Politics of Industrial Change* (Boulder, Colo.: Westview Press, 1989), 97–128, and Gilbert Winham and I. Kabashima, "The Politics of U.S.-Japanese Auto Trade," in I. M. Destler and H. Sato, eds., *Coping with U.S.-Japanese Economic Conflicts* (Lexington, Mass.: D. C. Heath, 1982).

24. "An Auto Trade Dilemma for Reagan to Resolve," *Business Week*, March 23, 1981, 42–43.

25. On reciprocity, see Jagdish Bhagwati and Hugh T. Patrick, eds., *Aggressive Uni-*

lateralism: America's 301 Trade Policy and the World's Trading System (Ann Arbor: University of Michigan Press, 1990), and Thomas O. Bayard and Kimberly Ann Elliott, *Reciprocity and Retaliation in U.S. Trade* (Washington, D.C.: Institute for International Economics, 1994).

26. On export politics, see Destler, *American Trade Politics*, 17–18.

27. David Broder, "Top Democrats Struggle to Find Fuel for a Political Comeback," *Washington Post*, October 18, 1981.

28. See Commerce undersecretary Lionel Olmer's comments in *U.S. Import Weekly*, December 9, 1981, 247. See also Christopher Madison, "Flirting with Reciprocity—New U.S. Trade Policy Makes Some People Nervous," *National Journal*, February 20, 1982, 320–24.

29. Richard I. Kirkland Jr., "Washington's Trade War of Words," *Fortune*, April 5, 1982, 34–39.

30. For this and the next paragraph, see Taylor E. Dark, *The Unions and the Democrats* (Ithaca, N.Y.: Cornell University Press, 1999), 125–33; Andrew Battista, "Political Divisions in Organized Labor, 1968–1988," *Polity* 24, no. 2 (Winter 1991): 173–97; and Dom Bonafede, "Labor's Early Endorsement Will Prove a Psychological Boost and Then Some," *National Journal*, September 24, 1993, 1938–41.

31. Morton Kondracke, "The Democrats' New Agenda," *New Republic*, October 18, 1982, 15–17.

32. Howell Raines, "Move to Curb Competitiveness of Imports Rises as Focus at End of Campaign," *New York Times*, October 25, 1982. Gallup data showed an increase from 42 percent in 1980 to 50 percent in 1982 of Americans who said they were less inclined to buy foreign products. *Business and Public Affairs*, November 15, 1982, 7–8.

33. "The Momentum Builds for Protectionism," *Business Week*, October 4, 1982, 44.

34. Stuart Auerbach, "Brock Favors Longer Curbs on Auto Imports," *Washington Post*, October 20, 1982.

35. Lou Cannon and Stuart Auerbach, "Accord Reached with Europeans on Steel Exports," *Washington Post*, October 22, 1982.

36. On this episode, see Ernest H. Preeg, *Traders in a Brave New World: The Uruguay Round and the Future of the International Trading System* (Chicago: University of Chicago Press, 1995), 29–36.

37. In an interview conducted shortly before the GATT meeting, Brock complained that the "actions of the Democratic leaders, particularly Mondale and Kennedy, have cast the Democratic Party into a protectionist mold." Christopher Madison, "Brock Gambling That Trading Partners Will Go Beyond Mere Damage Control," *National Journal*, November 20, 1982, 1976.

38. The Democratic leadership was able to move the bill to the floor because it had given first jurisdiction over the multiply referred measure not to the pro–free-trade Ways and Means Committee but rather to the Energy and Commerce Committee, headed by the entrepreneurial John Dingell, of Michigan, a strong supporter of the auto industry. This guaranteed that the bill would go directly to the floor whether or not Ways and Means acted on it. This case demonstrates how the decentralizing House reforms of the 1970s opened up access to the trade policy process to formerly excluded protectionist interests, while the centralizing reforms of the same decade enhanced the power of the Democratic leadership, contributing to increased partisanship on trade

issues. See Martha L. Gibson, *Conflict amid Consensus in American Trade Policy* (Washington, D.C.: Georgetown University Press, 2000), 136–37.

39. Peter Trubowitz emphasizes this point in his discussion of the House vote. He also notes that due to intraregional economic differences, the South was split on trade issues, siding with the free-trade–oriented West on some measures, including domestic content, and with the protectionist North on others, especially textile quota legislation. Trubowitz, *Defining the National Interest: Conflict and Change in American Foreign Policy* (Chicago: University of Chicago Press, 1998), 207–9.

40. On this point, see G. Mustafa Mohatarem, "Trade Policy and the U.S. Auto Industry: Intended and Unintended Consequences," in Alan V. Deardorff and Robert M. Stern, eds., *Constituent Interests and U.S. Trade Policies* (Ann Arbor: University of Michigan Press, 1998), 125.

41. The bill was opposed by manufacturing and agricultural exporters who feared foreign retaliation, by domestic distributors of foreign cars, and even by the Big Three automakers, which imported cars from Japanese partners.

42. Business PACs did increase the absolute amount of their contributions to Democratic incumbents in order to maintain access to these lawmakers.

43. Total PAC spending on congressional races jumped from $4.8 million in 1974 to $49.1 million in 1982. The Republican share of business PAC dollars alone increased from 57 percent in 1976 to 66 percent in 1982. Total labor PAC spending rose from $6.3 million in 1974 to $20.2 million in 1982. Only about 5–6 percent of this went to Republican candidates during each election cycle. See Gary C. Jacobson, "Money in the 1980 and 1982 Congressional Elections," in Michael J. Malbin, ed., *Money and Politics in the United States: Financing Elections in the 1980s* (Washington, D.C.: American Enterprise Institute and Chatham House Publishers, 1984), 42–43.

44. Larry Sabato, "Parties, PACs, and Independent Groups," in Thomas E. Mann and Norman J. Ornstein, eds., *The American Elections of 1982* (Washington, D.C.: American Enterprise Institute, 1983), 88–89; Maxwell Glen, "Labor Tries to Bring Its Rebellious Members Back to the Democratic Fold," *National Journal*, October 30, 1982, 1837–40; Harold W. Stanley and Richard G. Niemi, eds., *Vital Statistics on American Politics*, 4th ed. (Washington, D.C.: CQ Press, 1998), 101–3.

45. Sabato, "Parties, PACs, and Independent Groups," 89; Alan Murray, "Trade, Defense Issues Fray U.S.-Japan Ties," *Congressional Quarterly Weekly Report*, November 27, 1982, 2904; Hobart Rowen, "Only Long-Shot Askew Sticks to Free-Trade Line," *Washington Post*, January 2, 1983.

46. Union support for the bill was so strong that it was generally viewed more as a labor than as a trade issue. Econometric analysis has shown that after controlling for members' closeness to labor, measured by their COPE ratings, the significance of party in voting on the bill disappears. Moreover, the higher the level of unionization in a member's district and the greater the labor share of a member's campaign contributions, the more likely he or she was to vote for the bill. Democrats were, of course, more likely to represent such districts. Ikuo Kabashima and Hideo Sato, "Local Content and Congressional Politics: Interest-Group Theory and Foreign-Policy Implications," *International Studies Quarterly* 30 (1986): 295–314; Cletus C. Coughlin, "Domestic Content Legislation: House Voting and the Economic Theory of Regulation," *Economic Inquiry* 23, no. 3 (July 1985): 437–48; John McArthur and Stephen V. Marks, "Empirical Determinants of Protection: A Survey and Some New Results," in John S. Odell and Thomas D.

Willett, eds., *International Trade Policies: Gains from Exchange between Economics and Political Science* (Ann Arbor: University of Michigan Press, 1990), 105–39.

47. Ronald Brownstein, "Business Moves Out, Labor Moves In—And the Two Parties Switch Sides," *National Journal*, September 19, 1987, 2329.

48. "New Politics of U.S. Protectionism."

49. Hodding Carter III, "Democrats Reach for Protectionist Snake Oil," *Wall Street Journal*, December 9, 1982.

50. "New Politics of U.S. Protectionism."

51. Chalmers Johnson has defined industrial policy as a "summary term for the activities of government that are intended to develop or retrench various industries in a national economy in order to maintain global competitiveness." Johnson, "The Idea of Industrial Policy," in Johnson, ed., *The Industrial Policy Debate* (San Francisco: Institute for Contemporary Studies, 1984), 7.

52. For the best account of this episode, see Otis L. Graham Jr., *Losing Time: The Industrial Policy Debate* (Cambridge: Harvard University Press, 1992).

53. Actually, this is not quite accurate. Industrial policy had already made a brief appearance during the 1980 presidential campaign, when Jimmy Carter, responding to crises in the auto and steel industries, political pressure from the labor movement, the "reindustrialization" plan proposed by Edward Kennedy during the Democratic primaries, and Ronald Reagan's supply-side tax cutting program, announced an "economic revitalization" program of his own. In the end, however, the plan played almost no part in the general election campaign. See Graham, *Losing Time*, 26–58.

54. The distinct early 1980s American use of the term "neoliberal" is not to be confused with its European meaning employed earlier, which signifies a post-Keynesian, laissez-faire approach to the economy. On American neoliberalism, see Randall Rothenberg, *The Neo-Liberals: Creating the New American Politics* (New York: Simon and Schuster, 1984); Ferguson and Rogers, *Right Turn*, chaps. 5–6; and Robert Kuttner, *The Life of the Party: Democratic Prospects in 1988 and Beyond* (New York: Viking, 1987), 151–54, 167–82.

55. See Ann M. Reilley with Henriette Sender, "Here Come the Atari Democrats," *Dun's Business Month*, January 1983, 32.

56. Rothenberg, *Neo-Liberals*, chap. 7; Kuttner, *Life of the Party*.

57. Elizabeth Drew, "The Democratic Party," *New Yorker*, July 19, 1982, 144; Jerry Hagstrom, "High-Tech Leaders Have Their Own Ideas of What Government Can Do for Them," *National Journal*, May 15, 1982, 865.

58. Stuart Auerbach, "Democrats Seek a Definition; 'Industrial Policy' Newest Buzzword," *Washington Post*, June 10, 1983.

59. I.e., Walter Mondale, Gary Hart, Alan Cranston, Ernest Hollings, and Reuben Askew.

60. Timothy B. Clark, "An Industrial Get-Well Card," *National Journal*, May 28, 1983, 1129; Alan Murray, "With an Eye on '84 Elections, Democrats Lay Foundations for National Industrial Policy," *Congressional Quarterly Weekly Report*, August 20, 1983, 1679–87.

61. Murray, "With an Eye on '84 Elections."

62. "Democrats Try Again on Industrial Policy," *Business Week*, September 26, 1983, 175.

63. Murray, "With an Eye on '84 Elections."

64. In late September, after summarizing polls of business leaders' views on the issue, William Schneider observed, "For a policy designed to 'help' the business sector, industrial policy has surprisingly little support among industry leaders themselves." Schneider, " 'Industrial Policy': It All Depends on How It's Sold to the Voters," *National Journal*, September 17, 1983, 1917.

65. For example, a poll taken in early November showed that whereas 52 percent of those surveyed liked the idea of an Economic Cooperation Council, only 6 percent favored a bank. Norman Jonas, "Why the Democrats Need to Come Up with an Industrial Policy," *Business Week*, November 21, 1983, 42–43.

66. "Industrial Policy Divides the Democrats," *Business Week*, May 14, 1984, 205.

67. *Congressional Quarterly Weekly Report*, October 20, 1984, 2717.

68. Niskanen, *Reaganomics*, 140.

69. "Fresh Troubles for Free Trade," *Fortune*, January 23, 1984, 35.

70. Clyde H. Farnsworth, "Administration Talks Free Trade, Acts to Protect Industry," *New York Times*, March 4, 1984.

71. Clyde H. Farnsworth, "Reagan Denies Import Protection to Domestic Producers of Copper," *New York Times*, September 17, 1984; *International Trade Reporter*, August 29, 1984, 230–31.

72. For other analyses of the background to the steel case, see Kent Jones, "Another Turn in the Protectionist Spiral," *World Economy* 8, no. 4 (September 1985): 393–408, and Michael O. Moore, "Steel Protection in the 1980s: The Waning Influence of Big Steel?," in Anne O. Krueger, ed., *The Political Economy of Trade Policy* (Chicago: University of Chicago Press, 1996), 101–7.

73. "Import Protection: Reagan Is on a Tightrope," *Business Week*, August 20, 1984, 153.

74. Steven Pressman, "Pressure Mounts on Protectionist Trade Bills," *Congressional Quarterly Weekly Report*, August 4, 1984, 1897.

75. "Import Protection"; Steven Pressman, "The Making of Fortress America," *New York Times*, August 5, 1984; Tom Wicker, "Damned Either Way," *New York Times*, August 31, 1984.

76. Hedrick Smith, "Power of the Incumbent," *New York Times*, September 19, 1984.

77. Niskanen, *Reaganomics*, 143–34.

78. Stuart Auerbach, "Free-Trade Protectionism," *Washington Post National Weekly Edition*, October 1, 1984, 33.

79. For analysis of the Trade and Tariff Act of 1984, see Destler, *American Trade Politics*, 84–89, and Pietro S. Nivola, *Regulating Unfair Trade* (Washington, D.C.: Brookings Institution, 1993), 97–101.

80. Stuart Auerbach, "House Caucus Platform on Trade Offered," *Washington Post*, March 2, 1984.

81. *U.S. Import Weekly*, June 27, 1984, 1162–63.

82. Clyde H. Farnsworth, "House Backs Broader Trade Curbs," *New York Times*, July 27, 1984.

83. "Mondale Moves to Shore Up Base," *New York Times*, September 27, 1984.

84. Clyde H. Farnsworth, "House Backs Steel Curbs and Israeli Free Trade Zone," *New York Times*, October 4, 1984.

85. For a quantitative study of the determinants of House voting on seven trade bills in 1983–84, see James M. Lutz, "Determinants of Protectionist Attitudes in the United States House of Representatives," *International Trade Journal* 5, no. 3 (Spring 1991): 301–28.

86. This may explain, for example, why the UAW never tried to attach a domestic content amendment to the bill.

87. By at least 1983, pro–free-trade import-using, retail, export-oriented, and transnational business interests had mobilized to oppose protectionist import relief petitions filed, and restrictive legislation backed, by the auto, steel, textile, and copper industries. Pressman, "Pressure Mounts on Protectionist Trade Bills"; Boyd France, "An Antiprotectionist Backlash Is Gathering Strength on the Hill," *Business Week*, September 17, 1984, 40. For more on the role of antiprotectionist business interests in the 1980s, see I. M. Destler and John S. Odell, *Anti-Protection: Changing Forces in United States Trade Politics* (Washington, D.C.: Institute for International Economics, 1987).

88. For more on Coelho's and other Democratic efforts to court business support during the 1980s, see Brooks Jackson, *Honest Graft: Big Money and the American Political Process* (New York: Knopf, 1988); Thomas B. Edsall, "A Funny Thing Happened to the Party of the Working Class," *Washington Post National Weekly Edition*, August 25, 1986, 28–38; Kuttner, *Life of the Party*; Ferguson and Rogers, *Right Turn*; Thomas Ferguson, *Golden Rule: The Investment Theory of Party Competition and the Logic of Money-Driven Politics* (Chicago: University of Chicago Press, 1995); and Thomas Gais, *Improper Influence: Campaign Finance Law, Political Interest Groups, and the Problem of Equality* (Ann Arbor: University of Michigan Press, 1996), 167–69.

89. This included both regulated or "hard" money donations to individual candidates and congressional party committees and increasing amounts of unregulated or "soft" money contributions to party committees that could be used to finance "party-building" activities—voter registration and education, getting out the vote, etc.—that did not directly advocate the election of specific candidates.

90. The business share of House Democrats' total PAC receipts increased from 41 to 45 percent during the same period (it increased to 54 percent by 1992), while the labor share dropped from 43 to 41 percent (it fell to 33 percent by 1992). Stanley and Niemi, *Vital Statistics on American Politics*, 101–3. See also Vogel, *Fluctuating Fortunes*, 271–72, and Maxwell Glen, "Democratic Candidates Got a Larger Share of the Corporate Pie in 1984," *National Journal*, January 19, 1985, 156–58. On the advantage in the receipt of PAC contributions enjoyed by members of the House majority party, see Thomas J. Rudolph, "Corporate and Labor PAC Contributions in House Elections: Measuring the Effects of Majority Party Status," *Journal of Politics* 61, no. 1 (February 1999): 195–206.

91. See the comments of several PAC officials and other close observers in Glen, "Democratic Candidates Got a Larger Share." See also Tom Kenworthy, "Are House Democrats Victims of Their Fund-Raising Success?," *Washington Post*, October 30, 1989; John R. Wright, "Interest Groups, Congressional Reform, and Party Government in the United States," *Legislative Studies Quarterly* 25, no. 2 (May 2000): 230–31; and R. Kenneth Godwin, *One Billion Dollars of Influence: The Direct Marketing of Politics* (Chatham, N.J.: Chatham House Publishers, 1988), 128–36. In a recent debate, Ronald Keith Gaddie argued that business was coerced to shift contributions back to the Democrats in 1984 and thereafter to avoid potentially hostile government action. Though not denying this, Dan Clawson, Tie-ting Su, and Alan Neustadtl replied—correctly, I think—that this was less significant than the fact that the Democrats themselves changed their positions and behavior to be more pro-business. See Gaddie, "Pragmatism and the Corporate Shift in Political Action: An Alternative Perspective," and Dan Clawson, Tie-ting Su, and Alan Neustadtl, "Shift Happens: Corporations and the Struggle over American Politics, 1976–1986," both in *Social Science Quarterly* 77, no. 4 (December 1996): 924–93.

92. Mondale downplayed his support for the domestic content bill, in part because as his campaign manager, Bob Beckel, explained, "Some of our major contributors were strong free traders, and we heard from them." Quoted in Bruce Stokes, "Trade May Be a Tricky Issue for GOP and Democrats in 1986," *National Journal*, November 9, 1995, 2527.

93. "Trade Talks May Not Head Off a Collision with Japan," *Business Week*, December 31, 1984, 39.

Chapter 4

1. Charles O. Jones, "Ronald Reagan and the U.S. Congress: Visible-Hand Politics," in Jones, ed., *The Reagan Legacy: Promise and Performance* (Chatham, N.J.: Chatham House Publishers, 1988), 30–59.

2. Ronald M. Peters Jr., *The American Speakership: The Office in Historical Perspective* (Baltimore: Johns Hopkins University Press, 1997), 255.

3. For the following discussion, see Barbara Sinclair, *Legislators, Leaders, and Lawmaking: The U.S. House of Representatives in the Postreform Era* (Baltimore: Johns Hopkins University Press, 1995), and David W. Rohde, *Parties and Leaders in the Postreform House* (Chicago: University of Chicago Press, 1991).

4. See John R. Wright, "Interest Groups, Congressional Reform, and Party Government in the United States," *Legislative Studies Quarterly* 25, no. 2 (May 2000): 230–31.

5. As southern blacks moved into the Democratic Party in the wake of the passage of the Voting Rights Act of 1965, conservative whites were driven out. This meant that fewer southern Democrats got elected to Congress, but those that did acted more like their liberal northern colleagues.

6. See Paul S. Herrnson and Kelly D. Patterson, "Toward a More Programmatic Democratic Party? Agenda-Setting and Coalition-Building in the House of Representatives," *Polity* 27, no. 4 (Summer 1995): 607–28.

7. For an explanation of the evolving trade policy preferences of high-tech firms based on "strategic trade theory," see Helen V. Milner and David B. Yoffie, "Between Free Trade and Protectionism: Strategic Trade Policy and a Theory of Corporate Trade Demands," *International Organization* 43, no. 2 (Spring 1989): 239–72.

8. As William Niskanen explained, "the reelection of the president finally led the administration not to seek renewal of the VRA in 1985." William A. Niskanen, *Reaganomics: An Insider's Account of the Policies and the People* (New York: Oxford University Press, 1988), 140.

9. Clyde H. Farnsworth, "Debate on Trade Affecting Parties," *New York Times*, April 11, 1985.

10. In May Republican free trader Representative Bill Frenzel of Minnesota ruefully noted that protectionism was no longer "union led"; it was now "management-led." Later that month Frenzel observed that the movement of high-tech companies away from free trade had had "an enormous impact on Congress." *International Trade Reporter*, May 1, 1985, 616; Stuart Auerbach, "Protectionist Mood Rising," *Washington Post*, May 12, 1985. Kevin Phillips provided survey evidence of business's hardening attitudes on trade policy in "The Politics of Protectionism," *Public Opinion* (April–May 1985): 42.

11. See the survey results compiled in Phillips, "Politics of Protectionism."

12. Mark Bisnow, *In the Shadow of the Dome: Chronicles of a Capitol Hill Aide* (New York: William Morrow, 1990), 281.

13. House Democrats' political interest in the trade issue was spurred at an early

March retreat by a speech given by Chrysler chairman Lee Iacocca, who harshly criticized the Reagan administration for its decision not to extend the auto VRA with Tokyo. Andy Plattner, "Democrats Gain Comraderie but No Consensus on Message," *Congressional Quarterly Weekly Report*, March 9, 1985, 456–88.

14. Farnsworth, "Debate on Trade Affecting Parties."

15. On business support for budget deficit reduction as the path toward bringing the dollar and thus the trade deficit down, see I. M. Destler and C. Randall Henning, *Dollar Politics: Exchange Rate Policymaking in the United States* (Washington, D.C.: Institute for International Economics, 1989), 128, 137, and Clyde H. Farnsworth, "Business Fear: Strong Dollar," *New York Times*, May 11, 1985.

16. Destler and Henning, *Dollar Politics*, 38, 105; Clyde H. Farnsworth, "Democrats Seek Currency-Intervention Policy," *New York Times*, April 25, 1985.

17. See Hedrick Smith, "Republicans See Opportunity," *New York Times*, February 4, 1985, and Dan Balz, "The GOP as Majority Party," *Washington Post National Weekly Edition*, January 28, 1985, 11–12.

18. Donald Regan, *For the Record: From Wall Street to Washington* (San Diego: Harcourt, Brace Jovanovich, 1988), 280–81.

19. On Republican hopes of consolidating a realignment through tax reform, see David Beam, Timothy Conlan, and Margaret Wrightson, *Taxing Choices: The Politics of Tax Reform* (Washington, D.C.: CQ Press, 1989).

20. Robert W. Merry, "Reagan's Tax Plan Is Part of His Family Theme to Win 'Final Backbone' of Democratic Party," *Wall Street Journal*, June 7, 1985.

21. Norman Jonas, "Reagan's Second Step Toward a Free-Market Economy," *Business Week*, June 17, 1985, 31. See also Cathie Jo Martin, *Shifting the Burden: The Struggle over Growth and Corporate Taxation* (Chicago: University of Chicago Press, 1991), 159–89.

22. Anna Cifelli Isgro, "Unwatched Trade Issues Come to a Boil," *Fortune*, July 22, 1985, 814. See also Bruce Stokes, "Trade Debate on Reagan Tax Proposal Centers on Jeopardy to U.S. Competitiveness," *National Journal*, July 6, 1985, 1580.

23. Harrison Donnelly, "Democrats Join Battle on Trade with an Import Surcharge Bill," *Congressional Quarterly Weekly Report*, July 20, 1985, 1436.

24. See Clyde H. Farnsworth, "Most in Poll Found to Favor Import Limits to Protect Jobs," *New York Times*, June 9, 1985.

25. Julia Malone, "From Washington to Texas, the Call Grows Louder for US Crackdown on Imports," *Christian Science Monitor*, July 16, 1985.

26. Peter W. Bernstein, "The Middlest Middle of the Road Democrat," *Fortune*, May 13, 1985, 108–9.

27. "Protection or Retaliation?," *National Journal*, July 7, 1985, 1765.

28. "Given a large budget deficit, it can be useful to have a strong dollar and an increased trade deficit," said Council of Economic Advisers chairman Martin Feldstein in early 1983. Christopher Madison, "Dollar Dilemma: An Economic Malady Searching in Vain for a Miracle Cure," *National Journal*, August 20, 1983, 1736. See also Destler and Henning, *Dollar Politics*, 27–28, and Benjamin Ginsberg and Martin Shefter, *Politics by Other Means: The Declining Importance of Elections in America* (New York: Basic Books, 1990), 127–28.

29. On this latter point, see William Greider, *Secrets of the Temple: How the Federal Reserve Runs the Country* (New York: Simon and Schuster, 1987), 597–98.

30. Steven Solomon, *The Confidence Game: How Unelected Central Bankers Are Governing the Changed World Economy* (New York: Simon and Schuster, 1995), 296. Baker

was also pressured by leaders of the Business Roundtable, the National Association of Manufacturers, and other groups and firms to take action to bring down the value of the dollar.

31. For academic discussion, see James M. Glaser, *Race, Campaign Politics, and the Realignment in the South* (New Haven: Yale University Press, 1996); Earl Black and Merle Black, *The Vital South: How Presidents Are Elected* (Cambridge: Harvard University Press, 1992); and John R. Petrocik, "Realignment: New Party Coalitions and the Nationalization of the South," in Eric M. Uslaner, ed., *American Political Parties: A Reader* (Itasca, Ill.: F. E. Peacock, 1993).

32. Thomas B. Edsall, "The GOP Pushes for Converts in Four States," *Washington Post National Weekly Edition*, May 27, 1985, 11.

33. Thomas B. Edsall, "Down South, Democrats Would Rather Switch Than Lose," *Washington Post National Weekly Edition*, May 13, 1985, 12–13; Brooks Jackson, *Honest Graft: Big Money and the American Political Process* (New York: Knopf, 1988), 265.

34. For analyses of the role of trade in the Texas race and its wider significance, see Glaser, *Race, Campaign Politics*, 88–89, 122; Paul Taylor, "GOP: The Nays of Texas," *Washington Post National Weekly Edition*, August 19, 1985, 11–12.

35. Clyde H. Farnsworth, "Tougher Trade Policy Looms," *New York Times*, August 5, 1985. For Fall 1985 survey evidence that confirms Albertine's view of business trade militance, see "A Reluctant Vote for Protection," *Business Week*, December 2, 1985, 18, and William Schneider, "Two Looks at the Problem of America's Perception of Japan: From the American Side," *JAMA Forum* 14, no. 2, December 13, 1985.

36. Steven V. Roberts, "Congress Trade Revolt," *New York Times*, September 19, 1985.

37. Margaret Shapiro, "Calls for Protectionism Put Republicans on Defensive," *Washington Post*, September 16, 1985.

38. Andy Plattner, "Democrats See Political Gold in Trade Issue," *Congressional Quarterly Weekly Report*, September 21, 1985, 1856 (quotations).

39. Don Bonker, *America's Trade Crisis: The Making of the U.S. Trade Deficit* (New York: Houghton Mifflin, 1988), 55–56.

40. Shapiro, "Calls for Protectionism."

41. "Dole Sees Congress Passing Import Curbs," *Los Angeles Times*, August 31, 1985.

42. For accounts of the process that produced the "Plaza Accord," see Art Pine, "To Avert a Trade War, U.S. Sets Major Push to Drive Down Dollar," *Wall Street Journal*, September 23, 1985, and Peter T. Kilborn, "Reagan's Turnabout on the Dollar," *New York Times*, September 29, 1985. See also Destler and Henning, *Dollar Politics*, 42, and Yoichi Funabashi, *Managing the Dollar: From the Plaza to the Louvre* (Washington, D.C.: Institute for International Economics, 1988).

43. Robert W. Merry, "Reagan Aides Split over His Trade Speech and Altered It Sharply," *Wall Street Journal*, September 24, 1985.

44. "The New Trade Strategy," *Business Week*, October 7, 1985, 94.

45. Bruce Stokes, "New Players Taking Center Stage," *National Journal*, November 9, 1985, 2528.

46. See, e.g., "Simple, Clear, and Wrong," *Washington Post National Weekly Edition*, September 9, 1985, 27. On the media's general role in the trade debate of the 1980s, see Susan C. Schwab, *Trade-Offs: Negotiating the Omnibus Trade and Competitiveness Act of 1988* (Boston: Harvard Business School Press, 1994), 57–59, 176–77.

47. Steven Pressman, "Conflicting Forces Buffet Members on Trade," *Congressional Quarterly Weekly Report*, October 5, 1985, 1013–16.

48. The *Wall Street Journal* reported that many in Congress saw the "specter" of Smoot-Hawley "weighing more and more heavily each day in the debate. It didn't go unnoticed that when a trade subcommittee drafted the textile measure in a secret session last week, Chairman Sam Gibbons (D., Fla.) sat under a portrait of Willis Hawley." David Shribman and Art Pine, "Congress May Take More Moderate Trade Stance as Protectionist Fever Shows Signs of Cooling," *Wall Street Journal*, September 25, 1985.

49. Roberts, "Congress Trade Revolt."

50. Indicative of the partisan tensions still surrounding the trade issue, sponsorship of a major omnibus Senate bill, drafted under Republican leadership but with broad Democratic support, was hotly debated in both party caucuses, as senators argued over the political merits of bipartisanship versus partisan line drawing. *International Trade Reporter*, November 6, 1985, 1390; Schwab, *Trade-Offs*, 71–72; Martha L. Gibson, *Conflict amid Consensus in American Trade Policy* (Washington, D.C.: Georgetown University Press, 2000), 105–6.

51. Tensions ran especially high between Dan Rostenkowski of Ways and Means and John Dingell of Energy and Commerce. In the latest episode of their long-running turf fight regarding trade policy, the two committee chairmen were battling over competing drafts of telecommunications legislation that Democratic leaders wanted included in any omnibus trade bill. A House aide described Wright's role as an "overseer with the stick and whip to try to keep everything in line." Steven Pressman, "Trade Tug of War: A Tale of Two Committees," *Congressional Quarterly Weekly Report*, March 8, 1986, 557.

52. John Gilmour, *Strategic Disagreement: Stalemate in American Politics* (Pittsburgh: University of Pittsburgh Press, 1995).

53. On the opposition party strategy of provoking "blame game" vetoes under divided government, see Tim Groseclose and Nolan McCarty, "The Politics of Blame: Bargaining before an Audience," *American Journal of Political Science* 45, no. 1 (January 2000): 100–119; Charles M. Cameron, "Bargaining and Presidential Power," in Robert Y. Shapiro, Martha Joint Kumar, and Lawrence R. Jacobs, eds., *Presidential Power: Forging the Presidency for the Twenty-First Century* (New York: Columbia University Press), 63–64. For a similar view, see Gilmour, *Strategic Disagreement*, 119–31, esp. 122–23.

54. Bruce Stokes, "Hot and Cold on New Trade Bill," *National Journal*, March 22, 1986, 710.

55. Richard Alm, "Trade Winds Blow Hot in Washington," *U.S. News & World Report*, February 17, 1986, 42.

56. Steven Pressman, "In the Capitol Marketplace: Trade Expansion Bills," *Congressional Quarterly Weekly Report*, March 8, 1986, 558.

57. *International Trade Reporter*, March 26, 1986, 394–95.

58. "Please, No Christmas Tree of a Trade Bill," *National Journal*, March 22, 1986, 709.

59. This was in retaliation for the EC's imposition of variable levies on U.S. agricultural imports into Spain and Portugal following those two countries' entry into the EC.

60. Steven Pressman, "Omnibus Trade Bill Portends Showdown with White House," *Congressional Quarterly Weekly Report*, April 26, 1986, 907.

61. Under the proposal, the president was required to swiftly negotiate trade agreements with these countries to cut their surpluses with the United States by 10 percent annually. Failure to reach this goal would produce mandatory retaliation by the president, unless such action would cause "substantial harm" to the U.S. economy.

62. *Business and Public Affairs*, March 1, 1986, 1.

63. According to participants in an early May meeting before an international eco-

nomic summit in Tokyo, the president and Donald Regan said they believed that every Democrat in the House was going to use trade as an issue in the elections. *International Trade Reporter*, May 7, 1986, 627.

64. When asked whether the timing of the announcement would blunt passage of the House bill, Secretary of Commerce Malcolm Baldridge half confirmed the skeptics' suspicions: "No, but I hope it helps," he replied. Stuart Auerbach, "Reagan to Seek Cutbacks on Machine-Tool Imports," *Washington Post*, May 21, 1986.

65. Niskanen, *Reaganomics*, 146–47.

66. Gerald M. Boyd, "Bush Urges Restraint by Canada," *New York Times*, June 13, 1986. The *Times* later editorialized that the administration's actions were intended "in an election year to fend off Democratic appeals to workers threatened by foreign competition." "Hammering Canada's Shingles," *New York Times*, June 27, 1986.

67. Democrats opposed the substitute 1–239; Republicans backed it by a 144–26 margin.

68. Steven Pressman, "Over Reagan's Protest, House Votes Trade Bill," *Congressional Quarterly Weekly Report*, May 24, 1986, 1156.

69. Jackson, *Honest Graft*, 149–57.

70. Bruce Stokes, "Everybody's in the Act," *National Journal*, April 18, 1987, 928–29.

71. David Broder, "Tony Coelho's Pyrrhic Victories," *Washington Post National Weekly Edition*, June 30, 1986, 4. Whereas House Republicans from agricultural areas had opposed the bill, House leaders were able to stave off major defections by Democrats from export-oriented agricultural states by convincing them that the bill would not pass.

72. Among these groups were the National Association of Manufacturers, the Business Roundtable, the U.S. Chamber of Commerce, and the Emergency Committee for American Trade. *International Trade Reporter*, June 11, 1986, 786, June 18, 1986, 810.

73. *American Political Report*, June 13, 1986, 1.

74. Peter Osterlund, "House Democrats Entering Debate on Trade Bill with '86 Elections in View," *Christian Science Monitor*, May 16, 1986.

75. Broder, "Coelho's Pyrrhic Victories."

76. See, e.g., Richard Moe, "The Democrats Are Going to Have to Start Whistlin' Dixie," *Washington Post National Weekly Edition*, April 7, 1986, 23–24. Moe was Vice President Mondale's chief of staff. See also Phil Gailey, "Frankly, Democrats Want the South," *New York Times*, January 6, 1986.

77. Amy Wilentz, "Seeking Political Protection," *Time*, June 9, 1986, 30.

78. Edward Walsh, "The Democrats Are Banking on Trade," *Washington Post National Weekly Edition*, June 9, 1986, 13.

79. On the South's mixed interests in international trade and trade policy in the 1980s, see Peter Trubowitz, *Defining the National Interest: Conflict and Change in American Foreign Policy* (Chicago: University of Chicago Press, 1998), 213–15.

80. Richard E. Cohen, "Democratic Leadership Council Sees Party Void and Is Ready to Fill It," *National Journal*, February 1, 1986, 267–70; Kenneth S. Baer, *Reinventing Democrats: The Politics of Liberalism from Reagan to Clinton* (Lawrence: University Press of Kansas, 2000), 76.

81. Indicative of the continuing growth of the Democratic leadership's influence on trade policy relative to that of the Ways and Means Committee was the ease with which the textile bill's backers overcame the opposition of the powerful Ways and Means chairman, Dan Rostenkowski, and the trade subcommittee chairman, Sam Gibbons. Faced with a bill backed by nearly three hundred cosponsors and pressured by the

Democratic leadership, Rostenkowski and Gibbons chose not to try to block the effort to bring the bill to the floor.

82. Albert R. Hunt, "No Democratic Majority in Assailing Imports," *Wall Street Journal*, September 24, 1985.

83. Steven V. Roberts, "The President's Hard Sell on Free Trade," *New York Times*, September 29, 1985.

84. Ibid.

85. The bill passed the House the first time by 262–159, with Democrats voting for it 187–62 and Republicans opposing it 75–97. The Senate passed the measure by a 60–30 vote; Democrats backed the bill 35–11; Republicans opposed it 25–28. Finally, the House passed the Senate-approved version of the bill by a 255–161 vote, with the Democrats in favor 180–61 and the Republicans opposed 75–100.

86. Jonathan Feuerbringer, "Anti-Import Bill Sent to President: Veto Expected," *New York Times*, December 4, 1985. For an econometric analysis of the first House vote stressing both its partisan and constituency-based, regional character, see Suzanne C. Tosini and Edward Tower, "The Textile Bill of 1985: The Determinants of Congressional Voting Patterns," *Public Choice* 54, no. 1 (1987): 19–25. For an analysis of the Senate vote that reaches similar conclusions, see Stanley D. Nollen and Harvey J. Iglarsh, "Explanations of Protectionism in International Trade Votes," *Public Choice* 66, no. 2 (August 1990): 137–53.

87. Richard E. Cohen, "Running without Reagan," *National Journal*, December 7, 1985, 2787.

88. The five-year agreement came only hours before the Commerce Department was due to issue a final antidumping ruling on certain Japanese semiconductors and before the president was to render a decision in a Section 301 chips case against Japan brought by the Semiconductor Association in June 1985. In the spring, the administration had reluctantly proposed such a market-sharing solution to head off congressional pressure. The agreement's political intent was evident when officials admitted privately that it would have been very difficult to pin down a dumping charge against Japan. Hobart Rowen, "Giving in on Semiconductors," *Washington Post National Weekly Edition*, August 18, 1986, 5. As for the other actions, in late July the United States settled intellectual property rights and insurance disputes with South Korea, and on August 1 the White House both threatened to take retaliatory measures against Taiwan for its customs practices and decided to reverse a long-standing Reagan policy to sell subsidized wheat to the Soviet Union.

89. Kathleen Bawn argues that congressional majority party leaders, to maintain that dominant status, will sometimes make procedural decisions about individual bills that are designed to help those members of their party for whom the intensity of the bills' electoral impact is likely to be greatest, even if this means going against the wishes of a less intense party majority. I would suggest that other leadership activities, including bargaining and persuasion of the kind employed by House Democratic leaders in the textile bill override fight to help their southern members, are also undertaken with party maintenance goals in mind. Bawn, "Congressional Party Leadership: Utilitarian versus Majoritarian Incentives," *Legislative Studies Quarterly* 23, no. 2 (May 1998): 219–43.

90. Richard Alm, "Death of a Bill, Birth of an Issue," *U.S. News & World Report*, August 18, 1986, 6.

91. On the Democrats' attempts to fuse populism and economic nationalism during the campaign, see Sidney Blumenthal, "The Democrats Are Going Back to Populism,"

Washington Post National Weekly Edition, September 15, 1986, 6–7, and Clyde H. Farnsworth, "Record Trade Deficit Seen as Election Issue," *New York Times*, August 30, 1986.

92. These included contests in Pennsylvania, North and South Carolina, Georgia, Louisiana, and North and South Dakota. Peter Bragdon, "Trade," *Congressional Quarterly Weekly Report*, October 18, 1986, 2603–4.

93. Bruce Stokes, "Trade Issues Aren't Stirring the Voters," *National Journal*, September 27, 1986, 2320.

94. *Inside U.S. Trade*, October 3, 1986, 1.

95. Niskanen, *Reaganomics*, 149. See also Peter T. Kilborn, "U.S. Puts 15% Tariff on Lumber," *New York Times*, October 17, 1986. The administration also initiated a Section 301 action against Taiwan for obstructing the distribution of U.S. beer, wine, and tobacco, and, reversing previous White House policy, announced a new $1.5 billion farm aid program to help Republican senators in North and South Dakota who were locked in tough reelection battles.

96. Michael Wines, "Reagan Demands Progress by Allies to End Trade Curbs," *Los Angeles Times*, September 14, 1986. On the launching of the Uruguay Round, see Ernest Preeg, *Traders in a Brave New World: The Uruguay Round and the Future of the International Trading System* (Chicago: University of Chicago Press, 1995), 51–63.

97. Only 7 percent of the voters saw trade as an important issue in the election. Of these, 47 percent voted Republican and 49 percent Democratic. Also depressing for the Democrats, most voters were not even aware of the parties' positions on the trade issue. William Schneider, "Return to Normalcy," *National Journal*, November 8, 1986, 2710; Matthew Greenwald and Ruy Teixeira, "Storm Warnings on the Trade Front," *JAMA Forum* 5, no. 1, November 12, 1986.

Chapter 5

1. On the incentives for congressional majority leaders to establish a strong collective party record to improve their members' reelection prospects, see Gary Cox and Matthew McCubbins, *Legislative Leviathan: Party Government in the House* (Berkeley: University of California Press, 1992).

2. On Democratic agenda setting in the House in the One-hundredth Congress, see David W. Rohde, *Parties and Leaders in the Postreform House* (Chicago: University of Chicago Press, 1991); Barbara Sinclair, *Legislators, Leaders, and Lawmaking: The U.S. House of Representatives in the Postreform Era* (Baltimore: Johns Hopkins University Press, 1995); and John B. Bader, *Taking the Initiative: Leadership Agendas in Congress and the "Contract with America"* (Washington, D.C.: Georgetown University Press, 1996).

3. Janet Hook, "Partisan Battles Stall Action on Capitol Hill," *Congressional Quarterly Weekly Report*, August 15, 1987, 1871.

4. Ann Reilly Dowd, "Protectionism in Disguise," *Fortune*, December 8, 1986, 102.

5. See Taylor E. Dark, *The Unions and the Democrats: An Enduring Alliance* (Ithaca, N.Y.: Cornell University Press, 1999), chap. 7.

6. On this kind of choice and the considerations that underlie it, see John B. Gilmour, *Strategic Disagreement: Stalemate in American Politics* (Pittsburgh: University of Pittsburgh Press, 1995), esp. 15–50.

7. "Too tough a bill could wind up looking irresponsible," said one congressional source. *Inside U.S. Trade*, November 7, 1986, 2.

8. Tom Redburn, "Backing Fades for Trade Bill Protectionism," *Los Angeles Times*, February 16, 1987.

9. On this episode, see Otis L. Graham Jr., *Losing Time: The Industrial Policy Debate* (Cambridge: Harvard University Press, 1992), 219–22; Max Holland, *The CEO Goes to Washington* (Knoxville, Tenn.: Whittle (Direct) Books, 1994), 12–13; and John B. Judis, *The Paradox of American Democracy: Elites, Special Interests, and the Betrayal of Public Trust* (New York: Pantheon, 2000), 183–85.

10. Lee Smith, "The Democrats' Desperate Search for the Big Idea," *Fortune*, September 29, 1986, 108–16.

11. The White House also took a number of new administrative trade actions intended in part to undermine politically motivated Democratic efforts to pass a tough trade bill. These included imposing duties on various European products in response to the loss of sales of U.S. feed grains to Spain when it joined the EC; successfully pressuring Canada to impose a tax on lumber exports to the United States, where the lumber industry had been hurt by subsidized Canadian exports; and ending the duty-free status of imports from Taiwan, South Korea, and other newly industrialized countries.

12. On the role of the leadership's retention of control in exacerbating partisanship over the bill, see Martha L. Gibson, *Conflict amid Consensus in American Trade Policy* (Washington, D.C.: Georgetown University, 2000), 106–7, 138.

13. "The Evolution of a U.S. Trade Bill: Rostenkowski Explains the Paths Taken by Controversial Legislation on Capitol Hill," *Washington Post*, March 22, 1987.

14. According to one key Reagan adviser, the president "felt he had to make a preemptive strike, lest Congress take things entirely into its own hands and leave us with little to say about what happens." R. W. Apple Jr., "U.S. Move a Departure from the Norm," *New York Times*, March 28, 1987.

15. Hobart Rowen, "Chip Shot at Japan," *Washington Post*, March 31, 1987.

16. Hobart Rowen, "Japanese Warned on Trade," *Washington Post*, April 20, 1987. *Business Week* reported that House Majority Whip Tony Coelho believed that "even a losing confrontation with a weakened President would be better for the party's 1988 prospects than producing a watered-down bill." Douglas A. Harbrecht and Bill Javetski, "Trade: The Democrats Come Out Swinging—At One Another," *Business Week*, March 30, 1987, 41.

17. "Evolution of a U.S. Trade Bill." Jim Wright similarly observed that "it was the experience with Smoot-Hawley that caused people to cringe at the word protectionist. . . . It shows the manner in which labels can frighten people." Jonathan Feuerbringer, "Fear of Protectionism Softens Trade Bill," *New York Times*, May 4, 1987. Gephardt himself insisted, "There are no protectionists in the United States Congress." Edward Walsh, "Trade Debaters Wary of '88 Impact," *Washington Post*, May 1, 1987.

18. John M. Barry, *The Ambition and the Power: The Fall of Jim Wright: A True Story of Washington* (New York: Viking Penguin, 1989), 267.

19. Ibid., 272–73.

20. For the next two paragraphs, see Barry, *The Ambition and the Power*, 272; John Cranford, "Confrontation Likely over Trade Amendment," *Congressional Quarterly Weekly Report*, April 11, 1987, 678–79; Michael J. Gilligan, *Empowering Exporters: Reciprocity, Delegation, and Collective Action in American Trade Policy* (Ann Arbor: University of Michigan Press, 1997), 80–81; Helen Milner, "The Political Economy of U.S. Trade Policy: A Study of the Super 301 Provision," in Jagdish Bhagwati and Hugh T. Patrick,

eds., *Aggressive Unilateralism: America's 301 Trade Policy and the World Trading System* (Ann Arbor: University of Michigan Press, 1990), 170–72; and Stephen V. Marks, "Economic Interests and Voting on the Omnibus Trade Bill of 1987," *Public Choice* 75 (January 1993): 26–27.

21. In the industrial belt running from Illinois to Massachusetts, the Democratic vote for the amendment was 74–10. Of the seventeen Republicans who supported the measure, thirteen were from this area. On the other hand, a slim majority of Democrats from the three Pacific Coast states joined all the region's Republicans in opposing the measure. Southerners generally voted along party lines. Some farm state legislators were against the amendment, fearing retaliation against agricultural exports. Walsh, "Trade Debaters Wary."

22. Marks found that political party was the dominant factor in the vote on the amendment. Marks, "Economic Interests," 35. For another statistical analysis of the vote highlighting both its regional and partisan aspects, see Larry L. Wade and John B. Gates, "A New Tariff Map of the United States (House of Representatives)," *Political Geography Quarterly* 9, no. 3 (July 1990): 284–304.

23. For this kind of analysis of the differences in congressional voting on the 1985 textile bill and the 1987 omnibus bill, see Stanley D. Nollen and Harvey D. Iglarsh, "Explanations of Protectionism in International Trade Votes," *Public Choice* 66, no. 1 (1990): 137–53.

24. Jonathan Feuerbringer, "Tough Retaliatory Trade Measure Wins by 4-Vote Margin," *New York Times*, April 30, 1987. Marks found a strong association between the vote and labor contributions to individual members. Marks, "Economic Interests," 35.

25. Stuart Auerbach, "House Votes to Retaliate for Unfair Trade Practices," *Washington Post*, April 30, 1987. In a meeting of the House Democratic caucus shortly before the vote, Jim Wright had signaled those of his colleagues who wanted to produce a law, not a vetoed bill, but who for other reasons were willing to vote for Gephardt's measure, that he was willing to compromise with the Senate and not insist that the amendment be included in the final bill. Barry, *The Ambition and the Power*, 273.

26. Marks reports that the only independent variables that had statistically significant effects on the vote were political party and labor contributions. Marks, "Economic Interests," 37.

27. Sam Gibbons, a self-declared free trader, admitted that the bill was "a tough one to vote for." But, he said, "this is a bicameral organization, and there is hope that we can work out an acceptable bill before we are at the end of all this." John Cranford, "House Passes Comprehensive Trade Measure," *Congressional Quarterly Weekly Report*, May 2, 1987, 812.

28. John Cranford, "Debate over the Gephardt Amendment Masks Extent of Consensus on Trade Bill," *Congressional Quarterly Weekly Report*, May 2, 1987, 815.

29. "The greatest change in the last year is the tremendous shift in business," noted Dick Gephardt. "Companies that were once adamant free traders unwilling to do anything to upset the apple cart are now for tough measures on trade." Alan Murray and Monica Langley, "A Tougher Trade Law Seems Likely as Anger Rises in Much of U.S.," *Wall Street Journal*, April 27, 1987. See also I. M. Destler and John S. Odell, *Anti-Protection: Changing Forces in United States Trade Politics* (Washington, D.C.: Institute for International Economics, 1987), 109–23.

30. Speaking of his party's move away from protectionism, one senior Democrat said, "Our position on trade is supposed to get us into the White House, not keep us out of it."

"Tough Guys Don't Call It Protection," *Economist*, July 11, 1987, 29. Polling and election results indicated that voter preferences—although ambiguous, uncertain, and prone to vary with the wording of survey questions—nevertheless seemed to lie somewhere between the extremes of pure free trade and outright protectionism. In a February 1987 poll taken for *Time* by Yankelovich Clancy Shulman, respondents voted 60 percent to 35 percent to limit the number of Japanese goods that could be sold in the United States. But when asked about charging a tariff that would make Japanese products more expensive, only 48 percent were in favor, whereas 44 percent were opposed. George J. Church, "A Mix of Admiration, Envy, and Anger," *Time*, April 13, 1987, 38–39. See also polling results reported in Murray and Langley, "A Tougher Trade Law Seems Likely," 17.

31. Hobart Rowen, "Some Cures Can Be Deadly," *Washington Post National Weekly Edition*, March 23, 1987, 5.

32. The Gephardt amendment would have required tariffs or quotas to achieve yearly 10 percent reductions in trade surpluses against certain countries that ran large chronic surpluses with the United States and refused to eliminate their unfair trade practices. The Riegle-Danforth measure required the USTR to identify countries that consistently erected barriers, to place a dollar value on the injury to U.S. exports, and to initiate steps to remove the barriers within fifteen to nineteen months. If the barriers had not been eliminated within three years, with a one-third reduction each year, dollar-for-dollar retaliation for the unfair practices would be initiated. The president could decide not to act when this would lead either to extreme damage to the U.S. economy or to "serious harm" to the U.S. national security.

33. Drew Douglas, "Senate Twice Retains Veto-Bait Provisions," *Congressional Quarterly Weekly Report*, July 11, 1987, 1510. See also Susan Schwab, *Trade-Offs: Negotiating the Omnibus Trade and Competitiveness Act* (Boston: Harvard Business School Press, 1994), 137, 151–52.

34. On the politics of this vote, see Schwab, *Trade-Offs*, 153–54, and John Cranford, "Trade Bill Passes Senate, Heads for Conference," *Congressional Quarterly Weekly Report*, July 25, 1987, 1633–36.

35. On the role of the supermajoritarian institutions of the filibuster and the veto in producing policy gridlock, see David W. Brady and Craig Volden, *Revolving Gridlock: Politics and Policy from Carter to Reagan* (Boulder, Colo.: Westview Press, 1998), and Keith Krehbiel, *Pivotal Politics: A Theory of U.S. Lawmaking* (Chicago: University of Chicago Press, 1998).

36. Janet Hook, "Speaker Jim Wright Takes Charge in the House," *Congressional Quarterly Weekly Report*, July 11, 1987, 1483–88; Richard E. Cohen, "Living with a Lame Duck," *National Journal*, August 1, 1987, 1956–60.

37. Douglas A. Harbrecht and Bill Javetski, "Getting a Trade Bill Is Going to Take a Lot of Trading," *Business Week*, September 28, 1987, 34.

38. Harbrecht and Javetski, "Getting a Trade Bill," 34.

39. See John R. Cranford, "Effects of 1930 Law Color Debate on Trade Bill," *Congressional Quarterly Weekly Report*, November 7, 1987, 2740, and Susan F. Rasky, "Stock Market Fall May Affect Trade Bill," *New York Times*, October 30, 1987.

40. David Rapp, "Elections Loom over Congressional Calendar," *Congressional Quarterly Weekly Report*, January 223, 1988, 139.

41. See Jonathan Rauch, "All Gain No Pain," *National Journal*, July 16, 1988, 1856–59, and Paul Blustein, "The Democrats' Great Debate," *Washington Post*, July 17, 1988.

42. Ronald Brownstein, "Tangling over Trade," *National Journal*, September 19, 1987,

2330; Susan F. Rasky, "Trade Debate Takes a Role in Campaigns," *New York Times*, July 27, 1987.

43. Douglas Harbrecht, "Howdy, I'm Dick Gephardt—Trade Warrior," *Business Week*, May 4, 1987, 9899. See also Edward Walsh, "Gephardt Is Riding the Trade Issue," *Washington Post National Weekly Edition*, May 11, 1987, 12–13.

44. Bruce Stokes, "Trade Bill: Bound for the Front Burner," *National Journal*, January 2, 1988, 30.

45. Harold Meyerson, "It's the Neo-Pops vs. the Neo-Libs in '88," *Los Angeles Herald-Examiner*, February 14, 1988. See also Fred Barnes, "The Man to Beat," *New Republic*, March 7, 1988, 13.

46. In his widely publicized and debated book, *The Rise and Fall of the Great Powers* (New York: Random House, 1988), Kennedy argued that the United States, following the path of Britain and other great powers before it, had entered into a period of relative economic decline due to its "imperial overstretch," i.e., its foreign military obligations exceeded its economic ability to pay for them. Kennedy's arguments were influential in Washington; according to Representative Tim Wirth (D-Colo.), they were "circulating everywhere in Congress." Peter Schmeisser, "Is America in Decline?," *New York Times Magazine*, April 17, 1988.

47. See Sidney Blumenthal, *Pledging Allegiance: The Last Campaign of the Cold War* (New York: HarperCollins Publishers, 1990), 164–66.

48. An NBC/ *Wall Street Journal* poll conducted between February 28 and March 1 seemed to confirm this, finding that 71 percent of Democratic voters said they would be more likely to vote for "a candidate who says the United States must get tougher with its foreign trading partners." For summaries of other late 1987 and early 1988 polls, all of which found substantial support for greater U.S. toughness on trade, see *American Political Report*, March 4, 1988, 3.

49. The critics maintained that despite earlier difficulties, much of the southern economy, including the textile industry, was thriving. See Ann Reilly Dowd, "No Longer the Solid South," *Fortune*, March 14, 1988, 99–105.

50. Peter T. Kilborn, "Economic Nationalism Shapes Democratic Campaign Debate," *New York Times*, March 22, 1988.

51. For more on the conference, see Schwab, *Trade-Offs*, 179–218; Stephen D. Van Beek, *Post-Passage Politics: Bicameral Resolution in Congress* (Pittsburgh: University of Pittsburgh Press, 1995), 79–119.

52. "Writ large, the Congress gave much more than the Administration," said William T. Archey, international vice president of the U.S. Chamber of Commerce. Bruce Stokes, "The Trade Debate's Winners and Losers," *National Journal*, April 16, 1988, 1010.

53. "The fingerprints of the Business Roundtable and the Emergency Committee for American Trade area are all over this bill," a Senate aide said. Stokes, "Winners and Losers," 1021. For more on the influence of business on the bill, see Schwab, *Trade-Offs*, 167–71.

54. In mid-November, for example, the White House had announced that the United States would retaliate against Brazil for excluding foreign firms from its computer market. And in late January Reagan announced that Taiwan, Hong Kong, South Korea, and Singapore would be ineligible for the duty-free treatment offered under the Generalized System of Preferences because they no longer need this assistance.

55. Notably, Tokyo's March 29 decision to open bidding on fourteen major con-

struction projects to U.S. companies staved off the trade sanctions against Japan that had been recommended by Reagan's Economic Policy Council two weeks earlier.

56. For example, the Chamber of Commerce was particularly effective in maintaining the president's authority in granting import relief. "Archey [the Chamber's international vice president] pulled our fat out of the fire on that one," said an administration official. Stokes, "Winners and Losers," 1021. See also Stuart Auerbach, "Big Business May Buck White House and Back Measure," *Washington Post*, March 10, 1988.

57. For a content analysis of *Washington Post*, *New York Times*, and *Wall Street Journal* editorials on the trade bill from 1986 to 1988, see Schwab, *Trade-Offs*, 176–75.

58. However, labor pressure was important in the inclusion of the Super 301 provision, which the unions preferred to nothing at all. And the unions won an expanded training and adjustment and assistance program, a tougher and expedited unfair trade practices procedure, including the designation of violation of workers' rights as an unfair trade practice, and, of course, the plant closing provision. Stokes, "Winners and Losers," 1021; Frank Swoboda, "Labor's Question: Did We Win or Did We Lose?," *Washington Post*, April 10, 1988. See also Schwab, *Trade-Offs*, 172–74.

59. Stuart Auerbach of the *Washington Post* evocatively described the new political environment in which House and Senate conferees considered the bill in the immediate wake of the crash: "The grim portrait of . . . Willis C. Hawley, glares down on House and Senate conferees, reminding them of the risks they face as they try to craft a sweeping revision of trade legislation in the midst of a global financial upheaval. Hawley . . . was the cosponsor with Sen. Reed Smoot of the 1930 bill that increased U.S. tariffs and is widely blamed for helping to trigger the Great Depression. As important to the politicians on Capitol Hill, both Smoot and Hawley . . . were defeated in the 1932 election. With their eyes on that grim history, Congress is treading cautiously with the trade bill." Auerbach, "Congress Treads Cautiously; Reminders Linger of Trade Bill Blamed for Depression," *Washington Post*, October 30, 1987.

60. Monica Langley, "Weary Lawmakers Use Summer Camp Tactics in an Attempt to Pass Long-Stalled Bill," *Wall Street Journal*, March 18, 1988. On the role of the super-majoritarian institution of the veto in forcing the construction of cross or bipartisan coalitions under divided government, see Brady and Volden, *Revolving Gridlock*, and Krehbiel, *Pivotal Politics*.

61. The rapid growth of foreign investment in the American economy had became a hot political issue by the spring of 1988. See Bruce Stokes, "Foreign Owners," *National Journal*, September 19, 1987, 2333–36.

62. Swoboda, "Labor's Question." On the whole spring battle over the plant closing issue, see Schwab, *Trade-Offs*, 173–74, 200–201, 204–5, 208–11, 215–17.

63. Elizabeth Wehr, "Congress May Yet Send Reagan a Veto-Proof Trade Measure," *Congressional Quarterly Weekly Report*, April 23, 1988, 1060. See also Gibson, *Conflict amid Consensus*, 108. This pressure from the Democratic leadership and the subsequent House vote for the omnibus bill can be viewed as an example of a successful leadership-facilitated, intra-Democratic logroll; as such, it is evidence that the congressional party can "matter" beyond simply aggregating its members' induced or personal preferences. On this dispute, see Keith Krehbiel, *Pivotal Politics* and "Paradoxes of Parties in Congress," *Legislative Studies Quarterly* 24, no. 1 (February 1999): 31–64; Cox and McCubbins, *Legislative Leviathan*; David W. Rohde, "Parties and Committees in the House: Member Motivations, Issues, and Institutional Arrangements," in Kenneth A. Shepsle

and Barry R. Weingast, eds., *Positive Theories of Congressional Institutions* (Ann Arbor: University of Michigan Press, 1995); and Steven S. Smith, "Positive Theories of Congressional Parties," *Legislative Studies Quarterly* 25, no. 2 (May 2000): 193–215.

64. Steven V. Roberts, "Playing the Numbers: Both Parties Looking for an Edge on the Economy," *New York Times*, May 1, 1988.

65. Richard E. Cohen, "Labor Comes Alive," *National Journal*, July 16, 1988, 1864–68.

66. A *Washington Post*/ABC News poll found 82 percent of the respondents in favor, with only 15 percent opposed. David S. Broder, "To Democrats, Reagan Veto a Blessing," *Washington Post*, May 25, 1988.

67. Stuart Auerbach, "To Democrats, Plant Closing Issue Is Sure-Win Issue," *Washington Post*, April 26, 1988.

68. Clyde H. Farnsworth, "Trade Bill Voted in Senate by 63–36 but Is Facing Veto," *New York Times*, April 28, 1988.

69. Elizabeth Wehr, "Omnibus Trade Bill to Get a Second Chance," *Congressional Quarterly Weekly Report*, June 18, 1988, 1668.

70. Most southern Democrats were persuaded to vote for the bill after word went out that textile quota legislation wanted badly by southerners would suffer if they defected. This was again, in effect, an intra-Democratic logroll facilitated by the Democratic leadership. Elizabeth Wehr, "Trade, Plant-Closing Bills Win Strong House Backing," *Congressional Quarterly Weekly Report*, July 16, 1988, 1991–92.

71. Tom Kenworthy, "Democrats See Plant-Closing Notice as Campaign Issue," *Washington Post*, July 14, 1988.

72. Steven V. Roberts, "Reagan Veto Is Seen as Less Likely," *New York Times*, August 2, 1988.

73. Steven V. Roberts, "Reagan Is Pressed on Plant Closings," *New York Times*, July 27, 1988.

74. See David Brady and Jongryn Mo, "The U.S. Congress and Trade Policy: An Institutional Approach," *Pacific Affairs* 5, no. 2 (Fall 1990): 5–25; Stanley D. Nollen and Dennis P. Quinn, "Free Trade, Fair Trade, Strategic Trade, and Protectionism in the U.S. Congress, 1987–88," *International Organization* 48, no. 3 (Summer 1994): 491–525.

75. Elizabeth Wehr, "Democrats Will Skip Conference to Speed Action on Textile Bill," *Congressional Quarterly Weekly Report*, September 17, 1988, 2582.

76. Richard Fly, "Meet Militant Mike, the Tough Talker on Trade," *Business Week*, October 24, 1988, 37.

77. *International Trade Reporter*, November 11, 1988, 1494–95.

78. *International Trade Reporter*, November 9, 1988, 1468.

79. A Cable News Network/*Los Angeles Times* exit poll found that only 5 percent of the respondents named foreign trade as the most important issue in their vote. Of this 5 percent, 57 percent voted for Bush and 42 percent for Dukakis. "Explaining Their Vote," *National Journal*, November 12, 1988, 2854.

80. See the comments of former Gephardt adviser Robert Shrum in "Democrats Need the Presidency," *New York Times*, November 21, 1988.

Chapter 6

1. Michael Nelson, "The Presidency: Clinton and the Cycle of Policy and Politics," in Nelson, ed., *The Elections of 1992* (Washington, D.C.: CQ Press, 1993), 143.

2. For the politics of U.S.-Japan trade relations, including during the Bush years, see

Leonard J. Schoppa, *Bargaining with Japan: What American Pressure Can and Cannot Do* (New York: Columbia University Press, 1997); I. M. Destler and Michael Nacht, "U.S. Policy toward Japan," in Robert J. Art and Seyom Brown, eds., *U.S. Foreign Policy: Search for a New Role* (New York: Macmillan, 1993), 289–314; and Stephen D. Cohen, *An Ocean Apart: Explaining Three Decades of U.S.-Japanese Trade Frictions* (Westport, Conn.: Greenwood Press, 1998).

3. Referring to a February 1989 ACTPN report, Maureen Smith, deputy assistant secretary of Commerce for Japan, said: "It's a landmark. Those are mainstream Establishment business people." Robert Neff and Paul Magnusson, "Rethinking Japan: The New, Harder Line toward Tokyo," *Business Week*, August 7, 1989, 52.

4. These intellectuals were associated with policy shops and think tanks like the Council on Competitiveness, Rebuild America, the Economic Policy Institute (EPI), and the Berkeley Roundtable on the International Economy (BRIE).

5. See Paul Kennedy, "Can the US Remain Number One?," *New York Review of Books*, March 16, 1989, 36–42. On the debate between "declinists" like Kennedy and "revivalists" like Samuel Huntington and Joseph Nye, see Aaron L. Friedberg, "The Strategic Implications of Relative Decline," *Political Science Quarterly* 104, no. 3 (Fall 1989): 402–6.

6. For the seminal revisionist texts by the "gang of four"—Prestowitz, University of California at Berkeley political scientist Chalmers Johnson, American journalist James Fallows, and Dutch journalist Karel van Wolferen—see Prestowitz, *Trading Places: How We Are Giving Our Future to Japan and How to Reclaim It* (New York: Basic Books, 1988); Johnson, *MITI and the Japanese Miracle: The Growth of Industrial Policy, 1925–1975* (Stanford: Stanford University Press, 1982); Fallows, "Containing Japan," *Atlantic*, May 1989, 40–54; and van Wolferen, *The Enigma of Japanese Power: People and Politics in a Stateless Nation* (New York: Knopf, 1989). See their collective statement in "Beyond Japan-Bashing," *U.S. News & World Report*, May 7, 1990.

7. For an influential early collection of essays on strategic trade theory, see Paul Krugman, ed., *Strategic Trade Policy and the New International Economics* (Cambridge: MIT Press, 1986). For a contemporary journalistic discussion, see Karen Pennar, "The Gospel of Free Trade Is Losing Apostles," *Business Week*, February 27, 1989, 89.

8. In an early February *Washington Post*/ABC News poll, 44 percent of the respondents considered Japan to be a bigger threat than the Soviet Union. A 69–30 percent majority favored restricting Japanese imports; of those in favor, 87 percent endorsed such curbs even if it meant higher prices for U.S. consumers. For these and similar findings, see *Business and Public Affairs*, March 15, 1989, 1–2. See also "What Americans Think of Japan Inc," *Business Week*, August 7, 1989, 51.

9. See the comments by Democratic consultants Robert Shrum, Tom Kiley, and Celinda Lake in Bruce Stokes, "Mr. Horton's Neighborhood?," *International Economy*, March–April 1989, 42–46.

10. Paul Magnusson and Douglas Harbrecht, "Trade Hawk Gephardt Pulls in His Claws—A Bit," *Business Week*, August 28, 1989, 39.

11. On this episode, in addition to the articles cited below, see Schoppa, *Bargaining with Japan*, 69–78; Steve Dryden, *Trade Warriors: USTR and the American Crusade for Free Trade* (New York: Oxford University Press, 1995), 357–60; Peter Truell and Alan Murray, "Bush Advisers Deeply Divided on Trade Policy," *Wall Street Journal*, May 22, 1989; Elizabeth Wehr, "Japan, India, Brazil Cited for Import Barriers," *Congressional Quarterly Weekly Report*, May 27, 1989, 1242–43; and Bill Powell, "Japan Makes the Hit List," *Newsweek*, June 5, 1989, 48–49.

12. Satellites and supercomputers were two competitive high-tech sectors widely thought to be strategic, because they were characterized by economies of scale, very high profits, beneficial spin-offs, and linkages to other sectors of the economy. On the choice of these industries, see Thomas O. Bayard and Kimberly Ann Elliott, *Reciprocity and Retaliation in U.S. Trade Policy* (Washington, D.C.: Institute for International Economics, 1994), 101–48, and Michael Mastanduno, "Setting Market Access Priorities: The Use of Super 301 in U.S. Trade with Japan," *World Economy* 15, no. 6 (November 1992): 729–53.

13. On the decision to launch the SII and the subsequent negotiations under its auspices, see Schoppa, *Bargaining with Japan*, and Michael Mastanduno, "Framing the Japan Problem: The Bush Administration and the Structural Impediments Initiative," *International Journal* 47, no. 2 (Spring 1992): 235–64.

14. For example, a May 18 letter from 72 House members to Carla Hills urging that Japan be cited as a priority country was signed by 56 Democrats, but only by 16 Republicans. *Inside U.S. Trade*, May 19, 1989, 1.

15. Art Pine, "Target Japan for Trade Sanctions, Senators Warn," *Los Angeles Times*, May 4, 1989.

16. Bush had served as Republican National Committee chairman during the Watergate scandal of the 1970s. See Sidney M. Milkis, "The Presidency and Political Parties," in Michael Nelson, ed., *The Presidency and the Political System*, 6th ed. (Washington, D.C.: CQ Press, 2000), 392–95.

17. Hobart Rowen, "Away from Free Trade," *Washington Post*, June 8, 1989.

18. Robert Shogan, "Making U.S. No. 1 Again by Remedying Ills at Home," *Los Angeles Times*, August 7, 1989.

19. See the following influential briefs in support of managed trade: Robert Kuttner, *Managed Trade and Economic Sovereignty* (Washington, D.C.: Economic Policy Institute, 1989); Laura D'Andrea Tyson, "Managed Trade: Making the Best of the Second Best," and Rudiger W. Dornbusch, "Policy Options for Freer Trade: The Case for Bilateralism," both in Robert Z. Lawrence and Charles L. Schultze, eds., *An American Trade Strategy: Options for the 1990s* (Washington, D.C.: Brookings Institution, 1990), 106–85; and "A Fresh Look at Trade Policy," by Kuttner, Pat Choate, Clyde Prestowitz, Howard D. Samuel (of the AFL-CIO), and Alan Wm. Wolff (a trade lobbyist), one of the twin statements published in *The Free Trade Debate: Reports of the Twentieth Century Fund Task Force on the Future of American Trade Policy* (New York: Twentieth Century Fund, 1989), 25–36. For contemporary journalistic discussion of the broadening debate on managed trade, see Hobart Rowen, "Defining the Danger of 'Managed Trade,' " *Washington Post*, October 29, 1989, and Anetta Miller, "What Is 'Managed Trade'—And Will It Work?," *Newsweek*, March 5, 1990, 26.

20. For example, a January NBC News/*Wall Street Journal* poll found that 73 percent of the respondents thought that Japan was in a stronger economic position than the United States, and they favored a limit on imports even if it would increase prices. Bruce Stokes, "Running on Nationalism," *National Journal*, March 3, 1990, 17. See also Michael Oreskes, "Poll Detects Erosion of Positive Attitudes toward Japan among Americans," *New York Times*, February 6, 1990.

21. Stokes, "Running on Nationalism," 514; Richard Moe, "Charge, Democrats, Charge!," *Washington Post*, January 30, 1990.

22. See Valerie Rice, "Democrats Talk High Tech; Some Valley Execs Like What They Hear," *San Jose Mercury*, February 26, 1990.

23. Bill Javetski, "Can They Douse the Flames?," *Business Week*, March 12, 1990, 36–37.

24. Ronald D. Elving, "Response Subdued to Removal of Japan from 'Super 301,'" *Congressional Quarterly Weekly Report*, May 5, 1990, 1333–32.

25. During the second half of 1990, the only other major trade issue to come up for a congressional vote was a new version of the textile quota bill that twice had been passed by Congress and successfully vetoed by Ronald Reagan. Despite efforts by the Bush administration to discourage passage, the Senate and House approved the bill, but the House once again narrowly failed to override a presidential veto. All of the congressional votes had both regional and partisan aspects.

26. Paul Magnusson, "Congress Is Storming into the Breach on Trade," *Business Week*, February 18, 1991, 49.

27. Ibid.

28. See Michael Hart with Bill Dymond and Colin Robertson, *Decision at Midnight: Inside the Canada-US Free-Trade Negotiations* (Vancouver: UBC Press, 1994).

29. For three excellent analyses of NAFTA, see George Grayson, *The North American Free Trade Agreement: Regional Community and the New World Order* (Lanham, Md.: University Press of North America, 1995); Frederick W. Mayer, *Interpreting NAFTA: The Science and Art of Political Analysis* (New York: Columbia University Press, 1998); and Maxwell A. Cameron and Brian W. Tomlin, *The Making of NAFTA: How the Deal Was Done* (Ithaca, N.Y.: Cornell University Press, 2000). For a lively journalistic account, see John R. MacArthur, *The Selling of "Free Trade": NAFTA, Washington, and the Subversion of American Democracy* (New York: Hill and Wang, 2000).

30. The fast-track provision had its origins in the 1974 Trade Act.

31. For a review of debates on the sources of regionalism and its relation to globalization, including whether (1) the world economy is dividing into regional blocs, (2) regional accords are trade creating or trade diverting, and (3) such pacts are "building blocks" or "stumbling blocks" toward further multilateral trade liberalization, see Helen V. Milner and Edward D. Mansfield, "The New Wave of Regionalism," *International Organization* 53, no. 3 (Summer 1999): 589–627.

32. Timothy McKeown argues that because the United States already has a large market and has been closely linked to Canada for many years, NAFTA is much less about optimal scale or increasing competition for American firms than it is about holding down wage costs for U.S. investors in Mexico. Timothy J. McKeown, "The Global Economy, Post-Fordism, and Trade Policy in Advanced Capitalist States," in Herbert Kitschelt, ed., *Continuity and Change in Contemporary Capitalism* (Cambridge: Cambridge University Press, 1998), 29.

33. Jeffrey H. Birnbaum and David Rogers, "Free Trade Treaty Is Key Issue in U.S. Presidential Election," *Wall Street Journal*, August 13, 1992.

34. Another Bush aide added: "[Secretary of State] James Baker and [Secretary of Commerce] Bob Mosbacher are both from Texas. Both are more interested in politics than policy. Both want to see George Bush campaigning in Mexican American neighborhoods in Chicago and New York saying he is the father of the free trade agreement. They both see an unbelievable opportunity." Michael Duffy and Dan Goodgame, *Marching in Place: The Status Quo Presidency of George Bush* (New York: Simon and Schuster, 1992), 239. One poll found that 77 percent of Hispanics thought that a free-trade agreement with Mexico would benefit them. David Marchick, "Democrats Flubbed Fast-Track," *Journal of Commerce*, June 25, 1991, 8A.

35. For the next six paragraphs, see Mayer, *Interpreting NAFTA*, 69–77; William P.

Avery, "Domestic Interests in NAFTA Bargaining," *Political Science Quarterly* 113, no. 2 (Summer 1998): 281–305; Ronald W. Cox, "Corporate Coalitions and Industrial Restructuring: Explaining Regional Trade Agreements," *Competition & Change* 1 (1995): 13–30; Bruce Stokes, "Trade Talks with Mexico Face Hurdles," *National Journal*, June 16, 1990, 1486–87; and David S. Cloud, "Congress Wary of Bush Plan to Open Doors to Mexico," *Congressional Quarterly Weekly Report*, February 23, 1991, 451–54.

36. Drawing on strategic trade theory, Helen Milner argues that support for NAFTA was most prevalent among firms characterized by increasing returns. See Helen V. Milner, "Industries, Governments, and the Creation of Regional Trade Blocs," in Edward D. Mansfield and V. Milner, eds., *The Political Economy of Regional Integration* (New York: Columbia University Press, 1998), 77–106.

37. On the business origins of NAFTA, see Henry Jacek, "Public Policy and NAFTA: The Role of Organized Business Interests and the Labor Movement," *Canadian-American Public Policy* no. 19 (October 1994): 5–6.

38. Recall Timothy McKeown's argument (n. 32 above) that given the large size of the U.S. market, NAFTA was more about holding down wage costs than achieving economies of scales.

39. As Sandra Masur, director of Public Policy Analysis for Eastman Kodak and leader of the Business Roundtable's efforts on behalf of NAFTA, explained, American business supported NAFTA, because "U.S. manufacturing must pursue joint production [with Mexico] to keep costs down and compete against European and Japanese competitors who pursue similar strategies." Masur, "The North American Free Trade Agreement: Why It's in the Interest of U.S. Business," *Columbia Journal of World Business*, June 22, 1991, 98. According to a 1992 Roper poll, 40 percent of about 450 U.S. corporate executives said that it was "very" or "somewhat" likely that their companies would "shift some production to Mexico . . . if NAFTA is ratified." For large companies, the figure was 55 percent. Samuel Bowles and Mehrene Larudee, "Nafta: Friend or Foe?," *New York Times*, November 15, 1993. On the role of Japanese competition in prompting and giving shape to U.S. business support for NAFTA, see Lorraine Eden and Maureen Appel Molot, "Fortress or Free Market? NAFTA and Its Implications for the Pacific Rim," in Richard Higgott, Richard Leaver, and John Ravenhill, eds., *Pacific Economic Relations in the 1990s: Cooperation or Conflict?* (Boulder, Colo.: Lynne Rienner, 1993).

40. In the same 1992 Roper poll, 24 percent of the executives surveyed admitted that it was either very or somewhat likely that "Nafta will be used by [their] company as a bargaining chip to keep wages down in the U.S." Bowles and Larudee, "Nafta: Friend or Foe?." On NAFTA as an element of a strategy of industrial restructuring at labor's expense, see Mark E. Rupert, "(Re)Politicizing the Global Economy: Liberal Common Sense and Ideological Struggle in the US NAFTA Debate," *Review of International Political Economy* 2, no. 4 (Autumn 1995): 658–92, and Kim Moody, "NAFTA and the Corporate Redesign of America," *Latin American Perspectives* 22, no. 1 (Winter 1995): 95–115.

41. Cox, "Corporate Coalitions"; Lorraine Eden and Maureen Appel Molot, *From Silent Integration to Strategic Alliance: The Political Economy of North American Free Trade* (Ottawa, Canada: Centre for Trade Policy and Law, Occasional Paper No. 17, 1991), esp. 11–4; Wieslaw Michalak and Richard Gibb, "Trading Blocs and Multilateralism in the World Economy," *Annals of the Association of American Geographers* 87, no. 2 (June 1997): 264–79; Charles Oman, *Globalisation and Regionalisation: The Challenge for Developing Countries* (Paris: OECD, 1994), esp. 17–18, 86–91; Allen J. Morrison and Kendall

Roth, "The Regional Solution: An Alternative to Globalization," *Transnational Corporations* 1, no. 2 (August 1992): 37–55.

42. I. M. Destler notes that in recent years, workers' interests have become "decoupled" from those of the firms where they work, due to the fact that capital is internationally mobile while labor is not. Destler, "U.S. Trade Governance in the New Global Economy," in Susan M. Collins and Robert Z. Lawrence, eds., *Brookings Trade Forum, 1999* (Washington, D.C.: Brookings Institution Press, 1999), 150. With respect to NAFTA on this issue, see McKeown, "Global Economy," 31–32.

43. On the growing role of environmental issues in trade policy, including in NAFTA, see David Vogel, "The Environment and International Trade," *Journal of Policy History* 12, no. 1 (2000): 72–100.

44. Robin Toner, "Democrat Session Previews '92 Race," *New York Times*, May 8, 1991.

45. "This is the most powerful political issue Democrats could have if you want to paint Republicans as representing big business," said Democratic consultant Frank Greer. Ronald Brownstein and Karen Tumulty, "Mexico Free-Trade Pact Faces Hard Sell in Congress," *Los Angeles Times*, April 6, 1991. See also John Dillin, "Democrats See Trade as Potent Election Issue," *Christian Science Monitor*, April 15, 1991.

46. Robert Shogan, "Democrats Map a Strategy for '92 Comeback," *Los Angeles Times*, March 24, 1991.

47. Amy Borrus and Paul Magnusson, "Trade Hawks Want Tokyo's Blood, Bush Wants a Few Concessions," *Business Week*, April 8, 1991, 24.

48. Peter Truell and Eduardo Lachica, "Administration Gets Tough on Trade as Congress Gets Set to Vote on Extending Negotiating Powers," *Wall Street Journal*, April 29, 1991; Paul Magnusson, "Bush Does More Slugging, Less Ducking, on Trade," *Business Week*, May 13, 1991, 41.

49. Bruce Stokes, "Gephardt Skates on Fast-Track," *National Journal*, May 18, 1991, 1191.

50. The House and Senate defeated resolutions to disallow fast-track authority by votes of 192–231 and 36–59 respectively.

51. At least in the House, only those Republicans with strong labor-oriented constituencies opposed fast track. Richard S. Conley, "Derailing Presidential Fast-Track Authority: The Impact of Constituency Pressures and Political Ideology on Trade Policy in Congress," *Political Research Quarterly* 52, no. 4 (December 1999): 785–89.

52. Many Democrats who were predisposed to support free trade were nevertheless able to vote against fast track so as not to unnecessarily alienate their labor backers once it was clear that the White House had the votes to win. In a statistical analysis of voting in both houses, Glen Sussman and Byron Daynes concluded that liberal Democrats representing the Rust Belt and blue-collar constituencies were more inclined to oppose fast track. They also found ideology to be more influential in the Senate, with its larger, more heterogeneous constituencies, than in the House. Sussman and Daynes, "The Impact of Political Ideology on Congressional Support for Presidential Policy Making Authority: The Case of the Fast Track," *Congress & the Presidency* 22, no. 2 (Fall 1995): 143–241. For a study of just the House vote that reaches similar conclusions, see Conley, "Derailing Presidential Fast-Track Authority."

In another statistical analysis of House and Senate voting, William Kaempfer and Stephen Marks show that union membership and labor contributions were negatively associated with votes in favor of fast track, whereas the likely sectoral employment effects of a free-trade agreement had little influence, due to the uncertainty of their incidence. William H. Kaempfer and Stephen V. Marks, "The Expected Effects of Trade Liberalisation: Evidence from US Congressional Action on Fast-Track Authority," *World Economy* 16, no. 6 (November 1993): 725–40. In still another econometric study, however, Leo Kahane found the influence of organized labor on Senate voting to be unimportant. Instead, the likely sectoral impact of a free-trade agreement on a state's employment was a significant predictor of the vote. Leo H. Kahane, "Senate Voting Patterns on the 1991 Extension of the Fast-Track Trade Procedures: Prelude to NAFTA," *Public Choice* 87, nos. 1–2 (April 1996): 35–53.

53. Thirty-nine of the 91 House Democratic fast-track supporters, or 42.9 percent, were from the South.

54. On this intra-Democratic division, see Janet Hook, "Budget Ordeal Poses Question: Why Can't Congress Be Led?," *Congressional Quarterly Weekly Report*, October 20, 1990, 3473, and Barbara Sinclair, "Governing Unheroically (and Sometimes Unappetizingly): Bush and the 101st Congress," in Colin Campbell, S.J., and Bert Rockman, eds., *The Bush Presidency: First Appraisals* (Chatham, N.J.: Chatham House Publishers, 1991), 163.

55. Fred Barnes, "Hill Potatoes," *New Republic*, May 20, 1991, 26–27. For a broader argument that during the 1980s congressional Democrats gave up the attempt to recapture the presidency, see Benjamin Ginsberg and Martin Shefter, *Politics by Other Means: The Declining Importance of Elections in America* (New York: Basic Books, 1990), 36.

56. For an overview, see Robert Neff and Bill Javetski, "The Japan That Can Say 'Get Lost,'" *Business Week*, October 14, 1991, 58–59.

57. Paul Tsongas and Bill Clinton stressed competitiveness rather than trade policy. Bruce Stokes, "The Democrats Find a Hot Topic," *National Journal*, October 19, 1921, 2571.

58. John Maggs, "Gephardt Announces Trade, Aid Initiatives," *Journal of Commerce*, September 11, 1991, 1A; Paul Magnusson, "Has Gephardt Found a Slingshot for the Democrats?," *Business Week*, September 30, 1991, 37.

59. John Maggs, "House Version of Super 301 Law Closes Trade Reciprocity Loopholes," *Journal of Commerce*, November 5, 1991, 1A.

60. Tim Shorrock, "Washington Urged to Focus on Problems at Home," *Journal of Commerce*, December 3, 1991, 12A.

61. R. W. Apple, "Majority in Poll Fault Focus by Bush on Global Policy, but Back New Order," *New York Times*, October 11, 1991.

62. John E. Yang and Ann Devroy, "Pay No Attention to That Foreign Policy behind the Curtain," *Washington Post National Weekly Edition*, December 23–29, 1991, 13.

63. Michael Wines, "Bush's Asian Trip Recast to Stress Jobs and Exports," *New York Times*, December 29, 1991.

64. Kevin Kearns, "Is Japan About to Do in the Big Three?," *Washington Post National Weekly Edition*, June 24–30, 1991, 23.

65. Bruce Stokes, "Protection—For a Price," *National Journal*, April 4, 1992, 795, quoting Charles E. Cook, editor and publisher of the *Cook Political Report*, a Washington-based newsletter.

66. John Maggs, "US Pushes for Auto Parts Pact with Japan," *Journal of Commerce*, November 15, 1991, 1A.

67. Don Oberdorfer, "Trading in Mistrust," *Washington Post National Weekly Edition*, March 9–15, 1992, 6.

68. For this typology, see Nicol Rae, "Party Factionalism, 1946–96," in Byron E. Shafer, ed., *Partisan Approaches to Postwar American Politics* (Chatham, N.J.: Chatham House Publishers, 1998), 63–64. See also John B. Judis, *The Paradox of Democracy: Elites, Special Interests, and the Betrayal of the Public Trust* (New York: Pantheon, 2000), chap. 8; David Frum, *Dead Right* (New York: Basic Books, 1995), 9–12; and Paul Starobin, "Right Fight," *National Journal*, December 9, 1995, 3022–26.

69. For the next three paragraphs, see Judis, *Paradox of Democracy*, 191–94, "The Tariff Party," *New Republic*, March 30, 1992, 23–25, and "White Squall," *New Republic*, March 11, 1996, 26–30; and Frum, *Dead Right*, 1995, 136–41.

70. See John P. Cregan, ed., *America Asleep: The Free Trade Syndrome and the Global Economic Challenge* (Washington, D.C.: U.S. Industrial Council Educational Foundation, 1991), with a forward by Pat Buchanan.

71. See Judis, "White Squall."

72. Mark Magnier, "Justification of Trip May Backfire on Bush," *Journal of Commerce*, December 31, 1991, 1A.

73. Jim Mann, "Bush's Tour Reflects New Realities in U.S.-Asia Ties," *Los Angeles Times*, January 7, 1992.

74. Andrew Rosenthal, "Bush Signals He's Prepared for Tough Campaign in '92," *New York Times*, January 3, 1992.

75. They were encouraged by a grassroots "Buy American" campaign that briefly swept parts of the country following George Bush's trip to Japan. Walter Shapiro, "Japan Bashing on the Campaign Trail," *Time*, February 10, 1992, 23–24.

76. Clinton's opposition to protectionism was strengthened by a June 1991 dinner with the top Democratic Wall Street executives, which aides described as an important step in his business education. The executives, in turn, were impressed with Clinton's willingness to embrace free trade and free markets. Nicholas D. Kristof with David Sanger, "Global Contagion: A Narrative," *New York Times*, February 16, 1999. On Clinton's support among internationalist business interests—the vast majority of whom at this time, however, still favored George Bush's reelection—see Thomas Ferguson, "The Democrats Deal for Dollars," *Nation*, April 13, 1992, 475–78; John B. Judis, "Clinton and the Lobbyists: Who Is Paying the Bill?," *In These Times*, March 11–17, 1992, 3; and Paul Starobin, "An Affair to Remember?," *National Journal*, January 16, 1993, 120–24.

77. Virginia Postrel, "Foreign Firms Enjoy Southern Hospitality," *Los Angeles Times*, March 6, 1992.

78. See R. W. Apple Jr., "Trade Warriors," *New York Times*, March 15, 1992.

79. Greg Steinmetz, "Electing to Get Tough on Japanese," *Newsday*, March 6, 1992, 45.

80. Stokes, "Protection—For a Price."

81. David S. Cloud, "Japan, Bush Are Targets of New Democratic Bill," *Congressional Quarterly Weekly Report*, May 9, 1992, 1240; Keith Bradsher, "Return of an Issue: Protectionism," *New York Times*, June 16, 1992.

82. Keith Bradsher, "House Votes Bill Tougher on Trade," *New York Times*, July 9, 1992.

83. Bradsher, "Return of an Issue."

84. Bradsher, "House Votes Tougher Bill on Trade."

85. Keith Bradsher, "Senate Democrats Forge an Economic Strategy," *New York Times*, July 2, 1992.

86. John Maggs, "Bentsen Sends Mixed Signal on House-Passed Trade Bill," *Journal of Commerce*, July 23, 1992, 2A.

87. The UAW's membership had fallen by more than 300,000 since 1978, while tens of

thousands of Americans now worked for U.S.-based Japanese auto and auto parts companies. Stokes, "Protection—For a Price."

88. Bruce Stokes, "Remember Trade?," *National Journal*, October 10, 1992, 2337.

89. Andrew Rosenthal, "The 1992 Campaign: Republicans," *New York Times*, September 12, 1992.

90. "Washington Wire," *Wall Street Journal*, March 13, 1992.

91. Paul Magnusson, "Bush Bulls Ahead on Free Trade with Mexico," *Business Week*, February 24, 1992, 46–47.

92. Birnbaum and Rogers, "Free Trade Treaty Is Key Issue."

93. Under the pact, about 65 percent of U.S. industrial and agricultural exports to Mexico were made eligible for duty-free treatment immediately or within five years; rules governing the operation of U.S. banks, securities, and insurance companies were liberalized; intellectual property rights were tightened; and domestic content, export requirements, and other investment rules were liberalized or eliminated. However, stiff North American content or rule of origin requirements, long phaseouts of protection, and other exemptions and provisions were included at the behest of, and as "side payments" to, the auto and auto parts, textile and apparel, and other manufacturing industries to preclude non–North American investors from using Mexico as a platform from which to export to the United States. Modest measures to mitigate the negative effects of NAFTA on workers and the environment were also added to the final draft of the treaty, signed in early October, or were separately promised by Bush. For "two-level game" analyses of the actual negotiations that produced the treaty, see Mayer, *Interpreting NAFTA*, 109–64; Cameron and Tomlin, *The Making of NAFTA*; and Avery, "Domestic Interests in NAFTA Bargaining," 294–99. See also Grayson, *North American Free Trade Agreement*, 73–107.

94. James Risen, "Dynamite Deal: Trade Pact Could Backfire on Bush in the Rust Belt," *Los Angeles Times*, August 7, 1992.

95. Greg McDonald, "Bush Woos Middle America with Vows of New Jobs, Markets," *Houston Chronicle*, August 24, 1992.

96. "We've identified Nafta as a wedge issue for the campaign in the Hispanic community," said Ernest Olivas, a senior outreach adviser to the Bush campaign. Tim Shorrock, "Bush to Woo Hispanic Voters with Trade Pact," *Journal of Commerce*, August 21, 1992, 1A.

97. For much of the following account of the role played by NAFTA in the 1992 presidential race, see Peter Behr, "Clinton's Path to NAFTA," *Washington Post National Weekly Edition*, September 27–October 3, 1993, 21. See also Grayson, *The North American Free Trade Agreement*, 109–28.

98. For the following account, see Behr, "Clinton's Path to NAFTA"; Mayer, *Interpreting NAFTA*, 167–68; Bob Woodward, *The Agenda: Inside the Clinton White House* (New York: Simon and Schuster, 1994), 55–56; Elizabeth Drew, *On the Edge: The Clinton Presidency* (New York: Simon and Schuster, 1994), 288; and MacArthur, *Selling of "Free Trade,"* 160–63.

99. Stokes, "Remember Trade?"; Bruce Stokes, "A Trade Pact That Could Rile Voters," *National Journal*, August 15, 1992, 1901.

Chapter 7

1. See Herbert Kitschelt, *The Transformation of European Social Democracy* (Cambridge: Cambridge University Press, 1994), and Carles Boix, *Political Parties, Growth, and*

Equality: Conservative and Social Democratic Economic Strategies in the World Economy (Cambridge: Cambridge University Press, 1997).

2. On the simultaneous movement since the 1970s of nonunionized blue-collar workers away from the Democrats and routine white-collar workers and professionals toward the party, see Jeff Manza and Clem Brooks, *Social Cleavages and Political Change: Voter Alignments and U.S. Party Coalitions* (New York: Oxford University Press, 1999).

3. Many observers who find "class" to be a useful category of social and political analysis insist on a production-level definition of the concept in which industrial and lower-level white-collar workers are part of the "working class" rather than an amorphous middle class. Other scholars, however, dispute altogether the utility of the concept of class to explain either social stratification or various forms of political behavior. An interesting way through this thicket has been proposed by Allin Cottrell, who accepts an economic notion of class but who also argues that classes as such are not political actors. He instead advances the concept of a "pertinent social collectivity," defined as a category of agents broadly sharing some aspect of culture and orientation to politics and susceptible to organization into a political constituency that acquires a certain salience or pertinence in relation to the dominant political issues of a given period. Such pertinent collectivities, whose preferences politicians both respond to and attempt to shape, are not likely to form exclusively along economic class lines. In the 1990s Clintonites tried to discursively construct the "middle class" as just such a pertinent social collectivity. Cottrell, *Social Classes in Marxist Theory* (London: Routledge and Kegan Paul, 1984), 194–97.

4. See Michael Lind, "The Radical Center or the Moderate Middle?," *New York Times Magazine*, December 3, 1995, 72–73.

5. For evolving Democratic and Republican factions since World War II, see Nicol C. Rae, "Party Factionalism, 1946–1996," in Byron E. Shafer, ed., *Partisan Approaches to Postwar American Politics* (New York: Chatham House Publishers, 1998), 41–74.

6. On the DLC, see Rae, "Party Factions" and *Southern Democrats* (New York: Oxford University Press, 1996); Kenneth Baer, *Reinventing Democrats: The Politics of Liberalism from Reagan to Clinton* (Lawrence: University Press of Kansas, 2000); Dan Balz and Ronald Brownstein, *Storming the Gates: Protest Politics and the Republican Revival* (Boston: Little, Brown, 1996); E. J. Dionne Jr., *They Only Look Dead: Why Progressives Will Dominate the Next Political Era* (New York: Simon and Schuster, 1996); and Jon F. Hale, "The Making of New Democrats," *Political Science Quarterly* 110, no. 2 (Summer 1995): 207–32.

7. On the DLC's business backing, see Baer, *Reinventing Democrats*, 187–88; Paula Dwyer, "The Democratic Right Shows It Knows How to Squabble, Too," *Business Week*, May 6, 1991; and Lloyd Grove, "Lobbyists Thermidor," *Washington Post*, December 9, 1992.

8. See Ruy Teixeira and Joel Rogers, *America's Forgotten Majority: Why the White Working Class Still Matters* (New York: Basic Books, 2000), 71.

9. See Dionne, *They Only Look Dead*, and John B. Judis, "From Hell," *New Republic*, December 19, 1994, 14–18.

10. For a useful overview of these disagreements, see Baer, *Reinventing Democrats*.

11. For academic and journalistic support for this view, see Baer, *Reinventing Democrats*; Balz and Brownstein, *Storming the Gates*; Paul R. Abramson, John H. Aldrich, and David W. Rohde, *Change and Continuity in the 1992 Election*, rev. ed. (Washington, D.C.: CQ Press, 1995); and Charles O. Jones, *Clinton and Congress, 1993–1996: Risk, Restoration, and Reelection* (Norman: University of Oklahoma Press, 1999).

12. For examples of this view, see Pippa Norris, "The Presidential Election, Voting Behavior, and Legitimacy," in Gillian Peele, Christopher J. Bailey, Bruce Cain, and B. Guy Peters, eds., *Developments in American Politics—2* (Chatham, N.H.: Chatham House Publishers, 1995), 18–44; Jeff Faux, *The Party's Not Over: A New Vision for the Democrats* (New York: Basic Books, 1996); and Ruy Teixeira, "Economic Change and the Middle-Class Revolt against the Democratic Party," in Stephen C. Craig, ed., *Broken Contract? Changing Relations between Americans and Their Government* (Boulder, Colo.: Westview Press, 1996), 67–84.

13. For this more balanced view, see Dionne, *They Only Look Dead*, and Judis, "From Hell."

14. Twenty-one percent of the voters from union households voted for Perot.

15. For the next two paragraphs, see Balz and Brownstein, *Storming the Gates*; Faux, *The Party's Not Over*; Dionne, *They Only Look Dead*; and Baer, *Reinventing Democrats*.

16. For an argument that this is how all presidents now govern, see Cary R. Covington and Lester G. Seligman, *The Coalitional Presidency* (Chicago: Dorsey Press, 1989).

17. Dick Morris, *Behind the Oval Office: Winning the Presidency in the Nineties* (New York: Random House, 1997), 84.

18. For a useful attempt to clarify the meaning of triangulation, see Gary Wills, "The Would-Be Progressives," *New York Review of Books*, July 11, 1996, 14. See also Nicol Rae, "Clinton and the Democratic Party," in Steven E. Schier, ed., *The Postmodern Presidency: Bill Clinton's Legacy in U.S. Politics* (Pittsburgh: University of Pittsburgh Press, 2000).

19. Stephen Skowronek, *The Politics Presidents Make: Leadership from John Adams to Bill Clinton* (Cambridge: Belknap/Harvard University Press, 1997), 447–64. See also John J. Coleman, "Clinton and the Party System in Historical Perspective," in Schier, *Postmodern Presidency*, and Sidney M. Milkis, "The Presidency and Political Parties," in Michael Nelson, ed., *The Presidency and the Political System*, 6th ed. (Washington, D.C.: CQ Press, 2000), 395–401. We may question, however, as I will below, whether the Republicans actually consolidated such a regime.

20. Bert A. Rockman, "Leadership Style and the Clinton Presidency," in Colin Campbell and Rockman, eds., *The Clinton Presidency: First Appraisals* (Chatham, N.J.: Chatham House Publishers, 1996), 325–62.

21. At the end of Clinton's presidency, Glenn Kessler of the *Washington Post* observed: "Like many of the president's policies, his position on trade has evolved over time. He has sometimes tacked left, sometimes right." Kessler, "Score One for Legacy," *Washington Post*, September 20, 2000.

22. On such "activation" strategies, which he distinguishes from partisan strategies of mass "mobilization" intended to stimulate high voter turnout, see Steven Schier, *By Invitation Only: The Rise of Exclusive Politics in the United States* (Pittsburgh: University of Pittsburgh Press, 2000).

23. See Jon R. Bond and Richard Fleisher, eds., *Polarized Politics: Congress and the President in a Partisan Age* (Washington, D.C.: CQ Press, 2000).

24. Democratic defections from Clinton's position on roll-call votes were actually more common than might have been expected in light of the heightened congressional partisanship. But such defections on trade issues were still more common. See Richard Fleisher and Jon R. Bond, "Partisanship and the President's Quest for Votes on the Floor of Congress," in Bond and Fleisher, *Polarized Politics*, 154–85.

25. The Clinton administration, however, did negotiate labor and environmental side agreements to accompany NAFTA and pushed for the inclusion of similar provisions in

a fast-track measure to be included in the GATT implementing bill. These were positions that both Reagan and Bush would have opposed.

26. See Michael Reich, "Social Structure of Accumulation Theory: Retrospect and Prospect," and Victor D. Lippit, "The Reconstruction of a Social Structure of Accumulation in the United States," both in *Review of Radical Political Economics* 29, no. 3 (September 1997): 1–21.

27. In addition to Skowronek's book, see Martin Shefter and Benjamin Ginsberg, "Institutionalizing the Reagan Regime," in Ginsberg and Alan Stone, eds., *Do Elections Matter?* (Armonk, N.Y.: M. E. Sharpe, 1986), 191–203. At one point Skowronek himself seems to doubt Reagan's success in consolidating a conservative regime. Skowronek, *The Politics Presidents Make*, 428.

28. On these points, see Larry M. Schwab, *The Illusion of a Conservative Reagan Revolution* (New Brunswick, N.J.: Transaction Publishers, 1991); Paul Pierson, *Dismantling the Welfare State? Reagan, Thatcher, and the Politics of Retrenchment* (Cambridge: Cambridge University Press, 1984); and Steven E. Schier, "American Politics after Clinton," in Schier, ed., *The Postmodern Presidency: Bill Clinton's Legacy in U.S. Politics* (Pittsburgh: University of Pittsburgh Press, 2000), 255–65.

29. See Robert B. Reich, *The Work of Nations: Preparing Ourselves for 21st-Century Capitalism* (New York: Vintage Books, 1992).

30. On Clinton's business support, see Kirk Victor, "The Long Hello," *National Journal*, December 12, 1992, 2829–32; Paul Starobin, "An Affair to Remember," *National Journal*, January 16, 1993, 120–24; and Thomas Ferguson, " 'Real Change'? 'Organized Capitalism,' Fiscal Policy and the 1992 Election," *The Golden Rule: The Investment Theory of Political Parties and the Logic of Money-Driven Political Systems* (Chicago: University of Chicago Press, 1995), 275–345.

31. Clinton's plan was based on a report prepared by the industry-backed Council on Competitiveness following several meetings between Clinton and top Silicon Valley electronics executives. See Lee Gomes, "How Clinton Captured Heart of Silicon Valley," *San Jose Mercury*, September 28, 1992, and Calvin Sims, "Silicon Valley Takes Partisan Leap of Faith," *New York Times*, October 29, 1992.

32. Victor, "The Long Hello," 2829–30.

33. Barry Bluestone and Bennett Harrison, *Growing Prosperity: The Battle for Growth with Equity in the 21st Century* (New York: Houghton Mifflin, 2000). On some Clintonites' support for deficit reduction to attract the support of Perot backers, see Fred Barnes, "The Undead," *New Republic*, February 1, 1993, 21–22. On Clinton's plan, see Viveca Novak, "Spending Spree?," *National Journal*, February 27, 1993, 509–11.

34. According to a CNN/*Time* magazine poll, the view that "Bill Clinton is a tax-and-spend liberal" rose from 41 percent in February to 58 percent at the end of May. William Schneider, "Whatever Happened to Clintonomics?," *National Journal*, June 26, 1993, 1680. On the DLC criticisms, see Paul Richter, "Clinton Hears Rumblings within Own Ranks," *Los Angeles Times*, May 16, 1993.

35. For further analysis of the entire budget fight, including the demise of Clinton's original investment strategy, see Paul Pierson, "The Deficit and the Politics of Domestic Reform," in Margaret Weir, ed., *The Social Divide: Political Parties and the Future of Activist Government* (Washington, D.C.: Brookings Institution, 1998), 126–78, and M. Stephen Weatherford and Lorraine M. McDonnell, "Clinton and the Economy: The Paradox of Policy Success and Political Mishap," *Political Science Quarterly* 111, no. 3 (Fall 1996): 403–36.

36. *Public Papers of the Presidents of the United States: William J. Clinton*, 1993, Book 2 (Washington, D.C.: U.S. Government Printing Office, 1994), 2114, 2141. See also pp. 2096, 2121.

37. According to longtime Clinton friend and adviser, Derek Shearer. Burt Solomon, "Clinton Ventures into Diplomacy with the Touch of a Politician," *National Journal*, April 3, 1993, 835.

38. Douglas Harbrecht and Owen Ullman, "Clinton's Trade Route," *Business Week*, July 26, 1993, 24.

39. Barry Bluestone and Bennett Harrison argue that Clinton's "real objective" in pursuing these free-trade agreements was not increased exports but rather the neoliberal goal of combating inflation by keeping "downward pressure on wages and prices by spurring even more global competition." Bluestone and Harrison, *Growing Prosperity*, 15. I think, however, that Clinton's commitment to export promotion during the slow-growth years of the early 1990s was genuine and that his appreciation of the positive effects of imports only emerged strongly in his second term, when their role in containing inflation during the economic boom of the second half of the decade had become clear.

40. Michael K. Frisby and Gerald F. Seib, "Clinton's Nafta Drive Belies Nagging Doubts on His Commitment," *Wall Street Journal*, November 2, 1993.

41. Bob Davis, "U.S. Sets Tough Trade Agenda for Trade Talks with Japan," *Wall Street Journal*, June 9, 1993. For further analysis of the evolution of the administration's Japan policy during the spring of 1993, see Keith Bradsher, "For Clinton, 'Managed Trade' Is Emerging as Policy Option," *New York Times*, March 30, 1993, and Bruce Stokes, "Wary Partners," *National Journal*, April 10, 1993, 868–72.

42. On the growing influence of revisionism, see T. R. Reid and Paul Blustein, "The U.S. and Japan: Going No's to No's," *Washington Post National Weekly Edition*, May 3–9, 1993, 14; John B. Judis, "Rougher Trade," *New Republic*, May 31, 1993, 24–29; and Matthew Cooper and Jim Impoco, "The Making of a Trade Hawk," *U.S. News & World Report*, July 12, 1993, 28–29.

43. See, e.g., C. Fred Bergsten and Marcus Noland, *Reconcilable Differences? United States–Japan Economic Conflict* (Washington, D.C.: Institute for International Economics, 1993). Other mainstream, Democrat-aligned economists like Treasury Undersecretary Lawrence Summers, Robert Lawrence of the Brookings Institution, and Alan Blinder of Princeton University reached similar conclusions.

44. At Derek Shearer's recommendation, Clinton read books and articles by authors like Prestowitz, economists Lester Thurow and Laura Tyson, economic journalist Robert Kuttner, former U.S. trade negotiator Glenn Fukushima, and novelist Michael Crichton. Judis, "Rougher Trade"; Cooper and Impoco, "The Making of a Trade Hawk."

45. Drawing on revisionism and strategic trade theory, in her major work, *Who's Bashing Whom: Trade Conflict in High-Technology Industries* (Washington, D.C.: Institute of International Economics, 1992), Tyson argued for the use of both subsidies and a results-oriented trade policy to strengthen America's high-tech industries in their competition with Japanese rivals.

46. I. M. Destler, "Foreign Economic Policy Making under Bill Clinton," in James M. Scott, ed., *After the End: Making U.S. Foreign Policy in the Post–Cold War World* (Durham, N.C.: Duke University Press, 1998), 107.

47. Stokes, "Wary Partners," 871.

48. Retaining labor support was of particular importance to USTR Mickey Kantor.

"He's the principal person in the Administration who has remembered who the Administration's constituents are," said an AFL-CIO official. Bruce Stokes, "In Your Face," *National Journal*, August 21, 1993, 2071.

49. Such hopes were again buoyed by a continuing stream of polling results. For a comprehensive fall 1993 review of public opinion polls on trade in the late 1980s and early 1990s that similarly concluded that most Americans preferred a tough trade stance and argued that the Democratic Party could more easily attract the support of Perot voters by stressing "economic nationalism" rather than budget deficit reduction, see Ruy A. Teixeira and Guy Molyneux, *Economic Nationalism and the Future of American Politics* (Washington, D.C.: Economic Policy Institute, 1993).

50. Reid and Blustein, "The U.S. and Japan."

51. For three excellent, book-length analyses of the 1993 NAFTA battle, see George W. Grayson, *The North American Free Trade Agreement: Regional Community and the New World Order* (Lanham, Md.: University Press of America, 1995); Frederick W. Mayer, *Interpreting NAFTA: The Nature of Politics and the Art of Political Analysis* (New York: Columbia University Press, 1998); and Maxwell A. Cameron and Brian W. Tomlin, *The Making of NAFTA: How the Deal Was Done* (Ithaca, N.Y.: Cornell University Press, 2000). See also William P. Avery and H. Richard Friman, "Who Got What and Why: Constructing North American Free Trade," in Kenneth P. Thomas and Mary Ann Tetreault, eds., *Racing to Regionalize: Democracy, Capitalism, and Regional Political Economy* (Boulder, Colo.: Lynne Rienner Publishers, 1999); and John R. MacArthur, *The Selling of "Free Trade": NAFTA, Washington, and the Subversion of American Democracy* (New York: Hill and Wang, 2000).

52. For this discussion of the side agreements negotiations, see Grayson, *North American Free Trade Agreement*, 129–50; Mayer, *Interpreting NAFTA*, 168–204; Cameron and Tomlin, *Making of NAFTA*, 179–207; MacArthur, *Selling of "Free Trade,"* 174, 183; Judis, "Rougher Trade," 26; and Bruce Stokes, "Mexican Roulette," *National Journal*, May 15, 1993, 1160–64.

53. See Cameron and Tomlin, *Making of NAFTA*, 205.

54. Elizabeth Newlin Carney, "Suiting Up for Combat on Trade Pact," *National Journal*, January 2, 1993, 31–33; Charles Lewis and Margaret Ebrahim, "NAFTA's Opposition," *Nation*, June 14, 1993, 828.

55. See Ken Kollman, *Outside Lobbying: Public Opinion and Interest Group Strategies* (Princeton, N.J.: Princeton University Press, 1998), and Darrell West and Burdett Loomis, *The Sound of Money* (New York: Norton, 1999). For a related discussion of broader "activation" strategies used by parties, interest groups, and candidates to "induce particular, finely targeted portions of the public to become active in elections, demonstrations, and lobbying," see Schier, *By Invitation Only*.

56. For example, a July 1992 *Time/CNN* poll showed that respondents supported a free-trade agreement with Mexico by a 45–39 percent margin. But in June 1993, they opposed it 35–46 percent. "Public Uncertain, Executives United," *American Enterprise*, September–October 1993, 83. See also Alec Gallup and David W. Moore, "Public Leery of New Trade Agreement," *Gallup Poll Monthly*, August 1993, 2, and Gerald Seib, "Clinton Needs to Sway the Public on Nafta Issues as Poll Shows That Many Oppose the Agreement," *Wall Street Journal*, September 15, 1993.

57. See Ann Devroy and Kenneth J. Cooper, "House Republicans Warn Clinton of Eroding Trade-Pact Support," *Washington Post*, September 10, 1993; Bruce Stokes, "If NAFTA's Bogging Down, Is Hillary to Blame?," *National Journal*, October 2, 1993, 2381;

Grayson, *North American Free Trade Agreement*, 138–39, 196–98; MacArthur, *Selling of "Free Trade,"* 184; and Elizabeth Drew, *On the Edge: The Clinton Presidency* (New York: Simon and Schuster, 1994), 285, 288–90.

58. Pointing to these centrist issues, a senior White House aide said, "After being beaten bloody around the head and shoulders as a tax-and-spend Democrat the past months, this will give the president the opportunity to be for something America is for." Ann Devroy, "Post-Vacation Clinton Swims toward Mainstream," *Washington Post*, September 6, 1993. For more on Clinton's New Democrat turn, see Dan Balz and David Broder, "One Down, Two to Go," *Washington Post National Weekly Edition*, August 16–22, 1993, 11.

59. Bob Woodward, *The Agenda: Inside the Clinton White House* (New York: Simon and Schuster, 1994), 318. Against those who argued that Clinton should back away from NAFTA to avoid alienating labor, Lloyd Bentsen insisted that Clinton could demonstrate political courage by battling the AFL-CIO over the treaty, a position surprisingly seconded by Mickey Kantor. Drew, *On the Edge*, 289.

60. MacArthur, *Selling of "Free Trade,"* 215. In deciding to push for NAFTA, Clinton "wanted to be sure he wasn't seen as hostile" to business, said Clinton aide George Stephanopoulos. Jeffrey H. Birnbaum and David Wessel, "Nafta: The Road Ahead," *Wall Street Journal*, November 19, 1993.

61. Daniel Wirls, "The Consequences of Equal Representation: The Bicameral Politics of NAFTA in the 103rd Congress," *Congress & the Presidency* 25, no. 2 (Autumn 1998): 129–45. Senators' lengthy terms, weak Senate party leadership, and the chamber's foreign policy responsibilities also contributed to the stronger support for NAFTA in the Senate than was found in the House.

62. On these cross-pressured members and attempts to woo them, see David S. Cloud, "'Undecideds' Are Final Target in Battle over Trade Pact," *Congressional Quarterly Weekly Report*, November 6, 1993, 3011–22. On the overall effort made by Clinton and other administration officials on behalf of NAFTA, see, among many sources, Gwen Ifill, "The Free Trade Accord: How Clinton Won," *New York Times*, November 19, 1993; and Daniel J. Palazzolo and Bill Swinford, "'Remember in November'?: Ross Perot, Presidential Power, and the NAFTA" (paper presented at the annual meeting of the American Political Science Association, New York, September 1–4, 1994).

63. On this "vote-buying," see MacArthur, *Selling of "Free Trade,"* 257–66.

64. Ken Jennings and Jeffrey W. Steagall, "Unions and NAFTA's Legislative Passage: Confrontation and Cover," *Labor Studies Journal* 21, no. 1 (Spring 1996): 72.

65. USA*NAFTA consisted of groups like the U.S. Council of the Mexico-U.S. Business Committee, the National Foreign Trade Council, the Business Roundtable, and the National Association of Manufacturers.

66. On the business role in the pro-NAFTA effort, see Mayer, *Interpreting NAFTA*, 234–35; Cameron and Tomlin, *Making of NAFTA*, 201–2; MacArthur, *Selling of "Free Trade,"* chap. 4; Carney, "Suiting Up for Combat"; Stokes, "Mexican Roulette"; Richard E. Cohen, "Democratic Salvage Operation on NAFTA," *National Journal*, September 18, 1993, 2259; and Michael C. Dreiling, "The Class Embeddedness of Corporate Political Action: Leadership in Defense of the NAFTA," *Social Problems* 48, no. 1 (February 2000): 21–48.

67. Individual corporations serving as "captains" in each state were responsible for selling NAFTA to the public.

68. Joshua Mills, "Business Lobbying for Trade Pact Appears to Sway Few in Congress," *New York Times*, November 12, 1993. On the business lobbying effort, see Kollman, *Outside Lobbying*, 133–54; Kevin Goldman, "Nafta Supporters and Foes Pitch Views to Public in Ad Campaign," *Wall Street Journal*, September 16, 1993; Bruce Stokes, "A Hard Sell," *National Journal*, October 16, 1993, 2472–76; and Peter Stone, "Lobbyists Lend a Hand on NAFTA," *National Journal*, October 30, 1993, 2595–96.

69. For the next several paragraphs, see Kollman, *Outside Lobbying*; Jennings and Steagall, "Unions and NAFTA's Legislative Passage"; Jack W. Germond and Jules Witcover, "Labor's Huge Stake in NAFTA Battle," *National Journal*, September 25, 1993, 2329; Peter T. Kilborn, "Unions Gird for War over Trade Pact," *New York Times*, October 4, 1993; and Jefferson Cowie, "National Struggles in a Transnational Economy: A Critical Analysis of US Labor's Campaign against NAFTA," *Labor Studies Journal* 21, no. 4 (Winter 1994): 3–32.

70. The hotly debated sources of this decline include the shift from manufacturing to services, the introduction of labor-saving technology, the relocation of production to nonunionized sites in the United States and abroad, new management techniques to avoid and combat unions, the reemergence of popular cultural hostility to unions, lax union organizing efforts, the spread of government-mandated benefits that have replaced union-provided benefits, and a more hostile labor law regime.

71. For the next two paragraphs, see Taylor Dark, *The Unions and the Democrats: An Enduring Alliance* (Ithaca, N.Y.: Cornell University Press, 1999), 158–65.

72. Labor lobbyists targeted freshman Democrats, who had received 44 percent of their PAC contributions from organized labor in the 1992 elections, compared to 31 percent for their more senior colleagues. Jennings and Steagall, "Unions and NAFTA's Legislative Passage."

73. Thomas Galvin, "PACs: Silence Speaks Volumes," *Congressional Quarterly Weekly Report*, September 18, 1993, 2437. Members who had voted for fast track in 1991 had already seen a decline in their contributions from labor PACs. Grayson, *North American Free Trade Agreement*, 191.

74. A survey by pollsters Mark Mellman and Celinda Lake of Mellman-Lake-Lazarus found that 58 percent of Perot voters opposed NAFTA, more than half of them strongly. Tim Curran, "NAFTA Holdouts Looking to 1994," *Roll Call*, November 8, 1993, 1.

75. On Republican divisions and maneuvers over NAFTA, see MacArthur, *Selling of "Free Trade,"* 252; Stokes, "Hard Sell"; David S. Cloud, "GOP Wants to See Democrats' Hand before Getting into Game," *Congressional Quarterly Weekly Report*, September 18, 1993, 2438–39; and Gerald F. Seib, "Nafta Vote Holds a Political Test for the GOP, Too," *Wall Street Journal*, November 3, 1993.

76. John Aloysius Farrell, "NAFTA Fraying Ties That Bind GOP," *Boston Globe*, September 26, 1993.

77. Cloud, "GOP Wants to See Democrats' Hand."

78. On the intra-Democratic split over NAFTA, see Dan Balz, "NAFTA Forces Each Party to Face Internal Divisions," *Washington Post*, November 17, 1993; Thomas B. Edsall, "NAFTA Debate Reopens Wounds in the Body of the Democratic Party," *Washington Post*, October 24, 1993; and David S. Broder, "NAFTAmath," *Washington Post*, November 19, 1993.

79. Edsall, "NAFTA Debate Reopens Wounds."

80. Representative Robert T. Matsui (D-Calif.), a leader of the pro-NAFTA forces who

represented a high-growth, prosperous Sacramento district, argued: "If Democrats want to reach out and remain the majority party in the 1990s, we are going to have to reach out to suburban America." Edsall, "NAFTA Debate Reopens Wounds."

81. John Aloysius Farrell, "Senate's OK Finalizes NAFTA Pact," *Boston Globe*, November 21, 1993.

82. Edsall, "NAFTA Debate Reopens Wounds."

83. A *Washington Post*/ABC News poll conducted on November 11–14 found 42 percent in favor of the pact and 42 percent opposed. A September 19 ABC News poll had determined that only 33 percent of those surveyed thought that NAFTA should be approved and 45 percent thought that it should be rejected. Peter Behr, "Poll Shows Nation Is Split on NAFTA," *Washington Post*, November 16, 1993. For similar poll results, see Gwen Ifill, "The Free Trade Accord: The Mood," *New York Times*, November 16, 1993; Mayer, *Interpreting NAFTA*, 315; and Kollman, *Outside Lobbying*, 152.

84. For the view that NAFTA supporters reduced the political pressure on House members by changing public opinion, members' perceptions of public opinion, and members' beliefs about NAFTA, see Mayer, *Interpreting NAFTA*, 320–34.

85. In the Senate, support for the pact was stronger in both parties than it had been in the House. Republican senators backed the agreement 34–10, and Democrats barely opposed it 27–28.

86. See Grayson, *North American Free Trade Agreement*, 219–20; Wirls, "Consequences of Equal Representation"; Palazzolo and Swinford, "'Remember in November'?"; Jennings and Steagall, "Unions and NAFTA's Legislative Passage"; John A. C. Conybeare and Mark Zinkula, "Who Voted against NAFTA? Trade Unions versus Free Trade," *World Economy* 19, no. 1 (January 1996): 1–12; Lawrence Mishel and Ruy A. Teixeira, "The Political Arithmetic of the NAFTA Vote" (Briefing Paper, Economic Policy Institute, Washington, D.C., November 18, 1993); Jon Healey and Thomas H. Moore, "Clinton Forms New Coalition to Win NAFTA's Approval," *Congressional Quarterly Weekly Report*, November 20, 1993, 3181–83; Charles F. Doran, "The NAFTA Vote and Political Party," in Doran and Gregory M. Marchildon, eds., *The NAFTA Puzzle: Political Parties and Trade in North America* (Boulder, Colo.: Westview Press, 1994), 247–62; Gordon L. Clark, "NAFTA—Clinton's Victory, Organized Labor's Loss," *Political Geography Quarterly* 13, no. 4 (July 1994): 377–84; Fred M. Shelley, J. Clark Archer, Fiona M. Davidson, and Stanley D. Brunn, *Political Geography of the United States* (New York: Guilford Press, 1996), 224–27; and Albert J. Menendez, *The Perot Voters and the Future of American Politics* (Amherst, N.Y.: Prometheus Books, 1996), 201–9.

Also Jeffrey W. Steagall and Ken Jennings, "Unions, PAC Contributions, and the NAFTA Vote," *Journal of Labor Research* 17, no. 3 (Summer 1996): 515–21; Leo H. Kahane, "Congressional Voting Patterns on NAFTA: An Empirical Analysis," *American Journal of Economics and Sociology* 55, no. 4 (October 1996): 395–409; Kenneth A. Wink, C. Don Livingston, and James C. Garand, "Dispositions, Constituencies, and Cross-Pressures: Modeling Roll-Call Voting on the North American Free Trade Agreement in the U.S. House," *Political Research Quarterly* 49, no. 4 (December 1996): 729–48; C. Don Livingston and Kenneth A. Wink, "The Passage of the North American Free Trade Agreement in the U.S. House of Representatives: Presidential Leadership or Presidential Luck?," *Presidential Studies Quarterly* 27, no. 1 (Winter 1997): 52–70; Janet Box-Steffensmeir, Laura W. Arnold, and Christopher J. S. Zorn, "The Strategic Timing of Position Taking in Congress: A Study of the North American Free Trade Agreement," *American Political Science*

Review 91, no. 2 (June 1997): 324–38; David B. Hollian, Timothy B. Krebs, and Michael H. Walsh, "Constituency Opinion, Ross Perot, and Roll-Call Behavior in the U.S. House: The Case of NAFTA," *Legislative Studies Quarterly* 22, no. 3 (August 1997): 369–92; and Willem Thorbecke, "Explaining House Voting on the North American Free Trade Agreement," *Public Choice* 92, nos. 3–4 (September 1997): 231–42.

Also see Sharyn O'Halloran, "Comment," in Susan M. Collins, ed., *Imports, Exports, and the American Worker* (Washington, D.C.: Brookings Institution Press, 1998), 412–20; David W. Brady and Craig Volden, *Revolving Gridlock: Politics and Policy From Carter to Clinton* (Boulder, Colo.: Westview Press, 1998), 126–30; Eric M. Uslaner, "Let the Chits Fall Where They May? Executive and Constituency Influences on Congressional Voting on NAFTA," *Legislative Studies Quarterly* 23, no. 3 (August 1998): 347–71; Eric M. Uslaner, "Trade Winds: NAFTA and the Rational Public," *Political Behavior* 20, no. 4 (December 1998): 341–60; In-Bong Kang and Kenneth Greene, "A Political Economic Analysis of Congressional Voting Patterns on NAFTA," *Public Choice* 98, nos. 3–4 (March 1999): 385–97; Robert E. Baldwin and Christopher S. Magee, *Congressional Trade Votes: From NAFTA Approval to Fast-Track Defeat* (Washington, D.C.: Institute for International Economics, 2000); and Robert E. Baldwin and Christopher S. Magee, "Is Trade Policy for Sale? Congressional Voting on Recent Trade Bills," *Public Choice* 105, nos. 1–2 (October 2000): 79–101.

87. Whereas studies using *state*-level data find no correlation between levels of unionization and member opposition to NAFTA (Wink, Livingston, and Garand; Kahane), analyses employing more appropriate *district*-level data do find such effects (Box-Steffensmeir, Arnold, and Zorn; Conybeare and Zinkula; Uslaner; Baldwin and Magee). In all studies, the correlation between labor PAC contributions as a percentage of a member's total PAC or overall contributions and the likelihood of that member's opposing NAFTA is very strong. In districts where Democratic members got 20 percent or more of their total campaign contributions from labor PACs, 77 percent of those members opposed the treaty. Or, according to the Center for Responsive Politics, 78 percent of House Democrats who voted against NAFTA received more campaign funds from unions than from business.

88. Calculated from Norman J. Ornstein, Thomas E. Mann, and Michael J. Malbin, eds., *Vital Statistics in Congress, 1999–2000* (Washington, D.C.: AEI Press, 2000), 103–5.

89. Democrats who received more money from business PACs than labor PACs voted 82–88 against NAFTA.

90. Surprisingly, anti- and pro-NAFTA Democrats did not differ significantly with respect to whether their constituents were predominantly urban or suburban, blue- or white-collar, low- or high-income, or noncollege or college-educated. Mishel and Teixeira, "Political Arithmetic."

91. See esp. Palazzolo and Swinford, "'Remember in November'?"; Uslaner, "Let the Chits Fall Where They May?."

92. Wink, Livingston, Garand, "Dispositions, Constituencies, and Cross-Pressures."

93. See Jon R. Bond and Richard Fleisher, *The President in the Legislative Arena* (Chicago: University of Chicago Press, 1990), and George C. Edwards III, *At the Margins: Presidential Leadership of Congress* (New Haven: Yale University Press, 1989).

94. In an analysis of House members who switched their positions between the 1991 fast-track and the 1993 NAFTA votes, David Brady and Craig Volden find little or no evidence that Clinton's bargaining and persuasive efforts won support for NAFTA.

Brady and Volden, *Revolving Gridlock*, 126–33. David Karol also minimizes the effectiveness of such presidential efforts, but he acknowledges that Clinton won over fifteen Democratic fast-track opponents while losing only seven Republican fast-track supporters, for a net gain of eight votes. Karol, "Divided Government and U.S. Trade Policy: Much Ado about Nothing?," *International Organization* 54, no. 4 (Autumn 2000): 834. As noted above, direct evidence of Clinton's successful lobbying has been provided by a number of authors, but Brady and Volden and Karol do not cite their findings. These analysts err in neglecting the fact that labor pressure on congressional Democrats to oppose NAFTA in 1993 was considerably stronger than it had been before the 1991 fast-track vote. Without Clinton's energetic and successful lobbying of fellow party members under unified government, NAFTA would have received still less Democratic support from labor-pressured members than it actually did, thus likely dooming the agreement. And had the 1993 level of labor opposition prevailed two years earlier with Bush presiding over a divided government, fast track might well have been defeated.

95. MacArthur, *Selling of "Free Trade,"* 18. The respected *National Journal* trade writer, Bruce Stokes, similarly reported that "most Capitol Hill handicappers believe that no Republican Administration could have persuaded Congress to pass the North American trade pact." Stokes, "Out for Kantor's Scalp? Take a Number," *National Journal*, December 10, 1994, 2915. For the same conclusion, see Doran, "The NAFTA Vote," 256, and Helen Milner, *Interests, Institutions, and Information: Domestic Politics and International Relations* (Princeton, N.J.: Princeton University Press), 214.

96. Barnaby Feder, "Business Chiefs Praise Clinton for Stand on Japan," *New York Times*, February 21, 1994.

97. A Gallup Poll taken on the eve of the House vote showed that the pact was disproportionately supported by affluent, college-educated, white-collar voters; it was opposed by less affluent, noncollege-educated, blue-collar voters. Teixeira and Michel, "Political Arithmetic," 4.

98. Clinton won nineteen states in the election that he did carry on the NAFTA vote.

99. See Ann Devroy and Dan Balz, "For President, Coalitions Are in Constant Flux," *Washington Post*, November 18, 1993.

100. David Broder, "Labor's NAFTA-Math: 1 Trade Pact = 3-Month Cut in Funds for Democrats," *Washington Post*, December 7, 1993.

101. Dark, *The Unions and the Democrats*, 170–72.

102. Paul Magnusson and Owen Ullman, "The Second Year," *Business Week*, January 24, 1994, 68–74.

103. Keith Bradsher, "Mickey Kantor," *New York Times Magazine*, December 12, 1993; Jim Hoagland, "Pushing Japan to the Brink," *Washington Post National Weekly Edition*, February 28–March 6, 1994, 29; Paul Blustein and Peter Behr, "U.S.-Japan Trade Talks: Trust Is the Biggest Gap," *Washington Post*, January 25, 1994.

104. This legislation was offered by House Majority Leader Dick Gephardt and Senator Jay Rockefeller (D-W.Va.) and separately by Senator Max Baucus (D-Mont.).

105. Hobart Rowen, "Wall Street's High Anxiety over Reviving 'Super 301,'" *Washington Post*, March 27, 1994.

106. Robert Neff, "The Japanese Are Hardly Heading for the Bunkers," *Business Week*, February 28, 1994, 29–31.

107. See Bruce Stokes, "The Money-Go-Round," *National Journal*, September 3, 1994, 2026–30. See also Thomas Friedman, "Trade Ties Bind, Indeed," *New York Times*, May 25, 1994, and Steven Pearlstein, "Wall Street's Wild Ride," *Washington Post*, March 5, 1994.

108. Friedman, "Trade Ties Bind"; Stokes, "The Money-Go-Round," 2026; Douglas Harbrecht, "Trade with Japan: Why the Doves Are Flying High Again," *Business Week*, July 4, 1994, 45.

109. Douglas Harbrecht, "Why Washington Backed Down at the Midnight Hour," *Business Week*, October 17, 1994, 46. See also R. Taggart Murphy, *The Weight of the Yen: How Denial Imperils America's Future and Ruins an Alliance* (New York: Norton, 1997), 293.

110. David S. Cloud, "Extension of Fast-Track Rules Seen Prodding GATT Talks," *Congressional Quarterly Weekly Report*, May 1, 1993, 1076.

111. Among the key changes in the new agreement were (1) tariff cuts on approximately 85 percent of world trade, including reductions in industrial tariffs averaging 40 percent, (2) the inclusion of farm commodities under GATT for the first time, with modest cuts in agricultural and export subsidies, (3) the phasing out of the Multi-Fiber Arrangement (MFA) on textile and apparel trade over ten years, (4) the preservation of American and European authority to use domestic antidumping laws against countries that exported goods at prices below cost, (5) a comprehensive agreement on trade safeguards, including the outlawing of voluntary export restraints, (6) the restriction of domestic industrial subsidies, except for government-supported research and development, (7) the extension of GATT rules to protect trade-related intellectual property rights (TRIPs), (8) a new General Agreement on Trade in Services (GATS) to govern the estimated $1 billion in world trade in services, (9) strengthened dispute settlement procedures, which removed the ability of a party found guilty to block a decision, and (10) the replacement of the GATT with a new World Trade organization (WTO), a permanent body with greater authority to force member nations to comply with Uruguay Round agreements. However, multilateral agreements to open markets in specific service sectors, such as shipping, banking, and insurance, proved elusive. For this summary, see I. M. Destler, *American Trade Politics*, 3d ed. (Washington, D.C.: Institute for International Economics and Twentieth Century Fund, 1995), 231–32.

112. Baldwin and Magee, *Congressional Trade Votes*, 42.

113. David S. Cloud with Heather M. Fleming, "Senate Panel Narrowly OKs GATT Financing Package," *Congressional Quarterly Weekly Report*, July 30, 1994, 2118–19.

114. See John Maggs, "Bill Ties Chile Talks to Labor, Environmental Issues," *Journal of Commerce*, May 10, 1994, 1A, and David S. Cloud, "Panels Tackle Fast Track, Financing," *Congressional Quarterly Weekly Report*, July 23, 1994, 2008.

115. On the administration's labor standards campaign, see Bruce Stokes, "The New Linkage," *National Journal*, June 25, 1994, 1509–14. More generally on the labor standards issue and its role at the WTO, see Robert O'Brien, Anne Marie Goetz, Jan Aart Scholte, and Marc Williams, *Contesting Globalization: Multilateral Economic Institutions and Global Social Movements* (Cambridge: Cambridge University Press, 2000).

116. Bruce Stokes, "Why a GATT Go-Ahead Is No Done Deal," *National Journal*, June 4, 1994, 1303.

117. Destler, *American Trade Politics*, 245.

118. More generally on such intrabranch sources of legislative gridlock, see Sarah Binder, "The Dynamics of Legislative Gridlock," *American Political Science Review* 93, no. 3 (September 1999): 519–33.

119. Bob Benenson, "With Health Care Receding, GATT Pact Gains Urgency," *Congressional Quarterly Weekly Report*, September 24, 1994, 2661–66; John Maggs, "Clinton May Use Trade Pact to Boost Candidates," *Journal of Commerce*, September 26, 1994.

120. The Alliance for GATT NOW had been formed the previous February by the Business Roundtable and included the National Association of Manufacturers and the U.S. Chamber of Commerce. Again as on NAFTA, the coalition mounted a three-pronged, $2 million campaign on behalf of the agreement involving Washington lobbying, grassroots mobilization, and advertising and public relations. On the business campaign in support of the GATT accord, see Robert Weissman, "GATT: The Final Act," *Multinational Monitor*, October 1994, 7–14, and Peter H. Stone, "Friends, after All," *National Journal*, October 22, 1994, 2440–45.

121. On opposition to the GATT deal, see Weissman, "GATT: The Final Act"; Keith Bradsher, "No Rest on Trade," *New York Times*, October 3, 1994; and Susan Aaronson, *Taking Trade to the Streets: The Lost History of Public Efforts to Shape Globalization* (Ann Arbor: University of Michigan Press, 2001), chap. 6.

122. Baldwin and Magee, *Congressional Trade Votes*, 29, 42; Martha L. Gibson, *Conflict amid Consensus in American Trade Policy* (Washington, D.C.: Georgetown University Press, 2000), 11–12; Aaronson, *Taking Trade to the Streets*.

123. On the parties' positions at this time, see Peter Behr, "Voter Shift Threatens Old Trade Coalition," *Washington Post*, October 7, 1994; Bob Davis and David Rogers, "Democrats Vow to Take Up Trade Pact Despite Attempt by Gingrich for Delay," *Wall Street Journal*, October 5, 1994; and Keith Bradsher, "The G.O.P. Looks Homeward on Trade," *New York Times*, October 16, 1994.

124. Ann Devroy, "GOP Taking Joy In Obstructionism," *Washington Post*, October 7, 1994; Behr, "Voter Shift Threatens Old Trade Coalition."

125. According to one set of exit polls, only 3 percent of those who voted listed trade as their top concern. Jeffrey H. Birnbaum, "Democrats, Seeking Path Back to Power, Fear Clinton Is Off Track with Focus on Free Trade," *Wall Street Journal*, November 21, 1994. See also Alan Murray, "Global Trade Fizzles as an Election Issue," *Wall Street Journal*, November 7, 1994. One reason for the apparently low salience of the trade issue was the failure of organized labor to effectively carry out its threat to retaliate against the 102 Democrats who had voted for NAFTA the previous year. Not one Democratic NAFTA supporter was denied renomination, and of the 35 Democrats who were defeated in the general election, 16 had supported the pact and 19 had opposed it. Jennings and Steagall, "Unions and NAFTA's Legislative Passage," 76–77; Heather M. Fleming, "Labor Working to Strengthen Weakened Political Muscle," *Congressional Quarterly Weekly Report*, September 24, 1994, 2718–20.

126. Joyce Price, "GATT Not Good for GOP, Poll Says," *Washington Times*, November 24, 1994; David E. Sanger, "New Status Puts Dole in Cross Currents on GATT," *New York Times*, November 18, 1994.

127. See ibid., and Alissa J. Rubin, "Dole, Clinton Compromise Greases Wheels for GATT," *Congressional Quarterly Weekly Report*, November 26, 1994, 3405.

128. Erik Gartzke and Mark Wrighton found that in both houses, the more liberal the members or senators or the more loyal they were to the AFL-CIO as measured by previous floor votes in support of federation positions, the more likely they were to oppose the GATT accord. Erik Gartzke and J. Mark Wrighton, "Thinking Globally or Acting Locally? Determinants of the GATT Vote in Congress," *Legislative Studies Quarterly* 23, no. 1 (February 1998): 33–55.

129. Birnbaum, "Democrats, Seeking Path Back to Power."

130. That most Democrats accepted this view is indicated by Baldwin and Magee's findings that (1) the degree of unionization did not significantly influence voting pat-

terns on the bill, (2) a high proportion of less-educated workers was actually associated with a greater likelihood of the lawmaker voting for the bill, and (3) there was a statistically significant negative relation between the unemployment rate in a House member's district and the possibility of a favorable GATT vote. Baldwin and Magee, *Congressional Trade Votes*, 42.

131. Gartzke and Wrighton ("Thinking Globally or Acting Locally?") suggest that such a Republican desire for partisan point scoring, combined with the concern of some Democrats to bolster the legislative record of a president from their own party, explains why normally free-trading House Republicans—though not their Senate colleagues—were more apt to oppose the GATT deal than were often protectionist-inclined Democrats.

132. Bruce Stokes, "Trade Deal Heads Down a Shaky Track," *National Journal*, November 26, 1994, 2784–85; David E. Sanger, "Senate Seems Set to Approve Trade Accord," *New York Times*, December 1, 1994; Douglas Harbrecht, " 'Delay Would Mean the Death of GATT,' " *Business Week*, December 5, 1994, 34–36.

133. Stokes, "Out for Kantor's Scalp?."

Chapter 8

1. On these points, see I. M. Destler and John S. Odell, *Anti-Protection: Changing Forces in United States Trade Politics* (Washington, D.C.: Institute for International Economics, September 1987); David Vogel, "The Triumph of Liberal Trade: American Trade Policy in the Postwar Period," in Morton Keller and R. Shep Melnick, eds., *Taking Stock: American Government in the Twentieth Century* (Cambridge: Woodrow Wilson Center Press and Cambridge University Press, 1999), 35–53; Michael Lusztig, "The Limits of Rent Seeking: Why Protectionists Become Free Traders," *Review of International Political Economy* 5, no. 1 (Spring 1998): 38–63; Oona A. Hathaway, "Positive Feedback: The Impact of Trade Liberalization on Industry Demands for Protection," *International Organization* 52, no. 3 (Summer 1998): 575–612; and John B. Goodman, Debora Spar, and David B. Yoffie, "Foreign Direct Investment and the Demand for Protection in the United States," *International Organization* 50, no. 4 (Autumn 1996): 565–91.

2. For additional discussion of the events covered in this chapter, see the following works by I. M. Destler: *Renewing Fast-Track Legislation* (Washington, D.C.: Institute for International Economics, 1997), 16–27; "Foreign Economic Policy Making under Bill Clinton," in James M. Scott, ed., *After the End: Making U.S. Foreign Policy in the Post–Cold War World* (Durham, N.C: Duke University Press, 1998); and with Peter J. Balint, *The New Politics of American Trade: Trade, Labor, and the Environment* (Washington, D.C.: Institute for International Economics, 1999).

3. John Maggs, "US Resolve Toughens on Japan Autos, Parts Trade," *Journal of Commerce*, April 17, 1995, 1A; Douglas Harbrecht, Mike McNamee, and Dean Foust, "Showdown Time for U.S.-Japan Trade?," *Business Week*, April 24, 1995, 48–49.

4. On the postelection debate, see James A. Barnes and Richard E. Cohen, "Seeking the Center," *National Journal*, November 12, 1994, 2622–24; John B. Judis, "From Hell," *New Republic*, December 19, 1994, 14–19; and Bill Turque and Bob Cohn, "Why Clinton Won't Play Class War," *Newsweek*, April 24, 1995, 31–32. See also Kenneth Baer, *Reinventing Democrats: The Politics of Liberalism from Reagan to Clinton* (Lawrence: University Press of Kansas, 2000), 231–33; E. J. Dionne, *They Only Look Dead: Why Progressives Will Dominate the Next Political Era* (New York: Simon and Schuster, 1996); and Jeff Faux,

The Party's Not Over: A New Vision for the Democrats (New York: Basic Books, 1996). For academic analysis of the 1994 election results, see David W. Brady, John F. Cogan, Brian J. Gaines, and Douglas Rivers, "The Perils of Presidential Support: How the Republicans Took the House in the 1994 Midterm Elections," *Political Behavior* 18, no. 4 (December 1996): 345–67, and Philip A. Klinkner, ed., *Midterm: The Elections of 1994 in Context* (Boulder, Colo.: Westview Press, 1996). The DLC based its views on a postelection poll conducted by liberal Clinton pollster Stanley Greenberg. Dan Balz, "Health Plan Was Albatross for Democrats," *Washington Post*, November 18, 1994.

5. On Reich's analysis of the predicament of the "anxious class," see Frank Swoboda, "Helping the 'Anxious Class,'" *Washington Post National Weekly Edition*, October 3–9, 1994, 19. See also Ruy Teixeira, *The Politics of the High-Wage Path: The Challenge Facing Democrats*, Working Paper 110 (Washington, D.C.: Economic Policy Institute, October 1994). Despite his polling work for the DLC, this was also largely the view of Clinton pollster Stanley Greenberg, who was exiled from the administration after the 1994 election, mainly for having overestimated the likely popular support for the Clinton health care plan. See Stanley B. Greenberg, "After the Republican Surge," *American Prospect*, Fall 1995, 66–72.

6. See, e.g., Jeff Faux, "A New Conversation: How to Rebuild the Democratic Party," *American Prospect*, Spring 1995, 35.

7. Judis, "From Hell"; Robert Marshall Wells, "A Longtime Voting Bloc Falls with Southern Democrats," *Congressional Quarterly Weekly Report*, December 31, 1994, 3627–29.

8. On the partisan shift in PAC contributions and its implications, see Thomas B. Edsall, "The Decline and Fall of the Democratic Party," *Washington Post National Weekly Edition*, November 28–December 4, 1994, 23, and Jonathan D. Salant and David S. Cloud, "To the '94 Election Victors Go the Fundraising Spoils," *Congressional Quarterly Weekly Report*, April 15, 1995, 1055–59.

9. On Gephardt's role, see Ronald Brownstein, "Gephardt Presents Risky Challenge to Clinton's Global Economic Vision," *Los Angeles Times*, February, 13, 1995, and David Corn, "Dick Gephardt: Working-Class Hero, On-the-Make Pol or Both?," *Nation*, July 7, 1997, 11–16.

10. David S. Broder, "Bill Clinton's Free Ride," *Washington Post National Weekly Edition*, December 25–31, 1995, 12–13.

11. On Kantor and Morris's roles, see John Maggs, "Dick Morris Helped Kantor Get Tough on Japan," *Journal of Commerce*, November 21, 1996, 1A.

12. John F. Harris, "Clinton Defends Free-Trade Record but Warns Japan," *Washington Post*, June 28, 1995. In the Midwest as a whole in 1994, the Republicans picked up 15 House seats, won all 4 open Senate races, and swept 8 of the 9 governorships, 6 of them with more than 60 percent of the vote.

13. Although the evidence is mixed, some observers suggested that several dozen Democratic lawmakers who had voted for NAFTA in 1993 lost to Republicans in 1994 partly because alienated union members stayed away from the polls. Jill Abramson with Steven Greenhouse, "The Trade Bill: Labor," *New York Times*, November 12, 1997. Gary Jacobson's statistical analysis of the 1994 House elections demonstrates that incumbent Democrats who voted for NAFTA were hurt by their positions. Gary C. Jacobsen, "The 1994 House Elections in Perspective," in Klinkner, *Midterm*. But David Brady and his coauthors find no such NAFTA effect. Brady et. al., "The Perils of Presidential Support."

14. Robert S. McElvaine, *What's Left? A New Democratic Vision for America* (Hol-

brook, Mass.: Adams Media Corporation, 1996), 121. See also Bob Davis, Angelo B. Henderson, and Michael Williams, "Getting Serious: U.S. Trade Flap Intensifies as U.S. Sets Early Date for Tariffs," *Wall Street Journal*, May 17, 1995, and Amy Borrus, "Your Move, Japan," *Business Week*, May 22, 1995, 38–40.

15. Paul Richter, "Pact Gives Clinton Pluses on the Political Front," *Los Angeles Times*, June 29, 1995. A *Wall Street Journal*/NBC News poll found that by a 72–19 percent margin, the public approved of the administration's sanction plan. Bob Davis, "U.S.'s Quick-Hit Strategy May Backfire in Long Run," *Wall Street Journal*, June 9, 1995.

16. John Maggs, "Gephardt Introduces Unfair-Trade Measure," *Journal of Commerce*, May 4, 1955, 1A.

17. David E. Sanger, "Sanctions of Japan: The Overview," *New York Times*, May 17, 1995.

18. David E. Sanger, "U.S. Plans to Threaten Japan with Tariffs in Trade Dispute," *New York Times*, April 13, 1995.

19. Maggs, "US Resolve Toughens on Japan Autos, Parts Trade"; Douglas Harbrecht, Mike McNamee, and Dean Foust, "Showdown Time for U.S.-Japan Trade?," *Business Week*, April 24, 1995, 48–49.

20. In fact, the May 10 announcement of the U.S. actions pushed the dollar up slightly against the yen. Big Three auto stocks also jumped.

21. The United States had won concessions from Japan in previous negotiations by finding allies inside that country who supported the American position. But in the auto case, Washington was attacking not only a core Japanese industry, but also the country's whole interlocking keiretsu system, which was widely believed to constitute one of Japan's major competitive advantages. See Leonard Schoppa, *Bargaining with Japan: What American Pressure Can and Cannot Do* (New York: Columbia University Press, 1997), 254–55, 268–74.

22. David Sanger, "U.S. Settles Trade Dispute, Averting Billions in Tariffs on Japanese Luxury Autos," *New York Times*, June 29, 1995; John B. Judis, "Dollar Foolish," *New Republic*, December 9, 1996, 23–24; R. Taggart Murphy, *The Weight of the Yen: How Denial Imperils America's Future and Ruins an Alliance* (New York: Norton, 1996) and "Japan's Economic Crisis," *New Left Review* 1 (January–February 2000): 25–52; Robert Brenner, "The Boom and the Bubble," *New Left Review* 6 (November–December 2000): 5–43.

23. Susan B. Garland with Brian Bremner, "Japan: Why Clinton's Trader Warriors Are Making Nice," *Business Week*, November 27, 1995, 50; Phred Dvorak, "Distress, Deregulation, and Diplomacy Breach Walls of Fortress Japan," *Wall Street Journal*, December 28, 2000. See also Michael Mastanduno, "Models, Markets, and Power: Political Economy and the Asia-Pacific, 1989–1999," *Review of International Studies* 26, no. 4 (October 2000): 493–507. Mastanduno argues that the reduction of U.S.-Japan trade tensions after mid-1995 was due mainly to the new priority given by the Clinton administration to security concerns in Asia. I maintain, however, that other factors mentioned in this paragraph were equally important.

24. On Clinton's increasing reliance on Penn and Schoen's polls, see John F. Harris, "A Clouded Mirror: Bill Clinton, Polls, and the Politics of Survival," in Steven E. Schier, ed., *The Postmodern Presidency: Bill Clinton's Legacy in U.S. Politics* (Pittsburgh: University of Pittsburgh Press, 2000), 87–105.

25. Thomas B. Edsall, "House Democrats, Clinton Are at a Fork in the Road," *Washington Post*, September 18, 1995. In August one Clinton adviser acknowledged: "Lately

we've been cowed into the position of not sticking up for working people, because we've been looking increasingly to wealthy interests in order to fund our campaign." Thomas Ferguson, "Impeachment, the Clinton Presidency, and the Politics of Division," in William Crotty, ed., *The State of Democracy in America* (Washington, D.C.: Georgetown University Press, forthcoming). See also Susan B. Garland, "A Hard Sell Called Clinton," *Business Week*, July 3, 1995, 26–28.

26. Burton Solomon, "Clinton: The Sequel," *National Journal*, August 24, 1996, 1788–93.

27. For more on this episode, see Destler, *Renewing Fast-Track Legislation*, 20–23.

28. "Rotten Tomatoes," *Economist*, February 10, 1996, 74–75; Helene Cooper, "Shift into Reverse: Ban on Mexican Trucks In U.S. Interior Shows Rise of Protectionism," *Wall Street Journal*, February 5, 1996.

29. Michael Kramer, "Flaw in the Formula," *Time*, March 4, 1996, 35. See also Richard Lacayo, "The Case against Buchanan," *Time*, March 4, 1996, 28, and "America's Professed Protectionists Are Really Free-Traders as Well," *Wall Street Journal*, March 8, 1995.

30. The United States had previously backed away from talks on liberalizing trade in banking, insurance, and securities and had refused to negotiate on maritime trade. Helene Cooper and Bhushan Bahree, "U.S. Is Signaling Radical Change in Trade Tactics," *Wall Street Journal*, May 2, 1996; Paul Lewis, "Is the U.S. Souring on Free Trade?," *New York Times*, June 25, 1996.

31. Burt Solomon, "Clinton: California on His Mind," *National Journal*, January 20, 1996, 134; Keith B. Richburg, "U.S. Withdraws Its Threat of Sanctions against China," *Washington Post*, June 18, 1996. The United States had threatened to impose $3 billion in tariffs on Chinese exports, including $2 billion on textile and apparel exports alone. The White House hoped that the move would score political points with labor unions and workers in the textile states, particularly in the South. Helene Cooper and Kathy Chen, "U.S. and China Announce Tariff Targets as Both Nations Step Up Trade Rhetoric," *Wall Street Journal*, May 16, 1996.

32. Michael K. Frisby, "Clinton to Press Hashimoto over Trade," *Wall Street Journal*, June 27, 1996.

33. David E. Sanger, "For U.S.-Japan Trade Pact, Less at Stake," *New York Times*, August 5, 1996.

34. Ben Wildavsky, "One Issue Whose Time Isn't Now," *National Journal*, October 5, 1996, 2125–26.

35. Ibid.

36. Paula L. Green, "USTR Slaps China with Textile Charges," *Journal of Commerce*, September 9, 1996, 1A; David E. Sanger, "President Wins Tomato Accord," *New York Times*, October 12, 1996. The United States also announced that it was taking a number of new complaints to the WTO, three of which involved the auto industry, a major employer in several politically crucial industrial states.

37. David E. Sanger, "Standing by His Man in Role after Role," *New York Times*, November 2, 1996.

38. For a typically enthusiastic *Business Week* discussion of the "New Economy," see Christopher Farrell with Michael Mandel, "Why Are We So Afraid of Growth?," *Business Week*, May 16, 1994, 62–72. For a recent academic debate on the reality and implications of the new economy, see the symposium on "Computers and Productivity," *Journal and Economic Perspectives* 14, no. 4 (Fall 2000): 3–74. This debate is certain to intensify in the wake of the 2000 Nasdaq collapse.

39. Baer, *Reinventing Democrats*, 166–68. The quotation on crumbling politics is by Will Marshall, president of the DLC-affiliated Progressive Policy Institute. Eliza Newlin Carney, "Party Pooper?," *National Journal*, April 6, 1996, 768. On the new knowledge workers, see the book by two California DLC activists: Morley Winograd and Dudley Buffa, *Taking Control: Politics in the Information Age* (New York: Henry Holt, 1996). The concept of "wired" workers was first introduced in a poll conducted in 1996 for the Institute for a New California, founded by Winograd and Buffa. See Buffa, Michael Hais, and Morley Winograd, "Wired Workers and the Digital Deal," *New Democrat*, November–December 1996, 28.

40. See Will Marshall et. al., *The New Progressive Declaration: A Political Philosophy for the Information Age* (Washington, D.C.: Progressive Foundation, July 1996). See also Baer, *Reinventing Democrats*, 234–35; John B. Judis, "Beyond the Clinton Presidency," *New Republic*, September 16, 23, 1996, 24–26; and Sara Miles, *How to Hack a Party Line: The Democrats and Silicon Valley* (New York: Farrar, Straus and Giroux, 2001).

41. On the familiar postelection debate, see Baer, *Reinventing Democrats*, 250, and Ronald Brownstein, "Democrats Are Split over What Sewed Up Win," *Los Angeles Times*, November 22, 1996. For academic analyses of the 1996 elections, see Michael Nelson, ed., *The Elections of 1996* (Washington, D.C.: CQ Press, 1997); Gerald M. Pomper et. al., *The Election of 1996* (Chatham, N.J.: Chatham House Publishers, 1997); and Paul R. Abramson, John H. Aldrich, and David W. Rohde, *Change and Continuity in the 1996 and 1998 Elections* (Washington, D.C: CQ Press, 1999).

42. Dionne, *They Only Look Dead*; Robert L. Borosage, "Clinton Needs to Act More Like Roosevelt—Teddy, That Is," *Washington Post National Weekly Edition*, September 29, 1997, 21; Faux, *The Party's Not Over*; Judis, "Beyond the Clinton Presidency."

43. See Ruy A. Teixeira, "Economic Change and the Middle-Class Revolt against the Democratic Party," in Stephen C. Craig, ed., *Broken Contract? Changing Relations between Americans and Their Government* (Boulder, Colo.: Westview Press, 1996), 67–84.

44. See Ruy A. Teixeira, "Who Joined the Democrats? Understanding the 1996 Election Results," *Economic Policy Institute Briefing Paper* (Washington, D.C.: Economic Policy Institute, November 1996). For a critique of Teixeira's analysis, see Jeff Manza and Clem Brooks, *Social Cleavages and Political Change: Voter Alignments and U.S. Party Coalitions* (New York: Oxford University Press, 1999), 205–16.

45. Clinton was particularly impressed by the book by DLC activists Morley Winograd and Dudley Buffa, *Taking Control: Politics in the Information Age*.

46. John F. Harris, "Winning a Second Term," *Washington Post*, January 20, 1997.

47. In September 1995 Clinton laid out his evolving perspective in a number of speeches and interviews. See *Public Paper of the Presidents of the United States: William J. Clinton, 1995*, book 2 (Washington, D.C.: U.S. Government Printing Office, 1994), 1412–13, 1441, 1458. See also John F. Harris, "After Season of Doubt, Clinton Says He's Charging Up for '96 Campaign," *Washington Post*, September 24, 1995. For a discussion of Clinton's 1997 inaugural address and its excited reception by Silicon Valley high-tech executives, see Miles, *How to Hack a Party Line*, 47–48.

48. By attracting foreign capital to the United States, the strong dollar helped compensate to some degree for the insufficiency of private savings, thus lowering interest rates and fueling the stock market boom in the same way as budget deficit reduction.

49. "The New Economy Needs Free Trade," *Business Week*, December 30, 1996, 196.

50. Douglas Harbrecht, "Gatt: 'It's Yesterday's Agreement,'" *Business Week*, December 27, 1993, 36.

51. For the next six paragraphs, see Corn, "Dick Gephardt"; Paul Blustein, "'Fast-Track' Trade Plan Pits White House against Top Congressional Democrats," *Washington Post*, March 22, 1997; John Maggs, "Trading Places," *New Republic*, April 14, 1997, 15–16; Dan Balz, "The Battle to Seize the Heart and Soul of the Democrats," *Washington Post National Weekly Edition*, June 9, 1997, 11–12; and Jonathan Cohn, "Hard Labor," *New Republic*, October 6, 1997, 21–26. More generally on the 1997 fast-track fight, in addition to the works by Destler cited earlier, see Karen E. Schnietz and Timothy Nieman, "Politics Matter: The 1997 Derailment of Fast-Track Trade Authority," *Business and Politics* 1, no. 2 (August 1999): 233–51.

52. Sweeney had complained privately that the federation had wasted resources fighting NAFTA that should have been used to elect more Democrats to Congress. Now Sweeney and his advisers reportedly worried that too rigid a stance on NAFTA expansion might threaten relations with the Clinton administration over what was probably a losing cause. Maggs, "Trading Places"; Cohn, "Hard Labor."

53. The industrial unions' resolve was heightened by the findings of a study that 60 percent of union organizing efforts in manufacturing after NAFTA were met by management threats to close the factories, compared with 29 percent before NAFTA. Kate Bronfenbronner, *Final Report: The Effects of Plant Closings or the Threat of Plant Closings on the Right of Workers to Organize* (Ithaca, N.Y.: New York State School of Industrial and Labor Relations, Cornell University, 1997).

54. Amy Borrus, "The Latest Trade War: Democrat vs. Democrat," *Business Week*, March 10, 1997, 43.

55. Nancy Dunne and Bruce Clark, "Clinton Starts Big Push on 'Fast-Track,'" *Financial Times*, September 10, 1997, 6.

56. Schnietz and Nieman, "Politics Matter"; Amy Borrus, "Business Is in a Hurry for Fast-Track," *Business Week*, September 15, 1997, 38–39; Peter H. Stone, "Business Pushes for Fast-Track," *National Journal*, September 27, 1903–4.

57. Andrew Taylor, "Clinton Loses First Opportunity after All-Out Fast-Track Push," *Congressional Quarterly Weekly Report*, November 8, 1997, 1754.

58. The coalition was organized in late 1996. See Christopher Georges, "Bypassing Leadership, 'New Democrats' Group Gives Clinton a Home in the House on Big Issues," *Wall Street Journal*, September 3, 1997.

59. This was Penn's interpretation of his findings. The DLC's spin notwithstanding, the poll actually recorded intense ambivalence among both Democrats and the public at large on fast track and the wider issue of globalization. See David S. Broder, "As the Democrats Turn," *Washington Post*, August 17, 1997.

60. See Baer, *Reinventing Democrats*, 253, and Jacob Heilbrunn, "The New New Democrats," *New Republic*, November 17, 1997, 20–21.

61. See Taylor Dark, *The Unions and the Democrats: An Enduring Alliance* (Ithaca, N.Y.: Cornell University Press, 1999), 178–84.

62. This labor mobilization, together with the similarly expanded efforts of business and other organizations and the increased activities of congressional party campaign committees signaled to some observers a challenge to the prevailing system of candidate-centered campaigning. See Paul Herrnson, "Parties and Interest Groups in Postreform Congressional Elections," in Allan J. Cigler and Burdett A. Loomis, eds., *Interest Group Politics*, 5th ed. (Washington, D.C.: CQ Press, 1998), 145–67. On labor's electoral efforts in 1996, see Julie Kosterlitz, "For Labor: No More Playing Defense," *National Journal*, August 24, 1996, 1799–1801; Dark, *The Unions and the Democrats*, 184–87; and Robin

Gerber, "Building to Win, Building to Last: The AFL-CIO Takes on the Republican Congress," in Robert Biersack, Paul S. Herrnson, and Clyde Wilcox, eds., *After the Revolution: PACs and Lobbies in the Republican Congress* (Boston: Allyn and Bacon, 1999).

63. The margin rises to a staggering 23–1 if "soft" money spending is included.

64. Norman J. Ornstein, Thomas E. Mann, and Michael J. Malbin, eds., *Vital Statistics in Congress, 1999–2000* (Washington, D.C.: AEI Press, 2000), 105–6.

65. Gerber, "Building to Win." Gary Jacobson provides statistical evidence that Republican incumbents targeted by the AFL-CIO did substantially worse than untargeted Republicans, particularly if they were freshmen. Gary C. Jacobson, "The 105th Congress: Unprecedented and Unsurprising," in Nelson, *Elections of 1996*, 157.

66. For a detailed account of the labor mobilization against fast track, see David Glenn, "How Fast Track Was Derailed: Lessons for Labor's Future," *Dissent* (Fall 1998): 47–52. See also Abramson with Greenhouse, "The Trade Bill"; Julie Kosterlitz, "Muddy Track," *National Journal*, August 9, 1997, 1594–97; and Frank Swoboda, "Labor Plans Ads, Lobbying on Trade Pacts," *Washington Post*, September 17, 1997.

67. "Labor is practicing the politics of intimidation either with outright threats or implied threats—that labor will withdraw any campaign support, either financial or otherwise" to fast-track supporters, said Representative Calvin M. Dooley (D-Calif.). Ronald Brownstein, "Trade Is Still the Exception to Clinton's Rule," *Los Angeles Times*, November 7, 1997. See also Richard E. Cohen, "Dems Feel the Squeeze on Fast Track," *National Journal*, October 18, 1997, 2085.

68. In December 1996 a group of researchers at the University of California in Los Angeles had concluded that NAFTA had almost no impact on U.S. employment during its first three years. In June the Economic Policy Institute and five other research groups issued a report asserting that NAFTA had cost the United States 400,000 jobs. Even a congressionally mandated White House study released in July claimed only a net gain of 180,000 U.S. jobs. Kosterlitz, "Muddy Track"; Richard W. Stevenson, "U.S. to Report to Congress NAFTA Benefits Are Modest," *New York Times*, July 11, 1997.

69. See esp. William Greider, *One World, Ready or Not: The Manic Logic of Global Capitalism* (New York: Simon and Schuster, 1997); Dani Rodrik, *Has Globalization Gone Too Far?* (Washington, D.C.: Institute for International Economics, 1997); and George Soros, "The Capitalist Threat," *Atlantic*, February 1997, 45–58. Rodrik tellingly pointed out that neoclassical Stolper-Samuelson models expect that in advanced industrial countries, unskilled labor, as a scarce production factor, will be harmed by free trade.

70. Again due to the large size of many states, the overrepresentation in the Senate of agricultural and less unionized states, senators' lengthy terms, weak party leadership, and the chamber's foreign policy responsibilities. Thus, in early November the Senate voted 69–31 (R 43–12, D 26–10) to invoke cloture on a motion to proceed to that chamber's version of the fast-track bill and then approved the motion to proceed the next day by a 68–31 vote. The measure was shelved when the House bill was withdrawn.

71. For these estimates, see Claude E. Barfield, "Politics of Trade and Fast Track in the United States" (paper presented at The First Academic Colloquium of the Americas, University of Costa Rica, March 12–14, 1998, *AEI Speeches*, http://www.aei.org/sp/spbarfld.htm, and Robert E. Baldwin and Christopher S. Magee, *Congressional Trade Votes: From NAFTA Approval to Fast-Track Defeat* (Washington, D.C.: Institute for International Economics, 2000), 11–12.

72. On these Republican nationalists, see John B. Judis, "White Squall," *New Republic*,

March 11, 1996, 26–30, and Ben Wildavksy, "Going Nativist?," *National Journal*, May 27, 1995, 1278–81. On the role of this group in the fast-track fight, see Peter Beinart, "The Nationalist Revolt," *New Republic*, December 1, 1997, 22–26. David Karol incorrectly states that Republicans first elected to the House in 1994 or 1996 were more supportive of fast track than other GOP House members. Karol, "Divided Government and U.S. Trade Policy: Much Ado about Nothing?," *International Organization* 54, no. 4 (Autumn 2000): 841.

73. The nine GOP NAFTA supporters in 1993 who switched to an anti–fast-track position four years later represented districts that were hard hit by such NAFTA-related job losses. Kedron Bardwell, "The Puzzling Decline in House Support for Free Trade: Was Fast Track a Referendum on NAFTA?," *Legislative Studies Quarterly* 25, no. 4 (November 2000): 591–610.

74. On this last point, see Bardwell, "The Puzzling Decline," and James A. Barnes, "How to Corner an Elusive White House," *National Journal*, November 1, 1997, 2205. On the multiple sources of GOP opposition to fast track, see Richard S. Conley, "Derailing Presidential Fast-Track Authority: The Impact of Constituency Pressures and Political Ideology on Trade Policy in Congress," *Political Research Quarterly* 52, no. 4 (December 1999), 785–99.

75. On the factors explaining GOP support for fast track, see Bardwell, "The Puzzling Decline." Bardwell, however, appears to underestimate the extent of Republican support for fast track, which correspondingly leads him to conclude that GOP opposition to the measure played a more central role in its defeat than I believe was the case. Relying on "head counts" taken by Public Citizen, an anti–fast-track interest group, and the AFL-CIO, Bardwell writes that only 131 GOP members (57.5 percent) supported fast track, whereas 72 (31.5 percent) opposed it and 25 (11 percent) were undecided (p. 593). Martha Gibson, drawing on a poll conducted by the *National Journal's CongressDaily*, similarly states that only 104 (45.8 percent) of GOP members supported or were leaning toward fast track, while 67 (29.5 percent) opposed or were leaning against it and 56 (24.7 percent) were undecided. These head counts may have been taken before GOP leaders put on their final press for fast-track support. According to a tally taken by the GOP leadership itself, 156 Republicans were solidly in favor of fast track, another 6–8 members would probably have voted for the measure (for a total of about 72 percent), and the addition of another dozen or more "Hail Marys" might have gotten the GOP total as high as 170. Taylor, "Clinton Loses First Opportunity," 2830. This falls within the previously cited 70–75 percent range of GOP support reported by Claude Barfield, who relied on the *National Journal* poll combined with additional information from outside sources. On the other hand, David Karol's estimate that "at least" 170 Republicans supported fast track is almost certainly too high. Karol, "Divided Government," 840.

Gibson argues that Republicans elected to Congress in 1994 and 1996 played a particularly important role in the defeat of fast track. Basing her view on a comparison of the projected 1997 vote with an earlier fast-track extension vote in 1993, Gibson demonstrates that many Democrats who supported fast track in 1993 were defeated by Republicans who opposed Clinton's bill four years later, thus suggesting the importance of the GOP "replacement" effect. But in addition to the problems with her 1997 data discussed above, the fast-track procedure approved in the 1993 bill applied only to the relatively uncontroversial Uruguay Round GATT, then being completed by the Clinton administration, and thus generated only modest congressional dissent. A more appropriate comparison would have been with the more salient NAFTA vote. Many Democratic fast-track supporters in 1993 who were later defeated also voted *against* NAFTA, thus reducing the importance of the Republican replacement effect. Martha L. Gibson, *Conflict amid Consensus in American Trade Policy* (Washington, D.C.: Georgetown University Press, 2000), 176.

76. On these points, see Beinart, "The Nationalist Revolt"; Conley, "Derailing Presidential Fast-Track Authority"; and James A. Barnes and Richard E. Cohen, "Divided Democrats," *National Journal*, November 15, 1997, 2304–7;

77. Since 1991, the number of white Democratic House members from the thirteen southern states had declined from 79 to 42. In the 1993 NAFTA vote, House Democrats from the South backed the deal 53–32, whereas the rest of the caucus opposed it by almost a 3–1 margin. Overall, more than half of the 102 Democrats who had voted for NAFTA in 1993 no longer served in the House in 1997. Put another way, only 28 percent of Democrats still in the House in 1997 who had voted on NAFTA had voted yes, compared to the 40 percent of the Democratic caucus who had favored the agreement when the vote was cast.

78. See Schnietz and Nieman, "Politics Matter."

79. John Maggs, "Before and NAFTA," *New Republic*, September 1, 1997, 11–12; Joel Millman, "Nafta's Do-Gooder Side Deals Disappoint," *Wall Street Journal*, October 15, 1997.

80. Conley, "Derailing Presidential Fast-Track Authority"; Thomas B. Edsall, "Big Labor Flexes Its Muscle Once Again," *Washington Post National Weekly Edition*, November 24, 1997, 11.

81. A July *Wall Street Journal*/NBC News poll showed that 42 percent of Americans believed that NAFTA had had a negative impact on the United States—up from 35 percent in mid-1994—while only 32 percent believed it had had a positive impact. Respondents opposed granting Clinton new fast-track authority by a 62–32 percent margin. For these and other polling results on NAFTA and fast track, see Kosterlitz, "Muddy Track"; *American Political Report*, October 3, 1997, 1–2.

82. John F. Harris and Peter Baker, "The Public Wasn't Sold on Fast Track," *Washington Post National Weekly Edition*, November 17, 1997, 11.

83. Many lawmakers who opposed fast track had studied what happened to several dozen Democratic members of Congress who voted for NAFTA in 1993. They were defeated in 1994 partly because alienated union members stayed away from the polls. Abramson with Greenhouse, "The Trade Bill."

84. For the next two paragraphs, see Thomas Gais, *Improper Influence: Campaign Finance Law, Political Interest Groups, and the Problem of Equality* (Ann Arbor: University of Michigan Press, 1996), 167–69; Dan Clawson, Alan Neustadtl, and Mark Weller, *Dollars and Votes: How Business Campaign Contributions Subvert Democracy* (Philadelphia: Temple University Press), 150–57; and Brooks Jackson, *Honest Graft: Big Money and the American Political Process* (New York: Knopf, 1988).

85. In 1982 business PACs gave only about 39 percent of their contributions in House races to Democrats. By 1992 this share had jumped to about 55 percent. Thanks to this new influx of business money, from 1982 to 1992, the business share of House Democrats' total PAC receipts jumped from 41 to 54 percent, while labor's share fell from 43 to 33 percent. Ornstein, Mann, and Malbin, *Vital Statistics*.

86. See Cohen, "Dems Feel the Squeeze"; Barnes and Cohen, "Divided Democrats"; Beinart, "The Nationalist Revolt"; Abramson with Greenhouse, "The Trade Bill"; and Edsall, "Big Labor Flexes Its Muscle."

87. For Democratic challengers who won Republican-held seats in 1996, the dependence on union money was even greater. More than 60 percent of the PAC contributions made to these candidates came from labor (the figure for all Democratic challengers— both winners and losers—was 71 percent).

88. As the fast-track vote approached, Democrats took note of a recent special election on Staten Island. In that case, a strong Democratic candidate lost because the GOP was able to spend $800,000 on ads financed by soft money, whereas the Democratic Party lacked the funds to reply.

89. Bardwell ("The Puzzling Decline") argues that labor's "carrot" strategy of increasing PAC contributions to Democratic NAFTA supporters from 1992 to 1996 was more effective than the "stick" strategy of withholding funds in convincing such members to oppose fast track.

90. Brownstein, "Trade Is Still the Exception to Clinton's Rule" (senior House Democrat); Barnes and Cohen, "Divided Democrats," 2306 (Democratic leadership aide); John F. Harris, "Clinton Hits 'Fast-Track' Opponents," *Washington Post*, October 28, 1997 (another Democrat).

91. Abramson with Greenhouse, "The Trade Bill."

92. John E. Yang and Peter Baker, "Getting What He Asked For," *Washington Post National Weekly Edition*, December 15, 1997, 11.

93. Lee Walczak, Mike McNamee, and Richard S. Dunham, "The State of the Union? It's Flush," *Business Week*, February 2, 1998, 36.

94. Steven Greenhouse, "Two Feuding Democratic Voices Call a Truce," *New York Times*, August 9, 1998.

95. On the late summer and fall 1998 fast-track fight, in addition to the articles cited below, see Julie Kosterlitz, "A Vote the Dems Would Like to Trade In," *National Journal*, September 12, 1998, 2108, and David Hosansky, "House Vote Signals a Key Reversal of U.S. Support for Free Trade," *Congressional Quarterly Weekly Report*, September 26, 1998, 2603–4.

96. See Peter H. Stone, "Family Feud," *National Journal*, May 2, 1998, 986, and Richard S. Dunham and Amy Borrus, "Still the Party of Big Business?," *Business Week*, September 14, 1998, 150–60.

97. Stone, "Family Feud"; Thomas B. Edsall, "Business, GOP Chiefs Reconcile on Agenda," *Washington Post*, July 8, 1998.

98. "Some Republicans aren't going to be there on trade issues," said Dan Schnur, a California GOP consultant. "Ultimately, business is going to form relationships with elements of both parties." Dunham and Borrus, "Still the Party of Big Business?," 158.

99. See esp. "There's More Than One Party of Business," *Business Week*, May 4, 1988, 182. See also Dunham and Borrus, "Still the Party of Big Business?"; Richard S. Dunham, "Is the GOP the Only Party of Business?," *Business Week*, May 4, 1998, 154; and Thomas B. Edsall, "Giving Republicans the Business," *Washington Post National Weekly Edition*, June 22, 1998, 10.

100. "We want to create an alternative base of financial and political support for New Democratic candidates," said NDN cofounder and DLC chairman Senator Joseph Lieberman of Connecticut. Eliza Newlin Carney, "What? A Smiling 'New Democrat'?", *National Journal*, November 6, 1997, 2477.

101. Figures from the Center for Responsive Politics; Amy Borrus, "Mugging on K Street: The GOP Assault on Business Lobbyists," *Business Week*, November 9, 1998, 59.

102. Dunham and Borrus, "Still the Party of Big Business?," 152 (first quotation); Borrus, "Mugging on K Street" (second quotation).

103. For the whole 1997–98 election cycle, 34 percent of business PAC contributions went to Democratic House and Senate candidates, down from the late June figure of 37 percent. In the House alone, the proportion of business PAC money donated to Democrats rose only a little—from 32 percent in 1996 to 34 percent in 1998. The business share of House Democrats' total PAC receipts increased from 41 percent in 1996 to 42 percent in 1998. Ornstein, Mann, and Malbin, *Vital Statistics*, 106.

104. Edsall, "Business, GOP Chiefs Reconcile"; Dunham and Borrus, "Still the Party of Big Business?"; Juliet Eilperin, "House Leaders See Trade as a Key Issue," *Washington Post*, July 20, 1998 (quotation); Jonathan Peterson, "Democrats Call House Defeat of Fast-Track Bill Bid to Humiliate Them," *Los Angeles Times*, September 28, 1998.

105. *Inside U.S. Trade*, September 18 (p. 1), 28 (p. 1), 1998.

106. As of October 1, business had outspent labor by a margin of 12–1. For the full 1997–98 election cycle, the share of House Democrats' PAC money from labor fell to 43.6 percent, down from 48.4 percent two years earlier. Ornstein, Mann, and Malbin, *Vital Statistics*, 106.

107. While spending only about $5 million on TV ads in 1998, labor invested $18 million in a tightly targeted get-out-the-vote effort coordinated by 392 paid field activists, up from 135 in 1996, and focused on 8 Senate races and 45 tight House races, down from 105 House contests two years earlier. Steven Greenhouse, "Republicans Credit Labor for Success by Democrats," *New York Times*, November 6, 1998; Aaron Bernstein, "Labor Helps Turn the Tide—the Old Fashioned Way," *Business Week*, November 16, 1998, 45.

108. After the defeat of the House bill, a similar Senate Republican measure was shelved.

109. Baldwin and Magee, *Congressional Trade Votes*.

110. Ibid. Baldwin and Magee (p. 38) found that the increased dependence of Democrats on labor PAC campaign contributions relative to business contributions explained the behavior of about thirteen of the twenty-two "switcher" Democrats who voted for NAFTA in 1993 but opposed fast track in 1998.

111. Martha Gibson argues that the defeat of the 1997 and 1998 fast-track bills and an earlier 1995 Republican proposal were also due to the Republican takeover of the House in 1994, since the loss of key committee chairmanships prevented the Democrats from drafting "cover" legislation, including labor and environmental provisions of the kind that allegedly accompanied the NAFTA and GATT implementing bills, that might have won additional Democratic support. But such provisions in the NAFTA bill were very weak, no such provisions were included in the GATT bill, and such cover legislation was added to the measure for permanent normal trade relations (PNTR) in 2000, when the GOP controlled the House. Gibson, *Conflict amid Consensus*, 178.

112. "Daniel Patrick Moynihan: America's Free-Trade Coalition Is 'Shattered,'" *Rushford Report*, April 1999, 3.

113. A point acknowledged by I. M. Destler, "Congress, Constituencies, and U.S. Trade Policy," in Alan V. Deardorff and Robert M. Stern, eds., *Constituent Interests and U.S. Trade Policies* (Ann Arbor: University of Michigan Press, 1998), 102–3.

Chapter 9

1. Progressive Policy Institute, *The New Economy Index: Understanding America's Economic Transformation*, November 1998, http://www.neweconomyindex.org.

2. Al From and Will Marshall, "Building the Next Democratic Majority," and William A. Galston and Elaine C. Kamarck, "Five Realities That Will Shape 21st Century Politics," both in *Blueprint Ideas for a New Century*, Fall 1998, http://www.dlc.org/blueprint/fall/98.

3. On this familiar intra-Democratic debate, see Kenneth S. Baer, *Reinventing Democrats: The Politics of Liberalism from Reagan to Clinton* (Lawrence: University Press of Kansas, 2000), 260–61, and Adam Nagourney, "A Party So Happy It Could Burst," *New York Times*, November 15, 1998.

4. See Ruy Teixeira, "Waitress Moms and Technician Dads: The Story behind the 1998 Election Results," *EPI Briefing Paper*, November 5, 1998, http://epinet.org/briefing papers/election98.

5. See, for example, Clinton's introductory remarks to an early April 2000 White House economic summit on the New Economy, attended by scores of corporate leaders, economists, financial analysts, and high-tech entrepreneurs. Edward Chen, "Conferees Debate U.S. Prosperity," *Los Angeles Times*, April 6, 2000.

6. See the following important speech by Summers to a May 2000 conference of high-tech executives: "The New Wealth of Nations," *Treasury News*, May 10, 2000, http://www.treas.gov/press/releases/ps61/htm. In early 2000 Clinton joined Summers and other economic advisers in also beginning to speak more publicly about the benefits to the New Economy of imports as a source of innovation, competition, and low inflation. See Michael M. Phillips, "Clinton Is Beating the Drum for Imports as Trade Fights Loom," *Wall Street Journal*, February 4, 2000.

7. See Jason Zengerle, "Silicon Smoothies," *New Republic*, June 8, 1998, 19–23; Alan K. Ota, "High Tech Swarms the Hill as CEOs Turn Lobbyists," *Congressional Quarterly Weekly Report*, June 12, 1999, 1356–61; Neil Munro, "The New Conquerors," *National Journal*, October 2, 1999, 2796–99, 887; and esp. Sara Miles, *How to Hack a Party Line: The Democrats and Silicon Valley* (New York: Farrar, Straus and Giroux, 2001).

8. Paul Magnusson, "Clinton's Trade Crusade," *Business* Week, June 8, 1998, 34–36.

9. The bill passed the House in mid-March by a wide margin, supported by almost all voting Democrats and over 40 percent of Republicans, mostly from the Rust Belt. The Senate version of the bill was killed in late June, however—thanks in part to intensive White House lobbying—when a motion to limit the debate was rejected by a vote of 57–42, with Republicans opposing the cloture motion 15–39 and Democrats favoring it 27–18.

10. For various views of the issues and events surrounding the Seattle meeting, see Robert Weissman, "Welcome to Seattle," *Multinational Monitor* 20, nos. 10–11 (October–November 1999); Lori Nitschke, "U.S. Trading Partners at Crossroads in Seattle," *Congressional Quarterly Weekly Report*, November, 27, 1999, 2826–37; David Moberg, "Seattle Showdown: Citizens Stand Up to the WTO," *In These Times*, November 28, 1999, 22–24; Harold Meyerson, "The Battle in Seattle," *LA Weekly*, December 3–9, 1999, 15–16; Joseph Kahn and David E. Sanger, "Impasse on Trade Delivers a Stinging Blow to Clinton," *New York Times*, December 5, 1999; and Thomas B. Edsall, "Divisions on Trade Issues Leave Democrats Vulnerable," *Washington Post*, December 9, 1999.

11. On the New Democrats' support for a new round of trade talks, see Miles, *How to Hack a Party Line*, 204–5.

12. Neil Munro, "Click Here for Online Trade Dispute," *National Journal*, October 30, 1999, 3164; Helene Cooper and Johns Simons, "Dumping Issue May Foil E-Commerce Agenda at WTO," *Wall Street Journal*, November 23, 1999. A year later USTR Charlene Barshefsky announced a six-point "Networked World" initiative to further liberalize trade and investment in high-tech goods and services.

13. See Zogby International and Harris poll results reported in Keith Koffler, "Survey Shows U.S. Opinion Moving against Free Trade," *National Journal's CongressDaily*, December 15, 1999, and "A Survey of Discontent," *Business Week*, December 27, 1999, 54–55.

14. See Nicholas Bayne, "Why Did Seattle Fail? Globalization and the Politics of Trade," *Government and Opposition* 35, no. 2 (Spring 2000): 131–51.

15. Harold Meyerson, "Union Man," *American Prospect*, April 24, 2000, 18–22.

16. Steven Greenhouse, "Endorsement Brings Big Labor Test for Gore," *New York Times*, October 17, 1999.

17. For the next three paragraphs, see Kahn and Sanger, "Impasse on Trade"; Meyerson, "Battle in Seattle"; and Katharine Q. Seelye with Steven Greenhouse, "China Deal Adds a Sour Note to Gore's Sweet Labor Tune," *New York Times*, November 25, 1999.

18. Evelyn Iritani, "Upcoming WTO Talks Meet with Apathy, Anger," *Los Angeles Times*, November 21, 1999.

19. Kahn and Sanger, "Impasse on Trade."

20. Helene Cooper, Bob Davis, and Gregg Hitt, "WTO's Failure in Bid to Launch Trade Talks Emboldens Protesters," *Wall Street Journal*, December 6, 1999.

21. On the history of China's attempt to enter the WTO and the issues involved, see Mark A. Groombridge and Claude E. Barfield, *Tiger by the Tail: China and the World Trade Organization* (Washington, D.C.: AEI Press, 1999).

22. For the next two paragraphs, see David E. Sanger, "How Push by China and U.S. Business Won Over Clinton," *New York Times*, April 15, 1999; Steven Mufson and Robert G. Kaiser, "Missed U.S.-China Deal Looms Large," *Washington Post*, November 10, 1999; and Helene Cooper, Bob Davis, and Ian Johnson, "To Brink and Back: In Historic Pact, U.S. Opens Way for China to Finally Join WTO," *Wall Street Journal*, November 16, 1999.

23. The requirement for an annual vote stemmed from an expansion of the Jackson-Vanik Amendment to the Trade Act of 1974, which was intended to punish communist countries with spotty records on human rights. The law allows the president to issue a waiver and grant normal trade relations on a temporary basis, as long as he promises to press for human rights reforms in the affected country. Congress then votes on whether to approve or disapprove the presidential waiver.

24. Robert G. Sutter, *U.S. Policy toward China: An Introduction to the Role of Interest Groups* (Lanham, Md.: Rowman and Littlefield, 1998); John W. Dietrich, "Interest Groups and Foreign Policy: Clinton and the China MFN Debates," *Presidential Studies Quarterly* 29, no. 2 (June 1999): 280–96.

25. Richard E. Cohen and Eliza Newlin Carney, "A Do-Little Congress?," *National Journal*, February 13, 1999, 394–97; Andrew Taylor, "Issues Held Hostage in War between Action, Gridlock," *Congressional Quarterly Weekly Report*, February 26, 2000, 394–99; Deirdre Shesgreen, "Gephardt Nudges Democrats in Congress toward More Centrist Positions," *St. Louis Post-Dispatch*, April 2, 2000; Lizette Alvarez, "House Republicans Fret about 'Do-Nothing' Tag," *New York Times*, June 26, 2000.

26. Jeanne Cummings, "Clinton Goes All Out for Gore," *Wall Street Journal*, January 13, 2000.

27. "There's no question in our minds that we are subverting NAFTA," said a disgruntled senior trade official of the Mexican truck and bus decision, "and we are doing it purely because we don't want to upset the Teamsters." Esther Schrader, "U.S. Seeks Delay in Key NAFTA Issue with Mexico," *Los Angeles Times*, January 7, 2000.

28. "It's the legacy thing," said USTR Charlene Barshefsky, who negotiated the China agreement. "For the president, there's nothing bigger." David E. Sanger, "The Trade Deal: The Drama," *New York Times*, November 17, 1999.

29. On the White House campaign, see Robert O'Neill, "Dismantling the Great Wall," *National Journal*, March 25, 2000, 936–43; John Maggs, "Art of the Deal," *National Journal*, May 19, 2000; and Eric Schmitt and Joseph Kahn, "The China Trade Vote: A Clinton Triumph," *New York Times*, May 25, 2000.

30. According to a senior White House official, in contrast to the 1997 fast-track fight, when Clinton readily let Democrats off the hook for voting against him, on PNTR Clinton did not "give anybody a pass." O'Neill, "Dismantling the Great Wall," 939.

31. See Maggs, "Art of the Deal."

32. Katharine Q. Seelye, "Union Welcomes Gore, Despite China Views," *New York Times*, May 23, 2000.

33. Helene Cooper and Ian Johnson, "Opening Doors: Congress's Vote Primes U.S. Firms to Boost Investments in China," *Wall Street Journal*, May 25, 2000. A survey by the U.S. Business and Industry Council of the web sites of fifty American multinational corporations found that they barely mentioned selling from their U.S-based factories to China but talked instead about using the country as a production base. Alan Tonelson, "China's Mythic Market," *New York Times*, May 18, 2000. See also John Burgess, "For Many, China Trade Bill Isn't About Exports," *Washington Post*, May 27, 2000, and Joseph Kahn, "Playing the China Card," *New York Times*, July 7, 2000.

34. Earlier I noted Lawrence Summers's argument that high-tech firms seek enlarged export markets to help them achieve the economies of scale necessary to rapidly amortize high R&D and other fixed costs. But since such scale economies often exist at the firm rather than the plant level, companies can access foreign markets as efficiently through sales from foreign subsidiaries as they can via exports from their home bases. Hence, for U.S. high-tech supporters of the China deal, trade liberalization was also a less important goal than the liberalization of Beijing's investment rules. On this general point, see Stephen J. Kobrin, "An Empirical Analysis of the Determinants of Global Integration," *Strategic Management Journal* 12, Special Issue (1991): 17–31.

35. On the distinction between these two kinds of foreign investors in China, see Michael A. Santoro, *Profits and Principles: Global Capitalism and Human Rights in China* (Ithaca, N.Y.: Cornell University Press, 2000).

36. "The business community has really stepped up their effort on this as compared to the fast-track debate," said a top aide to a Republican lawmaker. John Bresnahan, "PNTR Votes Remain in Flux," *Roll Call*, May 1, 2000. On the business campaign for PNTR, see Peter H. Stone, "K Street Musters for the Middle Kingdom," *National Journal*, March 25, 2000, 944–45; Karen Foerstel, "Multi-Front NTR Lobbying Effort Seeks to Boost Public Support," *Congressional Quarterly Weekly Report*, April 15, 2000, 909; Ian Urbina, "The Corporate PNTR Lobby: How Business Is Paying Millions to Gain Billions in China," *Multinational Monitor* 21, no. 5 (May 2000); Helene Cooper, "On China Trade Bill, Business Shows It Learned Lessons," *Wall Street Journal*, May 19, 2000; Michael M.

Phillips, "Big Business Lobbies Hard as House China Vote Nears," *Wall Street Journal*, May 23, 2000; and Joseph Kahn, "Last-Ditch Effort by 2 Sides to Win China Trade Vote," *New York Times*, May 23, 2000. Spurred by labor's powerful anti-PNTR mobilization, the business campaign for the bill was a classic example of what has been termed "counteractive lobbying."

37. "In the past, our opposition argued the specifics of how trade legislation would hurt specific jobs, while we argued the general," said Cal Cohen, head of the Emergency Committee for American Trade. "So we reversed the process." Cooper, "On China Trade Bill." On the way uncertain, boundedly rational firms develop their political strategies by learning from their previous successes and failures, see Sandra I. Suarez, *Does Business Learn? Tax Breaks, Uncertainty, and Political Strategies* (Ann Arbor: University of Michigan Press, 2000).

38. "Unions have been superbly successful on trade issues and we have really learned from them," said Robert N. Burt, chairman and chief executive of FMC Corporation and head of the Business Roundtable. Kahn, "Last-Ditch Effort." The Roundtable focused on 88 districts, hiring 60 full-time "trade organizers," and the Chamber of Commerce focused on 66 districts.

39. Phillips, "Big Business Lobbies Hard." On the use of PAC contributions by Boeing Co., a major exporter and promoter of the China deal, to reward and punish waverers on PNTR, see Karen Foerstel, "PAC Man Bites Back," *Congressional Quarterly Weekly Report*, September 23, 2000, 2226. See also Michael M. Phillips, "Lawmakers Are Warned to Back China Trade or Lose Contributions," *Wall Street Journal Interactive Edition*, February 9, 2000.

40. See Stone, "K Street Musters"; Juliet Eilperin, "Electronics Lobby Focusing on China Trade," *Washington Post*, March 21, 2000; Jonathan Peterson, "High-Tech Firms Join Push for Trade Ties with China," *Los Angeles Times*, May 3, 2000; Jim Puzzanghera, "Tech Pushes Hard for China Trade," *San Jose Mercury News*, May 15, 2000; and Lizette Alvarez, "The China Trade Wrangle: The Silicon Lobby," *New York Times*, May 18, 2000.

41. "This is as mobilized as I have ever seen high tech on any issue," said Michael Mailbach, Washington lobbyist for semiconductor giant Intel. Carolyn Lochhead, "Unlikely Allies in Trade Fight," *San Francisco Chronicle*, May 12, 2000.

42. Sara Miles claims that with the prominent exception of America Online, the new Internet companies were much less involved in the PNTR fight than were the bigger, established high-tech firms. Miles, *How to Hack a Party Line*, 242–43.

43. Center for Responsive Politics, *Who's Paying for This Election?*, http://www.opensecrets.org/pubs/whospayoo/index.asp. See also Holly Bailey, "Silicon Valley Goes to Washington," *Public Perspective*, January–February 2000, 33–35; Amy Borrus and Richard S. Dunham, "Tech: The Virtual Third Party," *Business Week*, April 24, 2000, 74–78.

44. High-tech lobbyists told House members that their companies would use end-of-the-year scorecards of how lawmakers voted on eight to ten key high-tech issues in deciding whom to support with their campaign contributions. In some cases, the China vote was weighted three times more than the others. Puzzanghera, "Tech Pushes Hard for China Trade."

45. David Baumann, "A Republican Resurgence," *National Journal*, May 6, 2000, 1416. See also Philip Dine, "Gephardt's Split with White House over China Trade Delights Republicans," *St. Louis Post-Dispatch*, April 23, 2000.

46. Paul Magnusson, "China Trade: Will Clinton Pull It Off?," *Business Week*, May 29, 2000, 74.

47. Most of the members of the smaller, more conservative "Blue Dog" Coalition also backed PNTR.

48. Foerstel, "Multi-Front NTR Lobbying Effort"; "The New Democrat Coalition: 'A Modernizing Force,'" *Rushford Report*, February 2000, 8. See also Stone, "K Street Musters," and Juliet Eilperin, "House's New Democrats at Center of Influence," *Washington Post*, May 29, 2000.

49. "Associating yourself in the public's mind with these emerging technologies and emerging industries is a huge political benefit," said Republican strategist Dan Schnur. Carla Marinucci and Marc Sandalow, "Silicon Valley Emerges as a Force in Politics," *San Francisco Chronicle*, May 10, 1999. See also Miles, *How to Hack a Party Line*; Amy Borrus, "Seeking Geeks Bearing Gifts, the GOP Courts Silicon Valley," *Business Week*, July 27, 1998, 39; "New Democrats Emerge as Brokers on High Tech Bills," *National Journal's CongressDaily*, November 16, 1999; Thomas B. Edsall, "GOP Vies for Backing of High-Tech Leaders," *Washington Post*, June 13, 1999; "House Dems Go to School on High Technology Issues," *National Journal's CongressDaily*, February 8, 2000; and Susan Milligan, "High-Tech Companies Plug into Politics," *Boston Globe*, April 13, 2000.

50. Ceci Connolly, "New Democrat Dinner Is Record Fund-Raiser," *Washington Post*, February 14, 1999. See also Miles, *How to Hack a Party Line*.

51. See Steven Greenhouse, "U.S. Labor Leaders Push Hard to Kill China Bill," *New York Times*, May 14, 2000. In a widely cited study based on figures produced by the International Trade Commission, Robert Scott, EPI's chief trade economist, found that if PNTR was approved by Congress, over the next decade the U.S.-China trade deficit would expand, resulting in the elimination of 872,091 jobs; this would include sizable job losses in every state and in virtually every sector of the economy. Robert E. Scott, "Booming Trade Deficit with China Will Accelerate Job Destruction in Next Decade with Losses in Every State," EPI Briefing Paper, May 2000, http://www.epinet.org/brief ingpapers/chinastates/chinastates.html.

52. Helene Cooper, Bob Davis, and Greg Hitt, "Up in Smoke: WTO's Failure in Bid to Launch Trade Talks Emboldens Protesters," *Wall Street Journal*, December 6, 1999.

53. See Greenhouse, "U.S. Labor Leaders Push Hard"; Helene Cooper and Glenn Burkins, "Unions Debate How Fiercely to Protest China Bill," *Wall Street Journal*, April 7, 2000; and Joseph Kahn with Steven Greenhouse, "Unions Prepare to Hit the Street in Washington," *New York Times*, April 12, 2000.

54. On the basis of exit polls, labor leaders claimed that the proportion of union household members in the electorate rose from 14 percent in 1994 to 23 percent in 1998. According to a survey of union members by Peter D. Hart Research Associates, 71 percent of union members voted for Democratic congressional candidates in 1998, up from just over 60 percent in 1994. Steven Greenhouse, "Republicans Credit Labor for Success by Democrats," *New York Times*, November 6, 1998.

55. In Iowa, voters from union families made up a third of all caucus goers, backing Gore by nearly 3 to 1. In New Hampshire, the efforts of labor activists likely produced the 4 percent margin by which Gore beat Bill Bradley. Meyerson, "Union Man."

56. As in 1998, but unlike in 1996, the emphasis was to be on the "ground" rather than the "air" war. The AFL-CIO planned to put 650 full-time workers in the field and to enlist another 5,000 unpaid "local coordinators" to organize grassroots voter registration and get-out-the-vote activities. Steven Greenhouse, "A.F.L.-C.I.O. Vows to Spend More Than Ever Before on Candidates," *New York Times*, February 16, 2000.

57. As of June 30, 2000, labor unions had donated nearly $15 million in soft money, 50

percent more than their entire soft-money giving for each of the preceding two elections. Ruth Marcus and Mike Allen, "Democrats' Donations from Labor Up Sharply," *Washington Post*, July 18, 2000.

58. Frank Swoboda and Matthew Vita, "For Labor, China Bill Makes Tough Litmus Test," *Washington Post*, April 12, 2000. The force of labor's threats was driven home by the fate of nine-term Democratic incumbent Representative Matthew G. "Marty" Martinez of suburban Los Angeles, who was defeated in a March 7 primary by a labor-backed candidate who was thought to be a more solid union supporter.

59. See Richard E. Cohen, "Trade Winds Swirling over China Vote: Congressional Republicans," *National Journal*, December 18, 1999, 3619.

60. Lori Nitschke with Matthew Tully, "Big Victory for China Trade Needs Senate's Blessing," *Congressional Quarterly Weekly Report*, May 27, 2000, 1249.

61. The Center for Responsive Politics found that House members who voted for PNTR received an average of $44,000 in PAC and individual contributions from members of the Business Roundtable, whereas members who voted no received only $25,000. But Republicans who voted yes received an average of $47,000 each, whereas Democratic PNTR supporters got only about $37,000. Holly Bailey, "A Passage to China Update: House Approves PNTR," *Center for Responsive Politics*, May 24, 2000, http://www.open secrets.org/news/china—house.htm. Since Republican candidates in general and GOP PNTR supporters in particular continue to receive both more campaign money and a larger percentage of their total funds from business interests than do the Democrats, business donations contributed to the greater GOP support for PNTR.

62. While the China deal almost certainly meant more apparel imports from China, the African-Caribbean bill, although it allowed more clothing imports from Africa and Latin America, required them to be made with American cotton. Maggs, "Art of the Deal." Space limitations prevent a more detailed discussion of this long-stalled bill, but its passage was hailed as an important free-trade victory for Clinton and, as intended by the White House, added momentum to the pro-PNTR drive.

63. PNTR opponent Lori Wallach, director of Public Citizens Global Trade Watch, claimed that such pressure from the GOP leadership caused seventeen Republicans to switch their votes from no to yes toward the end of the fight. Mark Egan, "U.S. Foe of China Trade Pact Considers Revenge," *Yahoo! News*, May 26, 2000, http://dailynews. yahoo.com/h/nm/20000526/pl/wto—china—105.html.

64. Owen Ullman, "A Labor Liberal's Efforts to Make the Difference," *USA Today*, May 24, 2000.

65. Helene Cooper, "Eclectic Grass-Roots Campaign Emerges in China Trade," *Wall Street Journal*, March 13, 2000.

66. Nitschke with Tully, "Big Victory for China Trade," 1249. Of the fifty-six Democrats who hailed from seven key industrial states—New Jersey, Pennsylvania, Illinois, Ohio, Michigan, Wisconsin, and Missouri—only four voted for PNTR. Harold Meyerson, "Clinton's Wedge: China Cracks the Democrats," *LA Weekly*, June 2–8, 2000, 15.

67. Of the 108 House Democrats, or 52 percent of the caucus, who received at least 20 percent of their total campaign contributions for their most recent campaigns from labor PACs, 86 voted against PNTR. Nitschke with Tully, "Big Victory for China Trade," 1249. According to the Center for Responsive Politics, House Democrats who opposed the China bill received an average of $76,000 in PAC and individual contributions from unions, whereas lawmakers voting yes received only about $59,000 from labor. Bailey, "Passage to China Update."

68. Based on "dozens" of visits to House members, DLC president Al From observed that "having spent the last six years in the minority, all House Democrats want to win back the majority this year. Most of them see labor money and manpower as crucial. So, even if their own seats are safe, many Democrats have concluded that antagonizing organized labor over trade with China is too big a risk. Moreover, they're pretty certain that the business community . . . won't be lining up to replace any campaign contributions to Democrats that labor unions might withhold. In fact, most Democrats expect, with good reason, that most of the business community will back Republicans for House seats, even against Democrats who vote to make China's trade status permanent." Al From, "National vs. Special Interests: The PNTR Vote Is All About Election Year Politics," *New Democrat Online*, June 1, 2000, http://www.ndol.org/ndol—ci.cfm.?kaid=86&subid=84&contentid=485. Democratic fears regarding business were aroused in early March when the Chamber of Commerce endorsed the Republican challengers to pro-PNTR incumbent Democrats Baron Hill of Indiana and Earl Pomeroy of North Dakota. Before the vote, the Chamber eventually did announce the endorsements of seven Democrats.

69. For a wide range of polling results, see the publication of the University of Maryland's Program on International Policy Attitudes, "Americans on Globalization: A Study of U.S. Public Attitudes, March 28, 2000, Appendix A: Americans on U.S.-China Trade," http://www.pipa.org/Online-Reports/Globalization/appendixa/appendixa.htm; "International Trade," *PollingReport.com*, http://www.pollingreport.com/tradee/htm; and "2000 Polling on China," *Poll Track*, http://www.nationaljournal.com/members/polltrack/2000/issues/00china.htm.

70. Respondents favored PNTR 54–43 percent in mid-November, 50–40 in late January, *opposed* it 43–45 in early April, and backed it again 56–37 the weekend before the vote. Frank Newport, "Public Favors Passage of China Trade Bill," *The Gallup Organization: Poll Releases*, May 23, 2000, http://www.gallup.com/poll/releases/pr000523.asp.

71. Juliet Eilperin and David Broder, "Despite UAW Threat, Low Risk Seen on China Vote," *New York Times*, May 24, 2000. According to the Gallup Poll, in early May, by the weekend before the vote, only 41 percent said they had been following the issue very or somewhat closely, a much lower figure than the 70 percent who were paying close attention to the NAFTA debate on the eve of the vote on that agreement. Newport, "Public Favors Passage."

72. See, e.g., Aaron Bernstein, "Backlash: Behind the Anxiety over Globalization," *Business Week*, April 24, 2000, 38–46, and the Harris Poll on globalization included therein.

73. Baer, *Reinventing Democrats*, 252; Eilperin, "House's New Democrats."

74. "I never worshiped at the altar of a balanced budget before this president," said Bonior. "But through that fiscal discipline we have been able to blunt the Republicans' main charge against us. And we have built an economic climate that let us thrive as a nation. To convince someone like me is an accomplishment." David Broder, "Democrats' Image Changes," *Washington Post*, August 13, 2000.

75. See Eilperin, "House's New Democrats"; Eric Pianin, "Learning from Their Mistakes," *Washington Post National Weekly Edition*, January 3, 2000, 12–13; and Jonathan Cohn, "Change for a Buck: Gephardt Abandons the Left," *New Republic*, August 21, 2000, 26–31.

76. Ethan Wallison, "Unions Mull Primary Challenges in 2000," *Roll Call*, June 22, 2000.

77. For example, when the United Food and Commercial Workers polled its members' priorities, trade and China were far down the list. John B. Judis, "Disunion: Gore's Labor Pains," *New Republic*, August 21, 2000, 22.

78. See Laurence McQuillan, "Labor Unions Split over Proposed China Trade Agreement," *USA Today*, April 12, 2000, and Paul Bedard, Warren P. Strober, Suzi Parker, and Nancy Bentrup, "A Labor Mutiny on China Trade," *U.S. News & World Report*, May 22, 2000, 11.

79. See Guy de Jonquieres, "Against the Tide," *Financial Times*, May 11, 2000; Maggs, "Art of the Deal"; and Karen Foerstel, "Unions and Pro-Trade Democrats: Estrangement but No Divorce," *Congressional Quarterly Weekly Report*, May 27, 2000, 1251.

80. GOP leaders acknowledged this. See Nitschke with Tully, "Big Victory for China Trade," 1252.

81. Ullman, "A Labor Liberal's Efforts." Support for the China bill, especially from nine of the thirty-six members of the Congressional Black Caucus (CBC), was also secured by (1) the decision by Representative Charles Rangel, the influential liberal black lawmaker from New York, to support the measure, (2) a deal reached between the White House and GOP leaders on legislation to use tax breaks and public investment to help distressed urban and rural communities, and (3) the passage in early May by bipartisan majorities of the long-stalled, administration-backed African-Caribbean trade bill, which was overwhelmingly supported by the CBC.

82. On business's lobbying advantage over labor, see Eric Schmitt, "China Trade Bill Is Edging Closer to Approval in House," *New York Times*, May 20, 2000.

83. Juliana Greenwald, "High-Tech Industry Plays Big Role in PNTR Passage," *Technology Daily*, May 24, 2000.

84. Lee Walczak, "Can Bush Heal the Nation?," *Business Week*, December 25, 2000, 44.

85. Figures from the Center for Responsive Politics; Mike Allen, "Democrats Gain as Business Hedges Bets," *Washington Post*, October 17, 2000. More dramatic still, looking only at the flow of soft money, Common Cause found that whereas the DCCC received about 29 percent of total business soft-money contributions to the two House party committees in 1997–98, that figure rose to 47 percent for the whole of 1999. Jim Vande-Hei, "Democrats Close the 'Soft Money' Gap with Republicans," *Wall Street Journal*, March 14, 2000.

86. Center for Responsive Politics, *Who's Paying?*

87. Susan Crabtree, "Democrats Download High-Tech Money in L.A.," *Roll Call*, August 21, 2000.

88. The figures are from the Center for Responsive Politics. Greg Hitt, "Democrats Move Ahead in Soft-Money Race," *Wall Street Journal*, August 17, 2000.

89. Louis Jacobson, "For Friends in Need, Business Money Indeed," *National Journal*, June 3, 2000, 1764–65. Minority Leader Dick Gephardt, who in the spring of 2000 was intensively courting business support, observed that "the business community is beginning to think, to some extent, that the Democratic Party is more fiscally conservative than the Republican Party. It's almost disorienting." Hitt, "Democrats Move Ahead."

90. According to the Center for Responsive Politics, Democrats voting for PNTR received an average of $37,000 in contributions from members of the Business Roundtable whereas those voting against it got only about $22,000. Bailey, "Passage to China Update." Regarding the influence of campaign donations from the high-tech sector, an aide to Representative Nancy Pelosi (D-Calif.), a leading PNTR opponent, said, "Silicon

Valley is a gold mine for campaign contributions. Now that they're in on [the China issue], a lot of politicians are really hustling." Urbina, "The Corporate PNTR Lobby."

91. Cooper, "On China Trade Bill." On the role of this kind of learning in the evolution of business political strategy, see Suarez, *Does Business Learn?*

92. Kristin Brainerd, "With an Eye toward Speakership, Gephardt May Soon Spurn Presidential Bid," *Congressional Quarterly Weekly Report*, January 23, 1999, 1979.

93. Eilperin, "House's New Democrats" (first Gephardt quotation); Albert R. Hunt, "Gephardt Sets the Agenda for November House Contest," *Wall Street Journal*, June 15, 2000 (second Gephardt quotation); Cohn, "Change for a Buck," 30; Shesgreen, "Gephardt Nudges Democrats" (Roemer).

94. See Susan B. Glasser, " 'Soft Money' Paves the Way," *Washington Post National Weekly Edition*, October 25, 1999, 6–8.

95. On the increased fund-raising role of the congressional party committees, see Paul Herrnson, "Parties and Interest Groups in Post-Reform Congressional Elections," in Allan Cigler and Burdett Loomis, eds., *Interest Group Politics*, 5th ed. (Washington, D.C.: CQ Press, 1998), 145–67, and Marianne Holt, "The Surge in Party Money in Competitive 1998 Congressional Elections," in David B. Magleby, ed., *Outside Money: Soft Money and Issue Advocacy in the 1998 Congressional Elections* (Lanham, Md.: Rowman and Littlefield Publishers, 1999), 17–40.

96. Juliet Eilperin, "Congress Is Open for Business," *Washington Post National Weekly Edition*, April 17, 2000, 13; VandeHei, "Democrats Close the 'Soft Money' Gap."

97. Lizette Alvarez, "Gephardt Courts the Technology Industry," *New York Times*, March 29, 2000.

98. Ibid.

99. Ethan Wallison, "Labor Criticizes Gephardt's Role," *Roll Call*, May 22, 2000; Cohn, "Change for a Buck."

100. For the next two paragraphs, see Eric Schmitt, "G.O.P. Tries to Delay Vote in the Senate on China Bill," *New York Times*, July 12, 2000, and Joseph Kahn, "Playing for (Political) Time on China Trade," *New York Times*, July 28, 2000.

101. "Should this vote get tangled up in the politics of nuclear proliferation and other amendments to the extent that it might not be passed," Donohue said, "I think that that would have a very serious political implication for those who were a party to that action." Eric Schmitt, "Wavering Senators Feeling Pressure on China Bill," *New York Times*, September 13, 2000.

102. Twenty-three Republicans and nine Democrats voted for the amendment.

103. "The House-Senate difference has been clear for years," said AFL-CIO director of legislative affairs Peggy Taylor. "The Senate has been more free-trade-oriented." Senator Max Baucus (D-Mont.) explained part of the reason for this: "Senators represent states, not congressional districts. They generally have a wider array of interests to consider.... Every state has considerable farm interests. Most House Democrats don't." Richard E. Cohen, "A Cease-Fire in the Trade War," *Congressional Quarterly Weekly Report*, September 16, 2000, 2876–77.

104. Even the UAW and the Teamsters, the two most vociferous labor opponents of the China deal, had made their peace with and endorsed Al Gore.

105. "We've got a lot at stake in this election," said the AFL-CIO's Peggy Taylor. "It's not just trade policy." Matthew Vita, "Senate Approves Normalized Trade with China," *Washington Post*, September 20, 2000. See also Eric Schmitt, "Senate Votes to Lift Curbs on U.S. Trade with China," *New York Times*, September 20, 2000.

106. Nick Anderson, "Permanent Trade Status for China Clears Congress," *Los Angeles Times*, September 20, 2000.

107. Due to a number of disagreements between China and various WTO members, as of this writing (late April 2001) negotiations on Beijing's entry into the organization were not expected to be concluded until later in the year or perhaps even 2002.

Conclusion

1. See *Competitive Enterprise Index* (Washington, D.C.: Competitive Enterprise Institute, 1985–94).

2. Data not reproduced here also show that the parties split over trade in all regions of the country. In other words, such differences were not due simply to greater Democratic representation in the protectionist-oriented industrial heartland combined with disproportionate Republican strength in the free-trade–inclined Sun Belt. In Figures A.2 and A.3, the graphic indicators of House and Senate partisan division over trade issues, reproduced from an article by Michael Hiscox, show less clear patterns of partisan division during this same period than the CEI indexes due to the smaller sample of bills that Hiscox examined.

3. Looking only at the House, John Coleman shows that after declining throughout the post–World War II era, party voting on trade increased from 1983 to 1992. During this period 72 percent of all trade-related votes were "party votes," i.e., where a majority of one party opposed a majority of the other. This was up from 60 percent from 1947 to 1964, 49 percent from 1965 to 1975, and 44 percent from 1976 to 1982. John J. Coleman, *Party Decline in America: Policy, Politics, and the Fiscal State* (Chicago: University of Chicago Press, 1996), 26–28.

4. Keith T. Poole and Howard Rosenthal, *Congress: A Political-Economic History of Roll Call Voting* (New York: Oxford University Press, 1997).

5. Morris Fiorina has recently argued that parties matter in Congress mainly because lawmakers' preferences reflect those of their core partisan electoral constituencies. In advancing this view, he is partly taking issue with scholars like John Aldrich and David Rohde, who maintain that a principal source of party influence in Congress is pressure from party leaders, who use rewards and punishments to discipline their followers, and with other authors like Keith Krehbiel, who deny that parties have effects in Congress, since partisan differences are due not to party discipline, but rather only to differences in lawmakers' induced preferences, the sources of which are not specified. Both groups of analysts, Fiorina argues, pay too little attention to the influence of the party-in-the-electorate. Morris P. Fiorina, *"Keystone" Reconsidered*," in Lawrence C. Dodd and Bruce I. Oppenheimer, eds., *Congress Reconsidered*, 7th ed. (Washington, D.C.: CQ Press, 2001), 141–62; John H. Aldrich and David W. Rohde, "The Consequences of Party Organization in the House: The Role of the Majority and Minority Parties in Conditional Party Government," in Jon R. Bond and Richard Fleisher, eds., *Polarized Politics: Congress and the President in a Partisan Era* (Washington, D.C.: CQ Press, 2000), 31–72; Keith Krehbiel, *Pivotal Politics: A Theory of U.S. Lawmaking* (Chicago: University of Chicago Press, 1998).

6. During the Clinton presidency, the inclination of Republican members of Congress to posture on behalf of tougher trade policy was tempered by their constituency- and ideologically induced preferences for free trade.

7. I. M. Destler, *American Trade Politics*, 3d. ed. (Washington, D.C.: Institute for Inter-

national Economics and Twentieth Century Fund, 1995), 182–84; William Schneider, "The Old Politics and the New World Order," in Kenneth A. Oye, Robert J. Lieber, and Donald Rothschild, eds., *Eagle in a New World: American Grand Strategy in the Post–Cold War Era* (New York: HarperCollins Publishers, 1991); Ruy A. Teixeira and Guy Molyneux, *Economic Nationalism and the Future of American Politics* (Washington, D.C.: Economic Policy Institute, 1993).

8. This analysis does support the views of "conditional party government" theorists like John Aldrich and David Rohde and contradicts the perspectives of authors like Keith Krehbiel, cited in n. 5. As I have tried to demonstrate, the heresthetical, agenda-setting, and cohesion-fostering activities of congressional Democratic leaders, especially in the House, had significant influence on their members' conduct as well as on actual trade policy choices and outputs.

9. See various issues of the *Gallup Poll*, 1981–90.

10. Destler, *American Trade Politics*; Judith Goldstein, *Ideas, Interests, and American Trade Policy* (Ithaca, N.Y.: Cornell University Press, 1993), 182.

11. I. M. Destler, "U.S. Trade Policy-Making in the Eighties," in Alberto Alesina and Geoffrey Carliner, eds., *Politics and Economics in the Eighties* (Chicago: University of Chicago Press, 1991), 256–57.

12. David Vogel stresses this point in "The Triumph of Liberal Trade: American Trade Policy in the Postwar Period," in Morton Keller and R. Shep Melnick, eds., *Taking Stock: American Government in the Twentieth Century* (Cambridge: Woodrow Wilson Center Press and Cambridge University Press, 1999), 35–53. For more on the activities of anti-protectionist interests during this period, see I. M. Destler and John S. Odell, *Anti-Protection: Changing Forces in United States Trade Politics* (Washington, D.C.: Institute for International Economics, 1987).

13. Stephen J. Majeski, "An Alternative Approach to the Generation and Maintenance of Norms," in Karen Schweers Cook and Margaret Levi, eds., *The Limits of Rationality* (Chicago: University of Chicago Press, 1990), 273–81. For other work on the reliance of policymakers on historical lessons, precedents, and analogies, see Richard Rose, *Lesson-Drawing in Public Policy: A Guide to Learning across Time and Space* (Chatham, N.J.: Chatham House Publishers, 1993), and Yuen Foong Khong, *Analogies at War: Korea, Munich, Dien Bien Phu, and the Vietnam Decisions of 1965* (Princeton, N.J.: Princeton University Press, 1991).

14. On political time horizons and discount rates, see Paul Pierson, "Increasing Returns, Path Dependence, and the Study of Politics," *American Political Science Review* 94, no. 2 (June 2000): 261–62.

15. R. Douglas Arnold, *The Logic of Congressional Action* (New Haven: Yale University Press, 1990); Keith Krehbiel, *Information and Legislative Organization* (Ann Arbor: University of Michigan Press, 1991); Richard L. Hall, "Heterogeneous Preferences and the Practice of Group Representation in U.S. Trade Policy," in Alan V. Deardorff and Robert M. Stern, eds., *Constituent Interests and U.S. Trade Policies* (Ann Arbor: University of Michigan Press, 1998), 109–19.

16. See James M. Lindsay, "Congress and Foreign Policy: Why the Hill Matters," *Political Science Quarterly* 107 (1992–93): 607–28.

17. On such "anticipated reactions," see James M. Lindsay and Randall B. Ripley, "How Congress Influences Foreign and Defense Policy," in Lindsay and Ripley, eds., *Congress Resurgent: Foreign and Defense Policy on Capitol Hill* (Ann Arbor: University of Michigan Press, 1993).

18. Given that sixty-two House Republicans voted for the 1986 immigration bill, whereas fifty-nine GOP members supported the 1986 draft of what became the 1988 Trade Act, Ronald Peters points out the seeming anomaly that the trade bill was politically defined as a Democratic bill whereas the immigration bill was not. He concludes that "a bill is bipartisan in the politically relevant sense when it draws substantial votes from both sides of the aisle and is not used as an instrument for one party to club the other." Clearly, House Democrats tried to use the 1986 trade bill to club their Republican rivals. Ronald M. Peters Jr., *The American Speakership: The Office in Historical Perspective*, 2d ed. (Baltimore: Johns Hopkins University Press, 1997), 366.

19. This substantial opposition to a president of their own party, by the way, provides further evidence that House Democrats' toughness on trade during the Reagan-Bush era was not just posturing of the kind predicted by incumbency-focused theories.

20. In general, however, party conflict in the Senate remained intense throughout the Clinton years.

21. Martha Gibson maintains that the House reforms of the 1970s also contributed to increased partisanship on trade. She argues that the decentralizing reforms of that decade opened up access to the trade policy process to formerly excluded protectionist interests, while the centralizing reforms of the same decade enhanced the power of the Democratic leadership. See Martha L. Gibson, *Conflict amid Consensus in American Trade Policy* (Washington, D.C.: Georgetown University Press, 2000), 136–37. In an econometric analysis, John Coleman uses a dummy variable to test the impact of the 1970s reforms on levels of party conflict over trade in the House. Unlike Gibson, Coleman finds no significant effects for the reforms. John J. Coleman, "Bipartisan Order and Partisan Disorder in Postwar Trade Policy" (unpublished paper, University of Wisconsin at Madison, 1997).

22. Along with many other scholars, Pomper argues that the partisan nature of the presidency has been diminished by the growth of the administrative state and candidate-centered campaigning, whereas congressional party divisions have widened due to the strengthening of the leadership's powers and the greater homogeneity of the parties' respective voting coalitions. Gerald M. Pomper, "The Alleged Decline of American Parties," in John Geer, ed., *Politicians and Party Politics* (Baltimore: Johns Hopkins University Press, 1998), 14–39.

23. For the interbranch view, see Destler, *American Trade Politics*, and Robert A. Pastor, "The Cry-and-Sigh Syndrome: Congress and Trade Policy," in Allen Schick, ed., *Making Economic Policy in Congress* (Washington, D.C.: American Enterprise Institute, 1983), 158–95.

24. On the role of intervening variables in "amplifying" the effects of other variables, see John S. Odell, "Understanding International Trade Policies: An Emerging Synthesis," *World Politics* 43 (October 1990): 139–67.

25. Destler, *American Trade Politics* and "U.S. Trade Policy-Making in the Eighties."

26. The growing scholarly literature on "ideas" rarely specifies in any detail how policy ideas become institutionalized and are reproduced, but anecdotes from the process of drafting the 1988 Trade Act illuminate one interesting mechanism. Recall that House Trade Subcommittee members and later House and Senate conferees who worked on the bill were very conscious of the symbolism of the visage of Willis Hawley, coauthor of the Smoot-Hawley Tariff Act, who gazed down on them from the walls of the committee rooms in which they labored.

27. Destler advances this argument in I. M. (Mac) Destler, "Congress, Constituencies, and U.S. Trade Policy," in Deardorff and Stern, *Constituent Interests*, 100.

28. As Republican House Minority Leader Robert Michel warned during the intense autumn of 1985, speaking for members of both parties, "We've got to get some results. People have constituents to satisfy." David Shribman, "Congress Is Relieved by Efforts on Dollar, but Some Stress Need to See Fast Results," *Wall Street Journal*, September 23, 1985.

29. Pietro Nivola, *Regulating Unfair Trade* (Washington, D.C.: Brookings Institution Press, 1993), 17 (Baker); David Hale, "Global Finance and the Retreat to Managed Trade," *Harvard Business Review* (January–February 1990): 152; Anne O. Krueger, "Comment," in Alesina and Carliner, *Politics and Economics in the Eighties*, 283–84—a critique of Destler's article in the same volume. Thomas Bayard and Kimberly Elliott show that in 1985–89 the number of Section 301 investigations had increased by 50 percent over the previous five-year period, with an even sharper rise in the proportion of cases involving public threats, including cases self-initiated by the U.S. Trade Representative. Thomas O. Bayard and Kimberly A. Elliott, *Reciprocity and Retaliation in U.S. Trade Policy* (Washington, D.C.: Institute for International Economics, 1994).

30. Andreas Falke argues that since 1980, the United States has seen a partial or incomplete "paradigm shift" toward fair trade. Falke, "American Trade Policy after the End of the Cold War," in Michael Minkenberg and Herbert Dittgen, eds., *The American Impasse: U.S. Domestic and Foreign Policy after the Cold War* (Pittsburgh: University of Pittsburgh Press, 1996), 264–97. For other judgments that the trade policy changes of the Reagan-Bush era were of greater consequence than analysts like Destler would have it, see the comment by Thomas E. Mann on another article by Destler in Susan M. Collins and Robert Z. Lawrence, eds., *Brookings Trade Forum, 1999* (Washington, D.C.: Brookings Institution Press, 1999), 162, and Richard Higgott, "Beyond Embedded Liberalism: Governing the International Trade Regime in an Era of Economic Nationalism," in Philip Gummett, ed., *Globalization and Public Policy* (Brookfield, Vt.: Edward Elgar, 1996), 18–45.

31. On the more general process of institutional transformation via recombination with other institutions, see Kathleen Thelen, "Timing and Temporality in the Analysis of Institutional Evolution and Change," *Studies in American Political Development* 14, no. 1 (Spring 2000): 101–8.

32. The volatility of global financial markets and other factors led the Clinton administration to retreat from its tough stance toward Tokyo after mid-1995.

33. In different ways, Stephen Skowronek's and William Mayer's analyses are somewhat consistent with this view. See Skowronek, *The Politics Presidents Make: Leadership from John Adams to Bill Clinton* (Cambridge: Belknap/Harvard University Press, 1997), and Mayer, "Changes in Elections and the Party System: 1992 in Historical Perspective," in Bryan D. Jones, ed., *The New American Politics: Reflections on Political Change and the Clinton Administration* (Boulder, Colo.: Westview Press, 1995), 19–50.

34. See John B. Judis, "The Spirit of '76: Why W. Won't Stop an Emerging Democratic Majority," *New Republic*, November 6, 2000, 27–29. Taylor Dark goes further to argue that, although weakened, the electoral coalition and institutions of the New Deal Order never really died, due largely to the continuity in labor's role in the Democratic Party at the national level. Dark, *The Unions and the Democrats: An Enduring Alliance* (Ithaca, N.Y.: Cornell University Press, 1999), 195–201.

35. Peter F. Nardulli, "The Concept of a Critical Realignment, Electoral Behavior, and

Political Change," *American Political Science Review* 89, no. 1 (March 1995): 10–22; T. J. Pempel, *Regime Shift: Comparative Dynamics of the Japanese Political Economy* (Ithaca, N.Y.: Cornell University Press, 1998), 126; John H. Aldrich, "Political Parties in a Critical Era," *American Politics Quarterly* 27, no. 1 (January 1999): 9–32; David G. Lawrence, *The Collapse of the Democratic Presidential Majority: Realignment, Dealignment, and Electoral Change from Franklin Roosevelt to Bill Clinton* (Boulder, Colo.: Westview Press, 1997), 169–90. Of course, some analysts find the whole party system/realignment framework either misguided or outmoded. See many of the articles in Bryon E. Shafer, ed., *The End of Realignment? Interpreting American Electoral Eras* (Madison: University of Wisconsin Press, 1991).

36. In this respect at least, I agree with DLC president Al From, who argues that "a new political order for the Information Age has not yet been formed to replace the New Deal order that dominated Industrial Age America. Until a new order takes shape, it is likely that no clear electoral pattern will emerge—and different coalitions will decide each election." From, "The Parties at Parity: The True Story of the 2000 Election Was That It Was a Tie," *New Democrat*, December 20, 2000.

37. On this question, see Jim VandeHei and Shailagh Murray, "Bush's Ability to Exploit Democrats' Rifts Could Be Key to Advancing His Agenda," *Wall Street Journal*, January 3, 2001, and Dana Milbank, "Bipartisanship's Lesson: It's Easy Come, Easy Go," *Washington Post*, January 9, 2001.

38. The House New Democrat Coalition grew from 65 to at least 72 members in the new Congress, while the overlapping Blue Dog group has about 30 members. The recently formed Senate New Democratic Coalition increased from 16 to as many as 23 members.

39. Steven Pearlstein, "U.S. Trade Debate Heats Up with Steel at Its Core," *Washington Post*, November 24, 2000.

40. The groundbreaking deal with Jordan, consistent with the position taken by the Clinton administration at the Seattle WTO meeting in late 1999, commits both countries to enforce existing laws on labor and the environment. It is the first trade agreement in U.S. history that includes labor and environmental standards as part of the main text and the first agreement negotiated during the Clinton years that has the support of organized labor. Some business interests, especially the U.S. Chamber of Commerce, their conservative GOP congressional allies, and, it appears, the Bush administration oppose these enforceable standards, and the agreement may be modified. Steven Pearlstein, "Leftover Trade Issues on Bush's Plate," *Washington Post*, January 2, 2001; Edward Alden, "Bush Faces Huge Free Trade Divide," *Financial Times*, January 3, 2001.

41. Bush initially planned to demote the USTR from cabinet status, but pressure from business and the wider trade policy community led him to abandon the idea.

42. For the following discussion of the prospects for a new fast-track bill, see Pearlstein, "Leftover Trade Issues"; Alden, "Bush Faces Huge Free Trade Divide"; Anthony DePalma, "Latin America Is Priority on Bush Trade Agenda," *New York Times*, December 18, 2000; Edward Alden, "Companies Seek to Resolve Trade Issues," *Financial Times*, January 30, 2001; David Moberg, "FTAA, Eh?: A Bigger, Badder Trade Deal," *In These Times*, April 16, 2001, 16–19; Daniel Schorr, "Bush's Back Door to Latino Vote?," *Christian Science Monitor*, April 27, 2001; Steven Greenhouse, "Labor Leaders Joining Forces in Opposition to Trade Plan," *New York Times*, April 29, 2001; and Morton Kondracke, "Bush Walks Fine Line on 'Sanctions' to Win Trade Fight," *Roll Call*, April 30, 2001.

43. In mid-December 2000, House New Democrat Coalition cochairman Cal Dooley

said that it would be "very, very difficult" for Bush to win fast-track approval without Republicans and business groups agreeing to some kind of compromise on labor and environmental issues. Doug Palmer, "Barshefsky Urges Bush to Be 'Pragmatic' on Trade," *Excite News*, www.news.excite.com. In an early January letter to President-Elect Bush, members of both House and Senate New Democrat coalitions wrote that they were inclined to support new fast-track authority to help Bush negotiate the FTAA, but they also called for "provisions that will provide for reasonable consideration of issues relating to labor and the environment." The text of the letter is available on the Democratic Leadership Council's website at www.ndol.org.

44. In early 2001 a group of top U.S. companies, including Boeing, Motorola, Kodak, and Caterpillar, sought just such an accommodation. Frank Vargo, a vice president for international economic affairs at the National Association of Manufacturers, which organized the initiative, said that the outlines of a compromise might be found in a recent free-trade deal between Canada and Chile, in which side agreements provided that fines rather than trade sanctions be used to penalize infractions of labor and environmental laws. But other powerful business interests, including the U.S. Chamber of Commerce and textile and apparel makers, remained opposed to any linkage between trade and labor and environmental issues. Pearlstein, "Leftover Trade Issues"; Alden, "Companies Seek to Resolve Trade Issues."

45. In the last few weeks of the 2000 campaign, for example, the Business Roundtable undertook a $6 million trade-centered issue ad offensive on behalf of thirty-five House members and four senators, one-third of whom were Democrats, thanking them for their support of PNTR with China. In addition, the U.S. Chamber of Commerce and the Business-Industry Political Action Committee (BIPAC) stayed clear of races in which pro-PNTR Democratic incumbents were running. Charlie Mitchell, "House Races," *CongressDailyAM*, October 27, 2000; Susan Schmidt, "Businesses Ante Up $30 million," *Washington Post*, October 26, 2000.

46. DLC leaders, including Al From and Will Marshall, based their views on yet another survey by former Clinton and Gore pollster, Mark Penn. Liberal Democrats replied that Gore lost not because of his populist appeals, which were actually quite effective, but rather because of the centrality to voters of cultural (guns, abortion, etc.) rather than economic issues, some voters' revulsion against the scandals and moral crises of the Clinton administration, Bush's success in blurring his policy differences with Gore, and the vice president's poorly run campaign. Once again the liberals based their arguments on a survey conducted for the Campaign for America's Future by former Clinton pollster Stanley Greenberg, who replaced Penn as Gore's pollster in the summer of 2000. See Thomas B. Edsall, "Fissures Widening among Democrats after Gore's Loss," *Washington Post*, December 16, 2000, and Morton Kondracke, "Left-Center Rift Re-emerges for Democratic Leaders," *Roll Call*, January 11, 2001. Cal Dooley indicated in late January that he might accept a compromise in which labor and environmental provisions would not be enforced through trade sanctions. Bob Davis, "Trade May Soon Top Bush's List of Issues," *Wall Street Journal*, January 31, 2001.

47. In the 2000 elections labor fielded more than 1,000 full-time grassroots campaign coordinators, who mobilized 100,000 union members to make 8 million phone calls, send out 12 million pieces of mail, and pass out more than 14 million leaflets. As a consequence of these efforts, union members and their families comprised 26 percent of the electorate in 2000, up from 19 percent in 1992 and 23 percent in 1996. Sixty-three percent of these union voters cast their ballots for Al Gore; only 32 percent voted for

George Bush. Aaron Bernstein, "Labor's Labors Aren't Lost," *Business Week*, November 7, 2000, 86–90.

48. Shortly after the PNTR fight, Thomas J. Donohue, president of the U.S. Chamber of Commerce, remarked: "Anybody who stands up and says, 'We won this thing by a couple of votes and therefore labor is weak,' they don't know how to count. Labor has a lot of money. Labor has a lot of forces on the ground. Anyone who wants to declare them weak, just look out for the next fight." Steven Greenhouse, "Despite Defeat on China Bill, Labor Is on Rise, *New York Times*, May 30, 2000. For the influence of labor on the dynamics and politics of the international economy, see Mark Rupert, *Producing Hegemony: The Politics of Mass Production and American Global Power* (Cambridge: Cambridge University Press, 1995); Andrew Herod, "Labor as an Agent of Globalization and as a Global Agent," in Kevin Cox, ed., *Spaces of Globalization* (New York: Guilford Press, 1997); and Robert O'Brien, "Labour and IPE: Rediscovering Human Agency," in Ronen Palan, ed., *Global Political Economy: Contemporary Theories* (London: Routledge, 2000), 89–99.

49. John F. Harris, "Indispensable or Irrelevant?," *Washington Post*, January 18, 2001. See also Robert Wright, "Clinton's One Big Idea," *New York Times*, January 16, 2001.

50. After climbing by 240,000 in 1999, the largest such increase in more than a decade, union membership declined by 200,000 in 2000 to 13.5 percent of the workforce, its lowest point in six decades (its peak was 35 percent in the 1950s).

Brazil, 98, 103, 107, 141
Breglio, Vince, 145
Bretton Woods agreements (1944), 57
Brock, William, 13, 82, 92
Brookings Institution, 179
Brown, Jerry, 155, 176
Bryan, William Jennings, 51
Buchanan, Patrick, 152–55, 158, 176, 181–
  82, 192, 207; supporters of, 193, 208, 218,
  243
Bull Moose Party, 52
Bush, George H. W., 4, 7, 8, 168, 169; trade
  policy, 2, 8, 10, 30, 137–60, 255–61, 264–
  66; fast-track bills, 5, 137, 144–49, 160,
  261; reelection bid, 8, 22, 154–55, 157–
  60, 162; political orders and, 43; as vice
  president, 107, 134; presidential campaign, 132, 135–36; foreign policy, 140,
  149, 150; Structural Impediments Initiative, 141, 142, 143, 160; China and,
  148, 155, 157, 234. *See also* Japan: Bush
  and
Bush, George W., 269–71
Business Coalition for U.S.-China Trade,
  237
Business conflict theory, 2, 55
Business-Industry Political Action Committee, 223
Business Roundtable, 130, 146, 195, 214,
  237–38, 252
Business sector, 13, 270–72; politics and, 6,
  7, 13–15, 62, 71, 75–77, 83, 86–87, 101,
  108, 117, 119, 120, 130, 147, 163, 222–24,
  240–41, 248–50, 257, 259, 261, 270–72;
  China PNTR status and, 9, 228, 234–39,
  247–49, 251, 253–54, 263, 268; swing interests, 16; Order of '96, 51–52; New
  Deal Order, 54, 56, 62; Reagan and, 71,
  75–77, 83, 86, 96, 108, 109, 130, 132;
  post-Fordism and, 72–73, 99; Bush
  and, 138, 141–42, 145–46, 151; NAFTA
  and, 145–46, 176, 179, 183, 262, 267;
  Clinton and, 166, 169–70, 172, 174, 186,
  191–93, 196, 205, 214, 218–19, 232; GATT
  and, 192–95. *See also* Campaign contributions: by business sector; Multinational corporations
Byrd, Robert, 117, 118, 125, 126, 127, 131, 132

Campaign contributions, 13; by business
  sector, 15, 16, 21, 83, 92–93, 180, 184, 202,
  216, 220, 223–24, 230, 238–41, 248–51,
  254, 262–63, 268; by labor, 16, 83, 84,
  108, 148, 184, 187, 202, 208, 215, 216,
  220–21, 225, 242, 248; by PACs, 83, 92,
  180, 184, 202, 216, 220–21, 223–24, 248.
  See also Democratic Party; Republican
  Party
Campaign for America's Future, 211
Canada, 80, 107, 110, 114, 155; NAFTA and,
  137, 144, 159, 175–76; WTO complaint
  against, 207–8
Canada-U.S. Free Trade Agreement
  (1988), 4, 144, 260
Capital, 13–14, 39; mobility of, 35, 72; New
  Deal Order, 54, 57, 68; post-Fordism
  and, 73, 99
Capitalism, 48, 51, 73, 212
Carter, Hodding, III, 85
Carter, Jimmy, 69, 71–72, 78, 81, 99, 162
Cerny, Philip, 73
Chapman, Jim, 100
Chile, 198, 213, 270
China, 4, 223, 224; PNTR status, 2, 4, 5, 9,
  15, 21, 23, 27, 29, 30, 33, 166–68, 228,
  231–55, 262, 263, 268, 271; Clinton and,
  2, 9, 23, 27, 30, 166–68, 172, 205, 208,
  209, 227–28, 231–54, 268, 271; WTO
  and, 2, 198, 227, 232, 233, 241; Reagan
  and, 88–89; Bush and, 148, 155, 157, 234;
  textile quotas and, 209, 234
China Trade Relations Working Group,
  235
Chrysler, 156
Citizens Trade Campaign, 176, 181, 192,
  217, 242
Civil rights movement, 71, 100
Civil War Order, 42, 47–51
Class, 53, 162–63
Cleveland, Grover, 50
Clinton, Bill, 4, 43, 147; trade policy, 2, 5,
  7–10, 23, 30, 154, 158, 161–256, 261–63,
  266–68; Seattle WTO meeting and, 5, 9,
  30, 33, 227, 230–33, 256, 267–68; reelection bid, 9, 199, 205–9, 211, 267; cross-
  partisan coalitions, 27, 165, 166, 177,
  186, 262; 1992 election campaign, 154–

Foley, Tom, 121, 177, 178
Ford, Gerald, 69
Fordism, 43, 44, 54, 65, 67, 68–69, 258;
    transition from, 72–75, 269
Ford Motor Company, 78, 156
Fordney-McCumber Tariff Act (1922), 53
Foreign aid, 54
Foreign investment, 66, 73, 131, 138, 143
Foreign policy, 20, 23, 25, 52, 140, 149, 150
France, 103
Free trade: liberalization initiatives, 1–5,
    54, 111, 144–45, 146, 180, 199, 206, 265–
    67; U.S. presidents and, 4–10, 20, 23–
    24, 27–31, 77–79, 103–4, 114, 154, 158,
    161–62, 166–69, 172, 175, 195–97, 198–
    221, 225–56, 261, 266–68; Republicans
    and, 5–8, 13, 15, 19, 60, 113, 167, 181, 191,
    193, 195, 208, 243, 256–57, 261–62, 267,
    271; Democrats and, 7–8, 15, 23–25, 48,
    119, 124, 167, 243, 253, 262; Congress
    and, 24–25, 27–29, 256–57; policy
    choice issues, 30–33; international mar-
    ket integration, 34–35; New Deal
    Order, 54–68; Fordism and, 73; Bush
    and, 145; intra-Democratic divisions
    and, 148, 167–68; future prospects,
    270–72
Free trade agreements, 2–5, 144, 172, 231,
    260, 270
Free Trade Area of the Americas, 191, 198,
    270
Frenzel, Bill, 107
Friedman, Thomas, 188
Friends of the Earth, 242
From, Al, 183, 221

GATT, 4, 5, 21, 30, 36, 243, 255, 262; Clin-
    ton and, 2, 8, 23, 33, 165–68, 172, 185,
    189–96, 198, 201, 212, 266; Uruguay
    Round, 15, 21, 114, 129–30, 139, 143, 144,
    167, 185, 189–96, 212, 234, 267; Reagan
    and, 23, 82, 106, 114, 129–30; Bush and,
    23, 139, 143, 144, 189–90, 195, 196; cre-
    ation of, 54, 57; escape clause provi-
    sions, 58; New Deal Order and, 59,
    61; Kennedy Round, 64, 66; Tokyo
    Round, 69
Gaurini, Frank, 142

General Agreement on Tariffs and Trade.
    See GATT
Gephardt, Dick: Reagan policies and, 87,
    98–99, 107, 119–23, 127–30, 135; Bush
    and, 140, 142, 143, 148, 150, 152, 156, 159;
    Clinton policies and, 176–77, 182, 190,
    193, 202, 203, 213, 217, 221, 246; China
    PNTR status and, 249–51
Germany, 103, 107, 157, 204
Gibbons, Sam, 91, 92, 132
Gilmour, John, 22, 105
Gingrich, Newt, 182, 214, 222, 224, 225
Glenn, John, 87
Globalization, 1, 2, 34–35, 72, 144, 175, 217;
    post-Fordism and, 73, 169, 182; labor
    sector and, 180; Seattle WTO meeting
    and, 231
Gold standard, 48, 52, 57
Goldstein, Judith, 18, 19, 259
Gore, Al, 127, 169, 179, 221; presidential
    bid, 9, 33, 213, 219, 222, 227, 231–32, 235,
    242, 247, 250, 256, 268, 271; China
    PNTR status and, 236, 239
Gourevitch, Peter, 14
Gramm, Phil, 194
Gramm-Rudman-Hollings bill, 94, 109
Grassroots organizations, 13, 176, 181
Great Britain, 57, 103, 152
Great Depression, 18, 43, 53, 54, 56, 59
Great Society, 65
Greenberg, Stanley, 211
G-7, 175, 190
Gulf War, 144, 147

Harding, Warren, 53
Harkin, Tom, 154, 158, 180
Harris, John F., 203
Harrison, Benjamin, 50
Harrison, Bennett, 170
Hart, Gary, 163
Hashimoto, Ryutaro, 208
Hegemonic projects, 38
Heinz, John, 90, 141
Helms, Jesse, 112, 152, 192
Herethetics, 7, 20–22, 32, 41, 53, 77, 85,
    95–104, 134, 145, 161, 222–24, 258–59,
    264
Heritage Foundation, 179

High-technology sector, 2, 16, 96, 145; Japan and, 2, 120, 138; New Deal Order, 65, 68, 69; Republicans and, 68; post-Fordism and, 72, 73, 86, 99; Democrats and, 86–87, 111, 240–41, 248; in Bush era, 138, 139, 141, 145; strategic trade theory and, 139; Clinton and, 169–70, 172, 174, 190, 208, 214, 228–31, 234; PACs, 230, 248; China PNTR status and, 238–41, 248–49, 251, 254

Hills, Carla, 139, 140, 148

Hiscox, Michael, 14

Hoffa, James P., 242

Hollings, Ernest, 135

Home market thesis, 50

Hong Kong, 112

Hook, Janet, 117

Hoover, Herbert, 53

Hosokawa, Morihiro, 185–86

House of Representatives, U.S., 2, 5, 6, 9, 50; 1970s reforms, 94. *See also* Congress, U.S.

House Trade and Competitiveness Task Force, 140

House Ways and Means Committee, 65, 66, 105–7, 119, 122, 129, 156, 191–92, 206–7, 214

Hufbauer, Gary, 212

Hull, Cordell, 55

Human rights groups, 146–47, 231, 242

Hunter, Duncan, 152

Iacocca, Lee, 98

Immigration, 48, 181

Imports, 1, 2, 13, 43; voluntary restraint agreements, 1, 33, 58, 79, 82, 88, 90, 96, 107, 135–36; nontariff barriers, 4, 66, 69, 79–80; free trade and, 34–35; Civil War Order, 49; Order of '96, 52, 53; New Deal Order, 56–58, 61, 64, 65, 67; Carter and, 72; Reagan and, 77, 78–79, 89, 95–96, 114, 265–66; surcharge proposal, 98–99, 101, 103, 104; Bush and, 138, 142. *See also* Quotas

India, 141, 148

Industrialization, 48–52

Industrial policy, 85–88, 138–39

Industry-led policy, 138, 140

Inflation, 35, 65, 66, 72, 75, 99, 188

Information technology paradigm, 72–73

Institute for International Economics, 179

Institute for Policy Studies, 181

Interest groups, 13, 18, 169, 176

Interest rates, 35, 72, 79, 170, 171, 188

International Bank for Reconstruction and Development, 57

International Monetary Fund, 54, 57, 223, 224

International structures and institutions, 12, 33–36

International Trade Commission, U.S., 58, 78, 89, 100, 129

Internet, 229–30, 231

Internet Coalition for China PNTR, 238

Investment economics, 128

Investment strategy, 168–71

Investor blocs, 14

Iran-Contra scandal, 117, 119

Iraq, 144

Jackson, Jesse, 127, 129, 132, 202

Japan, 1, 105, 256; Bush and, 2, 5, 33, 137–44, 147–57, 160, 256, 266; closed markets, 2, 79–80, 82, 95–96, 151, 172, 185; high-technology sector and, 2, 120, 138; Clinton and, 5, 8, 9, 22, 24, 30, 33, 35, 164, 166, 168, 172–75, 185–89, 195–96, 199–205, 208, 256, 266, 267; Reagan and, 5, 33, 78–79, 82, 85, 88, 93, 95–96, 99–100, 103, 107, 113, 114, 120–21, 130, 256, 266; New Deal Order and, 58–59, 64–65, 69; auto industry, 78–79, 82, 88, 96, 137, 150, 151, 153, 156, 157, 189, 199–205, 267; dollar valuation issues, 103, 188, 204–5; managed trade agreements, 113, 138, 142, 173; Structural Impediments Initiative, 141–43, 160; European Community and, 143

Jasinowski, Jerry, 253

Jessop, Bob, 38, 73–74

Johnson, Lyndon, 65–66

Jordan, 270

Kaifu, Toshiki, 142–43

Kantor, Mickey, 174–76, 185–89, 192, 200, 202, 206–9, 225

47, 154, 159, 175–76, 179, 181, 235; peso
  collapse, 204
Michel, Robert, 182
Microsoft, 230, 238
Military spending, 76, 170
Mimicking, 22, 161, 261
Mitchell, Denise, 241
Mitchell, George, 157
Modes of regulation, 37–39, 41, 43; Civil
  War Order, 48; Order of '96, 51–52;
  New Deal Order, 54, 68–69; post-
  Fordism and, 73, 261
Modisett, Jeff, 251
Mondale, Walter, 24, 33, 81, 85, 87, 88, 90–
  93, 97, 118, 163, 179, 256
Monetary policy, 75, 79, 103, 104, 188
Monetary regimes, 54, 57
Morphogenetic approach, 37, 45
Morris, Dick, 22, 165–66, 202, 205, 206
Mosbacher, Robert, 139, 140, 151
Motorola, 186, 238
Moynihan, Daniel Patrick, 191, 226
Multi-Fiber Arrangement, 111, 112, 113
Multilateral Agreement on Investment,
  231
Multinational corporations, 34, 43, 73,
  199, 211; New Deal Order, 65, 68;
  NAFTA and, 145, 146; Clinton and, 172,
  188, 230

Nader, Ralph, 181, 192, 268
NAFTA, 4, 32, 33, 220, 235, 243, 255; Clinton and, 2, 5, 8, 23, 27, 28, 30, 32, 33, 137,
  154–55, 157–60, 164–68, 172, 175–85,
  196, 198, 201, 203, 213, 256, 262, 266–67;
  Bush and, 8, 23, 32, 137, 144–49, 157–60,
  185, 196, 267; party positions and, 15,
  21–23, 27, 28, 262; Chile and, 198, 213;
  future expansion of, 270
Nasdaq, 73
National Association of Manufacturers,
  146, 214, 237
National Economic Council, 173, 176
National economic strategy, 164, 168–71
National Farmers Union, 242
National Industrial Development Bank,
  87
National Industrial Strategy Act (1983), 87

Neocorporatism, 73–74
Neoliberalism, 73–75, 86–87, 145, 163, 210,
  212
Neomercantilism. *See* Economic na-
  tionalism
Neostatism, 73–74, 86, 138, 140, 169
New Deal, 14, 57, 67
New Deal Order, 43, 44, 53–71
New Democrat Coalition, 215, 218, 221,
  240, 241, 244, 246, 247, 249
New Democrat Network, 223, 240, 241,
  246, 249
New Economy, 210, 212, 213, 228–31, 269,
  271
New Economy Task Force, 228, 241
New Nationalism, 211
Niskanen, William, 78, 88, 90, 107, 114
Nixon, Richard, 66–67, 69
Nollen, Stanley D., 18–19
Nontariff barriers, 4, 66, 69, 79–80
North American Development Bank, 178
North American Free Trade Agreement.
  See NAFTA
North Atlantic Treaty Organization, 233
North Korea, 205

O'Halloran, Sharyn, 30–31, 63
Oil shocks (1973, 1979), 72, 78
Omnibus Trade and Competitiveness Act
  (1988), 4, 5, 15, 17, 256, 257; Super 301
  provision, 2, 125, 129, 137, 140–43, 150,
  154, 156, 160, 186–88, 266; policy contagion and, 7, 29, 32, 116, 119, 134, 137;
  development and passage of, 26, 95,
  116–34, 260–61, 264, 265; plant closings
  and, 125, 130–34
O'Neill, Tip, 105, 110, 111, 113
Operation Desert Storm, 144
Orderly marketing agreements, 58
Order of '96, 42, 51–54
Ottinger, Richard, 80

Packwood, Robert, 125
PACs, 83, 92–93, 180, 184, 202, 216, 220–21,
  223, 230, 248
Pak, Kyoungsan, 32
Partisan regimes. *See* Political orders
Paster, Howard, 177